Informationen für die Benutzung

Inhalt

3–4	Einführung (gibt Informationen über dieses Buch)
5–8	Ausführliches Inhaltsverzeichnis (nach Sachthemen)
9–316	Wortschatz in thematischer Ordnung
317–339	Englische Kurzgrammatik
340–356	ABC der Sprachgebrauchsprobleme
357–410	Register Englisch
411–456	Register Deutsch
Umschlag	Die Zeichen der Lautschrift

Verwendete Abkürzungen

AE = Amerikanisches Englisch
BE = Britisches Englisch

adj. = *adjective* = Adjektiv = Eigenschaftswort
adv. = *adverb* = Adverb = Umstandswort
dt. = deutsch
n. = *noun* = Substantiv = Hauptwort
Pl. = Plural = Mehrzahl
prep. = *preposition* = Präposition = Verhältniswort
pron. = *pronoun* = Pronomen = Fürwort
sb. = *somebody* = jemand
sth. = *something* = etwas
v. = *verb* = Zeitwort / Tätigkeitswort

Verwendete Zeichen

™ = trademark (= Warenzeichen)
Mit diesem Zusatz werden als Markenzeichen geschützte Namen ge-
kennzeichnet. Das Fehlen dieser Kennzeichnung bietet allerdings keine
Gewähr dafür, dass ein Wort kein eingetragenes Warenzeichen ist.

* Sternchen
Es weist bei unregelmäßigen Verbformen darauf hin, dass auch die
regelmäßige Form gebräuchlich ist. Beispiel: learnt* = Es gibt auch
die regelmäßige Form learned.

/ Schrägstrich
Er steht vor alternativen Ausdrucksmöglichkeiten.

– Gedankenstrich
Er findet Verwendung bei Gegenüberstellungen oder zur Trennung
von zwei Worteinträgen, die zum Zweck der Platzersparnis auf eine
Zeile gesetzt sind.

 Dieses Symbol kennzeichnet Erklärungen zu Grammatik,
Wortgebrauch und Aussprache.

 Unter diesem Zeichen werden sprachliche Erläuterungen mit
landeskundlichen Informationen verknüpft.

Großer
Lernwortschatz

Englisch *aktuell*

15 000 Wörter zu 150 Themen

Erweiterte und aktualisierte Neuausgabe

Hans G. Hoffmann
Marion Hoffmann
Patrick Hoffmann

Hueber Verlag

Hans G. Hoffmann: Englischlehrer und Autor zahlreicher englischer Lehrwerke, Selbstlernkurse, Grammatiken, Übungsbücher und Wörterbücher.

Marion Hoffmann: Englischlehrerin, Autorin, Oberstudiendirektorin des Victor-Klemperer-Kollegs in Berlin.

Patrick Hoffmann, BA Hons. (Cantab.), englischer Schul- und Universitätsabschluss, Lehrerfahrung in Deutschland, Myanmar und Tansania.

5.	4.	3.			Die letzten Ziffern
2022	21	20	19	18	bezeichnen Zahl und Jahr des Druckes.

Alle Drucke dieser Auflage können, da unverändert, nebeneinander benutzt werden.
© 2013 Hueber Verlag GmbH & Co. KG, 85737 Ismaning, Deutschland
1. Ausgabe © 1997 Hueber Verlag – Originaltitel «Großer Lernwortschatz Englisch»
Erweiterte und aktualisierte Neuausgabe © 2003 Hueber Verlag
Redaktion: Valerio Vial, Kerstin Zülsdorf, Hueber Verlag GmbH & Co. KG, Ismaning
Umschlaggestaltung: creative partners gmbh, München
Fotogestaltung Cover: wentzlaff I pfaff I güldenpfennig kommunikation gmbh, München
Coverfoto: © Getty Images/Stockbyte
Zeichnungen: Katja Lechthaler, München
Kolorierung der Zeichnungen: creative partners gmbh, München
Layout: Kerstin Rieger, Hueber Verlag, Ismaning;
    Sieveking · Agentur für Kommunikation, München
Druck und Bindung: Friedrich Pustet GmbH & Co. KG, Regensburg
Printed in Germany
ISBN 978-3-19-109493-5

Art. 530_16539_001_03

Einführung

Mit dem *Großen Lernwortschatz Englisch* steht Ihnen ein neuartiges Lern- und
Nachschlagewerk zur Verfügung, das außer einem enorm umfangreichen
Wortschatz auch viele Idioms, Sprichwörter, Erklärungen zum Sprachge-
brauch, unterhaltsame Texte sowie eine auf das Wesentliche konzentrierte
Grammatik enthält. In Schule und Hochschule, Beruf und Alltag bietet
dieses Buch vielseitige Nutzungsmöglichkeiten:

- Als thematischer „Sprachgenerator", mit dem Sie sich gezielt und syste-
  matisch auf ein bestimmtes Sachgebiet vorbereiten können (Politik, Rechtswesen, Soziales, Wirtschaft, Fremdenverkehr, Religion, Kunst, Literatur,
  Technik, Wissenschaft, Computer usw. – es sind 150 Themen!). Sie finden
  direkt verwertbares sprachliches Material für Schülerarbeiten, Präsentatio-
  nen, Vorträge, Sachdiskussionen, Mediennutzung, berufliche Aufgaben
  und private Interessen.
- Als englisch-deutsches und deutsch-englisches Wörterbuch. Über die beiden umfangreichen Register können Sie ein benötigtes englisches oder
  deutsches Wort schnell auffinden und sich über Bedeutung, Aussprache,
  Gebrauchsbesonderheiten und verwandte Ausdrücke informieren. Sie werden feststellen, dass dieses Buch auch ganz aktuelle Begriffe enthält, die
  erst in den letzten Jahren Teil der Alltagssprache geworden sind.
- Als universaler *companion*, der Ihnen über zahlreiche sprachliche und lan-
  deskundliche „Extras", Zitate, Lesetexte, eine „Kurzgrammatik" und ein
  „ABC der Sprachgebrauchsprobleme" wichtige Kenntnisse und mancherlei
  food for thought vermittelt.

Wie finden Sie benötigtes Sprachmaterial?

Zugang zum thematisch geordneten Wortschatz haben Sie über
das Inhaltsverzeichnis (S. 5–8), das englische (S. 341–392) und
das deutsche (S. 393–436) Register.

Angenommen, Sie suchen Wortschatz zum Thema *Schule*.
Im Inhaltsverzeichnis stoßen Sie schnell auf Kapitel 9 *Education* = *Bildungswesen*. In den fünf Unterkapiteln 9.1 bis 9.5 können Sie gezielt das finden,
was Sie interessiert.

Was tun Sie, wenn Sie „Ihr" Thema nicht im Inhaltsverzeichnis finden? *Schule*
Versuchen Sie es mit dem Stichwort *school* über das englische Register.
Dort finden Sie 10 Seitenverweise – vielleicht ein bisschen viel, denn Sie 148 - 154
haben keine Lust, alle genannten Seiten aufzuschlagen, um das für Sie
relevante Kapitel zu finden?

Jetzt hilft Ihnen das „Eingrenzen": Sie sehen, dass sich die Verweise auf die
Seiten 148 bis 154 (vielleicht noch 159) konzentrieren, d.h. die Wahrscheinlichkeit
ist groß, dass in diesem Teil des Buches das Thema *school* schwerpunktmäßig
behandelt wird. In der Tat: die Seiten 148 und 149 sind den *educational
facilities* = *Bildungseinrichtungen* gewidmet, Sie sind also mitten im Thema.

Aber wie helfen Sie sich, wenn Sie unter zahlreichen Seitenverweisen keinen
Schwerpunkt ausmachen können?
Suchen Sie ein Stichwort, das zu Ihrem Thema gehört, aber zu speziell ist,
um an vielen Stellen vorzukommen – zum Beispiel den Begriff *Gymnasium*.
Da es sich um ein deutsches Wort handelt, suchen Sie es im deutschen
Register. Dort gibt es nur eine Fundstelle: Seite 148. Sie schlagen diese Seite
auf und finden so die ausführliche Behandlung des Themas, die Sie suchen.

Wie prägen Sie sich neuen Wortschatz ein?

Dafür gibt es viele individuelle Methoden, unter denen die folgenden die am häufigsten angewandten sind:

- Sie lernen den spaltenweise angeordneten Wortschatz nach Möglichkeit laut, erst links – rechts und dann rechts – links.

- Sie testen sich, indem Sie zunächst die deutsche Entsprechung des englischen Eintrags abdecken, die deutsche Übersetzung aus dem Gedächtnis sprechen und dann das Blatt nach unten schieben, um die Übersetzung für die Überprüfung Ihrer Eigenleistung „freizugeben".

- Später verfahren Sie entsprechend mit der englischen Spalte, d.h. Sie sprechen die englische Übersetzung, während der Eintrag in der linken Spalte abgedeckt ist, und überprüfen dann durch Herabschieben des Blattes Ihre Antwort.

- Nehmen Sie sich nie einen zu langen Abschnitt vor! Mehr als acht Einträge sollten Sie nicht auf einmal lernen.

- Begrenzen Sie Ihre Lernsitzungen. Jeden Tag eine Viertelstunde ist besser als einmal die Woche zwei Stunden üben.

Was machen Sie mit „hartnäckigen Verweigerern", d.h. Wörtern oder Wortfolgen, die Sie sich nicht merken können? Schreiben Sie sie auf Zettel im Format DIN A7 – das Englische auf die eine Seite, das Deutsche auf die andere. Legen Sie die Zettel an auffälliger Stelle in Ihrer Wohnung aus oder tragen Sie sie bei sich, damit Sie immer wieder einmal üben oder sich testen können.

Schließlich: Wörter lernen sich am besten und nachhaltigsten in der Gesellschaft anderer Wörter. Also nicht einfach *speech = Rede*, sondern *make / give / deliver a speech* (S. 103), damit Sie die idiomatisch üblichen „Begleiter" gleich mitlernen.

Features dieser Neuausgabe

Im vorhandenen Text wurden ca. 500 Zeilen durch neues, zumeist aktuelleres Material ersetzt.

12 bisher freie Seiten wurden mit ergänzendem Text gefüllt, wobei erstmals auch zusammenhängende Dialoge mit zahlreichen Neuwörtern aufgenommen wurden.

Das Kapitel „ABC der Sprachgebrauchsprobleme" wurde neu aufgenommen. Die über 400 farblich gekennzeichneten „Extras" geben Ihnen – wie schon in früheren Ausgaben – Hinweise zur Grammatik, zur Begriffsdifferenzierung, zur Landeskunde, zu Idiomatik und Slang, zu Stilebenen, Wortfamilien, Begriffsfeldern und Ausspracheproblemen.

Auf Abweichungen zwischen britischem (BE) und amerikanischem (AE) Englisch wird durchweg hingewiesen.

Englische Kurzgrammatik und „ABC der Sprachgebrauchprobleme" sind übergreifende Hilfen für die Wahl der richtigen Wortformen, die Bildung korrekter Sätze und das Vermeiden von Fehlern.

Verfasser und Verlag

Inhaltsverzeichnis

1	**Human beings**	**Der Mensch**	9
1.1	Personal data	Angaben zur Person	10
1.2	Parts of the body	Körperteile	12
1.3	Outward appearance	Äußere Erscheinung	15
1.4	Childhood and youth	Kindheit und Jugend	17
1.5	Middle age and old age	Mittlere Jahre und Alter	20
1.6	Personality and behaviour	Persönlichkeit und Verhalten	22
1.7	Senses and sensations	Sinne und Sinneseindrücke	25
1.8	Feelings and attitudes	Gefühle und Einstellungen	28
1.9	Morality and immorality	Moral und Unmoral	31
1.10	Human relations	Menschliche Beziehungen	33
1.11	Sexuality	Sexualität	36
1.12	Personal hygiene	Körperpflege	38
1.13	Death	Tod	40
	The creativity of language		44

2	**The family**	**Die Familie**	45
2.1	Family relations	Verwandtschaftliche Beziehungen	46
2.2	Marriage and divorce	Ehe und Ehescheidung	48
2.3	Parents and children	Eltern und Kinder	50
	Parents-and-children proverbs		52

3	**Eating, drinking, clothing**	**Essen, Trinken, Kleidung**	53
3.1	Foods	Nahrungsmittel	54
3.2	Beverages	Getränke	57
3.3	Kitchen and cooking	Küche und Kochen	58
3.4	Meals	Mahlzeiten	60
3.5	Eating out	Auswärts essen	61
3.6	Clothing	Kleidung	64

4	**Health care**	**Gesundheitspflege**	67
4.1	Illnesses and symptoms	Krankheiten und Symptome	68
4.2	Accidents and injuries	Unfälle und Verletzungen	71
4.3	Disabilities	Behinderungen	73
4.4	At the doctor's	Beim Arzt	75
4.5	At the dentist's	Beim Zahnarzt	78
4.6	In hospital	Im Krankenhaus	80
4.7	Healthy living	Gesunde Lebensweise	82
	Gym talk		84

5	**The home**	**Die Wohnung**	85
5.1	Flats and houses	Wohnungen und Häuser	86
5.2	Furniture, fittings, etc.	Möbel, Ausstattung etc.	89
5.3	Housework	Hausarbeit	92
	Wortverkürzungen, Abkürzungen, Akronyme		94

6	The social order	Die Sozialordnung	95
6.1	Communities	Gemeinschaften	96
6.2	Social movements	Gesellschaftliche Bewegungen	98
6.3	Political systems	Politische Systeme	99
6.4	Parties and politics	Parteien und Politik	100
6.5	The legislature	Die gesetzgebende Gewalt	102
6.6	Government	Regierung	105
6.7	Antigovernment activity	Aktivitäten gegen die Regierung	107
6.8	Law and police	Rechtswesen und Polizei	109
6.9	Taxation	Steuern	113
6.10	Social security	Soziale Sicherheit	115
6.11	International relations	Internationale Beziehungen	116
6.12	Defence, war, military	Verteidigung, Krieg, Militär	118
6.13	Titles, forms of address	Titel, Anredeformen	121

7	Social problems	Soziale Probleme	123
7.1	Housing shortage	Wohnungsmangel	124
7.2	Unemployment	Arbeitslosigkeit	126
7.3	Drug and alcohol abuse	Drogen- und Alkoholmissbrauch	128
7.4	Poverty	Armut	130
7.5	Crime and violence	Verbrechen und Gewalttätigkeit	131
7.6	Xenophobia and racism	Ausländerfeindlichkeit und Rassismus	134
7.7	Sexism	Sexismus	136

8	Social sciences	Sozialwissenschaften	137
8.1	Anthropology	Anthropologie	138
8.2	History	Geschichte	140
8.3	Political science	Politische Wissenschaft	142
8.4	Psychology	Psychologie	143
8.5	Sociology	Soziologie	145
	The language of research		146

9	Education	Bildungswesen	147
9.1	Educational facilities	Bildungseinrichtungen	148
9.2	Subjects and skills	Fächer und Fertigkeiten	150
9.3	Exams and qualifications	Prüfungen und Qualifikationen	152
9.4	Teaching and learning	Lehren und Lernen	154
9.5	In the classroom	Im Klassenzimmer	155

10	"Weltanschauung"	Weltanschauung	157
10.1	Religions and denominations	Religionen und Konfessionen	158
10.2	God and divinity	Gott und Göttlichkeit	160
10.3	Religious doctrines, practices, institutions	Religiöse Lehren, Bräuche, Institutionen	162
10.4	Nonreligious beliefs	Nichtreligiöse Überzeugungen	164
10.5	Philosophy	Philosophie	165

11	Art and literature	Kunst und Literatur	167
11.1	Painting and sculpture	Malerei und Bildhauerei	168
11.2	Graphic art	Grafische Kunst	170

11.3	Photography	Fotografie	171
11.4	Music and dance	Musik und Tanz	173
11.5	Theatre and cinema	Theater und Film	175
11.6	Architecture	Architektur	177
11.7	Literature	Literatur	179

12	**Leisure and recreation**	**Freizeit und Erholung**	181
12.1	Holidays	Feiertage und Urlaub	182
12.2	Festive occasions	Festliche Anlässe	184
12.3	Socializing	Gesellschaftlicher Umgang	185
12.4	Entertainments	Vergnügungen	187
12.5	Travel and tourism	Reisen und Tourismus	188
12.6	Accommodation	Unterkunft	191
12.7	Shopping	Einkaufen	193
12.8	Sports	Sport	195
12.9	Hobbies	Hobbys	198
12.10	Drinking and smoking	Trinken und Rauchen	200
Social media			202

13	**The universe**	**Das Weltall**	203
13.1	Stars and planets	Sterne und Planeten	204
13.2	Space exploration	Raumforschung	206
Idioms			208

14	**The earth**	**Die Erde**	209
14.1	Geology	Geologie	210
14.2	Metals and gemstones	Metalle und Schmucksteine	212
14.3	Geographical divisions	Geografische Einteilungen	214
14.4	Oceans, lakes, rivers	Meere, Seen, Flüsse	216
14.5	The countryside	Die Landschaft	218
14.6	The farming world	Die Welt der Landwirtschaft	220
14.7	The city	Die Stadt	223
14.8	The environment	Die Umwelt	225
14.9	Weather and climate	Wetter und Klima	227
14.10	Natural disasters	Naturkatastrophen	229

15	**Living things**	**Lebewesen**	231
15.1	Animals	Tiere	232
15.2	Plants	Pflanzen	235
15.3	Simpler life forms	Einfachere Lebewesen	237
Idioms			238

16	**Science**	**Wissenschaft**	239
16.1	Physics	Physik	240
16.2	Chemistry	Chemie	242
16.3	Medicine	Medizin	244
16.4	Mathematics	Mathematik	246
16.5	Numbers	Zahlen	248
16.6	Measures and weights	Maße und Gewichte	250
Zur Aussprache längerer Wörter			252

17	**Technology**	**Technik**	253
17.1	Materials, tools, machines	Werkstoffe, Werkzeuge, Maschinen	254
17.2	Manufacturing	Fabrikproduktion	257
17.3	Electricity and electronics	Elektrizität und Elektronik	259
17.4	Containers	Behälter	261
At the cutting edge			262

18	**Information and communications**	**Information und Kommunikation**	263
18.1	Reference sources	Nachschlagemöglichkeiten	264
18.2	Books and publishing	Bücher und Verlagswesen	266
18.3	The press	Die Presse	268
18.4	Radio and television	Rundfunk und Fernsehen	270
18.5	The postal service	Der Postdienst	272
18.6	Telephone and fax	Telefon und Fax	274
18.7	Computers	Computer	276
Going portable			282

19	**Means of transport**	**Transportmittel**	283
19.1	Motor vehicles and road traffic	Kraftfahrzeuge und Straßenverkehr	284
19.2	Rail transport	Beförderung mit der Eisenbahn	287
19.3	Air transport	Beförderung mit dem Flugzeug	289
19.4	Water transport	Beförderung auf dem Wasserweg	291
19.5	Public transport	Öffentlicher Nahverkehr	293

20	**The economy**	**Die Wirtschaft**	295
20.1	Economic theory and policy	Wirtschaftstheorie und -politik	296
20.2	Business	Das Geschäftsleben	298
20.3	Money and finance	Geld und Finanzwesen	302
20.4	Advertising	Werbung	305
20.5	Insurance	Versicherung	307
20.6	Real estate	Immobilien	308
20.7	Occupations and job titles	Berufe und Funktionsbezeichnungen	309
20.8	In the office	Im Büro	312
20.9	Labour relations	Beziehungen zwischen den Tarifpartnern	314

Englische Kurzgrammatik	318
ABC der Sprachgebrauchsprobleme	340
Register Englisch	357
Register Deutsch	411

Human beings
Der Mensch

1   **Personal data**
    Angaben zur Person

2   **Parts of the body**
    Körperteile

3   **Outward appearance**
    Äußere Erscheinung

4   **Childhood and youth**
    Kindheit und Jugend

5   **Middle age and old age**
    Mittlere Jahre und Alter

6   **Personality and behaviour**
    Persönlichkeit und Verhalten

7   **Senses and sensations**
    Sinne und Sinneseindrücke

8   **Feelings and attitudes**
    Gefühle und Einstellungen

9   **Morality and immorality**
    Moral und Unmoral

10 **Human relations**
    Menschliche Beziehungen

11 **Sexuality**
    Sexualität

12 **Personal hygiene**
    Körperpflege

13 **Death**
    Tod

The creativity of language

Personal data
Angaben zur Person

There are three things I always forget. Names, faces, and – the third
I can't remember. (*Italo Svevo, Italian novelist, 1861–1928*)

name [neɪm]
What's your name?
Her maiden name is Smith.
Sarah Smith, née [neɪ] Welsh
**first name / forename / given
name / Christian** [ˈkrɪstʃən] **name**

Name
Wie heißt du / ist Ihr Name?
Ihr Mädchenname ist Smith.
Sarah Smith, geb. Welsh
Vorname

In der heutigen multikulturellen Gesellschaft (= *multicultural society*)
wird *Christian name* auf Formularen etc. weitgehend vermieden, da
Nichtchristen (= *non-Christians*) und Atheisten (= *atheists* [ˈeɪθiɪsts]) ihre
Vornamen nicht als *Christian names* auffassen. Die Bezeichnung *given
name* ist besonders sinnvoll bei Angehörigen von Kulturgemeinschaften,
in denen der „Vorname" auf den Familiennamen folgt, wie etwa bei
Chinesen, Japanern, Koreanern etc.

**surname / last name / family
name**
middle name [mɪdl ˈneɪm]
George Bush's middle name is
Walker.

Familienname; Nachname; Zuname

mittlerer Name; zweiter Vorname
George Bushs zweiter Vorname
ist Walker.

Idiom: *Courtesy* [ˈkɜːtəsi] *is his middle name.* (= Er ist die Höflichkeit in
Person.)

nickname [ˈnɪkneɪm]
date of birth [bɜːθ]
She was born on the sixth of May /
on May (the) sixth, nineteen sixty-two
(on 6 May, 1962 / May 6, 1962).
When is / When's your birthday?

It's his birthday today.
She has a birthday next Monday.

Spitzname
Geburtsdatum
Sie ist am sechsten Mai neunzehn-
hundertzweiundsechzig / am 6. Mai
1962 geboren.
Wann hast du / haben Sie Geburts-
tag?
Er hat heute Geburtstag.
Sie hat nächsten Montag Geburtstag.

Vermeiden Sie die abgekürzte Form:
6/5/62 heißt BE 6. Mai, AE dagegen 5. Juni!

age [eɪdʒ]
What age are you? / What's your age?
place of birth [bɜːθ]
place of residence [ˈrezɪdəns]

Alter
Wie alt bist du / sind Sie?
Geburtsort
Wohnort

nationality [næʃə'næləti] | **Nationalität; Staatsangehörigkeit**
What nationality are you? | Welche Staatsangehörigkeit haben Sie?

marital status ['mærɪtl steɪtəs] | **Familienstand**
Married, single, or divorced? | Verheiratet, ledig oder geschieden?
sex: male [meɪl] – **female** ['fi:meɪl] | **Geschlecht: männlich – weiblich**
height [haɪt] – **weight** [weɪt] | **Größe – Gewicht**
What height are you? | Wie groß sind Sie / bist du?
What weight are you? | Was wiegen Sie / wiegst du?
religion [rɪ'lɪdʒən] – **religious affiliation** [əfɪli'eɪʃn] | **Religion – Religionszugehörigkeit**
What's his religious affiliation? | Was ist seine Religion(szugehörigkeit)?

address [ə'dres] | **Adresse; Anschrift**
He can be reached at this address. | Er ist unter dieser Adresse zu erreichen.
What's your e-mail address? | Wie ist deine E-Mail-Adresse?

Courtesy is his middle name.

Parts of the body
Körperteile

The body is a machine of the nature of an army, not of that of a watch, or of a hydraulic apparatus. Of this army each cell is a soldier, each organ a brigade. (Thomas Henry Huxley, English biologist, 1825–1895)

head [hed]
from head to toe [təʊ]
skull [skʌl]
brain [breɪn]
He died of a brain tumour ['tjuːmə].
hair [heə]
I had my hair cut.
face [feɪs]
eye [aɪ]
She's blind [blaɪnd] in one eye.
nose [nəʊz]
He's got a runny nose.
mouth [maυθ]
tooth [tuːθ] – **teeth** [tiːθ]
tongue [tʌŋ]
lip [lɪp]
He kissed [kɪst] her lips.
ear [ɪə] – **eardrum** ['ɪədrʌm]
an infection of the middle ear
neck [nek]
He broke his neck.
throat [θrəʊt]
I've got a sore [sɔː] throat.
shoulder ['ʃəʊldə]
He just shrugged [ʃrʌgd] his shoulders.
arm [ɑːm]
She has broken her arm.
elbow ['elbəʊ]
hand [hænd]
He injured ['ɪndʒəd] his hand.
finger ['fɪŋgə]
(finger)nail [('fɪŋgə)neɪl]
leg [leg]
I need to stretch my legs a bit.

knee [niː]
My left knee hurts [hɜːts].
foot [fʊt] – **feet** [fiːt]

Kopf
von Kopf bis („Zeh") Fuß
Schädel
Gehirn
Er starb an einem Gehirntumor.
Haar; Haare
Ich ließ mir die Haare schneiden.
Gesicht
Auge
Sie ist auf einem Auge blind.
Nase
Ihm läuft die Nase.
Mund; Maul
Zahn – Zähne
Zunge
Lippe
Er küsste sie auf die Lippen.
Ohr – Trommelfell
eine Mittelohrentzündung
Hals *(von außen gesehen)*
Er brach sich das Genick.
Kehle; Hals *(von innen gesehen)*
Ich habe Halsschmerzen.
Schulter
Er zuckte nur mit den Achseln.
Arm
Sie hat sich den Arm gebrochen.
Ell(en)bogen
Hand
Er verletzte sich an der Hand.
Finger
(Finger-)Nagel
Bein
Ich muss mir ein bisschen die Beine
    vertreten.

Knie
Mir tut das linke Knie weh.
Fuß – Füße

Sentences with body idioms

*I'd keep him at **arm's** length* [leŋθ]. (= Ich würde ihn mir vom Leibe halten.)
*Get off my **back**!* (= Lass mich endlich in Ruhe!)
*I've got a **bone** to pick with you.* (= Ich habe mit dir ein Hühnchen zu rupfen.)
*I must get this off my **chest**.* (= Ich muss mir das von der Seele reden.)
*I'm up to the **eyes** in work.* (= Ich stecke bis über beide Ohren in Arbeit.)
*He wouldn't raise a **finger*** [ˈfɪŋgə] *to help us.* (= Er würde keinen Finger krumm machen, um uns zu helfen.)
*I really put my **foot** in it.* (= Ich bin ganz schön ins Fettnäpfchen getreten.)
*She's been living from **hand** to **mouth** these last six months.* (= Sie lebt seit einem halben Jahr von der Hand in den Mund.)
*I can't make **head** or tail of it.* (= Ich werde daraus nicht schlau.)
*I couldn't find it in my **heart*** [hɑːt] *to tell her the truth* [truːθ]. (= Ich konnte es nicht übers Herz bringen, ihr die Wahrheit zu sagen.)
*The company is on its last **legs**.* (= Die Firma pfeift auf dem letzten Loch.)
*She's a real pain in the **neck**.* (= Sie geht mir schwer auf den Wecker.)
*He had the **nerve** to call me a miser* [ˈmaɪzə]. (= Er besaß die Frechheit, mich einen Geizhals zu nennen.)
*We paid through the **nose**.* (= Wir haben einen Wahnsinnspreis bezahlt.)
*That remark really went under my **skin**.* (= Diese Bemerkung ist mir wirklich unter die Haut gegangen.)
*It's on the tip of my **tongue*** [tʌŋ]. (= Es liegt mir auf der Zunge.)
*She's got a sweet **tooth**.* (= Sie isst gern Süßigkeiten / ist ein Süßschnabel.)

chest [tʃest]	**Brust(korb)**
breast [brest] – **breasts**	**Brust – Brüste**
Breast milk is best for babies.	Muttermilch ist für Babys am besten.
rib [rɪb]	**Rippe**
heart [hɑːt]	**Herz**
He's had a heart condition for years.	Er ist seit Jahren herzkrank.
lung [lʌŋ] – **lungs**	**Lungenflügel – Lunge**
liver [ˈlɪvə]	**Leber**
kidney [ˈkɪdni]	**Niere**
perform [pəˈfɔːm] a kidney transplant	eine Nierentransplantation durchführen
stomach [ˈstʌmək]	**Magen; Bauch**
on an empty stomach	auf nüchternen Magen
abdomen [ˈæbdəmən]	**Unterleib**
the bowels [ˈbaʊəlz] / **the intestines** [ɪnˈtestɪnz]	**der Darm**
When did you last have a bowel movement [ˈmuːvmənt]?	Wann hatten Sie das letzte Mal Stuhlgang?
faeces [ˈfiːsiːz] – **stools** – **motions**	**Stuhl; Kot**
He's got blood [blʌd] in his faeces / motions.	Er hat Blut im Stuhl.
buttocks (*Mit Pluralverb!*) [ˈbʌtəks]	**Gesäß; Hintern; Hinterteil**
a smack on the buttocks	ein Schlag / Klaps auf den Po
anus [ˈeɪnəs]	**After; Anus**

bladder ['blædə]	Blase
urine ['jʊərɪn] – **urinate** ['jʊərɪneɪt]	Urin / Harn – urinieren
genitals ['dʒenɪtəlz]	Genitalien; Geschlechtsteile
the male / female genitals	die männlichen / weiblichen Genitalien
vagina [və'dʒaɪnə]	Vagina; Scheide
ovary ['əʊvəri]	Eierstock
womb [wuːm] / **uterus** ['juːtərəs]	Gebärmutter / Uterus
penis ['piːnɪs]	Penis
prostate (gland) ['prɒsteɪt (glænd)]	Prostata; Vorsteherdrüse

Euphemismen

Ein Euphemismus ist eine beschönigende, „verhüllende" Umschreibung für etwas, das man sich scheut direkt auszusprechen, etwa wenn man dahinscheiden (= *pass away*) statt sterben (= *die* [daɪ]) sagt.
Für bestimmte Körperteile, Ausscheidungen etc. werden – z.B. beim Arzt (= *at the doctor's*) – häufig solche „indirekten" Ausdrücke gebraucht. Beispiele:
anus ['eɪnəs]: *back passage* • ***breast*** [brest]: *bust / chest* • ***buttocks:*** *behind / bottom / seat* • ***defecate*** ['defəkeɪt] (= Kot ausscheiden): *have the bowels opened* • ***faeces*** ['fiːsiːz] / ***stools:*** *motions* • ***genitals*** ['dʒenɪtəlz]: *private parts* • ***penis*** ['piːnɪs]: *private part(s) / privates* • ***urinate*** ['jʊərɪneɪt]: *pass water* • ***vagina*** [və'dʒaɪnə]: *down below, front passage, private (part)* • ***vomit*** ['vɒmɪt] (= erbrechen): *be sick*
Mit *Little Bill has had an accident* ['æksɪdənt] kann euphemistisch ausgedrückt werden, dass ihm ein Malheur passiert ist, er sich also in die Hose gemacht hat.
Beachten Sie in diesem Zusammenhang den Unterschied zwischen *my back* (= mein Rücken) und *my backside* (= mein Hintern)!

circulation [sɜːkju'leɪʃn]	(der) Kreislauf
blood [blʌd]	Blut
blood donor ['blʌd dəʊnə]	Blutspender(in)
vein [veɪn] – **artery** ['ɑːtəri]	Vene – Arterie
Varicose ['værɪkəʊs] veins are caused by poor circulation.	Krampfadern werden durch schlechte Durchblutung verursacht.
skeleton ['skelətən]	Skelett
bone [bəʊn]	Knochen
He's all skin and bone.	Er ist nur noch Haut und Knochen.
joint [dʒɔɪnt]	Gelenk
painful / swollen ['swəʊlən] joints	schmerzende / geschwollene Gelenke
skin [skɪn]	Haut
muscle ['mʌsl]	Muskel
gland [glænd]	Drüse
nerve [nɜːv]	Nerv
She has good / bad nerves.	Sie hat gute / schlechte Nerven.
He gets on my nerves.	Er geht mir auf die Nerven.
nervous ['nɜːvəs]	nervös; ängstlich; Nerven-
She is a nervous type [taɪp].	Sie ist ein nervöser / ängstlicher Typ.
He had a nervous breakdown.	Er erlitt einen Nervenzusammenbruch.

Outward appearance
Äußere Erscheinung

The Lord does not see as a mortal sees; mortals see only appearances but the Lord sees into the heart. (*Bible, 1 Samuel 16:7*)

tall [tɔːl] – **short** [ʃɔːt]
groß – klein (gewachsen)
slender ['slendə] / **slim** [slɪm]
schlank
thin [θɪn]
dünn
a thin man with the upright bearing ['beərɪŋ] of the professional soldier ['səʊldʒə]
ein dünner Mann mit der aufrechten / geraden Haltung des Berufssoldaten
wiry ['waɪəri]
drahtig
the wiry figure of a runner
die drahtige Figur eines Läufers
skinny ['skɪni]
mager; dünn
lean [liːn] – **gaunt** [gɔːnt]
mager – ausgemergelt
a lean boy of seventeen
ein schmaler Siebzehnjähriger
haggard ['hægəd]
ausgezehrt; verhärmt; abgespannt
underweight [-weɪt] – **overweight**
untergewichtig – übergewichtig
well-built [wel'bɪlt]
kräftig
a well-built, muscular ['mʌskjʊlə] man
ein kräftiger, muskulöser Mann
plump [plʌmp]
rundlich; mollig; pummelig
stout [staʊt]
korpulent; beleibt; füllig
a matronly [eɪ] woman, slightly stout
eine matronenhafte Frau, etwas füllig
portly ['pɔːtli]
beleibt; korpulent
the landlord's portly figure ['fɪgə]
die beleibte Gestalt des Wirts
buxom ['bʌksəm]
drall
a buxom, rosy-cheeked woman
eine dralle, rotbackige Frau
broad(-shouldered) [brɔːd'ʃəʊldəd]
breit(schultrig)
husky ['hʌski] / **burly** ['bɜːli]
kräftig (gebaut)
a husky longshoreman
ein bärenstarker Hafenarbeiter
stocky ['stɒki] / **thickset** [θɪk'set]
stämmig; gedrungen
a thickset policeman [pə'liːsmən]
ein stämmiger Polizist
dashing ['dæʃɪŋ]
flott; fesch; schneidig
a dashing young officer ['ɒfɪsə]
ein flotter junger Offizier
strapping ['stræpɪŋ]
stramm
a strapping young fellow
ein strammer junger Bursche
stooped [stuːpt] (with old age)
(vom Alter) **gebeugt**

Attractiveness [ə'træktɪvnəs] (**= Attraktivität**)
cute [kjuːt]: *a cute little baby* (= ein niedliches kleines Baby)
lovely ['lʌvli]: *a lovely little girl* (= ein reizendes kleines Mädchen)
attractive [ə'træktɪv]: *an attractive man* (= ein attraktiver Mann)
handsome ['hænsəm]: *young and handsome* (= jung und gut aussehend)
good-looking: *a good-looking man* (= ein gut aussehender Mann)
shapely ['ʃeɪpli]: *She has shapely legs.* (= Sie hat wohlgeformte Beine.)
smart: *a smart, lightly built man* (= ein schicker Mann von schlankem Wuchs)
pretty ['prɪti]: *a pretty young girl* (= ein hübsches junges Mädchen)
beautiful ['bjuːtəfl]: *beautiful blue eyes* (= wunderschöne blaue Augen)

1

3

Unattractiveness [ˌʌnə'træktɪvnəs] **(= mangelnde Attraktivität)**
homely AE: *a plump, homely woman* (= eine rundliche, wenig attraktive Frau)
plain: *She was plain, almost ugly.* (= Sie war unansehnlich, beinahe hässlich.)
unattractive: *a hard, unattractive woman* (= eine harte, unattraktive Frau)
unpleasant: *an unpleasant-looking man* (= ein unangenehm wirkender Mann)
ugly ['ʌgli]: *a fat, ugly woman* (= eine dicke, hässliche Frau)

face [feɪs]	**Gesicht**
an oval ['əʊvl] face – a round face	ein ovales Gesicht – ein rundes Gesicht
a bloated ['bləʊtɪd] face	ein aufgedunsenes Gesicht
eye [aɪ]	**Auge**
dark eyes – bright eyes	dunkle Augen – strahlende Augen
He was pale and hollow-eyed.	Er war bleich und hohläugig.
complexion [kəm'plekʃn]	**Gesichtsfarbe**
a ruddy / pallid ['pælɪd] complexion	eine rosige / bleiche Gesichtsfarbe
radiant ['reɪdiənt]	**strahlend; leuchtend**
She was radiant with joy.	Sie strahlte vor Freude.
wrinkles ['rɪŋklz] – **wrinkled** ['rɪŋkld]	**Falten – runzlig / faltig**

Zur Beschreibung des Haares
a trendy hairstyle ['heəstaɪl] / *hairdo* ['heədu:] (= eine aktuelle Frisur)
his shining blond [blɒnd] *locks* (= seine leuchtenden blonden Locken)
her beautiful blonde [blɒnd] *hair* (= ihr schönes blondes Haar)
brunettes, blondes, and redheads (= Brünette, Blondinen und Rothaarige)
a dark-haired / white-haired woman (= eine dunkelhaarige / weißhaarige Frau)
She wears her hair in a ponytail ['pəʊni-]. (= Sie trägt einen Pferdeschwanz.)
a teenager with cute [kju:t] *pigtails* (= ein Teenager mit niedlichen Zöpfen)
straight, curly, and frizzy ['frɪzi] *hair* (= glattes, lockiges und krauses Haar)
a crew cut ['kru: kʌt] (= ein Bürstenschnitt)
His hair is thinning ['θɪnɪŋ]. (= Sein Haar lichtet sich langsam.)
He wears [weəz] *a wig.* (= Er trägt eine Perücke.)
He's in his fifties turning grey. (= Er ist in den Fünfzigern und wird langsam grau.)
He's balding ['bɔ:ldɪŋ]. (= Er bekommt langsam eine Glatze.)
He's bald [bɔ:ld]. (= Er hat eine Glatze.)

dress [dres] – **dressed** [drest]	**Kleidung – gekleidet**
stylishly / trendily dressed	elegant / modisch gekleidet
She was dressed in a blouse and skirt.	Sie trug eine Bluse und einen Rock.
He's a smart dresser.	Er geht immer schick / flott gekleidet.
well groomed [u:] – **badly groomed**	**gepflegt – ungepflegt**
dishevelled [dɪ'ʃevld]	**ramponiert; ungepflegt**
his dishevelled / unkempt appearance	seine ungepflegte Erscheinung
dirty ['dɜːti] – **grubby** ['grʌbi]	**schmutzig – schmuddelig**
a grubby shirt	ein schmutziges / schmuddeliges Hemd
shabby ['ʃæbi] – **scruffy** ['skrʌfi]	**schäbig – vergammelt**
rumpled ['rʌmpld]	**zerknittert; verwuschelt; zerzaust**
He was wearing [eə] a rumpled suit.	Er trug einen zerknitterten Anzug.

Childhood and youth
Kindheit und Jugend

→ 2.3 Parents and children

A torn jacket is soon mended; but hard words bruise the heart of a child.
(*Henry Wadsworth Longfellow, US poet, 1807–1882*)

child [tʃaɪld] – **children** [ˈtʃɪldrən]	**Kind – Kinder**
child labour [eɪ] – child abuse [əˈbjuːs]	Kinderarbeit – Kindesmisshandlung
children's wear [weə]	Kinderbekleidung
childminder / nanny / baby-minder [aɪ]	Tagesmutter
She's an only child.	Sie ist ein Einzelkind.
baby [ˈbeɪbi] – **babies**	**Baby – Babys**
a newborn [ˈnjuːbɔːn] (baby / child)	ein Neugeborenes
baby-sitter / sitter	Babysitter

Mit *the baby boom* bezeichnet man den enormen Anstieg der Geburtenrate in den USA nach dem 2. Weltkrieg. Die Angehörigen dieser geburtenstarken Jahrgänge heißen noch heute *baby boomers* oder einfach *boomers* und entsprechen soziologisch etwa den Achtundsechzigern in Deutschland.

toddler – **infant** [ˈɪnfənt] – **small child**	**Kleinkind**
infancy [ˈɪnfənsi]	**frühe Kindheit; Kindesalter**
cradle [ˈkreɪdl]	**Wiege**
from the cradle to the grave [greɪv]	von der Wiege bis zur Bahre
cot [kɒt] BE / AE **crib** [krɪb]	**Kinderbett**
pram [præm] BE / AE **baby carriage** [ˈkærɪdʒ]	**Kinderwagen**
pushchair [ʊ] BE / AE **stroller** [əʊ]	**Buggy**
dummy [ʌ] BE / AE **pacifier** [æ]	**Schnuller**
crèche [kreʃ] BE	**Kinderkrippe**
(day) nursery [ˈnɜːsəri] BE / AE **day-care center**	**Kindergarten / -tagesstätte** (für 2- bis 5-Jährige)
playgroup [ˈpleɪgruːp]	**Spielgruppe** (für 2- bis 5-Jährige)
a **toy** [tɔɪ]	ein **Spielzeug**
Every child needs toys.	Jedes Kind braucht Spielzeug.
toy car – toy train set	Spielzeugauto – Spielzeugeisenbahn

Dinge, mit denen sich Kinder beschäftig(t)en
play (with a) ball (= Ball spielen) • *play cards* (= Karten spielen) • *play at cops and robbers* (= Räuber und Gendarm spielen) • *play at mothers and fathers* (= Mutter und Vater spielen)
doll [dɒl] (= Puppe) • *doll's pram* BE / AE *doll carriage* [ˈkærɪdʒ] (= Puppenwagen) • *doll's house* BE / AE *dollhouse* (= Puppenstube) • *stuffed animal* (= Stofftier) • *teddy bear* [eə] (= Teddybär) • *hand puppet* (= Handpuppe) • *rocking horse* (= Schaukelpferd)

building blocks ['bɪldɪŋ blɒks] (= Bauklötze) • *marbles* (= Murmeln)
model ['mɒdl] *railway* BE / AE *model railroad* (= Modelleisenbahn) •
model aircraft (= Modellflugzeug)
comics [ɒ] / *comic books* (= Comic-Hefte) • *comic strips* • *picture book*
(= Bilderbuch) • *fairy tale* (= Märchen)
colouring ['kʌlərɪŋ] *book* (= Malbuch) • *colouring set* (= Mal- / Tuschkasten) • *crayons* ['kreɪənz] (= Buntstifte) • *wax crayons* (= Wachsmal-
stifte) • *paints* (= Farben)
board [ɔ:] *game* (= Brettspiel) • *puzzle* ['pʌzl] (= Rätsel, Denksportaufgabe) •
jigsaw ['dʒɪgsɔ:] *(puzzle)* (= Puzzle / Puzzlespiel)
fly a kite (= einen Drachen steigen lassen) • *sandpit* BE / AE *sandbox*
(= Sandkasten) • *pail and shovel* ['ʃʌvl] (= Eimerchen und Schaufel) •
seesaw (= Wippe) • *swing* (= Schaukel) • *roller* [əʊ] *skates* (= Rollschuhe) •
ice skates (= Schlittschuhe) • *skateboard* (= Skateboard / Rollbrett) •
bicycle ['baɪsɪkl] / *bike* (= Fahrrad) • *tricycle* (= Dreirad) • *sledge* BE /
AE *sled* (= Schlitten)

young [jʌŋ]	**jung**
young people ['pi:pl]	junge Leute; Jugendliche
young children ['tʃɪldrən]	kleine Kinder
for the young	für die Jugend; für die jungen Leute
youngster ['jʌŋstə]	**Jugendliche(r)**

Männliche Jugendliche sind *boys, guys* [gaɪz], *lads, youngsters, youths*
[ju:ðz].
Weibliche Jugendliche sind *girls* oder (besonders nordenglisch oder
schottisch) *lasses* ['læsɪz], auch *young ladies*. Von manchen Männern
gebrauchte Slangwörter wie *chick* oder *bird* werden von Frauen oft als
beleidigend (= *offensive* [ə'fensɪv]) empfunden.

youth [ju:θ]	(die) **Jugend(zeit)**
youth club – youth hostel [ɒ]	Jugendklub – Jugendherberge

Entsprechungen für „Jugend"

Jugend = Jugendzeit:
I spent my youth in Hull. (= Ich habe meine Jugend in Hull verbracht.)
Jugend = junge Menschen:
Young people are optimistic [ɒptɪ'mɪstɪk]. (= Die Jugend ist optimistisch.)
Today's youth has its own problems ['prɒbləmz]. (= Die heutige Jugend hat
  ihre eigenen Probleme.)
The party never had the trust of the young. (= Die Partei besaß nie das
  Vertrauen der Jugend.)

brat [bræt]	**Balg; Gör(e); Flegel**
She's a spoilt [spɔɪlt] brat.	Sie ist ein verwöhntes Balg.
schoolboy – schoolgirl	**Schüler – Schülerin**
adolescent [ædə'lesnt]	**Heranwachsende(r)**
adolescence [ædə'lesns]	**das Erwachsenwerden**
puberty ['pju:bəti]	(die) **Pubertät**

a teenager / a teen   **ein Teenager**
A lot of teen(ager)s are on drugs.   Viele Teenager nehmen Drogen.
She spent her teenage years in London. Ihre Teenager-Jahre verbrachte sie
                                    in London.
a teen(age) mother ['mʌðə]   eine Mutter im Teenalter
a girl in her early teens   ein Mädchen zwischen 13 und 14
minor ['maɪnə]   **Minderjährige(r)**
come / be of age [eɪdʒ]   **großjährig werden / sein**

Ein paar ungute Dinge, die Kinder und Jugendliche tun
They bully ['bʊli] *other children.* (= Sie schikanieren / tyrannisieren andere
  Kinder.)
They play truant ['truːənt] BE / AE *hook(e)y.* (= Sie schwänzen die Schule.)
They drop out of school [skuːl]. (= Sie brechen die Schule ab.)
They run away from home. (*– ran – run*) (= Sie laufen von zu Hause weg.)
They go on joyrides. (= Sie machen Spritztouren mit gestohlenen Autos.)
They take / do drugs. (= Sie nehmen Drogen.)
They get into trouble ['trʌbl] *with the police* [pə'liːs]. (= Sie kriegen Ärger
  mit der Polizei.)

juvenile ['dʒuːvənaɪl]   **Jugend-**
juvenile court   Jugendgericht
juvenile delinquent [dɪ'lɪŋkwənt] (JD) jugendliche(r) Straftäter(in)
juvenile detention [dɪ'tenʃn] center *AE* Jugendstrafanstalt

Violence ['vaɪələns] **(= Gewaltanwendung)**
Why did you kick me? (= Warum hast du mich getreten?)
Dad! Peter keeps hitting me! (= Papi! Der Peter haut mich immer!)
He thumped her in the stomach ['stʌmək]. (= Er schlug ihr / sie in den
  Magen.)
Corporal punishment of children is illegal [ɪ'liːgl] *in some countries.* (= Die kör-
  perliche Züchtigung von Kindern ist in manchen Ländern rechtswidrig.)
Kids got beaten ['biːtn] *a lot in the old days.* (= Die Kinder bekamen früher
  oft Schläge.)
I don't like to smack my child. (= Ich haue mein Kind nicht gern.)
If you don't stop it, you'll get a spanking / a thrashing ['θræʃɪŋ] */ a good
  hiding.* (= Wenn du nicht aufhörst, kriegst du 'ne Tracht Prügel.)

adult ['ædʌlt]   **erwachsen; Erwachsene(r)**
a programme intended to appeal   ein Programm, das junge Erwachsene
  to young adults   ansprechen soll
grown-up [grəʊn'ʌp / 'grəʊnʌp] **erwachsen**
They have two grown-up ['grəʊnʌp] Sie haben zwei erwachsene Söhne.
  sons.
grownup ['grəʊnʌp]   Erwachsene(r) *(aus der Sicht von
                          Kindern)*

You grownups don't understand   Ihr Erwachsenen versteht uns
  us kids.   Kinder nicht.

Middle age and old age
Mittlere Jahre und Alter

The only time you really live fully is from thirty to sixty. ... The young are slaves to dreams; the old servants of regrets. (*Hervey Allen, US novelist, 1889–1949*)

middle age [mɪdl 'eɪdʒ]	das mittlere Lebensalter (ca. 40–65)
mid-life crisis [mɪdlaɪf 'kraɪsɪs]	Krise in der Lebensmitte (um die 40)
mature [mə'tʃʊə] – **maturity**	(*körperlich, geistig*) **reif** – **Reife**
a mature student *BE*	Student(in) über 25
prime [praɪm]	**Höhepunkt; Krönung**
She's in her prime.	Sie ist in den besten Jahren.
She's past her prime.	Sie ist über die besten Jahre hinaus.
spring chicken [sprɪŋ 'tʃɪkən]	**junges Huhn**
She's no spring chicken.	Sie ist nicht mehr die Jüngste.
life expectancy [ɪk'spektənsi]	(die) **Lebenserwartung**
ageing ['eɪdʒɪŋ] *BE* / *AE* **aging**	das Altern
menopause / **the change of life**	die Wechseljahre
the onset of menopause ['menəpɔːz]	das Einsetzen der Wechseljahre
grow old / **get old**	alt werden
get on (in years) (– got – got)	(langsam) älter werden
We're getting on (in years).	Wir werden langsam älter.
elderly ['eldəli]	ältere(r, s)
poverty ['pɒvəti] among the elderly	Armut unter älteren Menschen

☞ Die Adjektive *elderly* und *older* haben nicht die gleiche Bedeutung! *Elderly* bezeichnet Menschen, die (absolut) alt sind: *elderly people* ['piːpl] (= ältere / alte Leute / Menschen). *Older people* dagegen sind relativ älter als andere, aber nicht notwendigerweise alt: *older people are more experienced* [ɪk'spɪəriənst] (= ältere Menschen haben mehr Erfahrung). – In *the older generation* [dʒenə'reɪʃn] (= die ältere Generation) z.B. kann *older* nicht durch *elderly* ersetzt werden.

the old folk [fəʊk]	die alten Leute
old folk's home / old people's home	Altenheim; Altersheim
veteran ['vetərən]	(*auch* Kriegs-)**Veteran(in)**
a veteran diplomat / teacher	ein altgedienter Diplomat / Lehrer
of pensionable ['penʃənəbl] **age**	im Renten- / Pensionsalter
(old-age) pensioner *BE* / *AE* **retiree**	Rentner(in)
retire [rɪ'taɪə]	in den Ruhestand treten
a retired civil servant [sɪvl 'sɜːvənt]	ein pensionierter Beamter / eine pensionierte Beamtin
occupation [ɒkjə'peɪʃn]: retired	Beruf: Rentner(in)
retirement [rɪ'taɪəmənt]	**Ausscheiden aus dem Arbeitsleben**
when she reaches retirement age	wenn sie das Rentenalter erreicht
at an advanced [əd'vɑːnst] **age**	in vorgerücktem Alter
old age [əʊld 'eɪdʒ]	das Alter
the approach [ə'prəʊtʃ] of old age	das Herannahen des Alters
She lived to a ripe old age.	Sie erreichte ein hohes Alter.

Wenn von *old age* oder *elderly people* die Rede ist, werden oft Euphemismen (= beschönigende / verhüllende Ausdrücke) verwendet: *women of a certain age* sind in mittleren Jahren, *a distinguished* [dɪˈstɪŋgwɪʃt] *professor* ist einer, der schon älter ist, das Alter selbst wird oft als *the golden years, her sunset years* oder *his twilight years* umschrieben. Ein *old people's home* BE / AE *old-age home* erhält solche weniger „direkt" klingenden Namen wie *nursing home, rest home, convalescent* [kɒnvəˈlesnt] *home* (eigentlich = Genesungsheim) oder schlicht *home,* wenn es nicht angedeutet wird mit so etwas wie *somewhere (s)he can be looked after* (= wo man sich um ihn / sie kümmern kann). Die deutschen Senioren sind auf Englisch *senior citizens*; vorher ist man *middle-aged* und sagt zuweilen scherzhaft, man sei *on the wrong side of forty*.

longevity [lɒnˈdʒevəti]	**Langlebigkeit**
decline [dɪˈklaɪn]	**Verfall; abnehmen**
declining physical energy [ˈenədʒi]	nachlassende körperliche Energie
in his declining years	in seinen letzten Lebensjahren
decrepit [dɪˈkrepɪt]	**altersschwach**
a decrepit old man	ein hinfälliger alter Mann

Weitere Adjektive, die Schwäche (= *weakness / feebleness*) bzw. Gebrechlichkeit (= *infirmity* [ɪnˈfɜːməti]) ausdrücken: *weak* (= schwach) • *feeble* (= matt / schwach) • *frail* (= schwach / gebrechlich / zart) • *infirm* [ɪnˈfɜːm] (= gebrechlich / hinfällig)

senile [ˈsiːnaɪl] – **senility** [sɪˈnɪləti]	**senil – Senilität**
Alzheimer's [ˈæltshaɪməz] **disease**	**die Alzheimerkrankheit**
suffer from Alzheimer's (disease)	an der Alzheimerkrankheit leiden

Unfreundliche, diskriminierende Ausdrücke, die auf ältere Menschen angewandt werden: *gaga* [ˈgɑːgɑː] (= verkalkt / senil) • *fuddy-duddy* [ˈfʌdidʌdi] (= verknöchert / verkalkt) • *doddering / doddery* (= tatterig / vertrottelt) • *(s)he's past it* (= er / sie bringt's nicht mehr)

in poor health [helθ]	**bei schlechter Gesundheit**
meals on wheels [miːlz ɒn ˈwiːlz]	**Essen auf Rädern**
nursing home [ˈnɜːsɪŋ həʊm]	**Pflegeheim**
admit someone to a nursing home	jemand in ein Pflegeheim aufnehmen

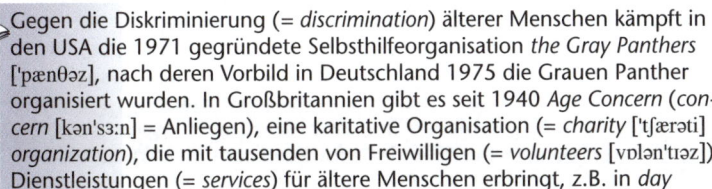

Gegen die Diskriminierung (= *discrimination*) älterer Menschen kämpft in den USA die 1971 gegründete Selbsthilfeorganisation *the Gray Panthers* [ˈpænθəz], nach deren Vorbild in Deutschland 1975 die Grauen Panther organisiert wurden. In Großbritannien gibt es seit 1940 *Age Concern* (*concern* [kənˈsɜːn] = Anliegen), eine karitative Organisation (= *charity* [ˈtʃærəti] *organization*), die mit tausenden von Freiwilligen (= *volunteers* [vɒlənˈtɪəz]) Dienstleistungen (= *services*) für ältere Menschen erbringt, z.B. in *day centres* und *lunch clubs* sowie durch *visits to the elderly in their homes*.

Personality and behaviour
Persönlichkeit und Verhalten

Although aloof, egotistical and imperious, MacArthur could also be warm-hearted, human, and witty. Most people agreed that he was courageous and highly intelligent ... (*Charakterisierung des US-Generals Douglas MacArthur, 1880–1964, in The Academic American Encyclopedia*)

behave [bɪ'heɪv]
He behaved like a bull [bʊl] in a china ['tʃaɪnə] shop.
personality [pɜːsə'næləti]
She has an appealing personality.
temper ['tempə]
She has a quick / violent temper.
She lost her temper.

sich benehmen / verhalten
Er benahm sich / führte sich auf wie ein Elefant im Porzellanladen.
Persönlichkeit
Sie besitzt ein sympathisches Wesen.
Wesen; Naturell
Sie hat ein heftiges Naturell.
Sie verlor die Beherrschung.

Adjektive, die menschliche Eigenschaften ausdrücken, mit ihrem Gegenteil
Die Antonyme (= Gegensatzwörter) werden hier durch Vorsetzen von *dis-, im-, in-, ir-* oder *un-* gebildet.
contented [kən'tentɪd] (= zufrieden) – *discontented* (= unzufrieden)
honest ['ɒnəst] (= ehrlich) – *dishonest* [dɪs'ɒnəst] (= unehrlich)
mature [mə'tʃʊə] (= reif) – *immature* [ɪmə'tʃʊə] (= unreif)
patient ['peɪʃnt] (= geduldig) – *impatient* [ɪm'peɪʃnt] (= ungeduldig)
polite [pə'laɪt] (= höflich) – *impolite* [ɪmpə'laɪt] (= unhöflich)
considerate [kən'sɪdərət] (= rücksichtsvoll) – *inconsiderate* (= rücksichtslos)
decent ['diːsnt] (= anständig) – *indecent* [ɪn'diːsnt] (= unanständig)
efficient [ɪ'fɪʃnt] (= fähig) – *inefficient* [ɪnɪ'fɪʃnt] (= unfähig)
experienced [ɪk'spɪəriənst] (= erfahren) – *inexperienced* (= unerfahren)
flexible ['fleksəbl] (= flexibel) – *inflexible* [ɪn'fleksəbl] (= unflexibel)
sincere [sɪn'sɪə] (= aufrichtig) – *insincere* [ɪnsɪn'sɪə] (= unaufrichtig)
tolerant ['tɒlərənt] (= duldsam) – *intolerant* [ɪn'tɒlərənt] (= unduldsam)
responsible (= verantwortungsbewusst) – *irresponsible* (= verantwortungslos)
civilized ['sɪvəlaɪzd] (= kultiviert) – *uncivilized* [ʌn'sɪvəlaɪzd] (= unkultiviert)
cooperative [kəʊ'ɒprətɪv] (= entgegenkommend) – *uncooperative* (= wenig entgegenkommend)
fair [feə] (= fair / gerecht) – *unfair* [ʌn'feə] (= unfair / ungerecht)
inhibited [ɪn'hɪbɪtɪd] (= gehemmt) – *uninhibited* (= ungehemmt)
pleasant ['pleznt] (= sympathisch) – *unpleasant* [ʌn'pleznt] (= unsympathisch)
reliable [rɪ'laɪəbl] (= zuverlässig / verlässlich) – *unreliable* (= unzuverlässig)
selfish ['selfɪʃ] (= selbstsüchtig) – *unselfish* [ʌn'selfɪʃ] (= selbstlos)
sophisticated [sə'fɪstɪ-] (= anspruchsvoll) – *unsophisticated* (= anspruchslos)
sympathetic [sɪmpə'θetɪk] (= mitfühlend) – *unsympathetic* (= wenig mitfühlend)
Beachten Sie, dass – anders als im Deutschen – die negativen Vorsilben *dis-, im-, in-, ir-, un-* etc. im Englischen nicht betont werden.
Deutsch: Sie ist ja so 'unfair / 'unduldsam / 'unzufrieden.

Englisch: *She is so un'fair / in'tolerant / discon'tented.*
Die Adjektivendung *-ful* wird im Antonym häufig durch *-less* ersetzt:
careful ['keəfl] (= vorsichtig) – *careless* ['keələs] (= unvorsichtig)
tactful ['tæktfl] (= taktvoll) – *tactless* ['tæktləs] (= taktlos)

good [gʊd] – **bad** [bæd]   gut – schlecht
benevolent [-'nev-] – **malevolent**   gütig – boshaft
a benevolent master / god / ruler   ein gütiger Herr / Gott / Herrscher
a malevolent [-'lev-] look / neighbour   ein boshafter Blick / Nachbar
compassionate [kəm'pæʃnət] –   mitfühlend – mitleidlos
  pitiless ['pɪtɪləs]
He's pitiless in exploiting others.   Er nutzt andere erbarmungslos aus.
honest ['ɒnəst] – **corrupt** [kə'rʌpt]   ehrlich – korrupt
a plain, honest man   ein schlichter, ehrlicher Mensch
a corrupt politician [pɒlə'tɪʃn]   ein(e) korrupte(r) Politiker(in)

Viele der hier aufgeführten Adjektive werden durch Anhängen von *-ly*
zu häufig gebrauchten Adverbien:
He acted foolishly / unselfishly / irresponsibly / immaturely. (= Er handelte
  töricht / selbstlos / verantwortungslos / unreif.)
She behaved tactfully / wisely / courageously / sensibly. (= Sie verhielt sich
  taktvoll / klug / mutig / vernünftig.)

industrious [ɪn'dʌstriəs] – **lazy** ['leɪzi]   fleißig – faul
courteous ['kɜːtiəs] – **rude** [ruːd]   höflich – unhöflich
No need to be rude.   Warum denn gleich grob werden?
clever ['klevə] – **stupid** ['stjuːpɪd]   klug – dumm
sensible ['sensəbl] – **foolish** ['fuːlɪʃ]   vernünftig – töricht

Achtung, „falsche Freunde" (= *false* [fɔːls] *friends*)!
sensitive ['sensətɪv] = sensibel, *sensible* ['sensəbl] = vernünftig!
Self-conscious [self'kɒnʃəs] heißt gehemmt; selbstbewusst dagegen ist
self-confident [self'kɒnfɪdənt] oder *self-assured* [selfə'ʃʊəd].

excitable [ɪk'saɪtəbl] – **even-**   leicht erregbar – ausgeglichen
  tempered [iːvn'tempəd]
conservative [kən'sɜːvətɪv] –   konservativ – progressiv
  progressive [prə'gresɪv]
broad-minded – **narrow-minded**   tolerant – engstirnig
very broad-minded views about sex   sehr freie Ansichten über Sex
generous ['dʒenərəs] – **stingy** [dʒ]   großzügig – geizig / knauserig
easygoing [iːzi'gəʊɪŋ] – **fussy** ['fʌsi]   lax / lässig – pingelig

Das vollkommene Fehlen einer Eigenschaft kann durch *devoid* [dɪ'vɔɪd] *of*
ausgedrückt werden:
She's completely devoid of ambition / courage / humour / pity / talent.
(= Es mangelt ihr vollkommen an Ehrgeiz / Mut / Humor / Mitleid / Talent.)

charming – **devoid of charm** [tʃɑːm]   charmant – ohne Charme
She's devoid of any charm.   Sie besitzt keinerlei Charme.

1

6

optimistic [ˌɒptɪˈmɪstɪk] – **pessimistic**	optimistisch – pessimistisch
outgoing – **reserved** [rɪˈzɜːvd]	kontaktfreudig – zurückhaltend
cheerful [ˈtʃɪəfl] – **gloomy** [ˈgluːmi]	gut gelaunt – trübsinnig
Jack was looking rather gloomy.	Jack schaute recht bedrückt drein.
interesting [ˈɪntrəstɪŋ] – **boring** [ɔː]	interessant – langweilig

> **Fairly, rather, pretty als Entsprechungen für „ziemlich"**
> *Fairly* steht vorzugsweise bei „wünschenswerten" Eigenschaften: *She's
> fairly attractive. He remained fairly calm. Their behaviour was fairly civilized.*
> *Rather* wird bei „nicht wünschenswerten" Eigenschaften bevorzugt:
> *He was rather aggressive* [əˈgresɪv]. *That was a rather stupid thing to do.
> The new secretary proved* [pruːvd] *to be rather inefficient* [ˌɪnɪˈfɪʃnt].
> *Pretty* [ˈprɪti] ist umgangssprachlicher als *fairly* und *rather* und wird
> gleichermaßen bei „wünschenswerten" und „nicht wünschenswerten"
> Eigenschaften gebraucht: *She's pretty good / bad. He's pretty clever / stupid.*

strong [strɒŋ] – **weak** [wiːk]	stark – schwach
tough [tʌf] – **weak** [wiːk]	zäh / hart – schwach
a tough guy [gaɪ]	ein harter Bursche / Typ
My grandmother was a tough cookie – she buried [ˈberid] three husbands.	Meine Großmutter war ein zäher Typ – sie hat drei Männer überlebt.
brave / **courageous** – **cowardly**	mutig – feige
a brave soldier [ˈbreiv ˈsəʊldʒə]	ein(e) tapfere(r) Soldat(in)
a cowardly attack [ˈkaʊədli əˈtæk]	ein feiger Anschlag
a craven coward [ˈkreivn ˈkaʊəd]	eine feige Memme
relaxed [rɪˈlækst] – **tense** [tens]	entspannt – angespannt
calm [kɑːm] – **agitated** [ˈædʒɪteɪtɪd]	ruhig – aufgeregt
He was very calm before the operation.	Er war vor der Operation sehr ruhig.
respectful – **cheeky** *BE* / *AE* **sassy**	respektvoll – frech
Don't be sassy with your parents.	Sei nicht frech zu deinen Eltern.
humble [ˈhʌmbl] – **conceited** [-ˈsiːtɪd]	demütig / bescheiden – eingebildet

Für die Beschreibung von Menschen gibt es eine Reihe von *idioms* mit *as …
as* (= so … wie). Beispiele:
*He's **as bold as brass** [brɑːs].* (= kühn wie Messing = frech wie Oskar)
*He was **as brave as a lion** [ˈlaɪən].* (= so tapfer / mutig wie ein Löwe)
*She's **as busy** [ˈbɪzi] **as a bee**.* (= emsig wie eine Biene, bienenfleißig)
*He's **as clever as they make them**.* (= schlau wie sonst was)
*She's **as cold as charity**.* (= kalt wie eine Hundeschnauze)
*He was **as cool as a cucumber** [ˈkjuː-].* (= kühl wie eine Gurke = seelenruhig)
*His agent is **as cunning as a fox**.* (= schlau wie ein Fuchs)
Lincoln [ˈlɪŋkən] *was **as honest** [ˈɒnəst] **as the day is long**.* (= grundehrlich)
*He's **as mad as a hatter**.* (= verrückt wie ein Hutmacher = total verrückt)
*He was **as meek as a lamb** [læm].* (= sanft wie ein Lamm = lammfromm)
*He's **as stubborn as a mule**.* (= störrisch wie ein Maultier = ein sturer Bock)
*Her teacher is **as patient** [ˈpeɪʃnt] **as Job** [dʒəʊb].* (= so geduldig wie Hiob)
*He was **as proud as a peacock** [ˈpiːkɒk].* (= stolz wie ein Pfau)
*The man's **as thick as two planks**.* (= „dumm wie Bohnenstroh")
*He's **as timid as a mouse** [maʊs].* (= scheu / schüchtern wie eine Maus)

Senses and sensations
Sinne und Sinneseindrücke

A fool sees not the same tree that a wise man sees.
(*William Blake, English poet, artist, and mystic, 1757–1827*)

sense [sens]
the five senses ['sensɪz]
the sense of sight / hearing
the sense of smell / taste / touch

sensation [sen'seɪʃn]
such sensations as pain and thirst

eye [aɪ]
see [siː] (– saw [sɔː] – seen)
She saw that nobody was looking.
look [lʊk]
Did you look in the kitchen?
I'm looking for my glasses.
Have a look at this one.
perceive [pə'siːv] – **perception**
Can all animals perceive light?
notice ['nəʊtɪs]
No one noticed the theft [θeft].
She took no notice of them.
noticeable ['nəʊtɪsəbl]
a noticeable increase ['ɪŋkriːs]
watch [wɒtʃ]
She watched the dog eat(ing).
We watched a video ['vɪdiəʊ].
observe [əb'zɜːv]

sight [saɪt]
It was love at first sight.
shortsighted *BE* / *AE* nearsighted
He's longsighted *BE* / *AE* farsighted.
view [vjuː]
Slowly the train came into view.
a fine view of the city
visible ['vɪzəbl] – **invisible**
The lighthouse was clearly visible.
invisible to the naked ['neɪkɪd] eye
visual ['vɪʒuəl]
visual aids [vɪʒuəl 'eɪdz]
video ['vɪdiəʊ]
glance [glɑːns]
You can see it at a glance.
He glanced through the paper.

Sinn
die fünf Sinne
der Gesichts- / Gehörsinn
der Geruchs- / Geschmacks- /
    Tastsinn
Gefühl; Empfindung; Sinneseindruck
Empfindungen wie Schmerz und
    Durst
Auge
sehen (– sah – gesehen)
Sie sah, dass niemand hinschaute.
sehen; schauen; Blick
Hast du in der Küche nachgesehen?
Ich suche meine Brille.
Schau dir doch mal dies hier an.
wahrnehmen – Wahrnehmung
Können alle Tiere Licht wahrnehmen?
bemerken; wahrnehmen
Niemand bemerkte den Diebstahl.
Sie nahm keine Notiz von ihnen.
erkennbar; deutlich
eine deutliche / merkliche Zunahme
beobachten; sich (etw.) **ansehen**
Sie sah zu, wie der Hund fraß.
Wir sahen uns ein Video an.
**beobachten; bemerken; wahr-
    nehmen**

(das) **Sehvermögen**
Es war Liebe auf den ersten Blick.
kurzsichtig
Er ist weitsichtig.
Sicht; Aussicht
Langsam kam der Zug in Sicht.
ein schöner Ausblick auf die Stadt
sichtbar – unsichtbar
Der Leuchtturm war deutlich sichtbar.
mit bloßem Auge nicht erkennbar
visuell; Seh-
visuelle Hilfsmittel / Medien
Video(-)
(kurzer) Blick; (kurz) sehen / blicken
Man sieht es auf einen Blick.
Er warf einen Blick in die Zeitung.

glimpse [glɪmps]
We just caught a glimpse of him.
I just glimpsed through the article.
(kurzer) Blick; (kurz) sehen
Wir bekamen ihn nur kurz zu Gesicht.
Ich habe den Artikel nur überflogen.
ear [ɪə]
I'll keep my ears open.
Ohr
Ich werde die Ohren offen halten.
hear [hɪə] (– heard [ɜː] – heard)
Did you hear that noise [nɔɪz]?
hören (– hörte – gehört)
Hast du das Geräusch gehört?
hearing ['hɪərɪŋ]
He's a little hard of hearing.
Gehör
Er ist ein bisschen schwerhörig.
hearing aid ['hɪərɪŋ eɪd]
deaf [def]
a deaf-mute [def'mjuːt]
He's deaf and dumb [dʌm].
Hörhilfe; Hörgerät
taub
ein(e) Taubstumme(r)
Er ist taubstumm.

Bestimmte Adjektive können durch vorangestelltes *the* zu Pluralnomen
gemacht werden:
guide dogs for the blind (= „Führerhunde für die Blinden" = Blindenhunde)
a school for the deaf (= eine Schule für Taube / taube Menschen)
aids for the hard-of-hearing (= Hilfen für Schwerhörige)

listen ['lɪsn]
I listened hard but couldn't hear it.
(zu)hören
Ich lauschte angestrengt, konnte es
  aber nicht hören.
listen to the radio ['reɪdiəʊ]
sound [saʊnd]
the sound of an approaching car
It sounds like a diesel engine.
a soundproof booth [buːð]
tone [təʊn]
I don't like your tone (of voice).
loud [laʊd] – **loudness** ['laʊdnəs]
Try to speak louder / more loudly.
volume ['vɒljuːm]
turn the volume up / down
audible ['ɔːdəbl] – **inaudible**
a scarcely ['skeəsli] audible sound
audio ['ɔːdiəʊ]
CD players and other audio equipment
noise [nɔɪz]
What was that loud noise?
I can't stand the noise.
noisy ['nɔɪzi] – **noiseless** ['nɔɪzləs]
The air-conditioning is too noisy.
Radio hören
Geräusch; Laut; Klang; klingen
das Geräusch eines nahenden Autos
Es klingt wie ein Dieselmotor.
eine schalldichte Kabine
Ton
Mir gefällt dein Ton nicht.
laut – „Lautheit" / Lautstärke
Versuchen Sie lauter zu sprechen.
Lautstärke
das Gerät lauter / leiser stellen
hörbar – unhörbar
ein kaum wahrnehmbarer Laut
Audio-; Ton-
CD-Spieler und andere Audiogeräte
Geräusch; Lärm; Krach
Was war das für ein lautes Geräusch?
Ich kann den Lärm nicht aushalten.
geräuschvoll / laut – geräuschlos
Die Klimaanlage ist zu laut.

Entsprechungen für „ruhig"
*We live in a **quiet** neighbourhood.* (= Wir leben in einer ruhigen Gegend.)
*Business is **quiet** ['kwaɪət] at the moment.* (= Das Geschäft ist zurzeit ruhig.)
*She's always so **silent** ['saɪlənt], as if she had nothing to say.* (= Sie ist immer
  so ruhig, als ob sie nichts zu sagen hätte.)
*The sea was absolutely **calm** [kɑːm].* (= Das Meer war vollkommen ruhig.)

She has difficulty ['dɪfɪkəlti] *sitting **still**.* (= Es fällt ihr schwer, ruhig zu sitzen.)
*At last a **peaceful** evening at home.* (= Endlich ein ruhiger Abend zu Hause.)
*We had a **smooth*** [smuːð] *crossing.* (= Wir hatten eine ruhige Überfahrt.)
*You need a **steady*** ['stedi] *hand.* (= Man braucht eine ruhige Hand.)

nose [nəʊz]	Nase
a nose for profitable ['prɒfətəbl] deals	eine Nase für lohnende Geschäfte
smell [smel]	**riechen; Geruch**
Can't you smell the gas [gæs]?	Riechst du nicht das Gas?
The soup smells delicious [dɪ'lɪʃəs].	Die Suppe riecht köstlich.

Idiom: *I can smell a rat here.* (= Hier ist doch irgendetwas faul.)
Wenn allerdings Hamlet sagt: „Etwas ist faul im Staate Dänemark", dann
heißt das in Shakespeares Original: *Something is rotten in the state of Denmark.*
Rotten heißt faul im Sinn von verdorben: *a rotten egg / tooth / apple* (= ein
faules Ei / ein fauler Zahn / Apfel). *Rotten apple* wird auch in übertragenem
Sinn gebraucht: *Our police as a whole are OK, but there are a few rotten apples among them.* (= Unsere Polizei als Ganzes ist in Ordnung, aber es
sind ein paar schwarze Schafe darunter.)

odour ['əʊdə]	**Geruch; Gestank**
stink [ɪ] (– stank [æ] – stunk [ʌ])	**stinken** (– stank – gestunken)
fragrance ['freɪgrəns]	**(Wohl-)Geruch; Duft**
the unique fragrance of these roses	der besondere Duft dieser Rosen
scent [sent]	**Duft; Geruch;** *BE auch* **Parfüm**
the scent of lemons ['lemənz]	der Geruch von Zitronen
perfume ['pɜːfjuːm]	**Parfüm; Duft; parfümieren**
aroma [ə'rəʊmə]	**Aroma; Duft**

Engl. ***aroma*** wird gerochen und als angenehm empfunden, ist also *Duft*.
Dt. **Aroma** wird geschmeckt und als angenehm empfunden, engl. =
flavour / taste: the aroma of fresh-ground coffee (= der Duft frisch gemahlenen Kaffees) *These tomatoes have no flavour / taste at all.* (= Diese Tomaten
haben überhaupt kein Aroma / keinen Geschmack.)

taste [teɪst]	**Geschmack; schmecken**
It has a bitter taste.	Es hat einen bitteren Geschmack.
It tastes sweet / salty ['sɔːlti] / sour.	Es schmeckt süß / salzig / sauer.
flavour ['fleɪvə]	**Aroma; Geschmack**
appetite ['æpətaɪt]	**Appetit**
It has spoilt my appetite.	Es hat mir den Appetit verdorben.
touch [tʌtʃ]	**berühren; Berührung; (Tast-)Gefühl**
Please do not touch.	Bitte nicht berühren.
The material has a very soft touch.	Der Stoff fühlt sich sehr weich an.
handle ['hændl]	**anfassen; berühren**
Please do not handle the goods.	Die Waren bitte nicht berühren.
feel [fiːl] (– felt – felt)	**fühlen** (– fühlte – gefühlt)
She didn't feel the pain.	Sie spürte den Schmerz nicht.

Feelings and attitudes
Gefühle und Einstellungen

It is not that the Englishman can't feel – it is that he is afraid to feel. He has been taught at his public school that feeling is bad form. He must not express great joy or sorrow, or even open his mouth too wide when he talks – his pipe might fall out if he did. (*E.M. Forster, English novelist, 1879–1970*)

attitude ['ætɪtjuːd]
her attitude to(wards) foreigners
feeling ['fiːlɪŋ]
I didn't mean to hurt your feelings.
feel [fiːl] (– felt – felt)
She was feeling tired and depressed.
I feel like a drink.
emotion [ɪ'məʊʃn]
emotions such as joy and fear
emotional [ɪ'məʊʃnəl]
a highly emotional moment
people who are emotionally disturbed
mood [muːd]
I'm not in the mood for joking.
She isn't in a good mood.
temper ['tempə]
He was in a good / bad temper.
urge [ɜːdʒ]
He felt an urge to pray [preɪ].
love [lʌv]
I love swimming in the sea.
I'd love to stay here.
like [laɪk]
I don't like wine.
I like travelling by train.
Would you like a drink?
I'd (= I would) like to stay longer.
his likes and dislikes ['dɪslaɪks]
enjoy [ɪn'dʒɔɪ]
I enjoy being with you.
fancy ['fænsi]
He fancies cars.
care for somebody
She really cares for us.
I don't much care for rap.
adore [ə'dɔː]
She adores Brahms.

Einstellung; Haltung
ihre Einstellung gegenüber Ausländern
Gefühl
Ich wollte dich nicht verletzen.
fühlen (– fühlte – gefühlt)
Sie fühlte sich müde und deprimiert.
Mir ist nach einem Drink zumute.
Gefühl; Emotion
Gefühle wie Freude und Furcht
emotional
ein sehr bewegender Augenblick
Menschen, die seelisch gestört sind
Stimmung
Mir ist nicht nach Spaßen zumute.
Sie ist nicht in guter Stimmung.
Laune
Er hatte gute / schlechte Laune.
Bedürfnis; Drang
Er fühlte den Drang zu beten.
(es) lieben; Liebe
Ich liebe es, im Meer zu schwimmen.
Gern würde ich hier bleiben.
mögen; gern haben
Ich mag keinen Wein.
Ich reise gern mit dem Zug.
Hätten Sie gern was zu trinken?
Ich würde gern länger bleiben.
seine Neigungen und Abneigungen
genießen
Ich bin sehr gern mit dir zusammen.
gern haben (wollen)
Autos haben es ihm angetan.
jemand gern haben
Sie ist uns wirklich zugetan.
Ich mache mir nicht viel aus Rap.
anbeten
Sie schwärmt für Brahms.

Wie man Liebe, Zuneigung, Gernhaben ausdrückt
We immediately took a liking to her. (= Sie war uns sofort sympathisch.)
I'm very fond of wine. (= Ich trinke sehr gern Wein.)

I'm not wildly keen on fish. (= Auf Fisch bin ich nicht so versessen.)
The idea had caught her fancy. (= Der Gedanke hatte es ihr angetan.)
He enjoys everyone's affection. (= Er genießt die Zuneigung aller.)
This task would appeal to me. (= Diese Aufgabe würde mich reizen.)
Old books fascinate ['fæsmeɪt] *me.* (= Alte Bücher faszinieren mich.)

desire [dɪ'zaɪə]	Wunsch; Begehren; begehren
the desire for peace / love	das Verlangen nach Frieden / Liebe
the desired effect [ɪ'fekt]	die erwünschte Wirkung
long for [lɒŋ]	**sich sehnen nach**
They all long for peace.	Sie sehnen sich alle nach Frieden.
crave (for) [kreɪv] – **craving**	**sich sehnen nach – Verlangen**
She craves (for) recognition.	Sie giert nach Anerkennung.
She has a craving for pickles.	Sie hat einen Heißhunger auf Gewürzgurken.
interest – interesting ['ɪntrəstɪŋ]	**Interesse – interessant**
He read [red] it with great interest.	Er las es mit großem Interesse.

Verwechseln Sie nicht *interested* (= interessiert) mit *interesting* (= interessant)! Und beachten Sie, dass *Ich interessiere mich für …* auf Englisch mit *I'm interested in …* ausgedrückt wird:
I'm interested in history. (= Ich interessiere mich für Geschichte.)

prefer [prɪ'fɜ:]	**(es) vorziehen**
I prefer the CD-ROM to the book.	Ich ziehe die CD-ROM dem Buch vor.
I prefer travelling by train.	Ich reise lieber mit dem Zug.
I'd prefer to go by train.	Ich würde lieber mit dem Zug fahren.

Sehr heißt in Bezug auf Verben nicht *very*, sondern *very much*:
He loves / admires her very much. (= Er liebt / bewundert sie sehr.)

bear [beə] (– bore [ɔ:] – borne)	**ertragen** (– ertrug – ertragen)
He can't bear being criticized.	Er verträgt keine Kritik.
stand [stænd]	**ertragen; aushalten**
I can't stand the heat.	Ich halte die Hitze nicht aus.
tolerate ['tɒləreɪt]	**tolerieren; dulden**
I wouldn't tolerate that.	Das würde ich nicht hinnehmen.
put up with (– put – put) [pʊt]	**sich abfinden mit; sich gefallen lassen**
That's something I won't up with.	So etwas lasse ich mir nicht bieten.
dislike [dɪs'laɪk]	**nicht mögen; nicht leiden können**
She dislikes him intensely [ɪn'tensli].	Er ist ihr äußerst unsympathisch.
hate [heɪt]	**(es) hassen; Hass**
I hate having to rush [rʌʃ].	Ich hasse es, wenn ich hetzen muss.
Her eyes were full of hate.	Ihre Augen waren voller Hass.
hatred ['heɪtrɪd]	**Hass**
Stalin's hatred of intellectuals	Stalins Hass auf Intellektuelle

Verben, die starke Abneigung ausdrücken

She detests / loathes [ləʊðz] *him.* (= Sie verabscheut ihn.)
She can't stand him. (= Sie kann ihn nicht ausstehen.)
I abhor [əb'hɔ:] *violence.* (= Ich verabscheue Gewalttätigkeit.)

optimism [ˈɒptɪmɪzm] – **pessimism**	Optimismus – Pessimismus
optimistic [ɒptɪˈmɪstɪk] – **pessimistic**	optimistisch – pessimistisch
hope [həʊp]	hoffen; Hoffnung
I hope she likes it.	Hoffentlich gefällt es ihr.
Will he help us? – I hope so.	Wird er uns helfen? – Ich hoffe es.
Is it broken? – I hope not.	Ist es kaputt? – Ich hoffe nicht.
our hopes and fears	unsere Hoffnungen und Befürchtungen
despair [dɪˈspeə]	Verzweiflung; verzweifeln
He looked at her in despair.	Er sah sie verzweifelt an.
touching [ʌ] / **moving** [uː]	rührend; bewegend; ergreifend
a touching / moving moment	ein bewegender Augenblick
prejudice [ˈpredʒədɪs] – **prejudiced**	Vorurteil – voreingenommen
prejudice against foreigners [ˈfɒrənəz]	Vorurteile gegen Ausländer
They're prejudiced against us.	Sie haben Vorurteile gegen uns.
subjective [səbˈdʒektɪv] – **objective**	subjektiv – objektiv
sentimental [sentɪˈmentl]	sentimental

Adjektive, mit denen Verärgerung ausgedrückt wird
She was angry / cross / annoyed [əˈnɔɪd] *because I had kept her waiting.*
  (= böse / ärgerlich / verärgert)
The boss was furious [ˈfjʊəriəs] / *livid* [ˈlɪvɪd]. (= wütend / fuchsteufelswild)

be afraid of [əˈfreɪd]	Angst haben vor
Are you afraid of the dog?	Hast du Angst vor dem Hund?
He was afraid to jump.	Er traute sich nicht zu springen.
She's afraid of flying.	Sie fürchtet sich vor dem Fliegen.
proud [praʊd] – **pride** [praɪd]	stolz – (der) Stolz
We're proud of this achievement.	Auf diese Leistung sind wir stolz.
jealous (of) [ˈdʒeləs] – **jealousy**	eifersüchtig (auf) – Eifersucht
Are you jealous of him?	Bist du eifersüchtig auf ihn?
He killed her out of jealousy [ˈdʒeləsi].	Er hat sie aus Eifersucht umgebracht.
envy [ˈenvi]	Neid; beneiden
I envy you this job.	Ich beneide dich um diesen Job.
despise [dɪˈspaɪz]	verachten
surprise [səˈpraɪz]	Überraschung; überraschen
She looked at me in surprise.	Sie sah mich überrascht an.
I'm surprised to see you here.	Ich bin überrascht dich hier zu sehen.
astonished [əˈstɒnɪʃt] – **amazed**	erstaunt – verblüfft
We were amazed at / by the result.	Wir waren über das Ergebnis verblüfft.
cry [kraɪ]	weinen; schreien
Listen – the baby's crying.	Hör doch mal – das Baby schreit.
weep (– wept – wept) [wiːp]	weinen

Verben, die Lächeln oder Lachen ausdrücken
smile (= lächeln) • *grin* (= grinsen) • *chuckle* (= leise vor sich hin lachen) •
giggle [ˈgɪgl] (= kichern) • *laugh* (= lachen) • *guffaw* [gəˈfɔː] (= schallend lachen)

Morality and immorality
Moral und Unmoral

What is moral is what you feel good after, and what is immoral is what you feel bad after. (*Ernest Hemingway, US writer, 1898–1961*)

moral ['mɒrəl]	**moralisch; sittlich**
moral principles / standards	moralische Prinzipien / Maßstäbe
That would be morally objectionable.	Das wäre moralisch nicht in Ordnung.
That's a question of morals.	Das ist eine Frage der Moral.
immoral [ɪ'mɒrəl]	**unmoralisch; unsittlich**
immorality [ɪmə'ræləti]	**Unmoral; Unsittlichkeit**
ethical ['eθɪkl]	**ethisch; moralisch**
unethical behaviour [bɪ'heɪvjə]	unmoralisches Verhalten
good [gʊd] (– better – best)	**gut** (– besser – beste); **Gute(s)**
Eat your soup, there's a good boy.	Sei schön brav und iss deine Suppe.
It's never too late to do good.	Es ist nie zu spät, Gutes zu tun.
It was for your own good.	Es geschah zu deinem Besten.
bad [bæd] (– worse – worst)	**schlecht** (– schlechter – schlechteste)
right [raɪt]	**richtig; recht**
You've done the right thing.	Du hast richtig / recht gehandelt.
wrong [rɒŋ]	**falsch; schlecht; unrecht**
I know I was in the wrong.	Ich weiß, dass ich im Unrecht war.
evil ['iːvl]	**böse; das Böse**
good and evil deeds [diːdz]	gute und böse Taten
the conflict between good and evil	der Konflikt zwischen Gut und Böse
sin [sɪn] – **sinful** ['sɪnfl]	**Sünde – sündhaft / sündig**
It would be a sin to do that.	Es wäre eine Sünde, das zu tun.
conscience ['kɒnʃəns]	**Gewissen**
a clear / guilty ['gɪlti] conscience	ein reines / schlechtes Gewissen
ideal [aɪ'dɪəl]	**Ideal; ideal**
He lived up to his ideals.	Er lebte entsprechend seinen Idealen.
virtue ['vɜːtʃuː] – **vice** [vaɪs]	**Tugend – Laster**
Truthfulness is her greatest virtue.	Wahrhaftigkeit ist ihre größte Tugend.
Smoking is his only vice.	Das Rauchen ist sein einziges Laster.
quality ['kwɒləti]	(positive) **Eigenschaft**
She has many good qualities.	Sie hat viele gute Eigenschaften.
generosity [dʒenə'rɒsəti]	**Großzügigkeit; Freigebigkeit; Edelmut**
wisdom ['wɪzdəm]	**Weisheit**
bravery ['breɪvəri]	**Tapferkeit**

From the letter of Paul to the Galatians [gə'leɪʃnz] in the Bible (= Aus dem Brief des Paulus an die Galater in der Bibel): *But the harvest of the spirit is love, joy, peace, patience, kindness, goodness, faithfulness, gentleness, and self-control.* (= Die Frucht aber des Geistes ist Liebe, Freude, Friede, Geduld, Freundlichkeit, Güte, Treue, Sanftmut und Selbstbeherrschung.)

innocence [ˈɪnəsns] – **innocent** [-snt]	**Unschuld – unschuldig**
integrity [ɪnˈtegrəti]	**Integrität; Redlichkeit**
He's a man of integrity.	Er ist ein integrer / redlicher Mensch.
justice [ˈdʒʌstɪs] – **injustice**	**Gerechtigkeit – Ungerechtigkeit**
just [dʒʌst] – **unjust** [ʌnˈdʒʌst]	**gerecht – ungerecht**
fight in a just cause (– fought – fought)	für eine gerechte Sache kämpfen
honesty [ˈɒnəsti] – **dishonesty**	**Ehrlichkeit – Unehrlichkeit**
Honesty is the best policy [ˈpɒləsi].	Ehrlich währt am längsten.
obedience [əˈbiːdiəns] –	**Gehorsam – Ungehorsam**
disobedience	
obedience to the law	Gehorsam gegenüber dem Gesetz

The Seven Virtues (= die sieben Tugenden): *faith* (= Glaube), *hope* (= Hoffnung), *charity* (= Liebe), *justice* (= Gerechtigkeit), *fortitude* (= Tapferkeit), *prudence* (= Klugheit), *temperance* (= Mäßigkeit).
The Seven Deadly Sins (= die sieben Todsünden): *pride* (= Hochmut), *wrath* [rɒθ] (= Zorn), *envy* (= Neid), *lust* (= Unkeuschheit), *gluttony* (= Unmäßigkeit), *avarice* [ˈævərɪs] (= Geiz), *sloth* [sləʊθ] (= Trägheit).

decency [ˈdiːsnsi] – **decent** [ˈdiːsnt]	**Anständigkeit – anständig**
I'm sure he's a decent guy [gaɪ].	Sicherlich ist er ein anständiger Kerl.
indecent [ɪnˈdiːsnt]	**unanständig; anstößig; unsittlich**
faithful [ˈfeɪθfl] – **faithfulness** [-nəs]	**treu – Treue**
He swore to remain faithful to her.	Er schwor, ihr treu zu bleiben.
trustworthy [ˈtrʌstwɜːði]	**vertrauenswürdig**
upright [ˈʌpraɪt]	**aufrecht; rechtschaffen**
an upright character / citizen	ein aufrechter Charakter / Bürger
greed [griːd] – **greedy** [ˈgriːdi]	**(Hab-)Gier; Habsucht – habgierig**
his greed for money [ˈmʌni] / power	seine Geldgier / Machtgier
corruption [kəˈrʌpʃn]	**Korruption; Bestechlichkeit**
worthless [ˈwɜːθləs]	**wertlos; nichtswürdig; nichtsnutzig**
a worthless character [ˈkærəktə]	ein nichtswürdiger Mensch
hypocrite [ˈhɪpəkrɪt]	**Scheinheilige(r); Heuchler(in)**
liar [ˈlaɪə]	**Lügner(in)**
He's a bloody [ˈblʌdi] liar.	Er ist ein verdammter Lügner.
troublemaker [ˈtrʌblmeɪkə]	**Unruhestifter(in)**
good-for-nothing [ˈgʊdfənʌθɪŋ]	**Nichtsnutz; Tunichtgut**
crook [krʊk]	**Gauner**
swine [swaɪn] (Pl. swine / swines)	**Schwein(ehund)**
You've cheated [iː] me, you swine.	Du Schwein hast mich betrogen.
scruple [ˈskruːpl]	**Skrupel**
She didn't have the slightest scruples.	Sie hatte nicht die leisesten Skrupel.
fault [fɔːlt]	**Fehler**
It's all my fault.	Es ist alles meine Schuld.
None of us is faultless / without fault.	Keiner von uns ist ohne Fehler.
ashamed [əˈʃeɪmd]	**beschämt**
You should be ashamed of yourself.	Du solltest dich schämen.
It's nothing to be ashamed of.	Das braucht dir nicht peinlich zu sein.
obscene [əbˈsiːn]	**obszön; unzüchtig**
obscene words / pictures / books	unzüchtige Worte / Bilder / Bücher
pornography [pɔːˈnɒgrəfi]	**(die) Pornografie**

Menschliche Beziehungen

It is explained that all relationships require a little give and take. This is untrue. Any partnership demands that we give and give and give and at the last, as we flop into our graves exhausted, we are told that we didn't give enough.
(*Quentin Crisp, British-born writer, performer and critic, 1908–99*)

relations [rɪˈleɪʃnz]	Beziehungen
relations between the races [ˈreɪsɪz]	die Beziehungen zwischen den Rassen
relationship [rɪˈleɪʃnʃɪp]	Beziehung
her relationships with men	ihre Beziehungen zu Männern
terms [tɜːmz]	(≈ relations = Beziehungen)
I'm on good terms with him.	Ich (ver)stehe mich gut mit ihm.
associate [əˈsəʊʃieɪt] with other people	mit anderen Menschen Umgang haben
get along (– got – got) [get əˈlɒŋ]	zurechtkommen
She gets along well with him.	Sie kommt gut mit ihm aus.
get on (– got – got) [get ˈɒn]	sich verstehen; auskommen
They get on well with each other.	Sie kommen gut miteinander zurecht.
mutual [ˈmjuːtʃuəl]	gegenseitig; beiderseitig
mutual support / respect [rɪˈspekt]	gegenseitige Unterstützung / Achtung
crowd [kraʊd]	(Menschen-)Menge
the crowd outside the building	die Menschenmenge vor dem Gebäude
group [gruːp]	Gruppe
all the members of the group	alle Mitglieder der Gruppe
class [klɑːs]	Klasse
We were in the same class.	Wir waren in derselben Klasse.
the upper / middle / lower class	die Ober- / Mittel- / Unterklasse
a middle-class family	eine bürgerliche Familie
club [klʌb]	Klub; Verein
join [dʒɔɪn] a club	einem Verein beitreten
gang [gæŋ]	Bande
a gang of criminals [ˈkrɪmɪnəlz]	eine Verbrecherbande

Jemand, mit dem man zusammen ist, etwas gemeinsam hat oder tut

playmate (= Spielkamerad/in), *schoolmate* (= Schulkamerad/in)
fellow citizens (= Mitbürger/innen), *fellow passengers* (= Mitreisende)
my pal / chum BE / *mate* BE / *buddy* AE (= mein Kumpel)
colleague [ˈkɒliːg] (= Kollege / Kollegin), *comrade* [ˈkɒmreɪd] (= Kamerad/in)
companion [kəmˈpænjən] (= Gefährte / Gefährtin), *competitor* [kəmˈpetɪtə]
(= Konkurrent/in), *accomplice* [əˈkʌmplɪs] (= Komplize / Komplizin)

member [ˈmembə] – **membership**	Mitglied – Mitgliedschaft
partner [ˈpɑːtnə] – **partnership**	Partner(in) – Partnerschaft
leader [ˈliːdə] – **leadership**	(An-)Führer(in) – Führung

supporter [sə'pɔːtə]	Anhänger(in)
supporters of the president ['prezɪdənt]	Anhänger des Präsidenten
friend [frend]	Freund(in)
They're close [kləʊs] friends.	Sie sind eng befreundet.
boyfriend – girlfriend	Freund – Freundin
He doesn't have a steady girlfriend.	Er hat keine feste Freundin.
friend and foe [fəʊ]	Freund und Feind
friendship ['frendʃɪp]	Freundschaft
a close [kləʊs] / warm friendship	eine enge / herzliche Freundschaft
company ['kʌmpəni]	Gesellschaft
She keeps him company.	Sie leistet ihm Gesellschaft.
I like your company.	Ich bin gern mit dir zusammen.
companionship [kəm'pænjənʃɪp]	Gesellschaft
He's longing for companionship.	Er sehnt sich nach Gesellschaft.
acquaintance [ə'kweɪntəns]	Bekanntschaft; Bekannte(r)
I made her acquaintance in London.	Ich habe sie in London kennen gelernt.
She's an acquaintance of mine.	Sie ist eine Bekannte von mir.
acquainted [ə'kweɪntɪd]	bekannt; vertraut
We got acquainted during the war.	Wir lernten uns im Krieg kennen.
get to know [nəʊ] (– got – got)	kennen lernen
She gradually got to know him better.	Allmählich lernte sie ihn besser kennen.
neighbour ['neɪbə] – **neighbour-hood**	Nachbar(in) – Nachbarschaft
Love your neighbour as yourself.	Liebe deinen Nächsten wie dich selbst.
indifferent [ɪn'dɪfrənt] – **indifference**	gleichgültig – Gleichgültigkeit
close [kləʊs]	nahe
We were always very close.	Wir standen uns immer sehr nahe.
She's a close friend of mine.	Sie ist eine enge Freundin von mir.
intimate ['ɪntɪmət]	intim; vertraut; vertraulich
sympathy ['sɪmpəθi]	Mitgefühl; Mitleid
They deserve no / our sympathy.	Sie verdienen kein / unser Mitgefühl.
support [sə'pɔːt]	unterstützen; Unterstützung
They offered ['ɒfəd] us their support.	Sie boten uns ihre Unterstützung an.
cooperation – **cooperate** [kəʊ'ɒpəreɪt]	Zusammenarbeit – zusammen-arbeiten
solidarity [sɒlɪ'dærəti]	Solidarität
affection [ə'fekʃn]	Zuneigung
love [lʌv]	Liebe; lieben
She's in love with him.	Sie ist in ihn verliebt.
She fell in love with her teacher.	Sie verliebte sich in ihren Lehrer.
There's no love lost between them.	Sie können sich nicht ausstehen.
agreement [ə'griːmənt] – **disagree-ment**	Einvernehmen – Uneinigkeit
There's agreement on this.	Hierüber herrscht Einverständnis.
disagreements among [ə'mʌŋ] them	Meinungsverschiedenheiten unter ihnen
tension ['tenʃn]	Spannung
tensions within the group [gruːp]	Spannungen innerhalb der Gruppe

conflict ['kɒnflɪkt] — Konflikt
clash [klæʃ] — Konflikt; zusammenstoßen
a clash of interests — ein Interessenkonflikt
We often clashed [klæʃt]. — Wir gerieten oft aneinander.
quarrel ['kwɒrəl] — **Streit; sich streiten**
They seem to have settled their quarrel. — Sie scheinen ihren Streit beigelegt zu haben.
They often quarrelled. — Sie stritten sich oft.
animosity (towards) [ænɪ'mɒsəti] — **Animosität / Feindseligkeit (gegenüber)**
antipathy (to / towards) [æn'tɪpəθi] — **Antipathie / Abneigung** (gegen)
contempt [kən'tempt] — **Verachtung**
hostile ['hɒstaɪl] – **hostility** [hɒ'stɪləti] — **feindselig – Feindseligkeit**
They are hostile to foreigners. (→7.6) — Ausländern sind sie feindlich gesinnt.
bad blood [bæd 'blʌd] — **„böses Blut"**
There's bad blood between them. — Sie haben ein gestörtes Verhältnis.
enemy ['enəmi] — **Feind(in)**
She made a lot of enemies there. — Sie hat sich dort viele Feinde gemacht.

opponent [ə'pəʊnənt] — **Gegner(in)**
grudge [grʌdʒ] — **Groll; nicht gönnen**
So that's why she bears me a grudge. — Deshalb also ist sie mir böse.
I don't grudge you your success. — Ich gönne dir deinen Erfolg.

Behaviour towards others (= **Verhalten anderen gegenüber**)
courtesy ['kɜːtəsi] / *politeness* [pə'laɪtnəs] (= Höflichkeit), *respect* (= Achtung), *kind(li)ness* / *friendliness* (= Freundlichkeit), *consideration* [kənsɪdə'reɪʃn] (= Rücksicht), *decency* ['diːsnsi] (= Anständigkeit), *tact* (= Takt), *tactfulness* (= Takt)
impoliteness / *rudeness* (= Unhöflichkeit), *disrespect* (= Respektlosigkeit), *unfriendliness* (= Unfreundlichkeit), *thoughtlessness* (= Rücksichtslosigkeit), *tactlessness* (= Taktlosigkeit), *impudence* ['ɪmpjʊdəns] (= Unverschämtheit)

---

contact ['kɒntækt] — Kontakt
We must keep in contact. — Wir müssen in Kontakt bleiben.
We've lost contact. — Wir haben den Kontakt verloren.
touch [tʌtʃ] — **(≈ communication = Kommunikation)**
be in touch with someone — mit jemand in Verbindung stehen
He got in touch with her. — Er setzte sich mit ihr in Verbindung.
connection [kə'nekʃn] — **Verbindung**
She has good connections. — Sie hat gute Verbindungen / Beziehungen.

talk [tɔːk] — **Gespräch; Unterhaltung; Unterredung**
We've got to have a talk about it. — Wir müssen uns darüber unterhalten.
conversation [kɒnvə'seɪʃn] — **Gespräch; Unterhaltung; Konversation**
I overheard your conversation. — Ich habe Ihr Gespräch mit angehört.
dialogue ['daɪəlɒg] — **Dialog**
discussion [dɪ'skʌʃn] — **Diskussion**
There was much discussion about this. — Darüber gab es lange Diskussionen.

11 Sexuality
Sexualität

Sex is a conversation carried out by other means. If you get on well out of bed, half the problems of bed are solved. (*Sir Peter Ustinov, English actor, writer, and film director, born in 1921*)

marital ['mærɪtl] – **extramarital**	ehelich – außerehelich
erotic [ɪ'rɒtɪk]	erotisch
sex [seks]	Geschlecht; Sex; Sexualität; Sexual-
the opposite ['ɒpəzɪt] sex	das andere Geschlecht
sex education [edju'keɪʃn]	Sexualerziehung
sex crime – sex criminal ['krɪmɪnəl]	Sexualverbrechen – Sexualverbrecher
sex offender – sex maniac ['meɪniæk]	Sexualtäter(in) – Triebverbrecher(in)
sexual ['sekʃuəl]	sexuell; Sexual-; Geschlechts-
sexual harassment ['hærəsmənt]	sexuelle Belästigung
sexual abuse [ə'bju:s]	sexueller Missbrauch
sexy / **sexually attractive** [ə'træktɪv]	sexuell attraktiv
heterosexual [hetərə'sekʃuəl]	heterosexuell; Heterosexuelle(r)
homosexual [həʊmə'sekʃuəl]	homosexuell; Homosexuelle(r)
homosexuality [həʊməsekʃu'æləti]	Homosexualität
gay [geɪ]	schwul; Schwule(r)
lesbian ['lezbiən]	lesbisch; Lesbierin / Lesbe
come out (– came – come) [kʌm 'aʊt]	sich als Homosexuelle(r) bekennen

---

Ausdrücke für *(sexual) intercourse* ['ɪntəkɔ:s] (= Geschlechtsverkehr)
make love to someone, sleep with someone, go to bed with someone, have sex with someone, have sexual relations with someone (= mit jemand sexuelle Beziehungen haben), *be intimate* ['ɪntɪmət] *with someone* (= mit jemand intim sein), *the sexual act* (= der Geschlechtsakt), *sexual union* ['ju:niən] (= sexuelle Vereinigung), *coitus* ['kəʊɪtəs] (= Koitus), *have carnal knowledge of someone* (Rechtssprache: „fleischliche Kenntnis" von jemand haben)

---

petting ['petɪŋ]	Petting
arouse [ə'raʊz] – **arousal** [ə'raʊzl]	(sexuell) erregen – Erregung
climax ['klaɪmæks] – **peak** [pi:k]	Höhepunkt
orgasm ['ɔ:gæzm]	Orgasmus
have (an) / reach / achieve orgasm	einen Orgasmus haben
penis ['pi:nɪs] – **clitoris** ['klɪtərɪs]	Penis – Klitoris / Kitzler
erect [ɪ'rekt] – **erection** [ɪ'rekʃn]	erigiert / steif – Erektion
ejaculation [ɪdʒækju'leɪʃn]	Ejakulation; Samenerguss
semen ['si:mən] – **sperm** [spɜ:m]	Samen(flüssigkeit); Sperma
vagina [və'dʒaɪnə]	Vagina; Scheide

 Cultural note (= kulturelle Anmerkung): *The "man-above position" in intercourse is often called the missionary position, a term that originated in Polynesia, where Christian missionaries taught it as the only "correct" position to the Polynesians, who traditionally preferred other positions.*

frigid ['frɪdʒɪd] – **frigidity** [frɪ'dʒɪdəti] frigide – Frigidität
impotent ['ɪmpətənt] – **impotence** impotent – Impotenz
the potency ['pəʊtnsi] drug Viagra™ das Potenzmittel Viagra™
conception [kən'sepʃn] Empfängnis

Ausdrücke für *contraception* [kɒntrə'sepʃn] **(= Empfängnisverhütung)**
birth control (= Geburtenkontrolle) • *family planning* (= Familienplanung) •
planned parenthood (= geplante Elternschaft)
Contraceptive methods ['meθədz] **(= Verhütungsmethoden)**
condom ['kɒndəm] (= Kondom / Präservativ) • *cap* (= Pessar) •
intrauterine [ɪntrə'juːtəraɪn] *device / IUD* (= Intrauterinpessar) • *diaphragm*
['daɪəfræm] (= Scheidendiaphragma) • *coil / loop* (= Spirale) • *the pill* •
the morning-after pill (= die Pille am Morgen danach) • *the male pill* (= die
Pille für den Mann) • *the rhythm* ['rɪðm] *method* (= die Knaus-Ogino
Methode) • *withdrawal / coitus interruptus* [ɪntə'rʌptəs] (= Coitus interruptus) • *sterilization* [sterəlaɪ'zeɪʃn] (= Sterilisation) • *vasectomy* [və'sektəmi]
(= Vasektomie)

---

pregnant ['pregnənt] – **pregnancy** schwanger – Schwangerschaft
abortion [ə'bɔːʃn] Schwangerschaftsabbruch
have an abortion eine Abtreibung vornehmen lassen
masturbation [mæstə'beɪʃn] Masturbation; Selbstbefriedigung
masturbate ['mæstəbeit] masturbieren; onanieren
sleep around (– slept – slept) die Sexualpartner häufig wechseln
prostitute ['prɒstɪtjuːt] – **prostitution** Prostituierte(r) – Prostitution
rent boy *BE / AE* **hustler** ['hʌslə] Strichjunge; Stricher
whore [hɔː] Hure
call girl ['kɔːl gɜːl] Callgirl
hooker ['hʊkə] *AE* Nutte
brothel ['brɒθəl] Bordell; Puff

Adult ['ædʌlt] **(= erwachsen / für Erwachsene)**
Adult bookshops = euphemism ['juːfəmɪzm] (= beschönigende Umschreibung)
for shops specializing in the sale of pornographic books, magazines, videos, etc.
Adult films, videos, magazines, etc. are not suitable for young people.

---

soft porn [sɒft 'pɔːn] – **hard porn** weicher Porno – harter Porno
sadism [eɪ] – **masochism** ['mæsəkɪzm] Sadismus – Masochismus
exhibitionism [eksɪ'bɪʃənɪzm] – Exhibitionismus – Exhibitionist(in)
  exhibitionist
rape [reɪp] – **rapist** ['reɪpɪst] Vergewaltigung – Vergewaltiger(in)

Venereal [və'nɪərɪəl] *diseases* (= Geschlechtskrankheiten) *and other sexually
transmitted diseases* (= durch Geschlechtsverkehr übertragene Krankheiten):
The two most serious venereal diseases are syphilis ['sɪfəlɪs] (= Syphilis / Lues)
and gonorrhea [gɒnə'riːə] (= Gonorrhöe / Tripper). – *AIDS is often transmitted through anal* ['eɪnl] *intercourse* (= Aids wird oft durch Analverkehr
übertragen).

Personal hygiene
Körperpflege

Man does not live by soap alone; and hygiene, or even health, is not much good unless you can take a healthy view of it – or, better still, feel a healthy indifference to it. (*G.K. Chesterton, English writer, 1874–1936*)

hygiene ['haɪdʒiːn]	**Hygiene**
cleanliness ['klenlɪnəs]	**Reinlichkeit**
wash [wɒʃ]	**(sich) waschen; Wäsche**
Did you wash your hands?	Hast du dir die Hände gewaschen?
Your green shirt is in the wash.	Dein grünes Hemd ist in der Wäsche.
(a bar of) **soap** [səʊp]	(ein Stück) **Seife**
brush [brʌʃ]	**Bürste; bürsten**
hairbrush, nailbrush, toothbrush	Haarbürste, Nagelbürste, Zahnbürste
Did you brush your teeth [tiːθ]?	Hast du dir die Zähne geputzt?
bath [bɑːθ]	**Bad**
Did you have *BE* / *AE* take a bath?	Hast du gebadet?
shower ['ʃaʊə]	**Dusche; sich duschen**

Kollokationen mit *have a* ...

have a bath (= ein Bad nehmen) • *have a shower* (= duschen) • *have a wash* (= sich waschen) • *have a sauna* ['sɔːnə] (= in die Sauna gehen) • *have a shave* (= sich rasieren) • *have a haircut* (= sich die Haare schneiden lassen) • *have a blow-dry* (= sich föhnen lassen) • *have a shampoo* [ʃæm'puː] *and set* (= sich die Haare waschen und legen lassen) • *have a massage* ['mæsɑːʒ] (= sich massieren lassen) • *have a shoeshine* (= sich die Schuhe putzen lassen)

flannel *BE* / *AE* **washcloth** [-klɒθ]	**Waschlappen**
sponge [spʌndʒ]	**Schwamm**
towel ['taʊəl]	**Handtuch**
Wait – I'm just towelling myself down.	Warte – ich trockne mich nur noch ab.
rub (oneself) down [rʌb]	**(sich) abrubbeln / abfrottieren**

Die *of*-Konstruktion bei Behälter- und Mengenangaben

a bottle of aftershave / *cologne* [kə'ləʊn] / *shampoo* / *mouthwash* (= eine Flasche Aftershave / Kölnischwasser / etc.) • *a bar of soap* (= ein Stück Seife) • *a box of cotton buds* / *toothpicks* (= eine Schachtel Wattestäbchen / Zahnstocher) • *a pack of tissues* ['tɪʃuːz] (= eine Packung Papiertaschentücher) • *a roll of toilet paper* (= eine Rolle Toilettenpapier) • *a jar of cream* (= eine Dose Creme) • *a tube of toothpaste* (= eine Tube Zahnpasta)

mouthwash – dental floss	**Mundwasser – Zahnseide**
shave [ʃeɪv]	**(sich) rasieren**
shaving cream	Rasiercreme
electric [ɪ'lektrɪk] **razor** / **shaver**	**Elektrorasierer**
shampoo [ʃæm'puː]	**Haarwaschmittel; Haarwäsche**

shampoo and (hair) conditioner	Shampoo und Pflegespülung
I'm going to shampoo my hair.	Ich will mir die Haare waschen.
hairdryer ['heə draɪə]	**Haartrockner; Föhn**
comb [kəʊm]	**Kamm; kämmen**
hairdresser ['heə dresə]	**Friseur(in)**
She's at the hairdresser's.	Sie ist beim Friseur.
barber ['bɑːbə]	**(Herren-)Friseur**
I'm going to the barber('s).	Ich gehe zum Friseur.
make-up ['meɪk ʌp]	**Make-up; Schminke**
apply [ə'plaɪ] / remove make-up	Make-up auftragen / entfernen

Some cosmetics [kɒz'metɪks] **(= Kosmetika)**
cream (= Creme) • *cleansing* ['klenzɪŋ] *cream* (= Reinigungscreme) •
moisturizing ['mɔɪstʃəraɪzɪŋ] *cream* (= Feuchtigkeitscreme) • *face powder*
(= Gesichtspuder) • *lipstick* (= Lippenstift) • *eye shadow* (= Lidschatten) •
eyebrow pencil (= Augenbrauenstift) • *cologne* [kə'ləʊn] (= Eau de Cologne;
Kölnischwasser) • *perfume* (= Parfüm) • *deodorant* [di'əʊdrənt] (= Deodorant)

manicure ['mænɪkjʊə] – **pedicure**	**Maniküre – Pediküre**
nail polish / *BE also* **nail varnish**	**Nagellack**
(a pair of) nail scissors ['sɪzəz]	**(eine) Nagelschere**

Lotions ['ləʊʃnz] sind Pflegeflüssigkeiten für die Haut: *body lotion, face lotion,
hand lotion, skin lotion, aftershave lotion, pre-shave lotion, suntan lotion*
(= Sonnenöl), *baby lotion* etc. – *Rub in some of this lotion twice a day.*
(= Reiben Sie sich zweimal täglich mit dieser Flüssigkeit ein.)

cotton wool [wʊl] *BE* / *AE* **cotton** [ɒ]	**Watte**
cotton bud *BE* / *AE* **Q-tip**™ [kjuː]	**Wattestäbchen**
handkerchief ['hæŋkətʃɪf] / **hanky**	**Taschentuch**
tissue ['tɪʃuː] / **Kleenex**™ ['kliːneks]	**Papier- / Tempo™-Taschentuch**
blow [bləʊ] (– blew [bluː] – blown)	**blasen**
Blow your nose, that's a good girl.	Sei schön brav und putz dir die Nase.
sanitary ['sænətri] **towel** *BE* / *AE*	**(Damen-)Binde**
sanitary napkin	
toilet paper / **lavatory paper** /	**Toilettenpapier**
toilet tissue	
the toilet – the loo *BE* / *AE* **the john**	**die Toilette – das Klo**
Jamie is in the loo [luː] *BE* / *AE* john.	Jamie ist auf dem Klo.
lavatory ['lævətri]	*(ebenfalls ein Ausdruck für)* **Toilette**
laundry ['lɔːndri]	**Wäscherei; Wäsche**
I'm doing the laundry / washing today.	Ich mache heute die Wäsche.
laund(e)rette *BE* / *AE* **laundromat**™	**Waschsalon**
(dry) cleaners [draɪ 'kliːnəz]	**Reinigung**
My coat is at the cleaners.	Mein Mantel ist in der Reinigung.
I'll have it dry-cleaned [draɪ'kliːnd].	Ich werde es reinigen lassen.

Idiom: *We've been taken to the cleaners.* (= Man hat uns ganz schön
geschröpft.)

Death
Tod

It is impossible that anything so natural, so necessary, and so universal as death should ever have been designed by providence as an evil to mankind. (*Jonathan Swift, Irish clergyman and satirist, 1667–1745*)

death [deθ]
Aren't you afraid of death?
death by hanging / firing squad [ɒ]
There were a number of deaths.
death certificate [sə'tıfıkət]
death camp – death cell
die [daɪ]
He died of cancer ['kænsə] / old age.
She died from an overdose ['əʊvədəʊs].
They died a natural death.

(der) **Tod; Todesfall**
Hast du keine Angst vor dem Tod?
Tod durch Erhängen / Erschießen
Es gab einige Todesfälle.
Sterbeurkunde; Totenschein
Vernichtungslager – Todeszelle
sterben
Er starb an Krebs / Altersschwäche.
Sie starb an einer Überdosis.
Sie starben eines natürlichen Todes.

Euphemismen (= verhüllende / beschönigende Ausdrücke) für „sterben"
go (= dahingehen) • *go to a better world* • *pass away* (= dahinscheiden) •
fall asleep (= einschlafen) • *he / she has closed his / her eyes*

perish ['perɪʃ]
Millions perished in the camps.
dying ['daɪɪŋ]
Dying is a very natural thing.
the dying
on his / **her deathbed** ['deθbed]
hospice ['hɒspɪs]
anointing [ə'nɔɪntɪŋ] **of the sick**
dead [ded]
The robber was shot dead.
a dead man / woman / person
drop dead
rise from the dead (– rose – risen)

umkommen
Millionen kamen in den Lagern um.
sterbend; das Sterben
Sterben ist etwas sehr Natürliches.
die Sterbenden
auf dem Sterbebett
Sterbeklinik
Krankensalbung
tot
Der Räuber wurde erschossen.
ein Toter / eine Tote
tot umfallen
von den Toten auferstehen

Euphemismen für „tot"
asleep (in Jesus) • *at peace* • *at rest* • *gone* [gɒn] • *in heaven* •
in the arms of Jesus • *with Jesus* • *with the Lord* • *with us no more*

(his) **demise** [dɪ'maɪz]
deceased [dɪ'siːst]
the widow ['wɪdəʊ] of the deceased

(sein) **Ableben / Hinscheiden**
verstorben
die Witwe des Verstorbenen

Bezeichnungen für tote Menschen oder Tiere
(dead) body (= Leiche) • *corpse* (= Leiche) • *stiff* (Slang = Leiche) •
cadaver [kə'dævə] (= Leiche) • *carcass* ['kɑːkəs] (= Tierkadaver)

autopsy ['ɔːtɒpsi] / **postmortem** (**examination**)	Obduktion; Leichenöffnung; Autopsie
perform an autopsy / a postmortem	eine Obduktion durchführen
coffin ['kɒfɪn] – **urn** [ɜːn]	**Sarg – Urne**
funeral ['fjuːnərəl]	**Begräbnis; Beerdigung; Beisetzung**
I was at her funeral.	Ich war auf ihrer Beerdigung.
funeral director / undertaker	Bestattungsunternehmer
funeral home	Bestattungsinstitut
funeral procession – funeral service	Trauerzug / Leichenzug – Trauerfeier

Idiom: *I don't think you'll get your money back, but that's your funeral.* (= Ich glaube nicht, dass du dein Geld zurückkriegst, aber das ist dein Problem.)

churchyard ['tʃɜːtʃjɑːd]	**Kirchhof; Friedhof** (bei der Kirche)
bury ['beri]	**begraben**
Where is she buried?	Wo liegt sie begraben?
She is / lies buried in this cemetery.	Sie ist auf diesem Friedhof begraben.
burial ['beriəl]	**Beerdigung; Bestattung**
burial at sea	Seebestattung
lay to rest (– laid – laid) [leɪ]	**zur letzten Ruhe betten**
cremate [krɪ'meɪt] – **cremation**	**einäschern – Einäscherung**
crematorium [kremə'tɔːriəm] *BE* / bes. *AE* **crematory** ['kremətəri]	**Krematorium**
grave [greɪv]	**Grab**
graveyard – gravedigger – gravestone	Friedhof – Totengräber – Grabstein
tomb [tuːm]	(großes, gemauertes) **Grab; Grabmal**
He laid a wreath [riːθ] at the Tomb of the Unknown Soldier.	Er legte am Grabmal des Unbekannten Soldaten einen Kranz nieder.
from womb [wuːm] to tomb	(*Idiom*) von der Wiege bis zur Bahre
epitaph ['epɪtɑːf]	**Grabinschrift; Epitaph**
RIP = **rest in peace** [piːs]	(*auf Grabsteinen*) **Ruhe in Frieden**
May he / she rest in peace.	Er / Sie ruhe in Frieden.

Aus der Bestattungsliturgie der *Church of England*
We brought nothing into the world, and we take nothing out. The Lord gives, and the Lord takes away: blessed ['blesɪd] *be the name of the Lord.* (= Wir haben nichts in die Welt gebracht und wir bringen nichts hinaus. Der Herr gibt, der Herr nimmt; der Name des Herrn sei gelobt.)
In the midst of life we are in death. (= In der Mitte des Lebens sind wir vom Tod umgeben.)
Earth to earth, ashes to ashes, dust to dust ... (= Erde zu Erde, Asche zu Asche, Staub zu Staub ...)

requiem mass [rekwiəm 'mæs]	**Totenmesse**
Kaddish ['kædɪʃ]	**Kaddisch** (= jüdisches Totengebet)
mortal ['mɔːtl]	**sterblich**
his mortal remains [rɪ'meɪnz]	seine sterblichen Überreste
mortal injuries ['ɪndʒəriz]	tödliche Verletzungen
the soul [səʊl]	**die Seele**
Do we have an immortal soul?	Haben wir eine unsterbliche Seele?

afterlife ['ɑːftəlaɪf]	Leben nach dem Tode
bereaved – bereavement	leidtragend – Trauerfall
[bɪˈriːvmənt]	
the bereaved [bɪˈriːvd]	die Hinterbliebenen
mourn [mɔːn] – **mourning**	(be)trauern – Trauer
Thousands mourned for her.	Tausende trauerten um sie.
She's still in mourning.	Sie ist immer noch in Trauer.
obituary [əˈbɪtʃuəri] / **obit** [ˈɒbɪt]	(*Zeitung*) **Nachruf, Todesanzeige**
the late ...	**der / die verstorbene** ...
the son of the late Frank Bell	der Sohn des verstorbenen Frank Bell

Der / Die Verstorbene wird euphemistisch auch als *the loved one* (= der /
die Geliebte), *the dear departed* (= der / die liebe Dahingeschiedene) oder
the late lamented [ləˈmentɪd] (*lament* = beklagen / beweinen) bezeichnet.

starve [stɑːv] – **starvation**	verhungern – Verhungern
Millions have starved to death.	Millionen sind verhungert.
die of starvation [stɑːˈveɪʃn]	hungers sterben
drown [draʊn]	**ertrinken; ertränken**
She (was) drowned.	Sie ertrank.
death by drowning	Tod durch Ertrinken
terminal [ˈtɜːmɪnl]	**End-; unheilbar**
terminal cancer [ˈkænsə]	unheilbarer Krebs
She is terminally ill.	Sie ist unheilbar krank.
euthanasia [juːθəˈneɪziə]	**Euthanasie; Sterbehilfe**
practise / perform passive euthanasia	passive Sterbehilfe leisten
suicide [ˈsuːɪsaɪd]	**Selbstmord; Selbsttötung; Freitod**
She committed [kəˈmɪtɪd] suicide.	Sie beging Selbstmord.

In *obituaries* (= Todesanzeigen / Nachrufen) wird *suicide* häufig durch
die verhüllende Umschreibung *after a brief* [briːf] *illness* (= nach kurzer
Krankheit) angedeutet. *After a long illness* dagegen deutet auf *cancer*
(= Krebs).

kill someone [kɪl]	**jemand töten / umbringen**
The crash killed [kɪld] 96 people.	Bei dem Absturz kamen 96 Menschen ums Leben.
liquidate someone [ˈlɪkwɪdeɪt]	**jemand liquidieren**
lynch someone [lɪntʃ]	**jemand lynchen**
The mob tried to lynch him.	Die Menge versuchte ihn zu lynchen.
poison someone [ˈpɔɪzn]	**jemand vergiften**
Did Napoleon die of poisoning?	Starb Napoleon an einer Vergiftung?

Die Endsilbe *-cide* [-saɪd] **bedeutet „Mord / Tötung"**
infanticide [ɪnˈfæntɪsaɪd] (= Kindesmord) • *matricide* [ˈmeɪtrɪsaɪd]
(= Muttermord) • *patricide* [æ] / *parricide* (= Vatermord) • *fratricide* [æ]
(= Geschwistermord) • *regicide* [ˈredʒɪsaɪd] (= Königsmord) • *suicide*
[ˈsuːɪsaɪd] (= Selbstmord) • *genocide* [ˈdʒenəsaɪd] (= Völkermord)

do away with someone (– did – done) | **jemand umbringen**
The witness has been done away with. | Den Zeugen hat man umgebracht.
bump someone off | **jemand umlegen / kaltmachen**
He was bumped off by the gang. | Er wurde von der Bande kaltgemacht.

Mit zahllosen *slang*-Ausdrücken wird *die* und *kill* drastisch ausgedrückt, z.B. „ins Gras beißen", „abkratzen", „den Löffel abgeben" etc.:
bite the dust (= „in den Staub beißen") • *kick the bucket* (= „den Eimer wegtreten") • *go west* (= „nach Westen fahren") • *cash in one's chips* (= „seine Chips einlösen") • *knock off* („Feierabend machen") • *pop off* (= verschwinden) • *buy the farm* (= „die Farm kaufen")
„Abmurksen", „kaltmachen", „fertigmachen", „um die Ecke bringen" etc.:
knock someone off • *finish someone off* (= jemand fertigmachen) • *do someone in* • *take care of someone* (= „sich um jemand kümmern") • *let someone have it* (= es jemand geben) • *give someone the works* • *send someone up the river*

execute ['eksɪkjuːt] – **execution** | **hinrichten – Hinrichtung**
execution by firing squad / by shooting | Hinrichtung durch Erschießen

Methods of inflicting [ɪn'flɪktɪŋ] ***the death penalty*** ['deθ penlti]
(= Hinrichtungsmethoden)
hanging (= Erhängen) • *electrocution / electric chair* (= elektrischer Stuhl) • *gas chamber* [eɪ] (= Gaskammer) • *firing squad* [ɒ] (= Erschießungs-kommando / Erschießen) • *lethal* ['liːθl] *injection* (= Todesspritze) • *beheading* (= Köpfen) • *guillotine* ['gɪlətiːn] (= Guillotine / Fallbeil) • *crucifixion* [kruːsə'fɪkʃn] (= Kreuzigung) • *stoning* (= Steinigung) • *burning at the stake* (= Scheiterhaufen)

will / testament ['testəmənt] | **Testament**
my last will and testament | mein letzter Wille

"You wouldn't have any single rooms, would you?

The creativity of language

Language is an anonymous, collective and unconscious art, the result of the creativity of thousands of generations. (*Edward Sapir, US linguist, 1884–1939*)

Sapir traf den Nagel auf den Kopf: Sprache ist kreativ, gerade auch das Englische. Eines der vielen Mittel sprachlicher Kreativität sind *prefixes* und *suffixes*, d. h. Vor- und Nachsilben, die die Bedeutung von Adjektiven, Verben und Nomen verändern.

Viele *prefixes* dienen der Bedeutungsverstärkung und sind mitunter *colloquial* (= umgangssprachlich), wie z. B. *mega*- ['megə] in *megastar* und *mega-rich*) und *super*- in *super-excited* (= mordsaufgeregt).
„Super" findet sich natürlich auch im Deutschen, etwa zur Panikmache in der kuriosen Wortbildung „Super-GAU" (GAU = größter anzunehmender Unfall = *worst case scenario*). Und selbst ansonsten eher nüchterne Wissen-schaftler gebrauchen *super*, wenn sie z. B. von einem *Super Large Hadron Collider* sprechen.

Ein häufig verwendetes englisches *prefix* ist *out*-, das bei Verben oft ein „Übertreffen" ausdrückt: *People are* **outnumbered** (= zahlenmäßig unter-legen), **outgunned** (= waffenmäßig unterlegen) or **outwitted** (= werden ausgetrickst). Bei amerikanischen Wahlen, in denen das Eintreiben von Spenden eine große Rolle spielt, gilt die Regel: *If you* **outraise** *and* **outspend** *your opponent you win*. (= Wenn du mehr Spenden sammelst und mehr Geld ausgibst als dein Gegner, siegst du.)

Zwei gern verwendete und gerade auch im Alltag flexibel benutzte Suffixe sind *-ish* und *-y*. Mit *-ish* drückt man bei Adjektiven eine Annäherung aus, ein „in etwa" bzw. „ungefähr" (*green – greenish*); Nomen werden durch Anhängen von *-ish* zu Adjektiven, die Eigenschaften des Nomens haben (*baby – babyish*):

We'll be arriving **sevenish**.	Wir werden so gegen sieben ankommen.
It was **darkish** by the time we arrived.	Es war schon recht dunkel, als wir ankamen.
Women loved his **boyish** charm.	Den Frauen gefiel sein jungen-hafter Charme.
She drives a **newish** sports car.	Sie fährt einen ziemlich neuen Sportwagen.

Auch *-y* bezeichnet Eigenschaften des jeweiligen Nomens oder Verbs: *A river is* **muddy** (= schlammig), *roads are* **icy** (= vereist), *she gives you an* **icy** *look* (= schaut dich eisig an), *the boy has a* **runny** *nose* (= dem Jungen läuft die Nase), *my hands are* **sticky** (= klebrig), *the weather is* **sticky** (= schwül), *her dream man is* **outdoorsy** (= ein Naturbursche), *and the sauce is nice and* **garlicky** (= schmeckt schön nach Knoblauch) ... *Let's stop here before it gets too* **lengthy**!

The family
Die Familie

1 **Family relations**
Verwandtschaftliche Beziehungen

2 **Marriage and divorce**
Ehe und Ehescheidung

3 **Parents and children**
Eltern und Kinder

Parents-and-children proverbs

2

Family relations
Verwandtschaftliche Beziehungen

God gives us relatives; thank God we can choose our friends. (*Proverb*)

relation [rɪ'leɪʃn]	**Verwandte(r)**
She's no relation of mine.	Sie ist nicht mit mir verwandt.
relative ['relətɪv]	**Verwandte(r)**
Do you have any relatives in this country?	Haben Sie hier in England etc. Verwandte?
ancestor ['ænsestə]	**Vorfahr**
Her ancestors came from Ireland.	Ihre Vorfahren kamen aus Irland.
descent [dɪ'sent]	**Abstammung; Herkunft**
They're of Irish descent.	Sie sind irischer Abstammung.
stock [stɒk]	**Abstammung; Herkunft**
Americans of European stock	Amerikaner europäischer Herkunft
family ['fæməli]	**Familie**
Our family has lived here for generations [dʒenə'reɪʃnz].	Unsere Familie lebt seit Generationen hier.
We're thinking of starting a family.	Wir wollen uns jetzt Kinder zulegen.
family tree [fæməli 'triː]	Stammbaum
my folks [fəuks]	**meine Leute / Verwandten / Familie**
next of kin [nekst əv 'kɪn]	**nächste(r) Verwandte(r)**
Have the next of kin been notified ['nəutɪfaɪd]?	Sind die nächsten Verwandten benachrichtigt worden?

Family wird im BE gern als Plural konstruiert, wenn mehr an die einzelnen Mitglieder als an die Gesamtheit gedacht wird; das AE bevorzugt stets die Singularkonstruktion:
*My family **are** / **is** scattered all over the globe.* (= Meine Familie ist über den ganzen Erdball verstreut.)

father ['fɑːðə] – **mother** ['mʌðə]	**Vater – Mutter**

Zusammensetzungen mit *step-*
stepfather (= Stiefvater) • *stepmother* (= Stiefmutter) • *stepparents* (= Stiefeltern) • *stepson* (= Stiefsohn) • *stepdaughter* (= Stieftochter) • *stepchildren* (= Stiefkinder) • *stepbrother* (= Stiefbruder) • *stepsister* (= Stiefschwester)

son [sʌn] – **daughter** ['dɔːtə]	**Sohn – Tochter**
brother ['brʌðə] – **sister** ['sɪstə]	**Bruder – Schwester**
half-brother – half-sister	Halbbruder – Halbschwester

in-laws
father-in-law ['fɑːðər ɪn lɔː] (= Schwiegervater) • *mother-in-law* (= Schwiegermutter) • *parents-in-law* (= Schwiegereltern) • *son-in-law* (= Schwiegersohn) • *daughter-in-law* (= Schwiegertochter) • *brother-in-law* (= Schwager) • *sister-in-law* (= Schwägerin)

My in-laws are coming to see us next weekend. (= Meine Schwiegereltern / angeheirateten Verwandten kommen uns nächstes Wochenende besuchen.)

uncle ['ʌŋkl] – **aunt** [ɑːnt]	**Onkel – Tante**
nephew ['nefjuː] – **niece** [niːs]	**Neffe – Nichte**
cousin ['kʌzn]	**Cousin / Vetter; Cousine**
Brenda is a cousin of mine.	Brenda ist eine Cousine von mir.

Zusammensetzungen mit *grand*- [grænd-] **und *great*-** [greɪt-]
grandfather (= Großvater) • *grandmother* (= Großmutter) • *grandparents* (= Großeltern) • *grandson* (= Enkel) • *granddaughter* (= Enkelin) • *grandchildren* (= Enkelkinder)
great-aunt / grandaunt (= Großtante) • *great-uncle / granduncle* (= Großonkel) • *great-nephew / grandnephew* (= Großneffe) • *great-niece / grandniece* (= Großnichte)
great-grandfather (= Urgroßvater) • *great-grandmother* (= Urgroßmutter) • *great-grandparents* (= Urgroßeltern) • *great-grandson* (= Urenkel) etc.
great-great-grandfather (= Ururgroßvater) etc.

"My in-laws are coming."

2 Marriage and divorce
Ehe und Ehescheidung

An ideal wife is any woman who has an ideal husband.
(Booth Tarkington, US novelist and playwright, 1869–1946)

marriage ['mærɪdʒ] — Ehe; Heirat
She has a daughter by a previous marriage. — Sie hat eine Tochter aus einer früheren Ehe.
The marriage took place in church. — Die Trauung fand in der Kirche statt.
marriage certificate [sə'tɪfɪkət] — Trauschein; Heiratsurkunde
marriage (guidance) counsellor — Eheberater(in)
marry ['mæri] — **heiraten; trauen**
Will you marry me? — Willst du mich heiraten?
They were married by the bishop. — Sie wurden vom Bischof getraut.
She's married to an artist. — Sie ist mit einem Künstler verheiratet.
They got married in 1994. — Sie haben 1994 geheiratet.
married couple [mærid 'kʌpl] — Ehepaar
matrimony ['mætrɪməni] — *(förmliches Wort für)* (die) **Ehe**
bachelor ['bætʃələ] — **Junggeselle**
He stayed a bachelor all his life. — Er blieb sein Leben lang Junggeselle.
common-law marriage ['kɒmən] — **eheähnliche Lebensgemeinschaft**
Ted and his common-law wife — Ted und seine Lebensgefährtin
propose to someone [prə'pəʊz] — **jemand einen Heiratsantrag machen**
He proposed to her. — Er machte ihr einen Heiratsantrag.
proposal (of marriage) [prə'pəʊzl] — **(Heirats-)Antrag**
engaged (to be married) [ɪn'geɪdʒd] — **verlobt**
They've just got engaged. — Sie haben sich gerade verlobt.
engagement [ɪn'geɪdʒmənt] — **Verlobung**
her **fiancé** – his **fiancée** [fi'ɒnseɪ] — ihr **Verlobter** – seine **Verlobte**
wedding ['wedɪŋ] — **Trauung; Hochzeit**
wedding ceremony ['serəməni] — Trauung; Eheschließung
wedding dress – wedding ring — Hochzeitskleid – Trauring / Ehering
She wants (to have) a church wedding. — Sie möchte sich kirchlich trauen lassen.
shotgun wedding — („Schrotflintenheirat") Mussheirat
It was a shotgun wedding. — Sie mussten heiraten.
silver / golden wedding (anniversary) — silberne / goldene Hochzeit
We celebrated our silver wedding last year. — Wir haben voriges Jahr unsere Silberhochzeit gefeiert.
wed [wed] — *(in Boulevardzeitungen)* **heiraten**
Prince to wed dancer — Prinz wird Tänzerin heiraten
registry office / register office BE — **Standesamt**
registry-office wedding / civil wedding — standesamtliche Trauung
the banns [bænz] — **das Aufgebot**
bride and (bride)groom [gruːm] — **Braut und Bräutigam**
bridesmaid ['braɪdzmeɪd] — **Brautjungfer**
best man [best 'mæn] — **Trauzeuge** (des Bräutigams)
honeymoon ['hʌnimuːn] — **Flitterwochen; Hochzeitsreise**
The newlyweds went to Rome for their honeymoon. — Ihre Flitterwochen verbrachten die Neuvermählten in Rom.

husband [ˈhʌzbənd] **and wife**	**(Ehe-)Mann und (Ehe-)Frau**
(Give) My regards to your wife.	Grüßen Sie Ihre Frau.
her ex-husband	ihr Exmann
spouse [spaʊs]	(*förmlich*) **(Ehe-)Gatte / Gattin**
partner [ˈpɑːtnə]	**Partner(in); Lebensgefährte / -gefährtin**
gay marriage [geɪ ˈmærɪdʒ]	**Homo-Ehe**
wear [eə] **the pants** (– wore – worn)	**die Hosen anhaben**
She's the one who wears the pants.	Sie ist diejenige, die die Hosen anhat.
anniversary [ænɪˈvɜːsəri]	**Hochzeitstag**
our 20th wedding anniversary	unser 20. Hochzeitstag
legitimate [lɪˈdʒɪtəmət] – **illegitimate**	**ehelich – nichtehelich**
legitimate and illegitimate children	eheliche und nichteheliche Kinder
faithful [ˈfeɪθfl] – **unfaithful**	**treu – untreu**
I've never been unfaithful to you.	Ich bin dir nie untreu geworden.
infidelity [ɪnfɪˈdeləti]	**Untreue** (*in Ehe bzw. Partnerschaft*)
adultery [əˈdʌltəri]	**Ehebruch**
commit [kəˈmɪt] adultery	Ehebruch begehen
affair [əˈfeə]	(außereheliches) **Verhältnis; Affäre**
an extramarital (love) affair	ein außereheliches (Liebes-)Verhältnis
Did he have an affair with her?	Hatte er wohl ein Verhältnis mit ihr?
mistress [ˈmɪstrəs]	**Geliebte; Mätresse**
lover [ˈlʌvə]	**Liebhaber; Geliebter**
His wife had a lover.	Seine Frau hatte einen Liebhaber.
philanderer [fɪˈlændərə]	**Schürzenjäger; Frauenheld**
separate [ˈsepəreɪt]	**sich trennen**
His parents are separated.	Seine Eltern leben getrennt.
separation [sepəˈreɪʃn]	**Trennung**
break up (– broke – broken)	**in die Brüche gehen**
Their marriage has broken up.	Ihre Ehe ist gescheitert.
on the rocks [rɒks]	(*Ehe*) **gescheitert, kaputt**
divorce [dɪˈvɔːs]	**(Ehe-)Scheidung**
Sue has filed for divorce.	Sue hat die Scheidung eingereicht.
Ken wants a divorce.	Ken will sich scheiden lassen.
contested / uncontested divorce	streitige / einverständliche Scheidung
She wants to divorce him.	Sie will sich von ihm scheiden lassen.
They (got) divorced.	Sie ließen sich scheiden.
alimony [ˈælɪməni]	**Unterhalt** (nach der Scheidung)
He has to pay alimony to his former wife.	Er muss seiner früheren Frau Unterhalt zahlen.

Aus *pal* (= Gefährte / Gefährtin) und *alimony* hat man im AE umgangssprachlich das Wort *palimony* gebildet, mit dem Unterhalt(szahlung) nach der Auflösung einer eheähnlichen Lebensgemeinschaft bezeichnet wird.

custody [ˈkʌstədi]	**elterliche(s) Sorge(recht)**
She got custody of the children.	Die Kinder wurden ihr zugesprochen.
widow [ˈwɪdəʊ] – **widower** [ˈwɪdəʊə]	**Witwe – Witwer**
bigamy [ˈbɪgəmi] – **bigamist**	**Bigamie – Bigamist(in)**

Parents and children
Eltern und Kinder

→ 1.4 Childhood and youth

The thing that impresses me most about America is the way
parents obey their children. (*Edward, Duke of Windsor, king of Britain
Jan.– Dec. 1936, 1894–1972*)

pregnancy ['prɛgnənsi]	**Schwangerschaft**
morning sickness ['mɔːnɪŋ sɪknəs]	**morgendliche Übelkeit**

Dass eine Frau schwanger (= *pregnant*) ist, kann auf unterschiedliche Weise
ausgedrückt werden:
*She's going to have a baby. She's having a baby. She's expecting. She's in the
family way. – An expectant mother* ist eine werdende Mutter.

labour ['leɪbə]	(die) **(Geburts-)Wehen**
the onset of labour	das Einsetzen der Wehen
midwife ['mɪdwaɪf] *Pl.* midwives	**Hebamme**
delivery [dɪ'lɪvəri]	**Entbindung**
birth [bɜːθ]	**Geburt**
before / after birth	vor / nach der Geburt
give birth to a child (– gave – given)	ein Kind zur Welt bringen
birth certificate [sə'tɪfɪkət]	Geburtsurkunde
Caesarean (section) [sɪ'zeərɪən]	**Kaiserschnitt**
miscarriage ['mɪskærɪdʒ]	**Fehlgeburt**
premature ['premətʃə]	**vorzeitig**
The baby was ten weeks premature.	Das Baby kam zehn Wochen zu früh.
twin(s) [twɪn(z)]	**Zwilling(e)**
baptism / christening ['krɪsnɪŋ]	**Taufe**
godchild ['gɒdtʃaɪld] *Pl.* -children	**Patenkind**
godfather – godmother	**Patenonkel – Patentante**

Kosewörter (= *terms of endearment*)
Für *father: dad, daddy, pa* [pɑː], *papa* [pə'pɑː], *pop, my old man.*
Für *mother: ma, mum* BE, *mummy* BE, *mom* AE, *mommy* AE, *mam(m)a*
   ['mɑːmə] AE, *my old lady.*
Für *the child: the little one, the little guy* [gaɪ], *the kid, our darling, our little
   angel* ['eɪndʒl], *the moppet* (= *little girl:* der kleine Fratz), *the little bugger*
   (= der kleine Kerl), *you little rascal* ['rɑːskl] (= du kleiner Schlingel).

bottle-feed – breast-feed	mit der Flasche ernähren – stillen
(– fed – fed)	
nappy BE / AE **diaper** ['daɪəpə]	**Windel**
change the baby's nappy / diaper	das Baby wickeln
potty ['pɒti]	**Töpfchen**
Have you been to the potty?	Bist du auf dem Topf gewesen?
potty training / toilet training	Sauberkeitserziehung

bath [bɑ:θ] *BE* / *AE* **bathe** [beɪð] the baby — das Baby **baden**

lullaby [ˈlʌləbaɪ] — Wiegenlied; Schlaflied

bedtime story [bedtaɪm ˈstɔ:ri] — Gutenachtgeschichte

the terrible twos [terəbl ˈtu:z] — das **Trotzalter** (im 2. Lebensjahr)

Family wird oft in der Bedeutung *children* verwendet: *The couple doesn't / don't want to start a family yet.* (= Das Paar will zunächst noch keine Kinder.) Beachten Sie, dass hier *couple* sowohl als Singular (*doesn't*) als auch als Plural (*don't*) konstruiert werden kann.

---

care [keə] — Obhut; Pflege
An aunt took the child into care. — Eine Tante nahm das Kind in Pflege.

foster parents [ˈfɒstə peərənts] — **Pflegeeltern**

adopt – **adoption** [əˈdɒpʃn] — **adoptieren** – **Adoption**
an adopted child [əˈdɒptɪd] — ein adoptiertes Kind / Adoptivkind
put up for adoption (– put – put) — zur Adoption freigeben

guardian [ˈgɑ:diən] – **guardianship** — **Vormund** – **Vormundschaft**

orphan [ˈɔ:fn] – **orphanage** [ˈɔ:fnɪdʒ] — **Waise(nkind)** – **Waisenhaus**

bring up / **raise** / **rear** [rɪər] **a child** — **ein Kind großziehen**

upbringing [ˈʌpbrɪŋɪŋ] — **Erziehung; Kinderstube**
She had a strict upbringing. — Sie wurde streng erzogen.

single parent [sɪŋgl ˈpeərənt] — **allein Erziehende(r)**

working mother [wɜ:kɪŋ ˈmʌðə] — **berufstätige Mutter**

take after someone (– took – taken) — **jemand nachschlagen / ähnlich sein**
She takes after her mother. — Sie kommt nach ihrer Mutter.

educate [ˈedjukeɪt] — **erziehen; bilden**
She was educated at home. — Sie wurde zu Hause unterrichtet.

education [edjuˈkeɪʃn] — **Erziehung; Bildung**

gifted children [ˈgɪftɪd tʃɪldrən] — **besonders begabte Kinder**
special education for the gifted — Begabtenförderung

(mentally) retarded [rɪˈtɑ:dɪd] — **(geistig) zurückgeblieben**

pocket money *BE* / *AE* **allowance** — **Taschengeld**
We've increased his allowance. — Wir haben sein Taschengeld erhöht.

chores [tʃɔ:z] — (lästige) **häusliche Pflichten**
do chores around the house — Arbeiten im Hause verrichten

grownup [ˈgrəunʌp] — (*Kindersprache*) **Erwachsene(r)**
Don't tell the grownups. — Sag das nicht den Erwachsenen!

tell someone off (– told – told) — **jemand ausschimpfen**
She told him off for hitting Ken. — Sie schimpfte mit ihm, weil er Ken gehauen hatte.

She gave him a good telling-off. — Sie hat ihn ganz schön ausgeschimpft.

scold [skəuld] **a child** — ein Kind **ausschimpfen / schelten**

hit a child (– hit – hit) — ein Kind **schlagen / hauen**

spoil a child (– spoilt* – spoilt*) — ein Kind **verziehen / verwöhnen**

neglect [nɪˈglækt] **a child** — ein Kind **vernachlässigen**

abandon [əˈbændən] **a child** — ein Kind **aussetzen**

ill-treat [ɪlˈtri:t] **a child** — ein Kind **misshandeln**

child abuse [ˈtʃaɪld əbju:s] — **Kindesmisshandlung** / **-missbrauch**

Parents-and-children proverbs

1 One **father** is more than a hundred schoolmasters.	Ein Vater ist mehr als hundert Schulmeister.
2 The future of a **child** is the work of the **mother**.	Die Zukunft eines Kindes ist die Arbeit der Mutter.
3 Little **children**, little problems; big **children**, big problems.	Kleine Kinder, kleine Probleme; große Kinder, große Probleme.
4 A **child** without **parents** is like a ship without a rudder.	Ein Kind ohne Eltern ist wie ein Schiff ohne Ruder.
5 Like **father**, like **son**.	Wie der Vater, so der Sohn.
6 No **mother** has a homely **child**.	Keine Mutter hat ein unansehnliches Kind.
7 A **mother's** love never ages.	Mutterliebe altert nie.
8 What **children** hear at home, soon flies abroad.	Was Kinder zu Hause hören, fliegt bald nach draußen.
9 As the **twig** is bent, so is the tree inclined.	Wie der Zweig gebogen wird, so neigt sich der Baum.
10 Naughty **boys** sometimes make good men.	Aus ungezogenen Jungen werden manchmal gute Männer.
11 **Children** should be seen and not heard.	Kinder sollte man sehen und nicht hören.
12 When **children** stand quiet, they have done some ill.	Wenn Kinder still sind, haben sie etwas ausgefressen.
13 **Children** and fools tell the truth.	Kinder und Narren sprechen die Wahrheit.
14 Heaven protects **children**, sailors, and drunken men.	Der Himmel beschützt Kinder, Seeleute und Betrunkene.
15 A **child** needs love the most when he deserves it the least.	Ein Kind bedarf der Liebe am meisten, wenn es sie am wenigsten verdient.
16 If you lie upon roses when **young**, you'll lie upon thorns when old.	Wer in der Jugend auf Rosen liegt, wird im Alter auf Dornen liegen.
17 Spare the rod and spoil the **child**.	Spar die Rute und verdirb das Kind.
18 A **child** that won't hear will feel.	Wer nicht hören will, muss fühlen.
19 A burnt **child** dreads the fire.	Ein gebranntes Kind scheut das Feuer.
20 He that has no **children** brings them up well.	Wer keine Kinder hat, zieht sie gut auf.

Sprichwörter (= *proverbs*) sind alt und überliefern die Erfahrungen vieler Generationen.

An den obigen Sprichwörtern fällt auf, dass das männliche Element überwiegt. Heute würde sich die Gleichstellung der Geschlechter auch in der Sprache spiegeln:

1 *Mother and father are more than a hundred schoolmasters.*

10 *Naughty children sometimes make good adults.*

17 entspricht nicht unserer heutigen Auffassung, geht aber auf die Bibel zurück. Interessant hier, dass das Englische kein eigenes Wort für „verwöhnen" hat, sondern dies mit *spoil* (= verderben) ausdrückt.

11 war ein bekannter Erziehungsgrundsatz der viktorianischen Zeit.

Eating, drinking, clothing
Essen, Trinken, Kleidung

1 **Foods**
  Nahrungsmittel

2 **Beverages**
  Getränke

3 **Kitchen and cooking**
  Küche und Kochen

4 **Meals**
  Mahlzeiten

5 **Eating out**
  Auswärts essen

6 **Clothing**
  Kleidung

3

Foods
Nahrungsmittel

→15.1 Animals, 15.2 Plants

Tell me what you eat and I will tell you what you are. (*Proverb*)

food [fuːd] (= Nahrung / Futter / Essen / Kost) • *health food* (= Reform-kost) • *junk food* (= minderwertige Kost) • *fast food* (= Schnellgerichte) • *convenience food* (= Fertignahrung) • *low-cal food* (= kalorienarme Kost)

milk (= Milch) • *full-cream milk* BE / AE *whole* [həʊl] *milk* (= Vollmilch) • *low-fat milk / skim(med) milk* (= fettarme Milch)

butter (= Butter) • *cream* (= Sahne) • *sour cream* (= saure Sahne) • *whipped* [wɪpt] *cream* (= Schlagsahne) • *ice cream* (= Speiseeis) • *yoghurt* [ˈjɒgət] (= Joghurt)

cheese [tʃiːz] (= Käse) • *cottage cheese* (= Hüttenkäse) • *goat cheese* (= Zie-genkäse) • *sheep's milk cheese* (= Schafskäse) • *Swiss cheese* (= Schweizer Käse) • *American cheese* AE (= Chester)

egg (= Ei) • *boiled* [bɔɪld] *egg* (= gekochtes Ei) • *fried* [fraɪd] *eggs* (= Spie-geleier) • *scrambled* [ˈskræmbld] *eggs* (= Rührei)

bread [bred] (= Brot) • *white bread* (= Weißbrot) • *brown bread* (= Grau-brot) • *rye* [raɪ] *bread* (= Roggenbrot) • *wholemeal* [ˈhəʊlmiːl] *bread* BE / AE *whole-grain bread* / AE *whole-wheat* [wiːt] *bread* (= Vollkornbrot) • *baguette* [bəˈget] • *roll* (= Brötchen) • *bun* (= süßes Brötchen) • *scone* [skɒn] (= weicher kleiner Kuchen, der, mit Butter bestrichen, zum Tee gegessen wird) • *sandwich* (= „Klappstulle") • *open sandwich* (= belegtes Brot) • *club sandwich / double-decker* (= „Doppeldecker"-Sandwich)

pastries [ˈpeɪstriz] (= Gebäck) • *cake* (= Kuchen) • *gateau* [ˈgætəʊ] (= Torte) • *tart* (= Obstkuchen / -törtchen) • *pancake* (= Eierkuchen) • *omelette* [ˈɒmlət] (= Omelett) • *doughnut* [ˈdəʊnʌt] (= Berliner [Pfannkuchen]) • *waffle* [ˈwɒfl] (= Waffel) • *shortbread* (= schottischer Butterteigkeks) • *biscuit* [ˈbɪskɪt] BE / AE *cookie* (= Keks) • *cracker* (= ungesüßter Keks)

Fruitcake [ˈfruːtkeɪk] ist ein englischer Napfkuchen, der *raisins* (= Rosinen), *currants* (= Korinthen), *nuts* (= Nüsse) etc. enthält. – *Nut(s)* bezeichnet auch jemand, der ein bisschen verrückt ist: *He's a bit of a nut.* (= Er spinnt ein bisschen.) *You must be nuts.* (= Du spinnst wohl.) *She's as nutty as a fruitcake* heißt, dass sie total verrückt ist. Schließlich kann man auch eine Person selbst als *fruitcake* bezeichnen: *You're a fruitcake.* (= Du hast ja 'ne Macke.)

grain (= Getreide) • *rye* (= Roggen) • *wheat* [wiːt] (= Weizen) • *flour* [ˈflaʊə] (= Mehl) • *bran* (= Kleie) • *oats* (= Hafer) • *rice* (= Reis)

cereals ['sɪərɪəlz] (= Getreideflocken) • *cornflakes* • *rolled oats* (= Hafer-flocken) • *porridge* BE / AE *oatmeal* (= Haferbrei)

sweets (= Süßigkeiten) • *candy* AE (= Bonbon / Bonbons / Süßigkeiten) • *butterscotch* (= Karamellbonbons) • *toffee* (= Sahnebonbon) • *a bar of chocolate* ['tʃɒklət] (= ein Riegel / eine Tafel Schokolade)

pasta ['pæstə] (= Teigwaren / Nudeln) • *dough* [dəʊ] (= Teig) • *noodles* (= Nudeln) • *spaghetti* • *macaroni* • *ravioli* • *vermicelli* [vɜːmɪ'tʃeli] (= Fadennudeln) • *pizza* ['piːtsə] • *dumpling* (= Kloß / Knödel)

meat [miːt] (= Fleisch) • *beef* (= Rindfleisch) • *pork* (= Schweinefleisch) • *veal* (= Kalbfleisch) • *lamb* [læm] (= Lammfleisch) • *mutton* (= Hammelfleisch) • *bacon* ['beɪkən] (= Speck) • *ham* (= Schinken) • *meatball* (= Frikadelle / Bulette)

poultry ['pəʊltri] (= Geflügel) • *chicken* (= Huhn) • *duck* (= Ente) • *goose* [guːs] (= Gans) • *turkey* (= Truthahn / Pute) • *pheasant* ['feznt] (= Fasan)

game (= Wild) • *venison* ['venɪsn] (= Hirsch / Reh) • *hare* (= Hase) • *rabbit* (= Kaninchen) • *wild boar* [waɪld 'bɔː] (= Wildschwein)

sausage ['sɒsɪdʒ] (= Wurst) • *liver* ['lɪvə] *sausage* BE / AE *liverwurst* (= Leber-wurst) • *frank(furter)* ['fræŋk(fɜːtə)] (= Frankfurter Würstchen) • *hot dog* • *pâté* ['pæteɪ] (= Pastete)

seafood (= Meeresfrüchte) • *fish* (= Fisch) • *eel* (= Aal) • *haddock* (= Schellfisch) • *halibut* ['hælɪbət] (= Heilbutt) • *herring* (= Hering) • *kipper* (= Bückling) • *plaice* (= Scholle) • *salmon* ['sæmən] (= Lachs) • *smoked salmon* (= Räucherlachs) • *sole* (= Seezunge) • *trout* (= Forelle) • *tuna* ['tjuːnə] (= Thunfisch) • *shellfish* (= Schalentiere) • *lobster* (= Hummer) • *oyster* (= Auster) • *shrimps* (= kleinere Krabben / Garnelen) • *prawns* [prɔːnz] (= größere Krabben / Garnelen) • *scampi* ['skæmpi]

soup [suːp] (= Suppe) • *broth* [brɒθ] / *consommé* [kən'sɒmeɪ] (= klare Suppe / Brühe) • *stew* [stjuː] (= Eintopf)

sauce [sɔːs] (= Soße) • *Worcester* ['wʊstə] *sauce* BE / AE *Worcestershire sauce* (= Worcestersoße) • *gravy* ['greɪvi] (= Bratensoße)

fat (= Fett) • *oil* (= Öl) • *olive oil* [ɒlɪv 'ɔɪl] (= Olivenöl) • *margarine* [mɑːdʒə'riːn] • *lard* (= Schweineschmalz)

herbs [hɜːbz] (= Gewürzkräuter) • *spice* (= Gewürz) • *seasoning* ['siːznɪŋ] (= Gewürze) • *salt* [sɔːlt] (= Salz) • *pepper* (= Pfeffer) • *curry* ['kʌri] • *mustard* ['mʌstəd] (= Senf) • *garlic* (= Knoblauch) • *parsley* ['pɑːsli] (= Peter-silie) • *vanilla* [və'nɪlə] (= Vanille)

vegetable(s) ['vedʒtəbl(z)] (= Gemüse) • *asparagus* [ə'spærəgəs] (= Spargel) • *beans* (= Bohnen) • *peas* (= Erbsen) • *cabbage* (= Kohl) • *Brussels sprouts* (= Rosenkohl) • *cauliflower* (= Blumenkohl) • *spinach* ['spɪnɪtʃ] (= Spinat) • *maize* BE / AE *corn* (= Mais) • *mushroom* (= Speisepilz / Champignon) •

tomato [təˈmɑːtəʊ] Pl. *-oes* (= Tomate) • *cucumber* [ˈkjuː-] (= Gurke) •
onion [ˈʌnjən] (= Zwiebel) • *radish* [æ] (= Radieschen) • *horseradish*
(= Meerettich) • *lettuce* (= Kopfsalat) • *rhubarb* (= Rhabarber)

Zu den *vegetables* werden im Englischen auch ausdrücklich Kartoffeln (= *potatoes* [pəˈteɪtəʊz]) gerechnet. *Meat and two vegetables* wäre entsprechend als
Fleisch mit Kartoffeln und Gemüse zu verstehen. – Kartoffelgerichte: *boiled
potatoes* (= Salzkartoffeln) • *potatoes boiled in their skins* (= Pellkartoffeln) •
fried potatoes (= Bratkartoffeln) • *(potato) chips* BE / AE *French fried potatoes /
French fries* (= Pommes frites) • *baked potatoes* (= in der Schale gebackene
Kartoffeln) • *mashed potatoes* (= Kartoffelbrei) • *potato salad* (= Kartoffelsalat) • *potato pancakes* (= Kartoffelpuffer)

fruit [fruːt] (= Obst) • *apple* (= Apfel) • *pear* [peə] (= Birne) • *cherry* (= Kirsche) • *plum* (= Pflaume) • *peach* (= Pfirsich) • *grape* (= Weintraube) • *berries*
(= Beeren) • *strawberries* (= Erdbeeren) • *blackberries* (= Brombeeren) •
raspberries [ˈrɑːzbəriz] (= Himbeeren) • *blueberries* (= Blaubeeren) • *gooseberries* [ˈɡʊzbəriz] (= Stachelbeeren) • *black currants* (= schwarze Johannisbeeren) • *raisins* [ˈreɪznz] (= Rosinen) • *banana* [bəˈnɑːnə] (= Banane) •
orange [ˈɒrɪndʒ] (= Apfelsine) • *grapefruit* • *lemon* [e] (= Zitrone) • *pineapple*
(= Ananas) • *date* (= Dattel) • *olive* [ˈɒlɪv] (= Olive)

Dem deutschen Schlagwort Bio- entspricht bei Lebensmitteln in der Regel das
Adjektiv *organic* [ɔːˈɡænɪk]: *organic food* (= Biokost / Biolebensmittel), *organic
vegetables* (= Biogemüse), *organic fruits* (= Bioobst), *organic milk* (= Biomilch),
organic products [ˈprɒdʌkts] (= Bioerzeugnisse).
Der Abfall, der von Biolebensmitteln übrig bleibt, heißt *organic waste* (= Biomüll). Die Landwirte, die biologischen Anbau betreiben, nennt man folgerich-
tig *organic farmers* (= Biobauern / Ökobauern), die Anbaumethode *organic farming* (= Bioanbau / biologischer Anbau). Wenn ein Bauernhof zu ökologischem
Landbau übergeht, so gebraucht man dafür häufig das Verb *go*: *The farm went
fully organic ten years ago.* (= Vor zehn Jahren stellte der Hof vollkommen auf
Bioanbau um.) Auch *bio-* [baɪəʊ] findet sich im Englischen, allerdings in anderen Zusammensetzungen: *bio bin* (= Biotonne), *biodegradable* [baɪəʊdɪˈɡreɪdəbl]
(= biologisch abbaubar), *bioengineering* [baɪəʊenʒɪˈnɪərɪŋ] (= Biotechnik), *biofuel*
[baɪəʊˈfjuːəl] (= Biotreibstoff), *bioethics* [baɪəʊˈeθɪks] (= Bioethik), *bioweapons*
[baɪəʊˈwepnz] (= biologische Waffen).
Den Bioläden entsprechen im Englischen in etwa *wholefood* [ˈhəʊlfuːd] *shops*
oder *organic food shops*.

nut (= Nuss) • *walnut* [ˈwɔːlnʌt] (= Walnuss) • *hazelnut* [ˈheɪzlnʌt] (= Haselnuss) • *peanut* (= Erdnuss) • *chestnut* [ˈtʃesnʌt] (= Kastanie)

salad [ˈsæləd] (= Salat) • *salad dressing* (= Salatsoße) • *mixed salad / tossed sa-
lad* (= gemischter Salat) • *green salad* (= grüner Salat) • *tomato salad* (= Tomatensalat) • *coleslaw* [ˈkəʊlslɔː] (= Kohl- / Krautsalat) • *fruit salad* (= Obstsalat)

Zum Ausdruck der Frische (*freshly caught fish, freshly baked bread*) wird häufig die
Form ohne *-ly* verwendet: *fresh-caught trout* (= fangfrische Forellen), *fresh-baked
bread* (= frisch gebackenes Brot), *fresh-picked strawberries* (= frisch gepflückte Erdbeeren), *fresh-squeezed orange juice* (= frisch ausgepresster Orangensaft), *fresh-brewed
coffee* (= frisch zubereiteter Kaffee), *new-laid / fresh-laid eggs* (= frisch gelegte Eier).

Beverages
Getränke

→ 12.10 Drinking and smoking

Pure water is better than bad wine. (*Proverb*)

soft drinks [sɒft 'drɪŋks]	alkoholfreie Getränke
(still mineral ['mɪnərəl]**) water**	(stilles Mineral-)Wasser
sparkling / fizzy water	Sprudel
drinking water – tap water	Trinkwasser – Leitungswasser
tonic [ɒ] (water) / *AE* quinine ['kwaɪnaɪn] water	Tonic
seltzer (water) ['seltsə]	Selters(wasser)
soda (water) / *AE auch* **club soda**	Soda(wasser)
soda ['səʊdə] **(pop)** *AE / BE* **pop**	Limo(nade); Brause
Soda (pop) / Pop is a sweet fizzy drink.	Limonade ist ein süßer Sprudel.
cream soda [kriːm 'səʊdə] *AE*	(kohlensäurehaltiges Vanillegetränk)

Dass ein Getränk kohlensäurehaltig ist, kann mit den Adjektiven *carbonated* ['kɑːbəneɪtɪd], *fizzy* ['fɪzi] oder *gassy* ['gæsi] ausgedrückt werden: *Colas are carbonated / fizzy soft drinks. American beers are too gassy for my taste.*

lemonade [leməˈneɪd]	(Zitronen-)Limonade
cola ['kəʊlə]	(Coca-Cola™, Coke™, Pepsi™ etc.)
ginger ale [dʒɪndʒə 'eɪl]	(kohlensäurehaltiges alkoholfreies Getränk mit Ingwergeschmack)
ginger beer [dʒɪndʒə 'bɪə]	(leicht alkoholhaltiges) Ingwerbier
root beer ['ruːt bɪə] *AE*	Limonade (aus Wurzelextrakten)
(fruit) juice [('fruːt) dʒuːs]	(Frucht-)Saft
apple / pineapple juice	Apfel- / Ananassaft
grape / grapefruit juice	Trauben- / Grapefruitsaft
squash [skwɒʃ] *BE*	Fruchtsaft (aus Konzentrat + Wasser)
a glass of orange squash	ein Glas Orangensaft
milkshake ['mɪlkʃeɪk]	Milchshake; Milchmixgetränk

Getränke können durch Vorsetzen von *a(n)* / *one* oder ein Zahlwort „portioniert" werden: *A coffee* (= *a cup of coffee*) *and a grapefruit juice* (= *a glass of grapefruit juice*)*, please. Two sodas* (= *bottles of soda*)*, please.*

(decaffeinated [diːˈkæfɪneɪtɪd]) **coffee**	(koffeinfreier) Kaffee
Sanka™ ['sæŋkə] *AE*	Sanka™ (= koffeinfreier Kaffee)
(black / green) **tea** [tiː]	(schwarzer / grüner) Tee
herb(al) tea [hɜːb(l) 'tiː]	Kräutertee
the cup that cheers [tʃɪəz] *BE*	„die Tasse, die aufmuntert" (= Tee)
cocoa ['kəʊkəʊ]	Kakao
hot / drinking chocolate ['tʃɒklət]	(heiße / Trink-)Schokolade; Kakao

Kitchen and cooking
Küche und Kochen

Everyone who runs a kitchen can, in the choice and preparation of food, decisively influence family health and happiness. (*From:* Joy of Cooking *by I.S. Rombauer and M. Rombauer Becker, a popular American cookbook*)

cooking ['kʊkɪŋ]	**Kochen**
French cooking / cuisine [kwɪˈziːn]	die französische Küche
home cooking / plain cooking	Hausmannskost
cookery book *BE* / *AE* **cookbook**	**Kochbuch**
clean the vegetables ['vedʒtəblz]	**das Gemüse putzen**
peel the potatoes [pəˈteɪtəʊz]	**die Kartoffeln schälen**
dress the salad ['sæləd]	**den Salat anmachen**
garnish ['gɑːnɪʃ] **the fish**	**den Fisch garnieren**
sieve [sɪv]	**Sieb; sieben**
stir [stɜː]	**(um)rühren**
beat (– beat – beaten) / **whip**	(*Ei / Sahne*) **schlagen**
slice [slaɪs]	**Scheibe; (in Scheiben) schneiden**
sliced bread [slaɪst 'bred]	geschnittenes Brot
chop [tʃɒp]	**klein schneiden; Kotelett**
mince [mɪns]	**durch den Fleischwolf drehen**
minced meat / mince	Hackfleisch; Gehacktes

Idioms mit „Küchenausdrücken"

*He didn't **mince** his words.* (= Er nahm kein Blatt vor den Mund.)
*The boss will make **mincemeat** of me if he hears that.* (= Der Chef macht Hackfleisch aus mir / macht mich zur Schnecke, wenn er das hört.)
*We fell / jumped out of the **frying pan** into the fire.* (= Wir kamen vom Regen in die Traufe.)
*We decided to let him **stew** [stjuː] in his own juice* [dʒuːs]. (= Wir beschlossen, ihn in seinem eigenen Saft schmoren zu lassen.)
*I can't afford a holiday – have to keep the **pot** / **kettle boiling**.* (= Ich kann mir keinen Urlaub leisten – muss dafür sorgen, dass der Schornstein raucht.)

grind [graɪnd] (– ground – ground)	(*z.B. Kaffee*) **mahlen**
coffee grinder / **coffee mill**	**Kaffeemühle**
boil [bɔɪl]	**kochen; sieden**
a soft-boiled / hard-boiled egg	ein weich gekochtes / hart gekochtes Ei
parboil ['pɑːbɔɪl]	**halbgar kochen; ankochen**
bake a cake [keɪk]	**einen Kuchen backen**
fry [fraɪ]	**(in der Pfanne) braten**
fried eggs [fraɪd 'egz]	Spiegeleier
sunny-side up *AE*	(*Ei*) **nur auf einer Seite gebraten**
stew [stjuː]	(*Fleisch*) **schmoren**; (*Obst*) **dünsten**
roast [rəʊst]	**braten; Braten**
roast pork / beef / duck	Schweine- / Rinder- / Entenbraten
roast chicken [rəʊst 'tʃɪkən]	Brathähnchen

grill [grɪl] *BE / AE* **broil** [brɔɪl]	grillen
barbecue [ˈbɑːbəkjuː] **a steak**	ein Steak grillen / auf dem Rost braten
rare [reə]	nur schwach gebraten
I want my steak [steɪk] rare.	Ich möchte mein Steak „englisch".
medium [ˈmiːdiəm]	halb durchgebraten; halb durch
well done [wel ˈdʌn]	durchgebraten
toast [təʊst] – **toaster**	Toast / toasten – Toaster
pots and pans [pɒts n ˈpænz]	Töpfe und Pfannen
teapot – **coffeepot** [ˈkɒfipɒt]	Teekanne – Kaffeekanne
frying pan *BE / AE* **skillet** [ˈskɪlət]	Bratpfanne
saucepan [ˈsɔːspən]	Kochtopf
kettle [ˈketl]	Kessel
Shall I put the kettle on?	Soll ich Kaffee / Tee machen?
dish [dɪʃ]	Schüssel; Gericht (= *Speise*)
do the dishes [ˈdɪʃɪz] (– did – done)	das Geschirr abwaschen
vegetarian [vedʒəˈteəriən] dishes	vegetarische Gerichte
bowl [bəʊl]	Schüssel; Schale
salad / soup [suːp] bowl	Salat- / Suppenschüssel
cup and saucer [ˈsɔːsə]	Tasse und Untertasse
plate [pleɪt]	Teller
jar [dʒɑː]	(Marmeladen-)**Glas; Topf / Krug / Gefäß** (aus Glas, Ton etc.)
a jar of English marmalade	ein Glas englischer Orangen-marmelade
jug [dʒʌg] *BE / AE* **pitcher**	(Ton- / Glas-)**Kanne / Krug**
a jug of fresh milk	ein Krug mit frischer Milch
can [kæn]	**einmachen; eindosen; einwecken**
can opener [ˈkæn əʊpnə]	Büchsenöffner; Dosenöffner
canned beans [kænd ˈbiːnz]	Bohnen in der Dose / Büchse

Können Sie das enträtseln?
After a record [ˈrekɔːd] *harvest, a Californian bean farmer was asked what the farmers were doing with such vast quantities* [ɒ] *of beans. His answer: "We eat what we can, and what we can't eat we can."*

bottle opener [ˈbɒtl əʊpnə]	**Flaschenöffner**
corkscrew [ˈkɔːkskruː]	**Korkenzieher**
nutcracker [ˈnʌtkrækə]	**Nussknacker**
knife [naɪf] **and fork** *Pl.* knives	**Messer und Gabel**
spoon [spuːn]	**Löffel**
soupspoon – teaspoon	Suppenlöffel – Teelöffel
two teaspoonfuls of sugar	zwei Teelöffel Zucker
measuring [ˈmeʒərɪŋ] **cup / spoon**	**Messbecher / -löffel**
cooker *BE / AE* **stove** [stəʊv]	**(Koch-)Herd**
pressure cooker [ˈpreʃə kʊkə]	Schnellkochtopf
oven [ˈʌvn]	**Backofen**
microwave (oven) [ˈmaɪkrəweɪv]	**Mikrowelle(nherd)**
coffeemaker [ˈkɒfimeɪkə]	**Kaffeemaschine**
tray [treɪ]	**Tablett**
blender [ˈblendə]	**(Küchen-)Mixer**

Meals
Mahlzeiten

At a dinner party one should eat wisely but not too well, and talk well but not too wisely. (*W. Somerset Maugham, British writer, 1874–1965*)

breakfast [ˈbrekfəst]
What time are we having breakfast?
I have coffee for breakfast.
a working breakfast

Frühstück
Wann frühstücken wir?
Ich trinke zum Frühstück Kaffee.
ein Arbeitsfrühstück

 Continental breakfast: ein „kleines" Frühstück, das aus *bread* (= Brot), *rolls* (= Brötchen), *croissants* [ˈkwæsɑːnts] (= Hörnchen), *butter, jam* (= Marmelade) und *coffee* besteht.
English breakfast: ein „großes" Frühstück bestehend aus *bacon* [ˈbeɪkən] *and eggs* (= Speck und Eiern), *cereals* [ˈsɪərɪəlz] wie *cornflakes* oder *muesli* [ˈmjuːzli], *toast and marmalade* [ˈmɑːməleɪd] (= Orangenmarmelade) sowie *fruit* [fruːt] (= Obst) oder *fruit juice* [dʒuːs] (= Fruchtsaft) etc.
Power breakfast (= „Kraftfrühstück" / Arbeitsfrühstück): ein kräftiges Frühstück, das Geschäftsleute in einem Restaurant oder Hotel einnehmen, wobei sie gleichzeitig geschäftliche Gespräche führen.

brunch [brʌntʃ]
We had a lie-in and then had brunch with the Smiths.

Frühstück und Mittagessen in einem
Wir haben uns ausgeschlafen und haben dann mit den Smiths „gebruncht".

lunch [lʌntʃ] / *förmlich* **luncheon** [ˈlʌntʃən]
We had lunch in the canteen [kænˈtiːn].

Mittagessen (*wenn die Hauptmahlzeit am Abend eingenommen wird*)
Wir haben in der Kantine zu Mittag gegessen.

 „Mahlzeit!" als Grußformel und „Guten Appetit!" haben im Englischen keine direkten Entsprechungen. Statt des Ersteren verwendet man so etwas wie *hello!, hi!* oder *(good) afternoon!*, während das Letztere durch *enjoy* [ɪnˈdʒɔɪ] *your meal!* oder das französische *bon appetit!* [bɒn apeˈti] ausgedrückt werden kann.

tea [tiː]
We had tea at the Savoy [səˈvɔɪ].

(Nachmittags-)Tee / Kaffee
Wir haben im Savoy Kaffee getrunken.

Eat your tea, Bobby.
dinner [ˈdɪnə]

Bobby, iss dein Essen auf!
Abend- / Mittagessen (*als Haupt-mahlzeit*)

We're having people for dinner.
We're going out to dinner tonight.
supper [ˈsʌpə]
She gave the kids their supper and then put them to bed.

Wir haben Gäste zum Essen.
Wir gehen heute Abend essen.
Abendessen; Abendbrot
Sie gab den Kindern ihr Abendbrot und brachte sie dann ins Bett.

Eating out
Auswärts essen

New Yorkers are fanatical about eating out, largely because they tend
to live in apartments with kitchens too small to toss an omelette in.
(*The Time Out New York Guide*)

guest [gest] / *förmlich* **patron** [eɪ]	**Gast**
Patrons are requested … [rɪˈkwestɪd]	Wir bitten unsere verehrten Gäste …
patronize [ˈpætrənaɪz]	**(als Kunde / Kundin) besuchen**
a restaurant patronized by artists	ein Restaurant, in dem Künstler verkehren
our **regulars** [ˈreɡjələz]	unsere **Stammgäste**

Kinds of restaurants [ˈrestrɒnts] (= **Arten von Restaurants**)
bistro [ˈbiːstrəʊ] (= Bistro) • *café* [ˈkæfeɪ] (= kleines Restaurant) • *cafeteria* [kæfəˈtɪəriə] (= Selbstbedienungsrestaurant) • *canteen* [kænˈtiːn] (= Kantine) • *chip shop / chippy* (BE = Fritten- / Pommesbude) • *deli(catessen)* [ˈdeli] (AE = Feinkostgeschäft mit Schnellimbiss) • *coffee bar* (BE = Café) • *coffee shop* (AE = kleines Restaurant, oft in Hotels) • *diner* (AE = Restaurant, das typisch amerikanische Kost in traditionellem Ambiente bietet) • *dining car* (= Speisewagen) • *drive-in* (= Drive-in-Restaurant) • *eatery* (= Esslokal) • *fish and chip shop* (BE = Fischbraterei) • *greasy spoon* [ɡriːsi ˈspuːn] (= „schmieriger Löffel" = kleines, billiges, oft schmuddeliges Esslokal) • *grillroom* (= Restaurant für Grillspezialitäten, oft in Hotels) • *hamburger place* (= Hamburger-Restaurant) • *lunch counter / luncheonette* (AE = Imbissstube) • *pizzeria* [piːtsəˈriːə] • *pull-in* (BE = Raststätte) • *restaurant* • *sandwich bar* • *self-service* (= Selbstbedienungsrestaurant) • *snack bar* (= Imbissstube) • *steakhouse* [ˈsteɪkhaʊs] • *takeaway* BE / AE *carryout / takeout* (= Restaurant für Außer-Haus-Verkauf) • *tearoom* (= Teestube / Café) • *transport café* [ˈtrænspɔːt kæfeɪ] BE / AE *truck stop* (= Fernfahrerraststätte) • *wine bar* (BE = Weinstube)

cloakroom *BE* / *AE* **checkroom**	**Garderobe**

Mit dem Wort *cloakroom* [ˈkləʊkrʊm] fragt man im BE in Theater oder
Restaurant auch nach der Toilette – ein Euphemismus (= verhüllender
Ausdruck).

snack [snæk]	**Imbiss; Kleinigkeit zu essen**
We'll just have a quick snack.	Wir essen nur rasch eine Kleinigkeit.
to take away *BE* / *AE* **to go**	**zum Mitnehmen**
a bag of chips to take away *BE* / *AE* a bag of French fries to go	eine Tüte Fritten / Pommes zum Mitnehmen
book [bʊk]	**buchen; reservieren; vorbestellen**
We'd better book a table.	Wir sollten besser einen Tisch reservieren.
reservation [rezəˈveɪʃn]	**Reservierung**
Have you a reservation, sir?	Haben Sie einen Tisch reserviert?

reserve [rɪˈzɜːv]
I have a table reserved in the name of Smith.
menu [ˈmenjuː]
Waiter, can I have the menu, please?
wine list [ˈwaɪn lɪst]
meal [miːl]
Would you care for a drink before your meal, sir?
a four-course meal
order [ˈɔːdə]
Do you wish to order now, sir?
Can I take your order, sir?
starter [ˈstɑːtə]
What would you like for a starter?
soup of the day / **soup du jour** [suːp dy ʒuːr]
We've **run out of** eel pie [iːl ˈpaɪ].
have (– had – had)
I think I'll have the smoked salmon [ˈsæmən], please.
side dish [ˈsaɪd dɪʃ] / **side order**
decide [dɪˈsaɪd]
Have you decided on a wine, sir?

recommend [rekəˈmend]
I'd recommend a dry Riesling.

choose [tʃuːz] (– chose – chosen)
Have you chosen a sweet, madam?
sweet *BE* / *AE* **dessert** [dɪˈzɜːt]
Can we have some fresh fruit for dessert?
do (– did – done [dʌn])
Do you do tiramisu?
to follow [tə ˈfɒləʊ]
with a coffee to follow
bill [bɪl] *BE* / *AE* **check** [tʃek]
Waiter, the bill / check, please.
service (charge) [ˈsɜːvɪs (tʃɑːdʒ)]
Service (is) not included [ɪnˈkluːdɪd].
cover charge [ˈkʌvə tʃɑːdʒ]
tip / *förmlich* **gratuity** [grəˈtjuːəti]
How much did you tip the maître d' [meɪtrə ˈdiː]?
Gratuities are at the discretion [dɪˈskreʃn] of our clients.
manager [ˈmænɪdʒə]
I'd like to see the manager, please.

reservieren (lassen)
Ich habe einen Tisch auf den Namen Smith reservieren lassen.
Speisekarte
Herr Ober, bitte die Speisekarte.
Weinkarte
Mahlzeit; Essen
Hätten Sie gern einen Drink vor dem Essen?
ein Essen mit vier Gängen
bestellen; Bestellung
Möchten Sie jetzt bestellen?
Kann ich Ihre Bestellung aufnehmen?
Vorspeise
Was hätten Sie gern als Vorspeise?
Tagessuppe

Uns ist die Aalpastete **ausgegangen**.
essen; nehmen
Ich glaube, ich nehme den Räucherlachs.
Beilage
(sich) entscheiden
Haben Sie sich für einen Wein entschieden?
empfehlen
Ich würde einen trockenen Riesling empfehlen.
(aus)wählen
Haben Sie ein Dessert ausgewählt?
Nachtisch
Können wir als Nachtisch frisches Obst haben?
(auf der Karte / im Angebot) **haben**
Haben Sie auch Tiramisu?
danach
und danach einen Kaffee
Rechnung
Herr Ober, bitte zahlen!
Bedienung(sgeld)
Bedienung nicht inbegriffen / extra.
(Preis für das) **Gedeck**
Trinkgeld
Wie viel Trinkgeld hast du dem Oberkellner gegeben?
Trinkgelder sind in das Belieben unserer Gäste gestellt.
Geschäftsführer(in)
Ich möchte bitte mal den Geschäftsführer sprechen.

People working in a restaurant

hostess ['həʊstəs] (= Empfangsdame) • *cloakroom attendant* [ə'tendənt] BE /
AE *checkroom attendant* (= Garderobenfrau) • *waiter* (= Kellner) • *waitress*
(= Kellnerin) • *headwaiter* (= Oberkellner) • *wine waiter* BE / AE *wine*
steward ['stjuːəd] (= Weinkellner) • *busboy* ['bʌsbɔɪ] (AE = Hilfskellner) •
barman BE / AE *barkeeper* / *bartender* (= Barkeeper) • *barmaid* (= Bardame) •
cook (= Koch / Köchin) • *chef* [ʃef] / *chief cook* (= Küchenchef) • *short-order*
cook (AE = Koch / Köchin für Schnellgerichte) • *pastry* ['peɪstri] *cook* (= Konditor / Konditorin) • *dishwasher* (= Geschirrspüler)

buffet ['bʊfeɪ] | **Büfett**
The hotel does an excellent breakfast buffet. | Das Hotel bietet ein ausgezeichnetes Frühstücksbüfett.
salad bar ['sæləd bɑː] | **Salattheke**
serving / **helping** / **portion** ['pɔːʃn] | **Portion**

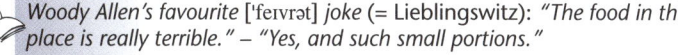

Woody Allen's favourite ['feɪvrət] *joke* (= Lieblingswitz): *"The food in this*
place is really terrible." – "Yes, and such small portions."

cuisine [kwɪ'ziːn] | **Küche**
excellent French cuisine | ausgezeichnete französische Küche

In der gehobenen Gastronomie geläufige französische Ausdrücke

à la carte (= nach der Speisekarte) • *carte du jour* (= Tageskarte) • *entrée*
(AE = Hauptgericht) • *hors d'oeuvres* (= Vorspeisen) • *nouvelle cuisine*
(= „neue Küche" = moderne, d.h. kalorienarme französische Küche) • *plat*
du jour (= Tagesmenü) • *soup du jour* (= Tagessuppe) • *maître d'(hôtel)*
[meɪtrə 'diː] (= Oberkellner) • *spécialité de la maison* (= Spezialität des
Hauses) • *table d'hôte* (= Tagesmenü / -gedeck)

to go with | **passend zu**
I'd like a dry wine to go with the fish. | Zum Fisch hätte ich gern einen trockenen Wein.
hot [hɒt] | **scharf** (gewürzt)
Is this curry ['kʌri] very hot? | Ist dieser Curry sehr scharf?

"And that's our Slimmer's Special."

Clothing
Kleidung

Good clothes open all doors. (*Proverb*)

clothes [kləʊðz]	Kleidung; (Anzieh-)Sachen; Klamotten
I need some new clothes.	Ich brauche was Neues zum Anziehen.
We don't spend a lot on clothes [kləʊðz].	Wir geben nicht viel für Kleidung aus.
casual ['kæʒuəl] clothes	legere Kleidung
smart casual ['kæʒuəl]	sportlich elegant; gepflegte Freizeitkleidung
dress [dres]	Kleidung; sich anziehen / kleiden
She always dresses well.	Sie zieht sich immer gut an.
She was dressed in black.	Sie war schwarz gekleidet.
wear [weə] (– wore – worn)	**tragen**
I never wear a hat.	Ich trage nie einen Hut.
put on (– put – put) [pʊt]	(*Kleidung*) **anziehen**; (*Hut*) **aufsetzen**
You'd better put a coat on.	Du ziehst besser einen Mantel an.
take off (– took – taken)	(*Kleidung*) **ausziehen**; (*Hut*) **abnehmen**
He took off his hat and coat.	Er legte Hut und Mantel ab.
She took her clothes off / undressed.	Sie zog sich aus.

Coats, jackets, and suits (= Mäntel, Jacken und Anzüge)
coat (= Mantel / AE auch Jackett / Sakko) • *overcoat* / *topcoat* (= Mantel) • *raincoat* / BE auch *mackintosh* / *mac* (= Regenmantel) • *fur coat* (= Pelzmantel) • *trench coat* • *anorak* ['ænəræk] • *parka* ['pɑːkə] • *jacket* (= Jacke / Jackett / Sakko) • *sports jacket* BE / AE *sport coat* (= Sportsakko) • *blazer* ['bleɪzə] • *cardigan* ['kɑːdɪɡən] (= Strickjacke) • *suit* [suːt] (= Anzug / Kostüm) • *lounge suit* [laʊndʒ] BE / AE *business suit* ['bɪznəs] (= Straßenanzug) • *pinstripe suit* (= Nadelstreifenanzug) • *trouser suit* BE / AE *pantsuit* (= Hosenanzug) • *waistcoat* ['weɪskəʊt] BE / AE *vest* (= Weste) • *dinner jacket* BE / AE *tuxedo* [tʌk'siːdəʊ] (= Smokingjacke / Smoking) • *tails* / *tailcoat* / *evening dress* (= Frack) • *jogging suit* (= Jogginganzug) *Jackets* oder *suits* können *single-breasted* [sɪŋɡl'brestɪd] (= einreihig) oder *double-breasted* (= zweireihig) sein.
Bei *suits* wird unterschieden zwischen *two-piece suit* (= jacket + trousers) und *three-piece suit* (jacket + waistcoat + trousers).
Bei sehr förmlichen Anlässen wird unterschieden zwischen *black-tie* (= „schwarze Fliege" = Smoking) und *white-tie* (= „weiße Fliege" = Frack).

Dresses (= Kleider)
dress (= Kleid) • *slit dress* (= Kleid mit Gehschlitz) • *wedding dress* / *wedding gown* [gaʊn] (= Hochzeitskleid) • *evening dress* / *evening gown* (= Abendkleid)

Tops (= Oberteile)
blouse [blaʊz] (= Bluse) • *sweater* ['swetə] / *pullover* ['pʊləʊvə] / *jersey* [z] / nur BE *jumper* (= Pullover / Pulli) • *V-neck(ed) sweater* (= Pullover mit

V-Ausschnitt) • *shirt* (= Oberhemd / Hemdbluse) • *long-sleeved – short-sleeved – sleeveless* (= langärmelig – kurzärmelig – ärmellos) • *sweatshirt* (= weit geschnittener Pullover) • *polo shirt* (= Polohemd) • *T-shirt*

Trousers, skirts, etc. (= **Hosen, Röcke** usw.)
trousers / pants (= Hose) • *slacks* (AE = locker sitzende Hose) • *corduroys* ['kɔːdərɔɪz] / *cords* (= Cordhose) • *(blue) jeans / denims* ['denɪmz] (= Jeans) • *shorts* (= kurze Hose) • *Bermuda shorts / Bermudas* [bəˈmjuːdəz] • *skirt* (= Rock) • *pleated skirt* (= Faltenrock) • *kilt* (= Schottenrock)

Bei *trousers, pants, tights* etc. entspricht dem deutschen Singular ein englischer Plural:
These trousers / pants are too tight. (= Diese Hose ist zu eng.)
Where are my tights / pantyhose ['pæntihəʊz]? (= Wo ist meine Strumpfhose?)
My trousers / pants are in this wardrobe ['wɔːdrəʊb]. (= Meine Hose ist / Meine Hosen sind in diesem Schrank.)
„Ein Exemplar" wird unmissverständlich mit *a pair of* ausgedrückt:
I'm looking for a pair of trousers / a pair of pants to match this jacket. (= Ich suche eine Hose, die zu dieser Jacke passt.)

Underwear and swimwear (= **Unterwäsche und Badekleidung**)
(under)pants / AE auch *undershorts* (= Unterhose) • *briefs* [briːfs] (= Slip) • *Jockey™ shorts / BVD's™* [biːviːˈdiːz] nur AE (= Herrenunterhose) • *boxer shorts / boxers* (= Boxershorts) • *long johns* ['lɒŋ dʒɒnz] (= lange Unterhose) • *panties* ['pæntiz] / nur BE *knickers* ['nɪkəz] (= Damenschlüpfer) • *vest* BE / AE *undershirt* (= Unterhemd) • *slip / underskirt* (= Unterrock) • *petticoat* (= Petticoat) • *tights* BE / AE *pantyhose* ['pæntihəʊz] (= Strumpf-hose) • *corset* ['kɔːsət] / BE auch *stays* (= Korsett) • *girdle* ['gɜːdl] (= Hüft-halter / Hüftgürtel) • *bra* [brɑː] (= BH) • *trunks* (= Badehose) • *swimsuit / bathing* ['beɪðɪŋ] *suit* (= Badeanzug) • *bikini* [bɪˈkiːni]

Night clothes [kləʊðz] (= **Nachtwäsche**)
nightdress BE / AE *nightgown* / BE+AE umgangssprachl. *nightie* ['naɪti] (= Damennachthemd) • *nightshirt* (= Herrennachthemd) • *pyjamas* [pəˈdʒɑːməz] BE / AE *pajamas* (= Schlafanzug) • *jammies* BE / AE *Pj's* ['piːdʒeɪz] (umgangssprachl. = Schlafanzug) • *dressing gown* [gaʊn] (= Morgenrock) • *bathrobe* ['bɑːθrəʊb] (= Bademantel)

Footwear ['fʊtweə] (= **Fußbekleidung**)
shoes [ʃuːz] (= Schuhe) • *oxfords* ['ɒksfədz] (= geschnürte Halbschuhe) • *casuals* ['kæʒuəlz] / *slip-on shoes / slip-ons* (= Slipper) • *court shoes* BE / AE *pumps* (= Pumps) • *(high) heels* (= hochhackige Schuhe) • *flats* (= flache Schuhe) • *Loafers™* (= bequeme mokassinartige Halbschuhe) • *wellington boots / wellingtons / wellies* alle BE / AE *rubber boots* (= Gummistiefel) • *sandals* ['sændəlz] (= Sandalen) • *slippers* (= Hausschuhe) • *trainers* BE / AE *sneakers* ['sniːkəz] (= Turnschuhe) • *flip-flops* (= Badesandalen / Flipflops)

Headgear ['hedgɪə] (= Kopfbedeckung)

hat (= Hut) • *top hat / topper* (= Zylinder) • *bowler (hat)* ['bəʊlə] BE /
AE *derby* ['dɑːbi] (= Melone) • *stetson* ['stetsn] / *ten-gallon hat* (= Arten
von Cowboyhut) • *(straw) boater* (BE = steifer Strohhut / Kreissäge) •
deerstalker ['dɪəstɔːkə] (= Sherlock-Holmes-Mütze) • *cap* (= Mütze) •
baseball cap (= Baseballmütze) • *peaked cap* [piːkt] (= Schirmmütze) •
helmet (= Helm) • *crash helmet* (= Sturzhelm) • *headscarf* (= Kopftuch)

Other articles of clothing ['kləʊðɪŋ] and accessories [ək'sesəriz] (= andere Kleidungsstücke und Zubehör)

tie / AE auch *necktie* (= Schlips) • *bow tie* [bəʊ 'taɪ] (= Fliege) • *scarf* (= Schal /
Halstuch) • *gloves* [glʌvz] (= Handschuhe) • *cufflinks* (= Manschettenknöpfe) • *cummerbund* ['kʌməbʌnd] (= Kummerbund) • *stockings*
(= Strümpfe) • *nylons* ['naɪlɒnz] (= Nylonstrümpfe) • *socks* (= Socken) •
apron ['eɪprən] (= Schürze) • *overalls* BE / *boiler suit* BE / AE *overall* / AE
jumpsuit (= Overall) • *belt* (= Gürtel) • *braces* ['breɪsɪz] BE / AE
suspenders [sə'spəndəz] (= Hosenträger) • *button* (= Knopf) • *zip* BE / AE
zipper (= Reißverschluss)

"I definitely need some new clothes."

Health care
Gesundheitspflege

1 **Illnesses and symptoms**
Krankheiten und Symptome

2 **Accidents and injuries**
Unfälle und Verletzungen

3 **Disabilities**
Behinderungen

4 **At the doctor's**
Beim Arzt

5 **At the dentist's**
Beim Zahnarzt

6 **In hospital**
Im Krankenhaus

7 **Healthy living**
Gesunde Lebensweise

Gym talk

4

Illnesses and symptoms
Krankheiten und Symptome

→ 4.4 At the doctor's, 4.6 In hospital, 16.3 Medicine

Sometimes the remedy is worse than the disease. (*Proverb*)

disease [dɪˈziːz] — (*bestimmte*) **Krankheit, Erkrankung**
Alzheimer's / Parkinson's disease — die Alzheimer- / Parkinsonkrankheit
infectious / tropical diseases — Infektions- / Tropenkrankheiten
sickness [ˈsɪknəs] — **Krankheit** (*allgemein*); **Übelkeit**
I had just four days of sickness. — Ich hatte nur vier Krankheitstage.
radiation [eɪ] sickness / injuries — Strahlenkrankheit / -schäden
seasickness – airsickness — Seekrankheit – Luftkrankheit
He easily gets carsick. — Ihm wird beim Autofahren leicht übel.

symptom [ˈsɪmptəm] — **Symptom; Anzeichen**
the typical symptoms of rabies [eɪ] — die typischen Symptome der Tollwut
withdrawal [wɪðˈdrɔːəl] symptoms — Entzugserscheinungen
attack [əˈtæk] — **Anfall**
an attack of asthma – a migraine attack — ein Asthma- / Migräneanfall

Ausdrücke für „Krankheit etc."
serious [ˈsɪəriəs] *diseases* (= ernste Krankheiten) • *a serious illness* (= eine ernste Erkrankung) • *contract* [kənˈtrækt] *a disease / an illness* (= sich eine Krankheit zuziehen) • *mental illness / disorder / disease* (= Geisteskrankheit) • *a respiratory* [rɪˈspɪrətri] *disease / ailment* (= eine Atemwegserkrankung) • *in sickness and in health* [helθ] (= in kranken und gesunden Tagen) • *a heart* [hɑːt] *condition* (= eine Herzkrankheit) • *a common* [ɒ] *complaint* [kəmˈpleɪnt] / *affliction* [əˈflɪkʃn] (= ein häufiges Leiden)

fever [ˈfiːvə] — **Fieber**
have a fever / run a temperature — Fieber / Temperatur haben
low-grade fever *AE* — erhöhte Temperatur
hay fever – scarlet fever — Heuschnupfen – Scharlach
typhoid (fever) [ˈtaɪfɔɪd] — Typhus
bug [bʌg] — **Bazillus; Infekt(ion)**
I suppose I've picked up your bug. — Ich habe mich wohl bei dir angesteckt.

nausea [ˈnɔːziə] — **Übelkeit**
vomiting [ˈvɒmɪtɪŋ] / **throwing up** — **Erbrechen**
chronic [ˈkrɒnɪk] — **chronisch**
stroke [strəʊk] — **Schlaganfall**
He suffered [ˈsʌfəd] a mild stroke. — Er erlitt einen leichten Schlaganfall.
heatstroke – sunstroke — (ein) Hitzschlag – (ein) Sonnenstich
collapse [kəˈlæps] — **zusammenbrechen; kollabieren**
He collapsed on the street. — Er brach auf der Straße zusammen.
heart [hɑːt] — **Herz**
She has a heart condition. — Sie ist herzkrank.
He suffered / had a heart attack. — Er erlitt einen Herzanfall / -infarkt.

heart trouble – heart failure	Herzbeschwerden – Herzversagen
palpitations [pælpɪ'teɪʃnz]	**Herzklopfen; Herzjagen**
coronary (thrombosis) [kɒrənri θrɒm'bəʊsɪs]	**(Herz-)Infarkt**
He has survived two coronaries.	Er hat zwei Infarkte überlebt.
cold [kəʊld]	**Erkältung; Schnupfen; Grippe**
Have you caught (a) cold?	Hast du dir einen Schnupfen geholt?
(the) **flu** [fluː]	(die) **Grippe**
She came down with (the) flu.	Sie kriegte die Grippe.
bird flu ['bɜːd fluː]	Vogelgrippe
swine flu ['swaɪn fluː]	Schweinegrippe
a sore throat [sɔː 'θrəʊt]	**Halsschmerzen**
I've got a sore throat.	Ich habe Halsschmerzen.
cough [kɒf]	**husten; Husten**
She has a bad cough.	Sie hat einen schlimmen Husten.
sneeze [sniːz]	**niesen**
(the) **measles** ['miːzlz]	(die) **Masern**
German measles	Röteln
smallpox ['smɔːlpɒks] – **chickenpox**	(die) **Pocken** – (die) **Windpocken**
Smallpox leaves deep scars on the skin.	Die Pocken hinterlassen auf der Haut tiefe Narben.
smallpox vaccination [væksɪ'neɪʃn]	Pocken(schutz)impfung
whooping cough ['huːpɪŋ kɒf]	**Keuchhusten**
pneumonia [njuː'məʊniə]	**Lungenentzündung**
rupture ['rʌptʃə] / **hernia** ['hɜːniə]	**Bruch; Hernie**
a ruptured appendix [ə'pendɪks]	ein geplatzter Blinddarm
blood [blʌd]	**Blut**
high / low blood pressure ['blʌd preʃə]	hoher / niedriger Blutdruck
blood poisoning / toxaemia [tɒk'siːmiə]	Blutvergiftung
Large boils can cause blood poisoning.	Große Furunkel können zu einer Blutvergiftung führen.
food poisoning ['fuːd pɔɪznɪŋ]	**Lebensmittelvergiftung**
indigestion [ɪndɪ'dʒestʃən]	**Verdauungsstörung**
stomach ['stʌmək]	**Magen**
stomach trouble ['stʌmək trʌbl]	Magenbeschwerden
He has an upset ['ʌpset] stomach / a stomach upset ['ʌpset].	Er hat sich den Magen verdorben.
constipation [kɒnstɪ'peɪʃn]	**Verstopfung**
diarrhoea [daɪə'rɪə]	**Durchfall**
dysentery ['dɪsəntri]	(die) **Ruhr**
(stomach) ulcer ['ʌlsə]	**(Magen-)Geschwür**
gallstone ['gɔːlstəʊn] – **kidney stone**	**Gallenstein – Nierenstein**
jaundice ['dʒɔːndɪs]	**Gelbsucht**
tumour ['tjuːmə]	**Tumor; Geschwulst**
a benign [bɪ'naɪn] / malignant [mə'lɪgnənt] tumour	eine gutartige / bösartige Geschwulst
cancer ['kænsə]	**Krebs**
stomach / lung / breast cancer	Magen- / Lungen- / Brustkrebs
She died of cancer.	Sie starb an Krebs.

tuberculosis [tjuːbɜːkjuˈləʊsɪs] / früher **consumption**
She contracted tuberculosis / TB.
AIDS [eɪdz]
There's no cure or vaccine ['vӕksiːn] for AIDS.
A person can be HIV positive [eɪtʃ aɪ viː ˈpɒzətɪv] for about five years before developing full-blown AIDS.
Ebola fever [iːˈbəʊlə fiːvə]

Tuberkulose / (früher) **Schwindsucht**
Sie erkrankte an Tuberkulose / Tbc.
Aids
Für Aids gibt es kein Heilmittel und keinen Impfstoff.
Man kann etwa fünf Jahre lang HIV-positiv sein, bevor man am Vollbild AIDS erkrankt.
(das) Ebola-Fieber

Die Endung -*itis* [-aɪtɪs] **bedeutet** *inflammation* (= -entzündung)
appendicitis [əpendəˈsaɪtɪs] (= Blinddarmentzündung) • *bronchitis* [brɒŋˈkaɪtɪs] (= Bronchitis) • *gastritis* [gӕˈstraɪtɪs] (= Magenschleimhautentzündung) • *laryngitis* [lӕrɪnˈdʒaɪtɪs] (= Kehlkopfentzündung) • *meningitis* [menɪnˈdʒaɪtɪs] (= Hirnhautentzündung) • *neuritis* [njuˈraɪtɪs] (= Nervenentzündung) • *phlebitis* [flɪˈbaɪtɪs] (= Venenentzündung) • *tonsillitis* [tɒnsəˈlaɪtɪs] (= Mandelentzündung)

---

cramp [krӕmp]
I've got a cramp in my leg.
tennis elbow [tenɪs ˈelbəʊ]
gout [gaʊt] – **rheumatism** [ˈruːmətɪzm]
sciatica [saɪˈӕtɪkə]
lumbago [lʌmˈbeɪgəʊ]
Lumbago is best treated by a chiropractor [ˈkaɪrəprӕktə].
allergic [əˈlɜːdʒɪk] – **allergy** [ˈӕlədʒi]
She's allergic to cats.
allergy sufferer [ˈsʌfərə]
rash [rӕʃ]
come out / break out in a rash
itching [ˈɪtʃɪŋ]
a (slight) **swelling** [ˈswelɪŋ]
The swelling is going down.
hangnail [ˈhӕŋneɪl] – **corn** [kɔːn]
athlete's foot [ӕθliːts ˈfʊt]
pus [pʌs]
The wound was oozing [ˈuːzɪŋ] pus.
haemorrhoids [ˈhemərɔɪdz] / **piles**
an ointment for haemorrhoids / piles
varicose veins [vӕrɪkəʊs ˈveɪnz]
Varicose veins are swollen and painful veins in the legs.

sleeplessness / **insomnia** [ɪnˈsɒmniə]
unconscious [ʌnˈkɒnʃəs] – **un-consciousness**
She became unconscious.

Krampf
Ich habe einen Krampf im Bein.
Tennisarm; Tennisellbogen
Gicht – Rheuma(tismus)

Ischias
Hexenschuss
Hexenschuss wird am besten von einem Chiropraktiker behandelt.
allergisch – Allergie
Sie ist gegen Katzen allergisch.
Allergiker(in)
Ausschlag
einen Ausschlag bekommen
Jucken; Juckreiz
eine (leichte) Schwellung
Die Schwellung geht zurück.
Niednagel – Hühnerauge
Fußpilz
Eiter
Die Wunde eiterte.
Hämorriden
eine Salbe für Hämorriden
Krampfadern
Krampfadern sind geschwollene und schmerzende Venen in den Beinen.

Schlaflosigkeit
bewusstlos – Bewusstlosigkeit

Sie wurde bewusstlos.

Accidents and injuries
Unfälle und Verletzungen

→ 4.6 In hospital

Accidents will happen. (*Proverb*)

accident ['æksɪdənt]
when an accident happens / occurs
There's been an accident in Hill Street.
She was injured in an accident.
crash [kræʃ]
The thief [θiːf] crashed the car into
a wall.
Six people died [daɪd] in the crash.

Unfall; Unglück
wenn es zu einem Unfall kommt
In der Hill Street war ein Unfall.
Sie wurde bei einem Unfall verletzt.
zusammenstoßen; abstürzen
Der Dieb fuhr mit dem Auto gegen
eine Mauer.
Bei dem Zusammenstoß / Absturz
kamen sechs Menschen ums Leben.

collide [kə'laɪd] – **collision** [kə'lɪʒn]
A taxi had collided with / crashed into
a bus.
a head-on collision
hit (– hit – hit) [hɪt]
The car hit a wall.

zusammenstoßen – Zusammenstoß
Ein Taxi war mit einem Bus
zusammengestoßen.
ein Frontalzusammenstoß
(*Auto*) **prallen gegen**
Das Auto prallte gegen eine Mauer.

Dass jemand angefahren wird, kann mit *knock down, knock over, hit (– hit
– hit), strike (– struck – struck)* ausgedrückt werden, das Überfahrenwerden
mit *run over (– ran – run)*:
She was knocked down / knocked over / hit / struck by a bus. (= Sie wurde
von einem Bus angefahren.)
She was run over by a bus. (= Sie wurde von einem Bus überfahren.)

unharmed / **unhurt** / **unscathed**
hurt (– hurt – hurt) [hɜːt]
She was hurt in the fire.
injure ['ɪndʒə] – **injuries** ['ɪndʒəriz]
He was seriously / critically injured.
She suffered head injuries.
break [breɪk] (– broke – broken)
He's broken his / a leg.
fracture ['fræktʃə]
She fractured her arm in the accident.

unverletzt
verletzen
Sie wurde bei dem Brand verletzt.
verletzen – Verletzungen
Er wurde schwer verletzt.
Sie erlitt Kopfverletzungen.
brechen
Er hat sich das / ein Bein gebrochen.
(Knochen-)Bruch; Fraktur
Sie brach sich bei dem Unfall den
Arm.

concussion [kən'kʌʃn]
She suffered concussion *BE* /
AE a concussion.
burns [bɜːnz]
He suffered second-degree burns.

(eine) **Gehirnerschütterung**
Sie erlitt eine Gehirnerschütterung.
Verbrennungen
Er erlitt Verbrennungen zweiten
Grades.

suffocate ['sʌfəkeɪt] – **suffocation**
The animals (were) suffocated.
Six people died of suffocation [-'keɪʃn].

ersticken – Ersticken
Die Tiere erstickten.
Sechs Menschen erstickten.

4

2

dislocate ['dɪsləkeɪt]
He dislocated his shoulder ['ʃəʊldə].
twist [twɪst]
I've twisted my arm.
She has twisted her ankle ['æŋkl].
sprain [spreɪn]
She has sprained her ankle.
strain [streɪn]
He strained his back playing squash
  [skwɒʃ].
bruise [bruːz]
cuts and bruises ['bruːzɪz]
She was badly bruised [bruːzd].
grazes / **abrasions** [ə'breɪʒnz]
bleed [bliːd] (– bled – bled)
The man was bleeding profusely
  [prə'fjuːsli].
dress a wound [wuːnd]
dressing ['dresɪŋ]
plaster [ɑː] / **Elastoplast™**
  [ɪ'læstəplɑːst] BE / AE **Band-Aid™**
Give me a plaster, quick.
casualty ['kæʒuəlti]
shock [ʃɒk]
She was obviously in shock.
exposure [ɪk'spəʊʒə]
The two survivors [sə'vaɪvəz] were
  suffering from exposure.
die of exposure
administer first aid [əd'mɪnɪstə]
resuscitate [rɪ'sʌsɪteɪt]
mouth-to-mouth resuscitation
  [rɪsʌsɪ'teɪʃn]
treat [triːt]
The victims were treated at the scene
  [siːn].
ambulance ['æmbjələns]
call / phone for an ambulance
stretcher ['stretʃə]
take [teɪk] (– took – taken)
They were taken to BE / AE to the
  hospital ['hɒspɪtl].
emergency [ɪ'mɜːdʒənsi]
emergency doctor
casualty ['kæʒuəlti] BE / AE
  emergency room
He was taken to casualty / to the
  emergency room.
condition [kən'dɪʃn]
She's still in (a) critical condition.

ausrenken; auskugeln; verrenken
Er kugelte sich die Schulter aus.
verdrehen; verrenken
Ich habe mir den Arm verrenkt.
Sie hat sich den Fuß vertreten.
verstauchen; Verstauchung
Sie hat sich den Fuß verstaucht.
(z.B. Muskel-)**Zerrung; zerren**
Er hat sich beim Squashspielen eine
  Rückenzerrung zugezogen.
blauer Fleck; Prellung; Bluterguss
Schnittwunden und Prellungen
Sie hatte überall blaue Flecken.
Schürfwunden
bluten
Der Mann blutete stark.

eine Wunde verbinden
Verband
(Heft-)Pflaster

Gib mir schnell mal ein Pflaster.
(Unfall-)Opfer; Verletzte(r)
Schock
Sie stand offensichtlich unter Schock.
Unterkühlung
Die beiden Überlebenden litten an
  Unterkühlung.
an Unterkühlung sterben; erfrieren
erste Hilfe leisten
wiederbeleben
Mund-zu-Mund-Beatmung

(ärztlich) behandeln
Die Opfer wurden an der Unfallstelle
  ärztlich versorgt.
Krankenwagen
einen Krankenwagen rufen
Tragbahre
bringen
Sie wurden ins Krankenhaus
  gebracht.
Notfall
Notarzt / Notärztin
Notaufnahme

Er wurde in die Notaufnahme
  gebracht.
Zustand; Verfassung
Ihr Zustand ist immer noch kritisch.

Disabilities
Behinderungen

The lame man who keeps the right road outstrips the runner who keeps the wrong one. (*Proverb*)

disability [dɪsə'bɪləti]	**Behinderung; Invalidität; Erwerbsunfähigkeit**
physical ['fɪzɪkl] / mental disability	körperliche / geistige Behinderung
He's afflicted [ə'flɪktɪd] with a serious physical disability.	Er leidet unter einer schweren körperlichen Behinderung
disorder [dɪs'ɔːdə]	**(Funktions-)Störung**
He suffers from a mental disorder.	Er leidet an einer Geisteskrankheit.
children with learning disorders	lernbehinderte Kinder
defect [dɪ'fekt]	**Fehler**
speech defect / disorder	Sprachfehler
congenital [kən'dʒenɪtl] defect	Geburtsfehler
disabled [dɪs'eɪbld]	**behindert**
She's mentally disabled.	Sie ist geistig behindert.
the disabled	die Behinderten
make buildings accessible [ək'sesəbl] to the disabled	Gebäude behindertengerecht machen
a disabled person	ein behinderter Mensch
handicap ['hændikæp]	**Behinderung**
handicapped ['hændikæpt]	behindert
a handicapped person	ein behinderter Mensch
physically / mentally handicapped	körperlich / geistig behindert

In „politisch korrekter" Sprache (PC = *political correctness*) wird „behindert" mitunter durch *challenged* ['tʃælɪndʒd] (= herausgefordert) ausgedrückt: *physically challenged* (= körperlich behindert), *mentally challenged* (= geistig behindert), *visually challenged* ['vɪʒuəli] (= sehbehindert) etc.

impair [ɪm'peə] – **impairment**	**beeinträchtigen – Beeinträchtigung**
impaired hearing	Schwerhörigkeit
She has a visual impairment.	Ihre Sehkraft ist eingeschränkt.
unable [ʌn'eɪbl] – **inability** [ɪnə'bɪləti]	**außerstande – Unfähigkeit**
He's unable to speak / walk.	Er kann nicht sprechen / laufen.
the inability to recognize colours	die Unfähigkeit, Farben zu erkennen
invalid ['ɪnvəlɪd]	**invalide; körperbehindert; Invalide**
A riding accident left her an invalid.	Ein Reitunfall machte sie zur Invalidin.
cripple ['krɪpl]	**Krüppel; verkrüppelt**
Though crippled by polio, Franklin Roosevelt became one of America's greatest presidents.	Obwohl die Kinderlähmung ihn zum Krüppel gemacht hatte, wurde Franklin Roosevelt einer der größten Präsidenten Amerikas.
(mentally) retarded [rɪ'tɑːdɪd]	**(geistig) zurückgeblieben**

Disabilities (= Behinderungen)

blindness ['blaɪndnəs] (= Blindheit) • *cleft palate* ['pælət] (= Gaumenspalte) • *clubfoot* [klʌb'fʊt] (= Klumpfuß) • *deafness* ['defnəs] (= Taubheit) • *deaf-muteness* [def'mjuːtnəs] (= Taubstummheit) • *Down's syndrome* ['daʊnz sɪndrəʊm] (= Down-Syndrom / Mongolismus) • *dyslexia* [dɪs'leksiə] (= Legasthenie) • *epilepsy* ['epɪlepsi] (= Epilepsie) • *hunchback / humpback* (= Buckel) • *mental deficiency* [dɪ'fɪʃnsi] (= Schwachsinn) • *paralysis* [pə'ræləsɪs] (= Lähmung / Paralyse) • *paraplegia* [pærə'pliːdʒə] (= doppel-seitige Lähmung) • *senile dementia* [siːnaɪl dɪ'menʃə] (= senile Demenz) • *spina bifida* [spaɪnə 'bɪfɪdə] (= offene Wirbelsäule) • *stuttering* (= Stottern)

deaf [def]	taub
She's deaf in one ear.	Sie ist auf einem Ohr taub.
He's almost totally deaf.	Er ist fast völlig taub.
a young deaf-and-dumb [dʌm] man	ein junger Taubstummer
She has been deaf-mute [def'mjuːt] from birth.	Sie ist von Geburt an taubstumm.
paralysed ['pærəlaɪzd]	gelähmt
control [kən'trəʊl]	Kontrolle; kontrollieren
She has no control of her arm or neck muscles ['mʌslz].	Sie kann ihre Arm- und Nacken-muskeln nicht kontrollieren.
hereditary [hə'redɪtri]	erblich; Erb-
hereditary disease / condition	Erbkrankheit
wheelchair (user) ['wiːltʃeə]	Rollstuhl(fahrer/in)
He's confined [kən'faɪnd] to a wheelchair.	Er ist an den Rollstuhl gefesselt.

Verben, die mit den Namen von Krankheiten oder Behinderungen „kollokieren", d. h. kombiniert werden:

*If you **catch** a serious cold, you should keep warm and stay in bed.* (= Wenn man eine schwere Erkältung bekommt, sollte man sich warm halten und im Bett bleiben.)

*A hundred years ago only one out of 25 people **developed** cancer.* (= Vor hundert Jahren erkrankte nur einer unter 25 Menschen an Krebs.)

*About 11,500 Australians **come down with** food poisoning every day.* (= Jeden Tag ziehen sich etwa 11.500 Australier eine Lebensmittelvergiftung zu.)

*My sister **contracted** meningitis when she was two years old.* (= Meine Schwester erkrankte mit zwei Jahren an einer Hirnhautentzündung.)

*My father recently **suffered** a stroke.* (= Mein Vater hat kürzlich einen Schlag-anfall erlitten.)

*During her final years, she **suffered from** Alzheimer's.* (= In ihren letzten Lebensjahren litt sie an Alzheimer.)

*Each year about 25,000 people **go** blind from the disease.* (= Jedes Jahr erblinden infolge der Krankheit etwa 25.000 Menschen.)

*Whipped cream makes me **break out in** a rash.* (= Von Schlagsahne bekomme ich Ausschlag.)

At the doctor's
Beim Arzt

→ 4.1 Illnesses and symptoms, 4.6 In a hospital, 16.3 Medicine

God heals, and the doctor takes the fee. (*Proverb*)

Doctor ist das allgemeine, umgangssprachliche Wort für Arzt / Ärztin und auch die Anredeform (*Thank you, doctor.*). *Physician* [fɪ'zɪʃn] ist die förmliche Berufsbezeichnung, wird aber nie als Anrede verwendet.

GP [dʒiː'piː] (= **general practitioner**)   praktischer Arzt / praktische Ärztin;
  [præk'tɪʃənə]   Arzt / Ärztin für Allgemeinmedizin
family doctor [fæməli 'dɒktə]   Hausarzt / Hausärztin

Some specialists (= Einige Fachärzte)
ear, nose, and throat specialist (= Hals-Nasen-Ohren-Arzt / -Ärztin) •
gynaecologist [gaɪnə'kɒlədʒɪst] (= Frauenarzt / -ärztin) • *ophthalmologist*
[ɒfθæl'mɒlədʒɪst] / *eye specialist* (= Augenarzt / -ärztin) • *orthopaedist*
[ɔːθə'piːdɪst] / *orthopaedic surgeon* / *specialist* (= Orthopäde / Orthopädin) •
paediatrician [piːdiə'trɪʃn] (= Kinderarzt / -ärztin) • *psychiatrist* [saɪ'kaɪətrɪst]
(= Psychiater/in) • *psychotherapist* [saɪkəʊ'θerəpɪst] (= Psychotherapeut/in) •
surgeon ['sɜːdʒən] (= Chirurg/in)
Im BE ist die korrekte Bezeichnung und Anrede für Chirurgen nicht *Dr* /
doctor, sondern *Mr, Mrs* oder *Ms*: *Mr Kelly is a very experienced surgeon.*
(= Herr Dr. Kelly ist ein sehr erfahrener Chirurg.)

Could you **refer** [rɪ'fɜː] me to   Könnten Sie mich an einen Lungen-
  a lung specialist?   arzt überweisen?
letter of referral [rɪ'fɜːrəl]   **Überweisungsschein**
surgery ['sɜːdʒəri]   *BE* **Sprechzimmer, Sprechstunde**
No Wednesday ['wenzdeɪ] surgery   Mittwochs keine Sprechstunde

BE **surgery** = AE **office**
Arztpraxis = BE (*doctor's*) *surgery* / AE (*doctor's*) *office*
Sprechstunde = BE *surgery hours* / AE *office hours*

receptionist [rɪ'sepʃənɪst]   **Sprechstundenhilfe** (*am Empfang*)
appointment [ə'pɔɪntmənt]   **Termin**
Have you (got) an appointment?   Haben Sie einen Termin?
patient ['peɪʃnt]   **Patient(in)**
trouble ['trʌbl]   **Beschwerden; Leiden**
What's the trouble?   Was haben Sie für Probleme?
I've got stomach ['stʌmək] trouble.   Ich habe Magenbeschwerden.
My back is giving me trouble.   Mein Rücken macht mir zu schaffen.
Do you have trouble passing (your)   Haben Sie Schwierigkeiten beim
  water?   Wasserlassen?
throat [θrəʊt]   **Rachen; Hals; Kehle**
I've got a sore throat.   Ich habe Halsschmerzen.

a stomach **upset** ['stʌmək ʌpset]	eine Magen**verstimmung**
emotional [ɪ'məʊʃnəl] upsets	seelische Erschütterungen
weight [weɪt]	**Gewicht**
I've put on weight / lost weight.	Ich habe zugenommen / abgenommen.
pain [peɪn]	**Schmerz(en)**
a dull / sharp / burning / stabbing pain	ein dumpfer / heftiger / brennender / stechender Schmerz
How long have you been having these pains?	Wie lange haben Sie diese Schmerzen schon?
-ache [-eɪk]	**-schmerzen**
I have backache / stomachache ['stʌmәkeɪk] / earache.	Ich habe Rückenschmerzen / Bauchschmerzen / Ohrenschmerzen.
headache ['hedeɪk]	**Kopfschmerzen**
Do you suffer from headaches?	Leiden Sie unter Kopfschmerzen?

Headache – headaches

Die Einzahl *a headache* steht für „Kopfschmerzen im konkreten Einzelfall":
I have / I had a headache. (= Ich habe / Ich hatte Kopfschmerzen.)
Die Mehrzahl *headaches* steht für „wiederholt auftretende Kopfschmerzen":
I often have headaches. (= Ich habe oft Kopfschmerzen.)

appetite ['æpətaɪt]	**Appetit**
How is your appetite?	Wie ist es mit Ihrem Appetit?
sick [sɪk]	**krank**
Do you feel sick?	Ist Ihnen übel?
I was sick (= I vomited ['vɒmɪtɪd] / threw up) three times last night.	Ich habe mich vorige Nacht dreimal übergeben.
period ['pɪəriəd]	**Periode; Monatsblutung**
Are your periods regular ['regjələ]?	Bekommen Sie Ihre Regel pünktlich?
bowels ['baʊəlz]	**Eingeweide; Gedärm**
Are your bowels regular ['regjələ]?	Haben Sie regelmäßig Stuhlgang?

Im Gegensatz zum Deutschen steht bei Dingen, die zum Körper des Menschen gehören, in der Regel das Possessivpronomen (= besitzanzeigende Fürwort):
*I have a pain in **my** chest.* (= Ich habe Schmerzen in der Brust.)
*She has trouble with **her** legs.* (= Sie hat Probleme mit den Beinen.)
*Just hold **your** breath for a moment.* (= Halten Sie mal den Atem an.)

breathe [briːð]	**atmen**
Breathe through your nose / mouth.	Atmen Sie durch die Nase / den Mund.
breath [breθ]	**Atem**
Take a deep breath.	Holen Sie tief Luft.
I'm easily out of / short of breath.	Ich gerate schnell außer Atem.
fever ['fiːvə]	**Fieber**
Does she have a fever?	Hat sie Fieber?
temperature ['temprətʃə]	**Temperatur**
Has he got a temperature?	Hat er Temperatur?

Fragekonstruktionen mit *have*: Wenn *have* im weitesten Sinn „besitzen / (etwas) an sich haben" bedeutet, so können Sie die Frageform grundsätzlich auf dreierlei verschiedene Weise bilden:

Have you any worries ['wʌriz]?
Have you got any worries?
Do you have any worries?
} (= Haben Sie [irgendwelche] Sorgen?)

Wir empfehlen Ihnen, die Frageform bei *have* immer mit *do / does / did* zu bilden – außer natürlich bei den Perfektformen:
Has your skin altered [ɔ:]? (Nicht *Does …*) (= Hat sich Ihre Haut verändert?)

blood pressure ['blʌd preʃə]	**Blutdruck**
Nurse will take your blood pressure.	Die Schwester wird Ihren Blutdruck messen.
X-ray ['eks reɪ]	**Röntgenaufnahme**
We'll have an X-ray to make sure.	Wir werden sicherheitshalber röntgen.
ECG [i:si:'dʒi:] *BE / AE auch* **EKG**	**EKG** (= **Elektrokardiogramm**)
ultrasound scan ['ʌltrəsaʊnd skæn]	**Ultraschalluntersuchung / -aufnahme**
do an ultrasound (scan)	eine Ultraschalluntersuchung durchführen
injection [ɪn'dʒekʃn]	**Injektion; Spritze**
The doctor gave her an injection.	Der Arzt gab ihr eine Spritze.
take off (– took – taken)	**ausziehen**
Would you mind taking off all your clothes [kləʊðz].	Würden Sie sich bitte ganz ausziehen.
get dressed (– got – got) [drest]	**sich anziehen**
You can get dressed now.	Sie können sich jetzt wieder anziehen.
examine [ɪg'zæmɪn]	**untersuchen**
Will you lie here, please, so I can examine you.	Wollen Sie sich bitte hier hinlegen, damit ich Sie untersuchen kann.
drug [drʌg]	**Medikament; Arzneimittel**
a pain-killing drug	ein Schmerzmittel
medication [medɪ'keɪʃn]	**Medikamente; Verordnung**
Don't forget to take your medication.	Vergiss nicht, deine Medikamente einzunehmen.
medicine ['medsn]	**Medizin; Medikament; Arznei**
Are you taking any medicines?	Nehmen Sie Medikamente ein?
pill [pɪl]	**Pille**
She's been on the pill for years.	Sie nimmt seit Jahren die Pille.
remedy ['remədi]	**(Heil-)Mittel**
There is no remedy for colds.	Es gibt kein Mittel gegen Erkältungen.
ointment ['ɔɪntmənt]	**Salbe**
The ointment is to be applied [ə'plaɪd] twice daily.	Die Salbe ist zweimal täglich aufzutragen.
prescription [prɪ'skrɪpʃn]	**Rezept**
available on prescription only	nur auf Rezept erhältlich
certificate [sə'tɪfɪkət]	**Bescheinigung**
a doctor's certificate [sə'tɪfɪkət]	ein ärztliches Attest
sick note ['sɪk nəʊt] *BE*	**Krankenschein**
checkup ['tʃekʌp]	**(ärztliche) Untersuchung**
have a checkup	sich untersuchen lassen
home visit *BE / AE* **house call**	**Hausbesuch**

At the dentist's
Beim Zahnarzt

For there was never yet philosopher / That could endure the toothache patiently. (William Shakespeare, English dramatist and poet, 1564–1616)

dentist ['dentɪst] / **dental surgeon**	**Zahnarzt / Zahnärztin**
dental clinic ['klɪnɪk] / **hospital**	**Zahnklinik**
dental treatment ['dentl tri:tmənt]	**Zahnbehandlung**
toothache ['tu:θeɪk]	**Zahnschmerzen**
I have toothache *BE* / *AE* a toothache.	Ich habe Zahnschmerzen.
sensitive ['sensətɪv]	**empfindlich**
The tooth is sensitive to cold.	Der Zahn ist kälteempfindlich.
hurt [hɜ:t]	**wehtun**
The tooth hurts only when I bite on it.	Der Zahn tut nur weh, wenn ich auf ihn beiße.

Pain – ache = Schmerz(en)
Pain ist das allgemeinere Wort für Schmerzen:
He was out of breath and had a pain in his side. (= Er war außer Atem und hatte Schmerzen in der Seite.) • *the pain caused by an ulcer* (= die Schmerzen, die durch ein Magengeschwür verursacht werden) • *I have a pain in my foot* [fʊt]. (= Ich habe Schmerzen im Fuß.) • *She was obviously in pain.* (= Sie hatte offensichtlich Schmerzen.) • *It's more of a piercing* ['pɪəsɪŋ] *pain.* (= Es ist eher ein stechender Schmerz.)
Ache [eɪk] bezeichnet in der Regel anhaltende, dumpfe, nicht genau lokalisierbare oder beschreibbare Schmerzen:
He has (an) earache / (a) backache / (a) toothache / (a) stomachache / a headache. (= Er hat Ohrenschmerzen / Rückenschmerzen / Zahnschmerzen / Bauchschmerzen / Kopfschmerzen.) • *The dull ache in her shoulder was almost unbearable* [ʌn'beərəbl]. (= Der dumpfe Schmerz in ihrer / der Schulter war fast unerträglich.) • *My head / back aches.* (= Mir tut der Kopf / Rücken weh.) • *aching muscles* ['mʌslz] (= schmerzende Muskeln)

tongue [tʌŋ]	**Zunge**
Do you feel the pain when you touch your tooth with your tongue?	Spüren Sie den Schmerz, wenn Sie den Zahn mit der Zunge berühren?
gum(s) [gʌm(z)]	**Zahnfleisch**
My gums bleed when I brush my teeth.	Mein Zahnfleisch blutet, wenn ich mir die Zähne putze.
You'll just feel a little prick in the gum.	Sie werden nur einen leichten Stich im Zahnfleisch spüren.

loose [lu:s]	**lose**
The tooth is loose.	Der Zahn wackelt.
lower jaw [dʒɔ:] – **upper jaw**	**Unterkiefer – Oberkiefer**
lean back (– leant* [lent] – leant*)	**sich zurücklehnen**
Will you lean back, please.	Lehnen Sie sich bitte zurück.
rinse [rɪns]	**spülen; Spülung**
Rinse thoroughly ['θʌrəli], please.	Bitte gründlich (aus)spülen.

tooth [tu:θ] – **teeth** [ti:θ]	**Zahn – Zähne**
pull out / take out / extract [ɪkˈstrækt] a tooth	einen Zahn ziehen
I've had a wisdom [ˈwɪzdəm] tooth out.	Mir ist ein Weisheitszahn gezogen worden.
fill [fɪl]	**füllen; plombieren**
This tooth needs filling.	Dieser Zahn muss plombiert werden.
filling [ˈfɪlɪŋ]	**Füllung; Plombe; Inlay**
This filling needs to be replaced.	Diese Füllung muss ersetzt werden.
a temporary [ˈtemprəri] filling	eine provisorische Füllung
decay [dɪˈkeɪ]	**Verfall; Zerfall; Karies**
I'll have to drill some more to remove [rɪˈmuːv] the decay.	Ich muss noch etwas bohren, um die Karies zu entfernen.
crown [kraʊn]	**Krone**
crown a tooth	einen Zahn überkronen
bridge [brɪdʒ]	**Brücke**
fit a bridge	eine Brücke anbringen
denture(s) [ˈdentʃə(z)]	**Zahnprothese; künstliches Gebiss**
a complete / partial [ˈpɑːʃl] denture	eine Voll- / Teilprothese
(a set of) dentures	Zahnersatz
braces [ˈbreɪsɪz] (*Plural*)	**Zahnspange**
root treatment [ˈruːt triːtmənt]	**Wurzelbehandlung**
impression [ɪmˈpreʃn]	**Abdruck**
take an impression for an inlay	einen Abdruck für ein Inlay machen
injection [ɪnˈdʒekʃn]	**Injektion; Spritze**
Could you give me an injection?	Können Sie mir eine Spritze geben?
tartar [ˈtɑːtə]	**Zahnstein**
There's a lot of tartar there.	Sie haben viel Zahnstein.
plaque [plɑːk]	**Zahnbelag**
Use dental floss to remove plaque from between your teeth.	Benutzen Sie Zahnseide, um den Belag zwischen den Zähnen zu entfernen.
water jet [ˈwɔːtə dʒet]	**Munddusche**

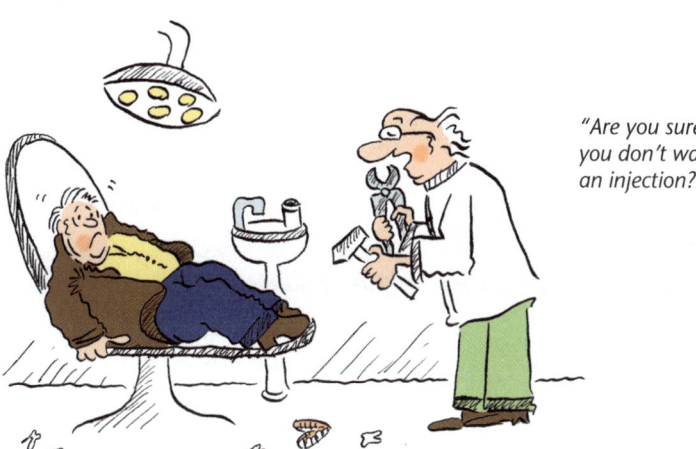

"Are you sure
you don't want
an injection?"

In hospital
Im Krankenhaus

→ 4.2 Accidents and injuries

Life is much more relaxed in hospitals today than ever before and the days of lying to attention in bed as the consultant comes round have, thankfully, gone for good. (*Dr Andrew Stanway, A Dictionary of Operations*)

hospital ['hɒspɪtl]	**Krankenhaus; Klinik; Hospital**
field hospital ['fi:ld hɒspɪtl]	(Feld-)Lazarett
hospital chaplain ['tʃæplɪn]	Krankenhauspfarrer(in)

Im BE wird *hospital* ohne *the* gebraucht, wenn es um „die Inanspruchnahme der Institution Krankenhaus" geht; im AE steht hier immer *the*.
He went into hospital. = Er ging (als Patient) ins Krankenhaus.
They went to the hospital. = Sie gingen in das Krankenhaus (z.B. um einen Kranken zu besuchen).
She was taken to hospital / AE *to the hospital.* = Sie wurde ins Krankenhaus gebracht.
He left hospital / AE *the hospital last Friday.* = Er hat das Krankenhaus vorigen Freitag verlassen.

hospitalization [hɒspɪtlaɪ'zeɪʃn]	**Einweisung ins Krankenhaus**
She was hospitalized ['hɒs-] for weeks.	Sie war wochenlang im Krankenhaus.
outpatient ['aʊtpeɪʃnt]	**ambulante(r) Patient(in)**
outpatient treatment	ambulante Behandlung
outpatient surgical centre	chirurgische Ambulanz
inpatient ['ɪnpeɪʃnt]	**stationär behandelte(r) Patient(in)**
doctor [ɒ] / **physician** [fɪ'zɪʃn]	**Arzt / Ärztin**
the doctor on duty ['dju:ti]	der / die Dienst habende Arzt / Ärztin
the attending [ə'tendɪŋ] physician	der / die behandelnde Arzt / Ärztin
consultant [kən'sʌltənt] *BE*	**(leitender) Facharzt** (*am Krankenhaus*)
senior ['si:niə] consultant *BE*	Chefarzt / -ärztin
houseman *BE* / *AE* **resident** ['rezɪdənt]	**Assistenzarzt**
senior registrar [redʒɪ'strɑ:] *BE* / *AE* **chief resident**	**Oberarzt / -ärztin**
medical *BE* / *AE* **physical** ['fɪzɪkl]	**ärztliche Untersuchung**
have a medical ['medɪkl] / physical	sich einer ärztlichen Untersuchung unterziehen
medical history ['hɪstri] / **case history**	**Krankengeschichte; Anamnese**
round [raʊnd]	**Visite**
The consultant [kən'sʌltənt] is doing his morning round.	Der Chefarzt macht gerade seine Morgenvisite.
ward [wɔ:d]	(*Krankenhaus*) **Station**
maternity [mə'tɜ:nəti] ward	Entbindungsstation
the medical ['medɪkl] ward	die innere Abteilung / Station
the surgical ['sɜ:dʒɪkl] ward	die chirurgische Station / Chirurgie

ward doctor ['dɒktə]	Stationsarzt / -ärztin
ward sister / charge nurse *BE*	Stationsschwester
nurse [nɜ:s]	**(Kranken-)Schwester / Pfleger**
student nurse [stju:dnt 'nɜ:s]	Lernschwester
senior nursing officer / senior nurse	Oberschwester
casualty *BE* / *AE* **emergency room**	**Notaufnahme**
He was taken to casualty ['kæʒuəlti] / to the emergency [ɪ'mɜ:dʒənsi] room.	Er wurde in die Notaufnahme gebracht.
trauma ['trɔ:mə]	**Verletzung;** *AE* **Schwerverletzte(r)**
trauma center *AE*	Unfallstation
operation [ɒpə'reɪʃn]	**Operation**
have / undergo an operation	sich einer Operation unterziehen
operate on someone ['ɒpəreɪt]	**jemand operieren**
I was operated on for appendicitis.	Ich wurde am Blinddarm operiert.
operable – inoperable [ɪn'ɒpərəbl]	**operabel – inoperabel**
an inoperable brain tumour ['tju:mə]	ein nicht operierbarer Gehirntumor
operating theatre *BE* / *AE* **operating room**	**Operationssaal**
theatre nurse *BE*	Operationsschwester; OP-Schwester
surgeon ['sɜ:dʒən] – **surgery**	**Chirurg(in) – (die) Chirurgie**
He specializes in heart surgery.	Er ist auf Herzchirurgie spezialisiert.
I had to have / undergo surgery.	Ich musste mich operieren lassen.
Caesarean (section) [si'zeəriən]	**Kaiserschnitt**
The baby was born by Caesarean.	Das Baby wurde mit Kaiserschnitt entbunden.
an organ transplant ['trænsplɑ:nt]	**eine Organtransplantation**

Wörter, die chirurgische Eingriffe bezeichnen, haben häufig die Endung *-ectomy* (= Herausschneidung / Entfernung) – die Betonung liegt auf dem *-e-*: *appendectomy* [æpn'dektəmi] (= Blinddarmoperation), *gastrectomy* [gæ'strektəmi] (= operative Entfernung des Magens), *hysterectomy* [hɪstə'rektəmi] (= operative Entfernung der Gebärmutter), *mastectomy* [mæ'stektəmi] (= Brustamputation), *nephrectomy* (= operative Entfernung einer Niere), *tonsillectomy* [tɒnsə'lektəmi] (= Mandeloperation), *vasectomy* [və'sektəmi] (= teilweise Entfernung des Samenleiters) etc.

anaesthetist [ə'ni:sθətɪst]	**Anästhesist(in); Narkosearzt / -ärztin**
anaesthesia [ænəs'θi:ziə]	**Narkose; Betäubung; Anästhesie**
anaesthetic [ænəs'θetɪk]	**Anästhetikum; Narkosemittel**
general anaesthetic	Vollnarkose
local anaesthetic	örtliche Betäubung
recovery room [rɪ'kʌvri ru:m]	**Wachraum; Wachstation**
intensive care unit [ɪn'tensɪv] / **ICU**	**Intensivstation**
She's in intensive care now.	Sie liegt jetzt „auf Intensiv".
drip [drɪp]	**Tropf; Infusion(sapparat)**
She's still on a drip.	Sie hängt immer noch am Tropf.
He's on strong **painkillers**.	Er bekommt starke **Schmerzmittel**.
terminal (patient) ['tɜ:mɪnl]	**unheilbar (Kranke / Kranker)**
terminal ward [wɔ:d]	Sterbestation
people who are terminally ill	Menschen, die unheilbar krank sind

Healthy living
Gesunde Lebensweise

An apple a day keeps the doctor away – but only if it's organically grown.
(*Variation of an old proverb*)

health [helθ]
Swimming is good for your health.
Smoking is a health hazard ['hæzəd].
health farm / *AE auch* fat farm
health resort [rɪ'zɔːt]
health food(s) ['helθ fuːd(z)]
health food shop *BE* / *AE* store

health freak ['helθ friːk]
health-conscious ['helθ kɒnʃəs]
diet ['daɪət]
Many people are dieting to control
  their cholesterol [kə'lestərɒl] intake.
regimen ['redʒɪmən]
I'm on a vegetarian regimen at the
  moment.
fast [fɑːst]
It's good to fast occasionally
  [ə'keɪʒnəli].
vegetarian [vedʒə'teəriən]
organic food(s) [ɔːgænɪk 'fuːd(z)]
organically grown [grəʊn]
additive-free [ædətɪv 'friː]
fibre ['faɪbə]
food high in fibre and low in fat

roughage ['rʌfɪdʒ]
Roughage is an essential element in
  the diet even though it provides no
  nutrients ['njuːtriənts].
oat bran ['əʊt bræn] – oatmeal
Oat bran is supposed to bring down
  the cholesterol level.
polyunsaturated [pɒliʌn'sætʃ-] **fats**
wholefood(s) ['həʊlfuːd(z)]
wholemeal bread [həʊlmiːl 'bred]
free-range eggs [friː reɪndʒ 'egz] *BE*
herb(al) tea(s) [hɜːb(l) 'tiː(z)]
vitamin(s) ['vɪtəmɪn(z)]
slimming pills / reducing pills
spa [spɑː]

Baden-Baden has been a spa since
  Roman times.

Gesundheit
Schwimmen ist gesundheitsfördernd.
Rauchen gefährdet die Gesundheit.
Gesundheitsfarm
Kurort
Reform(haus)kost; Naturkost
Reformhaus; Bioladen; Natur-
  kostladen
Gesundheitsfanatiker(in) / -apostel
gesundheitsbewusst
Diät; (eine) Schlankheitskur (machen)
Viele Leute leben Diät, um ihre Cho-
  lesterinaufnahme zu beschränken.
Heilprogramm; Diätplan; Kur
Ich lebe zurzeit nach einem vegetari-
  schen Diätplan.
fasten
Es ist gut, wenn man gelegentlich
  fastet.
vegetarisch; Vegetarier(in)
Biokost, Biolebensmittel (→ S. 56)
aus ökologischem Anbau (→ S. 56)
frei von chemischen Zusätzen
Faser; Ballast(stoffe)
Kost, die ballaststoffreich und
  fettarm ist
Ballaststoffe
Ballaststoffe sind für die Ernährung
  wichtig, obwohl sie keine
  Nährstoffe liefern.
Haferkleie – Haferbrei
Haferkleie soll den Cholesterinspiegel
  senken.
mehrfach ungesättigte Fettsäuren
Vollwertkost
Vollkornbrot
Eier von frei laufenden Hühnern
Kräutertee(s)
Vitamin(e)
Schlankheitspillen
Bade(kur)ort; Kurort; Wellnesscenter;
  AE auch Whirlpool
Baden-Baden ist schon seit der
  Römerzeit ein Badekurort.

physiotherapy [fɪziəʊ'θerəpi] | Physiotherapie
massage ['mæsɑːʒ] | Massage; massieren
The massage did me a world of good. | Die Massage hat mir enorm gut getan.

sauna ['sɔːnə] | Sauna
We're having a sauna tonight. | Wir gehen heute Abend in die Sauna.
steam room – Turkish bath | Dampfbad – türkisches Bad
sunbathing ['sʌnbeɪðɪŋ] | Sonnenbaden
sunlamp ['sʌnlæmp] | Höhensonne
solarium BE / AE **tanning salon** ['sælɒn] | Bräunungsstudio
jacuzzi™ [dʒə'kuːzi] / **whirlpool (bath)** AE auch **spa** | Whirlpool
exercise ['eksəsaɪz] | Bewegung; Übung
You need more exercise. | Sie brauchen mehr Bewegung.
exercises to strengthen your back muscles | (gymnastische) Übungen zur Stärkung der Rückenmuskulatur
You don't exercise enough. | Du bewegst dich nicht genug.
work out – workout ['wɜːkaʊt] | trainieren – Training
We work out at a gym [dʒɪm] once a week. | Einmal in der Woche machen wir in einer Turnhalle Fitnesstraining.
gymnastics [dʒɪm'næstɪks] | Turnen
gymnastic exercises ['eksəsaizɪz] | Turnübungen
aerobics [eə'rəʊbɪks] | Aerobic
Aerobics stimulate heart and lung activity [æk'tɪvəti]. | Aerobicübungen regen die Herz- und Lungenaktivität an.

Wörter auf -ics (→ S. 240) werden als Singular konstruiert, wenn sie eine Wissenschaft, ein Programm etc. ausdrücken; mit einem Pluralverb erscheinen sie, wenn es um die „praktische Anwendung" geht: *Aerobics / Gymnastics is a form of exercise. – Aerobics / Gymnastics are a good way to improve your fitness.* • *Athletics* (= Leichtathletik) *is called track and field in American English. – The athletics* (= Leichtathletikwettbewerbe) *were interesting to watch.* • *Politics* (= Politik) *is the art of the possible. – My politics* (= politischen Auffassungen) *are my own affair.*

yoga ['jəʊgə] | Yoga
Yoga exercises are supposed to relax your mind and improve your physical fitness. | Yogaübungen sollen den Geist entspannen und die körperliche Verfassung verbessern.
walking ['wɔːkɪŋ] | Spazierengehen; Wandern
jog [jɒg] | joggen; (einen) Dauerlauf (machen)
Shall we go for a jog? | Wollen wir einen Dauerlauf machen?
Jogging is slow running. | Joggen ist langsames Laufen.
bodybuilding exercises | muskelkräftigende Übungen
A lot of girls are into bodybuilding. | Viele Mädchen machen Bodybuilding.
breathing ['briːðɪŋ] **exercises** | Atemübungen
press-up BE / AE **push-up** ['pʊʃʌp] | Liegestütz
I do fifty push-ups every morning to stay fit. | Ich mache jeden Morgen fünfzig Liegestütze, um fit zu bleiben.
squat [skwɒt] | Kniebeuge

treadmill ['tredmɪl]	Laufband
cardio training ['kɑːdiəʊ treɪnɪŋ]	Cardiotraining
weightlifting ['weɪtlɪftɪŋ]	Gewichtheben
circuit training ['sɜːkɪt treɪnɪŋ]	Zirkeltraining
free weights / **dumb** [dʌm] **bells**	freie Hanteln
improve core stability [stə'bɪləti]	die „Kernstabilität" (d.h. die Muskulatur der Körpermitte) verbessern
isometric [aɪsəʊ'metrɪk] **exercises**	isometrisches Training
Arm wrestling is a form of isometric exercise.	Armdrücken ist eine Art isometrisches Training.
set [set]	Satz; Set
rest period ['pɪəriəd] / **rest day**	Ruhezeit / Ruhetag
flexion ['flekʃn]	Beugung

Gym talk

Chris I hear you're into **bodybuilding** as well now?

John A little. I've just been feeling rather **unfit** lately (= *ich fühle mich in letzter Zeit ziemlich schlecht in Form*). I used to do a lot of **bodyweight exercises** (= *Eigengewichtsübungen*) but now I'm doing machines every other day. One **gym** day (= *Tag im Fitnessstudio*), one rest day.

Chris Some **bodyweight exercises** are really good. If you want to define your **abs** (= *Bauchmuskeln*), **sit-ups** (= *Rumpfheben*) are still the way to go (= *die richtige Vorgehensweise*).

John Well, who wouldn't want to be **ripped** (= *muskulös*)? How many **reps** (= *Wiederholungen*) would you recommend?

Chris As many as you can do, and then a few more. It's **working to failure** (= *so lange man kann*), really.

John I've been meaning to ask you (= *ich wollte dich schon immer mal fragen*), what is your **chest training** (= *Brusttraining*) like?

Chris If you want to **work on** your chest, the **bench press** (= *Bankdrücken*) would be the thing to do (= *das, was man machen muss*), in my opinion.

John Oh, that's the one they impress the women with, isn't it? I doubt any girl watching me **pressing** (= *drücken*) my twenty pounds would go (= *sagen*), "Check out that guy (= *Schau dir den Typ mal an*) in the baggy (= *ausgeleiert*) T-shirt, it must be Schwarzenegger himself."

Chris Look, John. What counts is that you're going at all. My brother used to say, "My **gym membership** (= *Mitgliedschaft im Fitnessstudio*) is like my Catholicism. I belong, but I don't go."

John Easy for you to say. How much do you **press** on the **bench**?

Chris 120 pounds. So, what are you going to be **working on** today (= *woran wirst du heute arbeiten*), John?

John Just my self-esteem (= *Selbstachtung*), I guess.

The home
Die Wohnung

1   Flats and houses
Wohnungen und Häuser

2   Furniture, fittings, etc.
Möbel, Ausstattung etc.

3   Housework
Hausarbeit

Wortverkürzungen, Abkürzungen, Akronyme

5

Flats and houses
Wohnungen und Häuser

→ 7.1 Housing shortage, 11.6 Architecture, 20.6 Real estate

Home is the place where, when you have to go there, / They have to take you in. (*Robert Frost, US poet, 1874–1963*)

flat *BE* / *AE* **apartment** [ə'pɑːtmənt]	**(Etagen-)Wohnung**
a block of flats *BE* / *AE* an apartment building	ein Wohnblock

---

***Kinds of flats* / *apartments* (= Arten von Wohnungen)**
studio ['stjuːdiəʊ] (= Einzimmerwohnung) • *maisonette* [meizə'net] (= zweistöckige Einliegerwohnung) • *penthouse* (= Penthouse / Dach-terrassenwohnung) • *bedsit(ter)* BE (= Wohnschlafzimmer) Eine Eigentumswohnung ist im BE *an owner-occupied flat*, im AE *a condo(minium)* [kɒndə'mɪniəm] oder *a cooperative* [kəʊ'ɒprətɪv] *(apartment)* / *a co-op. Our apartment building is going co-op.* (= Die Wohnungen in unserem Block / Haus werden in Eigentumswohnungen umgewandelt.)

---

my home [maɪ 'həʊm]	**mein Heim / Haus; meine Wohnung**
We're never away from home long.	Wir sind nie lange von zu Hause weg.
my place ['maɪ pleɪs]	**meine Wohnung; mein Haus**
Shall we go to my place?	Wollen wir zu mir gehen?
This place is a dump.	Diese Wohnung ist ein Dreckloch.
house [haʊs] *Pl.* houses ['haʊzɪz]	**Haus**
We met at her parents' house.	Wir trafen uns im Haus ihrer Eltern.
house [haʊz]	**unterbringen**
efforts to house the homeless	Bemühungen, die Obdachlosen unterzubringen
housing ['haʊzɪŋ]	**Wohnungen** (*als kollektiver Begriff*)
a shortage of affordable [ə'fɔːdəbl] housing	ein Mangel an erschwinglichem Wohnraum

 Council ['kaʊnsl] *housing* ist BE für sozialen Wohnungsbau; *council houses* sind Mietshäuser mit *council flats* (= Sozialwohnungen). – *Housing estate* [ɪ'steɪt] ist BE für Wohnsiedlung; *a council estate* ist ein Wohnkomplex, der im sozialen Wohnungsbau errichtet wurde.

lodgings ['lɒdʒɪŋz]	**möblierte(s) Zimmer**
For years I lived in lodgings.	Jahrelang lebte ich in Untermiete.
quarters ['kwɔːtəz]	**Quartier; Unterkunft**
Our company ['kʌmpəni] took up quarters in a little village.	Unsere Kompanie bezog Quartier in einem kleinen Dorf.
shelter ['ʃeltə]	**Obdach; (Not-)Unterkunft**
residence ['rezɪdəns]	**(Wohn-)Haus; Residenz**
the prime minister's official residence	der Amtssitz des Premierministers
castle ['kɑːsl]	**Burg; Schloss**

palace ['pæləs']
Buckingham Palace is the Queen's
  main residence.

Palast
Der Buckingham-Palast ist die
  Hauptresidenz der Königin.

high-rise (building) ['haɪ raɪz]
high-rise flats BE / AE high-rise
  apartment house

Hochhaus
Wohnhochhaus

prefab(ricated house) ['priːfæb]
penthouse ['penthaʊs]

Fertighaus
Dachwohnung; Penthouse

Kinds of buildings ['bɪldɪŋz] **(= Arten von Gebäuden)**
hut (= Hütte) • *shack* (= ärmliche Hütte) • *shanty / hovel* ['hɒvl]
(= Bruchbude) • *blockhouse* (= Blockhaus) • *cabin* (= Holzhütte) •
log cabin (= Blockhütte) • *bungalow* [ʌ] (= Bungalow) • *cottage* [ɒ]
(= Häuschen) • *thatched* [θætʃt] *cottage* (= Häuschen mit Strohdach) •
farmhouse (= Bauernhaus) • *manor* [æ] *(house)* (= Herrenhaus) •
mansion ['mænʃn] (= Villa) • *duplex* ['djuːpleks] *(house)* (AE = Zweifami-
lienhaus) • *semidetached* [semɪdɪ'tætʃt] *house* BE / AE *attached house*
(= Doppelhaushälfte) • *terrace(d)* ['terəs(t)] *house* BE / AE *row* [əʊ] *house*
(= Reihenhaus) • *tenement* ['tenəmənt] *(house / block)* (= Mietshaus /
Mietskaserne) • *tower block* (= Wohn- / Bürohochhaus) • *skyscraper*
(= Wolkenkratzer)

tent [tent]
caravan ['kærəvæn] BE / AE **trailer**
mobile home BE / AE **house trailer**
houseboat ['haʊsbəʊt]

Zelt
Wohnwagen
Wohnmobil
Hausboot

Brownstones sind Altbauten mit rötlich-brauner Sandsteinfront (= *fronted
with reddish-brown sandstone*) – häufig anzutreffen und begehrt in *New
York City.*

floor [flɔː] / **storey** ['stɔːri]
They live on the third floor.
a six-storey house

Stock(werk); Etage
Sie wohnen im dritten Stock.
ein sechsgeschossiges Haus

Beachten Sie die in BE und AE abweichende Zählung der Stockwerke:
BE *ground floor*   = AE *first floor*   (= Erdgeschoss)
BE *first floor*   = AE *second floor*   (= erster Stock)
BE *second floor*   = AE *third floor*   (= zweiter Stock) etc.

(in the) **loft** [lɒft]
hall [hɔːl]
entrance hall ['entrəns hɔːl]
the hall at the bottom of the stairs

(auf dem) **Boden / Speicher**
Diele; Korridor; Saal
Eingangshalle; Hausflur
die Diele am unteren Ende der Treppe

Parts of a house or flat **(= Teile eines Hauses oder einer Wohnung)**
room (= Zimmer / Raum) • *bedroom* (= Schlafzimmer) • *living room /*
BE auch *sitting room* / BE auch *lounge* [laʊndʒ] (= Wohnzimmer) • *dining
room* (= Esszimmer) • *guestroom / spare room* (= Gästezimmer) • *study*
(= Arbeitszimmer) • *bathroom* (= Badezimmer) • *kitchen* (= Küche) •

kitchen-cum-dining room [-kʌm-] (= Essküche) • *kitchen-cum-living room* (= Wohnküche) • *larder / pantry* [æ] (= Speisekammer) • *doorway* (= Eingang) • *corridor* ['kɒrɪdɔː] (= Korridor / Flur) • *cellar* ['selə] (= Keller) • *landing* (= Treppenabsatz / Gang / Flur) • *basement* [s] (= Untergeschoss / Souterrain) • *attic / loft* (= Dachboden / Speicher / Mansarde) • *attic room* (= Dachzimmer) • *multipurpose* [mʌltiˈpɜːpəs] *room* (= Mehrzweckraum) • *utility* [juːˈtɪləti] *room* (= Nebenraum für Waschmaschine etc.) • *balcony* ['bælkəni] (= Balkon) • *porch* (= Vorbau / Vordach) • *veranda* [vəˈrændə] BE / AE *porch* (= Veranda) • *terrace* ['terəs] BE / AE *patio* ['pætiəʊ] (= Terrasse) • *conservatory* [kənˈsɜːvətri] (= Wintergarten)

☞ Beachten Sie: *A three-bedroom house* ist ein Haus mit vier Zimmern, nämlich: *three bedrooms + one living room*. *A two-bedroom flat / apartment* ist entsprechend eine Dreizimmerwohnung (*two bedrooms + one living room*).

door [dɔː]	**Tür**
There's someone at the door.	Es ist jemand an der Tür.
front door [frʌnt ˈdɔː] – back door	Haustür – Hintertür
revolving [-ˈvɒlv-] door – sliding door	Drehtür – Schiebetür
window ['wɪndəʊ]	**Fenster**
sash window [sæʃ ˈwɪndəʊ]	(*typisch englisches*) Schiebefenster
French windows [frentʃ ˈwɪndəʊz]	Verandatür (*zweiteilig, aus Glas*)
potted plants on the windowsill	Topfpflanzen auf dem Fensterbrett
the shutters ['ʃʌtəz]	**die Fensterläden**
chimney – open fire(place)	**Schornstein – offener Kamin**
roof [ruːf]	**Dach**
I was glad to have a roof over my head.	Ich war froh, ein Dach über dem Kopf zu haben.
lift *BE* / *AE* **elevator** ['eləveɪtə]	**Aufzug; Fahrstuhl; Lift**

☞ Der Garten beim Haus ist im BE *garden*, im AE *yard*.
Entsprechend: *front garden* BE / AE *front yard* (= Vorgarten), *back garden* BE / AE *back yard* (= Garten hinter dem Haus).
We've stopped mowing the lawn in our garden BE / AE *yard*. (= Wir mähen den Rasen in unserem Garten nicht mehr.)

yard [jɑːd]	**Hof**; *AE auch* **Garten** (beim Haus)
backyard [bækˈjɑːd]	**Hinterhof**
a backyard surrounded by a wall	ein von einer Mauer umgebener Hinterhof

What's outside the house (= Was außerhalb des Hauses ist)

shed (= Schuppen) • *toolshed* (= Geräteschuppen) • *woodshed* (= Holzschuppen) • *barn* (= Scheune) • *stable* (= Pferdestall) • *kennel* BE / AE *doghouse* (= Hundehütte) • *greenhouse* (= Gewächshaus / Treibhaus) • *outhouse* (AE = Außentoilette) • *cesspit / cesspool* ['ses-] (= Fäkaliengrube) • *(swimming) pool* (= Schwimmbad) • *garage* ['gærɑːʒ] (= Garage) • *carport* (= Carport) • *courtyard* ['kɔːtjɑːd] (= Hof) • *fence* (= Zaun) • *gate* (= Tor)

Furniture, fittings, etc.
Möbel, Ausstattung etc.

First build your house and then think of the furniture. (*Proverb*)

Dem deutschen Plural Möbel entspricht ein englischer Singular:
The furniture was expensive. (= Die Möbel waren teuer.)
Ein einzelnes Möbelstück ist *a piece / an item of furniture:*
Several pieces / items of furniture were missing. (= Mehrere Möbelstücke fehlten.)

cupboard ['kʌbəd] *BE / AE* **closet** ['klɒzɪt]	**Schrank**
built-in / fitted cupboard *BE / AE* closet	Einbauschrank
walk-in cupboard / closet	begehbarer Wandschrank / Einbau-schrank
kitchen cupboard *BE / AE* kitchen cabinet	Küchenschrank
a skeleton in her cupboard / closet	ein dunkler Punkt in ihrer Vergangen-heit
wardrobe ['wɔ:drəʊb]	**Kleiderschrank**

bed (= Bett) • *double bed* (= Doppelbett / französisches Bett) • *twin beds*
(= zwei gleiche Einzelbetten) • *folding / foldaway / collapsible* [kə'læpsəbl] *bed*
(= Klappbett) • *sofa* ['səʊfə] *bed / studio couch* (= Schlafcouch) • *mattress*
(= Matratze) • *pillow* (= Kopfkissen) • *cushion* [ʊ] (= [z.B. Sofa-]Kissen) •
sheet (= Laken) • *blanket* (= Decke) • *duvet* ['du:veɪ] (= Federbett / Plumeau)

Traditionell deckt man sich in britischen und amerikanischen Betten mit *sheets
and blankets* zu, die an drei Seiten unter die Matratze eingesteckt werden
(= *tucked* [tʌkt] *in*). Inzwischen wird das Zudecken nach kontinentaler Art,
with a duvet, immer häufiger. *Sheets and blankets, or a duvet?* ist die Frage.
Proverb ['prɒvɜːb] (= Sprichwort): *As you make your bed, so you must lie on
it.* (= Wie man sich bettet, so liegt man.)

shelf [ʃelf] *Pl.* shelves [ʃelvz]	**(Regal-)Brett; Bord**
shelves from floor to ceiling ['si:lɪŋ]	Regale vom Boden bis zur Decke
bookshelf *Pl.* -shelves	**Bücherbord; Bücherbrett**
bookcase ['bʊkkeɪs]	**Bücherregal; Bücherschrank**
chest of drawers [drɔ:z] *BE / AE* **bureau**	**Kommode**
bureau ['bjʊərəʊ]	*BE* **Sekretär;** *AE* **Kommode**
sideboard ['saɪdbɔ:d]	**Anrichte; Büfett; Sideboard**
tea trolley ['trɒli] *BE / AE* **tea wagon** ['wægən]	**Teewagen**

Tables, etc. (= Tische etc.)
table (= Tisch) • *coffee table* (= Couchtisch) • *dining table* (= Esstisch) •
kitchen table (= Küchentisch) • *bedside table BE / AE nightstand* (= Nachttisch) • *folding table* (= Klapptisch) • *(writing) desk* (= Schreibtisch) •
tablecloth ['teɪblklɒθ] (= Tischdecke)

toilet ['tɔɪlət] / **lavatory** ['lævətri]	**Toilette**
lav / **loo** *BE* / *AE* **john** [ɒ] / **can**	**Klo**
I'm just going to the loo / john / can.	Ich gehe nur mal schnell aufs Klo.
flush the toilet ['flʌʃ ðe 'tɔɪlət]	die Toilette **spülen**
bath [bɑ:θ] *BE* / *AE* **bathtub**	**Badewanne**
shower ['ʃaʊə]	**Dusche; Brause**
bathroom cabinet ['kæbɪnət]	**Badezimmerschrank**
bathroom scales *BE* / *AE* **scale** [skeɪl]	**Badezimmerwaage**
I'm looking for some bathroom scales	Ich suche eine Badezimmerwaage.
BE / *AE* a bathroom scale.	
tap *BE* / *AE* **faucet** ['fɔːsɪt]	**Wasserhahn**
turn the tap / faucet on / off	den Wasserhahn auf- / abdrehen
washbasin ['wɒʃbeɪsn] *BE* / *AE* **sink**	**Waschbecken**
(kitchen) sink [sɪŋk]	**Spülbecken; Spüle; Ausguss**

Electrical appliances [ə'plaɪənsɪz] (= **Elektrogeräte**)
refrigerator [rɪ'frɪdʒəreɪtə] / *fridge* (= Kühlschrank) • *freezer* (= Tiefkühltruhe / Gefrierschrank) • *cooker* BE / AE *stove* [stəʊv] (= Herd) • *toaster* (= Toaster) • *washing machine* (= Waschmaschine) • *dryer* ['draɪə] (= Trockner) • *dishwasher* ['dɪʃwɒʃə] (= Spülmaschine) • *vacuum* ['vækjuəm] *cleaner* (= Staubsauger) • *air conditioner* ['eə kəndɪʃənə] (= Klimaanlage) • *fan* (= Ventilator) • *water heater* (= Warmwasserbereiter) • *(electric) kettle* (= Wasserkocher)

lamp [læmp]	**Lampe**
standard lamp *BE* / *AE* floor lamp	Stehlampe
lampshade ['læmpʃeɪd]	Lampenschirm
light [laɪt]	**Licht; Lampe**
put / turn the lights on / off	die Lampen anmachen / ausmachen
(power) point *BE* / *AE* **(electric) socket**	**Steckdose**
Where's the telephone point?	Wo ist die Telefonsteckdose?
shaver point *BE* / *AE* shaver outlet	Steckdose für Elektrorasierer

Things to sit on or in (= **Dinge, auf oder in denen man sitzt**)
chair (= Stuhl / Sessel) • *armchair* / *easy chair* (= Sessel) • *collapsible* [kə'læpsəbl] *chair* / *folding chair* (= Klappstuhl) • *deck chair* (= Liegestuhl) • *rocking chair* (= Schaukelstuhl) • *swivel* [ɪ] *chair* (= Drehstuhl) • *sofa* ['səʊfə] / *settee* [se'tiː] / *couch* (= Sofa) • *stool* (= Hocker / Schemel)
You sit on a chair (= Stuhl) / *sofa* / *settee* / *couch* / *stool.*
You sit in a chair (= Sessel) / *an armchair* / *an easy chair* / *a rocking chair.*

(wall / grandfather) clock	**(Wand- / Stand-)Uhr**
alarm clock [ə'lɑːm klɒk]	Wecker
She set the alarm for ten.	Sie stellte den Wecker auf zehn Uhr.
put the clock forward an hour	die Uhr eine Stunde vorstellen
put the clock back an hour	die Uhr eine Stunde zurückstellen
The clock struck ten.	Die Uhr schlug zehn.
It's ten o'clock by the kitchen clock.	Nach der Küchenuhr ist es zehn Uhr.
Our kitchen clock is slow / fast.	Unsere Küchenuhr geht nach / vor.

Our (tele)phones are staffed [stɑːft] (a)round the clock. — Unsere Telefone sind rund um die Uhr besetzt.

mirror ['mɪrə] — **Spiegel**
look in(to) the mirror — in den Spiegel gucken
She looked at herself in the mirror. — Sie betrachtete sich im Spiegel.

curtains ['kɜːtnz] BE / AE **drapes** — **Vorhang / Vorhänge**
net curtain BE / AE curtain — Gardine
He pulled back the curtains. — Er zog die Vorhänge auf.
She drew [uː] / pulled [ʊ] the curtains. — Sie zog die Vorhänge zu.

blind BE / AE **(window) shade** — **Rollo; Jalousie; Rollladen**
We'd better pull the blinds down. — Wir lassen besser die Jalousien runter.
venetian blind [vəniːʃn 'blaɪnd] — Jalousie

carpet(ing) ['kɑːpɪt(ɪŋ)] — **Teppich(boden)**
have a carpet laid / fitted — einen Teppich verlegen lassen
fitted carpet BE / AE wall-to-wall — Teppichboden
roll out the red carpet — den roten Teppich ausrollen

rug [rʌg] — **Teppich; Läufer; Brücke**
parquet floor ['pɑːkeɪ] — **Parkettfußboden**
Parquet is easier to clean than carpeting. — Parkett lässt sich leichter sauber halten als Teppichboden.

(door)mat – bath mat — **(Fuß-)Matte – Badematte**
central heating [sentrəl 'hiːtɪŋ] — **Zentralheizung**
The house is centrally heated. — Das Haus hat Zentralheizung.

radiator ['reɪdieɪtə] — **Heizkörper**
boiler BE / AE **furnace** ['fɜːnɪs] — **Heizkessel**
boiler ['bɔɪlə] — Boiler; Warmwasserbereiter
tank [tæŋk] — **Tank; Wasserspeicher; (Wasser-)Kessel**
an 80-litre tank ['liːtə] — ein 80-Liter-Tank

Feines Porzellan(geschirr) ist *china* ['tʃaɪnə]; gröberes Geschirr ist BE *crockery,* AE *earthenware* ['ɜːθnweə]. Den sprichwörtlichen Elefanten im Porzellanladen gibt es im BE und AE ebenfalls: *She behaved like a bull* [ʊ] *in a china shop.*

wastepaper basket BE / AE **wastebasket** — **Papierkorb**
rubbish bin BE / **waste bin** BE / AE **garbage** ['gɑːbɪdʒ] **can** — **Mülleimer**
dustbin BE / AE **ashcan** / AE **garbage container** — **Mülltonne**
throw something in the dustbin (– threw [θruː] – thrown [θrəʊn]) — etwas in die Mülltonne werfen
When are the dustbins emptied? — Wann werden die Mülltonnen geleert?

(door)bell [('dɔː)bel] — **(Tür-)Klingel, Glocke**
ring the doorbell (– rang – rung) — klingeln
He didn't answer the door(bell). — Er reagierte nicht auf das Klingeln / machte nicht auf.

Housework
Hausarbeit

I hate housework! You make the beds, you do the dishes –
and six months later you have to start all over again.
(*Joan Rivers, US comedian, born in 1933*)

chore [tʃɔ:]
do the chores
clean [kli:n]
clean the windows ['wɪndəʊz]
This carpet doesn't clean very well.

It's time we gave the house a
  thorough ['θʌrə] cleaning.
clean out the drawers [drɔ:z]
I've cleaned up the bathroom.
wash [wɒʃ]
The tablecloth needs washing.

This material [mə'tɪəriəl] doesn't wash
  well.
I'm afraid the stains didn't wash out.

wash up / do the dishes
Your red shirt is in the wash.
wipe [waɪp]
wipe the crumbs [krʌmz] off the table
I've just wiped [waɪpt] the floor /
  washed the floor.

lästige Pflicht
die Haus(halts)arbeit erledigen
sauber machen; putzen
die Fenster putzen
Dieser Teppich lässt sich schlecht
  säubern.
Es wird Zeit, dass wir mal gründlich
  sauber machen.
die Schubladen sauber machen
Im Bad habe ich sauber gemacht.
waschen; aufwischen
Die Tischdecke müsste mal
  gewaschen werden.
Dieser Stoff lässt sich nicht gut
  waschen.
Die Flecken sind (beim Waschen)
  leider nicht rausgegangen.
(das) Geschirr abwaschen
Dein rotes Hemd ist in der Wäsche.
(auf)wischen
die Krümel vom Tisch wischen
Ich habe gerade aufgewischt / den
  Boden (feucht) gewischt.

Bildhaftes *idiom* ['ɪdiəm]: *The first time I played (against) her, she wiped the
floor with me.* (= Als ich das erste Mal gegen sie spielte, hat sie mich ganz
schön auseinandergenommen / vorgeführt.)

mop up [mɒp 'ʌp]
If you spill something, you might at
  least mop it up.

(auf)wischen
Wenn du etwas verschüttest, könntest
  du es wenigstens aufwischen.

Mrs Mop(p): In BE, nickname (= Spitzname) *for cleaning lady / cleaner*
(= Reinigungsfrau / Raumpflegerin).

scrub [skrʌb]
give the floor a good scrub
scour ['skaʊə]
scour a saucepan ['sɔ:spən]
sweep [swi:p] (– swept – swept)
I need a broom [bru:m] to sweep the
  kitchen with.

schrubben
den Fußboden gründlich schrubben
scheuern
einen Kochtopf scheuern
fegen
Ich brauche einen Besen, um die
  Küche zu fegen.

dust [dʌst] | Staub; abstauben
Did you dust the living room? | Hast du im Wohnzimmer Staub gewischt?

vacuum cleaner / *BE auch* **hoover** | Staubsauger
[uː] / *AE auch* **vacuum** ['vækjuəm]
vacuum / *BE auch* hoover a carpet | einen Teppich saugen
brush [brʌʃ] | **Bürste; bürsten**
clothes [kləʊðz] brush | Kleiderbürste
toilet / lavatory ['lævətri] brush | WC-Bürste; Toilettenbürste
He brushed the dust off his coat. | Er bürstete sich den Staub vom Mantel (ab).

Cleaning utensils [juː'tenslz], *cleaning agents* ['eɪdʒənts]
(= **Reinigungsutensilien, Reinigungsmittel**)
cloth [klɒθ] (= Tuch / Lappen) • *cleaning rag / cloth* (= Putzlappen) • *sponge* [spʌndʒ] (= Schwamm) • *tea towel* BE / *AE dish towel* (= Geschirrtuch) • *dish mop* (= Spülbürste) • *washing-up liquid* ['lɪkwɪd] BE / *AE dish liquid* (= Spülmittel) • *chamois* ['ʃæmwɑː] / *shammy* (= Fensterleder) • *duster* (= Staubtuch) • *broom* (= Besen) • *dustpan and brush* (= Müllschaufel und Handfeger) • *soap* (= Seife) • *detergent* [dɪ'tɜːdʒənt] (= Reinigungs- / Waschmittel) • *washing powder* BE / *AE laundry detergent* (= Waschpulver)

---

clear away [klɪər ə'weɪ] | abräumen; wegräumen
clear away the dirty dishes | das schmutzige Geschirr abräumen
tidy up [taɪdi 'ʌp] | aufräumen (in)
Tidy up your room / your room up. | Räum dein Zimmer auf.
straighten up [streɪtn 'ʌp] | aufräumen; in Ordnung bringen
My room's in a terrible mess / in quite a state, I've got to straighten it up. | In meinem Zimmer herrscht furchtbares Durcheinander, ich muss da mal Ordnung schaffen.

rinse [rɪns] | spülen
I'll just rinse the glasses. | Ich spüle nur schnell die Gläser ab.
dry (up) the dishes ['dɪʃɪz] | das Geschirr abtrocknen
Let me do the drying. | Lass mich abtrocknen.
laundry ['lɔːndri] | Wäsche
do the laundry / washing | (die) Wäsche waschen / machen
launder ['lɔːndə] | waschen und bügeln
iron ['aɪən] | bügeln
iron the shirts and press the trousers | die Hemden und Hosen bügeln
polish ['pɒlɪʃ] | polieren; putzen; bohnern
polish / clean / shine shoes [ʃuːz] | Schuhe putzen
floor polish – furniture polish | Bohnerwachs – Möbelpolitur
air a room / bed | ein Zimmer / Bett lüften
give a room a good airing | in einem Zimmer gründlich lüften
do [duː] (– did – done [dʌn]) | (*Zimmer, Bett etc.*) **machen**
do / make the beds | die Betten machen
Have you done the bathroom? | Haben Sie schon das Bad gemacht?
take the carpets up (– took – taken) | **die Teppiche hochnehmen**
beat the carpets (– beat – beaten) | **die Teppiche klopfen**

Wortverkürzungen, Abkürzungen, Akronyme

Wenn ein oft gebrauchtes Wort lang ist, kann man sicher sein, dass es im Alltagsgebrauch bald auf eine als erträglich empfundene Länge verkürzt wird. So wurde *spectacles* zu *specs* (= Brille), *influenza* zu *flu* (= Grippe), *advertisement* zu *advert* oder *ad* (= Anzeige / Werbespot), *zoological garden* zu *zoo* (= Zoo), *public house* zu *pub* (= Kneipe), *photograph* zu *photo* (= Foto), *veterinary surgeon* zu *vet* (= Tierarzt / -ärztin), *professional* zu *pro* (= Profi), *gymnasium* zu *gym* (= Turnhalle / Fitnesscenter), *bicycle* zu *bike* (= Fahrrad), *refrigerator* zu *fridge* (= Kühlschrank), *television* zu *telly* (= Fernseher / Fernsehen), *examination* zu *exam* (= Examen / Prüfung), *university* zu *uni* (= Uni[versität]), *vegetable(s)* zu *veg* [vedʒ] (= Gemüse), *modern conveniences* zu *mod cons* (= moderner Komfort), *air conditioning* zu *air con* (= Klimaanlage), *show business* zu *showbiz* (= das Showgeschäft), *president* zu *prez* (= Präsident), *abdominals* zu *abs* (= Bauchmuskeln) und *application* zu *app* (= Anwendung).

Abkürzungen (= *abbreviations*) gibt es von alters her, wie etwa *BC* (= *before Christ* = v. Chr.), *AD* (= *Anno Domini* [ˈænəʊ ˈdɒmɪnaɪ] = im Jahre des Herrn = unserer Zeitrechnung), *RIP* (= *rest in peace* = ruhe in Frieden), *RSVP* (= *répondez s'il vous plaît* = *please reply* = um Antwort wird gebeten), *i.e.* (= *id est* = *that is to say* = d. h.), *e.g.* (= *exempli gratia* = z. B.), *MD* (= *Doctor of Medicine* = Dr. med.), *ADHD* (= *attention deficit hyperactivity disorder* = Aufmerksamkeitsdefizit-Hyperaktivitäts-Syndrom) und *o.b.o.* (= *or best offer* = oder bestes Angebot [in Kleinanzeigen]).

Im 20. und 21. Jahrhundert sind zahllose neue Abkürzungen entstanden, von denen viele als Akronyme (= *acronyms*) benutzt werden, d. h. als Kombinationen von Anfangsbuchstaben, die als Wörter gesprochen werden: *NATO* (= *North Atlantic Treaty Organization* = Organisation des Nordatlantikvertrags [*NATO* im Englischen ohne *the*!]), *Aids* (= *acquired immune deficiency syndrome* = erworbenes Immunschwächesyndrom), *LED* (= *light-emitting diode* = Leuchtdiode), *CV* (= *curriculum vitae* = Lebenslauf), *DIY* (= *do-it-yourself* = Heimwerker(-) / Heimwerken), *aka* (= *also known as* = alias) und *nimby* [ˈnɪmbi] (= *not in my back yard* = Person, die z. B. Windräder befürwortet, aber nicht in der eigenen Nachbarschaft).

Der Zwang zur Kürze – in SMS, E-Mails, *chats*, Protokollen etc. – hat zu zahllosen Neuprägungen geführt, in denen mitunter auch Ziffern entsprechend ihrer Lautung integriert sind: *asap* (= *as soon as possible* = so bald wie möglich), *NP* (= *no problem* = kein Problem), *IMO* (= *in my opinion* = meiner Meinung nach), *AFAIK* (= *as far as I know* = soviel ich weiß), *FYI* (= *for your information* = zu Ihrer / deiner Information), *TBD* (= *to be done* = muss erledigt werden), *BRB* (= *be right back* = bin gleich zurück), *G2G* (= *got to go* = muss weg), *CUL8R* (= *see you later* = bis später), *XXX* (= *kisses* = Küsse), *2l8* (= *too late* = zu spät).

The social order
Die Sozialordnung

1   **Communities**
    Gemeinschaften

2   **Social movements**
    Gesellschaftliche Bewegungen

3   **Political systems**
    Politische Systeme

4   **Parties and politics**
    Parteien und Politik

5   **The legislature**
    Die gesetzgebende Gewalt

6   **Government**
    Regierung

7   **Antigovernment activity**
    Aktivitäten gegen die Regierung

8   **Law and police**
    Rechtswesen und Polizei

9   **Taxation**
    Steuern

10 **Social security**
    Soziale Sicherheit

11 **International relations**
    Internationale Beziehungen

12 **Defence, war, military**
    Verteidigung, Krieg, Militär

13 **Titles, forms of address**
    Titel, Anredeformen

6
1 Communities
Gemeinschaften

→ 14.7 The city

My country is the world. My countrymen are all mankind.
(*William Lloyd Garrison, US campaigner against slavery, 1805–1879*)

community [kə'mjuːnəti]	**Gemeinschaft**
serve the community	der Gemeinschaft dienen
people working in the community	Leute, die im Sozialbereich tätig sind
community work [kə'mjuːnəti wɜːk]	gemeinnützige Arbeit
the black community	die schwarze Bevölkerungsgruppe
union ['juːniən]	**Union; Vereinigung**
the European [jʊərə'piːən] Union	die Europäische Union
confederation [kənfedə'reɪʃn]	**Staatenbund; Konföderation**
the Swiss Confederation	die Schweizerische Eidgenossenschaft
commonwealth ['kɒmənwelθ]	**Commonwealth; Staatenbund**
the Commonwealth of Independent [ɪndɪ'pendənt] States (CIS)	die Gemeinschaft unabhängiger Staaten (GUS)

The Commonwealth (of Nations) is an association [əsəʊsi'eɪʃn] of Britain and 53 independent countries that were formerly part of the British Empire. The British monarch ['mɒnək] is the symbolic [sɪm'bɒlɪk] head of the Commonwealth.

empire ['empaɪə]	**Imperium; Weltreich**
the former British Empire	das frühere britische Weltreich
society [sə'saɪəti]	**(die) Gesellschaft**
the role of women in society	die Rolle der Frau in der Gesellschaft
society for the prevention [prɪ'venʃn] of cruelty ['kruːəlti] to animals	Tierschutzverein
country ['kʌntri]	**Land**
the eastern European countries	die osteuropäischen Länder
land [lænd]	(*bes. literarisch, feierlich*) **Land**
a land of unlimited opportunity	ein Land unbegrenzter Möglichkeiten
nation ['neɪʃn]	**Volk; Nation**
delegates ['delɪgəts] from 50 nations	Delegierte aus 50 Nationen / Staaten
state [steɪt]	**Staat;** (*Deutschland*) **(Bundes-)Land**
the rivalry ['raɪvəlri] of church and state	die Rivalität zwischen Kirche und Staat
the states that make up a nation	die Staaten, die eine Nation bilden
rogue state ['rəʊg steɪt]	Schurkenstaat

Beachten Sie den Gebrauch von *of* in Fügungen wie diesen:
the state of New York (= der Staat New York) • *the province of Ontario* (= die Provinz Ontario) • *the city of Toronto* (= die Stadt Toronto) • *the borough of Brooklyn* (= der Stadtteil Brooklyn) • *the district of Kreuzberg* (= der Bezirk Kreuzberg) • *the village of Steventon* (= das Dorf Steventon)

area ['eəriə]
a nice residential [rezɪ'denʃl] area
move (in)to an area
move away from an area
a socially deprived [dɪ'praɪvd] area
the area around Berlin
the Berlin metropolitan [metrə'pɒlɪtən] area
the Berlin area
region ['ri:dʒən] – **regional**
a remote [rɪ'məʊt] mountain region
a sparsely ['spɑ:sli] populated region
a regional war [wɔ:]
province ['prɒvɪns]
Ontario is Canada's most populous ['pɒpjələs] province.
county ['kaʊnti]
England is divided into counties.
district ['dɪstrɪkt]
New York's theatre ['θɪətə] district
city ['sɪti]
the largest city in the world
the city centre BE / AE downtown area
the inner city [ɪnə 'sɪti]

the City

municipality [mju:nɪsɪ'pæləti]

Hamburg is both a municipality and a state.
town [taʊn]
Are you going to town tomorrow?
his hometown of Palatine, Illinois

Gegend; Gebiet
eine schöne Wohngegend
in eine Gegend ziehen
aus einer Gegend wegziehen
ein sozial benachteiligtes Gebiet
das Gebiet um Berlin herum
das Stadtgebiet von Berlin

der Großraum Berlin
Region / Gebiet – regional
eine abgelegene Bergregion
ein dünn besiedeltes Gebiet
ein regionaler Krieg
Provinz
Ontario ist Kanadas bevölkerungs-reichste Provinz.
BE **Grafschaft;** AE **(Land-)Kreis**
England ist in Grafschaften unterteilt.
Gebiet; (Stadt-)Bezirk; Stadtteil
New Yorks Theaterviertel
(Groß-)Stadt
die größte Stadt der Welt
die Innenstadt; das Stadtzentrum
die Innenstadt (*als Brennpunkt sozialer Probleme*)
das Londoner Banken- und Börsen-viertel; die britische Finanzwelt
(Stadt-)Gemeinde; Gemeinde-verwaltung
Hamburg ist sowohl Stadt als auch Bundesland.
Stadt
Fährst du morgen in die Stadt?
seine Heimatstadt Palatine, Illinois

Downtown – uptown – midtown (alle AE)
In der Regel bezeichnet *downtown* die Innenstadt, das Geschäftsviertel und *uptown* die an der Peripherie gelegenen Wohnviertel; *midtown* liegt zwischen *downtown* und *uptown:*
The downtown restaurants ['restrɒnts] *are very busy* ['bɪzi] *at this time of day.*
(= Die Restaurants in der Innenstadt sind um diese Tageszeit sehr voll.)
They live in midtown Manhattan. (= Sie wohnen im mittleren Teil Manhattans.)

borough ['bʌrə]
Manhattan and Brooklyn are boroughs of New York City.
neighbourhood ['neɪbəhʊd]
We live in a nice neighbourhood.

village ['vɪlɪdʒ]
parish ['pærɪʃ]

(*London, New York*) **Bezirk, Stadtteil**
M. und B. sind Stadtteile / Bezirke von New York.
Gegend; Viertel; Kiez
Wir wohnen in einem schönen Viertel.
Dorf
(Kirchen-)Gemeinde

6
2 Social movements
Gesellschaftliche Bewegungen

Revolutionary movements attract the best and worst elements
in a given society. (*George Bernard Shaw, Irish writer, 1856–1950*)

active citizenship ['sɪtɪznʃɪp]   aktives / tätiges Staatsbürgertum
human ['hjuːmən] **rights movement**   Menschenrechtsbewegung

Affirmative action / positive discrimination / reverse discrimination
Dies sind *buzzwords* ['bʌzwɜːdz] (= Schlagworte) der aktuellen gesellschaftlichen
Diskussion. Sie bezeichnen das Prinzip der positiven Diskriminierung, d.h. Bevorzu-
gung von Mitgliedern benachteiligter Gruppen z.B. bei der Besetzung von Stellen.

Peace movements ['piːs muːvmənts] (= Friedensbewegungen):
antiwar movement (= gegen den Krieg) • *antinuclear* [ænti'njuːkliə] *movement*
(= gegen Kernwaffen oder Kernkraft) • *pacifism* ['pæsɪfɪzm] (= Pazifismus /
bedingungslose Friedensbereitschaft / grundsätzlicher Verzicht auf Krieg)

Racial equality [reɪʃl ɪ'kwɒləti] (= Gleichberechtigung der Rassen):
civil rights movement (= Bürgerrechtsbewegung) – *civil rights activist*
['æktɪvɪst] (= Bürgerrechtler / Bürgerrechtlerin) • *black (power) movement* –
black nationalism • *antiapartheid movement* (= gegen die früher in Südafrika bestehende Rassentrennung) • *abolitionist* [æbə'lɪʃənɪst] *movement*
(= zur Abschaffung der Sklaverei in den USA im 19. Jahrhundert)

Women's rights ['wɪmɪnz raɪts] (= Frauenrechte):
feminism ['femənɪzm] – *antifeminism* • *women's movement – women's
liberation / lib* (= Frauenbewegung) – *women's libber* (= Frauenrechtlerin /
Emanze) • *women's rights movement – women's rights activist* (= Frauenrechtlerin)

Abortion [ə'bɔːʃn] (= Abtreibung; Schwangerschaftsabbruch):
abortion movement – antiabortion movement • *pro-choice movement* (= für
die freie Entscheidung der Frau) – *anti-choice movement / right-to-life movement* (= Gegenbewegung zu *pro-choice*) • *pro-choicers* (= supporters of
pro-choice movement) – *right-to-lifers* (= supporters of right-to-life movement) •
birth-control movement (= für die Geburtenkontrolle) • *family planning /
planned parenthood* (= Familienplanung / geplante Elternschaft)

The LGBT movement (= die Lesben- und Schwulenbewegung):
LGBT – lesbian, gay, bisexual and transgender (= lesbisch, schwul, bisexuell und
transsexuell) • *LGBT rights* • *LGBT pride* • *gay pride parade* • *same-sex
marriage* (= gleichgeschlechtliche Ehe)

Youth movements ['juːθ muːvmənts] (= Jugendbewegungen):
counterculture („Gegenkultur", *in the US during the 1960s*) – *pop culture –
hippies – communes* ['kɒmjuːnz] – *the New Left* (= die neue Linke) • *student
protest* ['prəʊtest] *movement – student activism* [stjuːdnt 'æktɪvɪzm]

Political systems
Politische Systeme

→ 8.3 Political science

You can talk about capitalism and communism and all that sort of thing, but the important thing is the struggle everybody is engaged in to get better living conditions, and they are not interested too much in forms of government. (*Bernard Baruch, US businessman and statesman, 1870–1965*)

democracy [dɪ'mɒkrəsi]	(die) **Demokratie**
a parliamentary democracy	eine parlamentarische Demokratie
democratic [demə'krætɪk]	**demokratisch**
a democratically elected government	eine demokratisch gewählte Regierung
presidential form of government	**präsidentielles Regierungssystem**
republic [rɪ'pʌblɪk]	**Republik**
federation [fedə'reɪʃn]	**Zusammenschluss; Föderation**
the Russian ['rʌʃn] Federation	die Russische Föderation
federal ['fedərəl]	**Bundes-**
the Federal Republic of Germany	die Bundesrepublik Deutschland
authoritarian [ɔ:θɒrɪ'teəriən]	**autoritär**
police state [pə'li:s steɪt]	**Polizeistaat**
fascism ['fæʃɪzm]	(der) **Faschismus**
fascist ['fæʃɪst]	**faschistisch; Faschist(in)**
neofascist [ni:əʊ'fæʃɪst] groups	neofaschistische Gruppen
nazism ['nɑ:tsɪzm]	(der) **Nazismus**
Germany under the nazis ['nɑ:tsiz]	Deutschland unter den Nazis
neo-Nazi(s)	Neonazi(s)
communism ['kɒmjunɪzm]	(der) **Kommunismus**
socialism ['səʊʃəlɪzm]	(der) **Sozialismus**
capitalism ['kæpɪtəlɪzm]	(der) **Kapitalismus**
capitalist ['kæpɪtəlɪst]	**kapitalistisch; Kapitalist(in)**

Who governs ['gʌvnz]*? (= **Wer regiert?**)*
absolutism ['æbs-] (= Absolutismus): *an all-powerful monarch or dictator*
totalitarianism [-'teər-] (= totalitäres System): *an all-powerful dictator or party*
absolute monarchy ['mɒn-] (= absolute Monarchie): *an all-powerful monarch*
theocracy [θi'ɒkrəsi] (= Theokratie): *a priest or the priesthood*
aristocracy [ærɪ'stɒk-] (= Adelsherrschaft): *people of high birth – the nobility*
dictatorship [dɪk'teɪtəʃɪp] (= Diktatur): *a dictator*
oligarchy ['ɒlɪgɑ:ki] (= Oligarchie): *a small group of people with privileges and / or wealth*
meritocracy [-'tɒk-] (= Meritokratie): *people who have distinguished themselves through their ability*
constitutional monarchy [kɒnstɪ'tju:ʃnəl 'mɒnəki] (= konstitutionelle Monarchie): *the elected representatives* [reprɪ'zentətɪvz] *of the people*
democracy [dɪ'mɒk-] (= Demokratie): *the elected representatives of the people*

Parties and politics
Parteien und Politik

A statesman is a politician who's been dead ten or fifteen years.
(*Harry S. Truman, US president, 1884–1972*)

party ['pɑːti]	**Partei**
party leader [pɑːti 'liːdə]	Parteiführer(in)
the ruling party [ruːlɪŋ 'pɑːti]	die Regierungspartei
toe [təʊ] the party line	sich nach der Parteilinie richten
politics ['pɒlətɪks] – **a policy** ['pɒləsi]	(die) **Politik** – eine **Politik**

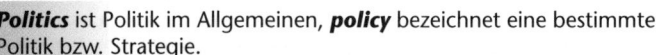 ***Politics*** ist Politik im Allgemeinen, ***policy*** bezeichnet eine bestimmte
Politik bzw. Strategie.
Die Mehrzahlform *policies* hat im Deutschen keine Entsprechung:
Politics *is the art of the possible.* (= Politik ist die Kunst des Möglichen.)
She went into ***politics***. (= Sie ging in die Politik.)
The two countries follow a common [ɒ] ***policy*** */ common* ***policies***. (= Die
beiden Länder verfolgen eine gemeinsame Politik.)
the government's economic [iːkə'nɒmɪk] */ domestic / defence* ***policy*** (= die
Wirtschafts- / Innen- / Verteidigungspolitik der Regierung)
British foreign ['fɒrən] ***policies*** *in the 1930s* (= die britische Außenpolitik
in den 30er-Jahren)
US ***policies*** *towards Latin America* [lætɪn ə'merɪkə] (= die amerikanische
Politik gegenüber Lateinamerika)

politician [pɒlə'tɪʃn]	**Politiker(in)**
a senior ['siːniə] Labour politician	ein(e) führende(r) Labour-Politiker(in)
political [pə'lɪtɪkl]	**politisch**
a political party	eine politische Partei
politically important [ɪm'pɔːtənt]	politisch wichtig / bedeutsam
power ['paʊə]	(die) **Macht**
the party now in power	die Partei, die jetzt an der Macht ist
if they come to power	falls sie an die Macht kommen
(party) member(ship)	**(Partei-)Mitglied(schaft)**
the centre ['sentə]	**die Mitte; das Zentrum**
a centre-left coalition [kəʊə'lɪʃn]	eine Mitte-Links-Koalition
the left / right wing	**der linke / rechte Flügel**
right-wing radicals / extremists	Rechtsradikale / -extremisten
a leftist – a rightist	**ein(e) Linke(r) – ein(e) Rechte(r)**
leftist parties	linke Parteien; Linksparteien
extreme rightist ideas [aɪ'dɪəz]	rechtsextremes Gedankengut
moderate ['mɒdərət]	**gemäßigt**
a moderate conservative [kən'sɜːvətɪv]	ein gemäßigter Konservativer
middle-of-the-road	**gemäßigt**
middle-of-the-road parties / policies	gemäßigte Parteien / Politik
radical ['rædɪkl]	**radikal; Radikale(r)**
radical parties / changes ['tʃeɪndʒɪz]	radikale Parteien / Veränderungen
the hawks and the doves [dʌvz]	**die Falken und die Tauben**
hawkish – dovish ['dʌvɪʃ] politicians	militante – gemäßigte Politiker

Die Parteienlandschaft (= *party-political scene*) in GB und den USA

(≈ bezeichnet die ungefähre Entsprechung in der Bundesrepublik Deutschland)

Britain:
the Conservative Party / the Conservatives [kən'sɜːvətɪvz] / the Tories ['tɔːriz]
  ≈ CDU/CSU
the Labour Party / (New) Labour ['leɪbə] ≈ SPD
the Liberal Democrats [lɪbərəl 'deməkræts] ≈ FDP
USA:
the Democratic [demə'krætɪk] Party / the Democrats ≈ SPD
the Republican [rɪ'pʌblɪkən] Party / the Republicans ≈ CDU/CSU

union ['juːniən]	**Union**
the Christian Democratic Union	die Christlich-Demokratische Union
socialist ['səuʃəlɪst]	**sozialistisch; Sozialist(in)**
a socialist party / movement	eine sozialistische Partei / Bewegung
communist ['kɒmjənɪst]	**kommunistisch; Kommunist(in)**
a communist party / government	eine kommunistische Partei / Regierung
grass roots [grɑːsˈruːts]	**(Partei-)Basis**
strengthen the party at the grass roots	die Partei an der Basis (ver)stärken
a grass-roots ['grɑːsruːts] movement	eine Bürgerinitiative
stand (– stood – stood) BE / AE **run** (– ran – run)	**kandidieren**
stand / run as an independent [-'pen-]	als Unabhängige(r) kandidieren
a **suitable** / **viable** candidate	ein(e) **geeignete(r)** Kandidat(in)
nominate ['nɒmɪneɪt] – **nomination**	**nominieren – Nominierung**
(election) platform ['plætfɔːm]	**(Wahl-)Plattform; Wahlprogramm**
The convention decides [dɪ'saɪdz] on the party's platform.	Der Parteitag entscheidet über das Wahlprogramm der Partei.

Sound bites sind griffige, von Politikern sorgfältig einstudierte Kurzaussagen, die sich gut für das Zitieren in Nachrichtensendungen (= *news programmes*) eignen. *Spin doctors* nennt man Mitarbeiter (= *aides*) eines Politikers, deren Aufgabe es ist, z.B. durch Beeinflussung der Medien (= *by influencing the media* ['miːdiə]) seine Handlungen und Äußerungen in dem von ihm gewünschten Licht erscheinen zu lassen. Allgemein nennt man Leute, die einem Kandidaten helfen, einen möglichst günstigen Eindruck zu machen, *imagemakers*.

opinion poll [ə'pɪnjən pəul]	**Meinungsumfrage**
The two candidates ['kændɪdəts] are neck and neck in the polls.	Die beiden Kandidaten liegen in den Meinungsumfragen Kopf an Kopf.
a **strong showing** in the election	ein **gutes Abschneiden** bei der Wahl
campaign finance ['faɪnæns]	**Wahlkampffinanzierung**
party financing [pɑːti faɪ'nænsɪŋ]	**Parteienfinanzierung**
slush funds ['slʌʃ fʌndz]	**schwarze Kassen**
slush-fund scandal ['skændl]	Schwarzgeldaffäre
reform [rɪ'fɔːm] **gridlock** / **reform logjam**	**Reformstau**

The legislature
Die gesetzgebende Gewalt

Democracy is good. I say this because other systems are worse.
(*Jawaharlal Nehru, Indian statesman, 1889–1964*)

the separation [sepə'reɪʃn] **of powers**	die Gewaltenteilung
chamber ['tʃeɪmbə]	Kammer

 The UK and the US both have two-chamber legislatures ['ledʒɪsleɪtʃəz].
Upper chamber: UK *House of Lords* (= Oberhaus), US *Senate* (= Senat).
Lower chamber: UK *House of Commons* ['kɒmənz] (= Unterhaus), US *House of Representatives* [repri'zentətɪvz] (= Repräsentantenhaus).

parliament ['pɑːləmənt] — Parlament
In the UK, parliament comprises the House of Commons and the House of Lords.
In Großbritannien umfasst das Parlament Unterhaus und Oberhaus.

congress ['kɒŋgres] — Kongress
The US Congress consists of the House of Representatives and the Senate.
Der amerikanische Kongress besteht aus Repräsentantenhaus und Senat.
Congressman / Congresswoman Smith
der / die Kongressabgeordnete Smith

MP (= Member of Parliament) — (Parlaments-)Abgeordnete(r)
When an MP has died, a by-election is held.
Wenn ein Abgeordneter stirbt, findet eine Nachwahl statt.

senate ['senət] – **senator** ['senətə] — Senat – Senator(in)
leader ['liːdə] — Führer(in)
the leader of the opposition [ɒpə'zɪʃn]
der / die Oppositionsführer(in)
the House Democratic leader *AE*
der / die Führer(in) der Demokraten (im Repräsentantenhaus)

 Als *whips* [wɪps] (= Einpeitscher) bezeichnet man in Parlamenten der englischsprachigen Länder Abgeordnete, die dafür zu sorgen haben, dass die Abgeordneten ihrer Partei bei wichtigen Abstimmungen zugegen sind und entsprechend der Parteilinie abstimmen – im deutschen Parlament entsprechen ihnen die parlamentarischen Geschäftsführer(innen).

majority [mə'dʒɒrəti] – **minority** — Mehrheit – Minderheit
the Senate majority leader *AE*
der Führer der Senatsmehrheit
speaker ['spiːkə] — (*Parlament*) Sprecher(in), Präsident(in)
the Speaker of the House of Representatives
der / die Sprecher(in) des Repräsentantenhauses
deputy ['depjʊti] — Stellvertreter(in); stellvertretend
backbenchers [bæk'bentʃəz] — Hinterbänkler(innen)
frontbenchers [frʌnt'bentʃəz] — führende Politiker(innen)
session ['seʃn] — Sitzung
The committee is in session now.
Der Ausschuss tagt gerade.
debate [dɪ'beɪt] — Debatte; debattieren
The Senate is debating the bill.
Der Senat berät über die Vorlage.

the **minutes** ['mɪnɪts] of a meeting
speech [spiːtʃ]
make / give / deliver a speech

das **Protokoll** einer Sitzung
Rede
eine Rede halten

The Queen's Speech ist die alljährlich zu Beginn der neuen *session*
(= Sitzungsperiode) des britischen Parlaments von der Königin verlesene,
jedoch vom Kabinett verfasste Thronrede mit Einzelheiten des Regierungs-
programms für das kommende Jahr.

filibuster ['fɪlɪbʌstə] *AE*
US senators sometimes try to block
legislation by filibustering.

Dauerrede; eine Dauerrede halten
US-Senatoren versuchen manchmal,
Gesetze durch Endlosreden zu
verhindern.

motion ['məʊʃn]
put forward / propose / make a motion
table a motion

Antrag
einen Antrag stellen
einen Antrag *BE* einbringen / *AE* auf
Eis legen

veto *Pl.* vetoes ['viːtəʊ(z)]
The president can veto a bill.

Veto
Der Präsident kann gegen ein Gesetz
sein Veto einlegen.

ratify ['rætɪfaɪ]
Treaties must be ratified by the Senate.

ratifizieren
Staatsverträge müssen durch den
Senat ratifiziert werden.

abstain [əb'steɪn]
abstention [əb'stenʃn]
seat [siːt]
Labour won [wʌn] 270 seats.
committee [kə'mɪti]
She is / sits on several committees.
Ways and Means Committee *AE*
constituency [kən'stɪtjuənsi]
the constituency he represents
law [lɔː] – **act** [ækt]
enact [ɪn'ækt] a law
amendment [ə'mendmənt]
Amendments to the Constitution of
the United States
The Senate **is in session** today.
The Commons **are in recess** [ri'ses]
this week.

sich (der Stimme) enthalten
Stimmenthaltung
(Parlaments-)Sitz; Mandat
Die Labour Party errang 270 Sitze.
Ausschuss
Sie ist / sitzt in mehreren Ausschüssen.
Haushalts- / Finanzausschuss
Wahlkreis
der Wahlkreis, den er vertritt
Gesetz
ein Gesetz erlassen
(Ab-)Änderung (eines Gesetzes)
Zusatzartikel zur Verfassung der
Vereinigten Staaten
Der Senat **tagt** heute.
Das (britische) Parlament **pausiert**
diese Woche.

Gesetz heißt allgemein *law: the laws of the United States* (= die Gesetze
der Vereinigten Staaten).
Ein „Gesetz in Vorbereitung" heißt *bill: give a bill its second reading* (= ein
Gesetz in zweiter Lesung beraten).
Verabschiedet, wird die *bill* zum *act*, wobei *act* vor allem in den Namen
bestimmter Gesetze zu finden ist: *the Clean Air Act of 1970* (= das
Luftreinhaltungsgesetz von 1970), *the Immigration Act of 1990* (= das
Einwanderungsgesetz von 1990), *the Hours of Trading Act* (= das
Ladenschlussgesetz).

Geschrieben vorliegende Gesetze heißen formell auch *statutes: enact a statute* (= ein Gesetz erlassen).
Gesetze heißen kollektiv auch *legislation: legislation enacted by (the) Congress* (= vom Kongress erlassene Gesetze).

budget [ˈbʌdʒɪt]	**Haushalt(splan); Etat**
balance [ˈbæləns] the budget	den Haushalt ausgleichen
lobbyist [ˈlɒbiɪst]	**Lobbyist(in)**
dissolve [dɪˈzɒlv]	**auflösen**
dissolve Parliament and call an election	das Parlament auflösen und eine Wahl ansetzen
referendum [-ˈren-] *Pl.* -dums / -da	**Referendum; Volksentscheid**
election [ɪˈlekʃn]	**Wahl**
the next general election	die nächste Unterhauswahl
He won / lost the election narrowly.	Er gewann / verlor die Wahl knapp.
(election) campaign [kæmˈpeɪn]	Wahlkampf
runoff (election) [ˈrʌnɒf]	Stichwahl
elect [ɪˈlekt]	**wählen**
Gore was elected to the Senate in 1984.	Gore wurde 1984 in den Senat gewählt.
vote [vəʊt]	**Stimme; Abstimmung; Wahl; wählen**
Let's take a vote on that.	Darüber sollten wir abstimmen.
a vote of no confidence [ˈkɒnfɪdəns]	ein Misstrauensvotum
I'm going to vote Labour [ˈleɪbə].	Ich werde die Labour Party wählen.
vote on a bill	über eine Vorlage abstimmen
She voted in favour of the reform.	Sie stimmte für die Reform.
voter [ˈvəʊtə]	**Wähler(in)**
swing voter [ˈswɪŋ vəʊtə]	**Wechselwähler(in)**
ballot [ˈbælət]	**(geheime) Abstimmung, Wahl**

Absentee [æbsənˈtiː] *voting enables voters to cast their ballots in an election without going to the polls.* (= Die Briefwahl ermöglicht es Wählern, bei einer Wahl ihre Stimme abzugeben, ohne zur Wahl zu gehen.)

candidate [ˈkændɪdət]	**Kandidat(in)**
What's the candidate's stand on abortion [əˈbɔːʃn]?	Wie steht der Kandidat zur Abtreibung?
run (– ran – run)	*AE* **kandidieren**
She ran for the Senate in 1994.	1994 kandidierte sie für den Senat.
incumbent [ɪnˈkʌmbənt]	**Amtsinhaber(in)**
primary [ˈpraɪməri]	*AE* (innerparteiliche) **Vorwahl**

In the US, each of the two major [ˈmeɪdʒə] *parties holds a series of primary elections to choose delegates to the party convention.* (= In den USA hält jede der beiden großen Parteien eine Reihe von Vorwahlen ab, um Delegierte für den Parteikonvent auszuwählen.)

term [tɜːm]	**Legislaturperiode; Amtszeit**
Members of the House of Representatives serve two-year terms.	Die Abgeordneten des Repräsentantenhauses werden auf zwei Jahre gewählt.

Government
Regierung

No man is good enough to govern another man without that other's consent.
(*Abraham Lincoln, US president, 1809–1865*)

government ['gʌvnmənt]   **Regierung**
the federal ['fedrəl] government   die Bundesregierung
form a government   eine Regierung bilden
NGO(s) (= non-governmental   Nichtregierungsorganisation(en)
  organization[s])
administration [ədmɪnɪ'streɪʃn]   **Verwaltung; Regierung**
the Obama administration   die Regierung Obama

Kollektivwörter wie *cabinet, government, committee* [kə'mɪti], *majority*
[mə'dʒɒrəti], *party* werden im BE mitunter als Plural aufgefasst:
*The cabinet / The government / The party **are** divided on the issue* ['ɪʃuː].
(= Das Kabinett / Die Regierung / Die Partei ist in dieser Frage zerstritten.)
*So far, the committee **have** been unable to reach a decision* [dɪ'sɪʒn].
(= Der Ausschuss hat sich noch nicht zu einer Entscheidung durchringen
können.)

the White House ['waɪt haʊs]   **(Amtssitz des US-Präsidenten)**
No 10 (Downing Street)   **(Amtssitz des brit. Premierministers)**
No 10 seems to be lukewarm on the   Der Premierminister scheint davon
  idea [aɪ'dɪə].   nur mäßig begeistert zu sein.
Whitehall ['waɪthɔːl]   **britische Regierungskreise**
president ['prezɪdənt]   **Präsident(in)**
vice president [vaɪs 'prez-] / **veep** [iː]   **Vizepräsident(in)**
chancellor ['tʃɑːnsələ]   *BE* **Schatzkanzler(in), Finanz-**
     minister(in)
Chancellor Merkel's government   die Regierung von Bundeskanzlerin
     Merkel
head of state [hed əv 'steɪt]   **Staatsoberhaupt**
The president of the US is both head   Der Präsident der USA ist sowohl
  of state and head of government.   Staatsoberhaupt als auch
     Regierungschef.
king [kɪŋ] – **queen** [kwiːn]   **König – Königin**
emperor ['empərə] – **empress**   **Kaiser – Kaiserin**
governor ['gʌvnə]   **Gouverneur(in)**
cabinet ['kæbɪnət]   **Kabinett**
cabinet reshuffle ['riːʃʌfl]   Kabinetts- / Regierungsumbildung
cabinet meeting   Kabinettssitzung
the shadow ['ʃædəʊ] cabinet   das Schattenkabinett (der Opposition)
chief of staff [stɑːf]   **Stabschef(in)**
counsellor ['kaʊnsələ]   **Berater(in)**
special adviser [əd'vaɪzə]   **Sonderberater(in)**
department [dɪ'pɑːtmənt]   **Ministerium**
the State Department *AE*   das Außenministerium

office ['ɒfɪs] | Amt; Dienststelle; Behörde
the president's term of office | die Amtszeit des Präsidenten
He took office on May 8. | Er trat am 8. Mai sein Amt an.
the Home Office *BE* / *AE* Department | das Innenministerium
of the Interior |
the Foreign Office ['fɒrən ɒfɪs] *BE* | das Außenministerium
secretary ['sekrətri] | **Minister(in)**
foreign secretary *BE* / *AE* secretary | Außenminister(in)
of state |
minister ['mɪnɪstə] | **Minister(in)**
minister of state *BE* | Staatssekretär(in)
prime minister [praɪm 'mɪnɪstə] | Premierminister(in)
the prime minister of Bavaria | der Ministerpräsident von Bayern
the German foreign minister | der deutsche Außenminister

Ein Minister, der einem der Hauptministerien vorsteht, heißt BE offiziell
secretary of state, AE einfach *secretary,* bei nicht englischsprachigen Staaten
minister. Zum Beispiel Verteidigungsminister(in) =
BE: *secretary of state for defence / defence secretary,*
AE: *secretary of defense / defense secretary,*
in Bezug auf andere Staaten: *minister of defence / defence minister.*

---

ministry ['mɪnɪstri] | **Ministerium**
appoint [ə'pɔɪnt] – **appointment** | **ernennen – Ernennung**
He was appointed secretary of state. | Er wurde zum Außenminister
 | ernannt.

step down [step 'daʊn] | **zurücktreten**
The prime minister has stepped down. | Der Premierminister ist zurück-
 | getreten.

resign [rɪ'zaɪn] – **resignation** | **zurücktreten – Rücktritt**
[rezɪg'neɪʃn] |
overthrow (– overthrew – overthrown) | (*die Regierung*) **stürzen**
succeed [sək'si:d] – **successor** | **nachfolgen – Nachfolger(in)**
[sək'sesə] |
Bush was succeeded by Obama. | Bushs Nachfolger war Obama.
lame-duck [leɪm 'dʌk] **president** | **Präsident am Ende seiner Amtszeit**
 | (*lame duck* = lahme Ente)

run out of steam [sti:m] | **den Schwung verlieren**
agency ['eɪdʒənsi] | **Behörde**
the Environmental Protection Agency | die (US-)Umweltschutzbehörde
the Central Intelligence Agency (CIA) | (der amerikanische Geheimdienst)
board [bɔ:d] | **Behörde**
The board has 33 regional ['ri:dʒənəl] | Die Behörde hat 33 Zweigstellen.
offices. |
bureau ['bjʊərəʊ] | **Amt; Behörde**
Federal Bureau of Investigation (FBI) | (US-)Bundeskriminalamt
commission [kə'mɪʃn] | **Kommission; Ausschuss**
the Commission on Civil Rights | der (US-)Ausschuss für Bürgerrechte
Who is going to chair the commission? | Wer wird in dem Ausschuss den
 | Vorsitz haben?

Antigovernment activity
Aktivitäten gegen die Regierung

The most radical revolutionary will become a conservative on the day after the revolution. (*Hannah Arendt, German-born US philosopher, 1906–1975*)

protest ['prəʊtest]	**Protest**
protest rally ['ræli] / demonstration	Protestkundgebung / -demonstration
protest [prə'test]	protestieren
They staged sit-ins to protest (against) racial segregation.	Sie veranstalteten Sit-ins als Protest gegen die Rassentrennung.
antiwar protesters [prə'testəz] / demonstrators	Antikriegsdemonstranten
antiwar rally [ænti'wɔː ræli]	**Antikriegsdemonstration**
civil rights [sɪvl 'raɪts]	**Bürgerrechte**
the civil rights movement ['muːvmənt]	die Bürgerrechtsbewegung
civil rights activist ['æktɪvɪst]	Bürgerrechtler(in)
civil disobedience [dɪsə'biːdiəns]	**ziviler Ungehorsam**
dissident ['dɪsɪdənt]	**Dissident(in); Regimekritiker(in)**
the persecution of dissidents	die Verfolgung von Regimekritikern
passive resistance [rɪ'zɪstəns]	**passiver Widerstand**
violence ['vaɪələns] – **nonviolence**	**Gewalt** – **Gewaltlosigkeit**
(acts of) political violence	politische Gewaltakte / Gewalttaten
demonstration [demən'streɪʃn]	**Demonstration**
take to the streets	**auf die Straße gehen**
Protesters were **dispersed** [dɪ'spɜːst].	Demonstranten wurden **auseinandergetrieben**.
denounce [di'naʊns] corruption	die Korruption **anprangern**
shout slogans ['sləʊgənz]	**Parolen / Slogans rufen**
strike [straɪk] – **strikers** ['straɪkəz]	**Streik** – **Streikende**
call a general strike	zum Generalstreik aufrufen
boycott ['bɔɪkɒt]	**Boykott; boykottieren**
sabotage ['sæbətɑːʒ]	**Sabotage; sabotieren**
acts of sabotage	Sabotageakte, -handlungen
agitator ['ædʒɪteɪtə] – **agitation**	**Agitator(in)** – **Agitation**
underground ['ʌndəgraʊnd]	**Untergrund-**
join the underground (movement)	sich der Untergrundbewegung anschließen
go underground [ʌndə'graʊnd] (– went – gone [gɒn])	in den Untergrund gehen; untertauchen
conspiracy [kən'spɪrəsi] – **conspirator** [kən'spɪrətə]	**Verschwörung** – **Verschwörer(in)**
a conspiracy / plot to overthrow the government	eine Verschwörung zum Sturz der Regierung
plot [plɒt]	**Komplott; Verschwörung**
They were accused [ə'kjuːzd] of plotting against the state.	Sie wurden angeklagt, sich gegen den Staat verschworen zu haben.
(political) unrest [ʌn'rest]	**(politische) Unruhen**
insurrection [ɪnsə'rekʃn]	**Aufstand**
The insurrection was put down.	Der Aufstand wurde niedergeschlagen.

suppress an uprising [sə'pres]	**einen Aufstand unterdrücken**
rebellion [rɪ'beljən]	**Rebellion; Aufstand**
rise in rebellion (– rose – risen) against	sich erheben gegen
suppress a rebellion [sə'pres]	einen Aufstand unterdrücken
revolt [rɪ'vəʊlt]	**Revolte; Aufstand; revoltieren**
The peasants ['peznts] rose in revolt against the landowners.	Die Bauern erhoben sich gegen die Grundbesitzer.
(high) treason ['tri:zn]	**(Hoch-)Verrat**
terrorism ['terərɪzm] – **terrorist**	**Terrorismus – Terrorist(in)**
terrorist acts [terərɪst 'ækts]	terroristische Handlungen
terrorist attacks against US citizens	Terroranschläge gegen US-Bürger
guer(r)illa [gə'rɪlə]	**Guerilla; Guerillakämpfer(in)**
fight a guer(r)illa war [wɔ:]	einen Guerillakrieg führen
revolution [revə'lu:ʃn]	**Revolution**
revolutionary [revə'lu:ʃnəri]	**revolutionär; Revolutionär(in)**
revolutionary activities [æk'tɪvətiz]	revolutionäre Aktivitäten
revolutionary leaders	Revolutionsführer(innen)
counterrevolution [kaʊntə revə'lu:ʃn]	**Konterrevolution**
coup [ku:]	**Staatsstreich**
The president was ousted in a bloodless ['blʌdləs] coup.	Der Präsident wurde durch einen unblutigen Staatsstreich abgesetzt.
putsch [pʊtʃ]	**Putsch**
the failed / abortive [ə'bɔːtɪv] putsch	der gescheiterte Putsch
assassinate [ə'sæsɪneɪt]	**ermorden**
Kennedy was assassinated.	K. fiel einem Attentat zum Opfer.
assassination [əsæsɪ'neɪʃn]	**Ermordung**
seize power [si:z 'paʊə]	**die Macht ergreifen**
(military) junta [mɪlɪtəri 'dʒʌntə]	**(Militär-)Junta**
The king was deposed [dɪ'pəʊzd] by a military junta.	Der König wurde von einer Militärjunta abgesetzt.
ringleader ['rɪŋli:də]	**Rädelsführer(in); Anführer(in)**
the ringleaders of the conspiracy [kən'spɪrəsi]	die Rädelsführer der Verschwörung

Law and police
Rechtswesen und Polizei

→ 7.5 Crime and violence

It may be true that the law cannot make a man love me, but it can keep him from lynching me, and I think that's pretty important. (*Martin Luther King, US clergyman and civil rights campaigner, 1929–1968*)

law [lɔː]	**Gesetz; Recht**
law and order [lɔː(r) ənd 'ɔːdə]	Recht und Ordnung
enforce [ɪnˈfɔːs] the law	dem Gesetz Geltung verschaffen
court [kɔːt]	**Gericht**
That's what he told the court.	Das hat er vor Gericht ausgesagt.
She threatened [ˈθretnd] to take him to court.	Sie drohte ihn zu verklagen.
an out-of-court settlement	ein außergerichtlicher Vergleich
(court) proceedings [prəˈsiːdɪŋz]	**(Gerichts-)Verfahren**
take (legal) proceedings against	gerichtlich vorgehen gegen

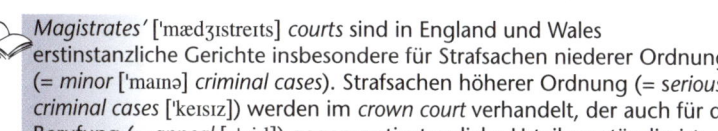

Magistrates' [ˈmædʒɪstreɪts] *courts* sind in England und Wales erstinstanzliche Gerichte insbesondere für Strafsachen niederer Ordnung (= *minor* [ˈmaɪnə] *criminal cases*). Strafsachen höherer Ordnung (= *serious criminal cases* [ˈkeɪsɪz]) werden im *crown court* verhandelt, der auch für die Berufung (= *appeal* [əˈpiːl]) gegen erstinstanzliche Urteile zuständig ist.

trial [ˈtraɪəl]	**(Gerichts-)Verfahren; Prozess**
She's on trial for perjury [ˈpɜːdʒəri].	Sie steht wegen Meineids vor Gericht.
(law)suit [(ˈlɔː)suːt]	**Prozess; Verfahren; Klage**
file / bring a suit against someone	gegen jemand Klage erheben
He lost the suit.	Er verlor den Prozess.
sue someone [suː]	**jemand verklagen**
They sued us for damages [ˈdæmɪdʒɪz].	Sie verklagten uns auf Schadenersatz.
judge [dʒʌdʒ]	**Richter(in)**
the jury [ˈdʒʊəri]	**die Geschworenen / Schöffen**
The jury found in her favour [ˈfeɪvə].	Die Jury entschied zu ihren Gunsten.

Mit *jury* gibt es ein modernes, häufig zu lesendes und zu hörendes *idiom*: *The jury is still out on this question.* (= Diese Frage ist noch nicht abschließend geklärt.) • *The jury is still out on global warming.* (= Hinsichtlich der weltweiten Klimaerwärmung sind noch viele Fragen offen.)

prosecute [ˈprɒsɪkjuːt]	**strafrechtlich verfolgen**
prosecuting counsel *BE* / *AE* prosecuting attorney [əˈtɜːni]	Staatsanwalt / Staatsanwältin
prosecution [prɒsɪˈkjuːʃn]	**Anklage(behörde); Staatsanwalt-schaft**
witness for the prosecution	Belastungszeuge / -zeugin
He escaped [ɪˈskeɪpt] prosecution.	Er entging der Strafverfolgung.

Staatsanwalt / Staatsanwältin heißt auch einfach *prosecutor* oder *the prosecution* (= die Staatsanwaltschaft), AE auch häufig *district attorney.*

charge [tʃɑːdʒ]	**Anklage; anklagen; beschuldigen**
The charge is murder ['mɜːdə].	Die Anklage lautet auf Mord.
release [rɪ'liːs] without charge	ohne Anklageerhebung freilassen
He was charged with manslaughter.	Er wurde des Totschlags angeklagt.
the defence [dɪ'fens]	**die Verteidigung**
witness for the defence	Entlastungszeuge / -zeugin
counsel ['kaʊnsl] for the defence	Verteidiger(in)

Rechtsanwalt: Die alltägliche, sowohl im BE als auch im AE übliche Bezeichnung ist *lawyer* ['lɔːjə]. Die offizielle Berufsbezeichnung für einen zugelassenen Anwalt dagegen ist im BE *solicitor* [sə'lɪsɪtə] und im AE *attorney* [ə'tɜːni]: *You ought to see a good lawyer / BE solicitor / AE attorney about this.* (= In dieser Sache sollten Sie sich von einem guten Anwalt beraten lassen.)
Darüber hinaus besteht im BE ein Unterschied zwischen *solicitor* und *barrister* ['bærɪstə]: *Barristers* werden von *solicitors* hinzugezogen bzw. beauftragt, wenn es um die Rechtsvertretung vor einem höheren Gericht oder Beratung in besonders komplizierten Rechtsfragen geht. Es gibt nur etwa 7000 *barristers* in Großbritannien, und dieser elitäre Kreis stellt das dar, was man *the Bar* (= die höhere Anwaltschaft) nennt.
Reformbestrebungen sehen vor, die Unterscheidung zwischen *solicitors* und *barristers* abzuschaffen.

witness ['wɪtnəs]	**Zeuge / Zeugin**
cross-examine a witness	einen Zeugen ins Kreuzverhör nehmen
misdemeanour [mɪsdɪ'miːnə]	**Vergehen; Übertretung**
offence [ə'fens]	**Straftat; Delikt**
It's an offence to drive a car without a licence ['laɪsns].	Autofahren ohne Führerschein ist strafbar.
crime [kraɪm]	**Verbrechen; Straftat**
commit [kə'mɪt] a crime	ein Verbrechen begehen
Violent ['vaɪələnt] crime has risen [ɪ] by 5 per cent.	Die Gewaltkriminalität hat um 5 Prozent zugenommen.
felony ['feləni]	**(schweres) Verbrechen**
homicide ['hɒmɪsaɪd]	*(juristisch)* **Tötung, Mord, Totschlag**
homicide squad [skwɒd]	Mordkommission

Murder (= Mord) – *manslaughter* (= Totschlag): Das amerikanische Recht unterscheidet bei Mord zwischen *first-degree murder* (keinerlei mildernde Umstände) und *second-degree murder* (gewisse mildernde Umstände).

innocent ['ɪnəsnt] – **guilty** ['gɪlti]	**unschuldig – schuldig**
You're assumed [ə'sjuːmd] to be innocent until proved [pruːvd] guilty.	Bis die Schuld erwiesen ist, gilt man als unschuldig.
temporary insanity [ɪn'sænəti]	**vorübergehende Unzurechnungs-fähigkeit**

Plea bargaining ['bɑ:gənɪŋ] nennt man die häufige Praxis, dass Verhandlungen (= *negotiations* [nɪgəʊʃi'eɪʃnz]) zwischen Anklage (= *prosecution*) und
Verteidigung (= *defence*) geführt werden mit dem Ziel, dass der / die Angeklagte (= *defendant* [dɪ'fendənt]) ein Schuldgeständnis (= *guilty plea*) ablegt
und dadurch eine Verminderung der Anklagepunkte (= *a reduction in
charges*) bzw. ein milderes Urteil (= *a more lenient* ['li:niənt] *sentence*) erwirkt.

diminished responsibility [dɪmɪnɪʃt rɪspɒnsə'bɪləti]	verminderte Zurechnungsfähigkeit
mitigating circumstances [mɪtɪgeɪtɪŋ 'sɜ:kəmstənsɪz]	mildernde Umstände
penalty ['penlti]	**Strafe**
He faces the death [e] penalty.	Ihm droht die Todesstrafe.
punishment ['pʌnɪʃmənt]	**Bestrafung; Strafe**
the debate over capital punishment	die Debatte über die Todesstrafe
fine [faɪn]	**Geldstrafe; Bußgeld; Verwarnungs-geld**
She was fined [faɪnd] £50.	Sie musste 50 Pfund Strafe zahlen.
remand [rɪ'mɑ:nd] *BE*	**Untersuchungshaft**
He's still on remand – he hasn't been convicted yet.	Er ist noch in Untersuchungshaft – er ist noch nicht verurteilt.
bail [beɪl]	**Kaution; Sicherheitsleistung**
The defendant was released on bail.	Der / Die Angeklagte wurde gegen Kaution freigelassen.
(on) probation [prə'beɪʃn]	**(auf) Bewährung**
probation officer	Bewährungshelfer(in)
prison ['prɪzn]	**Gefängnis**
He was sentenced to six years in prison.	Er wurde zu sechs Jahren Gefängnis verurteilt.
jail [dʒeɪl]	**Gefängnis**
She was jailed but freed for lack of evidence ['evɪdəns].	Sie wurde eingesperrt, aber aus Mangel an Beweisen wieder freigelassen.
appeal [ə'pi:l]	**Berufung; Revision(sverfahren)**
He appealed to the Supreme [su'pri:m] Court.	Er legte Berufung beim Obersten Bundesgericht ein.
The case has been appealed.	Es ist Berufung eingelegt worden.
law enforcement [ɪn'fɔ:smənt]	**Durchsetzung / Vollzug des Rechts**
law-enforcement officer	Polizeibeamte(r)
police [pə'li:s]	**Polizei**
The police are looking for a red Ford.	Die Polizei sucht einen roten Ford.
I'm a police officer.	Ich bin Polizist(in).

Police ist immer Plural. Also nicht *The police is / has / takes ...*, sondern
The police are / have / take ...
Police kann auch nicht mit *a(n)* konstruiert werden:
We have very good police. (= Wir haben eine sehr gute Polizei.)
„Zählbar", also mit *a* zu gebrauchen, ist dagegen *police force:*
We have an efficient [ɪ'fɪʃnt] *police force.* (= Wir haben eine effiziente Polizei.)

police station [pə'li:s steɪʃn]
state trooper ['tru:pə] *AE*

(Polizei-)Revier; (Polizei-)Wache
Polizist(in) (eines US-Staats)

Eine Anrede für Polizisten ist *officer: Excuse me, officer, can you ...?*

detective [dɪ'tektɪv]
detective superintendent
  [su:pərɪn'tendənt]
suspect ['sʌspekt]
warrant ['wɒrənt]

Detektiv(in); Kriminalbeamte(r)
Kriminalkommissar(in)

(Tat-)Verdächtige(r)
(richterlicher) **Haft- / Durchsuchungs-
  befehl**

We have a warrant for his arrest [ə'rest].

Wir haben einen Haftbefehl gegen
  ihn.

The prosecution obtained [əb'teɪnd]
  an arrest warrant against him.
offender [ə'fendə]
first offender – repeat [rɪ'pi:t] offender
juvenile ['dʒu:vənaɪl] / young offender
custody ['kʌstədi]
He was taken into custody.
The suspect ['sʌspekt] has been
  remanded [rɪ'mɑːndɪd] in custody.

Die Staatsanwaltschaft erwirkte einen
  Haftbefehl gegen ihn.
Straftäter(in); Verkehrssünder(in)
Ersttäter(in) – Rückfalltäter(in)
jugendliche(r) Straftäter(in)
(Polizei-)Gewahrsam; Haft
Er wurde in Haft genommen.
Der Verdächtige bleibt in
  Untersuchungshaft.

Der in Kriminalberichten britischer Zeitungen häufig zu findende Satz, dass
jemand *is helping the police with their inquiries* [ɪn'kwaɪəriz], bedeutet in der
Regel, dass die Polizei einen Tatverdächtigen verhört.

detain [dɪ'teɪn]
He was detained for questioning.

in Haft nehmen / halten
Er wurde zur Vernehmung fest-
  gehalten.

detention [dɪ'tenʃn]
One asylum [ə'saɪləm] seeker died
  in detention.
She was released [rɪ'li:st] from
  detention on medical grounds.

Festnahme; Haft
Ein Asylbewerber starb in der Haft.

Sie wurde aus medizinischen Gründen
  aus der Haft entlassen.

Praktisch jede der ca. 3000 *counties* ['kaʊntiz] in den USA hat ihre eigene
police force, die in der Regel einem *elected sheriff* (= gewählten Sheriff)
untersteht. Die Städte haben ebenfalls eigene *police departments*
[dɪ'pɑːtmənts]. Mit etwa 20 000 *police agencies* ['eɪdʒənsiz] (= Polizeibe-
hörden) haben die USA das dezentralisierteste Polizeisystem der Welt.
Das britische System hingegen ist – mit nur ca. 40 *law enforcement
agencies – highly centralized*. Die *London Metropolitan* [metrə'pɒlɪtən] *Police,*
nach ihrer früheren Adresse auch *Scotland Yard* genannt, ist die größte
Polizeibehörde des Landes und nimmt mit ihren *specialist departments*
auch überregionale Aufgaben – etwa *combating* ['kɒmbætɪŋ] *terrorism*
(= Terrorismusbekämpfung) – wahr; besonders bekannt ist ihr *CID =
Criminal Investigation Department* (= Kriminalpolizei).

Taxation
Steuern

Taxes, after all, are the dues that we pay for the privileges of membership in an organized society. (*Franklin D. Roosevelt, US president, 1882–1945*)

tax [tæks] – **taxes** ['tæksɪz]	**Steuer – Steuern**
raise / increase [ɪn'kriːs] taxes	die Steuern erhöhen
reduce [rɪ'djuːs] / lower / cut taxes	die Steuern senken
She is paid $611 a week before taxes.	Sie verdient wöchentlich 611 Dollar brutto.
tax increase ['ɪŋkriːs] – tax cut	Steuererhöhung – Steuersenkung
tax-free / free of tax	steuerfrei
tax evasion [ɪ'veɪʒn] / tax dodging	Steuerhinterziehung
tax haven ['heɪvn]	Steueroase; Steuerparadies
tax breaks for corporations that invest [ɪn'vest] at home *AE*	Steuervergünstigungen für Konzerne, die im Inland investieren
simplify ['sɪmplɪfaɪ] the tax code	das Steuersystem vereinfachen
tax [tæks]	**besteuern**
Taxpayers should be taxed in proportion to their ability to pay.	Die Steuerzahler sollten entsprechend ihrer finanziellen Leistungsfähigkeit besteuert werden.
the taxman ['tæksmæn]	(*personifizierend*) **das Finanzamt**
The taxman gets most of what I earn.	Den größten Teil meines Einkommens kriegt das Finanzamt.
income (tax) ['ɪnkʌm (tæks)]	**Einkommen(steuer)**
negative ['negətɪv] income tax	negative Einkommensteuer; Bürgergeld
net income – gross [grəʊs] income	Nettoeinkommen – Bruttoeinkommen
Income tax is collected by the Inland Revenue ['revənjuː] *BE* / *AE* Internal Revenue Service (IRS).	Die Einkommensteuer wird vom Finanzamt eingezogen.

PAYE [piː eɪ waɪ 'iː] = *pay as you earn* nennt man in GB den Direktabzug der Lohnsteuer durch den Arbeitgeber. Die amerikanische *payroll tax* ist eine Lohnsummensteuer, die der Arbeitgeber en bloc an das Finanzamt zahlt. Mangels eines spezialisierten Begriffs entspricht *income tax* allgemein auch der deutschen Lohnsteuer.

income tax return [rɪ'tɜːn]	**Einkommensteuererklärung**
prepare / complete [kəm'pliːt] an income tax return	eine Einkommensteuererklärung ausfüllen
file / submit an income tax return	eine Einkommensteuererklärung abgeben
value-added tax [væljuː 'ædɪd tæks] / **VAT** [væt] *BE*	**Mehrwertsteuer**
All prices are inclusive of VAT.	Alle Preise verstehen sich einschließlich Mehrwertsteuer.

6

9

Eine auf kommunaler Ebene erhobene (= *levied* ['levid]) Steuer war in
GB die unpopuläre Kopfsteuer (= *poll tax* ['pəʊl tæks] / *community charge*
[kə'mjuːnəti tʃɑːdʒ]), die 1991 abgeschafft und durch eine *council tax*
(*council* ist der Gemeinde- oder Stadtrat) ersetzt wurde.
In den USA gab es bis 1966 ebenfalls eine *poll tax,* die durch die Verknüpfung
mit dem Wahlrecht die Schwarzen benachteiligte und daher durch einen
Verfassungszusatz (= *amendment* [ə'mendmənt]) und eine höchstrichterliche
Entscheidung (= *Supreme Court decision* [dɪ'sɪʒn]) aufgehoben wurde.
Andere *local taxes* sind die *property tax* (= Vermögensteuer) und in den
USA die *sales tax,* die in fast allen 50 Bundesstaaten auf den Einzelhandels-
preis (= *retail price* ['riːteɪl praɪs]) aufgeschlagen wird.

tax-exempt [tæks ɪg'zemt]	**steuerbefreit; steuerfrei**
Books are exempt from VAT.	Bücher sind mehrwertsteuerfrei.
(non)taxable income ['tæksəbl]	**(nicht) steuerpflichtiges Einkommen**
(tax) refund ['riːfʌnd]	**(Steuer-)Erstattung**
You are entitled [ɪn'taɪtld] to a refund.	Sie haben Anspruch auf eine Erstattung.

Steuerberater sind *tax consultants* [kən'sʌltənts]; das Gemeinte wird aber
auch durch *accountant* [ə'kaʊntənt] (= Wirtschaftsprüfer) und *preparer*
(= *AE for someone trained to prepare tax returns for others*) ausgedrückt.

bookkeeping ['bʊkkiːpɪŋ]	**Buchführung; Buchhaltung**
accounting [ə'kaʊntɪŋ]	**Rechnungswesen; Buchhaltung**
the accounting department	die Buchhaltung(sabteilung)
audit ['ɔːdɪt]	**Buchprüfung; (die Bücher) prüfen**
assessment [ə'sesmənt]	**Veranlagung** (durch das Finanzamt)
charitable contribution [tʃærɪtəbl kɒntri'bjuːʃn]	**Spende**
Charitable contributions are deductible.	Spenden sind absetzbar.
depreciation [dɪpriːʃi'eɪʃn]	**Abschreibung**

Sozialabgaben sind *social-security contributions,* BE werden sie *NI contributions* genannt (*NI = National Insurance* [ɪn'ʃʊərəns]). Die AE-Entsprechung
ist *FICA tax* (*FICA = Federal Insurance Contributions Act*).

(customs) duty ['djuːti]	**Zoll(abgabe)**
Do you have to pay duty on this?	Muss man darauf Zoll bezahlen?

Deutsche Steuerbegriffe in Englisch
geringfügige Beschäftigung(sverhältnisse) / **Minijobs** (= *low-paid employment* /
low-paid jobs), **Gewerbesteuer** (= *business tax* / *trade tax*), **Grundfreibetrag**
(= *tax-free allowance*), **Grunderwerbsteuer** (= *real-estate* ['rɪəl ɪsteɪt] *transfer tax* /
property transfer tax), **Grundsteuer** (= *real-estate tax* / *property tax*), **Kapital-
ertrag(s)steuer** (= *capital-gains tax* / *withholding tax*), **Körperschaftssteuer**
(= *corporation tax*), **Lohnsteuer** (= *wage tax* / *salary tax*), **Lohnsteuerkarte**
(= *[wage-]tax card* / *salary-tax card*), **Schwarzarbeit** (= *illicit* [ɪ'lɪsɪt] *work*),
Solidaritätszuschlag (= *solidarity* [sɒlɪ'dærəti] *surcharge* / *solidarity tax*),
Steuersenkungsgesetz (= *tax reduction package* / *Tax Reduction Act*).

Social security
Soziale Sicherheit

If a free society cannot help the many who are poor, it cannot save
the few who are rich. (*John F. Kennedy, US president, 1917–63*)

Social security [sɪ'kjʊərəti] bedeutet allgemein soziale Sicherheit; speziell
bezeichnet der Begriff BE Sozialhilfe und AE Sozialversicherung:
Most workers are covered ['kʌvəd] *under social security.* AE (= Die meisten
  Arbeitnehmer sind sozial abgesichert.)
Social security is a form of social insurance [ɪn'ʃʊərəns]. AE (= ... ist eine Art
  Sozialversicherung.)
She's on social security BE / AE *on welfare.* (= Sie bezieht Sozialhilfe.)
Sozialamt ist BE *social security office* und AE *social welfare office.*

the social safety net ['seɪfti net]	das soziale Netz
welfare / public assistance *beide AE*	**Sozialhilfe**
her monthly welfare grant [ɑː] *AE*	ihre monatliche Sozialhilfezahlung
welfare cuts ['welfeə kʌts]	Streichung von Sozialleistungen
welfare reform ['welfeə rɪfɔːm]	Sozialreform
the welfare state [welfeə 'steɪt]	der Wohlfahrtsstaat / Sozialstaat
dismantle the social welfare system	Sozialabbau betreiben
maternity allowance / leave	**Mutterschaftsgeld / -urlaub**
housing benefit *BE /* AE **rent subsidy**	**Wohngeld**
sickness benefit ['sɪknəs benəfɪt] *BE*	**Krankengeld**

The National Health Service (NHS): Der grundsätzlich kostenlose, allen
Bürgern umfassende *medical care* (= medizinische Versorgung) bietende
staatliche Gesundheitsdienst des UK. – Ein *National Health doctor* ist so
etwas wie ein Kassenarzt, *National Health glasses* entsprechen einer
Kassenbrille. *I got it on the National Health.* (= Das hat die Kasse bezahlt.)

medical insurance / health insurance	**Krankenversicherung**
health-insurance company	Krankenkasse
curb [kɜːb] **(the) costs**	**(die) Kosten dämpfen**
nursing-care insurance ['nɜːsɪŋ]	(*Deutschland*) **Pflegeversicherung**
pension ['penʃn]	**Rente; Pension; Ruhegehalt**
retirement pension / old-age pension	(Alters-)Rente; Pension
You're **entitled** [ɪn'taɪtld] to benefit.	Sie haben Anspruch auf Beihilfe.
the **entitlement mentality** [-'tæləti]	das **Anspruchsdenken**

Medicare – Medicaid: Medicare ist das staatliche Krankenversicherungssys-
tem für ältere Bürger in den USA (= *a system of government-provided health
insurance for the elderly*), während *Medicaid* das Programm US-staatlicher
Gesundheitsfürsorge (= *health care*) für Einkommensschwache (= *people on
low incomes*) aller Altersstufen ist. – *Health-care reform* [rɪ'fɔːm] ist in den
USA ein zentrales politisches Thema (= *a major political issue* ['ɪʃuː]).

International relations
Internationale Beziehungen

I would like to see an international court established in which to settle disputes between nations, so that armies could be disbanded and the great navies allowed to rot in perfect peace. (*Robert G. Ingersoll, US orator, 1833–99*)

relations with other countries	**Beziehungen zu anderen Staaten**
strained relations [streɪnd rɪ'leɪʃnz]	gespannte Beziehungen
normalization of relations	Normalisierung der Beziehungen
sever ['sevə] / re-establish [riː'ɪ'stæblɪʃ] diplomatic relations / ties [taɪz]	die diplomatischen Beziehungen abbrechen / wiederherstellen
international affairs [ə'feəz]	**die internationale Politik**
international organizations	internationale Organisationen
the international community	die Völkergemeinschaft
the International Monetary Fund (IMF)	der Internationale Währungsfonds
foreign policy / foreign affairs	(die) **Außenpolitik**

Außenminister – Außenministerium
= UK: *foreign secretary* [fɒrən 'sekrətri] – *Foreign Office* ['fɒrən ɒfɪs]
= USA: *secretary of state* – *State Department* ['steɪt dɪpɑːtmənt]
= andere Staaten in der Regel: *foreign minister* ['mɪnɪstə] – *foreign ministry*

statesman [-mən] – **statesmanship**	**Staatsmann – Staatskunst**
state visit [steɪt 'vɪzɪt]	**Staatsbesuch**
summit meeting ['sʌmɪt miːtɪŋ]	**Gipfeltreffen**
diplomacy [dɪ'pləʊməsi]	(die) **Diplomatie**
shuttle diplomacy in the Middle East	Pendeldiplomatie im Nahen Osten
diplomatic recognition [rekəg'nɪʃn]	**diplomatische Anerkennung**
diplomat ['dɪpləmæt]	**Diplomat(in)**
ambassador [-'bæs-] – **embassy**	**Botschafter(in) – Botschaft**
the German embassy ['embəsi] in Paris	die deutsche Botschaft in Paris
envoy ['envɔɪ]	**Gesandter / Gesandtin**
special envoy	Sonderbeauftragte(r)
mission ['mɪʃn]	**Mission**
a diplomat on a secret [iː] mission	ein Diplomat in geheimer Mission
ally ['ælaɪ]	**Verbündeter; Bündnispartner**
the US and its allies	die USA und ihre Alliierten
the Allied ['ælaɪd] forces in Europe	die alliierten Streitkräfte in Europa
alliance [ə'laɪəns]	**Bündnis; Allianz**
nonaligned nations [nɒnə'laɪnd]	**blockfreie Staaten**
sovereign ['sɒvrɪn] – **sovereignity**	(*Staat*) **souverän – Souveränität**
territorial claims [terə'tɔːriəl]	**territoriale Ansprüche**

Die Grenze zwischen Staaten kann sowohl *border* als auch *frontier* ['frʌntɪə] heißen. *Border* ist das häufigere und daher „sicherere" Wort: *the Belgian border / frontier* (= die belgische Grenze), *border / frontier disputes* [dɪ'spjuːts] (= Grenzstreitigkeiten), *cross the border / frontier* (= die Grenze überqueren), *border clashes / conflicts* (= Grenzkonflikte).

crisis ['kraɪsɪs] *Pl.* crises ['kraɪsiːz]	**Krise**
a political solution to the crisis	eine politische Lösung der Krise
dispute [dɪ'spjuːt]	**Streit(igkeit); Auseinandersetzung**
The dispute might escalate ['eskəleɪt].	Der Streit könnte eskalieren.
armed intervention [ɪntə'venʃn]	**bewaffnete Intervention**
economic sanctions ['sæŋkʃnz]	**Wirtschaftssanktionen**
embargo [ɪm'bɑːgəʊ] *Pl.* embargoes	**Embargo**
impose [ɪm'pəʊz] / lift an embargo	ein Embargo verhängen / aufheben
intermediary [ɪntə'miːdiəri]	**Vermittler(in); Mittelsmann/-person**
mediate (in) a conflict ['miːdieɪt]	in einem Konflikt **vermitteln**
mediator ['miːdieɪtə]	**Vermittler(in)**
appeasement policy (towards)	**Beschwichtigungspolitik (gegen-**
	über)
reduce tensions ['tenʃnz]	(die) **Spannungen abbauen**
peace plan ['piːs plæn]	**Friedensplan**
settle a conflict ['kɒnflɪkt]	**einen Konflikt beilegen**
negotiate [nɪ'gəʊʃieɪt]	**verhandeln**
negotiate a treaty ['triːti]	einen (Staats-)Vertrag aushandeln
negotiations [nɪgəʊʃi'eɪʃnz]	**Verhandlungen**
achieve [ə'tʃiːv] **a breakthrough**	**einen Durchbruch erzielen**
reach a compromise ['kɒmprəmaɪz]	**einen Kompromiss erzielen**
issue a communiqué [kə'mjuːnɪkeɪ]	**ein Kommuniqué veröffentlichen**
agreement [ə'griːmənt]	**Abkommen**
a cease-fire ['siːs faɪə] agreement	ein Waffenstillstandsabkommen
reach an agreement	zu einer Einigung gelangen
accord [ə'kɔːd]	**Abkommen**
sign [saɪn] a peace accord	ein Friedensabkommen unter-
	zeichnen
the UN peacekeeping forces	**die UNO-Friedenstruppen**
(nuclear) nonproliferation treaty	**Atomwaffensperrvertrag**
disarmament conference ['kɒnfrəns]	**Abrüstungskonferenz**
pursue a policy of détente [deɪ'tɑːnt]	**eine Politik der Entspannung**
	verfolgen
free trade (area) ['eəriə]	**Freihandel(szone)**
trade barriers / barriers to free trade	Handelshemmnisse; Handels-
	schranken
trading partner ['treɪdɪŋ pɑːtnə]	Handelspartner
the European Union (EU)	**die Europäische Union**
apply for membership in the EU	die EU-Mitgliedschaft beantragen
enlargement of the EU	EU-Erweiterung
the Single European Market	**der Europäische Binnenmarkt**
European Monetary Union (EMU)	**Europäische Währungsunion** (EWU)
foreign aid – development aid	**Auslandshilfe – Entwicklungshilfe**
developing [dɪ'veləpɪŋ] **country**	**Entwicklungsland**
newly industrializing country (NIC)	**Schwellenland**

The United Nations / UN (= die Vereinten Nationen / UNO):
Security Council (= Sicherheitsrat) • *General Assembly* (= Vollversammlung) •
secretary-general (= Generalsekretär) • *UN resolution* [rezə'luːʃn] (= UNO-Beschluss)

6

12 Defence, war, military
Verteidigung, Krieg, Militär

Every gun that is made, every warship launched, every rocket fired signifies, in the final sense, a theft from those who hunger and are not fed, those who are cold and are not clothed. (*Dwight D. Eisenhower, US general and president, 1890–1969*)

defend [dɪˈfend] – **defence** [dɪˈfens]	**verteidigen – Verteidigung**
increased defence spending	erhöhte Verteidigungsausgaben
NATO [ˈneɪtəʊ]	(die) **NATO**
Spain joined [dʒɔɪnd] NATO in 1982.	Spanien trat 1982 der NATO bei.
arms control [ˈɑːmz kəntrəʊl]	**Rüstungskontrolle**
nonaggression pact	**Nichtangriffspakt**
deterrence [dɪˈterəns] – **deterrent**	**Abschreckung – Abschreckungsmittel**

Verteidigungsminister – Verteidigungsministerium
= UK: *secretary of state for defence – Ministry of Defence*
= USA: *secretary of defense – Department of Defense / the Pentagon*
= andere Staaten in der Regel: *minister of defence – ministry of defence*

conscription [kənˈskrɪpʃn] *BE / AE* **the draft**	die Wehrpflicht
conscripts [ˈkɒnskrɪpts] *BE / AE* **draftees** [drɑːfˈtiːz]	Wehrpflichtige
army [ˈɑːmi]	Armee; Heer
He's in the army.	Er ist beim Militär / „beim Bund".
military [ˈmɪlətri]	**Militär; Militär-; militärisch**
The military is against the plan.	Das Militär ist gegen den Plan.
He did his military service.	Er leistete seinen Wehrdienst ab.
the air force [ˈeə fɔːs]	**die Luftwaffe**
the navy [ˈneɪvi]	**die (Kriegs-)Marine**
officers – common soldiers [kɒmən ˈsəʊldʒəz]	**Offiziere – einfache Soldaten**
promote [prəˈməʊt]	**befördern**
He was promoted to captain [ˈkæptən].	Er wurde zum Hauptmann befördert.
general [ˈdʒenrəl] – **the general staff** [stɑːf]	**General – der Generalstab**
command [kəˈmɑːnd] – **commander**	**Kommando – Befehlshaber**
under Eisenhower's command	unter Eisenhowers Kommando
The president is commander-in-chief of the armed forces.	Der Präsident ist Oberkommandierender der Streitkräfte.
intelligence [ɪnˈtelɪdʒəns]	**Geheimdienst; Nachrichtendienst**
intelligence – counterintelligence	Spionage – Gegenspionage
information provided by US intelligence	Informationen, die der US-Geheimdienst liefert(e)

Military organizational units (= **militärische Organisationseinheiten**)
platoon [pləˈtuːn] (= Zug) • *company* [ˈkʌmpəni] (= Kompanie) • *regiment*

['redʒɪmənt] (= Regiment) • *unit* ['ju:nɪt] (= Einheit) • *battalion* [bə'tæliən]
(= Bataillon) • *brigade* [brɪ'geɪd] (= Brigade) • *division* [dɪ'vɪʒn] (= Division) •
corps [kɔ:] (= Korps) • *army* ['ɑ:mi] (= Armee)

war [wɔ:]	**Krieg**
the First / Second World War	der Erste / Zweite Weltkrieg
declare war on a country	einem Land den Krieg erklären
aggressor [ə'gresə] – **aggression**	**Aggressor – Aggression**
invade [ɪn'veɪd] – **invasion** [ɪn'veɪʒn]	**einmarschieren; überfallen – Invasion**
invade a neighbouring country	in ein Nachbarland einfallen
the German invasion of Poland	der deutsche Überfall auf Polen
attack [ə'tæk]	**Angriff; angreifen**
advance [əd'vɑ:ns] – **retreat** [rɪ'tri:t]	**Vormarsch – Rückzug**
occupy ['ɒkjupaɪ] **a country**	**ein Land besetzen**
occupation [ɒkju'peɪʃn]	**Besetzung**
the occupation of Poland	die Besetzung Polens
occupation forces	Besatzungstruppen
battle ['bætl]	**Schlacht**
He was killed in battle.	Er ist im Kampf gefallen.
battlefield – battleship	**Schlachtfeld – Schlachtschiff**
action ['ækʃn]	**Kampf; Gefecht**
He saw action in North Africa.	Er nahm an den Kämpfen in Nordafrika teil.
He was killed in action in 1944.	Er fiel 1944.
offensive [ə'fensɪv] – **counteroffensive**	**Offensive – Gegenoffensive**
plan / launch [lɔ:ntʃ] an offensive	eine Offensive planen / starten
resistance [rɪ'zɪstəns]	**Widerstand**
face heavy resistance	auf starken Widerstand stoßen
enemy troops / ships / attacks	**feindliche Truppen / Schiffe / Angriffe**
supplies [sə'plaɪz] **and ammunition** [æmju'nɪʃn]	**Nachschub und Munition**
infantry – artillery [-'tɪl-] – **tanks**	**Infanterie – Artillerie – Panzer**
missile ['mɪsaɪl] / **rocket**	**Rakete**
a missile / rocket attack on the city	ein Raketenangriff auf die Stadt
nuclear weapons [nju:klɪə 'wepnz]	**Kernwaffen**
weapons of mass destruction	Massenvernichtungswaffen
(nuclear) submarine [sʌbmə'ri:n]	**(Atom-)U-Boot**
bomb [bɒm]	**Bombe**
atom(ic) bomb ['ætəm bɒm / ətɒmɪk 'bɒm]	Atombombe
hydrogen bomb ['haɪdrədʒən bɒm]	Wasserstoffbombe
cluster bomb ['klʌstə bɒm]	Streubombe
They dropped bombs on the airfield.	Sie warfen Bomben auf den Flugplatz.
the bombing of industrial targets	das Bombardieren von Industrieanlagen
air base ['eə beɪs]	**Luftwaffenstützpunkt**
air raid ['eə reɪd]	**Luftangriff**
air-raid shelter	Luftschutzbunker, -keller, -raum
parachute ['pærəʃu:t] – **paratrooper**	**Fallschirm – Fallschirmjäger**

destroy – **destruction** [dɪˈstrʌkʃn]	zerstören – Zerstörung
destroyer [dɪˈstrɔɪə]	Zerstörer
court-martial [kɔːt ˈmɑːʃl]	**Kriegs- / Militärgericht**
He was court-martialled.	Er wurde vor ein Kriegsgericht gestellt.
capture [ˈkæptʃə]	**einnehmen; gefangen nehmen**
The town was captured after heavy fighting.	Die Stadt wurde nach schweren Kämpfen eingenommen.
conquer [ˈkɒŋkə] a city	eine Stadt **erobern**
withdraw (– withdrew – withdrawn)	**sich zurückziehen;** (*Truppen*) **abziehen**
guer(r)illa (fighters / warfare) [gəˈrɪlə]	**Guerilla(kämpfer / -krieg)**
partisan – **partisan war(fare)**	**Partisan(in)** – **Partisanenkrieg**
suicide [ˈsuːɪsaɪd] **attack / strike**	**Selbstmordanschlag**
rapid deployment [diˈplɔɪmənt]	**schnelles Eingreifen**
spy [spaɪ]	**Spion(in); spionieren**
casualties [ˈkæʒuəltiz]	**Verluste** (= Verwundete / Tote)
civilian [səˈvɪliən] casualties	Verluste in der Zivilbevölkerung
the wounded [ˈwuːndɪd] **and the dead**	**die Verwundeten und die Toten**
prisoners (of war) / POWs	**(Kriegs-)Gefangene**
They were taken prisoner [ˈprɪznə].	Sie wurden gefangen genommen.
victory [ˈvɪktəri] – **defeat** [dɪˈfiːt]	**Sieg – Niederlage**
surrender [səˈrendə]	**kapitulieren; Kapitulation**
war crime(s) [ˈwɔː kraim(z)]	**Kriegsverbrechen**
war criminal [ˈwɔː krɪmɪnəl]	Kriegsverbrecher(in)

"About turrrn!"

Titles, forms of address
Titel, Anredeformen

Emperors, kings, artisans, peasants, big people, little people –
at bottom we are all alike and all the same; all just alike on the inside,
and when our clothes are off, nobody can tell which of us is which.
(*Mark Twain, US writer, 1835–1910*)

duke [djuːk] – **duchess** ['dʌtʃɪs]	**Herzog – Herzogin**
the Duke of Edinburgh ['ednbərə]	der Herzog von Edinburgh
the Duchess of Kent	die Herzogin von Kent
(crown) prince [(kraʊn) 'prɪns]	**(Kron-)Prinz**
(crown) princess [(kraʊn) prɪn'ses]	(Kron-)Prinzessin

Sir / Dame – Lord / Lady:
Wenn ein einfacher *Mr John Brown receives a knighthood* ['naɪthʊd] (= „in
den Ritterstand erhoben", d.h. geadelt wird), wird er zu *Sir John Brown*,
abgekürzt *Sir John* (nicht: *Sir Brown*!).
Wird er später auch noch *raised to the peerage* ['pɪərɪdʒ] (als *peer* hat er
den Titel *Lord* und ist Mitglied des *House of Lords*), so wird er *Lord John
Brown*, abgekürzt *Lord Brown* (nicht: *Lord John*!).
Die entsprechenden weiblichen Titel sind: *Mrs Mary Brown – Dame Mary
Brown (Dame Mary) – Lady Mary Brown (Lady Brown)*.

Den Namen von Botschafter(inne)n (= *ambassadors* [æm'bæsədəz]) und
anderen hohen Würdenträgern (= *dignitaries* ['dɪgnətəriz]) wird häufig der
Titel *Excellency* ['eksələnsi] vorangestellt:
His Excellency the Ambassador of the United States of America ...
Die offizielle Anredeform ist entsprechend *Your Excellency:*
I hope Your Excellency had a pleasant journey ['dʒɜːni].
Der mächtigste Mann der Welt, *the US president,* wird dagegen schlicht
mit *Mr President* oder *sir* angeredet.
Anrede und Grußformel in einem Brief an den Präsidenten: *(Dear) Mr
President: ... (Very) Respectfully yours,*

In britischen Parlamentsdebatten gebraucht man *the Honourable* ['ɒnərəbl]
vor den Namen von Abgeordnetenkollegen:
Is the Honourable member aware that ...? (= Ist dem Herrn Abgeordneten /
   der Frau Abgeordneten bewusst, dass ...?)
Bei einem Kabinettsmitglied (= *Cabinet Minister*) steht the *Rt Hon* (= *the Right
Honourable* = der sehr ehrenwerte) vor dem Namen:
*Among those present was the Rt Hon Gordon Brown MP (Chancellor of the
   Exchequer* [ɪks'tʃekə])* ...
Anreden würde man den *Chancellor of the Exchequer* mit *Chancellor*
['tʃɑːnsələ]:
Yes, Chancellor, but don't you agree that ...? (= Jawohl, Herr Schatzkanzler,
   aber meinen Sie nicht auch, dass ...?)

Richter / Richterinnen (= *judges* ['dʒʌdʒɪz]) werden in GB und in den USA in der Regel mit *Your Honour* ['ɒnə] (= euer Ehren / hohes Gericht) oder *my Lord* angeredet:
Do I have to answer that question, Your Honour? That is correct, my Lord.

Bei Geistlichen (= *members of the clergy* ['klɜːdʒi]) wird gewöhnlich die Anrede *Reverend* ['revərənd] (= ehrwürdig / Hochwürden) verwendet:
Excuse me, Reverend, can I have a word with you? (= Entschuldigen Sie, Herr Pastor, kann ich Sie mal kurz sprechen?)
(In der Adresse:) *The Reverend John Brown* (= Herrn Pfarrer John Brown)

Vor den Namen „gewöhnlicher Sterblicher" (= *ordinary mortals* ['mɔːtəlz]) steht *Mr* (= Herr / Herrn), *Mrs* (= Frau), *Miss* (= Fräulein) oder *Ms* [mɪz] (= neutrale Anredeform für Frauen, die – entsprechend dem männlichen *Mr* – nicht zwischen „verheiratet" und „unverheiratet" unterscheidet).

Ein akademischer Grad ersetzt – anders als im Deutschen – den Titel *Mr / Mrs / Miss / Ms.* Entsprechend wäre Herr Prof. Dr. Peters im Englischen einfach *Professor Peters* bzw. – wenn er ein Chirurg ist – *Mr Peters.*
Über oder mit *Professor Peters* könnte man höflich so reden:
We have just heard from Dr Peters / Professor Peters that …
Excuse me, professor / Excuse me, sir, there's a student to see you …
Die Anrede *doctor* verwendet man nur bei Ärzten:
Goodbye, doctor, and thanks very much.

"Did your Excellency have a pleasant journey?"

Social problems
Soziale Probleme

1   **Housing shortage**
    Wohnungsmangel

2   **Unemployment**
    Arbeitslosigkeit

3   **Drug and alcohol abuse**
    Drogen- und Alkoholmissbrauch

4   **Poverty**
    Armut

5   **Crime and violence**
    Verbrechen und Gewalttätigkeit

6   **Xenophobia and racism**
    Ausländerfeindlichkeit und Rassismus

7   **Sexism**
    Sexismus

7
1 Housing shortage
Wohnungsmangel

→ 5.1 Flats and houses

Female, early 30s, nonsmoker, seeks quiet, clean and friendly flatshare in North or North East London. (*Classified ad in a London newspaper*)

housing ['haʊzɪŋ]	**Wohnungen; Wohnraum; Wohnungs-**
affordable [ə'fɔːdəbl] housing / living space	erschwinglicher Wohnraum
low-income housing	Wohnungen für Einkommens-schwache
construct / provide low-cost housing	preiswerten Wohnraum erstellen
the housing shortage ['ʃɔːtɪdʒ]	die Wohnungsknappheit / -not
the housing crisis ['kraɪsɪs]	die Wohnungsnot / -krise
the housing market ['mɑːkɪt]	der Wohnungsmarkt
study the housing ads [ædz]	die Wohnungsanzeigen studieren
promote housing construction	den Wohnungsbau fördern
housing programme ['prəʊɡræm]	Wohnungsbauprogramm
cuts in housing benefit ['benɪfɪt]	Wohngeldkürzungen
housing office ['haʊzɪŋ ɒfɪs]	Wohnungsamt
housing association [əsəʊsi'eɪʃn]	Wohnungs(bau)gesellschaft
housing cooperative [kəʊ'ɒprətɪv]	Wohnungsbaugenossenschaft

☞ Einer Sozialwohnung entspricht in Großbritannien ungefähr *a council flat* [kaʊnsl 'flæt]; allgemein könnte der deutsche Begriff mit *state-subsidized* ['sʌbsɪdaɪzd] *flat / apartment* wiedergegeben werden. Entsprechend: *council housing* BE / allg. *(state-)subsidized housing* (= Sozialwohnungen / sozialer Wohnungsbau). Sozialer Wohnungsbau wird auch mit *public housing construction* ausgedrückt. *Private sector housing* wäre der private Wohnungsmarkt / Wohnungsbau.

living space is difficult to find	**Wohnraum** ist schwer zu finden
the rise in rents	**das Ansteigen der Mieten**
the latest rent increase ['rent ɪŋkriːs]	die neueste Mieterhöhung
rent control [kən'trəʊl]	Wohnraumbewirtschaftung
(go) flat hunting BE	**(auf) Wohnungssuche (gehen)**
estate [ɪ'steɪt] **agent** BE / AE **real estate agent** / AE **realtor** ['riːəltə]	**Immobilien- / Wohnungsmakler(in)**
share a flat BE / AE **an apartment** [ə'pɑːtmənt]	**in einer Wohngemeinschaft leben**
Flat sharing is fairly common [ɒ] here.	Wohngemeinschaften gibt es hier ziemlich viele.
I'm looking for a nice flatshare. BE	Ich suche eine nette Wohngemein-schaft.
flatmate BE – **roommate**	**Mitbewohner(in) – Zimmer-genosse/in**
a place to live [pleɪs tə 'lɪv]	**eine Bleibe**

Tens of thousands don't have a decent ['di:snt] place to live.
Zehntausende haben keine anständige Bleibe.

give a tenant ['tenənt] **notice to quit**
einem Mieter **kündigen**

evict [ɪ'vɪkt] **a tenant**
einen Mieter zur Räumung zwingen

Tenants were evicted from / turned out of their homes because they fell behind with their rent.
Mieter wurden auf die Straße gesetzt, weil sie mit ihren Mietzahlungen in Rückstand geraten waren.

They now face **eviction** [ɪ'vɪkʃn].
Jetzt droht ihnen die **Zwangs-räumung**.

squat [skwɒt] (in a house)
ein Haus besetzt halten

They were evicted from the squat.
Sie mussten das besetzte Haus räumen.

squatter ['skwɒtə]
Hausbesetzer(in)

shantytown ['ʃæntitaʊn]
Barackensiedlung; (*Berlin*) **Wagen-burg**

homeless ['həʊmləs]
obdachlos

homeless people living in cardboard boxes
Obdachlose, die in Pappkartons leben

dormitories ['dɔ:mətriz] in homeless shelters
Schlafsäle in Obdachlosenheimen

ways to help the homeless
Möglichkeiten, den Obdachlosen zu helfen

a sharp increase ['ɪŋkri:s] in homeless-ness
eine starke Zunahme der Obdach-losigkeit

Homelessness is a pressing social problem (= ein brennendes soziales Problem), *it's The Big Issue* ['ɪʃu:] (= Das große Thema / Problem) – so der Name der von *homeless vendors* (= obdachlosen Verkäufern) auf den Straßen großer Städte verkauften Obdachlosenzeitung.

sleep rough [rʌf] / **outdoors** (– slept – slept)
im Freien übernachten

sleep / live on the streets
auf der Straße schlafen / leben

seek shelter (– sought [sɔ:t] – sought)
Zuflucht suchen

provide emergency [ɪ'mɜ:dʒənsi] shelter / accommodation
Notunterkünfte / eine Notunterkunft bereitstellen

provide temporary accommo-dation [əkɒmə'deɪʃn]
eine Behelfsunterkunft bieten

hostel ['hɒstl]
Wohnheim

rehouse [ri:'haʊz] homeless people
Obdachlosen wieder eine Wohnung geben

Unemployment
Arbeitslosigkeit

→ 20.9 Labour relations

It's a recession when your neighbour loses his job; it's a depression when you lose yours. (*Harry S. Truman, US president, 1884–1972*)

unemployed [ˌʌnɪmˈplɔɪd] / **jobless**	arbeitslos; erwerbslos
the long-term unemployed / jobless	die Langzeitarbeitslosen
bring the jobless rate down	die Arbeitslosenziffer senken
unemployment / **joblessness**	(die) **Arbeitslosigkeit** / **Erwerbs-losigkeit**
the unemployment rate is rising / falling	die Arbeitslosigkeit nimmt zu / geht zurück
cyclical [ˈsɪklɪkl] unemployment	konjunkturelle Arbeitslosigkeit
seasonal [ˈsiːznəl] unemployment	saisonbedingte Arbeitslosigkeit
structural [ˈstrʌktʃərəl] unemployment	strukturelle Arbeitslosigkeit
unemployment insurance [ɪnˈʃʊərəns]	Arbeitslosenversicherung
unemployment benefit *BE* / *AE* benefits	Arbeitslosengeld; Arbeitslosenhilfe
out of a job / **out of work**	**ohne Arbeit; arbeitslos**
I suddenly found myself out of a job.	Plötzlich stand ich ohne Arbeit da.
Millions are out of work.	Millionen sind ohne Arbeit.
redundant [rɪˈdʌndənt]	(*eigentlich*) **überflüssig**; *BE* **arbeitslos**
I'm going to be made redundant.	Ich werde meinen Arbeitsplatz verlieren.
redundancy [rɪˈdʌndənsi]	*BE* **Arbeitslosigkeit**
the threat [θret] of redundancy	der drohende Arbeitsplatzverlust
redundancy / severance pay(ment)	Abfindung
redundancy package / scheme [skiːm]	Sozialplan
downsizing [ˈdaʊnsaɪzɪŋ]	**Verschlanken; Stellen- / Personal-abbau**
restructuring [riːˈstrʌktʃərɪŋ]	(*Euphemismus für*) **Personalabbau**
job shedding [ˈdʒɒb ʃedɪŋ]	**Arbeitsplatzabbau; Stellenabbau**
short-time working	**Kurzarbeit**
We're on short time / working on short time at the moment.	Wir machen im Moment Kurzarbeit.

Das Entlassenwerden (= *being dismissed* [dɪsˈmɪst]) kann durch eine Reihe von Verben ausgedrückt werden, die von „direkt-brutal" bis „indirekt-euphemistisch" (= abschwächend-beschönigend) reichen:
He's been fired. / *BE* auch *He's been sacked.* / *He's been given the sack.* / *He got the sack.* (= Man hat ihn gefeuert / rausgeschmissen.)
Thousands of employees [ɪmˈplɔɪiːz] *were made redundant BE* / *AE were excessed* [ɪkˈsest] / *were surplused* [ˈsɜːpləst]. (= Tausende von Beschäftigten wurden freigesetzt.)
I've been laid off. (= Man hat mich entlassen.) *Lay off* bedeutete ursprünglich „vorübergehend entlassen", meint aber heute in der Regel das endgültige Aus.
He got his marching orders BE / *AE his walking papers* / *the pink slip* (= den rosa Zettel). (Burschikose Ausdrucksweise: „bekam seine Papiere".)

I'm afraid we're going to have to let you go. (Freundliches *understatement*.)
Erkundigt man sich nach jemand, der entlassen wurde, so hört man etwa:
I'm afraid Ms Ross is no longer with us.
Erwerbslose sind BE-umgangssprachlich *on the dole:*
Is she still on the dole? (= Geht sie immer noch stempeln?)
Dole money ['mʌni] ist entsprechend eine umgangssprachliche Alternative
zu *unemployment benefit.*
Schauspieler, die gerade kein Engagement haben, sagen scherzhaft von sich:
Right now, I'm between shows. Andere Arbeitslose beschönigen entsprechend:
I'm between jobs at the moment.

improve [ɪm'pruːv]	**sich bessern**
deteriorate [dɪ'tɪərɪəreɪt]	**sich verschlechtern**
upturn ['ʌptɜːn] – **downturn**	**Aufschwung – Abschwung**
an upturn in the economy [ɪ'kɒnəmi]	ein Wirtschaftsaufschwung
a downturn in economic activity [æk'tɪvəti]	ein Abflauen / Nachlassen der Konjunktur
the labour market ['leɪbə mɑːkɪt]	**der Arbeitsmarkt**
employ [ɪm'plɔɪ] – **employment**	**beschäftigen – Beschäftigung**
The employment situation has improved / deteriorated.	Die Beschäftigungssituation hat sich gebessert / verschlechtert.
self-employment [self ɪm'plɔɪmənt]	(berufliche) Selb(st)ständigkeit
self-employed [self ɪm'plɔɪd]	(beruflich) selb(st)ständig
go self-employed	sich selb(st)ständig machen

Für das sozial, rechtlich und steuerlich problematische Phänomen der
Scheinselb(st)ständigkeit gibt es im Englischen die bezeichnende Entsprechung *disguised employment* sowie eine Reihe von Übersetzungen, die den
deutschen Begriff genauer wiederzugeben versuchen: *apparent* [ə'pærənt] /
pretended [prɪ'tendɪd] / *phoney* ['fəʊni] / *pseudo* ['sjuːdəʊ] *self-employment.*

further vocational training	**berufliche Fortbildung**
retrain [riː'treɪn] – **retraining**	**umschulen – Umschulung**
job sharing – part-time work	**Arbeitsplatzteilung – Teilzeitarbeit**
job-creating schemes [skiːmz] / **job-creation programmes**	**Arbeitsbeschaffungsmaßnahmen / -programme**
labour / employment exchange	**Arbeitsamt**
jobcentre ['dʒɒbsentə] *BE*	**(staatliche) Arbeitsvermittlung**
employment agency ['eɪdʒənsi] / *BE auch* **recruitment consultants** [rɪ'kruːtmənt kənsʌltənts]	**(private) Arbeitsvermittlung**
jobhunter ['dʒɒbhʌntə]	**Arbeitssuchende(r)**
I'm still jobhunting / looking for a job.	Ich bin immer noch auf Arbeitssuche.
(re)hire [(riː)'haɪə] **workers**	**Arbeitskräfte (wieder) einstellen**
temp [temp] *BE*	**Zeitarbeitskraft**
I'm temping until I find something permanent.	Bis ich etwas für die Dauer finde, mache ich Zeitarbeit.

Der neudeutsche Begriff Ich-AG wird im BE mit *Me plc*, im AE mit *Me Inc.*
wiedergegeben.

Drug and alcohol abuse
Drogen- und Alkoholmissbrauch

→ 12.10 Drinking and smoking

I can't understand why anybody would want to devote their life to a cause like dope. It's the most boring pastime I can think of. It ranks a close second to television. (*Frank Zappa, US rock musician, 1940–93*)

drug [drʌg]	**Droge; Rauschmittel; Rauschgift**
narcotic [nɑːˈkɒtɪk] drug / substance	Rauschgift
hard / soft [sɒft] drugs	harte / weiche Drogen
mind-altering [ˈmaɪnd ɔːltərɪŋ] drugs	bewusstseinsverändernde Drogen
drug dependence / dependency	Drogenabhängigkeit
drug abuse [əˈbjuːs]	Drogenmissbrauch
drug addiction [əˈdɪkʃn]	Drogensucht; Rauschgiftsucht
a drug addict [ˈædɪkt]	ein(e) Drogensüchtige(r)
(drug) dealer / (drug) pusher [ʊ]	Dealer; Pusher
drug trafficker [ˈdrʌg træfɪkə]	Drogen- / Rauschgifthändler(in)
drug trafficking / the drug trade	der Drogen- / Rauschgifthandel
the drug / narcotics squad [skwɒd]	das Rauschgiftdezernat
legalization [liːgəlaɪˈzeɪʃn] of drugs	Legalisierung / Freigabe von Drogen
the number of drug-related deaths	die Zahl der Drogentoten
drugged / under the influence of drugs	unter Drogeneinfluss
high [haɪ]	**high** (= in einem Rauschzustand)
dope *Slang* / **stuff** *Slang*	**Stoff**
You still doing dope?	Fixt du immer noch?

Dass jemand rauschgiftsüchtig ist, kann man u.a. so ausdrücken:
She's addicted [əˈdɪktɪd] *to drugs.* • *She's a drug addict* [ˈædɪkt]. • *She's on / into drugs.* • *She's taking / doing drugs.* • *She's on the needle* [ˈniːdl].

fix [fɪks]	**Fix; fixen**
You can see kids fixing here.	Hier kann man Kinder fixen sehen.
shoot [ʃuːt] (– shot – shot) *Slang*	**schießen; drücken**
He shoots heroin twice a day.	Er drückt zweimal täglich Heroin.
shot [ʃɒt]	**Schuss** (= Drogeninjektion)
She gave herself a shot.	Sie setzte / drückte sich einen Schuss.
freak out [friːk ˈaʊt]	**ausflippen; auf einen Trip gehen**
uppers [ˈʌpəz] – **downers**	**Aufputschmittel – Beruhigungsmittel**
heroin [ˈherəʊɪn]	**Heroin**
She became addicted to heroin.	Sie wurde heroinsüchtig.
cocaine [kəʊˈkeɪn]	**Kokain**
inject [ɪnˈdʒekt] / sniff / smoke cocaine	Kokain spritzen / schnupfen / rauchen
crack [kræk]	**Crack** (= mit Backpulver aufgekochtes Kokain)
Crack is highly addictive [əˈdɪktɪv].	Crack ist extrem suchterzeugend.
hashish [ˈhæʃɪʃ] – **hash**	**Haschisch – Hasch**
LSD / *Slang* **acid** [ˈæsɪd]	**LSD**
He was on an LSD trip.	Er war auf einem LSD-Trip.

ecstasy ['ekstəsi]	Ecstasy
methadone ['meθədəʊn]	Methadon
dose [dəʊs] – **overdose** / **OD**	Dosis – Überdosis
Janis Joplin died of a heroin overdose.	J. J. starb an einer Überdosis Heroin.
the habit ['hæbɪt]	die Drogen- / Alkoholabhängigkeit
kick the habit	von der Sucht loskommen
cure [kjʊə]	heilen; kurieren; entwöhnen; Entzug
addicts who've been cured [kjʊəd]	Süchtige, die geheilt wurden
detoxification / **detox**	Entgiftung; Entwöhnung; Entzug
withdrawal (symptoms) [wɪð'drɔːəl]	Entzug(serscheinungen)
clean [kliːn]	clean (= nicht mehr drogenabhängig)
narcotics agent / **narc(o)** / **nark**	Rauschgiftfahnder(in)

Drogen-Slang

use drugs = shoot, fix, get off / up, hit / use the needle, blow coke / snow
drug user = junkie, junker, user, doper, freak, jabber, tripper, snifter
drugged = stoned, snowed (in / up), coked (up), loaded, joyriding, goofed
drug seller = (dope) dealer, (dope) pusher, dope peddler, connection, source
amphetamines = speed, uppers, whizz, driver, eye opener, splash
cocaine = blow, bouncing powder, (nose) candy, coke, snow, charlie
hashish = hash, heesh, sheesh, keef, candy
heroin = snow, sugar, fix, shit, hard stuff, white stuff, junk, (joy) powder
LSD = acid, candy, cube, trip, sunshine (pill), (instant) Zen
marijuana / cannabis = pot, dope, blow, grass, hay, weed, joint, tea

alcoholic [ælkə'hɒlɪk]	Alkoholiker(in)
Alcoholics Anonymous [ə'nɒnɪməs]	die Anonymen Alkoholiker

Die englischen Sprachbenutzer, stets neuerungsfreudig, bedienen sich seit etwa 1968 der von *alcoholic* abgeleiteten Endung *-aholic* um „Besessenheiten" auszudrücken: *a workaholic* (= ein arbeitswütiger Mensch), *a chocaholic* (= ein schokoladensüchtiger Mensch), *a milkaholic* (= jemand, der verrückt auf Milch ist), *a clothesaholic* (= jemand, der kleidungs- / modebesessen ist).

alcoholism ['ælkəhɒlɪzm]	Alkoholismus; Alkoholkrankheit
a drinker / **drunk** / **drunkard** [-kəd]	ein(e) Trinker(in) / Säufer(in)
liquor ['lɪkə]	*AE* Schnaps
go on a binge [bɪnʒ] / **drinking spree**	auf eine Sauftour gehen
(a little) tipsy ['tɪpsi]	(ein bisschen) beschwipst
drunk [drʌŋk]	betrunken; Betrunkene(r) / Trinker(in)
They were all blind [aɪ] drunk.	Sie waren alle sinnlos betrunken.
sleep it off (– slept – slept)	seinen Rausch ausschlafen
have a hangover ['hæŋəʊvə]	einen Kater haben

Alkohol-Slang

alcohol = booze, poison, juice [dʒuːs], sauce [sɔːs]
drink = hit the bottle / sauce / booze, go on a binge [bɪnʒ] / bender
drunk = tight, boozed, loaded, plastered, sozzled, stoned, pissed, blotto
drinker = boozer, lush, souse [saʊs], guzzler, dipso, rummy

Poverty
Armut

The big majority of Americans, who are comparatively well off, have developed an ability to have enclaves of people living in the greatest misery without almost noticing them. (*Gunnar Myrdal, Swedish sociologist and economist, 1898–1987*)

poverty ['pɒvəti]	**Armut**
fall into poverty (– fell – fallen)	in Armut geraten
the causes of poverty	die Ursachen der Armut
below the poverty line	unterhalb der Armutsgrenze
the poverty trap	die Armutsfalle
impoverished [ɪm'pɒvərɪʃt]	**verarmt**
poor [pʊə] – **the poor**	**arm – die Armen**
These people are desperately poor.	Diese Menschen sind schrecklich arm.
deprivation [deprɪ'veɪʃn]	**Entbehrung; Mangel**
deprived [dɪ'praɪvd] families / children	benachteiligte Familien / Kinder
disadvantaged [dɪsəd'vɑːntɪdʒd]	**benachteiligt**
the economically disadvantaged	die sozial Schwachen
the **precariat** [prɪ'keəriət]	das **Prekariat**
destitute (families) ['destɪtjuːt]	**mittellos(e Familien)**
an extremely low standard of living	**ein extrem niedriger Lebens-standard**
help the needy ['niːdi]	**den Bedürftigen helfen**
the basic ['beɪsɪk] **needs**	**die Grundbedürfnisse**
subsistence level [səb'sɪstəns levl]	**Existenzminimum**
live on the edge of subsistence	am Rand des Existenzminimums leben
a living wage [lɪvɪŋ 'weɪdʒ]	**ein zum Leben ausreichender Lohn**
set a minimum wage (– set – set)	einen Mindestlohn festsetzen
hunger ['hʌŋgə] – **hungry** ['hʌŋgri]	**Hunger – hungrig**
As a boy, he often went hungry.	Als Junge hat er oft gehungert.
starve [stɑːv] – **starvation**	**hungern – Hungern**
starve to death / die of starvation	verhungern
(poor) nutrition [njuː'trɪʃn]	**(Mangel-)Ernährung**
malnutrition due to poverty	durch Armut bedingte Fehlernährung
dependent on public assistance *AE*	**auf Sozialhilfe angewiesen**
soup kitchen ['suːp kɪtʃən]	**Suppenküche**
cuts in social services ['sɜːvɪsɪz]	**Sozialabbau**
low life expectancy [ɪk'spektənsi]	**niedrige Lebenserwartung**
a high infant mortality rate	**eine hohe Säuglingssterblichkeit**
illiteracy [ɪ'lɪtrəsi] **among the poor**	**Analphabetentum unter den Armen**
street children ['striːt tʃɪldrən]	**Straßenkinder**
child labour ['leɪbə] – child prostitution	Kinderarbeit – Kinderprostitution
(appalling) misery ['mɪzəri]	**(entsetzliches) Elend**
suffering ['sʌfərɪŋ]	**Leiden; Leid**
alleviate the suffering of the poor	das Leid(en) der Armen lindern
despair [dɪ'speə] – **hopelessness**	**Verzweiflung – Hoffnungslosigkeit**

Crime and violence
Verbrechen und Gewalttätigkeit

→ 6.8 Law and police

Americans are being murdered, raped, beaten, robbed and otherwise
terrorized in numbers suggesting that an extraordinary evil has been
loosed upon the society. (*Bob Herbert in The New York Times*)

crime [kraɪm]	**Verbrechen; Straftat**
violent ['vaɪələnt] crime	Gewaltverbrechen / -kriminalität
the struggle against crime	der Kampf gegen das Verbrechen
combating ['kɒmbætɪŋ] / fighting crime	Verbrechensbekämpfung
crime victims ['vɪktɪmz]	Opfer von Straftaten
crime prevention [prɪ'venʃn]	Verbrechensverhütung
the rising crime rate ['kraɪm reɪt]	das Zunehmen der Kriminalität
criminal ['krɪmɪnəl]	**kriminell; Verbrecher(in);**
	Straftäter(in)
a violent criminal	ein Gewaltverbrecher
habitual criminal – career criminal	Gewohnheits- – Berufsverbrecher

Häufig begangene Straftaten (= *criminal offences* [ə'fensɪz])
murder (= Mord) • *manslaughter* (= Totschlag) • *homicide* ['hɒmɪsaɪd]
(formell allgemein = Tötungsdelikt) • *bodily harm* (= Körperverletzung) •
rape (= Vergewaltigung) • *robbery* (= Raub) • *kidnapping / abduction*
(= Entführung) • *skyjacking* (= Flugzeugentführung) • *hostage* ['hɒstɪdʒ]
taking (= Geiselnahme) • *blackmail / extortion* (= Erpressung) • *arson* ['ɑːsn]
(= Brandstiftung) • *perjury* ['pɜːdʒəri] (= Meineid) • *counterfeiting*
['kaʊntəfɪtɪŋ] (= Fälschung) • *bribery* (= Bestechung) • *embezzlement*
[ɪm'bezlmənt] (= Unterschlagung / Veruntreuung) • *fraud* [frɔːd] (= Betrug) •
smuggling (= Schmuggel) • *poaching* (= Wilderei) • *vandalism* ['vændəlɪzm]
(= mutwillige Beschädigung / Zerstörung fremden Eigentums) • *trespassing*
['trespəsɪŋ] (= Hausfriedensbruch) • *pimping* (= Zuhälterei) • *prostitution*
(= Prostitution) • *causing a public nuisance* ['njuːsns] (= grober Unfug) •
resisting arrest [ə'rest] (= Widerstand gegen die Staatsgewalt) • *obstruction
of justice* ['dʒʌstɪs] (= Verdunkelung) •

TRESPASSERS WILL BE PROSECUTED (= Betreten bei Strafe verboten)

Bezeichnungen für Straftäter (= *offenders* [ə'fendəz])
murderer / killer (= Mörder) • *rapist* ['reɪpɪst] (= Vergewaltiger) • *assailant*
[ə'seɪlənt] / *attacker* [ə'tækə] (= Angreifer) • *crazed* [kreɪzd] *gunman*
(= Amokschütze) • *mugger* (= Straßenräuber) • *robber* (= Räuber) • *thug /
hoodlum* ['huːdləm] (= brutaler Rowdy) • *lager lout* ['lɑːgə laʊt] BE (= betrun-
kener Rowdy) • *football / soccer hooligan* (= Fußballrowdy) • *vandal* ['vændl]
(= mutwilliger Zerstörer) • *kidnapper* (= Entführer) • *skyjacker* (= Flugzeugentführer) • *blackmailer* (= Erpresser) • *gangster / mobster* (= Gangster) •
racketeer [rækə'tɪə] (= Ganove / Gangster / Erpresser) • *arsonist* ['ɑːsənɪst]
(= Brandstifter) • *counterfeiter* ['kaʊntəfɪtə] / *forger* ['fɔːdʒə] (= Fälscher) •

swindler / *con(fidence) man* / *con artist* / *confidence trickster* (= Betrüger / Hochstapler) • *smuggler* (= Schmuggler) • *poacher* (= Wilderer) • *pimp* (= Zuhälter) • *peeping Tom* / *voyeur* [vwaɪˈɜː] (= Spanner / Voyeur)

hijack [ˈhaɪdʒæk] **a plane**	**ein Flugzeug entführen**
They hijacked a bus.	Sie brachten einen Bus in ihre Gewalt.
bank robbery / *AE auch* **bank heist** [haɪst]	**Bankraub**
two armed and masked robbers	zwei bewaffnete und maskierte Räuber

Ein Überfall auf eine Person auf der Straße, in Verkehrsmitteln etc. ist *a mugging: She was mugged on the underground station.* (= Sie wurde auf dem U-Bahnhof überfallen.)
Ein tätlicher Angriff auf eine Person wird auch als *attack* [əˈtæk] oder *assault* [əˈsɔːlt] bezeichnet.
Ein Überfall auf eine Bank ist *a bank raid, a holdup* oder *a stickup.*

Stealing and thieves [θiːvz] (= **Stehlen und Diebe**)

stealing (= Stehlen) • *theft* (= Diebstahl) • *larceny* [ˈlɑːsəni] (juristisch = Diebstahl) • *pickpocketing* (= Taschendiebstahl) • *purse snatching* (AE = Handtaschenraub) • *shoplifting* (= Ladendiebstahl) • *thief* Pl. *thieves* (= Dieb / Diebin) • *pickpocket* (= Taschendieb / -diebin) • *purse snatcher* (AE = Handtaschendieb) • *joyriding* (= eine Spritztour mit einem gestohlenen Auto machen)
Ein Einbruch kann auf Englisch *a burglary* [ˈbɜːgləri] oder *a break-in* sein; die Juristen bezeichnen das Delikt auch als *breaking and entering* BE / AE *unlawful entry.* Ein Einbrecher ist *a burglar* oder *a housebreaker.*
In unser Haus wurde eingebrochen heißt *Our home / house was burgled* BE / AE *burglarized.*

(hand)gun – gun down [gʌn ˈdaʊn]	**(Hand-)Feuerwaffe – abknallen**
Two bystanders were gunned down.	Zwei Unbeteiligte („Dabeistehende") wurden niedergeschossen.
firearms [ˈfaɪərɑːmz]	**Schusswaffen**
He was fined for illegally possessing [pəˈzesɪŋ] a firearm / for possession [pəˈzəʃn] of an unlicensed handgun.	Er wurde wegen unerlaubten Waffenbesitzes zu einer Geldstrafe verurteilt.

Shoot someone (– shot – shot): He was shot and wounded [ˈwuːndɪd].
(= Er wurde angeschossen.)
He was shot and killed / shot dead. (= Er wurde erschossen.)
He was shot at. (= Es wurde auf ihn geschossen.)
Shoot allein für erschießen nur, wenn aus dem Zusammenhang deutlich ist, was gemeint ist:
Do you remember what you were doing on the night Kennedy was shot? (= Weißt du noch, was du an dem Abend gemacht hast, als Kennedy erschossen wurde?)

vigilant ['vɪdʒɪlənt] – **vigilance**   **wachsam – Wachsamkeit**

Wenn Bürger sich zum Schutz gegen Verbrechen organisieren:
In Amerika heißen solche Selbstschutzvereinigungen *vigilance committees*
[kə'mɪtiz], sonst allgemein auch *vigilante* [vɪdʒɪ'lænti] *groups* oder
neighbourhood watch groups.

riot ['raɪət]	**Aufstand; Aufruhr; Ausschreitungen**
rioting youths [ju:ðz]	randalierende Jugendliche
rioter ['raɪətə]	Aufrührer(in); Randalierer(in)
rampage ['ræmpeɪdʒ]	**Randale**
go on the rampage	Randale machen
rampage [ræm'peɪdʒ] through the streets	randalierend durch die Straßen ziehen
violence ['vaɪələns]	**Gewalt(tätigkeit)**
Violence broke out.	Es kam zu gewalttätigen Auseinandersetzungen.
violent ['vaɪələnt]	**gewalttätig**
fight [faɪt] / **brawl** [brɔ:l]	**Kampf; Prügelei; Schlägerei**
put [ʊ] up a fight	sich zur Wehr setzen
fight (– fought [ɔ:] – fought)	**kämpfen; sich prügeln / schlagen**
The children are always fighting.	Die Kinder prügeln sich ständig.

Verleumdung ist *defamation* [defə'meɪʃn]. Erfolgt sie mündlich, heißt sie
slander ['slɑ:ndə] (= üble Nachrede); erfolgt sie schriftlich, so handelt es
sich um *libel* ['laɪbl]. Üble Nachrede ist im Alltag auch *malicious* [mə'lɪʃəs]
gossip.

beat [i:] (– beat – beaten)	**schlagen; hauen**
He was beaten up by thugs [θʌgz].	Er wurde von Rowdys zusammengeschlagen.
stab someone [stæb]	**auf jemand einstechen**
She was stabbed to death [deθ].	Sie wurde erstochen.
strangle someone ['stræŋgl]	**jemand erwürgen / erdrosseln**
batter someone ['bætə]	**auf jemand einschlagen**
battered wife / baby	misshandelte(s) Ehefrau / Baby
bind [baɪnd] (– bound – bound)	**fesseln**
She was bound and gagged [gægd].	Sie wurde gefesselt und geknebelt.

Crimes against humanity [hju:'mænəti] **(= Verbrechen gegen die
Menschlichkeit)**
massacre ['mæsəkə] (= Massaker / Gemetzel) • *a pogrom* ['pɒgrəm] (= ein
Pogrom; Ausschreitungen besonders gegen Juden) • *atrocities* [ə'trɒsətiz]
(= Gräueltaten) • *concentration camp* (= Konzentrationslager) • *death camp*
(= Todeslager) • *liquidate* ['lɪkwɪdeɪt] (= liquidieren, d.h. ermorden) •
exterminate [ɪk'stɜ:mɪneɪt] (= ausrotten) • *extermination* (= Ausrottung) •
genocide ['dʒenəsaɪd] (= Völkermord) • *the slaughter* ['slɔ:tə] *of innocent*
['ɪnəsnt] *people* (= das Abschlachten unschuldiger Menschen)

*Holocaust, a word from the Old Testament, is used to describe the murdering
of over six million Jews* (= Juden) *by the Germans during World War II.*

6 Xenophobia and racism
Ausländerfeindlichkeit und Rassismus

Hostility to foreigners is the most stupid and most embarrassing thing in the world. (*Eberhard Diepgen, German politician, born in 1941*)

xenophobia [zenə'fəʊbiə]	Fremdenhass / -feindlichkeit / -furcht
xenophobic [zenə'fəʊbɪk]	fremden- / ausländerfeindlich

A phobia ist eine Phobie und damit eine krankhafte Angst: *claustrophobia* [klɔːstrə'fəʊbiə] (= Klaustrophobie = krankhafte Angst beim Aufenthalt in geschlossenen Räumen).
Angst erzeugt Abneigung, daher die Erweiterung des Begriffs in Zusammensetzungen wie *Anglophobia* (= Anglophobie = Englandfeindlichkeit), *Europhobia* (= Europafeindlichkeit), *Islamophobia* [ɪslæməʊ'fəʊbiə] (= Islamophobie = Islamfeindlichkeit) oder *homophobia* [həʊmə'fəʊbiə] (= Hass auf Homosexuelle).

foreign ['fɒrən] – **foreigner** ['fɒrənə]	**ausländisch – Ausländer(in)**
hostility [hɒ'stɪləti] to foreigners	Ausländerfeindlichkeit
hatred ['heɪtrɪd] of foreigners	Ausländerhass; Fremdenhass
Foreigners out!	Ausländer raus!
prejudice ['predʒudɪs]	**Vorurteil(e)**
hold prejudices towards other groups	Vorurteile gegen andere Gruppen hegen
stir up prejudice against foreigners ['fɒrənəz]	Vorurteile gegen Ausländer schüren
He's prejudiced ['predʒudɪst] against Arabs ['ærəbz].	Er hat Vorurteile gegen Araber / ist gegen Araber voreingenommen.
stereotypes ['steriətaips]	**stereotype Vorstellungen; gängige Klischees**
tackle sexist stereotypes	gegen sexistische Vorurteile angehen
negative stereotypes about foreign cultures	negative Klischeevorstellungen über andere Kulturen
asylum seeker [ə'saɪləm siːkə]	**Asylbewerber(in)**
grant [ɑː] someone asylum	jemand Asyl gewähren
limit / restrict the right of asylum	das Asylrecht einschränken
home / hostel for asylum seekers	Asylanten(wohn)heim
immigrants ['ɪmɪgrənts]	**Einwanderer; Zuwanderer**
(illegal) immigration [ɪmɪ'greɪʃn]	**(illegale) Einwanderung / Einreise**
victims of persecution [pɜːsə'kjuːʃn]	**politisch Verfolgte**
economic refugees [refju'dʒiːz]	**Wirtschaftsflüchtlinge**
bomb attack ['bɒm ətæk]	**Bombenanschlag; Sprengstoff- anschlag**
firebomb attack ['faɪəbɒm ətæk]	**Brandanschlag**
throw firebombs into buildings (– threw – thrown)	Brandbomben / -sätze in Gebäude werfen
a gang of skinheads ['skɪnhedz]	**eine Bande von Skin(head)s**
rightists ['raɪtɪsts]	**Anhänger der Rechten**
gangs of rightist youths [juːðz]	Banden rechtsradikaler Jugendlicher

right-wing radicals / extremists	Rechtsradikale; Rechtsextremisten
parties of the extreme right	rechtsextrem(istisch)e Parteien
right-wing extremism [ɪk'striːmɪzm]	Rechtsextremismus
nationalism – nationalist	**Nationalismus – nationalistisch**
chauvinism ['ʃəʊvənɪzm]	**Chauvinismus** (= übersteigerter Nationalismus)
jingoism ['dʒɪŋgəʊɪzm]	**militanter Nationalismus; Hurrapatriotismus**
ethnic group [eθnɪk 'gruːp]	**ethnische Gruppe; Volksgruppe**
ethnic minority [maɪ'nɒrəti]	ethnische Minderheit
ethnic cleansing ['klenzɪŋ]	ethnische Säuberung(en)
race – racism – racist ['reɪsɪst]	**Rasse – Rassismus – Rassist(in)**
the claim that some races are superior [suː'pɪəriə] to others	die Behauptung, dass manche Rassen anderen überlegen seien
race relations [rɪ'leɪʃnz]	(die) Beziehungen zwischen den Rassen
racial equality [reɪʃl ɪ'kwɒləti]	Gleichberechtigung der Rassen
race / racial discrimination [dɪskrɪmɪ'neɪʃn]	Rassendiskriminierung
race / racial hatred ['heɪtrɪd]	Rassenhass
(racial) segregation [segrɪ'geɪʃn]	(Rassentrennung in den USA bis 1954)
racial profiling [reɪʃl 'prəʊfaɪlɪŋ]	rassisches / ethnisches Profiling (= Fahndungsmethode, die sich an der Rassenzugehörigkeit orientiert)
racist remarks [rɪ'mɑːks]	rassistische Äußerungen
apartheid [ə'puːtaɪt]	**(Rassentrennung in Südafrika bis 1994)**
anti-Semitism [ænti'semətɪzm]	**Antisemitismus; Judenfeindlichkeit**
anti-Semitic [æntisə'mɪtɪk]	antisemitisch
anti-Semitic incidents ['ɪnsɪdənts]	antisemitische Vorfälle
anti-Semitic attacks [ə'tæks]	antisemitische Übergriffe
an anti-Semite [ænti 'siːmaɪt]	ein(e) Antisemit(in)
Aryan ['eəriən] – **non-Aryan**	(*Naziideologie*) **arisch – nichtarisch, Arier(in) – Nichtarier(in)**
gypsies ['dʒɪpsiz]	**Zigeuner(innen); Sinti; Roma**
the colour ['kʌlə] **of his skin**	**seine Hautfarbe**

Bezeichnungen für Menschen schwarzer Hautfarbe

Die Bezeichnungen *Negro(es)* ['niːgrəʊ(z)] und *coloured(s)* ['kʌləd(z)] sind nur noch in historischen Kontexten anzutreffen und würden heute Anstoß erregen (= *give offence* [ə'fens]). In der Alltagssprache ist heute die Bezeichnung *black(s)* gebräuchlich. In offiziellen Verlautbarungen, in der Presse und insbesondere im Sprachgebrauch führender Persönlichkeiten der *American black community* [kə'mjuːnəti] hat sich die Ende der 80er-Jahre aufgekommene Bezeichnung *African-American(s)* [æfrɪkən ə'merɪkən(z)] durchgesetzt.

Sexism
Sexismus

→ 6.2 Social movements

There are very few jobs that actually require a penis or vagina.
All other jobs should be open to everybody. (*Florynce R. Kennedy,
US civil rights activist, born in 1916*)

sexism ['seksɪzm] – **sexist**	**Sexismus** – **sexistisch** / **Sexist(in)**
sex discrimination [dɪskrɪmɪ'neɪʃn]	**sexuelle Diskriminierung**
sex roles / gender roles ['dʒendə rəʊlz]	Geschlechter- / Geschlechtsrollen
sex(ual) equality [ɪ'kwɒləti]	Gleichberechtigung der Geschlechter
sexual harassment ['hærəsmənt]	**sexuelle Belästigung**
sexual oppression [ə'preʃn]	sexuelle Unterdrückung
sexual violence [sekʃuəl 'vaɪələns]	sexuelle Gewalt

Sex ist Geschlecht im biologischen Sinn; *gender* ist Geschlecht im kulturellen
oder sprachlichen Sinn. Im Englischen versucht man heute, sich *gender-neutral*
(= geschlechtsneutral) auszudrücken, d.h. auf *linguistic sexism* / *sexist language*
("*he language*" / "*man language*") zu verzichten. Also z.B. kein *sex stereotyping*
['steriətaɪpɪŋ] bei Berufen! Nicht *clergymen* ['klɜːdʒimən] (= Geistliche), sondern
members of the clergy; nicht *businessmen* ['bɪznəsmen] (wenn Geschäftsleute
gemeint sind), sondern *(business) executives* [ɪg'zekjətɪvz]; nicht *firemen* (für
Feuerwehrleute), sondern *firefighters*.
Der früher übliche Gebrauch von *he, his* etc. als „neutrales" Pronomen wird
heute vermieden. Im folgenden Satz wäre das neutral gemeinte *his* durch *their*
zu ersetzen: *Everyone has his own problems.* (= Jeder hat seine eigenen Probleme.) In einem Sprichwort wie *You can tell a lot about a person by the way
he walks* ließe sich das männlich klingende *he* durch *they* ersetzen oder man
könnte sagen: *You can tell a lot about people by the way they walk.* Und die
männliche Personifizierung großer Tiere wäre zu unterlassen: *You can lead a
horse to the water, but you can't make him* (heute gender-neutral: *it*) *drink.*

feminist ['femənɪst]	**feministisch; Feminist(in)**
Most feminists support [sə'pɔːt] the right to abortion [ə'bɔːʃn].	Die meisten Feminist(inn)en befür- worten das Recht auf Abtreibung.
matriarchy ['meɪtriɑːki] – **patriarchy**	**Matriarchat – Patriarchat**
men's / **women's jobs** / **occupations**	**Männer- / Frauenberufe**
male superiority [supɪəri'ɒrəti]	**männliche Überlegenheit**
male chauvinism ['ʃəʊvənɪzm]	**männlicher Chauvinismus**
male chauvinist (pig)	Chauvi(nistenschwein)
macho ['mætʃəʊ]	**Macho; Chauvi**
A macho man wouldn't admit he cried.	Ein Macho würde nicht zugeben, dass er geweint hat.
misogyny [mɪ'sɒdʒəni]	**Frauenfeindlichkeit**

Social sciences
Sozialwissenschaften

1 **Anthropology**
Anthropologie

2 **History**
Geschichte

3 **Political science**
Politische Wissenschaft

4 **Psychology**
Psychologie

5 **Sociology**
Soziologie

The language of research

8

8

1 Anthropology
Anthropologie

Anthropology is the science which tells us that people are the same the whole world over – except when they are different. (*Nancy Banks-Smith, British journalist, born in 1929*)

anthropology [ænθrə'pɒlədʒi]	**Anthropologie; Lehre vom Menschen**
biological [baɪə'lɒdʒɪkl] anthropology	biologische / physische Anthropologie
social anthropology	Ethnosoziologie
anthropologist [ænθrə'pɒlədʒɪst]	**Anthropologe / Anthropologin**
anthropological [ænθrəpə'lɒdʒɪkl]	**anthropologisch**
ethnology [eθ'nɒlədʒi]	**Ethnologie; Völkerkunde**

Hinweise zur Aussprache
Bei Nomen auf -*ology* [-ɒlədʒi] oder -*ologist* [-ɒlədʒɪst] liegt die Hauptbetonung stets auf der -*ol*-Silbe: *archae'ology* [ɑːki'ɒlədʒi], *a'strology, chro'nology, crimi'nology, e'cology, phi'lology* etc.
Bei den entsprechenden Adjektiven liegt die Hauptbetonung auf -*log*-: *anthropo'logical, archaeo'logical* [ɑːkiə'lɒdʒɪkl], *astro'logical, chrono'logical, crimino'logical, eco'logical, ethno'logical, philo'logical* etc.

fieldwork ['fiːldwɜːk]	**Feldforschung**
human ['hjuːmən] – **humans**	**menschlich – Menschen**
human populations / races	menschliche Populationen / Rassen
human social life	das menschliche Gemeinschaftsleben
class humans into races	Menschen in Rassen einteilen
prehistoric [priːhɪ'stɒrɪk] humans	prähistorische / vorgeschichtliche Menschen
social structure ['strʌktʃə]	**Sozialstruktur**
social system ['sɪstəm] / order	Gesellschaftsordnung
political institutions [ɪnstɪ'tjuːʃnz]	**politische Einrichtungen / Institutionen**
culture – society [sə'saɪəti]	**Kultur – Gesellschaft**
early / ancient ['eɪnʃənt] societies and cultures	frühe / alte Gesellschaften und Kulturen
Native American cultures ['kʌltʃəz]	indianische Kulturen
the cultural ['kʌltʃərəl] **setting**	**der kulturelle Hintergrund**
a people's cultural heritage ['herɪtɪdʒ]	das kulturelle Erbe eines Volkes
cultural diversity [-'vɜː-] / differences	kulturelle Vielfalt / Unterschiede
folklore ['fəʊklɔː]	(mündliche) **Volksüberlieferung**
folk music ['mjuːzɪk] – folk song	Volksmusik – Volkslied
folk tale – folk medicine ['medsn]	Volksmärchen – Volksmedizin
folk art – primitive ['prɪmɪtɪv] art	Volkskunst – primitive Kunst
customs ['kʌstəmz]	**Sitten; Bräuche; Sitten und Gebräuche**
kinship ['kɪnʃɪp]	**(Bluts-)Verwandtschaft**
family structures ['strʌktʃəz]	**Familienstrukturen**
so-called primitive peoples	**sogenannte primitive Völker**

the Australian Aborigines [æbə'rɪdʒəniz]	die Ureinwohner Australiens
tribe [traɪb] – **tribal** ['traɪbl]	(Volks-)Stamm – Stammes-
symbol ['sɪmbl]	Symbol
symbolize ['sɪmbəlaɪz]	symbolisieren
symbolic(ally) [sɪm'bɒlɪk(li)]	symbolisch
ritual ['rɪtʃuəl]	Ritual; Zeremoniell
taboo [tə'buː]	Tabu; tabu
the incest ['ɪnsest] **taboo**	das Inzesttabu / Inzestverbot
totem ['təʊtəm] – **totemism**	Totem – Totemismus
semiotics [semi'ɒtɪks]	Semiotik; Lehre von den Zeichen
artefact ['ɑːtɪfækt]	Artefakt (= von vorgeschichtlichen Menschen geformter Gegenstand)
reciprocity [resɪ'prɒsəti]	Reziprozität; Gegenseitigkeit
gift exchange ['gɪft ɪkstʃeɪnʒ]	Gabentausch
patriarchal [peɪtri'ɑːkl] – **matriarchal** [meɪtri'ɑːkl]	patriarchal(isch) – matriarchal(isch)
human **agency** ['eɪdʒənsi]	menschliches **Tun**
cultural **hegemony** [hɪ'gemənɪ]	kulturelle **Hegemonie / Vorherrschaft**
westernization [westənaɪ'zeɪʃn]	**Verwestlichung; Westernisierung**
migration [maɪ'greɪʃn]	**Migration; Wanderung(en)**
adaptation to ecosystems	**Anpassung an Ökosysteme**
evolution [iːvə'luːʃn]	(die) Evolution
Darwin's theory of evolution	Darwins Evolutionstheorie
evolutionary [iːvə'luːʃənri]	**Evolutions-; Entwicklungs-**

*"**You** may be descended from the apes, but I'm not."*

History
Geschichte

That men do not learn very much from the lessons of history
is the most important of all the lessons that history has to teach.
(*Aldous Huxley, English writer, 1894–1963*)

history ['hɪstri]	Geschichte; Geschichtswissenschaft
ancient ['eɪnʃənt] history	(die) alte Geschichte
medieval [medi'i:vl] / modern history	mittelalterliche / neuere Geschichte
contemporary [kən'temprəri] history	(die) Zeitgeschichte
social / economic [i:kə'nɒmɪk] history	(die) Sozial- / Wirtschaftsgeschichte
ecclesiastical [ɪkli:zi'æstɪkl] history	(die) Kirchengeschichte
a cultural history of India	(eine) Kulturgeschichte Indiens
history of ideas [aɪ'dɪəz]	Geistesgeschichte; Ideengeschichte
local ['ləʊkl] history	(die) Heimatgeschichte
research [rɪ'sɜ:tʃ] into local history	Heimatforschung
historical [hɪ'stɒrɪkl]	**historisch; geschichtlich**
historical personalities [pɜ:sə'nælətiz]	historische Persönlichkeiten
a matter of historical interest ['ɪntrəst]	eine Sache von historischem Interesse
historical research [rɪ'sɜ:tʃ]	(die) Geschichtsforschung
historical records ['rekɔ:dz]	historische Zeugnisse / Belege

 Unterschied zwischen *historical* und *historic*

historical (= historisch / geschichtlich = zur Geschichte gehörig /
  geschichtlich nachgewiesen)
historic (= historisch / geschichtlich bedeutsam)
Was Jesus a historical figure? (= War Jesus eine geschichtliche Gestalt, d. h.
  eine Person, deren Existenz historisch nachgewiesen ist?)
The fall of the Berlin Wall was a historic event. (= Der Fall der Berliner Mauer
  war ein Ereignis von historischer Bedeutung.)
Der Fall der Berliner Mauer ist natürlich auch *a historical event,* insofern als
er Teil der Geschichte ist, also in diesem Sinn historisch / geschichtlich.

historian [hɪ'stɔ:riən]	**Historiker(in); Geschichtsforscher(in)**
a scholar ['skɒlə]	**ein(e) Gelehrte(r)**
prehistory [pri:'hɪstri] – **prehistoric**	**Vorgeschichte – vorgeschichtlich**
genealogy [dʒi:ni'ælədʒi]	**Genealogie; Ahnentafel / -forschung**
primary sources [praɪməri 'sɔ:sɪz]	**Primärquellen**
document ['dɒkjumənt]	**Dokument; Urkunde**
records ['rekɔ:dz]	**Aufzeichnungen; Zeugnisse; Belege**
contemporary [kən'temprəri] records	zeitgenössische Berichte
written records / sources ['sɔ:sɪz]	schriftliche Überlieferungen / Quellen
oral traditions ['ɔ:rəl trədɪʃnz]	**mündliche Überlieferungen**
archives ['ɑ:kaɪvz]	**Archive**
data from parish registers ['redʒɪstəz]	**Daten / Fakten aus Kirchenbüchern**
the deciphering [dɪ'saɪfərɪŋ] **of inscriptions**	das Entziffern von Inschriften
textual criticism [tekstʃuəl 'krɪtɪsɪzm]	**Textkritik**

chronicle ['krɒnɪkl] – **chronicler**
chronicle ['krɒnɪkl]
population figures ['fɪgəz]
population movements ['muːvmənts]
period (of history) ['pɪərɪəd]
during the Renaissance [rɪ'neɪsns]
  period
epoch ['iːpɒk]
the spirit of the / an age [eɪdʒ]
ancient ['eɪnʃənt]
ancient Rome [eɪnʃənt 'rəʊm]
in ancient times / in antiquity
  [æn'tɪkwəti]
the ancients ['eɪnʃənts]
antiquity / the ancient world [wɜːld]
the art of classical ['klæsɪkl] antiquity
the Crusades [kruː'seɪdz]
Crusaders [kruː'seɪdəz]
the Middle Ages [mɪdl 'eɪdʒɪz]
the Reformation [refə'meɪʃn]
the age of absolutism ['æbsəluːtɪzm]
the Enlightenment [ɪn'laɪtnmənt]
the French Revolution [revə'luːʃn]
the Industrial [ɪn'dʌstrɪəl] Revolution

Chronik – Chronist(in)
berichten; aufzeichnen
Bevölkerungszahlen
Bevölkerungsbewegungen
(Geschichts-)Epoche
während der Renaissance

Epoche; Zeitalter
der Zeitgeist
alt; antik
das alte Rom; das Rom der Antike
im Altertum; in der Antike

die Menschen der Antike
die Antike
die Kunst der Antike
die Kreuzzüge
Kreuzfahrer; Kreuzritter
das Mittelalter
die Reformation
das Zeitalter des Absolutismus
die Aufklärung
die Französische Revolution
die industrielle Revolution

"1066? 1066??? History just isn't my strong point."

Political science
Politische Wissenschaft

→ 6.3–6.7

Politics is not an exact science.
(*Otto von Bismarck, German statesman, 1815–98*)

political [pə'lɪtɪkl] – **politically**
political science ['saɪəns]

political scientist ['saɪəntɪst]
political attitudes ['ætɪtjuːdz]

political systems / institutions
the country's political culture ['kʌltʃə]
exercise political power
achieve [ə'tʃiːv] political aims

politisch – in politischer Hinsicht
politische Wissenschaft; Politikwissenschaft; Politologie
Politologe / Politologin
politische Einstellungen / Überzeugungen
politische Systeme / Institutionen
die politische Kultur des Landes
politische Macht ausüben
politische Ziele erreichen

Pressure group = Pressure-Group (= organisierte Interessengruppe, die Druck
auf Parteien, Regierung etc. ausübt, um Entscheidungen zu beeinflussen)

politically important / stable / active
go into **politics** ['pɒlətɪks]
international [ɪntə'næʃnəl] politics
policy ['pɒləsi]
policy document ['dɒkjumənt]
a predictable [-'dɪkt-] foreign policy
in the field of **foreign affairs** [ə'feəz]
(the) state [steɪt]
the nation state [neɪʃn 'steɪt]
international [ɪntə'næʃnəl]
international organizations
international relations [rɪ'leɪʃnz]
international law [lɔː]
decision-making processes
opinion poll [ə'pɪnjən pəʊl]
influence ['ɪnfluəns] public opinion
behaviour [bɪ'heɪvjə]
voting / voter behaviour
an analysis of electoral behaviour
patterns of political behaviour
social conflicts ['kɒnflɪkts]
civic education [edju'keɪʃn]
civics (*mit Singularverb*) ['sɪvɪks]

human rights [hjuːmən 'raɪts]
human rights violations / abuses
China's human rights record

politisch wichtig / stabil / aktiv
in die **Politik** gehen (→ *S. 100*)
(die) internationale Politik
(eine bestimmte) **Politik** (→ *S. 100*)
Grundsatzpapier
eine berechenbare Außenpolitik
auf dem Gebiet der **Außenpolitik**
(der) Staat
der Nationalstaat
international
internationale Organisationen
internationale Beziehungen
internationales Recht; Völkerrecht
Entscheidungsprozesse
Meinungsumfrage
die öffentliche Meinung beeinflussen
Verhalten
(das) Wählerverhalten
eine Analyse des Wählerverhaltens
politische Verhaltensmuster
soziale / gesellschaftliche Konflikte
politische Bildung
**Gemeinschafts- / (Staats-)Bürger-
   kunde**
Menschenrechte
Menschenrechtsverletzungen
Chinas Menschenrechtsbilanz;
   die Menschenrechtssituation in China

Psychology
Psychologie

Freud is the father of psychoanalysis. It had no mother.
(*Germaine Greer, Australian feminist, born in 1939*)

psychology [saɪˈkɒlədʒi]	**Psychologie**
applied [əˈplaɪd] psychology	angewandte Psychologie
clinical [ˈklɪnɪkl] psychology	klinische / medizinische Psychologie
comparative [kəmˈpærətɪv] psychology	vergleichende Psychologie
developmental [-ˈmentl] psychology	Entwicklungspsychologie
educational [edjuˈkeɪʃnəl] psychology	pädagogische Psychologie
learning psychology	Lernpsychologie

Hinweis zur Aussprache
Die folgenden viersilbigen Wörter werden auf der zweiten Silbe betont:
psyˈchology, paˈthology, psyˈchiatry, psyˈchologist, psyˈchiatrist, aˈnalysis.

psychologist [saɪˈkɒlədʒɪst]	**Psychologe / Psychologin**
psychological [saɪkəˈlɒdʒɪkl]	**psychologisch**
psychiatry [saɪˈkaɪətri] – **psychiatrist**	**Psychiatrie** – **Psychiater(in)**
psychoanalysis [saɪkəʊəˈnæləsɪs]	**Psychoanalyse**
psychoanalyst [saɪkəʊˈænəlɪst]	Psychoanalytiker(in)
psychopath [ˈsaɪkəpæθ]	**Psychopath(in)**
psychopathic [saɪkəˈpæθɪk]	psychopathisch
psychopathology [saɪkəʊpəˈθɒlədʒi]	**Psychopathologie**
psychotherapy [saɪkəʊˈθerəpi]	**Psychotherapie**
psychotherapist [saɪkəʊˈθerəpɪst]	Psychotherapeut(in)
behaviour [bɪˈheɪvjə]	**Verhalten**
abnormal [æbˈnɔːml] behaviour	abnormes / a(b)normales Verhalten
behavioural research [rɪˈsɜːtʃ]	Verhaltensforschung
behaviourism [bɪˈheɪvjərɪzm]	Behaviorismus; Verhaltens- psychologie
condition [kənˈdɪʃn] – **conditioning**	**konditionieren** – **Konditionierung**
conditioned reflex [ˈriːfleks]	bedingter Reflex
stimulus [ˈstɪmjələs] **and response**	**Reiz und Reaktion**
positive / negative reinforcement	**positive / negative Verstärkung**
personality [pɜːsəˈnæləti]	**Persönlichkeit**
the human mind [hjuːmən ˈmaɪnd]	**der menschliche Verstand / Geist**
the conscious [ɒ] / unconscious mind	das Bewusste / Unbewusste
perception [pəˈsepʃn]	**Wahrnehmung**
memory [ˈmeməri]	**Gedächtnis**
short-term memory	Kurzzeitgedächtnis
long-term memory	Langzeitgedächtnis
thinking [ˈθɪŋkɪŋ]	**(das) Denken**
reasoning [ˈriːznɪŋ]	**(logisches) Denken**
problem solving [ˈprɒbləm sɒlvɪŋ]	**Problemlösen**
intelligence [ɪnˈtelɪdʒəns]	**Intelligenz**
intelligence quotient [ˈkwəʊʃnt] / IQ	Intelligenzquotient / IQ

8

4

creativity [kriːerˈtɪvəti]	**Kreativität**
motivation [məʊtɪˈveɪʃn]	**Motivation; Verhaltensantrieb**
self-actualization / self-realization	**Selbstverwirklichung**
emotion [ɪˈməʊʃn]	**Gefühl**
emotions such as joy and anger [ˈæŋɡə]	Gefühle wie Freude und Zorn
repressed [rɪˈprest] emotions	unterdrückte Gefühle
pent-up emotions	aufgestaute Gefühle
subconscious [sʌbˈkɒnʃəs]	**unterbewusst**
unconscious [ʌnˈkɒnʃəs]	**unbewusst**
dream [driːm] – **dreaming**	**Traum – (das) Träumen**
nightmare [ˈnaɪtmeə]	**Albtraum**
anxiety [æŋˈzaɪəti]	**Angst**
troubled by feelings of anxiety	von Angstgefühlen geplagt

Der Begründer der Psychoanalyse wurde auch in der Umgangssprache verewigt. *Don't go all Freud on me!* ist eine häufige Reaktion, wenn sich Engländer zu eindringlich analysiert fühlen. Wenn man in einem *Freudian slip* (= *freudscher Versprecher*) einen unbewussten Gedankengang preisgibt, wird oft nur kommentiert: *That was pretty Freudian.*

mental disorders [dɪsˈɔːdəz]	**geistig-seelische Störungen**
(mentally) disturbed [dɪˈstɜːbd]	(geistes)gestört
mentally ill [mentəli ˈɪl]	geisteskrank; psychisch krank
(mentally) retarded [rɪˈtɑːdɪd]	(geistig) zurückgeblieben
learning disabilities [dɪsəˈbɪlətiz]	**Lernbehinderungen**
psychosis [saɪˈkəʊsɪs] – **neurosis**	**Psychose – Neurose**
neurotic behaviour [bɪˈheɪvjə]	neurotisches / krankhaftes Verhalten
He's a neurotic [njuˈrɒtɪk]	Er ist ein Neurotiker.
schizophrenia [skɪtsəˈfriːniə]	**Schizophrenie**
schizophrenic [skɪtsəˈfrenɪk]	schizophren; Schizophrene(r)
group therapy [gruːp ˈθerəpi]	**Gruppentherapie**
occupational [ɒkjuˈpeɪʃənl] therapy	Beschäftigungstherapie
therapist / counsellor [ˈkaʊnsələ]	**Therapeut(in)**

Das spaßhaft-umgangssprachliche Wort *shrink* bezeichnet *a psychotherapist, psychoanalyst or psychiatrist: She sees her shrink once a week.* (= Sie geht einmal wöchentlich zum Psychiater / zu ihrem Therapeuten.)

marriage counselling [ˈkaʊnsəlɪŋ]	**Eheberatung**
interview [ˈɪntəvjuː]	(psychodiagnostisches) **Gespräch**
case study [ˈkeɪs stʌdi]	**Fallstudie**
psychological testing / tests	**psychologische Tests**
intelligence testing / tests	Intelligenztests
ability [əˈbɪləti] test	Eignungstest / -prüfung
aptitude [ˈæptɪtjuːd] test	Eignungstest
achievement [əˈtʃiːvmənt] test	Leistungstest
standardized [ˈstændədaɪzd] test	standardisierter Test
validity (of a test) [vəˈlɪdəti]	**Validität / Gültigkeit** (eines Tests)
reliability [rɪlaɪəˈbɪləti]	**Zuverlässigkeit; Reliabilität**
standard deviation [diːviˈeɪʃn]	**Standardabweichung**

Sociology
Soziologie

8
5

A sociologist is a scientist who blames crime on everything and everyone, except the person who commits it. (*Laurence J. Peter, Canadian writer and teacher, 1910–90*)

sociology [səʊʃiˈɒlədʒi] – **sociologist**	Soziologie – Soziologe / Soziologin
sociological [səʊʃiəˈlɒdʒɪkl]	soziologisch
social [ˈsəʊʃl]	sozial; Sozial-; gesellschaftlich; Gesellschafts-
social change [tʃeɪndʒ]	sozialer / gesellschaftlicher Wandel
social norms [nɔːmz]	soziale / gesellschaftliche Normen
social relations / relationships	soziale / gesellschaftliche Beziehungen
the social environment [ɪnˈvaɪrənmənt]	das soziale Umfeld
the social structure [ˈstrʌktʃə]	die Sozialstruktur
social engineering [endʒɪˈnɪərɪŋ]	angewandte Sozialwissenschaft
socialization [səʊʃəlaɪˈzeɪʃn]	**Sozialisation; Sozialisierung**
society [səˈsaɪəti]	(die) **Gesellschaft**
the poorest members of society	die ärmsten Mitglieder der Gesellschaft
a classless [ˈklɑːsləs] society	eine klassenlose Gesellschaft
demographic [deməˈɡræfɪk]	**demografisch**
empirical research [rɪˈsɜːtʃ]	**empirische Forschung**
public opinion [pʌblɪk əˈpɪnjən]	(die) **öffentliche Meinung**
influence [ˈɪnfluəns] public opinion	die öffentliche Meinung beeinflussen
survey [ˈsɜːveɪ]	**Umfrage; Untersuchung**
carry out / conduct a survey	eine Umfrage veranstalten
45% of those surveyed [səˈveɪd]	45% der Befragten
census [ˈsensəs]	**(Volks-)Zählung; Zensus**
conduct [kənˈdʌkt] a census	eine (Volks-)Zählung durchführen
statistics [stəˈtɪstɪks]	**Statistiken; Statistik** (als Wissenschaft)
These statistics are misleading.	Diese Statistiken sind irreführend.
Statistics is a branch of mathematics [mæθəˈmætɪks].	Die Statistik ist ein Teilgebiet der Mathematik. (→ S. 83 u. 240)
population [pɒpjuˈleɪʃn]	(statistische) **Gesamtzahl / Gesamtheit**
population growth [ɡrəʊθ]	(das) Bevölkerungswachstum
sample [ˈsɑːmpl]	**Auswahl; (Zufalls-)Stichprobe; Sample**
random sample [rændəm ˈsɑːmpl]	(Zufalls-)Stichprobe
representative [reprɪˈzentətɪv] sample	repräsentative Auswahl
behaviour pattern [ˈpætn]	**Verhaltensmuster**
codes of behaviour [bɪˈheɪvjə]	Verhaltensnormen
deviant [ˈdiːviənt] behaviour	abweichendes Verhalten
group dynamics [daɪˈnæmɪks]	**Gruppendynamik**
peer group [ˈpɪə ɡruːp]	(soziale Gruppe, der sich ein Individuum als zugehörig empfindet)
decision-making process [ˈprəʊses]	**Entscheidungsprozess**

The language of research

If we knew what it was we were doing, it would not be called research, would it? (*Albert Einstein, German-born US physicist, 1879–1955*)

research ['riːsɜːtʃ] **question**	Forschungsfrage
research grant [grɑːnt]	Forschungsstipendium
research proposal [prəˈpəʊzl]	Exposé (zu einem Forschungs- vorhaben)
assumption – axiom ['æksiəm]	Annahme – Axiom
hypothesis [haɪˈpɒθəsɪs]	Hypothese
abstract ['æbstrækt]	Zusammenfassung; Abriss; Abstract
conclusion [kənˈkluːʒn]	Schlussfolgerung; Fazit
model ['mɒdl]	Modell
limitations [lɪmɪˈteɪʃnz]	Begrenzungen
several variables ['veəriəblz]	mehrere Variable(n)
empirical [ɪmˈpɪrɪkl] **study**	empirische Untersuchung
raw data [rɔː ˈdeɪtə]	Rohdaten; Ursprungsdaten
reliability [rɪlaɪəˈbɪləti]	Zuverlässigkeit
methodology [meθəˈdɒlədʒi]	Methodik
framework ['freɪmwɜːk]	Bezugsrahmen
investigation [ɪnvestɪˈgeɪʃn]	Untersuchung
interpretation [ɪntɜːprɪˈteɪʃn]	Interpretation; Deutung
identify [aɪˈdentɪfaɪ] **the causes**	die Ursachen identifizieren
synthesis ['sɪnθəsɪs]	Synthese

Zu den akademischen Schriften der Sozialwissenschaften gehören *(case) studies* (= [Fall-]Studien), *papers* (= Abhandlungen), *essays* ['eseɪz] (= Aufsätze) *and, of course, books*.
Manchmal bezeichnet man ein Buch als das *seminal* ['semɪnl] *work in its field* (= grundlegende Arbeit auf ihrem Gebiet) oder einen Aufsatz als *influential* (= einflussreich) wegen seiner *persuasive analysis* [əˈnæləsɪs] *of the forces at work and the dynamics involved* (= überzeugende Analyse der obwaltenden Einflüsse und Dynamiken). *Drawing on a body of new evidence* (= aus neuen Erkenntnissen schöpfend) *a groundbreaking paper might shed new light on political, historical or sociological processes*. Weniger bahnbrechende Werke, die den Leser im Großen und Ganzen trotz *impeccable* (= tadellos) *research* unbegeistert (= *unenthused*) lassen, wer- den mitunter als *scholarly* ['skɒləli] *account* (= gelehrte Abhandlung) be- zeichnet – ein Beispiel für (= *an example of*) etwas, was die Engländer *damning* ['dæmɪŋ] *with faint praise* (= durch zurückhaltendes Lob verdam- men) nennen. Eine unmissverständliche Verdammung allerdings ist es, wenn Gelehrte einen Kollegen wegen *unsound method* (= unsolide Methode) kriti- sieren. Zu einer strengeren (= *harsher*) Bewertung als *strong on theory and speculation but rather weak on evidence and objective data* (= stark in Theorie und Spekulation, aber schwach im Beweis- und Zahlenmaterial) wür- den sich dagegen nur wenige *academics* (= Wissenschaftler) bereitfinden.

Education
Bildungswesen

1 Educational facilities
Bildungseinrichtungen

2 Subjects and skills
Fächer und Fertigkeiten

3 Exams and qualifications
Prüfungen und Qualifikationen

4 Teaching and learning
Lehren und Lernen

5 In the classroom
Im Klassenzimmer

Educational facilities
Bildungseinrichtungen

Human history becomes more and more a race between education and catastrophe. (*H.G. Wells, English writer, 1866–1946*)

go to **school** [skuːl]	in die **Schule** gehen
attend [əˈtend] a school	eine Schule besuchen
nursery school [ˈnɜːsri skuːl]	**Kindergarten**
kindergarten [ˈkɪndəgɑːtn]	*BE* **Kindergarten;** *AE* **Vorschule für 4- bis 6-Jährige**
primary school *BE* / *AE* **elementary** [eliˈmentri] **school** / *AE* **grade school**	**Grundschule**
secondary [ˈsekəndri] **school**	**höhere / weiterführende Schule**
secondary modern (school) *BE*	(*früher*) **Hauptschule / Realschule**
comprehensive [kɒmprɪˈhensɪv] **school** *BE*	**Gesamtschule**
grammar school [ˈgræmə skuːl] *BE*	**Gymnasium**
sixth form college [ˈkɒlɪdʒ] *BE*	**gymnasiale Oberstufe** (als selbstständige Schule)

Die *sixth form* ist im britischen allgemeinbildenden Schulsystem die oberste, zwei Jahre umfassende Klassenstufe. Im AE heißt Klasse(nstufe) *grade. He's in the third form* BE / AE *in (the) eighth grade now.* (= Er ist jetzt in der achten Klasse.)

prep(aratory) school [ˈprep / prɪˈpærətri skuːl] *BE*	(**Privatinternat zur Vorbereitung auf die Public School**)
public school [pʌblɪk ˈskuːl]	*BE* **private Internatsschule;** *AE* **öffentliche Schule**
state school / **maintained school**	*BE* **öffentliche Schule**
special school [ˈspeʃl skuːl]	**Sonderschule**
boarding school [ˈbɔːdɪŋ skuːl]	**Internat(sschule)**

middle school (= AE Schule für die Klassen 5/6–8)
junior high [dʒuːniə ˈhaɪ] *(school)* (= AE Schule für die Klassen 7–8/9)
senior high [siːniə ˈhaɪ] *school* (= AE Schule für die Klassen 10–12)
high school (= AE Schule für die Klassen 9/10–12)

vocational [vəʊˈkeɪʃənl] **school**	**Berufsschule; berufsbildende Schule**
vocational college / **trade school**	**Berufsfachschule**
commercial / **business school**	**Handelsschule**
commercial / **business college**	**höhere Handelsschule**
technical [ˈteknɪkl] **college** *BE*	**Fach(ober)schule**
advanced [ədˈvɑːnst] **technical college**	**Fachhochschule**
higher education [edjuˈkeɪʃn]	**Hochschul(aus)bildung**

college [ˈkɒlɪdʒ] = AE höhere Bildungseinrichtung, die zu einem ersten Hochschulabschluss (*bachelor's degree* [ˈbætʃələz dɪɡriː], z.B. *BA = Bachelor of Arts*) führt: *He's still at college.* (= Er ist noch auf dem College.) *I went to college here.* (= Ich bin hier aufs College gegangen.) *She graduated* [ˈɡrædʒueɪtɪd] *from college last year.* (= Sie hat voriges Jahr ihren College-Abschluss gemacht.)
college = BE Teil einer Universität: *Prince Charles studied at Trinity College, Cambridge* [ˈkeɪmbrɪdʒ].
Ansonsten bezeichnet *college* eine Hochschule, Fachschule, Fachhochschule, Akademie etc.: *secretarial* [sekrəˈteəriəl] *college* (= Sekretärinnenfachschule), *art college* (= Kunsthochschule), *teacher training college* BE / AE *teachers college* (= pädagogische Hochschule).

university [juːnɪˈvɜːsəti]	**Universität**
go to / study at university	an der Universität studieren
He's a professor [prəˈfesə] at the University of Denver.	Er ist Professor an der Universität Denver.
get a place at / in a university	einen Studienplatz bekommen
distance-learning university	Fernuniversität
the Open University *BE*	die (britische) Fernuniversität
campus [ˈkæmpəs]	**Universitätsgelände; Universitäts-**
on campus	an der Universität; auf dem Universitätsgelände
integrated degree programme	**duales Studium**

Graduate [ˈɡrædʒuət] *school* bezeichnet im AE eine Hochschulabteilung für *postgraduates* [pəʊstˈɡrædʒuəts], d.h. Studierende, die nach dem ersten Hochschulabschluss (*bachelor's degree*) weiterstudieren.

department [dɪˈpɑːtmənt]	**Abteilung; Fachbereich; Seminar**
the Department of English	der Fachbereich Anglistik
medical school [ˈmedɪkl skuːl]	**medizinische Fakultät**
art academy [ˈɑːt əkædəmi]	**Kunstakademie**
(theological) seminary [ˈsemɪnəri]	**theologische Hochschule**
research institute [ˈɪnstɪtjuːt]	**Forschungsinstitut**
Sunday school [ˈsʌndeɪ skuːl]	**(religiöse) Sonntagsschule**
enrol [ɪnˈrəʊl] on a **course**	sich für einen **Kurs(us)** anmelden /
BE / *AE* enroll in a **course**	einschreiben
correspondence [-ˈspɒn-] course	Fernkurs
night school [ˈnaɪt skuːl]	**Abendschule**

Weiterbildung heißt im BE *further education,* sonst auch *adult education* (= Erwachsenenbildung), *continuing education* oder *continued education.* Volkshochschulkurse sind *adult education classes* oder *evening classes.* Volkshochschule könnte man mit *adult education centre* oder *college for further adult education* übersetzen. *She did / took an evening class.* (= Sie machte / besuchte einen VHS-Kurs.)

Subjects and skills
Fächer und Fertigkeiten

By being so long in the lowest form (at Harrow, one of the best public schools) I gained an immense advantage over the cleverer boys. They all went on to learn Latin and Greek. ... But I was taught English. ... Thus I got into my bones the essential structure of the ordinary British sentence – which is a noble thing. (*Sir Winston Churchill, British statesman, 1874–1965*)

subject ['sʌbdʒɪkt]	**(Unterrichts-)Fach**
My favourite ['feɪvrət] subject is maths [mæθs].	Mein Lieblingsfach ist Mathe.
optional ['ɒpʃənl] subject	Wahlfach
compulsory [kəm'pʌlsəri] subject	Pflichtfach
elective [ɪ'lektɪv]	*AE* **Wahlfach / Zusatzfach**
course [kɔːs]	**Kurs(us); Lehrgang**
attend [ə'tend] / take / do a course	einen Kurs besuchen / machen

National Curriculum [kə'rɪkjələm] heißt in *England and Wales* der Kanon von *three core subjects* (= Kernfächern) und *seven foundation subjects* (= Grundfächern), die für 5–16-Jährige an *state schools* (= öffentlichen Schulen) *compulsory* [kəm'pʌlsəri] (= obligatorisch) sind.
Core subjects: English, mathematics [mæθə'mætɪks], *science* ['saɪəns].
Foundation subjects: technology [tek'nɒlədʒi], *history* ['hɪstri], *geography* [dʒi'ɒgrəfi], *music* ['mjuːzɪk], *art, physical education, and a modern foreign language* [fɒrən 'læŋgwɪdʒ] (= Fremdsprache).

mathematics – maths *BE* / *AE* **math**	**Mathematik – Mathe**
technology (education) [tek'nɒlədʒi]	**Technik**
history ['hɪstri]	**Geschichte**
art [ɑːt] – **fine arts** [faɪn 'ɑːts]	**Kunst – bildende Kunst**

Viersilbige Wörter, die auf der zweiten Silbe betont werden:
bi'ology (= Biologie), *com'pulsory, cur'riculum, ge'ography* (= Erdkunde), *phi'losophy* (= Philosophie), *psy'chology, tech'nology.*

physical ['fɪzɪkl] **education** / PE	**Sport; Leibesübungen**
health [helθ] **(education)**	**Gesundheit(slehre)**
sex education ['seks edjukeɪʃn]	**Sexualkunde**
religious instruction [ɪn'strʌkʃn] /	**Religion(slehre)**
education / RI / RE	
social studies ['səʊʃl stʌdiz]	**Sozialkunde; Sozialwissenschaften**
home economics [iːkə'nɒmɪks] /	**Hauswirtschaftslehre**
home ec [ek]	

Das Fach *science* ['saɪəns] (= Naturwissenschaft) umfasst *biology* [baɪ'ɒlədʒi] (= Biologie), *chemistry* ['kemɪstri] (= Chemie), *physics* ['fɪzɪks] (= Physik) und *geoscience* [dʒiː-] (= Geowissenschaft). *Computer science* ist Informatik.

curriculum [kə'rɪkjələm]	**Fächerkanon; Lehrplan; Curriculum**
syllabus ['sɪləbəs]	**Lehrplan; Stoffplan; Rahmenplan**
stick to the syllabus (– stuck – stuck)	sich an den Stoffplan halten
depart [dɪ'pɑːt] from the syllabus	vom Stoffplan abweichen
listening ['lɪsnɪŋ] **comprehension**	**Hörverstehen / -verständnis**
reading comprehension [kɒmprɪ'henʃn]	Leseverstehen / -verständnis
speed reading ['spiːd riːdɪŋ]	**Schnelllesen**
dictation [dɪk'teɪʃn]	**Diktat**
We're doing a dictation today.	Wir schreiben heute ein Diktat.
essay ['eseɪ] *BE* / *AE* **paper** / *AE* **theme** [θiːm] / **composition** [kɒmpə'zɪʃn]	**(Schul-)Aufsatz**
write an essay / paper / theme on homelessness	einen Aufsatz über Obdachlosigkeit schreiben
past paper ['pɑːst 'peɪpə]	**Altklausur**

Mit *the three Rs* [θriː 'ɑːz] – *reading, (w)riting, (a)rithmetic* [ə'rɪθmətɪk] (= Rechnen) – bezeichnet man traditionell die Grundlagen der Schulbildung. Auch übertragen gebraucht: *the three Rs of good government* (= die Grundregeln guten Regierens).

Physical education.

Exams and qualifications
Prüfungen und Qualifikationen

In examinations those who do not wish to know ask questions of those who cannot tell. (*Sir Walter Raleigh, British academic, 1861–1922*)

Prüfungen sind *examinations* [ɪgzæmɪˈneɪʃnz] oder kurz *exams* [ɪgˈzæmz]: *oral* [ˈɔːrəl] / *written exam* (= mündliche / schriftliche Prüfung), *final exam* (= Abschlussprüfung). *I'm taking my finals in June.* (= Im Juni mache ich die Abschlussprüfung.) – *Students prepare for* (= bereiten sich vor auf) *or cram for* (= büffeln / pauken für) *an exam. They take / sit an exam* (= machen eine Prüfung / unterziehen sich einer Prüfung), *they pass / fail an exam* (= bestehen eine Prüfung / bestehen eine Prüfung nicht). Besonders AE auch *flunk an exam* (= bei einer Prüfung durchfallen / durchrasseln).

cheat (in an exam) [tʃiːt]	**(bei einer Prüfung) täuschen / abschreiben**
copy / crib off / from a neighbour	von einem Nachbarn **abschreiben**

Tests: *aptitude* [ˈæptɪtjuːd] *test* (= Eignungstest), *placement test* (= Einstufungstest), *achievement* [əˈtʃiːvmənt] *test* (= Leistungstest), *multiple-choice test* (= Antwortauswahltest), *cloze test* (= Lückentest, bei dem in einem Text z.B. jedes fünfte Wort zu ergänzen ist), *SAT™ AE = Scholastic* [skəˈlæstɪk] *Aptitude Test* (= standardisierter Qualifikationstest für das Studium an amerikanischen Universitäten und Colleges), *SAT BE = Standard Assessment* [əˈsesmənt] *Task* (= standardisierter Lernfortschrittskontrolltest in einem *core subject* des *National Curriculum*).

credit [ˈkredɪt]	**Schein** (als Leistungsausweis)
I've got two credits in Eng. Lit. [ɪŋ ˈlɪt]	Ich habe zwei Scheine in englischer Literatur.
pass [pɑːs]	(Prüfung) **bestehen**
get a pass in history [ˈhɪstri]	die Geschichtsprüfung (ohne Prädikat) bestehen
He passed with honours [ˈɒnəz].	Er bestand mit Auszeichnung.

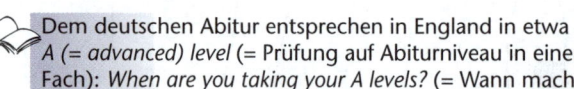

Dem deutschen Abitur entsprechen in England in etwa *A levels* [ˈeɪ levlz]. *A (= advanced) level* (= Prüfung auf Abiturniveau in einem bestimmten Fach): *When are you taking your A levels?* (= Wann machst du dein Abitur?) *You need A levels if you want to go to university.* (= Um an der Universität zu studieren, braucht man das Abitur.)
In den USA ist das *high school diploma* [dɪˈpləʊmə] annähernd dem Abiturzeugnis gleichzusetzen: *She graduated* [ˈgrædʒueɪtɪd] *from high school last year.* (= Sie hat voriges Jahr das Abitur gemacht.)
Dem mittleren Schulabschluss entspricht in England ungefähr *the GCSE* (= *General Certificate* [səˈtɪfɪkət] *of Secondary Education*): *pupils preparing for GCSE* (= Schüler, die sich auf den mittleren Abschluss vorbereiten), *He's got six GCSEs.* (= Er hat den mittleren Abschluss in sechs Fächern.)

graduate ['grædʒuət]	**(Hochschul-)Absolvent(in)**
university graduates	Akademiker(innen)
high school graduate *AE*	(*etwa:*) Abiturient(in)
graduate ['grædʒueɪt]	**das Studium abschließen**
She graduated last year.	Sie hat voriges Jahr ihren
	(Universitäts- / High School-)
	Abschluss gemacht.
graduation [grædʒu'eɪʃn]	**Graduierung; *AE* (Schul-)Entlassung**
graduation ceremony ['serəməni]	Abschlussfeier (mit Überreichung der
	Zeugnisse, Diplome etc.)

Noten, mit denen Leistungen bewertet werden, sind *marks* (BE) oder *grades* (AE, z.T. auch BE): *grades A to E* (= die Noten 1 bis 5); *She scored / gained / achieved top marks* BE / AE *grades in both papers.* (= Sie hatte in beiden Arbeiten eine Eins.) *Her science grades are less good.* (= In den Naturwissenschaften sind ihre Noten weniger gut.) *He achieved five straight As* [eɪz]. (= Er hatte fünf glatte Einsen.)

report [rɪ'pɔːt] *BE* / *AE* **report card**	(Zwischen- / Jahres- / etc.)**Zeugnis**
certificate [sə'tɪfɪkət]	(Prüfungs- / Abschluss-)**Zeugnis**

Als deutsche Schüler (= *German students*) bei den Prüfungen zum *Program(me) for International Student Assessment* (PISA) extrem schlecht abschnitten (= *did / performed extremely badly*), kam es in der deutschen Bildungsszene (= *educational scene*) zum PISA-Schock (= *PISA shock*). Warum hatten z.B. die Finnen so viel besser abgeschnitten als die Deutschen? (= *Why had the Finns, for example, done / performed so much better than the Germans?*)

diploma [dɪ'pləʊmə]	**Diplom**
He holds a diploma in economics.	(*etwa*) Er ist Diplomvolkswirt.

Um zu promovieren (= *do your / a doctorate* ['dɒktərət]), schreibt man u.a. eine Doktorarbeit oder Dissertation (= *doctoral thesis* ['θiːsɪs] / *dissertation*). Schließlich erlangt man die Doktorwürde (= *you gain / get your doctorate / doctor's degree*). Abkürzungen wie *PhD* (= Dr. phil.), *MD* (= Dr. med.) und *ScD* (= Dr. rer. nat.) werden nachgestellt: *Helen Jackson, PhD* (= Dr. phil. Helen Jackson). Andere akademische Grade (= *degrees* [dɪ'griːz]): *bachelor's* ['bætʃələz] *degree* (= niedrigster akademischer Grad): *BA / Bachelor of Arts* (= Bachelor der Geisteswissenschaften), *BSc / Bachelor of Science* (= Bachelor der Naturwissenschaften) *master's degree* (= Magister): *MA / Master of Arts* (= M.A. / Magister Artium), *MSc / Master of Science* (= M.Sc. / Magister der Naturwissenschaften). *He got his BA / bachelor's degree / MA / master's degree last year.* (= Er hat voriges Jahr seinen B.A. / M.A. gemacht.)

Teaching and learning
Lehren und Lernen

Nothing that is worth knowing can be taught.
(*Oscar Wilde, Irish writer, 1854–1900*)

teach (– taught [ɔː] – taught) | unterrichten; lehren
Who taught you that? | Wer hat dir das beigebracht?
teach English to children | Kindern Englischunterricht erteilen
foreign-language teaching | Fremdsprachenunterricht
train [treɪn] | **ausbilden; eine Ausbildung absolvieren**
well / poorly trained teachers | gut / schlecht ausgebildete Lehrer
He's training as a waiter. | Er macht eine Ausbildung als Kellner.
training programme ['prəʊgræm] | Ausbildungsprogramm
vocational [vəʊ'keɪʃənl] training | berufliche Bildung
apprenticeship [ə'prentɪsʃɪp] | **Lehre; Ausbildung**
instruction [ɪn'strʌkʃn] | **Unterricht**
instruction material(s) [mə'tɪəriəl(z)] | Lehrmaterial
self-instruction [self ɪn'strʌkʃn] | Selbstunterricht
instructor [ɪn'strʌktə] | **Lehrer(in); Ausbilder(in)**
driving instructor ['draɪvɪŋ ɪnstrʌktə] | Fahrlehrer(in)
lesson ['lesn] | **(Unterrichts-)Stunde**
give / take English lessons | Englischunterricht erteilen / nehmen
motivate ['məʊtɪveɪt] | **motivieren**
motivate the students to learn | die Schüler zum Lernen motivieren
motivation [məʊtɪ'veɪʃn] | **Motivation; Anreiz**
the students lack motivation | die Schüler sind nicht sehr motiviert
learn (– learnt* – learnt*) | **lernen**
I learnt / learned that at school. | Das habe ich in der Schule gelernt.
learn a poem by heart [hɑːt] | ein Gedicht auswendig lernen
learner ['lɜːnə] | **Lernende(r)**
She's a quick / slow learner. | Sie lernt schnell / langsam.
study ['stʌdi] (a subject) | (ein Fach) **studieren**
She's studying to be an engineer. | Sie macht ein Ingenieurstudium.
I'm studying for tomorrow's test. | Ich lerne für die morgige Arbeit.
I need more time for study. | Ich brauche mehr Zeit zum Studieren.
read [iː] (– read [e] – read [e]) | **lesen**
read the text silently ['saɪləntli] / aloud | den Text still / laut lesen
I'll read the text to you. | Ich werde euch den Text vorlesen.
She read philosophy at Oxford. *BE* | Sie hat in Oxford Philosophie studiert.
textbook ['tekstbʊk] | **Lehrbuch**
audiovisual aids [ɔːdiəʊvɪʒuəl 'eɪdz] | **audiovisuelle Hilfsmittel**
homework ['həʊmwɜːk] | **Hausaufgabe(n); Hausarbeit(en)**
set / assign [ə'saɪn] homework | Hausarbeiten aufgeben
She's given us a lot of homework. | Sie hat uns viel aufgegeben.
What have you got for homework? | Was hast du auf?
assignment [ə'saɪnmənt] | (z.B. Haus-)**Aufgabe; Hausarbeit**
homework assignments | Hausaufgaben; Hausarbeiten

In the classroom
Im Klassenzimmer

School: A house of discipline and instruction.
(*Definition in Dr Johnson's Dictionary, 1755*)

We have music in **period** ['pɪəriəd] three.	In der dritten **Stunde** haben wir Musik.
Who**'s absent** ['æbsənt] today?	Wer **fehlt** heute?
note it down in the **(class) register**	es im **Klassenbuch** vermerken
Let's **get started**.	Wir wollen **anfangen**.
(Can we have some) **Quiet**, please.	Bitte (etwas) **Ruhe**.
give out / **hand out** the books / texts	die Bücher / Texte **austeilen**
Take out your books.	Nehmt eure Bücher **heraus**.
Open your books at / to page 57.	Schlagt eure Bücher auf Seite 57 **auf**.
Shut / **Close** [z] your books, please.	Macht die Bücher bitte **zu**.
It's at the **top** / **bottom** of the page.	Es ist **oben** / **unten** auf der Seite.
act out a dialogue ['daɪəlɒg]	einen Dialog **spielen**
Will you **read** the part of the witch?	**Übernimmst** du die Rolle der Hexe?
Look at the third **paragraph**.	Schaut euch den dritten **Absatz** an.
Let's go on to the next paragraph.	Wir gehen weiter zum nächsten Absatz.
Better **make** / **take** some **notes**.	**Macht** euch besser ein paar **Notizen**.
summarize ['sʌməraɪz] the plot	die Handlung **zusammenfassen**
a brief / short **summary** of the text	eine kurze **Zusammenfassung** des Textes
find a **heading** for the story	für die Story eine **Überschrift** finden
I want you to **copy** this **down**.	Ich möchte, dass ihr das **abschreibt**.
Make sure you write **legibly** / **clearly**.	Bitte schreibt **leserlich** / **deutlich**.
Whose turn is it next?	**Wer** ist als Nächster **dran**?
Next (one), please.	Der **Nächste**, bitte.
Let's do this in **pairs**.	Das machen wir in **Partnerarbeit**.
work in **groups of four**	in **Vierergruppen** arbeiten
Speak up, please.	**Sprich** bitte **lauter**.
Could you speak a little **louder**.	Könntest du etwas **lauter** sprechen.
Try to speak more **clearly**.	Versuch **deutlicher** zu sprechen.
Say / **Repeat** [rɪ'piːt] after me …	**Sprecht** mir bitte **nach** …
Say it **once again**, please.	Sag das bitte **noch mal**.
No **prompting**, please.	Bitte nicht **vorsagen**.
Go to the **(black)board**, please.	Geh bitte zur **Tafel**.
a piece of **chalk** [tʃɔːk]	ein Stück **Kreide**
rub / **wipe** something **off**	etwas (von der Tafel) **abwischen**
clean the board	die Tafel **abwischen**
(overhead) projector / **OHP**	**Overhead-** / **Tageslichtprojektor**
Have you **finished**?	Seid ihr **fertig**?
Has everyone **handed in** their test?	Haben alle ihre Arbeit **abgegeben**?
I'll **return** the tests on Monday.	Ich **gebe** die Arbeit Montag **zurück**.
That'll do for today.	**Das wär's** für heute.
We'll **finish** it **off** next time.	Wir **machen** es nächstes Mal **zu Ende**.
For your **homework** would you do …	Als **Hausaufgabe** macht bitte …

homework (*stets Singular*) / **studies** (*stets Plural*)

Hausaufgaben

assess [ə'ses]

einschätzen; bewerten

How would you assess his academic ability [ə'bɪləti]?

Wie würden Sie seine akademische Begabung einschätzen?

continuous [kən'tɪnjuəs] **assessment**

fortlaufende Beurteilung

presentation [preznˈteɪʃn]

Präsentation

Next lesson, could you give us a presentation on / about the Roman conquest ['kɒŋkwest] of Britain?

Könnten Sie nächste Stunde eine Präsentation über die Eroberung Britanniens durch die Römer machen / halten?

analysis [ə'næləsɪs]

Analyse

Make sure to include plenty of analysis in your essays.

Denken Sie daran, ihren Aufsatz stark analytisch zu gestalten.

design [dɪ'zaɪn] a poster

ein Poster **gestalten**

The class is **well behaved** [bɪ'heɪvd]. They are a well-behaved class.

Die Klasse ist **diszipliniert.** Es ist eine disziplinierte Klasse.

set [set]

Leistungsgruppe

We have divided [dɪ'vaɪdɪd] the students into sets according [ə'kɔːdɪŋ] to their ability [ə'bɪləti].

Wir haben die Schüler entsprechend ihren Fähigkeiten in Leistungsgruppen eingeteilt.

He always used to be in the top set for maths and in the bottom set for history ['hɪstri].

In Mathematik war er immer in der obersten Gruppe und in Geschichte in der untersten.

What did you **put** for number 1?

Was hast du bei Nummer 1 **geschrieben?**

How did you **answer** question 3?

Wie hast du Frage 3 **beantwortet?**

term [tɜːm]

Trimester; Semester; Halbjahr

At the end of each term, teachers have to write **reports** [rɪ'pɔːts].

Zum Ende jedes Halbjahrs müssen die Lehrer **Zeugnisse** schreiben.

Students have to **revise** *BE* throughout exam [ɪg'zæm] term.

Während des ganzen Prüfungstrimesters / -semesters müssen die Schüler **Unterrichtsstoff wiederholen.**

I need to **revise** [rɪ'vaɪz] *BE / AE* **review** [rɪ'vjuː] for my exam tomorrow / for tomorrow's test.

Ich muss noch Sachen für die morgige Klausur / Klassenarbeit / Prüfung **wiederholen.**

revision [rɪ'vɪʒn] *BE /* *AE* **review** [rɪ'vjuː]

Wiederholung (von Unterrichtsstoff)

I should be doing some revision *BE / AE* review for the maths exam.

Ich müsste eigentlich noch etwas für die Matheprüfung wiederholen.

"Weltanschauung"
Weltanschauung

1 Religions and denominations
Religionen und Konfessionen

2 God and divinity
Gott und Göttlichkeit

3 Religious doctrines, practices, institutions
Religiöse Lehren, Bräuche, Institutionen

4 Nonreligious beliefs
Nichtreligiöse Überzeugungen

5 Philosophy
Philosophie

Weltanschauung ist eines von zahlreichen deutschen Wörtern, die ihren Weg in die englische Sprache gefunden haben – der Plural lautet *weltanschauungs* oder *weltanschauungen*.

Weitere Beispiele: *ablaut, abseil, affenpinscher, angst, auf Wiedersehen, aufgabe, Aufklärung, auslander, Auslese, autobahn, Bauhaus, Biedermeier, Bierstube, Bildungsroman, blitz, blitzkrieg, bratwurst, dachshund, Deutschmark, diktat, Ding an sich, doppelgänger, dreck, dummkopf, echt, ersatz, faltboat, Festschrift, flak, Fraktur, frankfurter, Fräulein, Führer, Gastarbeiter, gegenschein, Geisteswissenschaft, Gemeinschaft, gemütlich, Gemütlichkeit, Gesamtkunstwerk, Gesellschaft, gestalt, Gestapo, gesundheit, glockenspiel, Götterdämmerung, hausfrau, Heiligenschein, Heilsgeschichte, Heimweh, Heldentenor, Herrenvolk, hinterland, Jugendstil, kaffeeklatsch, kapellmeister, kaput, katzenjammer, kindergarten, kitsch, kraut, kriegspiel, krummholz, kümmel, lager, Lebensform, Lebenslust, Lebensraum, Lebensspur, Lebenswelt, leberwurst, Lebkuchen, lederhosen, leitmotif, lied, Luftwaffe, lumpenproletariat, mensch, Mensur, Methodenstreit, muesli, Mutti, poltergeist, pretzel, prosit, prost, putsch, rat(h)skeller, realpolitik, rinderpest, rucksack, sauerkraut, schadenfreude, schmaltz, schnap(p)s, schnauzer, schnitzel, Schupo, schuss, schwärmerei, Schweinerei, schwein(e)hund, Schwerpunkt, Schwung, sitz bath, Sitzfleisch, Sitz im Leben, sitzkrieg, Spätlese, spiel, Spielraum, Sprachgefühl, Sturm und Drang, Übermensch, U-boat, Vaterland, verboten, Verfremdung, Verfremdungseffekt, Völkerwanderung, völkisch, volkslied, waldhorn, Waldsterben, wanderlust, Wandervogel, Wehmut, Weinstube, Weisswurst, Weltbild, Weltgeist, weltschmerz, Wirtschaftswunder, Wirtshaus, wunderkind, zeitgeist, zugzwang.*

Religions and denominations
Religionen und Konfessionen

There is only one religion, though there are a hundred versions of it.
(*George Bernard Shaw, Irish writer, 1856–1950*)

religion [rɪˈlɪdʒən]
freedom of religion
He is English by birth but Greek Orthodox [ˈɔːθədɒks] by religion.

Religion
Religionsfreiheit
Von Geburt ist er Engländer, der Religion nach aber griechisch-orthodox.

religious [rɪˈlɪdʒəs]
religious beliefs [bɪˈliːfs]
a deeply religious person

religiös
religiöse Überzeugungen
ein (zu)tief(st) religiöser Mensch

Christianity [krɪstiˈænəti]
The cross is the symbol [ˈsɪmbl] of Christianity.

Christenheit
Das Kreuz ist das Symbol des Christentums.

Christian [ˈkrɪstʃən]
Christians believe that Jesus [ˈdʒiːzəs] is the Messiah [məˈsaɪə].
the early Christians

christlich; Christ(in)
Die Christen glauben, dass Jesus der Messias ist.
die Urchristen

Islam [ˈɪzlɑːm]
Adherents [ədˈhɪərənts] of Islam are called Muslims [ˈmʊzləmz].
Almsgiving [ˈɑːmzgɪvɪŋ] is one of the Five Pillars of Islam.

(der) Islam
Anhänger des Islam heißen Muslime.

Almosengeben ist eine der fünf Säulen des Islam.

Islamic [ɪzˈlæmɪk]
islamisch

Hinduism [ˈhɪnduɪzm]
The cow is revered [rɪˈvɪəd] in Hinduism.

(der) Hinduismus
Die Kuh wird im Hinduismus verehrt.

Hindu [ˈhɪnduː]
In a Hindu's eyes, everything is sacred [ˈseɪkrɪd].

hinduistisch; Hindu(-)
In den Augen eines Hindu ist alles heilig.

Buddhism [ˈbʊdɪzm]
Buddhism has spread [spred] in the West.

(der) Buddhismus
Der Buddhismus hat sich im Westen ausgebreitet.

Buddhist [ˈbʊdɪst]
buddhistisch; Buddhist(in)

Judaism [ˈdʒuːdeɪɪzm]
Judaism is the religion of the Jews.

(das) Judentum; (der) Judaismus
Der Judaismus ist die Religion der Juden.

Jew [dʒuː]
Jewish [ˈdʒuːɪʃ]
centres of Jewish culture [ˈkʌltʃə]
He's / She's Jewish.

Jude / Jüdin
jüdisch
Zentren jüdischer Kultur
Er ist Jude. / Sie ist Jüdin.

convert [kənˈvɜːt]
He converted to Roman Catholicism [kəˈθɒləsɪzm].

konvertieren; bekehren
Er konvertierte zum Katholizismus / trat zum katholischen Glauben über.

They were converted to Christianity [krɪstiˈænəti].

Sie wurden zum Christentum bekehrt.

Beachten Sie den Gebrauch des Artikels *a(n)*:
He's a Christian ['krɪstʃən] / *a Roman Catholic* ['kæθlɪk] / *a Protestant*
['prɒtɪstənt] / *a Jew* [dʒu:] / *etc.*
(= Er ist Christ / Katholik / Protestant / Jude / etc.)

denomination [dɪnɒmɪ'neɪʃn]	**Konfession; Glaubensgemeinschaft**
What denomination are you?	Welche Konfession haben Sie?
denominational school	Konfessions- / Bekenntnisschule
(Roman) Catholicism [kə'θɒləsɪzm]	(der) **Katholizismus**
In Poland, Roman Catholicism is the	In Polen ist der Katholizismus die
predominant [prɪ'dɒmɪnənt] religion.	vorherrschende Religion.
Roman Catholic [rəʊmən 'kæθlɪk]	**(römisch-)katholisch; Katholik(in)**
He was received [rɪ'si:vd] into the	Er wurde in die katholische Kirche
Roman Catholic church.	aufgenommen.
She became a (Roman) Catholic.	Sie wurde katholisch.
Protestantism ['prɒtɪstəntɪzm]	(der) **Protestantismus**
Luther(an)ism ['lu:θər(ən)ɪzm] is one	Das Luthertum ist eine der Haupt-
of the major branches of	richtungen des Protestantismus.
Protestantism.	
Protestant ['prɒtɪstənt]	**protestantisch; evangelisch**
Protestant churches ['tʃɜ:tʃɪz]	protestantische / evangelische
	Kirchen
He's / She's a Protestant.	Er / Sie ist Protestant(in) /
	evangelisch.
evangelical [i:væn'dʒelɪkl] Christians	**evangelikale** (= streng bibeltreue
	protestantische) Christen
Calvinism ['kælvənɪzm]	(der) **Kalvinismus**
Reformed [rɪ'fɔ:md] **churches**	**reformierte Kirchen**
Lutheran ['lu:θərən]	**lutherisch; Lutheraner(in)**
Lutheran churches	lutherische Kirchen
Baptist ['bæptɪst]	**Baptist(in)**
Methodist ['meθədɪst]	**methodistisch; Methodisten-**
She's a Methodist / Baptist.	Sie ist Methodistin / Baptistin.
Anglican ['æŋglɪkən]	**anglikanisch; Anglikaner(in)**
the Anglican Church	die anglikanische Kirche

Zur *Anglican Communion* [kə'mju:niən] (= anglikanischen Kirchengemein-
schaft) gehören u. a. *the Church of England, the Church in Wales, the Episcopal*
[ɪ'pɪskəpl] *Church in Scotland, the Church of Ireland* und in den USA *the Protestant Episcopal Church.* Alle zehn Jahre treffen sich die *Anglican bishops* ['bɪʃəps]
(= Bischöfe) zur *Lambeth Conference* [læmbəθ 'kɒnfrəns].

Presbyterian [prezbɪ'tɪəriən]	**presbyterianisch**
He's / She's a Presbyterian.	Er / Sie ist Presbyterianer(in).
Puritan ['pjʊərɪtən]	**puritanisch; Puritaner(in)**
Many Puritans emigrated ['emɪgreɪtɪd]	Viele Puritaner wanderten in die
to the New World.	Neue Welt aus.
the **Salvation Army** [sælveɪʃn 'ɑ:mi]	die **Heilsarmee**
Orthodox ['ɔ:θədɒks] (churches / Jews)	**orthodox**(e Kirchen / Juden)

God and divinity
Gott und Göttlichkeit

Everything is possible, even God. (*Ernest Renan, French philosopher, historian, and scholar of religion, 1823–1892*)

god [gɒd]
Fear God, and keep his command-ments [kəˈmɑːndmənts].
I believe in God the Father Almighty [ɔːlˈmaɪti], Maker of heaven [ˈhevn] and earth.
You shall have no other gods before me.
the Lord (God)
creator [kriˈeɪtə] / **maker**
the creator of the universe [ˈjuːnɪvɜːs]
Jesus Christ [dʒiːzəs ˈkraɪst]
our Lord Jesus Christ
the Messiah [məˈsaɪə]
the Holy [ˈhəʊli] **Spirit** / **Ghost**
the Holy Trinity [ˈtrɪnəti] (= Father, Son and Holy Spirit)

almighty [ɔːlˈmaɪti]
Let us pray to Almighty God / to the Almighty.
goddess [ˈgɒdes]
Artemis [ˈɑːtɪmɪs] was a Greek goddess.
Allah [ˈælə]
There is no God but Allah, and Muhammad [mʊˈhæməd] is his messenger.
the **Prophet Muhammad** [prɒfɪt mʊˈhæməd]
Vishnu and Shiva [ˈvɪʃnuː ənd ˈʃiːvə]
Vishnu and Shiva are the two principal [ˈprɪnsəpl] Hindu gods.
Krishna [ˈkrɪʃnə]
Buddha [ˈbʊdə]
Buddha means "the enlightened one".
Yahweh [ˈjɑːweɪ]
In the Jewish Bible, God was called YHWH, which was probably pronounced Yahweh.
deity [ˈdeɪəti]
Atheists [ˈeɪθiɪsts] deny the existence of a deity.
Jesus' humanity [hjuˈmænəti] and deity

Gott
Fürchte Gott und halte seine Gebote.

Ich glaube an Gott den Vater, den Allmächtigen, den Schöpfer des Himmels und der Erde.

Du sollst keine anderen Götter haben neben mir.
(Gott) der Herr
Schöpfer
der Schöpfer des Weltalls
Jesus Christus
unser Herr Jesus Christus
der Messias
der Heilige Geist
die Heilige Dreifaltigkeit / **Dreieinigkeit** (= Vater, Sohn und Heiliger Geist)

allmächtig
Lasst uns zum allmächtigen Gott / zum Allmächtigen beten.
Göttin
Artemis war eine griechische Göttin.
Allah (arabischer Name für Gott)
Es gibt keinen Gott außer Allah, und Mohammed ist sein Bote.

der **Prophet Mohammed**

Wischnu und Schiwa
Wischnu und Schiwa sind die beiden hinduistischen Hauptgötter.
Krischna (hinduistische Gottheit)
Buddha
Buddha heißt „der Erleuchtete".
Jahve / Jahwe
In der jüdischen Bibel hieß Gott YHWH, was wahrscheinlich Jahve ausgesprochen wurde.
Gottheit; Göttlichkeit
Atheisten leugnen die Existenz eines Gottes / einer Gottheit.
Jesu Menschlichkeit und Göttlichkeit

divine [dɪˈvaɪn]	göttlich
divine revelation [revəˈleɪʃn]	göttliche Offenbarung
by divine intervention [ɪntəˈvenʃn]	durch das Eingreifen / Einwirken Gottes
divinity [dɪˈvɪnəti]	**Göttlichkeit**
the divinity of Christ [kraɪst]	die Göttlichkeit Christi
believe in a **supreme** [suˈpriːm] **being**	an ein **höchstes Wesen** glauben
omnipotent [ɒmˈnɪpətənt]	**allmächtig**
omnipresent [ɒmnɪˈpreznt]	**allgegenwärtig**
omniscient [ɒmˈnɪsiənt]	**allwissend**
polytheism [ˈpɒliθiːɪzm]	**Polytheismus** (= Glaube an viele Götter)
monotheism [ˈmɒnəʊθiːɪzm]	**Monotheismus** (= Glaube an einen einzigen Gott)

"If only God hadn't made them so damned fast."

10

3 Religious doctrines, practices, institutions

Religiöse Lehren, Bräuche, Institutionen

There was never a century nor a country that was short of experts who knew the Deity's mind and were willing to reveal it.
(*Mark Twain, US writer, 1835–1910*)

doctrine ['dɒktrɪn]	**Lehre; Lehrmeinung; Grundsatz**
dogma ['dɒgmə]	**Dogma** (= kirchlicher Glaubenssatz)
exegesis [eksɪ'dʒiːsɪs]	**Exegese; (Bibel-)Auslegung**
theology [θi'ɒlədʒi]	**Theologie**
the Old / New Testament ['testəmənt]	**das Alte / Neue Testament**
the **parables** ['pærəblz] of Jesus	die **Gleichnisse** Jesu
the **gospel** ['gɒspl]	das **Evangelium**
psalm [sɑːm]	**Psalm**
heaven ['hevn]	(der) **Himmel**
ascend [ə'send] (in)to heaven	in den / zum Himmel auffahren
hell [hel]	(die) **Hölle**
angel ['eɪndʒəl]	**Engel**
saint [seɪnt]	**Heilige(r)**
St George [snt 'dʒɔːdʒ]	der heilige Georg / Sankt Georg
devil ['devl]	**Teufel**
the Ten Commandments [kə'mɑːndmənts]	**die Zehn Gebote**
the Resurrection [rezə'rekʃn]	**die Auferstehung** (Christi)
(original) **sin** [ərɪdʒənl 'sɪn]	(die) (Erb-)**Sünde**
a deadly / mortal ['mɔːtl] sin	eine Todsünde
church [tʃɜːtʃ]	**Kirche**
go to / attend [ə'tend] church	in die Kirche gehen
in / after church	in / nach der Kirche
cathedral [kə'θiːdrəl]	**Dom; Kathedrale**
attend a **service** ['sɜːvɪs]	an einem **Gottesdienst** teilnehmen
worship ['wɜːʃɪp]	**(am) Gottesdienst (teilnehmen)**
She regularly attended worship.	Sie ging regelmäßig zum Gottesdienst.

Christians worship in a church, Jews in a synagogue ['sɪnəgɒg], *and Muslims* ['mʊzlɪmz] *in a mosque* [mɒsk]. (= Christen halten Gottesdienst in einer Kirche, Juden in einer Synagoge und Muslime in einer Moschee.)

mass [mæs]	(die) **Messe**
go to / attend [ə'tend] mass	zur Messe gehen
preach [priːtʃ] – **preacher**	**predigen – Prediger(in)**
sermon ['sɜːmən] / **homily** ['hɒməli]	**Predigt**
the Sermon on the Mount [maʊnt]	die Bergpredigt

Religious doctrines, practices, institutions

altar [ˈɔːltə]	**Altar**
a **sacrament** [ˈsækrəmənt]	ein **Sakrament**
confession [kənˈfeʃn]	(die) **Beichte**
absolution [æbsəˈluːʃn]	**Absolution; Lossprechung** (von Sünden)
(Holy) Communion [kəˈmjuːniən]	die **(heilige) Kommunion**
the Last / the Lord's Supper	das **(heilige) Abendmahl**
prayer [preə]	**Gebet**
the Lord's Prayer [the lɔːdz ˈpreə]	das Vaterunser
the Creed [kriːd]	das **Glaubensbekenntnis**
amen [ɑːˈmen / eɪˈmen]	**amen; Amen**
christen [ˈkrɪsn] / **baptize** [bæpˈtaɪz]	**taufen**
He was christened / baptized Patrick.	Er wurde Patrick getauft.
confirmation [kɒnfəˈmeɪʃn]	**Konfirmation; Einsegnung; Firmung**
catechism [ˈkætəkɪzm]	**Katechismus**
congregation [kɒŋgrɪˈgeɪʃn]	**Gemeinde** (beim Gottesdienst)
parish [ˈpærɪʃ]	**(Kirchen-)Gemeinde**
parish council [pærɪʃ ˈkaʊnsl]	Gemeinderat
the clergy [ˈklɜːdʒi]	die **Geistlichkeit; der Klerus**
The clergy are against the law [lɔː].	Der Klerus ist gegen das Gesetz.

Pfarrer (→ S.122) hat im Englischen eine Vielzahl von Entsprechungen, u. a.:
(katholisch) *priest* [priːst] (= Priester)
(anglikanisch) *priest, minister* [ˈmɪnɪstə], *vicar* [ˈvɪkə], *rector* [ˈrektə], *pastor* [ˈpɑːstə]
(evangelisch) *pastor* [ˈpɑːstə], *minister, vicar*
(Krankenhaus- / Hochschul- / Militär- / Gefängnis-Pfarrer:) *chaplain* [ˈtʃæplɪn]
(allgemein) *clergyman* [ˈklɜːdʒimən] / *clergywoman* (= Geistlicher / Geistliche)

(arch)bishop [(ɑːtʃ)ˈbɪʃəp]	**(Erz-)Bischof**
cardinal [ˈkɑːdɪnl]	**Kardinal**
pope [pəʊp]	**Papst**
monk [mʌŋk] – **nun** [nʌn]	**Mönch – Nonne**
monastery [ˈmɒnəstri]	**(Mönchs-)Kloster**
Israel [ˈɪzreɪl]	**Israel**
the Torah [ˈtɔːrə]	die **Thora** (jüd. = die 5 Bücher Mose)
the Talmud [ˈtælmʊd]	der **Talmud** (= Sammelwerk der jüd. Lehre und Überlieferung)
temple [ˈtempl]	**Tempel**
rabbi [ˈræbaɪ]	**Rabbi(ner)**
kosher [ˈkəʊʃə]	**koscher**
circumcision [sɜːkəmˈsɪʒn]	**Beschneidung**
Sabbath [ˈsæbəθ]	**Sabbat**
the Koran [kɔːˈrɑːn]	der **Koran**
Ramadan [ræməˈdɑːn]	**Ramadan** (= islam. Fastenmonat)
fatwa [ˈfætwə]	**Fetwa** (= islam. Rechtsgutachten)
jihad [dʒɪˈhæd]	**Dschihad; Heiliger Krieg** (wörtl.: „eifernde Anstrengung für die Sache Gottes")
sharia [ʃəˈriːə] **(law)**	**Scharia(-Recht)** (= das religiöse Gesetz im Islam)
infidel [ˈɪnfɪdl]	**Ungläubige(r)**
fundamentalism [fʌndəˈmentəlɪzm]	**Fundamentalismus**

Nonreligious beliefs
Nichtreligiöse Überzeugungen

*The mystery of the beginning of all things is insoluble by us;
and I for one must be content to remain an agnostic.*
(*Charles Darwin, English scientist, 1809–1882*)

transcendent [træn'sendənt]	**transzendent** (= jenseits der sinnlichen Erfahrung liegend)
believe in the existence [ɪg'zɪstəns] of a transcendent being	an die Existenz eines transzendenten Wesens glauben
metaphysical [metə'fɪzɪkl]	**metaphysisch**
scepticism ['skeptɪsɪzm]	**Glaubenszweifel; Skeptizismus**
the sceptics of ancient ['eɪnʃnt] Greece	die Skeptiker des alten Griechenland
doubt [daʊt]	**zweifeln; Zweifel**
He doubts the existence of God.	Er bezweifelt die Existenz Gottes.
doubting Thomas [daʊtɪŋ 'tɒməs]	der ungläubige Thomas

 Jesus said to Thomas: "Be unbelieving no longer, but believe."

unbelief [ʌnbɪ'li:f]	(religiöser) **Unglaube**
reason ['ri:zn]	(die) **Vernunft**
Kant's critique [krɪ'ti:k] of pure reason	Kants Kritik der reinen Vernunft
rationalism ['ræʃnəlɪzm]	(der) **Rationalismus**
enlightenment [ɪn'laɪtnmənt]	**Aufklärung; Erleuchtung**
the Age of Enlightenment	das Zeitalter der Aufklärung
agnosticism – agnostic [æg'nɒstɪk]	**Agnostizismus – Agnostiker(in)**
atheism ['eɪθiɪzm] **– atheist**	**Atheismus – Atheist(in)**

 Question: Is there a God? – The believer's answer: Yes, there is. – The atheist's answer: No, there isn't. – The agnostic's answer: I don't know.

materialist [mə'tɪəriəlɪst]	**materialistisch; Materialist(in)**
a materialist view of the world	eine materialistische Weltsicht
nihilism ['naɪɪlɪzm] **– nihilist**	**Nihilismus – nihilistisch / Nihilist(in)**
anthroposophy [ænθrə'pɒzəfi]	**Anthroposophie**
superstition [su:pə'stɪʃn] **– superstitious** [su:pə'stɪʃəs]	**Aberglaube – abergläubisch**
esoteric [esə'terɪk]	**esoterisch** (= nur für Eingeweihte)
occult ['ɒkʌlt] **– the occult**	**okkult – das Okkulte**
New Age [nju: 'eɪdʒ]	**New Age** (= „neues Zeitalter")
meditation [medɪ'teɪʃn]	**Meditation**
astrology [ə'strɒlədʒi] **– astrologer**	**Astrologie – Astrologe / Astrologin**
horoscope ['hɒrəskəʊp]	**Horoskop**
fortunetelling – fortuneteller	**Wahrsagerei – Wahrsager(in)**
witch – witchcraft ['wɪtʃkrɑ:ft]	**Hexe – Hexerei**
sorcerer ['sɔ:sərə] **– sorcery**	**Zauberer – Zauberei**
(black / white) **magic** ['mædʒɪk]	(schwarze / weiße) **Magie**

Philosophy
Philosophie

Science is what you know, philosophy is what you don't know.
(*Bertrand Russell, English philosopher and mathematician, 1872–1970*)

philosophy [fə'lɒsəfi]	(die) **Philosophie**
ancient ['eɪnʃənt] philosophy	(die) antike Philosophie
linguistic [lɪŋ'gwɪstɪk] philosophy	(die) Sprachphilosophie
in Western philosophy	in der abendländischen Philosophie
philosophical [fɪlə'sɒfɪkl]	**philosophisch**
a philosophical problem / issue ['ɪʃuː]	ein philosophisches Problem / Thema
basic philosophical concepts ['kɒn-]	philosophische Grundbegriffe
philosopher [fə'lɒsəfə]	**Philosoph(in)**
philosophize [fə'lɒsəfaɪz] (about / on)	**philosophieren** (über)
think (– thought [ɔː] – thought)	**denken**
thinker – thinking	Denker(in) – (das) Denken
the Greek thinkers	die griechischen Denker
scientific [saɪən'tɪfɪk] thinking	(natur)wissenschaftliches Denken
Western thought	das abendländische Denken
understand (– understood – understood)	**verstehen**
understanding [ʌndə'stændɪŋ]	Verständnis
analysis [ə'næləsɪs] *Pl.* analyses [-siːz]	**Analyse**
analyse ['ænəlaɪz]	**analysieren**
define [dɪ'faɪn] – **definition** [defə'nɪʃn]	**definieren** – **Definition**
argument ['ɑːgjumənt] (for / against)	**Argument** (für / gegen)
develop a **theory** ['θɪəri]	eine **Theorie** entwickeln
consistent [kən'sɪstənt]	**konsistent; widerspruchsfrei**
a consistent theory	eine in sich stimmige Theorie
rational ['ræʃnəl]	**rational; vernunftmäßig**
explain something in rational terms	etwas auf rationale Weise erklären
idea [aɪ'dɪə]	**Idee**
The World [ɜː] as Will and Idea	Die Welt als Wille und Vorstellung
experience [ɪk'spɪəriəns]	(die) **Erfahrung**
experience shows that …	die Erfahrung lehrt, dass …
empirical [ɪm'pɪrɪkl]	**empirisch; erfahrungsmäßig**
empirical knowledge ['nɒlɪdʒ]	Erfahrungswissen
causality [kɔː'zæləti]	**Kausalität**
the law of causality	das Kausalgesetz
verify ['verɪfaɪ] – **verification**	**verifizieren** – **Verifikation**
falsify ['fɔːlsɪfaɪ] – **falsification**	**falsifizieren** – **Falsifikation**
logic ['lɒdʒɪk]	(die) **Logik**
the laws of logic	die Gesetze der Logik
logical ['lɒdʒɪkl]	**logisch; die Logik betreffend**
logical reasoning ['riːznɪŋ]	logisches Denken / Argumentieren
epistemology [ɪpɪstɪ'mɒlədʒi]	(die) **Epistemologie / Erkenntnislehre**
ontology [ɒn'tɒlədʒi]	(die) **Ontologie** (= Seinswissenschaft)

hermeneutics [hɜːməˈnjuːtɪks]
Hermeneutics is the art of interpretation.
ethics [ˈeθɪks]
It's a question of ethics.
aesthetics [iːsˈθetɪks]
Aesthetics is a branch of philosophy.

metaphysics [metəˈfɪzɪks]
the nature [ˈneɪtʃə] of metaphysics
Russell developed [dɪˈveləpt] a metaphysics of his own.
metaphysical [metəˈfɪzɪkl]
scholastic [skəˈlæstɪk]
the scholastics
dialectical [daɪəˈlektɪkl]
 materialism

(die) **Hermeneutik**
Die Hermeneutik ist die Kunst der Auslegung.
(die) **Ethik**
Das ist eine Frage der Ethik.
(die) **Ästhetik**
Die Ästhetik ist ein Teilgebiet der Philosophie.

(die) **Metaphysik**
das Wesen der Metaphysik
Russell entwickelte eine eigene Metaphysik.
metaphysisch
scholastisch
die Scholastiker
dialektischer Materialismus

Philosophische „Ismen": *exiˈstentialism* (= Existenzialismus) • *iˈdealism* (= Idealismus) • *maˈterialism* (= Materialismus) • *ˈpositivism* (= Positivismus) • *ˈpragmatism* (= Pragmatismus) • *ˈrationalism* (= Rationalismus) • *ˈrealism* (= Realismus) • *ˈscepticism* (= Skeptizismus)

„Ismen"-Adjektive: *exiˈstentialist* (= existenzialistisch) • *iˈdealist / ideaˈlistic* (= idealistisch) • *maˈterialist / materiaˈlistic* (= materialistisch) • *ˈpositivist* (= positivistisch) • *pragˈmatic* (= pragmatisch) • *ˈrationalist / rationaˈlistic* (= rationalistisch) • *reaˈlistic* (= realistisch) • *ˈsceptical* (= skeptisch)

Ahänger von „Ismen": *exiˈstentialist* (= Existenzialist/in) • *iˈdealist* (= Idealist/in) • *maˈterialist* (= Materialist/in) • *ˈpositivist* (= Positivist/in) • *ˈpragmatist* (= Pragmatiker/in) • *ˈrationalist* (= Rationalist/in) • *ˈrealist* (= Realist/in) • *ˈsceptic* [ˈskeptɪk] (= Skeptiker/in)

eclectic [ɪˈklektɪk]
Eclectics combine ideas from different sources [ˈsɔːsɪz] to form a new whole.
true [truː] – **truth** [truːθ]
the self [self]
Socrates' [ˈsɒkrətiːz] search for the self
thing-in-itself – things-in-themselves
appearance [əˈpɪərəns] **and reality**
cause and effect [ɪˈfekt]
mind [maɪnd] **and matter**
(the) **body** and (the) **mind**
time and space [speɪs]
the **beautiful** [ˈbjuːtəfl] and the **ugly**
good and evil [iːvl]
moral [ˈmɒrəl]
moral values / principles [ˈprɪnsəplz]

eklektisch; Eklektiker(in)
Eklektiker verbinden Ideen aus verschiedenen Quellen zu einem neuen Ganzen.
wahr – (die) **Wahrheit**
das Ich
Sokrates' Suche nach dem Ich
Ding an sich – Dinge an sich
Erscheinung und Wirklichkeit
Ursache und Wirkung
Geist und Materie
(der) **Körper** und (der) **Geist**
Zeit und Raum
das **Schöne** und das **Hässliche**
Gut und Böse
moralisch; sittlich; Moral-; Moral
moralische Werte / Grundsätze

Art and literature
Kunst und Literatur

11

1 **Painting and sculpture**
Malerei und Bildhauerei

2 **Graphic art**
Grafische Kunst

3 **Photography**
Fotografie

4 **Music and dance**
Musik und Tanz

5 **Theatre and cinema**
Theater und Film

6 **Architecture**
Architektur

7 **Literature**
Literatur

Painting and sculpture
Malerei und Bildhauerei

I paint objects as I think them, not as I see them.
(*Pablo Picasso, Spanish-born artist, 1881–1973*)

paint [peɪnt]	Farbe; malen
apply paint to a surface ['sɜːfɪs]	auf eine Fläche Farbe auftragen
paint a portrait ['pɔːtrət]	ein Porträt malen
painter ['peɪntə]	**Maler(in)**
painting ['peɪntɪŋ]	(die) **Malerei; Bild; Gemälde**
Painting is a wonderful hobby.	Malen ist ein herrliches Hobby.
The painting depicts a landscape.	Das Bild zeigt eine Landschaft.
picture ['pɪktʃə]	**Bild**
There are three women in the picture.	Auf dem Bild sind drei Frauen.
artist ['ɑːtɪst]	**Künstler(in)**
drawing ['drɔːɪŋ]	**Zeichnung**
do / make a drawing of something	eine Zeichnung von etwas anfertigen
draughtsman ['drɑːftsmən]	**Zeichner**
Picasso as (a) draughtsman	Picasso als Zeichner
draughtswoman ['drɑːftswʊmən]	**Zeichnerin**
watercolour ['wɔːtəkʌlə]	**Aquarell**
an exhibition of British watercolours	eine Ausstellung englischer Aquarelle
studio ['stjuːdiəʊ]	**Atelier**
out-of-doors, not in the studio	im Freien, nicht im Atelier
canvas ['kænvəs]	**Leinwand**
He works directly on the canvas.	Er malt direkt auf die Leinwand.
brush [brʌʃ]	**Pinsel**
with a few strokes of the brush	mit wenigen Pinselstrichen
oil(s) [ɔɪl(z)]	**Öl**
He usually ['juːʒəli] painted in oils.	Meistens malte er in Öl.
a large oil painting	ein großes Ölgemälde
subject (matter) ['sʌbdʒɪkt (mætə)]	**Gegenstand**
the subject (matter) of a painting	der Gegenstand eines Bildes
landscape ['lændskeɪp]	**Landschaft**
portrait ['pɔːtrət]	**Porträt; Bildnis**
She had her portrait painted.	Sie ließ sich porträtieren.
a self-portrait [self'pɔːtrət]	ein Selbstporträt / Selbstbildnis
still life [stɪl 'laɪf] *Pl.* still lifes	**Stillleben**
nude [njuːd]	**Akt**
nude painting	Aktmalerei
draw [drɔː] / paint from the nude	einen Akt zeichnen / malen
sitting / standing / reclining nude	sitzender / stehender / liegender Akt
arrangement [ə'reɪndʒmənt]	**Anordnung**
the arrangement of the figures ['fɪgəz]	die Anordnung der Personen
perspective [pə'spektɪv]	**Perspektive**
in / out of perspective	perspektivisch richtig / falsch
composition [kɒmpə'zɪʃn]	**Komposition**
the picture's perfect composition	die vollendete Komposition des Bildes
reproduction [riːprə'dʌkʃn]	**Reproduktion**

reproductions of famous paintings	Reproduktionen berühmter Bilder
a work of art [wɜːk əv 'ɑːt]	**ein Kunstwerk**
ancient ['eɪnʃənt] works of art	antike Kunstwerke
exhibit [ɪɡ'zɪbɪt]	**ausstellen; Ausstellungsstück**
the pictures exhibited here	die hier ausgestellten Bilder
exhibition [eksɪ'bɪʃn]	**Ausstellung**
(art) gallery ['ɡæləri]	**(Kunst-)Galerie**
the National Gallery [næʃnəl 'ɡæləri]	die Nationalgalerie
museum [mjuˈzɪəm]	**Museum**
the Museum of Modern Art	das Museum für moderne Kunst

Art movements ['muːvmənts] *and styles* (= **Kunstrichtungen und -stile**)
abstract ['æbstrækt] *art* (= abstrakte Kunst) • *art nouveau* [ɑːt nuːˈvəʊ] /
Jugendstil • *baroque* [bəˈrɒk] (= Barock) • *cubism* ['kjuːbɪzm] (= Kubismus) •
expressionism [ɪkˈspreʃənɪzm] (= Expressionismus) • *Gothic* ['ɡɒθɪk] *art*
(= gotische Kunst) • *impressionism* [ɪmˈpreʃənɪzm] (= Impressionismus) •
junk [dʒʌŋk] *art* • *neoclassicism* [niːəʊˈklæsɪsɪzm] (= Klassizismus) •
performance [pəˈfɔːməns] *art* • *pop art* • *realism* ['rɪəlɪzm] (= Realismus) •
Renaissance [rɪˈneɪsns] *art* • *representational* [reprɪzenˈteɪʃnəl] *art* (= gegen-
ständliche Kunst) • *Romanesque* [rəʊməˈnesk] *art* (= romanische Kunst) •
rococo [rəˈkəʊkəʊ] (= Rokoko) • *surrealism* [səˈrɪəlɪzm] (= Surrealismus)

Entsprechende Adjektive und Nomen:
expressionist / impressionist / realist / surrealist / Renaissance painters
junk / neoclassical / performance / pop / rococo artists
the expressionists / neoclassicists / realists / surrealists / cubists

sculpture ['skʌlptʃə]	**Skulptur; Plastik; Bildwerk; Bildhauerkunst; Bildhauerei**
a marble ['mɑːbl] sculpture	eine Marmorskulptur / -plastik
sculptures fashioned from ivory ['aɪvəri]	aus Elfenbein gearbeitete Plastiken
the history ['hɪstri] of sculpture	die Geschichte der Bildhauerei
a **sculptured** frieze [friːz]	ein **skulptierter** / **mit Skulpturen verzierter** Fries
a portrait bust **sculpted** by X	eine von X **geschaffene** Porträtbüste
sculptural ['skʌlptʃərəl]	**plastisch; bildhauerisch**
the sculptural works of Michelangelo	Michelangelos plastisches Werk
sculptor ['skʌlptə]	**Bildhauer(in)**
carve [kɑːv]	(*Holz*) **schnitzen;** (*Stein*) **meißeln**
stone carving	Steinskulptur / -plastik
wood carving	Holzschnitzerei
carved from limestone	aus Kalkstein gehauen / gearbeitet
a statuette **cast** in bronze [brɒnz]	eine in Bronze **gegossene** Statuette
a figurine **modelled** ['mɒdld] in clay	eine in Ton modellierte Figurine
a marble **statue** ['stætʃuː]	eine Marmor**statue**
a bronze **bust** [bʌst]	eine Bronze**büste**
a plaster ['plɑːstə] **figure**	eine Gips**figur**
relief [rɪ'liːf]	**Relief**
high / low relief	Hoch- / Flachrelief
mosaic [məʊˈzeɪɪk]	**Mosaik**
adorned [əˈdɔːnd] with marble **inlays**	mit Marmor**intarsien** verziert

Graphic art
Grafische Kunst

You use a glass mirror to see your face; you use works of art to see your soul.
(*George Bernard Shaw, Irish writer, 1856–1950*)

graphic art(s) / graphic design	(die) **Grafik** (= *grafisches Schaffen*)
Slevogt's graphic designs [dɪ'zaɪnz]	Slevogts Grafiken
after the artist's original designs	nach Originalentwürfen des Künstlers
graphic artist [græfɪk 'ɑːtɪst]	**Grafiker(in)** (*als Künstler*)
the graphic artist Käthe Kollwitz	die Grafikerin Käthe Kollwitz
commercial art [kəmɜːʃl 'ɑːt]	**Gebrauchs- / Werbegrafik**
commercial artist	**Gebrauchs- / Werbegrafiker(in)**
graphic designer [dɪ'zaɪnə]	**Grafikdesigner(in)**
book illustrations [ɪlə'streɪʃnz]	**Buchillustrationen**
printmaking ['prɪntmeɪkɪŋ]	**Druckgrafik**
plate [pleɪt]	**(Bild-)Tafel** (*in Buch*)
artwork ['ɑːtwɜːk]	(*Buch*) **Illustrationen, Bildmaterial**
poster ['pəʊstə]	**Plakat; Poster**
cartoon [kɑː'tuːn]	**Karikatur; Cartoon; Witzzeichnung**
Cartoons are humorous drawings.	Cartoons sind witzige Zeichnungen.
ink [ɪŋk]	**Tinte; Tusche; Druckfarbe**
drawing ['drɔːɪŋ]	**(Hand-)Zeichnung**
chalk [tʃɔːk] drawing	Kreidezeichnung
pen-and-ink drawing	Tuschzeichnung
engrave [ɪn'greɪv] – **engraver**	**(ein)gravieren – Graveur(in)**
engraving [ɪn'greɪvɪŋ]	(Kupfer- / Stahl-)Stich; Holzschnitt
woodcut ['wʊdkʌt] / wood engraving	Holzschnitt
copperplate print / engraving	Kupferstich
lithography [lɪ'θɒɡrəfi]	**Lithografie** (= *Verfahren*)
lithographer [lɪ'θɒɡrəfə]	Lithograf(in)
lithograph ['lɪθəɡrɑːf]	**Lithografie** (= *Kunstblatt*)
etching ['etʃɪŋ]	**Ätzung; Radierung**
Rembrandt as an etcher	Rembrandt als Radierer
linocut ['laɪnəʊkʌt]	**Linolschnitt**
facsimile [fæk'sɪməli]	**Faksimile**
collage ['kɒlɑːʒ]	**Collage**
monotone ['mɒnətəʊn] –	**einfarbig(es Bild) –**
duotone ['djuːətəʊn]	**zweifarbig(es Bild)**
screen [skriːn]	**Raster**
a 50-line screen	ein 50er-Raster
halftone ['hɑːftəʊn]	**Halbton- / Rasterbild**
(printing) block [('prɪntɪŋ) blɒk]	**Druckstock**
printing process ['prəʊses] /	**Druckverfahren**
method	
letterpress (printing) ['letəpres]	**Hochdruck** (= *Verfahren*)
offset (lithography / printing)	**Offset(druck)**
['ɒfset]	
gravure (printing) [ɡrə'vjʊə]	**Tiefdruck**

Photography
Fotografie

The camera is an instrument that teaches people how to see without a camera. (*Dorothea Lange, US photographer, 1895–1979*)

photography [fə'tɒgrəfi]
available-light photography

photographer [fə'tɒgrəfə]
photo(graph) ['fəʊtəʊ / 'fəʊtəgrɑːf]
mount / put photos in an album ['ælbəm]
photograph something ['fəʊtəgrɑːf]
She doesn't photograph very well.
photographic [fəʊtə'græfɪk]
my photographic equipment [ɪ'kwɪpmənt]
take pictures (– took – taken) ['pɪktʃəz]
snap(shot) ['snæpʃɒt]
take a few snaps / snapshots
This shot is overexposed [-ɪk'spəʊzd].
(colour / black-and-white) **prints**
standard ['stændəd] print
glossy ['glɒsi] (print)
flash [flæʃ]
I don't like to use flash.
a flash shot
camera ['kæmərə]
a fully automatic [ɔːtə'mætɪk] camera
disposable [dɪ'spəʊzəbl] **camera**
camera accessories [ək'sesəriz]
(camera) body
lens [lenz]
change [tʃeɪndʒ] the lens
mount / remove [rɪ'muːv] the lens
interchangeable [ɪntə'tʃeɪndʒəbl] lenses
telephoto lens [telifəʊtəʊ 'lenz]
wide-angle lens [waɪd æŋgl 'lenz]
single-lens reflex (camera) / SLR
lens cap [lenz 'kæp]
focal length [fəʊkl 'leŋθ]
zoom (button) [zuːm]
filter ['fɪltə]
load [ləʊd] **the film**
speed [spiːd]
the speed of the lens [lenz]
share photos online
image review [ɪmɪdʒ rɪ'vjuː]

(die) **Fotografie** (*Kunst / Verfahren*)
Fotografieren ohne Kunstlicht bei ungünstigen Lichtverhältnissen
Fotograf(in)
Foto(grafie); Aufnahme
Fotos in ein Album kleben / tun

etwas fotografieren
Sie ist nicht sehr fotogen.
fotografisch; Foto-
meine Fotoausrüstung

Aufnahmen machen

Schnappschuss
ein paar Schnappschüsse machen
Diese Aufnahme ist überbelichtet.
(Farb- / Schwarzweiß-)**Abzüge**
Standardvergrößerung
Hochglanzabzug / -vergrößerung
Blitz(licht)
Ich blitze nicht gern.
eine Blitzlichtaufnahme
Kamera; (Foto-)Apparat
eine vollautomatische Kamera
Einwegkamera; Wegwerfkamera
Kamerazubehör
(Kamera-)Gehäuse
Objektiv
das Objektiv wechseln
das Objektiv einsetzen / abnehmen
auswechselbare Objektive
Teleobjektiv
Weitwinkelobjektiv
einäugige Spiegelreflexkamera
Objektivkappe
Brennweite
Zoom(schalter)
Filter
den Film einlegen
Empfindlichkeit; Lichtstärke
die Lichtstärke des Objektivs
Fotos im Internet **teilen**
Bildbetrachtung

a **fast** lens [lenz]	ein **lichtstarkes** Objektiv
subject ['sʌbdʒɪkt]	**(Aufnahme-)Objekt / Motiv**
(view)finder ['vjuːfaɪndə]	**Sucher**
rangefinder ['reɪndʒfaɪndə]	**Entfernungsmesser**
focus ['fəʊkəs]	**die Entfernung einstellen**
Focusing is easy with this camera.	Die Scharfeinstellung ist bei dieser Kamera einfach.
The subject must be in focus / sharp.	Der Aufnahmegegenstand muss scharf sein.
The foreground is out of focus.	Der Vordergrund ist unscharf.
autofocus [ɔːtəʊ'fəʊkəs]	**Autofokus**
(in) **close-up** ['kləʊsʌp]	(in) **Nahaufnahme**
exposure (speed) [ɪk'spəʊʒə]	**Belichtung(szeit)**
exposure meter ['miːtə]	Belichtungsmesser
overexposure [əʊvərɪk'spəʊʒə]	Überbelichtung
Slides are best when they're slightly underexposed.	Dias sind am besten, wenn sie etwas unterbelichtet sind.
set the **shutter speed** ['ʃʌtə spiːd]	die **(Verschluss-)Zeit** einstellen
aperture ['æpətʃə]	**Blende(nöffnung)**
set the aperture	die Blende einstellen
set the aperture to 8	die Blende auf 8 stellen
depth of field [depθ əv 'fiːld]	**Tiefenschärfe; Schärfentiefe**
shutter / release (button) [rɪ'liːs]	**Auslöser**
Say cheese! / Smile please!	**Bitte recht freundlich!**
negative ['negətɪv]	**Negativ**
enlargement / blow-up ['bləʊʌp]	**Vergrößerung**
enlarge it [ɪn'lɑːdʒ] / **blow** it **up** to …	es auf … **vergrößern**
glossy [ɒ] **or matt** [mæt]?	**glänzend oder matt?**
colour slide / colour transparency [træns'pærənsi]	**Farbdia**
insert [ɪn'sɜːt] **a new battery**	**eine neue Batterie einsetzen**
accessories [ək'sesəriz]	**Zubehör**
ever-ready case [keɪs]	**Bereitschaftstasche**
digital ['dɪdʒɪtl] **camera**	**Digitalkamera; digitale Kamera**
sensor ['sensə]	**Sensor**
(mega)pixels [('megə)pɪkslz]	**(Mega-)Pixel**
a resolution of 3.2 megapixels	eine Auflösung von 3,2 Megapixeln
compress [kəm'pres] **an image** ['ɪmɪdʒ]	**ein Bild komprimieren**
compression [kəm'preʃn]	**Kompression; Komprimierung; Verdichtung**
store a picture / an image	ein Bild **speichern**
memory card ['meməri kɑːd]	**Speicherkarte**
image **editing** ['edɪtɪŋ]	**Bildbearbeitung**
photoshop ['fəʊtəʊʃɒp] a picture	ein Foto **mit Photoshop bearbeiten**
crop [krɒp] a photo	ein Foto **zuschneiden**
adjust [ə'dʒʌst] **brightness**	**die Helligkeit anpassen**
saturation [sætʃə'reɪʃn]	**Sättigung**
vibrance ['vaɪbrəns]	**Lebendigkeit**
frame rate ['freɪm reɪt]	**Bildfrequenz**
frames per second ['sekənd]	**Bilder pro Sekunde**

Music and dance
Musik und Tanz

People whose sensibility is destroyed by music in trains,
airports, lifts cannot concentrate on a Beethoven quartet.
(*Witold Lutoslawski, Polish composer, 1913–1994*)

music ['mjuːzɪk]	**Musik; Noten**
classical ['klæsɪkl] / light music	klassische / leichte Musik
I listen ['lɪsn] to music a lot.	Ich höre viel Musik.
Shall I put on some music?	Soll ich ein bisschen Musik auflegen?
a piece of music	ein Musikstück
Can you read music?	Kannst du Noten lesen?
musical ['mjuːzɪkl]	**musikalisch; Musik-; Musical**
musical instrument ['ɪnstrəmənt]	Musikinstrument
I'm not very musical.	Ich bin nicht sehr musikalisch.
musician [mjuˈzɪʃn]	**Musiker(in)**
muzak ['mjuːzæk]	**Musikberieselung** (*in Kaufhäusern etc.*)
sing (– sang – sung) – **singer** ['sɪŋə]	singen – Sänger(in)
singing ['sɪŋɪŋ]	**Singen; Gesang**
He takes singing lessons.	Er nimmt Gesangstunden.
I'm afraid I've a poor singing voice.	Leider kann ich nicht gut singen.
song [sɒŋ]	**Lied; Song; Chanson**

„**Text**": *the words of a song* (= der Text eines Liedes), *the lyrics* ['lɪrɪks] *of
a pop song* (= der Text eines Schlagers), *the libretto* [lɪˈbretəʊ] *of an opera*
['ɒprə] (= der Text einer Oper).

chorus ['kɔːrəs]	(*Oper, Oratorium*) **Chor; Refrain**
the final chorus of Beethoven's Ninth Symphony ['sɪmfəni]	der Schlusschor von Beethovens Neunter Sinfonie
(church / school) **choir** ['kwaɪə]	(Kirchen- / Schul-)**Chor**
soprano [səˈprɑːnəʊ] – **contralto** [kənˈtræltəʊ]	Sopran – Alt
tenor ['tenə] – **bass** [beɪs]	**Tenor – Bass**
tune [tjuːn] / **melody** ['melədi]	**Melodie**
You can sing it to the tune / melody of "Greensleeves".	Man kann es nach der Melodie von „Greensleeves" singen.
sing in tune / out of tune	richtig / falsch singen
The piano [piˈænəʊ] is out of tune.	Das Klavier ist verstimmt.
play (the piano / the violin [vaɪəˈlɪn])	(Klavier / Geige) **spielen**
He played it to me on the piano.	Er spielte es mir auf dem Klavier vor.
pianist ['pɪənɪst]	**Pianist(in)**
accompany [əˈkʌmpəni]	(instrumental) **begleiten**
He accompanied her on the piano.	Er begleitete sie auf dem Klavier.
composer [kəmˈpəʊzə]	**Komponist(in)**
composition [kɒmpəˈzɪʃn]	**Komposition; (das) Komponieren**
arrangement [əˈreɪndʒmənt]	**Arrangement; Bearbeitung**
orchestra ['ɔːkɪstrə]	**Orchester**
chamber ['tʃeɪmbə] orchestra / music	Kammerorchester / -musik

band [bænd]
brass band [brɑːs 'bænd]
conductor [kənˈdʌktə]
conduct [kənˈdʌkt] a concert
the Berlin Philharmonic [filɑːˈmɒnɪk]
  conducted by Sir Simon Rattle
concert [ˈkɒnsət]
We were at a concert.
concerto [kənˈtʃɜːtəʊ]
Beethoven's violin [vaɪəˈlɪn] concerto
sonata [səˈnɑːtə]
string quartet [strɪŋ kwɔːˈtet]
overture [ˈəʊvətjʊə]

Kapelle; Band
Blaskapelle
Dirigent(in)
ein Konzert **dirigieren**
die Berliner Philharmoniker unter
  der Leitung von Sir Simon Rattle
Konzert (= *Veranstaltung*)
Wir waren in einem Konzert.
Konzert (= *Komposition*)
Beethovens Violinkonzert
Sonate
Streichquartett
Ouvertüre

Notes (= Noten): *semibreve* [ˈsemibriːv] BE / AE *whole note* (= ganze Note) •
minim BE / AE *half note* (= halbe Note) • *crotchet* BE / AE *quarter note* (= Viertelnote) • *quaver* [eɪ] BE / AE *eighth note* (= Achtelnote).

a (whole / half) **tone** [təʊn]
pitch [pɪtʃ]
She has perfect pitch.
chord [kɔːd] – **harmony** [ˈhɑːməni]

ein (ganzer / halber) **Ton**
Tonhöhe / -lage; Stimmlage
Sie hat das absolute Gehör.
Akkord – Harmonie

„Takt": Takt als „Einheit" ist *bar*: *He just played the first few bars.* (= Er
spielte nur die ersten Takte.) Als rhythmisches Element ist Takt *time* oder
beat (= Taktschlag): *in three-four time* (= im Dreivierteltakt), *stay in time*
(= im Takt bleiben), *lose the beat* (= aus dem Takt kommen), *beat time*
(= den Takt schlagen). – Rhythmus ist *rhythm* [ˈrɪðm].

scale [skeɪl]
the scale of C
major [ˈmeɪdʒə] – **minor** [ˈmaɪnə]
in a major / minor key [kiː]

Tonleiter
die C-Dur-Tonleiter
Dur – Moll
in einer Dur- / Molltonart

Keys (= Tonarten): *C major* (= C-Dur) • *C minor* (= c-Moll) • *C sharp
minor* (= cis-Moll) • *E flat major* (= Es-Dur) • *F sharp minor* (= fis-Moll).
Dis / dis wäre entsprechend *D sharp*; Des / des dagegen *D flat*. Beachten
Sie besonders: *B flat major* (= B-Dur) – *B minor* (= h-Moll).

dance [dɑːns]
She loved dancing the waltz [wɔːls].
dance band – dance floor
dance studio / school
dancer [ˈdɑːnsə]
dancing [ˈdɑːnsɪŋ]
tap dancing – tap dancer
Sometimes we went dancing.
ballet [ˈbæleɪ]

Tanz(-); tanzen
Sie tanzte furchtbar gern Walzer.
Tanzkapelle – Tanzfläche
Tanzstudio / -schule
Tänzer(in)
Tanzen; Tanz-
Steppen – Stepptänzer(in)
Manchmal sind wir tanzen gegangen.
(das) **Ballett**

Theatre and cinema
Theater und Film

You need three things in the theatre – the play, the actors, and the audience, and each must give something. (*Kenneth Haigh, British actor, born in 1931*)

theatre [ˈθɪətə]   **Theater**
go to the theatre   ins Theater gehen

Als *fringe* [frɪndʒ] *theatre* (AE *off-off-Broadway theater*) bezeichnet man experimentelles, avantgardistisches Theater, das sich an ein jugendliches, oft studentisches Publikum wendet – deutsch Off-Theater.

cinema *BE* / *AE* **movie theater**   **Kino**
(film / movie [ˈmuːvi]) **star**   (Film-)**Star**
a film / movie starring / featuring   ein Film mit Hugh Grant (in der
  Hugh [hjuː] Grant   Hauptrolle)
film / **movie** / **motion picture**   **(Kino-)Film**
The film's still showing at the Plaza.   Im Plaza läuft der Film noch.
We went to the movies [ˈmuːviz].   Wir sind ins Kino gegangen.
feature film [ˈfiːtʃə fɪlm]   Spielfilm
filmgoer / moviegoer   Kinogänger(in)
the film / motion-picture industry   die Filmindustrie
the screen [skriːn]   **die Leinwand; der Film; das Kino**
adapt [əˈdæpt] a novel for the screen   einen Roman für den Film bearbeiten
write for the screen (– wrote – written)   für den Film / das Fernsehen
                                                   schreiben
screenplay / script [skrɪpt]   (*Film*) Drehbuch
screen a film / movie   einen Film zeigen / vorführen
dub [dʌb] a film / movie   einen Film **synchronisieren**
I'd rather watch a film with subtitles   Ich sehe mir lieber einen Film mit
  than one that's been dubbed.   Untertiteln an als einen, der
                                                   synchronisiert ist.

show [ʃəʊ]   **Show; Aufführung; Vorstellung**
We're going to a show tomorrow.   Morgen gehen wir in eine Show.
performance [pəˈfɔːməns]   **Aufführung; Vorstellung**
The performance was well attended.   Die Vorstellung war gut besucht.
the first night / first performance   die Uraufführung
premiere [ˈpremieə]   **Premiere; Ur- / Erstaufführung**
The premiere was a flop.   Die Uraufführung war ein Reinfall.
matinée [ˈmætɪneɪ]   **Matinee;** (*nachmittags*) **Frühvor-
                                                   stellung**
We've got tickets for the matinée.   Wir haben Karten für die Nachmit-
                                                   tagsvorstellung.

box office [ˈbɒks ɒfɪs]   **(Theater- / Kino-)Kasse**
seat [siːt]   **(Sitz-)Platz**
two seats in the front stalls [stɔːlz]   zwei Plätze vorne im Parkett
Are there any seats left for tonight?   Gibt's noch Karten für heute Abend?
row [rəʊ]   **Reihe**
What row are we in?   In welcher Reihe sitzen wir?

produce – production [prə'dʌkʃn]
a well-produced [prə'dju:st] play
(not) a very convincing production

inszenieren – Inszenierung
ein gut inszeniertes Stück
(k)eine sehr überzeugende
  Inszenierung

critically acclaimed [ə'kleɪmd]
director [də'rektə]
directed by Steven Spielberg
the stage [steɪdʒ]
She went on the stage.
the scenery ['si:nəri]
Scenery was limited to a few props.

von der Kritik hoch gelobt
(Film- / Theater-)Regisseur(in)
Regie Steven Spielberg
die Bühne; das Theater
Sie ging zur Bühne / zum Theater.
die Bühnendekoration / Kulissen
Das Bühnenbild beschränkte sich
  auf ein paar Requisiten.

costume ['kɒstju:m]
play [pleɪ]
the plays of Shakespeare ['ʃeɪkspɪə]
The play is set in post-war Rome.
What is the play about?
What film is playing at the Odeon?
playwright ['pleɪraɪt]
thriller ['θrɪlə]
Act 1, Scene 3 [si:n]
plot [plɒt]
The plot is as follows: ...
action ['ækʃn]
The action of the play takes place in ...
There's not much action in the play.
theme [θi:m]
character (in a play) ['kærəktə]
character actress ['æktrəs] / part
hero ['hɪərəʊ] – **villain** ['vɪlən]
monologue ['mɒnəlɒg] / **soliloquy**
Hamlet's famous soliloquy [sə'lɪləkwi]
actor ['æktə] – **actress** ['æktrəs]
the cast [kɑ:st]
Who's in the cast / in it?
part [pɑ:t]
play the part of the villain ['vɪlən]
act [ækt]
She acts the part convincingly [-'vɪns-].
The acting was excellent ['eksələnt].

Kostüm
spielen; (Theater-)Stück
die Dramen Shakespeares
Das Stück spielt im Nachkriegs-Rom.
Wovon handelt das Stück?
Was für ein Film läuft im Odeon?
Stückeschreiber(in); Dramatiker(in)
(Buch / Film) Thriller, Krimi, Reißer
1. Akt, 3. Szene / Auftritt
Handlung
Die Handlung ist folgendermaßen: ...
Handlung; Action
Das Stück spielt in ...
In dem Stück passiert nicht viel.
Thema
(handelnde) Person (in einem Stück)
Charakterdarstellerin / -rolle
Held – Schurke
Monolog
Hamlets berühmter Monolog
Schauspieler – Schauspielerin
die Besetzung / Mitwirkenden
Wer spielt mit?
Rolle
die Rolle des Schurken spielen
(eine Rolle) spielen; schauspielern
Sie spielt die Rolle überzeugend.
Man sah hervorragende schauspie-
  lerische Leistungen.

the audience ['ɔ:diəns]
The audience was / were enthusiastic.
applause [ə'plɔ:z]
critic ['krɪtɪk]
a review [rɪ'vju:]
hit [hɪt] – **flop** [flɒp]
a smash hit – a total ['təʊtl] flop
an Academy Award [əkædəmi
  ə'wɔ:d] / **an Oscar**
He won [ʌ] / received an Oscar for ...

das Publikum; die Zuschauer
Das Publikum war begeistert.
Applaus; Beifall; Klatschen
(Theater- / Film-)Kritiker(in)
eine Kritik / Besprechung
Erfolg – Reinfall
ein Riesenerfolg – ein totaler Reinfall
ein Oscar (Filmpreis)

Er bekam / erhielt einen Oscar für ...

Architecture
Architektur

The physician can bury his mistakes, but the architect can only advise his client to plant vines. *(Frank Lloyd Wright, US architect, 1867–1959)*

architect ['ɑːkɪtekt]	**Architekt(in)**
the (architect's) **client** ['klaɪənt]	der / die **Bauherr(in)**
architecture ['ɑːkɪtektʃə]	(die) **Architektur**
architectural [ɑːkɪ'tektʃərəl]	**architektonisch**
architectural style [staɪl]	Baustil

Styles of architecture (= **Baustile**)
art deco [ɑːt 'dekəʊ] • *art nouveau* [ɑːt nuːˈvəʊ] (= Jugendstil) • *baroque* [bəˈrɒk] (= Barock) • *Bauhaus* ['baʊhaʊs] • *Colonial* [kəˈləʊniəl] (= amerik. Kolonialstil des 17.–18. Jahrhunderts) • *Edwardian* [edˈwɔːdiən] (= aus der Regierungszeit Edward VII., 1901–10) • *Georgian* ['dʒɔːdʒən] (= aus der Regierungszeit George I., II., III., IV., 1714–1830) • *Gothic* ['gɒθɪk] (= gotisch) • *Gothic Revival* [rɪˈvaɪvl] / *neo-Gothic* [niːəʊˈgɒθɪk] (= neugotisch) • *neoclassical* [niːəʊˈklæsɪkl] (= klassizistisch) • *postmodern* [pəʊstˈmɒdn] (= spätes 20. Jahrhundert) • *Regency* ['riːdʒənsi] (= Regencystil 1811–20) • *Renaissance* [rɪˈneɪsns] • *Romanesque* [rəʊməˈnesk] (= romanisch) • *Tudor* ['tjuːdə] (= Tudorstil 1485–1558) • *Victorian* [vɪkˈtɔːriən] (= aus der Regierungszeit Victorias, 1837–1901)

design [dɪˈzaɪn]	**Entwurf; Gestaltung; entwerfen**
the designs for the new building	die Entwürfe für das neue Gebäude
Wright designed the Guggenheim [ʊ] Museum in New York.	Wright entwarf / gestaltete / schuf das Guggenheim Museum in New York.
win a competition (– won – won) [kɒmpəˈtɪʃn]	**einen Wettbewerb gewinnen**
planning ['plænɪŋ]	(die) **Planung**
in / at the planning stage [steɪdʒ]	im Planungsstadium
planning permission [pəˈmɪʃn]	(die) **Baugenehmigung**
Planning permission was granted [ɑː].	Die Baugenehmigung wurde erteilt.
the planners ['plænəz]	**die Planer**
blueprint ['bluːprɪnt]	**Plan; Entwurf**
ground plan ['graʊnd plæn]	**Grundriss**
build [bɪld] (– built [bɪlt] – built)	**bauen**
building ['bɪldɪŋ]	**Gebäude; Bau(-); (das) Bauen**
building materials [məˈtɪəriəlz]	Baumaterialien / -stoffe
building operations [ɒpəˈreɪʃnz]	Baumaßnahmen
building / construction work [wɜːk]	Bauarbeiten
the building plans [plænz]	die Baupläne
building site [saɪt]	Baustelle
(master) builder ['bɪldə]	**Baumeister**
construct [kənˈstrʌkt] – **construction**	**bauen – Bau**
(the) construction of the bridge	der Bau / das Bauen der Brücke
the construction industry ['ɪndəstri]	die Bauindustrie

construction time [kən'strʌkʃn]	(die) Bauzeit
The building is still under construction.	Das Gebäude ist noch in Bau.
steel skeleton ['skelɪtn] construction	Stahlskelettbauweise
structural ['strʌktʃərəl]	**Bau-; baulich; statisch**
The building is structurally sound.	Die Bausubstanz ist in Ordnung.
(property) developer [dɪ'veləpə]	(*etwa*) **Grundstücksspekulant(in)**
(building) contractor [kən'træktə]	**Bauunternehmer / -unternehmung**
house [haʊs] *Pl.* houses ['haʊzɪz]	**Haus**
facade [fə'sɑ:d]	**Fassade**
wall [wɔ:l]	**Wand; Mauer**
window ['wɪndəʊ]	**Fenster**
masonry ['meɪsnri]	**Mauerwerk**
brick [brɪk]	**Ziegelstein; Backstein**
stone – **stucco** ['stʌkəʊ] – **glass**	**Stein** – **Stuck** – **Glas**
mortar ['mɔ:tə]	**Mörtel**
(reinforced) concrete [(ri:ɪnfɔ:st) 'kɒŋkri:t]	**(Stahl-)Beton**
prefabricated [pri:'fæbrɪkeɪtɪd]	**in Fertigbauweise errichtet**
tower ['taʊə]	**Turm**
tower block ['taʊə blɒk] *BE*	Hochhaus
(triumphal) **arch** [(traɪʌmfl) 'ɑ:tʃ]	(Triumph-)**Bogen**
(Corinthian / Doric) **column** [(kə'rɪnθiən / 'dɒrɪk) 'kɒləm]	(korinthische / dorische) **Säule**
pillar ['pɪlə]	**Pfeiler; Stütze**

Church architecture (= **Kirchenarchitektur**)
nave (= Haupt- / Mittel- / Längsschiff) • *transept* ['trænsept] (= Querschiff) •
chancel ['tʃɑ:nsl] (= Altarraum / Chor) • *aisle* [aɪl] (= Seitenschiff) • *dome*
(= Kuppel) • *steeple* (= spitzer Kirchturm) • *spire* (= Turmspitze)

"It was designed by a famous architect."

Literature
Literatur

Great literature is simply language charged with meaning to the utmost possible degree. (*Ezra Pound, US poet, 1885–1972*)

literature ['lɪtrətʃə]	(die) **Literatur**
literary ['lɪtərəri]	**literarisch**
literary criticism ['krɪtɪsɪzm]	Literaturkritik / -wissenschaft
literary history / history of literature	Literaturgeschichte
literary genre [lɪtərəri 'ʒɑːnrə]	Literaturgattung
narrative ['nærətɪv]	**erzählend; Erzähl-; Erzählung**
first-person narrator [nə'reɪtə]	Ich-Erzähler(in)
fiction ['fɪkʃn]	**Erzähl- / Romanliteratur; Belletristik**

Kinds of fiction (= **Arten von Erzählliteratur**)

novel [ɒ] (= Roman) • *historical novel* (= historischer Roman) • *Gothic* [ɒ] *novel* (= Schauerroman) • *detective novel* (= Kriminalroman) • *detective story* (= Detektivgeschichte) • *whodunit* [huː'dʌnɪt] (= Krimi) • *thriller / cliffhanger* (= Thriller) • *novella* [nə'velə] (= Novelle) • *short story* [ʃɔːt 'stɔːri] (= Kurzgeschichte) • *short short story* • *anecdote* ['ænɪkdəʊt] (= Anekdote) • *light fiction* (= Trivialliteratur) • *science fiction* (= wissenschaftlich-utopische Literatur) • *pulp fiction* (= Schundliteratur) • *pulp novel* (= Schundroman) • *penny dreadful* BE (= Groschenheft) • *fantasy* ['fæntəsi] *novel* (= Fantasy-Roman)

fairy tale – folk tale ['fəʊk teɪl]	**Märchen**
Grimm's fairy tales ['feəri teɪlz]	Grimms Märchen
legend ['ledʒənd]	**Legende; Sage**
biography [baɪ'ɒgrəfi]	**Biografie; Lebensbeschreibung**
autobiography [ɔːtəbaɪ'ɒgrəfi]	Autobiografie
biographer [baɪ'ɒgrəfə]	Biograf(in)
(auto)biographical [(ɔːtə)baɪə'græfɪkl]	(auto)biografisch
diary ['daɪəri]	**Tagebuch**
an **essay** on … ['eseɪ]	ein **Essay** über …
drama ['drɑːmə]	(das) **Drama**
the development of modern drama	die Entwicklung des modernen Dramas
comedy ['kɒmədi] – **tragedy** ['trædʒ-]	**Komödie – Tragödie**
comic ['kɒmɪk] – tragic ['trædʒɪk]	komisch – tragisch
comic relief [kɒmɪk rɪ'liːf]	befreiende Komik
satire ['sætaɪə] – **satirical** [sə'tɪrɪkl]	**Satire – satirisch**
parody ['pærədi]	**Parodie**
prose [prəʊz]	(die) **Prosa; Prosa-**
lyric poet [lɪrɪk 'pəʊɪt] – **lyric poetry**	**Lyriker(in) – (die) Lyrik**
poetry ['pəʊətri]	(die) **Lyrik / (Vers-)Dichtung**
an anthology [æn'θɒlədʒi] of modern poetry	eine Anthologie moderner Lyrik
epic ['epɪk]	**Epos; episch**
epic poetry [epɪk 'pəʊətri]	(die) Epik

Kinds of poetry (= Arten von Lyrik)
poem (= Gedicht) • *occasional poem* (= Gelegenheitsgedicht) • *ballad* ['bæləd] (= Ballade) • *sonnet* ['sɒnɪt] (= Sonett) • *limerick* ['lɪmərɪk] (= witziges fünfzeiliges Gedicht, Reimschema aabba)

refrain [rɪ'freɪn] / **chorus** ['kɔːrəs]	Refrain
verse [vɜːs]	Vers; Strophe; Gedichte; Poesie
written in verse	in Versform
(the first / final) **stanza** ['stænzə]	(die erste / letzte) **Strophe**
rhyme [raɪm]	Reim; (sich) reimen
"Kind" rhymes with "find".	„Kind" reimt sich auf „find".
rhyme scheme [skiːm] / **pattern**	Reimschema
metre ['miːtə]	Metrum; Versmaß
poet ['pəʊɪt] – **poetic** [pəʊ'etɪk]	Dichter(in) – dichterisch / poetisch
Poet Laureate *BE*	Hofdichter(in)
writer ['raɪtə]	Schriftsteller(in)
author ['ɔːθə]	Autor(in); Verfasser(in)
novelist ['nɒvəlɪst]	Romanautor(in)
interpretation [ɪntɜːprɪ'teɪʃn]	Interpretation; Auslegung
interpret [ɪn'tɜːprɪt] a text	einen Text interpretieren
content ['kɒntent] **and form**	Inhalt und Form
(deep) structure ['strʌktʃə]	(Tiefen-)Struktur
plot – **subplot** ['sʌbplɒt]	Handlung – Nebenhandlung
setting ['setɪŋ]	Schauplatz; Zeit und Ort der Handlung
atmosphere ['ætməsfɪə]	Atmosphäre
local colour [ləʊkl 'kʌlə]	Lokalkolorit
point of view [pɔɪnt əv 'vjuː]	Erzählperspektive
stage directions ['steɪdʒ dərekʃnz]	Bühnenanweisungen
flashback ['flæʃbæk]	Rückblende
suspense [sə'spens]	Spannung
climax ['klaɪmæks]	Höhepunkt
surprise [sə'praɪz] **ending**	überraschender Schluss
a **rhetorical device** [rɪtɒrɪkl dɪ'vaɪs]	ein rhetorisches Mittel
imagery ['ɪmɪdʒəri]	Bilder(sprache); Metaphorik
metaphor ['metəfə]	Metapher
use a word metaphorically [-'fɒrɪkli]	ein Wort metaphorisch gebrauchen
irony ['aɪrəni]	(die) Ironie
pun [pʌn]	(ein) Wortspiel (machen)
bowdlerize ['baʊdləraɪz] a book	ein Buch von (angeblich) anstößigen Stellen befreien
plagiarize ['pleɪdʒə-] – **plagiarism**	plagiieren – Plagiat
He's been accused of plagiarism.	Man hat ihn des Plagiats beschuldigt.
romantic [rəʊ'mæntɪk]	romantisch; Romantiker(in)

Literary -isms (= literarische „Ismen")
romanticism [-'mæn-] (= Romantik) • *realism* (= Realismus) • *naturalism* (= Naturalismus) • *expressionism* [ɪk'spreʃənɪzm] (= Expressionismus)

Leisure and recreation
Freizeit und Erholung

1   **Holidays**
    Feiertage und Urlaub

2   **Festive occasions**
    Festliche Anlässe

3   **Socializing**
    Gesellschaftlicher Umgang

4   **Entertainments**
    Vergnügungen

5   **Travel and tourism**
    Reisen und Tourismus

6   **Accommodation**
    Unterkunft

7   **Shopping**
    Einkaufen

8   **Sports**
    Sport

9   **Hobbies**
    Hobbys

10 **Drinking and smoking**
    Trinken und Rauchen

Social media

Holidays
Feiertage und Urlaub

Term, holidays, term, holidays, till we leave school, and then work, work, work till we die. (C.S. Lewis, British writer, 1898–1963)

holiday ['hɒlədeɪ]
bank holiday *BE* / *AE* legal [iː] holiday
Good Friday is a public holiday.

Are you here on business ['bɪznəs]? – No, on holiday.
holidays ['hɒlədeɪz] *Pl.*
What are you doing in the summer holidays?
vacation [vəˈkeɪʃn]
Dr Gore is on vacation.
The summer vacation starts on July 28.

leave [liːv]
Captain Brown is on leave.
She's been on sick leave for two weeks.

break [breɪk]
I think we ought [ɔːt] to have / take a break.
They've gone [gɒn] away for a weekend break.
The children are still at break.
have time off [taɪm ˈɒf]
I'm going to take some time off.
Why don't you take a day off?

We were given a day off from school.
weekend [wiːkˈend]
We usually meet at the / *AE auch* on the weekend.
We're going to be away for the weekend.

Feiertag; Urlaub
(gesetzlicher) Feiertag
Karfreitag ist ein (gesetzlicher) Feiertag.
Sind Sie geschäftlich hier? – Nein, auf Urlaub.
BE **Ferien**
Was machst du in den Sommerferien?

AE **Urlaub / Ferien**
Herr Dr. Gore ist auf / in Urlaub.
Die Sommerferien beginnen am 28. Juli.
Urlaub
Hauptmann Brown ist auf Urlaub.
Sie ist seit zwei Wochen krankgeschrieben.
Pause; Unterbrechung
Ich denke, wir sollten mal (eine) Pause machen.
Sie sind übers Wochenende verreist.

Die Kinder sind noch in der Pause.
frei haben
Ich werde mir etwas frei nehmen.
Warum nehmen Sie sich nicht einen Tag frei?
Wir bekamen einen Tag schulfrei.
Wochenende
Meist sehen wir uns am Wochenende.
Wir sind übers Wochenende weg / verreist.

Important [ɪmˈpɔːtnt] *holidays* (= **wichtige Feiertage**)
New Year's Eve [iːv] (= Silvester), *New Year's Day* (= Neujahr)
Easter (= Ostern): *Good Friday* (= Karfreitag), *Easter Sunday* (= Ostersonntag), *Easter Monday* (= Ostermontag)
May Day (= Maifeiertag – 1. Mai) / *AE Labor* ['leɪbə] *Day* (= Tag der Arbeit – erster Montag im September)
Whitsun ['wɪtsn] (= Pfingsten): *Whit Sunday* (= Pfingstsonntag), *Whit Monday* (= Pfingstmontag)
Independence [ɪndɪˈpendəns] *Day AE* (= Unabhängigkeitstag – 4. Juli, bedeutendster nationaler Feiertag der USA)

Election [ɪˈlekʃn] *Day* AE (= Wahltag – erster Dienstag nach dem ersten
  Montag im November; an diesem Tag finden in den USA in jedem
  geraden Jahr Wahlen zum Kongress und in jedem zweiten geraden Jahr
  Präsidentschaftswahlen statt)
Thanksgiving Day AE (= Erntedanktag – am 4. Donnerstag im November)
Christmas [ˈkrɪsməs] (= Weihnachten): *Christmas Eve* (= Heiligabend),
  Christmas Day (= 1. Weihnachtstag), *Boxing Day* BE (= 1. Wochentag
  nach *Christmas Day*)
→ Seite 236: *Poppy Day* / *Remembrance Day*

Christmas [ˈkrɪsməs]	**Weihnachten**; (das) **Weihnachtsfest**
Merry / Happy Christmas!	Frohe / Fröhliche Weihnachten!
We wish you a merry / happy Christmas.	Wir wünschen euch ein frohes / schönes Weihnachtsfest.
Did you have a good / nice Christmas?	Hattet ihr schöne Weihnachten?
What did you get for Christmas?	Was hast du zu Weihnachten bekommen?

"Why don't you take a day off?"

Festive occasions
Festliche Anlässe

That everyone should eat and drink and enjoy himself,
in return for all his labours, is a gift of God. (*The Bible*)

celebration [selə'breɪʃn]
The victory was cause for celebration.
Weddings are marked by celebration.

Feier; Feierlichkeit
Der Sieg war Grund zum Feiern.
Hochzeiten werden feierlich begangen.

celebrate ['seləbreɪt]
celebrate a birthday / an anniversary
ceremony ['serəməni]
the opening ceremony
the wedding ceremony

feiern; begehen
einen Geburtstag / ein Jubiläum feiern
Zeremonie; Feier
die Eröffnungsfeier
die feierliche Trauung / Trauzeremonie

festivity [fe'stɪvəti]
public and private festivities
festival ['festɪvl]
the Berlin Film Festival
an international sports festival
feast [fiːst]
a wedding feast
carnival ['kɑːnɪvl]
Rio was celebrating carnival just then.
parade [pə'reɪd]
victory parade – farewell parade
a ticker-tape parade
birthday ['bɜːθdeɪ]
He had a birthday yesterday.
What are you giving her for her
birthday?
Many happy returns (of the day)!

Feier
öffentliche und private Festlichkeiten
Fest(ival); Festspiele; Festwoche(n)
die Berliner Filmfestspiele
ein internationales Sportfest
Festessen; Festmahl
ein Hochzeitsmahl
Volksfest; Karneval
Rio feierte damals gerade Karneval.
Parade; Umzug
Siegesparade – Abschiedsparade
eine Konfettiparade
Geburtstag
Er hatte gestern Geburtstag.
Was schenkst du ihr zum Geburtstag?

Herzlichen Glückwunsch zum
Geburtstag!

anniversary [ænɪ'vɜːsri]
We're celebrating our fiftieth
anniversary.
on their tenth wedding anniversary
the tenth anniversary of her death
jubilee ['dʒuːbɪliː]
Queen Elizabeth's Silver Jubilee in 1977

Jahrestag
Wir feiern unser fünfzigjähriges
Jubiläum / Bestehen.
an / zu ihrem zehnten Hochzeitstag
ihr zehnter Todestag
Jubiläum
Königin Elisabeths silbernes Thronjubiläum 1977

silver wedding – golden wedding
They've just celebrated their golden
wedding.
a red-letter day [red 'letə deɪ]
The day we moved into our own
home was a red-letter day for us.

Silberhochzeit – Goldhochzeit
Sie haben gerade ihre goldene
Hochzeit gefeiert.
ein besonderer Tag
Der Tag, an dem wir ins eigene Heim
einzogen, war ein besonderer Tag
für uns.

Socializing
Gesellschaftlicher Umgang

Show me your company, and I'll tell you who you are. (*Proverb*)

company ['kʌmpəni]
Her niece [niːs] keeps her company.
the people he keeps company with
She's good company.

Oh, you're expecting company?
visit ['vɪzɪt]
We were planning to pay you a visit.
We had a visit from him last summer.

I'm going on a visit to Brighton.
She regularly visits her old aunt.

call on [kɔːl]
May I call on you the next time I'm in town?
get together [get tə'geðə]
get-together ['get təgeðə]
We have a get-together every two weeks.
meet up with sb. [miːt 'ʌp]
go out [gəʊ 'aʊt]

I feel like going out.
go out with someone
He used to ['juːstə] go out with her.
date [deɪt]
I have a date with Bill.
The girls were talking about their dates.
Is she still dating him? *AE*
party ['pɑːti]
give / have / throw [θrəʊ] a party
gatecrash a party
They had a big party to celebrate ['seləbreɪt] the win.
Were you at June's New Year's party?
In London we did a lot of partying.
housewarming (party)
reunion [riːˈjuːnɪən]
class / family reunion
dance [dɑːns]
There's a dance at the club tonight.
May I have the next dance?

Gesellschaft; Umgang
Ihre Nichte leistet ihr Gesellschaft.
die Leute, mit denen er verkehrt
Es ist schön, mit ihr zusammen zu sein.

Ach, du erwartest wohl Besuch?
Besuch; besuchen
Wir hatten vor, dich zu besuchen.
Er war vorigen Sommer bei uns zu Besuch.
Ich fahre nach Brighton zu Besuch.
Sie besucht regelmäßig ihre alte Tante.

besuchen; aufsuchen
Darf ich Sie aufsuchen, wenn ich das nächste Mal in der Stadt bin?
zusammenkommen; sich treffen
Zusammenkunft; Treffen
Wir treffen uns alle vierzehn Tage.

sich mit jemand **treffen**
ausgehen, weggehen (zum Vergnügen)
Mir ist nach Ausgehen zumute.
mit jemand (aus)gehen
Sie war mal seine Freundin.
Verabredung; *AE auch* **Freund(in)**
Ich bin mit Bill verabredet.
Die Mädchen unterhielten sich über ihre Freunde.
Geht sie noch mit ihm?
Party
eine Party geben / machen
uneingeladen zu einer Party kommen
Sie feierten den Sieg mit einer großen Party.
Warst du auf Junes Silvesterparty?
In London waren wir viel auf Partys.
Einzugsparty
Treffen; Zusammenkunft
Klassen- / Familientreffen
Tanzveranstaltung / -abend / -party
Im Klub wird heute Abend getanzt.
Darf ich (Sie um den nächsten Tanz) bitten?

ball [bɔːl]
have / organize ['ɔːgənaɪz] a ball
We're going to a ball tonight.

Ball
einen Ball veranstalten
Wir gehen heute Abend auf einen
Ball.

reception [rɪ'sepʃn]
a reception in honour of the president

attend [ə'tend] a reception
host [həʊst] – **hostess** ['həʊstəs]
hospitality [hɒsprɪ'tælətɪ]
We appreciate [ə'priːʃieɪt] your
hospitality.
entertain [entə'teɪn]
We often entertain people to dinner.
They do a lot of entertaining.
guest [gest]
We have invited [ɪn'vaɪtɪd] six guests.
The guest of honour is served first.
If you want to use my phone, be my
guest.
toast [təʊst]
They drank a toast to the bride and
groom.

Empfang
ein Empfang zu Ehren des
Präsidenten
an einem Empfang teilnehmen
Gastgeber – Gastgeberin
Gastfreundschaft
Wir sind Ihnen für Ihre Gastfreund-
schaft dankbar.
bewirten; einladen
Wir haben oft Gäste zum Essen.
Sie haben häufig Gäste.
Gast
Wir haben sechs Gäste eingeladen.
Der Ehrengast wird zuerst bedient.
Wenn Sie mein Telefon benutzen
wollen – bitte!
Toast; Trinkspruch
Man trank (einen Toast) auf das
Brautpaar.

Common ['kɒmən] **toasts** (= gebräuchliche Trinksprüche)
Health! [helθ] / *Your health!* / *To your health!* (= Auf Ihr / dein Wohl!)
Cheers! [tʃɪəz] (= Prost! / Prosit! / Zum Wohl!)
Here's to you! / *Here's looking at you!* (= Auf dein Wohl!)
Here's to our collaboration [kəlæbə'reɪʃn] / *your new job!* (= Auf unsere
Zusammenarbeit / deinen neuen Job!)

"May I have the next dance?"

Entertainments
Vergnügungen

→ 11.5 Theatre and cinema

Hell is populated with the victims of harmless amusements. (*Proverb*)

circus ['sɜːkəs]	**Zirkus**
Every circus has a clown [klaʊn].	Jeder Zirkus hat einen Clown.
busker ['bʌskə]	**Straßenmusikant(in)**
Busking prohibited [prə'hɪbɪtɪd]	Musizieren verboten
band [bænd]	**Kapelle; Band**
They've got a live [laɪv] band there.	Die haben da eine richtige Kapelle.
dance [dɑːns]	**Tanz; tanzen**
We're going dancing. / We're going to a dance.	Wir gehen tanzen.
There's disco ['dɪskəʊ] dancing on Saturday nights.	Samstagabends ist Disko.
nightclub ['naɪtklʌb] / **nightspot**	**Nachtlokal; Nachtklub**
They watched the floor show at a nightclub.	Sie sahen sich die Show in einem Nachtklub an.
casino [kə'siːnəʊ]	**(Spiel-)Kasino; Spielbank**
Las Vegas is famous / notorious [nəʊ'tɔːriəs] for its gambling casinos.	Las Vegas ist wegen seiner Spielkasinos berühmt / berüchtigt.
contest ['kɒntest]	**(Wett-)Kampf; Wettbewerb**
beauty ['bjuːti] contest	Schönheitswettbewerb
fair [feə]	**(Jahr-)Markt; Volksfest**
funfair *BE* / *AE* amusement park	Jahrmarkt; Kirmes
merry-go-round / **roundabout**	**Karussell**
We had a ride on the merry-go-round.	Wir sind Karussell gefahren.

Funfair attractions (= **Jahrmarktsattraktionen**)
the Ferris ['ferɪs] *wheel* / *BE the Big Wheel* (= das Riesenrad) • *roller coaster* (= Achterbahn) • *shooting gallery* ['gæləri] (= Schießstand / Schießbude) • *sideshows* (= Nebenattraktionen / Schaubuden)

theme park ['θiːm pɑːk]	(thematisch gestalteter) **Freizeitpark**
Disneyland is a theme park.	Disneyland ist ein Vergnügungspark.
show [ʃəʊ]	**Schau**
fashion show ['fæʃn ʃəʊ]	Mode(n)schau
Punch-and-Judy show [pʌnʃ n 'dʒuːdi]	Kasperletheater
puppet show ['pʌpɪt ʃəʊ]	Puppenspiel; Marionettenspiel
wax museum / **waxworks (museum)** [wæks]	**Wachsfigurenkabinett**
Madame Tussaud's [tə'sɔːdz] waxworks museum is one of London's main tourist attractions.	Madame Tussauds Wachsfigurenkabinett gehört zu Londons Haupttouristenattraktionen.
race [reɪs]	**Rennen; Lauf**
They often go to the races ['reɪsɪz].	Sie gehen oft zum Pferderennen.

Travel and tourism
Reisen und Tourismus

→ 19 Means of transport

Travel broadens the mind. (*Proverb*)

travel ['trævl]	**reisen; Reisen**
travel (a)round the country	im Land herumreisen
go to the travel agent's / agency	zum Reisebüro gehen
travel brochures ['brəʊʃəz]	Reiseprospekte
tourist ['tʊərɪst]	**Tourist(in)**
The island ['aɪlənd] lives off tourists / on tourism.	Die Insel lebt von den Touristen / vom Tourismus.
tourist information office	Verkehrsamt
book [bʊk]	**buchen; reservieren**
book a room / flight [flaɪt]	ein Zimmer / einen Flug reservieren
book a package ['pækɪdʒ] holiday	einen Pauschalurlaub buchen
cancel ['kænsl]	**streichen; rückgängig machen**
We've cancelled the booking.	Wir haben die Reservierung rückgängig gemacht.
The flight has been cancelled.	Der Flug ist ausgefallen.
journey ['dʒɜːni]	(*oft* längere) **Reise**
a journey round the world	eine Weltreise
trip [trɪp]	**Reise; Fahrt**
Have a nice trip.	Gute Reise!
take a boat trip on the Thames [temz]	eine Bootsfahrt auf der Themse machen
the trip there and back	die Reise / Fahrt hin und zurück
day trip – day tripper *BE*	Ausflug – Ausflügler(in)
tour [tʊə]	**Tour; (Rund-)Fahrt; (Rund-)Reise**
go on a tour of Ireland ['aɪələnd]	eine Irland(rund)reise machen
a guided ['gaɪdɪd] tour of the palace	eine Führung durch den Palast
book a package tour	eine Pauschalreise buchen
the tour operator ['ɒpəreɪtə]	der Reiseveranstalter
excursion [ɪk'skɜːʃn]	**Ausflug**
go on an excursion	einen Ausflug machen
hike [haɪk]	**Wanderung; wandern**
go on a hike	eine Wanderung machen
hiker ['haɪkə]	Wanderer / Wanderin
visit ['vɪzɪt]	**besuchen; Besuch**
I'm just visiting here.	Ich bin hier nur zu / auf Besuch.
her last visit to London ['lʌndən]	ihr letzter Londonbesuch
stay [steɪ]	**Aufenthalt; wohnen**
the hotel [həʊ'tel] we were staying at	das Hotel, in dem wir wohnten
itinerary [aɪ'tɪnərəri]	**Reiseplan / -ablauf / -route**
draw [drɔː] up an itinerary	einen Reiseplan aufstellen
destination [destɪ'neɪʃn]	**Reiseziel; Zielbahnhof; Zielflughafen**
He has left the country for an unknown ['ʌnnəʊn] destination.	Er hat das Land mit unbekanntem Ziel verlassen.

resort [rɪˈzɔːt]
Brighton [ˈbraɪtn] is a seaside resort.
sightseeing [ˈsaɪtsiːɪŋ]
Today we're going sightseeing.

sightseeing tour [tʊə]
guide [gaɪd]
a guide to London
our tour guide
opening hours [ˈəʊpnɪŋ aʊəz]
What are the opening hours?
tip [tɪp]
How much did you tip him?

the Channel Tunnel [tʃænl ˈtʌnl]
The trip through the Channel Tunnel takes about 20 minutes.
arrival [əˈraɪvl]
the arrivals board [bɔːd]
departure [dɪˈpɑːtʃə]
the departures board [bɔːd]
delay [dɪˈleɪ]
The strike is causing enormous [ɪˈnɔːməs] delays.
customs [ˈkʌstəmz]
At (the) customs, take the green channel if you have nothing to declare [dɪˈkleə].
customs clearance [ˈklɪərəns]
(customs) duty [ˈdjuːti]
Do I have to pay duty on this?
duty-free [djuːtiˈfriː]
I've brought some duty-frees from Heathrow [hiːˈθrəʊ].

consulate (general) [ˈkɒnsjʊlət]
You can get your passport renewed [rɪˈnjuːd] at the consulate.
embassy [ˈembəsi]
the German embassy in London
apply [əˈplaɪ] for a visa [ˈviːzə]
application [æplɪˈkeɪʃn] for a visa
passport [ˈpɑːspɔːt]
My passport has expired [ɪkˈspaɪəd].
go through passport control [kənˈtrəʊl]
visa [ˈviːzə]
issue [ˈɪʃuː] a visa
valid [ˈvælɪd]
This visa is valid for 90 days.
identity [aɪˈdentəti] **card** / **ID card**

Urlaubsort
Brighton ist ein Seebad.
Besichtigungen
Heute schauen wir uns die Sehenswürdigkeiten an.

Besichtigungsfahrt; Stadtrundfahrt
(Fremden- / Reise-)Führer
ein Londonführer (= Buch)
unser(e) Reiseleiter(in)
Öffnungszeiten
Wann ist geöffnet?
Trinkgeld
Wie viel Trinkgeld hast du ihm gegeben?

der Kanaltunnel
Die Fahrt durch den Kanaltunnel dauert etwa 20 Minuten.
Ankunft
die Ankunftstafel / -anzeige
Abreise; Abfahrt; Abflug
die Abfahrtstafel / -anzeige
Verspätung; Verzögerung
Der Streik führt zu enormen Verspätungen.
Zoll
Gehen Sie am Zoll durch den grünen Ausgang, wenn Sie nichts anzumelden / zu verzollen haben.
Zollabfertigung
Zoll(abgabe)
Muss ich hierauf Zoll bezahlen?
zollfrei; zollfreie Ware
Ich habe einige zollfreie Sachen von Heathrow (= Londoner Flughafen) mitgebracht.

(General-)Konsulat
Man kann sich seinen Pass auf dem Konsulat verlängern lassen.
Botschaft
die deutsche Botschaft in London
ein Visum beantragen
Antrag auf ein Visum
(Reise-)Pass
Mein (Reise-)Pass ist abgelaufen.
durch die Passkontrolle gehen
Visum; Sichtvermerk
ein Visum ausstellen
gültig
Dieses Visum ist 90 Tage gültig.
Personalausweis

vaccination [væksɪ'neɪʃn] (Schutz-)Impfung
typhoid ['taɪfɔɪd] vaccination Typhus(schutz)impfung
vaccination certificate [sə'tɪfɪkət] Impfzeugnis, -ausweis
vaccination card Impfpass
insurance [ɪn'ʃʊərəns] **Versicherung**
luggage / baggage insurance (eine) Gepäckversicherung
trip cancellation insurance (eine) Reiserücktritt(s)versicherung
change [tʃeɪndʒ] **wechseln; umtauschen**
change euros into sterling Euro in britische Pfund
   ['stɜːlɪŋ] umtauschen
bureau de change **Wechselstube**
   [bjʊərəʊ də 'ʃɒndʒ]
exchange [ɪks'tʃeɪndʒ] (*Geld*) **Umtausch**
exchange rate / rate of exchange Wechselkurs
travellers cheque ['trævləz tʃek] **Reisescheck**
I'd like to cash a travellers cheque. Ich möchte einen Reisescheck
   einlösen.

luggage ['lʌgɪdʒ] / **baggage** **Gepäck**
   ['bægɪdʒ]
a piece / an item ['aɪtəm] of ein Gepäckstück
   luggage / baggage
(left-)luggage locker ['lɒkə] Gepäckschließfach
left-luggage office *BE* / *AE* baggage Gepäckaufbewahrung
   room
luggage trolley ['trɒli] *BE* / **Kofferkuli**
   AE **baggage cart**
bag [bæg] **Tasche**
a collapsible [kə'læpsəbl] bag eine zusammenfaltbare Tasche
Do you want to check your bags? Möchten Sie Ihr Gepäck aufgeben?
(suit)case [('suːt)keɪs] **Koffer**
There's space for four cases ['keɪsɪz]. Es ist Platz für vier Koffer.
holdall ['həʊldɔːl] *BE* / *AE* **carryall** **Reisetasche**

Group travel.

Accommodation
Unterkunft

The great advantage of a hotel is that it's a refuge from home life.
(*George Bernard Shaw, Irish writer, 1856–1950*)

accommodation [əkɒmə'deɪʃn] *BE* / *AE* **accommodations**
Unterkunft; (Nacht-)Quartier

Hotel accommodation is expensive.
Hotelzimmer sind teuer.

hotel [həʊ'tel]
Hotel

stay at / in a hotel
in einem Hotel wohnen

guesthouse ['gesthaʊs]
(Fremden-)Pension

Some guesthouses offer bed and breakfast only.
Manche Pensionen bieten nur Übernachtung und Frühstück.

motel [məʊ'tel]
Motel

inn [ɪn]
Gasthaus

Inns are pubs with accommodation and meals.
Inns sind Pubs, die Unterkunft und Mahlzeiten bieten.

youth hostel ['ju:θ hɒstl]
Jugendherberge

licensed ['laɪsnst] *BE*
zum Ausschank alkoholischer Getränke berechtigt

Is this place licensed?
Gibt es hier alkoholische Getränke?

vacancy ['veɪkənsi]
freies Zimmer

I'm afraid we haven't any vacancies at the moment.
Leider haben wir zurzeit keine Zimmer frei.

reservation [rezə'veɪʃn]
(Zimmer-)Reservierung

make a reservation
ein Zimmer bestellen

Reservations, please.
(*Tel.*) Bitte die (Zimmer-)Reservierung.

book [bʊk]
buchen; reservieren

We've booked a room at the Prince Hotel.
Wir haben ein Zimmer im Prince Hotel gebucht / reservieren lassen.

I'm afraid we're fully booked.
Leider sind wir total ausgebucht.

cancel ['kænsl]
stornieren; rückgängig machen

We've cancelled our reservation.
Wir haben unsere Zimmerbestellung rückgängig gemacht.

deposit [dɪ'pɒzɪt]
Anzahlung

Some hotels require a deposit on booking.
Manche Hotels verlangen bei der Zimmerbestellung eine Anzahlung.

supplement ['sʌpləmənt]
Aufschlag; Aufpreis

For seaview rooms, supplements apply [ə'plaɪ].
Für Zimmer mit Seeblick wird ein Aufpreis erhoben.

single ['sɪŋgl]
Einzel-

a single (room) with bath [bɑ:θ]
ein Einzelzimmer mit Bad

double ['dʌbl]
Doppel-

Do you want a double (room) or a twin(-bedded room)?
Möchten Sie ein Zimmer mit Doppelbett oder ein Zweibettzimmer?

board [bɔ:d]
Kost; Verpflegung

board and lodging ['lɒdʒɪŋ]
Kost und Logis

full board *BE* / *AE* American plan
Vollpension

half board
Halbpension

European [jʊərə'piːən] **plan** *AE*
check in [tʃek 'ɪn]
What time will you be checking in?

check out [tʃek 'aʊt]
When will you be checking out?
Checkout ['tʃekaʊt] time is 1100 hrs
['aʊəz].
reception desk [rɪ'sepʃn desk]
There was a message ['mesɪdʒ] for me
at reception.
hall porter / concierge ['kɒnsieəʒ]
Leave your keys [kiːz] at the hall
porter's desk.
cashier [kæ'ʃɪə]
There was a long queue [kjuː] *BE* /
AE line at the cashier's desk.
lounge [laʊndʒ]
Drinks are served in the lounge.
lobby ['lɒbi]
coffee shop ['kɒfi ʃɒp]
Breakfast is served in the coffee shop.
breakfast ['brekfəst]
What would you like for breakfast?
bed and breakfast / B&B
We stayed at a bed and breakfast.

(*Zimmer*) **ohne Mahlzeiten**
sich (am Empfang) anmelden
Um welche Zeit werden Sie ankommen?

abreisen
Wann werden Sie abreisen?
Das Zimmer muss bis 11 Uhr
geräumt sein.
Empfang
Am (Hotel-)Empfang war eine
Nachricht für mich.
(Hotel-)Portier
Lassen Sie Ihre Schlüssel beim Portier.

Kassierer(in)
An der Kasse war eine lange
Schlange.
(Hotel-)**Halle**
Drinks werden in der Halle serviert.
(*Hotel*) **Foyer**
kleines Restaurant; Frühstücksraum
Frühstück gibt es im Coffee Shop.
Frühstück
Was hätten Sie gern zum Frühstück?
Übernachtung mit Frühstück
Wir wohnten in einem Hotel garni.

 English or continental [kɒntɪ'nentl] ***breakfast?***
Das erstere ein „großes" Frühstück mit *orange juice* ['ɒrɪndʒ dʒuːs] (= Orangensaft), *porridge* (= Haferbrei), *cereals* ['sɪərɪəlz] (= Cornflakes, Müsli
usw.), *boiled eggs* (= gekochten Eiern), *fried eggs* (= Spiegeleiern) oder
scrambled eggs (= Rührei) vielleicht in Kombination mit *bacon* ['beɪkən]
(= Speck) oder *ham* (= Schinken), aber auch mit *sausage* ['sɒsɪdʒ]
(= Wurst), *mushrooms* (= Pilzen) oder *grilled tomatoes* (= gegrillten Tomaten). Dazu dann noch das, was auch zum *continental breakfast* gehört:
fresh breakfast rolls (= frische Frühstücksbrötchen), *hot croissants*
['kwæsɑːnts] (= heiße Croissants) und natürlich – hoffentlich jede Menge –
toast mit *marmalade* ['mɑːməleɪd] (= Orangen- bzw. Grapefruitmarme-
lade), *jam* (= Marmelade nicht aus Zitrusfrüchten) und *honey* ['hʌni]
(= Honig), vielleicht *lemon* ['lemən] *curd* (= Zitronencreme). In jedem Fall
selbstverständlich auch *coffee* (= Kaffee), *tea* (= Tee) oder *milk* (= Milch).

room service ['ruːm sɜːvɪs]
I called Room Service and ordered
a sandwich.
morning call / wake-up call
Could you wake us at six, please?

disturb [dɪ'stɜːb]
Please do not disturb.
hospitable [hɒ'spɪtəbl]

Zimmerservice
Ich rief den Zimmerservice an
und bestellte ein Sandwich.
Weckruf
Könnten Sie uns bitte um sechs
wecken?

stören
Bitte nicht stören.
gastfreundlich; gastlich

Shopping
Einkaufen

A good shop needs no sign. (*Proverb*)

Useful phrases (= **nützliche Redensarten**)

I'm looking for …	Ich suche …
Do you have / sell / stock …?	Haben / Führen Sie …?
Where do I find …?	Wo finde ich …?
How much is …?	Was kostet …?
Would you like it gift-wrapped?	Soll ich es als Geschenk einpacken?

shopping ['ʃɒpɪŋ] | **Einkaufen**
I'm doing my shopping today. | Heute mache ich meine Einkäufe.
I've got my shopping in the car. | Ich habe meine Einkäufe im Auto.
shopping bag – shopping basket [ɑː] | Einkaufstasche – Einkaufskorb
shopping trolley *BE* / *AE* shopping cart | Einkaufswagen
shopping centre *BE* / *AE* shopping mall | Einkaufszentrum
go on a shopping spree [spriː] | einen Einkaufsbummel machen

Shop – store: Im AE bezeichnet *store* auch einen (kleineren) Laden, der im BE als *shop* bezeichnet würde; BE *store* meint in der Regel *department store*, also „Kaufhaus". Entsprechend z.B. BE *bookshop* = AE *bookstore*.

department store [dɪˈpɑːtmənt stɔː] | **Kaufhaus; Warenhaus**
big stores like Harrods [ˈhærədz] | große Kaufhäuser wie Harrods
mail-order firm / **company** | **Versandhaus**
mail-order catalogue [ˈkætəlɒg] | Versandhauskatalog
buy something by mail order | etwas bei einem Versandhaus kaufen
customer [ˈkʌstəmə] | **Kunde** / **Kundin**
counter [ˈkaʊntə] | **Ladentisch**
medicines [ˈmedsnz] that you can buy over the counter | Medikamente, die man rezeptfrei bekommt
assistant [əˈsɪstənt] *BE* / *AE* **salesperson** | **Verkäufer(in)** (*in Laden, Kaufhaus etc.*)
service [ˈsɜːvɪs] | **(Kunden-)Dienst**
For customer service, call … | Unsere Kundenbetreuung erreichen Sie unter der Nummer …
our after-sales service | unser Kundendienst
bargain [ˈbɑːgən] | **günstiges Angebot; Sonderangebot**
It was a bargain. | Es war ein Schnäppchen.
save [seɪv] | **sparen**
You can save up to 40 per cent. | Sie können bis zu 40 Prozent sparen.
off [ɒf] | **„runter"**
25% off the retail [ˈriːteɪl] price | 25% unter dem Einzelhandelspreis
2 per cent off for cash | 2 Prozent Skonto bei Barzahlung
bill *BE* / *AE* **check** | **Rechnung**
a bill for £150 | eine Rechnung über 150 Pfund
deposit [dɪˈpɒzɪt] / **down payment** | **Anzahlung**
pay a deposit | eine Anzahlung leisten

instalment [ɪnˈstɔːlmənt]	**Rate**
payment by instalments	Ratenzahlung
We bought it on the installment plan	Wir haben es auf Raten gekauft.
AE / BE on hire purchase [ˈpɜːtʃəs] / HP.	
sale [seɪl]	**Verkauf**
clearance (sale) [ˈklɪərəns]	Räumungsverkauf
There's a sale on at Clark's.	Bei Clark läuft gerade ein Ausverkauf.
get it cheap at the sales	es billig im Ausverkauf bekommen
offer [ˈɒfə]	**Angebot; anbieten**
We have two models on offer.	Wir haben zwei Modelle im Angebot.
special offer	Sonderangebot
brand [brænd]	**Marke**
What brand of toothpaste [ˈtuːθpeɪst]?	Was für eine Zahnpasta(marke)?

Kinds of shop (AE statt *shop* oft *store*)

clothes [kləʊðz] *store* (= Konfektionshaus) • *fashion shop* (= Mode-geschäft) • *shoe shop* (= Schuhgeschäft) • *antique* [ænˈtiːk] *shop* (= Antiquitätengeschäft) • *gift shop* (= Geschenkladen) • *craft* [ɑː] *shop* (= Kunstgewerbeladen) • *antiquarian* [æntɪˈkweəriən] / *second-hand bookshop* (= Antiquariat) • *music shop* (= Musikalienhandlung / Musikladen) • *toy shop* (= Spielwarengeschäft) • *sports shop* (= Sportgeschäft) • *photographic shop* / *camera store* (= Foto-geschäft) • *electronics* [ɪlekˈtrɒnɪks] *shop* (= Elektronikgeschäft) • *newsagent* [ˈnjuːzeɪdʒənt] BE / AE *newsdealer* (= Zeitungshändler) • *art dealer* (= Kunsthändler) • *jeweller* [ˈdʒuːələ] (= Juwelier) • *hairdresser* (= Friseur)

stationer('s shop) [ˈsteɪʃnə]	Schreibwarenhandlung / -geschäft
florist('s shop) [ˈflɒrɪst]	Blumengeschäft
grocer('s shop) [ˈgrəʊsə]	Lebensmittelhändler
greengrocer('s shop) BE	Obst- und Gemüsehändler

 Lebensmittel bekommt man in Amerika außer *at the supermarket* oder *in a grocery* [ˈgrəʊsəri] auch *in a deli* [ˈdɛli] (= *delicatessen*). *Delis* bieten auch *sandwiches, hamburgers, salads* und kleine Spezialitätengerichte.

chemist [ˈkemɪst] *BE* /	**Apotheke**
AE&BE **pharmacy** [ˈfɑːməsi] /	
AE **drugstore**	
You'll get it at any chemist's /	Das bekommen Sie in jeder
pharmacy / drugstore.	Apotheke.

Apotheken sind in Großbritannien und Amerika in der Regel nicht so ausschließlich medizinisch ausgerichtet wie in den deutschsprachigen Ländern. Manche Filialen der britischen Pharmaziekette *Boots* führen fast alles *from toothpaste to computers*; amerikanische *drugstores* verkaufen nicht nur *drugs* (= Medikamente), sondern auch *toiletries* (= Toiletten-artikel), *cosmetics* (= Kosmetikartikel), *stationery* (= Schreibwaren) sowie *sweets* (= Süßigkeiten) und *refreshments* (= Erfrischungen).

Sports
Sport

True sport is always a duel: a duel with nature, with one's own fear, with one's own fatigue, a duel in which body and mind are strengthened.
(*Yevgeny Yevtushenko, Russian poet, born in 1933*)

sport [spɔːt]
Baseball ['beɪsbɔːl] is the USA's most popular ['pɒpjələ] sport.
What sports do you go in for / do?
Don't you do any sport?
game [geɪm]
Shall we have / play a game of chess?
match [mætʃ]
contest ['kɒntest] / **competition** [kɒmpəˈtɪʃn]
(track and field) meet [miːt]
tournament ['tʊənəmənt]
championship ['tʃæmpiənʃɪp]
challenge ['tʃælɪndʒ]
challenger ['tʃælɪndʒə]
win (– won [wʌn] – won)
lose [luːz] (– lost [lɒst] – lost)

Sport; Sportart
Baseball ist Amerikas beliebtester Sport.
In welchen Sportarten sind Sie aktiv?
Treibst du denn keinen Sport?
Spiel; Partie
Wollen wir eine Partie Schach spielen?
(Wett-)Spiel; Partie; (Wett-)Kampf
Wettbewerb

AE **(Leichtathletik-)Sportfest**
Turnier
Meisterschaft
herausfordern; Herausforderung
Herausforderer / Herausforderin
gewinnen (– gewann – gewonnen)
verlieren

Where sporting events take place (= **Orte sportlichen Geschehens**)
venue ['venjuː] (= Austragungsort) • *sportsground* (= Sportplatz) •
stadium ['steɪdɪəm] (= Stadion) • *football pitch* (Fußball: = Spielfeld) •
football ground (= Fußballplatz) • *cricket ground / pitch* (= Kricketfeld) •
handball court [kɔːt] (= Handballplatz) • *tennis court* (= Tennisplatz) •
golf course ['gɒlf kɔːs] (= Golfplatz) • *ballpark* (= Baseballstadion) •
gym [dʒɪm] (= Turnhalle)

(world) champion ['tʃæmpiən]
runner-up [rʌnər ˈʌp]
(world) record [(wɜːld) ˈrekɔːd]
set / break / hold a record

(Welt-)Meister(in)
Zweite(r); Zweitplatzierte(r)
(Welt-)Rekord
einen Rekord aufstellen / brechen / halten

favourite ['feɪvrət] – **underdog**
British fans want the underdog to win.

Favorit(in) – sichere(r) Verlierer(in)
Britische Fans wollen, dass der Schwächere / Außenseiter gewinnt.

amateur ['æmətə] – **professional**
sportsman – sportswoman
sportsmanlike behaviour [bɪˈheɪvjə]
race [reɪs]
the 100-metre race / dash / run
I ran a race with her.
relay race ['riːleɪ reɪs]
racing ['reɪsɪŋ]
motor racing *BE* / *AE* auto racing

Amateur(-) – Profi(-)
Sportler – Sportlerin
sportliches / faires Verhalten; Fairness
Rennen; (Wett-)Lauf
der 100-Meter-Lauf
Ich bin mit ihr um die Wette gelaufen.
Staffellauf
Rennen; Rennsport
Autorennsport

racing car – racing driver	Rennwagen – Rennfahrer(in)
track [træk]	**(Renn-)Bahn; Rennstrecke; Piste**
track event / running event [ɪ'vent]	(*Leichtathletik*) Laufwettbewerb
athletics [æθ'letɪks] *BE* / *AE* **track and field**	**Leichtathletik**
Track and field (athletics) is one of the oldest of sports.	Die Leichtathletik ist eine der ältesten Sportarten.
running – jumping – throwing	**Laufen – Springen – Werfen**
high / **long jump** [dʒʌmp]	**Hoch-** / **Weitsprung**
skating ['skeɪtɪŋ]	**Schlittschuh-** / **Rollschuhlauf(en)**
ice-skating	Schlittschuhlauf(en)
roller-skating	Rollschuhlauf(en)
figure ['fɪɡə] skating	Eiskunstlauf
skiing ['skiːɪŋ]	**Skilaufen; Skifahren**
In winter, we go skiing a lot.	Im Winter gehen wir oft Ski laufen.
yachting ['jɒtɪŋ]	**Segeln**
yachtsman – yachtswoman	Segler – Seglerin
swimming – diving ['daɪvɪŋ]	**Schwimmen – Tauchen**
boxing ['bɒksɪŋ] – **wrestling** ['reslɪŋ]	**Boxen – Ringen**

Fußball = *soccer* ['sɒkə] / **football** ['fʊtbɔːl] / *American football*
Im BE heißt Fußball *football* oder *soccer* (= *Association* [əsəʊsi'eɪʃn] *football*).
Die Amerikaner nennen „unsere" Art von Fußball *soccer*, während *football*
dort *American football* ist, bei dem ein eiförmiger Ball getragen oder
getreten wird (= *is carried or kicked* [kɪkt]). *American football* ist durch
große Härte gekennzeichnet und wird daher mit stark gepolsterter
Kleidung (= *heavily padded clothing* ['kləʊðɪŋ]), *Helmen* (= *helmets*) und
Gesichtsschutz (= *masks* [mɑːsks]) gespielt.

Some soccer terms	**Einige Fußballausdrücke**
striker ['straɪkə]	**Stürmer(in)**
midfield player / **midfielder**	**Mittelfeldspieler(in)**
defender [dɪ'fendə] – **defence**	**Verteidiger(in) – Verteidigung**
The **goalkeeper** ['ɡəʊlkiːpə] made an excellent save.	Der **Torwart** bot eine Glanzparade.
(team) captain ['kæptən]	**(Mannschafts-)Kapitän**
substitute ['sʌbstɪtjuːt]	**Ersatz-** / **Auswechselspieler(in)**
the England **manager** ['mænɪdʒə]	der englische **Nationaltrainer**
a strong English **side** / **team** / **squad** [skwɒd]	eine starke englische **Mannschaft**
a **friendly** ['frendli] against Wales	ein **Freundschaftsspiel** gegen Wales
a **home match** [həʊm 'mætʃ]	ein **Heimspiel**
an **away victory** ['vɪktəri]	ein **Auswärtssieg**
the **World Cup** [wɜːld 'kʌp]	die **Fußballweltmeisterschaft**
in the **first** / **second half**	in der **ersten** / **zweiten Halbzeit**
a **cross** from the right	eine **Flanke** von rechts
go into **extra time** (– went – gone [ɒ])	in die **Verlängerung** gehen
He **crossed** [krɒst] from the left.	Er **flankte** von links.
His **header** ['hedə] hit the **(cross)bar.**	Sein **Kopfball** ging an die **(Quer-)Latte.**

Neal **scored** [skɔ:d] the **equalizer** ['i:kwəlaɪzə].	Neal **erzielte** den **Ausgleichstreffer**.
a **set piece** [set 'pi:s]	eine **Standardsituation**
an **own goal** [əʊn 'gəʊl]	ein **Eigentor**
penalty ['penlti] **area – penalty kick**	**Strafraum – Strafstoß**
penalty shootout ['ʃu:taʊt]	**Elfmeterschießen**
golden goal [gəʊldn 'gəʊl]	erstes, das Spiel entscheidende und beendende Tor in der Verlängerung (*sudden death*)
He was **offside** [ɒf'saɪd].	Er war im **Abseits**.
They were awarded [ə'wɔ:dɪd] a **free kick** [fri: 'kɪk].	Sie erhielten einen **Freistoß**.
He was **sent off / shown the red card** for fouling Smith.	Er wurde wegen eines Fouls an Smith **vom Platz verwiesen / bekam** wegen … **die rote Karte**.
their first **win** in six **matches**	ihr erster **Sieg** in sechs **Spielen**
a **goalless draw** [drɔ:]	ein **torloses Unentschieden**
Premier League [premiə 'li:g] *BE*	**(oberste britische Liga)**
the German **league champion**	der deutsche **Fußballmeister**

Beachten Sie, dass nach Namen von Fußballmannschaften im BE die Pluralform des Verbs steht:
Everton ['evətn] *are at the bottom* ['bɒtəm] *of the Premier League.* (= Everton steht in der Ersten Liga an letzter Stelle.)
Southampton were lucky to win. (= Southampton hat mit Glück gewonnen.)
England have qualified ['kwɒlɪfaɪd] *for the World Cup.* (= England hat sich für die Weltmeisterschaft qualifiziert.)

Some tennis terms	**Etwas Tenniswortschatz**
tennis court ['tenɪs kɔ:t]	**Tennisplatz**
baseline ['beɪslaɪn] **– sideline**	**Grundlinie – Seitenlinie**
racket ['rækɪt]	**(Tennis-)Schläger**
play a **singles / doubles / mixed doubles**	ein **Einzel / Doppel / gemischtes Doppel** spielen
ace [eɪs]	**(Aufschlag-)Ass**
He served nine aces in the first set.	Im ersten Satz schlug er neun Asse.
double fault [dʌbl 'fɔ:lt]	**Doppelfehler**
forehand ['fɔ:hænd] **– backhand**	**Vorhand – Rückhand**
fifteen – love [lʌv]	**fünfzehn – null**
deuce [dju:s] **– advantage** [əd'vɑ:ntɪdʒ]	**Einstand – Vorteil**
set point – match point	**Satzball – Matchball**
The **score** is three – **zero** ['zɪərəʊ] in the **tiebreak** ['taɪbreɪk].	Es steht drei – null im Tiebreak.
a successful **tennis coach** [kəʊtʃ]	ein(e) erfolgreiche(r) **Tennistrainer(in)**

Achtung, Schiedsrichter – *referee* [refə'ri:] **oder** *umpire* ['ʌmpaɪə]?
In *basketball, boxing, football, hockey* ['hɒki], *rugby, snooker, squash* [skwɒʃ] und *wrestling* ['reslɪŋ] (= Ringen) ist Schiedsrichter(in) = *referee*.
In *badminton* (= Federball), *baseball* ['beɪsbɔ:l], *cricket* ['krɪkɪt], *swimming, tennis* und *volleyball* ['vɒlibɔ:l] ist Schiedsrichter(in) = *umpire*.

Hobbies
Hobbys

None but the wise man can employ leisure well. (*Proverb*)

My **hobbies** include [ɪn'klu:d] …
Beekeeping is a rewarding [rɪ'wɔ:dɪŋ]
  hobby.
Gardening is a hobby he's passionate
  ['pæʃnət] about.
pastime ['pɑ:staɪm]
my favourite ['feɪvrət] pastime
interest ['ɪntrəst]
What interests do you have?
My chief [tʃi:f] interests are music
  ['mju:zɪk] and tennis.
activity [æk'tɪvəti]
What's your favourite activity?
Cooking is a popular leisure ['leʒə]
  activity.
pursuits [pə'sju:ts]
artistic [ɑ:'tɪstɪk] pursuits
She now devotes [dɪ'vəʊts] most of her
  time to her literary ['lɪtərəri] pursuits.

Zu meinen **Hobbys** gehört …
Die Imkerei ist ein lohnendes /
  dankbares Hobby.
Die Gartenarbeit ist ein Hobby, dem
  er sich mit Leidenschaft widmet.
Zeitvertreib; Hobby
meine Lieblingsbeschäftigung
Interesse(ngebiet)
Was für Interessen haben Sie?
Meine Hauptinteressen sind Musik
  und Tennis.
Betätigung; Tätigkeit
Was ist deine Lieblingsbeschäftigung?
Kochen ist eine beliebte Freizeit-
  beschäftigung.
Beschäftigungen; Betätigungen
künstlerische Betätigungen
Den größten Teil ihrer Zeit widmet sie
  jetzt ihren literarischen Aktivitäten.

Crafts [krɑ:fts] **(= Handarbeit, Kunsthandwerk, Basteln)**
needlework ['ni:dlwɜ:k] (= Nadel- / Handarbeit) • *sewing* ['səʊɪŋ]
(= Nähen) • *knitting* ['nɪtɪŋ] (= Stricken) • *weaving* ['wi:vɪŋ] (= Weben) •
spinning (= Spinnen) • *embroidery* [ɪm'brɔɪdəri] (= Sticken) • *dressmaking*
(= Schneidern) • *flower arranging* [ə'reɪndʒɪŋ] (= Blumenstecken) •
pottery ['pɒtəri] (= Töpfern) • *basketry* ['bɑ:skɪtri] (= Korbflechten) •
woodworking (= Holzarbeiten) • *metalwork* ['metlwɜ:k] (= Metallarbeiten)

relaxation [ri:læk'seɪʃn]
The cinema is her relaxation.
Painting is his favourite ['feɪvrət]
  relaxation.
She listens to classical music for
  relaxation.
recreation [rekri'eɪʃn]
He repairs old clocks for recreation.
Chess is a wonderful ['wʌndəfl]
  recreation.
leisure ['leʒə]
spare time [speə 'taɪm]
What do you do in your spare time?
engage in something [ɪn'geɪdʒ]
She engages in all sorts of voluntary
  ['vɒləntri] work.

Entspannung; Freizeitbeschäftigung
Zur Entspannung geht sie ins Kino.
Beim Malen entspannt er sich am
  liebsten.
Zur Entspannung hört sie klassische
  Musik.
Erholung; Freizeitbeschäftigung
Zur Erholung repariert er alte Uhren.
Schach ist eine herrliche Freizeit-
  beschäftigung.
(die) Freizeit; Muße
Freizeit
Was machst du in deiner Freizeit?
sich mit etwas befassen
Sie widmet sich allen möglichen
  ehrenamtlichen Aufgaben.

take up a hobby (– took – taken)	**sich** ein Hobby **zulegen**
I've taken up photography [fə'tɒgrəfi].	Ich habe zu fotografieren ange-fangen.
pursue [pə'sju:] / **follow** a hobby	ein Hobby **betreiben**
go in for something (– went – gone [ɒ])	etwas **betreiben**
She doesn't go in for sports.	Mit Sport hat sie nichts im Sinn.
indulge [ɪn'dʌldʒ] **in** something	einer Sache **frönen; sich** einer Sache **hingeben**
For relaxation she indulges (in) her passion for riding.	Zur Entspannung gibt sie sich ihrer Leidenschaft für das Reiten hin.

What people collect [kə'lekt] (= **Was die Leute so sammeln**)
stamps (= Briefmarken) • *postcards* (= Postkarten) • *phonecards* (= Tele-fonkarten) • *coins* (= Münzen) • *autographs* ['ɔːtəgrɑːfs] (= Autogramme) •
antiques [æn'tiːks] (= Antiquitäten) • *fine old books* (= schöne alte Bücher) •
matchboxes (= Streichholzschachteln) • *beer mats* (= Bierdeckel) •
butterflies and moths [mɒθs] (= Schmetterlinge und Nachtfalter)

enjoy doing something [ɪn'dʒɔɪ]	etwas gern tun
I enjoy listening ['lɪsnɪŋ] to music.	Ich höre gern Musik.
She enjoys doing crossword puzzles.	Sie löst gern Kreuzworträtsel.
do-it-yourself / **DIY**	**Heimwerken**
Do-it-yourself is a popular ['pɒpjələ] pastime.	Heimwerken ist ein beliebter Zeitvertreib.
He's a keen **do-it-yourselfer**.	Er ist ein begeisterter **Heimwerker**.
She **does a lot of reading**.	Sie **liest viel**.
We spend a lot of time **playing cards**.	Wir verbringen viel Zeit beim **Kartenspiel**.
fishing ['fɪʃɪŋ]	**Angeln; Fischen**
He goes fishing for relaxation [riːlæk'seɪʃn].	Zur Entspannung geht er angeln.
play **video games** ['vɪdiəʊ geimz]	**Computerspiele** spielen
He's into video games at the moment.	Im Moment fährt er auf Computer-spiele ab.
She is a huge **movie buff** ['muːvi bʌf].	Sie ist ein großer **Filmfan**.

Outdoor activities [æk'tɪvətiz] (= **Aktivitäten im Freien**)
gardening (= Gartenarbeit) • *beekeeping* ['biːkiːpɪŋ] (= Imkern) •
jogging (= Joggen) • *hiking* (= Wandern) • *backpacking* (= Rucksack-wandern / -reisen) • *mountain climbing* ['maʊntən klaɪmɪŋ] / *mountaineering* [maʊntə'nɪərɪŋ] (= Bergsteigen) • *birdwatching* (= Vogelbeobachtung) •
cycling ['saɪklɪŋ] (= Radfahren) • *(horse-)riding* (= Reiten) • *hunting* (= Jagd) • *skiing* ['skiːɪŋ] (= Skilaufen) • *roller-skating* (= Rollschuh-laufen) • *ice-skating* (= Schlittschuhlaufen) • *sailing / yachting* ['jɒtɪŋ] (= Segeln) • *windsurfing* (= Windsurfen) • *water-skiing* (= Wasser-skilaufen) • *scuba-diving* ['skuːbə daɪvɪŋ] (= Sport- / Gerättauchen) •
skin-diving (= Sport- / Schnorcheltauchen) • *parachuting* ['pærəʃuːtɪŋ] /
skydiving (= Fallschirmspringen) • *hang-gliding* (= Drachenfliegen)

Drinking and smoking
Trinken und Rauchen

→ 7.3 Drug and alcohol abuse

We drink one another's healths and spoil our own.
(*Jerome K. Jerome, English writer, 1859–1927*)
The Surgeon General has determined that smoking cigarettes
is bad for your health. (*Health warning on cigarette packets*)

drink (– drank – drunk)	trinken
He drinks like a fish.	Er säuft wie ein Loch.
hard / soft [sɒft] drinks	harte / alkoholfreie Getränke
What about a drink?	Wie wär's mit 'nem Drink / Gläschen?
go out for a drink [fər ə 'drɪŋk]	auf einen Drink weggehen
(problem / serious ['sɪərɪəs]) drinker	Trinker(in)
drunk [drʌŋk]	Betrunkene(r); Trinker(in)
alcoholic [ælkə'hɒlɪk]	Alkoholiker(in)
booze [buːz]	Alkohol; Schnaps; saufen
boozer ['buːzə]	Säufer(in)
teetotaller [tiː'təʊtlə]	Abstinenzler(in)
have (– had – had)	haben; trinken
have a hangover ['hæŋəʊvə]	einen Kater haben
Have another drink.	Trinken Sie doch noch einen.
Let's have one for the road.	Trinken wir noch einen, bevor wir gehen.
drunk / **intoxicated** [ɪn'tɒksɪkeɪtɪd]	betrunken
(stone-cold) **sober** ['səʊbə]	(stock)nüchtern
beer (on draught [drɑːft] / on tap)	Bier (vom Fass)
I prefer [prɪ'fɜː] draught beer [bɪə].	Ich trinke lieber Bier vom Fass.

Types of beer (= **Biersorten**)
beer (neutraler Ausdruck für Bier) • *bitter* (goldgelb mit starkem Hopfen-
geschmack, das meistgetrunkene englische Fassbier) • *mild* [aɪ] (rotbraun,
schwächer, süßer als *bitter*) • *stout* [aʊ] (kräftiges dunkles Bier) • *pale ale*
(schwaches helles Bier) • *lager* (den deutschen hellen Bieren ähnlich)

(white / red) wine [waɪn]	(Weiß- / Rot-)Wein
sparkling wine [spɑːklɪŋ 'waɪn]	Schaumwein; Sekt
moselle [məʊ'zel]	Moselwein
champagne [ʃæm'peɪn]	Champagner; Sekt
vintage ['vɪntɪdʒ]	(Wein) Jahrgang
a vintage wine / champagne	ein edler / erlesener Wein / Sekt
liquor ['lɪkə] – **liqueur** [lɪ'kjʊə]	Schnaps – Likör
He can't hold his liquor ['lɪkə].	Der verträgt nichts.
shandy ['ʃændi]	„Radlermaß"; „Alsterwasser"

How to say prost! **in English** (= **Wie man auf Englisch** *prost!* **sagt**)
Cheers! [tʃɪəz] • *Skol!* [skɒl] • *Bottoms* ['bɒtəmz] *up!* • *Here's to you!* •
Your (very) good health [helθ]. • *Down the hatch!*

pint [paɪnt]	(BE = 0,57 Liter / AE = 0,47 Liter)
A pint of bitter, please.	Bitte ein großes Bitter.
A half [hɑːf] of bitter, please.	Bitte ein kleines Bitter.
double [ˈdʌbl]	**doppelt**
A double Scotch, please.	Bitte einen doppelten Scotch (Whisky).
barmaid [ˈbɑːmeɪd]	**Bardame**
barman BE / AE **bartender** [ˈbɑːtendə]	**Barmann**

To have a drink (= um einen zu trinken) geht man in England *to a pub* (= in einen Pub), in Amerika *to a bar* (= in eine Bar). *Saloons* [səˈluːnz] waren im 19. Jahrhundert *in the American West* verbreitet; heute gibt es sie fast nur noch in *westerns*. *Tavern* [ˈtævən] ist ebenfalls historisch, überlebt aber in den Namen von *pubs* und *bars* (*Railway Tavern, Trafalgar* [trəˈfælgə] *Tavern* etc.).

smoke [sməʊk]	**rauchen; Rauch**
I don't smoke.	Ich rauche nicht / bin Nichtraucher(in).
have a smoke	eine (Zigarette) rauchen
passive [ˈpæsɪv] smoking	passives Rauchen
No smoking	Rauchen verboten
(non-)smoking section / area	(Nicht-)Raucherbereich
(non-)smoking compartment	(Nicht-)Raucherabteil
(non-)smoker	(Nicht-)Raucher(in)
smoker's cough [kɒf]	Raucherhusten
chain-smoker [ˈtʃeɪn sməʊkə]	Kettenraucher(in)
cigarette [sɪgəˈret]	**Zigarette**
(filter-)tipped [tɪpt] / filter cigarette	Filterzigarette
high- / low-tar [tɑː] cigarettes	Zigaretten mit hohem / niedrigem Teergehalt
a pack(et) of cigarettes	eine Packung / Schachtel Zigaretten
a carton [ˈkɑːtən] of cigarettes	eine Stange Zigaretten
cigarette case [keɪs] / holder	Zigarettenetui / -spitze
cigarette paper BE / AE rolling paper	Zigarettenpapier
cigarette machine [məˈʃiːn]	Zigarettenautomat
roll-up BE / AE **roll-your-own**	**selbst gedrehte Zigarette**
cigar [sɪˈgɑː]	**Zigarre**
a box of cigars	eine Kiste Zigarren
pipe (cleaner) [paɪp]	**Pfeife(nreiniger)**
As always he was smoking his pipe.	Wie immer rauchte er seine Pfeife.
tobacco [təˈbækəʊ]	**Tabak**
The men chewed [tʃuːd] tobacco and spit a lot.	Die Männer kauten Tabak und spuckten viel.
tobacconist [təˈbækənɪst]	**Tabak(waren)laden**
nicotine [ˈnɪkətiːn]	**Nikotin**
He's addicted [əˈdɪktɪd] to nicotine.	Er ist nikotinsüchtig.
light a cigarette (– lit* – lit*)	(sich) eine Zigarette **anzünden**
light up [laɪt ˈʌp] (– lit* – lit*)	(sich) eine (Zigarette) **anzünden**
lighter [ˈlaɪtə] – **ashtray** [ˈæʃtreɪ]	**Feuerzeug – Aschenbecher**

Social media

You can buy attention (advertising). You can beg for attention from the media (PR). You can bug people one at a time to get attention (sales). Or you can earn attention by creating something interesting and valuable and then publishing it online for free. (*David Meerman Scott, online marketing strategist, born in 1961*)

like a **status** ['steɪtəs]	**einen** Status „**liken**" (= „gefällt mir" klicken)
Like my **page** [peɪdʒ].	„**Like**" meine **Seite**. (= Klick „gefällt mir".)
upload [ʌp'ləʊd] a picture	ein Bild **hochladen**
tag someone in a photo	jemand in einem Foto **markieren**
Remember to tag everyone in the photos.	Denk daran, alle auf den Fotos zu markieren.
poke [pəʊk] a person	jemand **anstupsen**
create an **event** [kri'eɪt ən ɪ'vent]	eine **Veranstaltung erstellen**
star a photo ['stɑːr ə fəʊtəʊ]	ein Foto **hervorheben**
share [ʃeə] a link	einen Link **teilen**
timeline ['taɪmlaɪn]	**Chronik**
wall [wɔːl]	**Pinnwand**

Die Namen mancher *messaging services* lassen sich im Englischen auch als Verben verwenden:
Get back in touch and **facebook**™ *him* (= Melde dich bei ihm und schreibe ihn bei Facebook™ an).
I'll **whatsapp**™ *him, maybe he has a moment for us* (= Ich werde ihn über WhatsApp™ anschreiben, vielleicht hat er ja etwas Zeit für uns).
Das Gleiche gilt für den BlackBerry Messenger™ (BBM™): *I'll have to* **BBM**™ *him later* (= Ich muss ihm später eine BBM schicken).
Bei Skype™ funktioniert das auch im Deutschen: *He was online, so I decided to* **skype**™ *him* (= Er war online, deshalb entschloss ich mich, ihn anzuskypen).

add a **contact** ['kɒntækt]	einen **Kontakt** hinzufügen
go **online** [ɒn'laɪn]	**online** gehen
video call ['vɪdɪəʊ kɔːl]	**Videoanruf**
group call ['gruːp kɔːl]	**Gruppenanruf**
Twitter™	**Twitter**™ (= ein soziales Netzwerk und Mikroblog)
tweet [twiːt]	**Tweet** (= ein Twitter™-Eintrag von bis zu 140 Zeichen)
compose [kəm'pəʊz] a new **tweet**	einen neuen **Tweet verfassen**
mention ['menʃn]	**Erwähnung**
user-generated content ['kɒntent]	**nutzergenerierte Inhalte**
The video-sharing website YouTube™ ['juːtjuːb] depends on user-generated content.	Das Videoportal YouTube™ ist auf nutzergenerierte Inhalte angewiesen.

The universe
Das Weltall

1   **Stars and planets**
    Sterne und Planeten

2   **Space exploration**
    Raumforschung

Idioms

Stars and planets
Sterne und Planeten

My own suspicion is that the universe is not only queerer than we suppose, but queerer than we *can* suppose. (*J.B.S. Haldane, British scientist, 1892–1964*)

the origin ['ɒrɪdʒɪn] of the **universe**	die Entstehung der **Welt**
The universe ['juːnɪvɜːs] has neither boundary ['baʊndəri] nor centre.	Das Weltall / Universum hat weder Grenze noch Mittelpunkt.
the **cosmos** ['kɒzmɒs]	der **Kosmos**; das **Weltall**
(outer) space [speɪs]	der **Weltraum**; das **(Welt-)All**
at light speed / **at the speed of light**	mit Lichtgeschwindigkeit
a distance ['dɪstəns] of … **light years**	eine Entfernung von … **Lichtjahren**
galaxy ['gæləksi]	**Galaxis**; **Galaxie**; **Milchstraße**
the Galaxy / the Milky Way	die Galaxis / Milchstraße
(galactic) **nebula** ['nebjʊlə]	(galaktischer) **Nebel**
Pl. nebulas / nebulae ['nebjʊliː]	
celestial [sə'lestiəl] **body** / **object**	**Himmelskörper**
(super)nova ['nəʊvə] *Pl.* novas / novae ['nəʊviː]	**(Super-)Nova**
pulsar ['pʌlsɑː] – **quasar** ['kweɪzɑː]	**Pulsar** – **Quasar**
comet ['kɒmɪt]	**Komet**
meteor ['miːtiə]	**Meteor**
meteorite ['miːtiəraɪt]	**Meteorit**
shooting star / **falling star**	**Sternschnuppe**
planet ['plænɪt]	**Planet**
(The) Earth [ɜːθ] is the third planet from the Sun.	Die Erde ist von der Sonne aus der dritte Planet.

The eight planets in the solar system (= **Die acht Planeten im Sonnensystem**)
Mercury ['mɜːkjəri] (= Merkur) • *Venus* ['viːnəs] • *Earth* [ɜːθ] (= Erde) • *Mars* [mɑːz] • *Jupiter* ['dʒuːpɪtə] • *Saturn* ['sætɜːn] • *Uranus* ['jʊərənəs] • *Neptune* ['neptjuːn] (= Neptun)

orbit ['ɔːbɪt]	**(Umlauf-)Bahn**; **(um)kreisen**
a circular ['sɜːkjələ] / an elliptical [ɪ'lɪptɪkl] orbit	eine kreisförmige / elliptische Bahn
The earth orbits (a)round the sun.	Die Erde umkreist die Sonne.
rotate [rəʊ'teɪt] on an axis ['æksɪs]	sich um eine Achse **drehen**
revolve [rɪ'vɒlv] (a)round the sun	sich um die Sonne **drehen**
satellite ['sætəlaɪt]	**Satellit**; **Trabant**
The moon is Earth's / the earth's satellite.	Der Mond ist der Trabant der Erde.
the **sun** – the **moon**	die **Sonne** – der **Mond**
waxing ['wæksɪŋ] moon	zunehmender Mond
waning ['weɪnɪŋ] moon	abnehmender Mond
solar eclipse [səʊlər ɪ'klɪps]	**Sonnenfinsternis**
lunar eclipse [luːnər ɪ'klɪps]	Mondfinsternis

"Moon" idioms

You're asking for the moon. (= Du verlangst Unmögliches.) • *He promised* ['prɒmɪst] *me the moon.* (= Er hat mir das Blaue vom Himmel herunter versprochen.) • *She writes once in a blue moon.* (= Sie schreibt nur alle Jubeljahre einmal.) • *She was over the moon about it.* (= Sie war überglücklich darüber.)

constellation [kɒnstə'leɪʃn]	Sternbild; Konstellation
The Big Dipper is a well-known constellation.	Der Große Wagen ist ein bekanntes Sternbild.
crater ['kreɪtə]	**Krater**
atmosphere ['ætməsfɪə]	**Atmosphäre**
asteroid belt [æstərɔɪd belt]	**Asteroidengürtel**
magnetic field [mægnetɪk 'fiːld]	**Magnetfeld**
gravity ['grævəti] / **gravitation**	**Gravitation; Schwerkraft**
Gravity at the equator [ɪ'kweɪtə] is lower than at the poles.	Die Schwerkraft ist am Äquator geringer als an den Polen.
Newton's theory ['θɪəri] of gravitation	Newtons Gravitationstheorie
the earth's **gravitational pull**	die **Anziehungskraft** der Erde
observatory [əb'zɜːvətri]	**Observatorium; Sternwarte**
astronomy [ə'strɒnəmi]	(die) **Astronomie**
cosmology [kɒz'mɒlədʒi]	(die) **Kosmologie**
the **creation** [kri'eɪʃn] **accounts** in the Bible ['baɪbl]	die **Schöpfungsberichte** in der Bibel (→ S. 139)
the **big bang theory** [bɪg 'bæŋ θɪəri]	die **Urknalltheorie**
a **black hole** [blæk 'həʊl]	ein **schwarzes Loch**
Einstein's **theory of relativity** [relə'tɪvəti]	Einsteins **Relativitätstheorie**

"I wonder why my phone bill is always so high."

Space exploration
Raumforschung

That's one small step for a man, one giant leap for mankind.
(Astronaut Neil Armstrong on stepping on the moon's surface, 20 July 1969)

(outer) space [(aʊtə) 'speɪs] — (der) **(Welt-)Raum**; (das) **(Welt-)All**
the space age ['speɪs eɪdʒ] — das Zeitalter der Raumfahrt
space travel ['speɪs trævl] — (die) **(Welt-)Raumfahrt**
space programme ['speɪs prəʊɡræm] — Raumfahrtprogramm
space mission ['mɪʃn] / spaceflight — (Welt-)Raumflug
spacesuit ['speɪssuːt] — Raumanzug
spacecraft ['speɪskrɑːft] — Raumfahrzeug
spaceship ['speɪsʃɪp] — Raumschiff
space capsule ['speɪs kæpsjuːl] — Raumkapsel
space shuttle ['speɪs ʃʌtl] — Raumfähre
space probe ['speɪs prəʊb] — Raumsonde
space station ['speɪs steɪʃn] — (Welt-)Raumstation
space junk ['speɪs dʒʌŋk] — Weltraummüll
space medicine ['speɪs medsn] — Raumfahrtmedizin
manned [mænd] – **unmanned** — bemannt – unbemannt
astronaut ['æstrənɔːt] — Astronaut(in)
cosmonaut ['kɒzmənɔːt] — Kosmonaut(in)
testing / **proving** [uː] **ground** — Versuchsgelände
launch a rocket [lɔːntʃ ə 'rɒkɪt] — eine Rakete **starten**
launching site ['lɔːntʃɪŋ saɪt] — (Raketen-)Abschussbasis
launchpad / launching pad [pæd] — Start- / Abschussrampe
launcher ['lɔːntʃə] — Trägerrakete
countdown ['kaʊntdaʊn] — Countdown
liftoff ['lɪftɒf] — (das) **Abheben**; (der) **Start**
We have liftoff. — Der Start ist erfolgt.
trajectory [trə'dʒektəri] — Flugbahn
rendezvous Pl. -vous ['rɒndɪvuː] — Rendezvous
docking manoeuvre [mə'nuːvə] — Kopplungsmanöver
circle (the moon) ['sɜːkl] — (den Mond) **umrunden**
fly-by (mission) ['flaɪbaɪ] — Vorbeiflug
lander ['lændə] — Landefahrzeug / -fähre
soft-land / **make a soft** [sɒft] — auf dem Mond **weich landen**
  landing on the moon
impact area ['ɪmpækt eəriə] — Landezone
lunar (excursion) module — Mond(lande)fähre
  ['mɒdjuːl] / LEM
collect **rock samples** ['sɑːmplz] — **Gesteinsproben** aufsammeln
abort [ə'bɔːt] a mission — einen (Raum-)Flug **abbrechen**
A thruster ['θrʌstə] failure aborted the — Ein Fehler am Korrekturtriebwerk
  flight. — führte zum Abbruch des Fluges.
The lunar landing had to be aborted / — Die Mondlandung musste ab-
  cancelled ['kænsəld]. — gebrochen / abgesetzt werden.
re-entry [ri'entri] — **Wiedereintritt** (*in die Erdatmosphäre*)
(ground) tracking station — Bodenstation

mission control [mɪʃn kən'trəʊl]   (das) **Kontrollzentrum**

Rakete: In der Raumfahrt *rocket* ['rɒkɪt], als militärische Waffe *missile* ['mɪsaɪl].

multistage ['mʌltisteɪdʒ] **rocket**	**Mehrstufenrakete**
retrorocket ['retrəʊrɒkɪt]	**Bremsrakete**
booster (rocket) ['buːstə]	**Booster; Startrakete**
propulsion system [prə'pʌlʃn sɪstəm]	**Antriebssystem**
(rocket) engine ['endʒɪn]	**(Raketen-)Triebwerk**
fuel ['fjuːəl]	**Treibstoff**
hydrogen ['haɪdrədʒən]	**Wasserstoff**
thrust [θrʌst] / **push** [pʊʃ]	**Schub**
command module [kə'mɑːnd mɒdjuːl]	**Kommandokapsel**
service module ['sɜːvɪs mɒdjuːl]	**Versorgungsteil**
life support [sə'pɔːt] **system**	**Lebenserhaltungssystem**
payload ['peɪləʊd]	**Nutzlast**
(artificial) **satellite** ['sætəlaɪt]	(künstlicher) **Satellit**
communications satellite	Nachrichtensatellit
weather satellite	Wettersatellit
orbit ['ɔːbɪt]	**Umlaufbahn; (um)kreisen**
put / place a satellite into orbit	einen Satelliten in eine Umlaufbahn bringen
orbit the earth [ɜːθ]	die Erde umkreisen
microgravity ['maɪkrəʊgrævəti] / **weightlessness**	**Schwerelosigkeit**
radiation [reɪdi'eɪʃn]	**Strahlung**
International Space Station (ISS)	**Internationale Raumstation**
(space) probe [prəʊb]	**(Raum-)Sonde**
commercial [kə'mɜːʃl] **spaceflight**	**kommerzieller Raumflug**

Space tourism in the year 2050.

Idioms

Die Begriffe *earth, sun, moon, stars, planet, sky* und *world* finden sich in mancherlei englischen *idioms*, also Redensarten, die das Gemeinte mit einem Bild ausdrücken:

It won't cost us **the earth** to pick up a cheap hire car and head for the Highlands.
His ideas are all **pie in the sky**. He needs to **come down to earth**.

Es wird uns nicht die Welt kosten, einen billigen Mietwagen zu nehmen und in die Highlands zu fahren.
Seine Ideen sind alles Luftschlösser (*wörtl.*: Pastete am Himmel). Er muss auf den Boden der Tatsachen runterkommen.

He's her hero. She thinks **the sun shines out of his backside**.

Er ist ihr Held. Sie denkt, dass ihm die Sonne aus dem Hintern scheint.

(Anstatt mit *backside* hört man dieses *idiom* auch mit *bum, behind, bottom* oder *ass* bzw. *arse*.)

Some cops **moonlight** as private eyes.

Manche Polizisten arbeiten nebenbei noch als Privatdetektive.

The pair had **done a moonlight flit**, leaving their cat in the empty flat.

Das Pärchen hatte sich bei Nacht und Nebel davongemacht und seine Katze in der leeren Wohnung zurückgelassen.

The whole story is just a load of **moonshine**.

Die ganze Geschichte ist totaler Quatsch.

He **reached for the stars** and saw his wildest dreams come true.

Er griff nach den Sternen und sah seine kühnsten Träume in Erfüllung gehen.

You should thank **your lucky stars** that you're still alive.
It seems she was born **under a lucky star**.
We are all in the gutter, but some of us are looking at **the stars**.

Du solltest deinem Glücksstern dankbar sein, dass du noch lebst.
Es scheint, dass sie unter einem glücklichen Stern geboren ist.
Wir liegen alle in der Gosse, aber manche von uns blicken zu den Sternen.

(Dies ist kein *idiom*, sondern ein Zitat aus einem Stück von Oscar Wilde.)

Rent a flat in Mayfair? **What planet are you on?**

In Mayfair eine Wohnung mieten? Wo denkst du hin?

(Mayfair ist ein besonders exklusiver und teurer Stadtteil von London.)

He's well educated, ambitious and good-looking. For him, **the sky's the limit**.

Er ist gebildet, ehrgeizig und gut aussehend. Für ihn gibt's nach oben keine Grenzen.

The food was **out of this world**.
There's **a world of a difference** between the two cities.

Das Essen war himmlisch.
Zwischen den beiden Städten liegen Welten.

The earth
Die Erde

1   **Geology**
    Geologie

2   **Metals and gemstones**
    Metalle und Schmucksteine

3   **Geographical divisions**
    Geografische Einteilungen

4   **Oceans, lakes, rivers**
    Meer, Seen, Flüsse

5   **The countryside**
    Die Landschaft

6   **The farming world**
    Die Welt der Landwirtschaft

7   **The city**
    Die Stadt

8   **The environment**
    Die Umwelt

9   **Weather and climate**
    Wetter und Klima

10 **Natural disasters**
    Naturkatastrophen

14

Geology
Geologie

The main activities of geology have been to map and classify the rocks exposed on the earth's surface and those accessible underground, and to explain their origin and distribution.
(*J.L.M. Lambert in The Fontana Dictionary of Modern Thought, 1977*)

geology [dʒi'ɒlədʒi]	(die) **Geologie**
structural ['strʌktʃərəl] geology / tectonics [tek'tɒnɪks]	Geotektonik
engineering [endʒɪ'nɪərɪŋ] geology	Ingenieurgeologie
marine [mə'riːn] geology	Meeresgeologie
historical [hɪ'stɒrɪkl] geology	historische Geologie
geologic(al) [dʒiː'ɒlɒdʒɪk(l)] processes	**geologische** Vorgänge
geologic(al) formation [fɔ:'meɪʃn]	geologische Formation
geologic(al) map [mæp]	geologische Karte
geological survey ['sɜːveɪ]	geologische Aufnahme
geologist [dʒi'ɒlədʒɪst]	**Geologe / Geologin**
geography [dʒi'ɒgrəfi]	**Geografie**

☞ *-ology* [-ɒlədʒi] und *-alogy* [-ælədʒi] – beachten Sie die Betonung:
geochro'nology [dʒiːəʊkrə'nɒlədʒi] (= Geochronologie) • *glaci'ology* [gleɪsi'ɒlədʒi] (= Glaziologie) • *mine'ralogy* [mɪnə'rælədʒi] (= Mineralogie) • *paleon'tology* [pælɪɒn'tɒlədʒi] (= Versteinerungskunde) • *pe'trology* [pə'trɒlədʒi] (= Petrologie) • *seis'mology* [saɪz'mɒlədʒi] (= Erdbebenkunde) • *volca'nology* [vɒlkə'nɒlədʒi] (= Vulkanologie)

(the) **history** ['hɪstri] **of the earth**	(die) **Erdgeschichte**
the **evolution** [iːvə'luːʃn] **of the earth**	die **Entwicklung der Erde**
the earth's **core** [kɔː]	der Erd**kern**
the earth's **interior** [ɪn'tɪərɪə]	das Erd**innere**
the earth's **crust** [krʌst]	die Erd**kruste** / Erd**rinde**
continental shelf [kɒntɪnentl 'ʃelf]	**Festland(s)sockel**
continental drift [kɒntɪnentl 'drɪft]	**Kontinentalverschiebung** / -drift
plate tectonics ['pleɪt tektɒnɪks]	**Plattentektonik**
sea- / ocean-floor spreading	**Erweiterung der Ozeane**
stratum ['strɑːtəm] *Pl.* strata ['strɑːtə]	**Schicht; Stratum**
fault [fɔːlt]	**Verwerfung; (Schichten-)Bruch**
rock(s) [rɒk(s)]	**Gestein(e)**
analyse **minerals** [ænəlaɪz 'mɪnərəlz]	**Mineralien** analysieren
mineral resources [rɪ'zɔːsɪz]	**Bodenschätze**
composition [kɒmpə'zɪʃn]	**Zusammensetzung**
the **formation** of crystals ['krɪstlz]	die **Bildung** von Kristallen
sedimentation – sediments ['sedɪ-]	**Sedimentation – Sedimente**
deposit [dɪ'pɒzɪt]	**Lagerstätte; Ablagerung**
deposits of oil and natural gas [gæs]	Öl- und Erdgasvorkommen

erosion [ɪˈrəʊʒn]	**Abtragung; Erosion**
weathering [ˈweðrɪŋ]	**Verwitterung**
fossil [ˈfɒsl]	**Fossil; Versteinerung**
index fossil [ˈɪndeks fɒsl]	Leitfossil
fossilize [ˈfɒsəlaɪz] / become fossilized	versteinern
fossilized remains [fɒsəlaɪzd rɪˈmeɪnz]	Versteinerung(en)
petrify [ˈpetrɪfaɪ] / **become petrified**	**versteinern**

☞ *Petrify* wird auch in der Alltagssprache benutzt: *He's petrified of speaking in public.* (= Er hat panische Angst davor, öffentlich zu reden.) *They were petrified to learn that there were snakes around.* (= Sie waren geschockt, als sie hörten, dass es in der Nähe Schlangen gab.)

(age-)dating [(eɪdʒ) ˈdeɪtɪŋ]	**Altersbestimmung**
radiocarbon dating [reɪdiəʊkɑːbn ˈdeɪtɪŋ]	Radiokarbondatierung
era [ˈɪərə]	**Ära; (Erd-)Zeitalter**
period [ˈpɪəriəd]	**Periode**
epoch [ˈiːpɒk]	**Epoche**
ice age [ˈaɪs eɪdʒ]	**Eiszeit**
glacier [ˈglæsiə]	**Gletscher**
meltwater [ˈmeltwɔːtə]	**Schmelzwasser**
(terminal / end) **moraine** [məˈreɪn]	(End-)**Moräne**
(earth)quake [(ˈɜːθ)kweɪk]	**(Erd-)Beben**
the **Richter scale** [ˈrɪktə skeɪl]	die **Richter-Skala**
volcano [vɒlˈkeɪnəʊ] *Pl.* -oes	**Vulkan**
(volcanic) eruption [ɪˈrʌpʃn]	(Vulkan-)Ausbruch
topography [təˈpɒgrəfi]	**Topografie**

"There are no active volcanoes in this part of the world."

Metals and gemstones
Metalle und Schmucksteine

Better have a friend on the road than gold or silver in your purse. (*Proverb*)

a **precious metal** [preʃəs 'metl]	ein **Edelmetall**
heavy / light metals	Schwer- / Leichtmetalle
gold [gəʊld]	**Gold; golden**

Beachten Sie den Unterschied zwischen den Adjektiven *gold* und *golden*:

gold = aus Gold:
a gold watch [gəʊld 'wɒtʃ] (= eine goldene Uhr), *a gold necklace* ['nekləs]
(= eine goldene Halskette), *a gold medal* ['medl] (= eine Goldmedaille)

golden ['gəʊldən] = golden im übertragenen Sinn:
golden wedding (= goldene Hochzeit), *the golden age* (= das goldene
Zeitalter), *a golden rule* (= eine goldene Regel)

silver ['sɪlvə]	**Silber; silbern**
mercury ['mɜːkjəri]	**Quecksilber**
iron ['aɪən]	**Eisen; eisern**
iron ore [aɪən 'ɔː]	Eisenerz
copper ['kɒpə]	**Kupfer; kupfern**
zinc [zɪŋk] – **tin** [tɪn]	**Zink – Zinn**
lead [led]	**Blei**
lead-free [led'friː] – unleaded [ʌn'ledɪd]	bleifrei – unverbleit
aluminium [ælə'mɪniəm] *BE* /	**Aluminium**
AE **aluminum** [ə'luːmɪnəm]	
alloy ['ælɔɪ]	**Legierung; legieren**
(stainless) **steel** [(steɪnləs) 'stiːl]	(Edel-)**Stahl**
bronze [brɒnz]	**Bronze; bronzen**
the Bronze Age ['brɒnz eɪdʒ]	die Bronzezeit
brass [brɑːs]	**Messing**

Idioms with gems [dʒemz] *and metals* ['metlz]
Be a gem and run me to the station. (= Sei ein Schatz und fahr mich zum
Bahnhof.) • *This CD is a real gem.* (= Diese CD ist wirklich Spitze.) • *He's
a rough diamond* [rʌf 'daɪəmənd]. (= Er hat eine raue Schale.) • *She had the
brass to say that to my face.* (= Sie besaß die Unverfrorenheit, mir das ins
Gesicht zu sagen.) • *Let's get down to brass tacks – how much do you want?*
(= Kommen wir doch zur Sache – wie viel wollen Sie?) • *As a secretary*
['sekrətri], *she's worth her weight in gold.* (= Als Sekretärin ist sie Gold wert.)

gem(stone) [dʒem]	**Schmuckstein; Edelstein**
The cutting of gems is an art.	Das Schleifen von Edelsteinen ist eine Kunst.
imitation [ɪmɪ'teɪʃn] gems	unechter Schmuck
synthetic [sɪn'θetɪk] gems / precious stones	künstliche Edelsteine

| **precious stone** [preʃəs 'stəʊn] | **Edelstein** |
| semiprecious [semi-] stone | Halbedelstein |

*This precious stone set in the silver sea … (= Dies Kleinod, in die Silbersee
gefasst …). So Shakespeare (1564–1616) in seinem Drama (= play)
Richard II (Richard the Second) in einem langen Hymnus auf England.*

rough [rʌf] / cut **diamond** ['daɪəmənd]	Roh**diamant** / geschliffener **Diamant**
jewel ['dʒuːəl]	**Juwel; Edelstein**
the British crown jewels	die britischen Kronjuwelen
She had to sell her jewels.	Sie musste ihren Schmuck verkaufen.
jewellery ['dʒuːəlri] *BE / AE* **jewelry**	**Schmuck**
She always wears expensive /	Sie trägt immer teuren /
valuable jewellery.	wertvollen Schmuck.
a precious ['preʃəs] piece of jewellery	ein kostbares Schmuckstück
Several pieces of jewellery were missing.	Mehrere Schmuckstücke fehlten.
costume jewellery ['kɒstjuːm dʒuːəlri]	Modeschmuck
emerald ['emərəld]	**Smaragd**
ruby ['ruːbi]	**Rubin**
sapphire ['sæfaɪə]	**Saphir**
pearl [pɜːl]	**Perle**
(a string of) pearls / a pearl necklace	eine Perlenkette
amber ['æmbə]	**Bernstein**

*"How do I
know they're
not fake?"*

Geographical divisions
Geografische Einteilungen

Boundary: In political geography, an imaginary line between two nations, separating the imaginary rights of one from the imaginary rights of the other. (*Definition in The Devil's Dictionary, by Ambrose Bierce, 1842–1914?*)

longitude ['lɒndʒɪtjuːd]	(geografische) **Länge**
5 deg(rees) [dɪ'griːz] east longitude	5 Grad östlicher Länge
latitude ['lætɪtjuːd]	(geografische) **Breite**
hemisphere ['hemɪsfɪə]	**Halbkugel; Hemisphäre**
time zone ['taɪm zəʊn]	**Zeitzone**
the **tropics** ['trɒpɪks]	die **Tropen**
the tropic of Cancer ['kænsə]	der Wendekreis des Krebses
the **Old / New World** [njuː 'wɜːld]	die **Alte / Neue Welt**
the **Third World** [θɜːd 'wɜːld]	die **Dritte Welt**
the **(Ant-)Arctic** [(ænt)'ɑːktɪk]	die **(Ant-)Arktis**
(at the) **equator** [ɪ'kweɪtə]	(am) **Äquator**
continent ['kɒntɪnənt]	**Kontinent; Erdteil**
on the Continent	auf dem Kontinent; in Europa
subcontinent [sʌb'kɒntɪnənt]	Subkontinent
continental [kɒntɪ'nentl]	**kontinental**
Britain's Continental neighbours	Großbritanniens europäische Nachbarn
Europe ['jʊərəp]	**Europa**
the old Europe	das alte Europa
European [jʊərə'piːən]	europäisch
Western Europe – Western European	Westeuropa – westeuropäisch
America – American [ə'merɪkən]	**Amerika – amerikanisch**
the Americas [ə'merɪkəz]	Nord-, Süd- und Mittelamerika
North / South America	Nord- / Südamerika
Latin America [lætɪn ə'merɪkə]	Lateinamerika
Australia [ɒ'streɪliə] – **Australian**	**Australien – australisch**
Africa ['æfrɪkə] – **African** ['æfrɪkən]	**Afrika – afrikanisch**
Asia ['eɪʒə] – **Asian** ['eɪʒn]	**Asien – asiatisch**
west [west]	**Westen; West-**
the Middle West / Midwest	der mittlere Westen (der USA)
western ['westən]	**westlich; West-**
the Western world [westən 'wɜːld]	die westliche Welt
Midwestern American small towns	Kleinstädte im mittleren Westen der USA

Beachten Sie den Unterschied:
They lived in West Germany (d.h. in der Bundesrepublik Deutschland vor der Wiedervereinigung von 1990).
They live in western Germany (d.h. im westlichen Teil Deutschlands).

east [iːst]	**Osten; Ost-**
the Middle / Far East	der Nahe / Ferne Osten

The Middle East is the region ['riːdʒən] where Asia, Africa, and Europe meet.	Der Mittlere (dt. ≈ Nahe) Osten ist das Gebiet, wo Asien, Afrika und Europa sich berühren.
the east coast [iːst 'kəʊst]	die Ostküste
the East Asian ['eɪʒn] countries	die ostasiatischen Länder
eastern ['iːstən]	**östlich; Ost-**
the eastern Mediterranean [medɪtə'reɪniən]	das östliche Mittelmeer
Eastern Europe – Eastern European	Osteuropa – osteuropäisch
the Middle Eastern nations	die Staaten im Nahen Osten
north [nɔːθ]	**Norden; Nord-**
the North-South divide [dɪ'vaɪd]	das Nord-Süd-Gefälle
the North / South Pole [pəʊl]	der Nord- / Südpol
They have moved [muːvd] up north.	Sie sind nach Norden gezogen.
northern ['nɔːðən]	**nördlich; Nord-**
Northern Ireland [nɔːðən 'aɪələnd]	Nordirland
Northern Irish [nɔːðən 'aɪrɪʃ]	nordirisch

Im BE heißt *north of Watford* ['wɒtfəd] (= nördlich von Watford) scherzhaft so viel wie „jwd" oder „auf dem Mond". Watford, eine *dormitory* ['dɔːmətri] *town* (= Schlafstadt) *northwest of London* (= nordwestlich von London) ist Endstation der U-Bahn – *civilization* [sɪvəlaɪ'zeɪʃn] *ends there!* AE-Entsprechungen sind *in the sticks* und *in the boondocks* ['buːndɒks].

south [saʊθ]	**Süden; Süd-**
south of the river ['rɪvə]	südlich des Flusses
Brighton is due [djuː] south of London.	Brighton liegt genau südlich von London.
Our living room faces south.	Unser Wohnzimmer liegt nach Süden.
The wind was coming from the southwest.	Der Wind kam von Südwesten.
southern ['sʌðən]	**südlich; Süd-**

Beachten Sie den Unterschied:
South Africa (= Südafrika) – *southern Africa* (= das südliche Afrika).

area ['eəriə]	**Gebiet; Gegend; Fläche**
The Dead Sea area is one of the hottest regions in the world.	Das Gebiet um das Tote Meer ist eine der heißesten Gegenden der Welt.
a mountainous ['maʊntənəs] area	eine bergige / gebirgige Gegend
Belgium ['beldʒəm] has a total area of 30,521 sq km [skweə 'kɪləmiːtəz].	Belgien hat eine Gesamtfläche von 30 521 km².
territory ['terətri]	**Gebiet; Territorium**
the occupied ['ɒkjupaɪd] territories	die besetzten Gebiete
on German territory	auf deutschem Staats- / Hoheitsgebiet
outside **territorial** [terə'tɔːriəl] waters	außerhalb der Hoheitsgewässer
terrain [tə'reɪn]	**Gelände; Terrain**
rough terrain [rʌf tə'reɪn]	unebenes Gelände
in mountainous ['maʊntənəs] terrain	in bergigem Gelände / Terrain
the **Midlands** ['mɪdləndz]	**Mittelengland**

Oceans, lakes, rivers
Meere, Seen, Flüsse

All the rivers flow into the sea, yet the sea never overflows; back to the place from which the rivers flowed they return to flow again. (*From the Book of Ecclesiastes in the Bible*)

the **sea** [siː]	die **See**; das **Meer**
the Mediterranean [medɪtə'reɪnɪən] Sea	das Mittelmeer
the Baltic Sea [bɔːltɪk 'siː]	die Ostsee
inland sea [ɪnlənd 'siː]	Binnenmeer
a holiday at the **seaside**	ein Urlaub an der **See**
the **seabed** / **seafloor** ['siːflɔː]	der **Meeresboden**
ocean ['əʊʃn]	**Ozean**; **Meer**
the Atlantic [ət'læntɪk] Ocean	der Atlantische Ozean
the Pacific [pə'sɪfɪk] Ocean	der Pazifische Ozean
strait [streɪt]	**Meerenge**
the Strait of Gibraltar [dʒɪ'brɔːltə]	die Straße von Gibraltar
gulf [gʌlf]	**Golf; Meerbusen**
the Persian Gulf [pɜːʃn 'gʌlf]	der Persische Golf
bay [beɪ]	**Bucht**
the southern portion of Hudson Bay	der südliche Teil der Hudson Bay
cape [keɪp]	**Kap**
the Cape of Good Hope	das Kap der Guten Hoffnung
the **coast(line)** [kəʊst]	die **Küste**
situated ['sɪtʃueɪtɪd] on the south coast	an der Südküste gelegen
(on the) **beach** [biːtʃ]	(am) **Strand**
a **lake** [leɪk]	ein **See**
Lake Constance ['kɒnstəns]	der Bodensee

Das schottische Wort für *lake* ist *loch* [lɒx]: *on the bonnie, bonnie banks of Loch Lomond* [lɒx 'ləʊmənd] (= „an den schönen, schönen Ufern des Lomond-Sees"). In irischen Namen dagegen *lough* [lɒx]: *Lough Gill* [lɒx 'gɪl] *is one of the prettiest Irish lakes.* (= Der Gill-See ist einer der hübschesten irischen Seen.)

reservoir ['rezəvwɑː]	**Stausee**
pond – **fishpond** ['fɪʃpɒnd]	**Teich – Fischteich**
pool [puːl]	**Schwimmbecken; Schwimmbad**
river ['rɪvə]	**Fluss**
the River Rhine *BE* / *AE* Rhine River	der Rhein
The river flows [fləʊz] across a plain.	Der Fluss fließt durch eine Ebene.
riverside ['rɪvəsaɪd]	**Flussufer**
down by the riverside	unten am Fluss
bank [bæŋk] (of a lake / river)	**Ufer** (eines Sees / Flusses)
on the banks of the Rhine	an den Ufern des Rheins
the **shore** [ʃɔː]	das **Ufer**; die **Küste**
two miles from / off (the) shore	zwei Meilen vom Ufer entfernt / vor der Küste

on the western shore of Lake Michigan ['mɪʃɪgən]	am Westufer des Michigansees
tributary (river) ['trɪbjətri]	**Nebenfluss**
The Moselle [məʊ'zel] is a tributary of the Rhine.	Die Mosel ist ein Nebenfluss des Rheins.
mouth [maʊθ] / **estuary** ['estʃʊəri]	(*Fluss*) **Mündung**
the Thames [temz] estuary	die Themsemündung

Als *Estuary English* bezeichnet man eine in den Städten des Mündungs-
gebiets der *Thames,* also in der Londoner Gegend, anzutreffende
Aussprache des Englischen. Es handelt sich um eine „veredelte" Form
des traditionellen Ostlondoner *cockney*-Dialekts, die sich seit den Sech-
zigerjahren des 20. Jahrhunderts ausbreitet.

channel ['tʃænl]	**Fahrrinne; (Fluss-)Bett**
the (English) Channel	der (Ärmel-)Kanal
canal [kə'næl]	(*künstlicher*) **Kanal**
the Panama / Suez ['suːɪz] Canal	der Panama- / Suezkanal
waterfall ['wɔːtəfɔːl]	**Wasserfall**
He crossed (the) Niagara [naɪ'ægərə] Falls on a tightrope.	Er überquerte die Niagarafälle auf einem Drahtseil.
stream [striːm] / **brook** [brʊk]	**Bach**
(hot) **spring** [sprɪŋ]	(Thermal-)**Quelle**
the **current** ['kʌrənt]	die **Strömung**
swim against the current (– swam – swum)	gegen den Strom schwimmen
the **tides** [taɪdz]	die **Gezeiten**
low [ləʊ] tide – high tide	Ebbe – Flut
iceberg ['aɪsbɜːg]	**Eisberg**
The Titanic [taɪ'tænɪk] struck an iceberg and sank.	Die Titanic rammte einen Eisberg und sank.
island ['aɪlənd]	**Insel**
Manhattan Island / the island of Manhattan [mæn'hætn]	die Insel Manhattan
Manhattan is a long narrow island.	Manhattan ist eine lange, schmale Insel.
peninsula [pə'nɪnsjʊlə]	**Halbinsel**

Isle [aɪl] (= Insel / Eiland) heute nur noch in Namen: *the British Isles* (= die
Britischen Inseln) • *the Isle of Man* (= die Insel Man) • *the Isle of Wight*
(= die Insel Wight).

port [pɔːt]	**Hafen(stadt)**
New York is one of the largest ports.	New York ist einer der größten Häfen.
harbour ['hɑːbə]	**Hafen**
a ship anchored ['æŋkəd] in the harbour	ein Schiff, das im Hafen vor Anker lag
the **docks** [dɒks]	die **Hafenanlagen**
Her husband works at / in the docks.	Ihr Mann arbeitet im Hafen.

14
5 The countryside
Die Landschaft

→ 14.6 The farming world, 15.1 Animals, 15.2 Plants

Each blade of grass has its spot on earth whence it draws its life, its strength; and so is man rooted to the land from which he draws his faith together with his life. (*Joseph Conrad, Polish-born British novelist, 1857–1924*)

countryside ['kʌntrisaid]	**Land(schaft)**
She loves the English countryside.	Sie liebt die englische Landschaft.
live in the country(side)	auf dem Land leben
walks in the surrounding [sə'raʊndɪŋ] countryside	Spaziergänge in der Umgebung
landscape ['lændskeɪp]	**Landschaft**
a hilly / rolling landscape	eine hügelige / wellige Landschaft
scenic ['siːnɪk] areas	landschaftlich schöne Gegenden
the beautiful **scenery** ['siːnəri] of the Highlands	die landschaftliche Schönheit des schottischen Hochlands
hills and **valleys** ['væliz]	**Berge** und **Täler**
mountain ['maʊntən]	**(hoher) Berg**
in the mountains	im Gebirge
a mountain range [reɪndʒ]	ein Gebirgszug

Mount [maʊnt] heute nur noch in Namen: *Alaska's highest peak* [piːk] *is Mount McKinley* [mə'kɪnli]. (= Alaskas höchster Berg ist Mount McKinley.)

peak [piːk] / **summit** ['sʌmɪt] / **top**	**(Berg-)Gipfel**
the **highland(s)** / **lowland(s)** ['ləʊləndz]	das **Hochland / Tiefland**
cliff [klɪf]	**Felswand** (am Meer)
the chalk [tʃɔːk] cliffs of Dover	die Kreidefelsen von Dover
the **Alps** [ælps]	die **Alpen**
canyon ['kænjən]	**Cañon** (= enges, tiefes Flusstal)
ravine [rə'viːn]	**Schlucht**
cave [keɪv]	**Höhle**
plateau ['plætəʊ] *Pl. -s od. -x*	**Hochebene; Plateau**
plain [pleɪn]	**Ebene; Flachland**
grassland ['grɑːslænd]	**Grasland; Weideland**
prairie ['preəri]	**(nordamerikanische Wiesenland-** schaft)
wasteland ['weɪstlænd]	**Ödland**
steppe [step]	**Steppe**
desert ['dezət]	**Wüste**
the Sahara [sə'hɑːrə] Desert in northern Africa	die Wüste Sahara in Nordafrika
wetlands ['wetlændz]	**Feuchtgebiete**
bog [bɒg]	**Moor; Sumpf**
marsh [mɑːʃ] / **swamp** [swɒmp]	**Sumpf**

moor [mʊə] — (Hoch-)Moor; Bergheide
More than 50 per cent [pə 'sent] of Scotland is moorland. — Mehr als die Hälfte Schottlands ist Heidemoor.
heath [hi:θ] — Heide
shrubs [ʃrʌbz] / **bushes** ['bʊʃɪz] — Sträucher; Gebüsch
a treeless area covered with low shrubs and heather ['heðə] — eine baumlose Gegend, in der niedrige Sträucher und Heidekraut wachsen

thicket(s) ['θɪkɪt(s)] — Dickicht; Büsche; Gebüsch
a sandy **beach** [bi:tʃ] — ein Sand**strand**
On hot days Brighton's pebble beach is jam-packed with sun-hungry Londoners. — An heißen Tagen ist Brightons Kieselstrand proppe(n)voll mit sonnenhungrigen Londonern.
(sand) dunes [dju:nz] — (Sand-)**Dünen**
forest ['fɒrɪst] — (größerer) **Wald**
a thick forest — ein dichter Wald
large forest areas / regions ['ri:dʒənz] — große Waldgebiete
Hansel ['hænsl] and Gretel ['gretl] were abandoned [ə'bændənd] in the forest. — Hänsel und Gretel wurden im Wald ausgesetzt.
the Black Forest [blæk 'fɒrɪst] — der Schwarzwald
rain forest ['reɪn fɒrɪst] — Regenwald
wood(s) [wʊd(z)] — (kleinerer) **Wald**
We walked through a dense [dens] wood. — Wir gingen durch einen dichten Wald.
We went for a walk in the woods. — Wir gingen im Wald spazieren.
Sometimes you can't see the wood BE / AE auch forest for the trees. — Manchmal sieht man den Wald vor lauter Bäumen nicht.
backwoods ['bækwʊdz] — **unerschlossene Waldgebiete**
backwoodsman ['bækwʊdzmən] — Hinterwäldler
grove [grəʊv] — **Wäldchen**
clearing ['klɪərɪŋ] — **Lichtung**
wilderness ['wɪldənəs] — **Wildnis**
jungle ['dʒʌŋgl] — **Dschungel; Urwald**
rural areas [rʊərəl 'eəriəz] — **ländliche Gegenden**
farmland ['fɑ:mlænd] — **Ackerland**
rich / fertile ['fɜ:taɪl] farmland — fruchtbares Ackerland
field [fi:ld] — **Feld; Acker; Weide**
the farmers working in the fields — die Bauern, die auf den Feldern arbeite(te)n

garden ['gɑ:dn] — **Garten**
the front [frʌnt] / back garden BE / AE yard — der Garten vor / hinter dem Haus
orchard ['ɔ:tʃəd] — **Obstgarten**
vineyard ['vɪnjəd] — **Weinberg**
hedge [hedʒ] — **Hecke**
park [pɑ:k] — **Park**
national park [næʃnəl 'pɑ:k] — (geschützter) Nationalpark
wildlife park ['waɪldlaɪf pɑ:k] — Wildpark
nature reserve ['neɪtʃə rɪzɜ:v] — **Naturschutzgebiet**
green belt ['gri:n belt] — **Grüngürtel**

The farming world
Die Welt der Landwirtschaft

→ 15.1 Animals, 15.2 Plants

There is no gilding of setting sun or glamour of poetry to
light up the ferocious and endless toil of the farmers' wives.
(*Hamlin Garland, US writer, 1860–1940*)

farm [fɑːm]	**Bauernhof; landwirtschaftlicher Betrieb**
farmhouse ['fɑːmhaʊs]	Farmhaus; Bauernhaus; Gutshaus
farm hand / farmworker	Landarbeiter(in)
farm products ['prɒdʌkts] / agricultural produce ['prɒdjuːs]	landwirtschaftliche Erzeugnisse
farming ['fɑːmɪŋ]	(die) **Landwirtschaft**
dairy farming ['deəri fɑːmɪŋ]	(die) Milchviehhaltung
fish farming ['fɪʃ fɑːmɪŋ]	(die) Fischzucht
factory farming ['fæktri fɑːmɪŋ]	(die) Massentierhaltung
farmer ['fɑːmə]	**Landwirt(in); Bauer / Bäuerin**

Peasants ['peznts] waren / sind arme, oft leibeigene Kleinbauern in früheren
Zeiten oder in der Dritten Welt.

agriculture ['ægrɪkʌltʃə]	(die) **Landwirtschaft**
agricultural [ægrɪ'kʌltʃərəl]	**landwirtschaftlich; Landwirtschafts-**
agricultural / farm machinery [mə'ʃiːnri]	Landmaschinen
ranch [rɑːntʃ] *AE*	(auf Viehzucht spezialisierter land-wirtschaftlicher Großbetrieb)
plantation [plɑː'teɪʃn]	**Pflanzung; Plantage**
a coffee / sugar ['ʃʊgə] plantation	eine Kaffee- / Zuckerplantage
the **soil** [sɔɪl]	die **Erde;** der **Boden**
fertile ['fɜːtaɪl] / poor [pʊə] soils	fruchtbare / karge Böden
(arable ['ærəbl]) **land**	(Acker-)**Land**
field [fiːld]	**Feld; Acker; Weide; Wiese**
a fallow ['fæləʊ] field	ein brachliegendes Feld; eine Brache
pasture ['pɑːstʃə]	**Weide(land)**
cattle grazing on green pastures	Rinder, die auf grünen Weiden grasen
irrigate ['ɪrɪgeɪt] – **irrigation**	**bewässern – Bewässerung**
manure [mə'njʊə]	**Mist; Dung; (natürlicher) Dünger**
fertilize ['fɜːtəlaɪz] – **fertilization**	**düngen – Düngung**
(chemical ['kemɪkl] / artificial [ɑːtɪ'fɪʃl]) fertilizer	(Kunst-)Dünger
pesticide ['pestɪsaɪd]	**Pestizid**
insecticide [ɪn'sektɪsaɪd]	**Insektizid**
weed [wiːd] (killer)	**Unkraut**(vertilgungsmittel)
cultivate ['kʌltɪveɪt]	**kultivieren; bestellen; anbauen**
Asparagus [ə'spærəgəs] is widely cultivated here.	Hier wird viel Spargel angebaut.

plant [plɑ:nt]
plant a field with rye [raɪ]

Pflanze; (an- / be)pflanzen
auf einem Feld Roggen anbauen /
säen

grow [grəʊ] (– grew [gru:] – grown)
Rice doesn't grow here.
We mainly grow maize BE / AE corn.
raise / grow wheat [wi:t] / vegetables
['vedʒtəblz]
raise / rear [rɪə] chickens / pigs

wachsen; anbauen; anpflanzen
Reis gedeiht hier nicht.
Wir bauen hauptsächlich Mais an.
Weizen / Gemüse anbauen

Hühner / Schweine züchten /
aufziehen

seed(s) [si:d(z)]
grain [greɪn] – grains
crop [krɒp]
Cotton ['kɒtn] is the leading crop.

Samen; Saat(gut)
Korn / Getreide – Körner
(das, was angebaut wird) Feldfrucht
Es wird hauptsächlich Baumwolle
angebaut.

The use of pesticides ['pestɪsaɪdz] has
increased crop yields [ji:ldz].
crop rotation [rəʊ'teɪʃn]
crop dusting ['dʌstɪŋ]
crop failure(s) ['feɪljə(z)]
harvest ['hɑ:vɪst]
Wheat [wi:t] harvest is in June.
Sugar beets [bi:ts] are harvested 20 to
30 weeks after the seeds are planted.

Der Einsatz von Pestiziden hat die
Ernteerträge erhöht.
Fruchtfolge; Fruchtwechsel
Schädlingsbekämpfung aus der Luft
Missernte(n)
Ernte; ernten
Die Weizenernte ist im Juni.
Zuckerrüben werden 20 bis 30
Wochen nach der Aussaat geerntet.

livestock ['laɪvstɒk] (Mit Pluralverb!)
(live)stock / cattle breeding
Many farms raise livestock.
cattle ['kætl] (Mit Pluralverb!)
Here the cattle are being fattened.
The cattle were grazing in the fields.
dairy cattle ['deəri kætl]
ox [ɒks] Pl. oxen ['ɒksn]
milk a cow [kaʊ]
mad cow disease [mæd 'kaʊ dɪzi:z] /
BSE

Vieh; Viehbestand / Viehbestände
Viehzucht
Viele Farmen betreiben Viehzucht.
(Rind-)Vieh; Rinder
Hier werden die Rinder gemästet.
Auf den Wiesen weidete das Vieh.
Milchvieh
Ochse
eine Kuh melken
Rinderwahnsinn / BSE

a herd [hɜ:d] of cattle
a flock [flɒk] of sheep
shepherd ['ʃepəd]
pig [pɪg] / AE auch hog [hɒg]
pigsty ['pɪgstaɪ] BE / AE pigpen /
AE hoghouse
horse [hɔ:s]
poultry ['pəʊltri] (farmer)
free-range hens [fri: reɪndʒ 'henz]
free-range eggs
fodder ['fɒdə] / animal feed [fi:d]
Corn is used for livestock ['laɪvstɒk]
feed. AE
hay [heɪ]
haystack ['heɪstæk]
straw [strɔ:]

eine Rinderherde
eine Schafherde
Schafhirte / -hirtin; Schäfer(in)
Schwein
Schweinestall

Pferd
Geflügel(züchter / -züchterin)
frei laufende Hühner
Eier von frei laufenden Hühnern
Viehfutter
Mais wird als Viehfutter verwendet.

Heu
Heuschober
Stroh

coop [ku:p] / **henhouse** ['henhaʊs]	**Hühnerstall; Geflügelkäfig**
barn [bɑ:n]	**Scheune; Stall**
(equipment [ɪ'kwɪpmənt]) **shed** [ʃed]	(Geräte-)**Schuppen**
cowshed ['kaʊʃed]	Kuhstall
lean-to shed	Anbauschuppen
stable ['steɪbl]	**(Pferde-)Stall**
manger ['meɪndʒə]	**Futtertrog;** (*Bibel*) **Krippe**
greenhouse ['gri:nhaʊs]	**Gewächshaus**
silo ['saɪləʊ] – **silage** ['saɪlɪdʒ]	**Silo – Silage**
mow [məʊ] – **mower** ['məʊə]	**mähen – Mäher**
plough [plaʊ] *BE* / *AE* **plow** [plaʊ]	**Pflug**
tractor ['træktə]	**Traktor**
thresh [θreʃ] – **thresher** ['θreʃə]	**dreschen – Drescher**
combine (harvester) ['kɒmbaɪn ('hɑ:vɪstə)]	**Mähdrescher**
genetic engineering [dʒənetɪk endʒɪ'nɪərɪŋ]	(die) **Gentechnik**
clone [kləʊn] a sheep	ein Schaf **klonen**

"Farming" idioms

The stuff isn't worth [wɜ:θ] *a bean.* (= Das Zeug ist keinen Pfifferling wert.) •
a chicken and egg situation [sɪtʃu'eɪʃn] (= eine Zwickmühle) • *hit the hay*
(= sich in die Falle hauen) • *It's like looking for a needle in a haystack.*
(= Es ist, wie wenn man eine Stecknadel im Heuhaufen sucht.) • *eat like
a horse* (= wie ein Scheunendrescher essen) • *put the cart before the horse*
(= das Pferd beim Schwanz aufzäumen) • *buy a pig in a poke* (= die Katze
im Sack kaufen) • *He's the black sheep of the family.* (= Er ist das schwarze
Schaf der Familie.) • *lock the stable door after the horse has bolted* ['bəʊltɪd]
(= den Brunnen erst zudecken, wenn das Kind hineingefallen ist) •
That was the last straw [strɔ:]. (= Das brachte das Fass zum Überlaufen.) •
catch at a straw (= sich an einen Strohhalm klammern)

The black sheep.

The city
Die Stadt

→ 6.1 Communities, 5.1 Flats and houses, 7.1 Housing shortage, 19.6 Traffic

People come to the city to find safety and happiness, to lead the good life.
(*Aristotle, Greek philosopher, 384–322 BC*)

city ['sɪti]	(größere) **Stadt**
the city and its residents ['rezɪdənts]	die Stadt und ihre Bewohner
go / travel to the city	in die Stadt fahren
a provincial [prə'vɪnʃl] city / town	eine Provinzstadt / Stadt in der Provinz
an industrial [ɪn'dʌstriəl] city	eine Industriestadt
satellite ['sætəlaɪt] city / town	Trabantenstadt
my native ['neɪtɪv] city / town	meine Geburtsstadt
the city centre [sɪti 'sentə]	das Stadtzentrum
within the city limits	innerhalb der Stadtgrenze
10 miles beyond the city boundaries ['baʊndəriz]	10 Meilen jenseits der Stadtgrenze
city / town planning	(die) Stadtplanung
the city / town council ['kaʊnsl]	der Rat der Stadt; die Stadtverwaltung

Als Gegensatz zu *city* bezeichnet *town* objektiv eine kleinere Stadt (*a small town* = eine Kleinstadt). Emotional und in bestimmten Wendungen wird *town* aber auch in Bezug auf Großstädte wie London und New York gebraucht: *Are you going into town?* (= Fährst du in die Stadt?) *You're from out of town, aren't you?* (= Sie sind wohl nicht von hier?) *Going up to town* heißt, dass man aus der Provinz nach London fährt, und *So-and-so is in town / out of town* bedeutet, dass der Betreffende gerade oder gerade nicht in London / New York / Chicago ist. Wer *out on the town* ist, der will dort was erleben, einen draufmachen, und in dem Film *On the Town* (1950) singen drei *sailors* (= Matrosen) auf Landurlaub in New York den *song* "New York, New York, a wonderful town".

city dweller ['dwelə]	**Stadtbewohner(in); (Groß-)Städter(in)**
slum / ghetto ['getəʊ] dweller	Slum- / Gettobewohner(in)
townsman – townswoman	**Städter – Städterin**
Townspeople are different ['dɪfrənt].	Leute aus der Stadt sind anders.

Garden cities [gɑːdn 'sɪtiz] (erste Gründung in GB war *Letchworth* ['letʃwəθ], 1903) sind auf dem Reißbrett (= *drawing board* ['drɔːɪŋ bɔːd]) entworfene, von Grüngürteln (= *green belts*) umgebene und von Grünflächen (= *green spaces / areas*) durchsetzte Gartenstädte.
Auch bei den seit dem Zweiten Weltkrieg in GB entstandenen ca. 30 *new towns* handelt es sich um *planned* [plænd] *cities*.

14

7

downtown [daʊn'taʊn] AE	**in der / in die Innenstadt**
Are you going downtown?	Fährst / Gehst du in die (Innen-)Stadt?
in the downtown ['daʊntaʊn] area	in der Innenstadt / City; im Zentrum
Munich's ['mjuːnɪks] downtown area	die Münchner Innenstadt
metropolis [mə'trɒpəlɪs]	**Metropole**
Vancouver [væn'kuːvə] is Canada's third largest metropolis.	Vancouver ist Kanadas drittgrößte Metropole.
the New York **metropolitan** [metrə'pɒlɪtn] **area**	der **Großraum** New York
the **central** ['sentrəl] **cities**	die **Innenstädte**
a map of central London	eine Karte / ein Plan der Londoner Innenstadt
the **suburbs** ['sʌbɜːbz]	die **Vororte**
on the **outskirts** ['aʊtskɜːts] of Berlin	am **Stadtrand** von Berlin
settle on the **periphery** [pə'rɪfəri]	sich an der **Peripherie** ansiedeln

„Städtisch" im Sinn von „zu einer bestimmten Stadt gehörend" = *municipal* [mjuː'nɪsɪpl]; im Sinn von „mit Städten allgemein zusammenhängend" = *urban* ['ɜːbən]:

the municipal parks / hospitals / theatres (= die städtischen Parks / Krankenhäuser / Theater) • *the municipal government* ['gʌvnmənt] (= die Stadtregierung / -verwaltung) • *municipal elections* (= Kommunalwahlen)

urban life (= das Leben in der Stadt) • *the urban population* (= die Stadtbevölkerung) • *urban planning* (= Stadtplanung) • *urban development* (= Stadtentwicklung) • *urban renewal* [rɪ'njuːəl] (= Stadterneuerung)

facilities [fə'sɪlətiz]	**Einrichtungen**
educational / research facilities	Bildungs- / Forschungseinrichtungen
cultural / medical facilities	kulturelle / medizinische Einrichtungen
a **run-down** / **blighted** ['blaɪtɪd] neighbourhood / area	eine **heruntergekommene** Gegend
demolish [dɪ'mɒlɪʃ] old buildings	alte Häuser / Altbauten **abreißen**
improve [ɪm'pruːv] (living) **conditions** in the cities	die **Lebensbedingungen** in den Städten verbessern

Unterschied zwischen *street* **und** *road*

Streets sind in der Stadt, zwischen Häusern – sie haben Bürgersteige (*pavements* ['peɪvmənts] BE / AE *sidewalks* ['saɪdwɔːks]), Geschäfte etc.: *We live in / on Russell* ['rʌsl] *Street.*
Der deutschen Hauptstraße entspricht BE *High Street* (*the shoe shop in the High Street*) und AE *Main Street* (*the shoe store on Main Street*).
Roads sind Verkehrswege, die irgendwo hinführen: *the Dover road* (= die Straße nach Dover). Viele *roads,* die sich ursprünglich zwischen Orten befanden, sind heute durch das Wachsen der Städte mitten in der Stadt. *Edgware* ['edʒweə] *Road* (= die Straße nach Edgware) z.B. ist heute ein Londoner Straßenname: *Her office is in / on Edgware Road.* (Londoner sagen auch: *in / on the Edgware Road.*)

The environment
Die Umwelt

The financial crisis is a result of our living beyond our financial means.
The climate crisis is a result of our living beyond our planet's means.
(*Yvo de Boer, climate expert and former UN official, born in 1954*)

the environment [ɪn'vaɪrənmənt]
You, too, can help protect [prə'tekt] the environment.
environmental [ɪnvaɪrən'mentl]
environmental pollution / protection / awareness [ə'weənəs]
environmental problems / disasters
environmental groups such as Greenpeace
environmentalism [ɪnvaɪrən'mentəlɪzm]
environmentalist [ɪnvaɪrən'mentəlɪst]
despite protests from environmentalists
environmentally friendly / ecofriendly ['iːkəʊfrendli]
ecological [iːkə'lɒdʒɪkl]
green [griːn]
green / environmental issues ['ɪʃuːz]
The Greens want all waste to be segregated.
forest ['fɒrɪst]
Tropical forests are being destroyed.
deforestation [diːfɒrɪ'steɪʃn]
desert ['dezət]
Deserts are spreading ['spredɪŋ].
the ozone layer ['əʊzəʊn leɪə]
CFCs destroy the ozone layer.
the greenhouse effect [ɪ'fekt]
pollution [pə'luːʃn]
air / water / soil pollution
radiation [reɪdi'eɪʃn] pollution
noise pollution ['nɔɪz pəluːʃn]
pollution control [kən'trəʊl]
pollutants [pə'luːtənts]

die Umwelt
Auch Sie können zum Umweltschutz beitragen.
Umwelt-
Umweltverschmutzung / -schutz / -bewusstsein
Umweltprobleme / -katastrophen
Umweltorganisationen wie etwa Greenpeace
Umweltschutz

Umweltschützer(in)
trotz der Proteste von Umweltschützern
umweltfreundlich

ökologisch; Umwelt-
grün; umweltfreundlich; ökologisch
Umweltthemen
Die Grünen setzen sich für eine umfassende Abfalltrennung ein.
Wald
Tropenwälder werden vernichtet.
Entwaldung
Wüste
Die Wüsten breiten sich aus.
die Ozonschicht
FCKW zerstören die Ozonschicht.
der Treibhauseffekt
Verschmutzung
Luft- / Wasser- / Bodenverschmutzung
radioaktive Verseuchung
Lärmbelästigung; Lärmbelastung
Vermeidung von Umweltbelastungen
Schadstoffe

Müll ist umgangssprachlich *rubbish* ['rʌbɪʃ], AE auch *garbage* ['gɑːbɪdʒ] oder *trash* [træʃ], in der Behördensprache allgemein *refuse* ['refjuːs]. Abfall / Abfälle heißt in theoretischen Zusammenhängen – etwa in der Ökologie – häufig *waste*, wobei die Pluralform *wastes* (= Abfälle / Abfallstoffe) mehr im AE zu finden ist: *Wastes are / Waste is burned at very high temperatures* ['temprətʃəz]. (= Abfälle werden / Müll wird bei sehr hohen Temperaturen verbrannt.)

waste disposal [dɪˈspəʊzl] (= Abfallbeseitigung / Abfallentsorgung) •
waste disposal site (= Mülldeponie) • *household / domestic* [dəˈmestɪk]
waste(s) (= Hausmüll) • *industrial* [ɪnˈdʌstriəl] *waste(s)* (= Gewerbeabfälle) • *hazardous* [ˈhæzədəs] / *toxic* [ˈtɒksɪk] / *nuclear* [ˈnjuːklɪə]
waste(s) (= Sonder- / Gift- / Atommüll) • *waste / refuse* [ˈrefjuːs] /
garbage incineration [ɪnsɪnəˈreɪʃn] (= Müllverbrennung) • *refuse tip* BE /
AE *garbage dump / landfill (site)* (= Müllkippe)

dump [dʌmp]	abladen; abkippen; Müllkippe; Müllabladeplatz
the dumping of radioactive waste in the ocean	die Versenkung / Verklappung von radioaktivem Müll im Ozean / Meer
an oil spill [ˈɔɪl spɪl]	eine Ölpest; ausgelaufenes Öl
oil slick [ˈɔɪl slɪk]	(ein) Ölteppich
overfertilization [əʊvəfɜːtəlaɪˈzeɪʃn]	Überdüngung
carbon dioxide [kɑːbn daɪˈɒksaɪd]	Kohlendioxid
reduce carbon dioxide emissions	den Kohlendioxidausstoß verringern
climate change [ˈklaɪmət tʃeɪndʒ]	(der) Klimawandel
global warming [gləʊbl ˈwɔːmɪŋ]	Erderwärmung
Exhaust fumes [ɪgˈzɔːst fjuːmz] contribute to global warming.	Auspuffgase tragen zur Erwärmung der Erdatmosphäre bei.
acid rain [æsɪd ˈreɪn]	saurer Regen
sustainable [səˈsteɪnəbl] **development**	nachhaltige Entwicklung
natural resources [rɪˈzɔːsɪz]	natürliche Ressourcen
an endangered species [ˈspiːʃiːz]	eine vom Aussterben bedrohte Art
the protection / preservation [prezəˈveɪʃn] of endangered species	der Artenschutz
fossil fuels [ˈfɒsl fjuːəlz]	fossile Brennstoffe / Energieträger
biofuel [ˈbaɪəʊfjuːəl]	Biokraftstoff; Biosprit
peak oil [ˈpiːk ɔɪl]	globales Ölfördermaximum
renewable [riˈnjuːəbl] **energy**	erneuerbare Energie
solar power – wind power	Sonnenenergie – Windkraft
solar panel [səʊlə ˈpænl]	Solarkollektor; Sonnenkollektor; Solarmodul, -zelle, -panel
recycle [riːˈsaɪkl]	wiederverarbeiten; recyceln
A lot of waste can be recycled.	Viele Abfallstoffe lassen sich wiederverwerten.
Recycling reduces the waste of raw materials [məˈtɪəriəlz].	Recycling reduziert die Verschwendung von Rohstoffen.
recycled paper [riːsaɪkld ˈpeɪpə]	Recyclingpapier
bottle bank [ˈbɒtl bæŋk] BE	Altglascontainer
unleaded petrol [ʌnledɪd ˈpetrəl] BE / AE **gas** [gæs]	bleifreies Benzin
returnable bottles [rɪtɜːnəbl ˈbɒtlz]	Mehrwegflaschen
nonreturnable [nɒn-] bottles	Einwegflaschen
packaging [ˈpækɪdʒɪŋ]	Verpackung
Companies are required [rɪˈkwaɪəd] to take back the packaging.	Die Firmen sind zur Rücknahme der Verpackungen verpflichtet.
compulsory deposit [kəmˈpʌlsəri dɪˈpɒzɪt]	Zwangspfand

Weather and climate
Wetter und Klima

When two Englishmen meet, their first talk is of the weather.
(*Samuel Johnson, known as Dr Johnson, British lexicographer, 1709–84*)

What's the **weather** like?	Wie ist denn das **Wetter?**
fair / foul weather	schönes / scheußliches Wetter
nice / dreadful ['dredfl] weather	schönes / furchtbares Wetter
weather permitting [pə'mɪtɪŋ]	wenn die Witterung es zulässt
a **fine** day	ein **schöner** Tag
Let's hope the **sun** comes out.	Hoffentlich kommt die **Sonne** heraus.
sunny periods / intervals / spells	**sonnige** Abschnitte; Aufheiterungen
sunshine ['sʌnʃaɪn]	**Sonnenschein**
We had a lot of sunshine.	Wir hatten viel Sonne.
on a **clear** day	bei **klarem** Wetter
hot – **cold**	**heiß** – **kalt**
heat [hiːt]	**Hitze**
a heat wave ['hiːt weɪv]	eine Hitzewelle
a **cold** / **warm front** [frʌnt]	eine **Kaltluft- / Warmluftfront**
fairly **warm** for the time of year	recht **warm** für die Jahreszeit
It seems to be getting warmer.	Es scheint wärmer zu werden.
warm and humid ['hjuːmɪd]	warm und feucht; feuchtwarm
humidity [hju'mɪdəti]	**(Luft-)Feuchtigkeit**
muggy ['mʌgi] / **sultry** ['sʌltri]	**schwül**
It's rather **close** [kləʊs] today.	Es ist heute ziemlich **drückend.**
It's turned [tɜːnd] **cooler.**	Es ist **kühler** geworden.
The evenings are **nice and cool**.	Die Abende sind **angenehm kühl.**
It's rather **chilly** ['tʃɪli] today.	Es ist heute recht **kühl** / **frisch.**
a chilly day	ein unfreundlicher Tag
It's a bit **nippy** ['nɪpi] this morning.	Es ist heute Morgen recht **frisch.**
biting / icy ['aɪsi] **cold**	schneidende / eisige **Kälte**
freeze [friːz] (– froze – frozen)	**(ge)frieren**
It'll probably freeze.	Es gibt wahrscheinlich Frost.
It's freezing (cold).	Es ist eiskalt.
above [ə'bʌv] / below freezing	über / unter dem Gefrierpunkt
frost [frɒst]	**Frost**
a **mild** [maɪld] / **severe** [sɪ'vɪə] winter	ein **milder** / **strenger** Winter
the **Met Office** ['met ɒfɪs] *BE* /	das **Wetteramt**
AE **weather bureau** ['bjʊərəʊ]	
the **weather map** ['weðə mæp]	die **Wetterkarte**
weather report [rɪ'pɔːt]	**Wetterbericht**
(tomorrow's) **weather forecast**	(die) **Wettervorhersage** (für morgen)
the **outlook** for tomorrow [tə'mɒrəʊ]	die **Vorhersage** für morgen
thermometer [θə'mɒmɪtə]	**Thermometer**
average **temperatures** ['temprətʃəz]	Durchschnitts**temperaturen**
above / below **zero** ['zɪərəʊ]	über / unter **null**
below-zero / subzero temperatures	Temperaturen unter null

Celsius ['selsiəs] – ***Fahrenheit*** ['færənhaɪt]
In GB hat sich bei Temperaturangaben *Celsius* inzwischen weitgehend durchgesetzt; in den USA ist in Wetterberichten noch ausschließlich *Fahrenheit* gebräuchlich. Entsprechungen:

°Fahrenheit	0	10	20	30	32	40	50	60	70	80	90	100
°Celsius	-18	-12	-7	-1	0	4	10	16	21	27	32	38

cloud [klaʊd]
Wolke
a cloudless sky [skaɪ]
ein wolkenloser Himmel
It'll cloud over in the afternoon.
Am Nachmittag wird es sich bewölken.

cloudy ['klaʊdi]
bewölkt; bedeckt; wolkig
It'll stay mostly cloudy.
Es bleibt überwiegend bewölkt.
overcast [əʊvə'kɑːst]
bedeckt; bewölkt
dull and **rainy** at first, **clearing up** later
zunächst **trübe** und **regnerisch**, später **aufheiternd**
dry – wet
trocken – nass
We're in for **rain.**
Es wird wohl **Regen** geben.
light / torrential [tə'renʃl] rain
leichter / wolkenbruchartiger Regen
It's pouring ['pɔːrɪŋ] (with rain).
Es gießt in Strömen.
It was raining heavily ['hevɪli].
Es regnete stark.
rainy weather ['weðə]
regnerisches Wetter / Regenwetter
a rainy day [reɪni 'deɪ]
ein verregneter Tag / Regentag
a **deluge** ['deljuːdʒ] / **downpour**
ein **(Regen-)Guss / Wolkenbruch**
(scattered ['skætəd]) **showers**
(vereinzelte) **Schauer**
drizzle ['drɪzl]
Nieselregen; Sprühregen
snow [snəʊ]
Schnee; schneien
precipitation [prɪsɪpɪ'teɪʃn]
Niederschlag
haze [heɪz] – **hazy** ['heɪzi]
Dunst – diesig
mist [mɪst]
(leichter) Nebel; Dunst
fog [fɒg] – **foggy** ['fɒgi]
Nebel – neb(e)lig
smog [smɒg]
Smog
dew [djuː]
Tau
a light / gentle [dʒentl] / fresh **breeze**
eine leichte / schwache / frische **Brise**
wind [wɪnd] – **windy** ['wɪndi]
Wind – windig
southerly ['sʌðəli] / easterly wind
Süd- / Ostwind
northerly ['nɔːðəli] / westerly winds
nördliche / westliche Winde
storm [stɔːm]
Unwetter; Gewitter; Sturm
thunderstorm ['θʌndəstɔːm]
Gewitter
a flash of **lightning** ['laɪtnɪŋ].
ein **Blitz**
There was thunder and lightning.
Es donnerte und blitzte.
gale (warning) ['geɪl (wɔːnɪŋ)]
Sturm(warnung)
climate ['klaɪmət]
Klima
a temperate / moderate climate
ein gemäßigtes Klima
maritime ['mærɪtaɪm] climate
Seeklima; Meeresklima
continental [kɒntɪ'nentl] climate
Kontinental- / Land- / Binnenklima
You could do with a change of climate.
Ein Klimawechsel würde Ihnen gut tun.

global climate change
globale / weltweite Klimaveränderung

Natural disasters
Naturkatastrophen

All the springs of the great deep burst out, the windows of the heavens were opened, and rain fell on the earth for forty days and forty nights.
(From the description of the Flood in the Bible)

the victims of **natural disasters** [nætʃərəl dɪ'zɑːstəz] — die Opfer von **Naturkatastrophen**

disaster area ['eəriə] — Katastrophengebiet

(earth)quake [('ɜː θ)kweɪk] — **(Erd-)Beben**

a minor ['maɪnə] / major ['meɪdʒə] earthquake — ein kleineres / größeres Erdbeben

if a quake hits downtown L.A. — wenn es in der Innenstadt von Los Angeles zu einem Erdbeben kommt

The quake caused [kɔːzd] a landslide. — Das Beben verursachte einen Erdrutsch.

epicentre ['epɪsentə] — **Epizentrum**

aftershock ['ɑːftəʃɒk] — **Nachbeben**

volcano [vɒl'keɪnəʊ] — **Vulkan**

a violent **eruption** [ɪ'rʌpʃn] of Mount Vesuvius [və'suːviəs] — ein gewaltiger **Ausbruch** des Vesuvs

lava ['lɑːvə] — **Lava**

The city was buried ['berɪd] under a thick layer ['leɪə] of lava and ash. — Die Stadt wurde unter einer dicken Lava- und Ascheschicht begraben.

avalanche ['ævəlɑːnʃ] — **Lawine**

whirlwind ['wɜːlwɪnd] — **Wirbelwind; Wirbelsturm**

a violent **cyclone** [vaɪələnt 'saɪkləʊn] — ein heftiger **Wirbelsturm**

tornado [tɔː'neɪdəʊ] *Pl.* tornadoes — **Tornado; Wirbelsturm**

hurricane ['hʌrɪkən] — **Hurrikan; Orkan**

The hurricane claimed 500 lives. — Der Hurrikan forderte 500 Todesopfer.

typhoon [taɪ'fuːn] — **Taifun**

The typhoon killed [kɪld] 300 people. — Dem Taifun fielen 300 Menschen zum Opfer.

flood [flʌd] — **Flut; Überschwemmung**

flood warning ['wɔːnɪŋ] — Hochwasser- / Flutwarnung

flood control [kən'trəʊl] — (der) Hochwasserschutz

flood-prone areas ['eəriəz] — hochwassergefährdete Gebiete

the Flood — die Sintflut

a millennium [mɪ'leniəm] flood — eine Jahrtausendflut

A large area was **flooded** ['flʌdɪd]. — Ein großes Gebiet wurde **überflutet / überschwemmt.**

The river **inundated** ['ɪnʌndeɪtɪd] a vast area. — Der Fluss **überflutete** ein riesiges Gebiet.

tidal wave [taɪdl 'weɪv] — **Flutwelle**

Hundreds of people **(were) drowned** [draʊnd]. — Hunderte von Menschen ertranken.

tsunami [tsuː'nɑːmi] — **Tsunami**

drought [draʊt] — **Dürre(periode)**

a period of devastating drought — eine verheerende Dürreperiode

fire ['faɪə]
a disastrous [dɪ'zɑːstrəs] fire / a fire disaster
Forest fires are often caused by lightning.
locust (plague) ['ləʊkəst (pleɪg)]
famine ['fæmɪn]
an impending [ɪm'pendɪŋ] famine
famine relief [rɪ'liːf]
Thousands died of famine.

Feuer; Brand
eine Brandkatastrophe
Waldbrände werden oft durch Blitzschlag verursacht.
Heuschrecke(nplage)
Hungersnot; Hungerkatastrophe
eine drohende Hungersnot
Hungerhilfe
Tausende verhungerten.

Eine der entsetzlichsten Hungerkatastrophen (= *One of the most horrific famines*) der europäischen Geschichte (= *in the history of Europe*) war die *Irish Famine* (1846–50). Die Iren (= *The Irish*) waren damals fast vollkommen abhängig von der Kartoffel (= *almost totally dependent on the potato*). Als die Kartoffelernte (= *the potato crop*) mehrere Jahre hintereinander durch einen Pilz vernichtet wurde (= *was destroyed by a fungus for several years in a row*), kam es zu einer Hungersnot, der über eine Million Menschen zum Opfer fielen (= *which killed over a million people*). Durch die Hungersnot, Krankheit und Auswanderung nach Amerika (= *Owing to the famine, disease, and emigration to America*) fiel Irlands Bevölkerungszahl (= *Ireland's population dropped*) damals von acht auf fünf Millionen (= *from eight to five million*).

crop failure ['krɒp feɪljə]
cracked soil [krækt 'sɔɪl]
climate disaster [dɪ'zɑːstə]
devastate ['devəsteɪt]
The city was devastated by an earthquake.
The city suffered a **devastating** earthquake.
cause great **devastation** [devə'steɪʃn]
the **aftereffects** ['ɑːftərɪfekts] of the disaster
The city of X was the hardest hit, with 34 **fatalities** [fə'tælətiz].
The **death toll** ['deθ təʊl] has risen to 68.
An estimated ['estɪmeɪtɪd] 600 people **lost their lives**.
rescue team ['reskjuː tiːm]

The rescue work is still going on.

They survived [sə'vaɪvd] the disaster **unscathed** [ʌn'skeɪðd].
The **damage** ['dæmɪdʒ] is estimated at $2 billion.
the Red Cross [red 'krɒs]
the Red Crescent ['kreznt]

Ernteausfall; Missernte
rissige Erde
Klimakatastrophe
verwüsten
Die Stadt wurde durch ein Erdbeben verwüstet.
Die Stadt wurde von einem **verheerenden** Erdbeben heimgesucht.
große **Verwüstungen** anrichten
die **Nachwirkungen** der Katastrophe
Die Stadt X war mit 34 **Todesopfern** am stärksten betroffen.
Die **Zahl der Todesopfer** hat sich auf 68 erhöht.
Die Zahl der Todesopfer wird auf 600 geschätzt.
Rettungsmannschaft; Bergungskommando
Die Bergungsarbeiten dauern noch an.
Sie überlebten die Katastrophe **unversehrt**.
Der **Sachschaden** wird auf 2 Milliarden Dollar geschätzt.
das Rote Kreuz
der Rote Halbmond (= muslimische Entsprechung des Roten Kreuzes)

Living things
Lebewesen

1   **Animals**
     Tiere

2   **Plants**
     Pflanzen

3   **Simpler life forms**
     Einfachere Lebewesen

Idioms

→ 3.1 Foods, 14.6 The farming world

We have enslaved the rest of the animal creation, and have treated our distant cousins in fur and feathers so badly that beyond doubt, if they were able to formulate a religion, they would depict the Devil in human form. (William Ralph Inge, British churchman, 1860–1954)

(tame / wild) **animal** [ˈænɪməl]	(zahmes / wildes) **Tier**
experimental [ɪkspeɪˈmentl] animals	Versuchstiere
cruelty [ˈkruːəlti] to animals	Tierquälerei
society [səˈsaɪəti] for the prevention of cruelty to animals	Tierschutzverein
animal welfare / rights	Tierschutz
animal rights activist [ˈæktɪvɪst]	Tierschützer(in)
the animal kingdom [ˈkɪŋdəm]	das Tierreich
beast [biːst]	**Tier; Bestie**
man and beast	Mensch und Tier
The lion [ˈlaɪən] is called the king of beasts.	Den Löwen nennt man den König der Tiere.
beast of burden [ˈbɜːdn]	Lasttier
pet [pet]	**(Haus-)Tier**
White mice are often kept as pets.	Weiße Mäuse werden oft als Haustiere gehalten.
mammal [ˈmæml]	**Säugetier**
fur [fɜː]	**Fell**
Many animals are hunted for their fur.	Viele Tiere werden wegen ihres Fells gejagt.

☞ Zur Bezeichnung von Tieren als Jagdwild steht häufig die Singularform. Vergleichen Sie:
*I've never shot **duck**.* (= Ich habe noch nie Enten geschossen / gejagt.)
*I've never seen **ducks** around here.* (= Ich habe hier noch nie Enten gesehen.)
*They're not allowed to shoot **elephant** [ˈelɪfənt] / **lion** [ˈlaɪən].* (= Elefanten / Löwen dürfen sie nicht schießen.)
*We didn't see any **elephants** / **lions**.* (= Elefanten / Löwen sahen wir nicht.)

dog [dɒg]	**Hund**
hunting dog – watchdog [ˈwɒtʃdɒg]	Jagdhund – Wachhund
fighting dog / killer dog	Kampfhund
hound [haʊnd] – **the hounds**	**Jagdhund – die Meute** (bei der Jagd)
bitch [bɪtʃ]	**Hündin; Weibchen** (= Füchsin etc.)
pup(py) [ˈpʌp(i)]	**Welpe; junger Hund**
Alsatian [ælˈseɪʃn] / **German shepherd** [ˈʃepəd]	**(deutscher) Schäferhund**
mongrel [ˈmʌŋgrəl]	**Bastard; Promenadenmischung**
cat [kæt]	**Katze**
tom(cat)	Kater

kitten ['kɪtn]	(Katzen-)Junges; Kätzchen
donkey ['dɒŋki] / **ass** [æs]	Esel
I've made an ass of myself.	Ich habe mich blamiert.
(big / small) **game** [geɪm]	(Groß- / Nieder-)**Wild**
game reserve [rɪ'zɜːv] / park	Wildreservat
deer [dɪə] Pl. deer	Hirsch(e); Reh(e)
fox [fɒks]	Fuchs
wolf [wʊlf] Pl. wolves [wʊlvz]	Wolf
monkey ['mʌŋki] – **ape** [eɪp]	Affe – Menschenaffe
Man is descended [dɪ'sendɪd] from the apes.	Der Mensch stammt vom Affen ab.
chimp / **chimpanzee** [tʃɪmpæn'ziː]	Schimpanse
lion ['laɪən] – **tiger** ['taɪɡə]	Löwe – Tiger
(brown / grizzly / polar) **bear** [beə]	(Braun- / Grisli- / Eis-)**Bär**
mouse [maʊs] Pl. mice [maɪs]	Maus
rat [ræt]	Ratte
You rat!	Du Miststück / (gemeiner) Hund!
guinea pig ['ɡɪni pɪɡ]	Meerschweinchen; Versuchs-kaninchen
hamster ['hæmstə]	Hamster
squirrel ['skwɪrəl]	Eichhörnchen
feather ['feðə]	Feder
Owls [aʊlz] have strong legs, sharp claws, and soft feathers.	Eulen haben kräftige Beine, scharfe Krallen und weiche Federn.
Fine feathers make fine birds.	Kleider machen Leute.
bird [bɜːd]	Vogel
migratory ['maɪɡrətri] bird – songbird	Zugvogel – Singvogel
bird of prey [preɪ]	Raubvogel; Greifvogel
bird's nest – birds' nests	Vogelnest – Vogelnester
The early bird catches the worm [ɜː].	Morgenstund hat Gold im Mund.
A bird in hand is worth two in the bush [bʊʃ].	Der Spatz in der Hand ist besser als die Taube auf dem Dach.
sparrow ['spærəʊ]	Sperling; Spatz
(blue / great) tit [tɪt]	(Blau- / Kohl-)Meise
swallow ['swɒləʊ] – **thrush** [θrʌʃ]	Schwalbe – Drossel
nightingale ['naɪtɪŋɡeɪl]	Nachtigall
woodpecker ['wʊdpekə]	Specht
crow [krəʊ]	Krähe
As the crow flies, it's about two miles.	Luftlinie sind es ungefähr zwei Meilen.
owl [aʊl]	Eule
dove [dʌv]	Taube
duck [dʌk]	Ente
goose [ɡuːs] Pl. geese [ɡiːs]	Gans
swan [swɒn] – **stork** [stɔːk]	Schwan – Storch
parrot ['pærət] – **canary** [kə'neəri]	Papagei – Kanarienvogel
budgerigar ['bʌdʒərɪɡɑː] / **budgie** ['bʌdʒi]	Wellensittich
penguin ['peŋɡwɪn]	Pinguin
fish [fɪʃ] Pl. fish / fishes ['fɪʃɪz]	Fisch
Fish are plentiful here.	Fische sind hier reichlich vorhanden.

Some fishes don't have ribs.	Manche Fische (= Fischarten) haben keine Rippen.
goldfish ['gǝʊldfɪʃ] *Pl.* goldfish	**Goldfisch**
shark [ʃɑːk] – **whale** [weɪl]	**Hai(fisch) – Wal(fisch)**
dolphin ['dɒlfɪn]	**Delphin**
seal [siːl]	**Seehund**
reptile ['reptaɪl]	**Reptil; Kriechtier**
tortoise ['tɔːtǝs] – **turtle** ['tɜːtl]	**Landschildkröte – Wasserschildkröte**
crocodile ['krɒkǝdaɪl]	**Krokodil**
shed / cry crocodile tears [tɪǝz]	Krokodilstränen vergießen / weinen

An Ivorian (= from the Ivory Coast) proverb says: "When in the middle of a river, do not insult the crocodile." (= Wenn man in der Mitte eines Flusses ist, sollte man nicht das Krokodil beleidigen.) Good advice, it seems. Come to think of it, perhaps one should never be disrespectful to any animal?

snake [sneɪk] – **snail** [sneɪl]	**Schlange – Schnecke**
frog [frɒg] – **toad** [tǝʊd]	**Frosch – Kröte**
(tape- / book)worm [wɜːm]	**(Band- / Bücher-)Wurm**
spider ['spaɪdǝ] – **insect** ['ɪnsekt]	**Spinne – Insekt**
cobweb / *AE auch* spiderweb	Spinnwebe
ant [ænt] – **bee** [biː] – **wasp** [wɒsp]	**Ameise – Biene – Wespe**
moth [mɒθ]	**Nachtfalter; Motte**
fly [flaɪ] – **butterfly** ['bʌtǝflaɪ]	**Fliege – Schmetterling**
midge [mɪdʒ] / **gnat** [næt] / **mosquito** [mǝ'skiːtǝʊ] *Pl.* -es	**Mücke**
midge / gnat / mosquito bite	Mückenstich
flea(bite) [fliː]	**Floh(biss / -stich)**
louse [laʊs] *Pl.* lice [laɪs]	**Laus**
cockroach ['kɒkrǝʊtʃ] / **roach**	**(Küchen-)Schabe; Kakerlake**
beetle ['biːtl]	**Käfer**
Colorado beetle / *AE auch* potato bug	(Kartoffel-)Käfer
ladybird (beetle) / *AE auch* ladybug	Marienkäfer
bug [bʌg]	**Wanze; Käfer; Insekt**
May bug *BE* / *AE* June bug	Maikäfer
tick [tɪk]	**Zecke**
tick bite ['tɪk baɪt]	Zeckenbiss
parasite ['pærǝsaɪt]	**Schmarotzer; Parasit**
pest [pest] – **pests**	**Schädling – Ungeziefer**
potato [pǝ'teɪtǝʊ] bugs and other pests	Kartoffelkäfer und andere Schädlinge
vermin ['vɜːmɪn]	**Ungeziefer**
vet [vet]	**Tierarzt / Tierärztin**
zoo [zuː] / **zoological** [zǝʊǝ'lɒdʒɪkl] **garden**	**Zoo / zoologischer Garten**
cage [keɪdʒ]	**Käfig; (Vogel-)Bauer**

Plants
Pflanzen

→ 14.5 The countryside, 14.6 The farming world, 3.1 Foods

Any fine morning a power saw can fell a tree that took a thousand years to grow. (*Edwin Way Teale, US naturalist and writer, 1899–1980*)

plant [plɑːnt]	Pflanze; (an)pflanzen
garden / cultivated / pot plant	Garten- / Kultur- / Topfpflanze
wild [waɪld] plant / flower	Wildpflanze / -blume
a hardy ['hɑːdi] plant	eine winterharte Pflanze
the plant kingdom ['kɪŋdəm]	das Pflanzenreich
tree [triː]	**Baum**
ash (tree) [æʃ]	**Esche**
beech (tree) [biːtʃ]	**Buche**
birch (tree) [bɜːtʃ]	**Birke**
(horse) **chestnut** (tree) ['tʃesnʌt]	(Ross-)**Kastanie**
pull the chestnuts out of the fire	die Kastanien aus dem Feuer holen
lime (tree) *BE* / *AE* **linden** (tree) ['lɪndən]	**Linde**
maple (tree) ['meɪpl]	**Ahorn**
mulberry (tree) ['mʌlbəri]	**Maulbeerbaum**
oak (tree) [əʊk] – **acorn** ['eɪkɔːn]	**Eiche** – **Eichel**
palm (tree) [pɑːm]	**Palme**
poplar ['pɒplə]	**Pappel**
(weeping) **willow** [(wiːpɪŋ) 'wɪləʊ]	(Trauer-)**Weide**
yew (tree) [juː]	**Eibe**
pine (tree) [paɪn]	**Kiefer**
Pines and firs are conifers ['kɒnɪfəz].	Kiefern und Tannen sind Nadelbäume.
(fir) cone [('fɜː) kəʊn]	**(Tannen-)Zapfen**
coniferous [kə'nɪfərəs] **forest**	**Nadelwald**
deciduous [dɪ'sɪdjuəs] **forest / tree**	**Laubwald / -baum**
flower ['flaʊə]	**Blume; Blüte**
The roses have just come into flower.	Die Rosen haben gerade zu blühen begonnen.
cut flowers	Schnittblumen
cornflower – sunflower	Kornblume – Sonnenblume
buttercup ['bʌtəkʌp]	**Butterblume**
daffodil ['dæfədɪl] / **daff** [dæf]	**Osterglocke**; (gelbe) **Narzisse**
daisy ['deɪzi]	**Gänseblümchen**
look (as) fresh as a daisy	frisch wie der junge Morgen aussehen
an ox-eye daisy / a marguerite [mɑːgə'riːt]	eine Margerite
dandelion ['dændɪlaɪən]	**Löwenzahn; Pusteblume**
lily ['lɪli]	**Lilie**
lily of the valley ['væli]	Maiglöckchen
thistle ['θɪsl] – **poppy** ['pɒpi]	**Distel – Mohn(blume)**

On Poppy Day (offiziell: Remembrance [rɪˈmembrəns] Day / Remembrance Sunday, jeweils der dem 11. November nächste Sonntag) gedenken die Briten ihrer Gefallenen beider Weltkriege. Als Zeichen der Trauer trägt man aus Papier oder Stoff gefertigte (corn / Flanders) poppies (= rote Mohnblumen), denn diese Blumen wuchsen auf den Schlachtfeldern (= battlefields) von Flanders [ˈflɑːndəz], wo im Ersten Weltkrieg (= First World War) so viele Soldaten verbluteten.

carnation [kɑːˈneɪʃn]	**Nelke**
tulip (bulb) [ˈtjuːlɪp (bʌlb)]	**Tulpe(nzwiebel)**
fuchsia [ˈfjuːʃə]	**Fuchsie**
rose [rəʊz] – **orchid** [ˈɔːkɪd]	**Rose – Orchidee**
cactus [ˈkæktəs] *Pl.* cacti [ˈkæktaɪ]	**Kaktus**
grass [grɑːs] – **grasses**	**Gras – Gräser**
sow [səʊ] grass	Gras (aus)säen
(– sowed – sown / sowed)	
sow the garden with grass	im Garten Gras (aus)säen
clover [ˈkləʊvə] – **moss** [mɒs]	**Klee – Moos**
herb [hɜːb]	**Kraut; Kräuter-**
fern [fɜːn]	**Farn(kraut)**
vine [vaɪn]	**Wein(rebe); Ranke**
weed(s) [wiːd(z)]	**Unkraut**
I've got to weed the garden.	Ich muss im Garten Unkraut jäten.
fungus [ˈfʌŋgəs] *Pl.* fungi [ˈfʌŋgiː]	**Pilz**
mushroom [ˈmʌʃrʊm]	(Speise- / essbarer) **Pilz; Champignon**
toadstool [ˈtəʊdstuːl]	**Giftpilz; nicht essbarer Pilz**
annual [ˈænjuəl]	**einjährig(e Pflanze)**
biennial [baɪˈeniəl]	**zweijährig(e Pflanze)**
an **evergreen** [ˈevəgriːn]	eine **immergrüne Pflanze**
root [ruːt]	**Wurzel**
stem [stem]	(*Blume, manchmal Baum*) **Stiel**
(tree) trunk [trʌŋk]	**(Baum-)Stamm**
branch [brɑːntʃ]	**Ast; (dickerer) Zweig**
twig [twɪg]	(kleiner / dünner) **Zweig**
bark [bɑːk]	**Borke; Rinde**
leaf [liːf] – **leaves** [liːvz]	**Blatt – Blätter / Laub**
The trees are shedding their leaves.	Die Bäume werfen ihr Laub ab.
bud [bʌd]	**Knospe**
The trees are in bud.	Die Bäume schlagen aus.
bloom [bluːm] / **blossom** [ˈblɒsəm]	**Blüte; blühen**
The trees are in full bloom / blossom.	Die Bäume stehen in voller Blüte.
The forget-me-not blooms from May to July.	Das Vergissmeinnicht blüht von Mai bis Juli.
yellow / fragrant [ˈfreɪgrənt] blossoms when the cherry trees blossom	gelbe / duftende Blüten wenn die Kirschbäume blühen
flora [ˈflɔːrə]	**Flora**
botany [ˈbɒtəni]	(die) **Botanik / Pflanzenkunde**
botanic(al) [bəˈtænɪk(l)] **garden(s)**	**botanischer Garten**

Simpler life forms
Einfachere Lebewesen

The Microbe is so very small / You cannot make him out at all. /
But many sanguine people hope / To see him through a microscope.
(*Hilaire Belloc, British writer, 1870–1953*)

organism [ˈɔːgənɪzm]	**Organismus**
microorganisms [maɪkrəʊˈɔːgənɪzmz]	Mikroorganismen; Kleinstlebewesen
single-cell(ed) organism(s)	Einzeller
gene [dʒiːn]	**Gen; Erbfaktor**
the **genetic code** [dʒənetɪk ˈkəʊd]	der **genetische Code**
hereditary [həˈredətri] **information**	**Erbinformation; genetische Information**
DNA [diː en ˈeɪ]	**DNA**
protein [ˈprəʊtiːn]	**Protein; Eiweiß(körper)**
amino acid [əmiːnəʊ ˈæsɪd]	**Aminosäure**
enzyme [ˈenzaɪm]	**Enzym**
cell [sel]	**Zelle**
cell division [dɪˈvɪʒn]	Zellteilung
stem cell [ˈstem sel]	Stammzelle
stem cell research [rɪˈsɜːtʃ]	Stammzell(en)forschung
unicellular [-ˈseljʊlə] – **multicellular**	**einzellig – mehrzellig**
protozoans / **protozoa** [prəʊtəˈzəʊə]	**Protozoen**
yeast [jiːst] – yeasts	**Hefe** – Hefen
mould [məʊld]	**Schimmel(pilz)**
mildew [ˈmɪldjuː]	**Mehltau(pilz)**
lichen [ˈlaɪkən]	**Flechte**
sponge [spʌndʒ]	**Schwamm**
microbe [ˈmaɪkrəʊb]	**Mikrobe**
virus [ˈvaɪrəs]	**Virus**
microbiology [maɪkrəʊbaɪˈɒlədʒi]	**Mikrobiologie**

Der Plural lateinischer und griechischer Wörter
Nur unregelmäßig: *bacillus* [bəˈsɪləs] – *bacilli* [bəˈsɪlaɪ] (= Bazillus – Bazillen) • *coccus* [ˈkɒkəs] – *cocci* [ˈkɒksaɪ] (= Kokke – Kokken) • *stimulus* [ˈstɪmjələs] – *stimuli* [ˈstɪmjəlaɪ] (= Stimulus – Stimuli) • *bacterium* [bækˈtɪəriəm] – *bacteria* [bækˈtɪəriə] (= Bakterie – Bakterien) • *alga* [ˈælgə] – *algae* [ˈældʒiː] (= Alge – Algen)
Regelmäßig oder unregelmäßig: *amoeba* [əˈmiːbə] – *amoebae* [əˈmiːbiː] / *amoebas* (= Amöbe – Amöben) • *cactus* [ˈkæktəs] – *cactuses* / *cacti* [ˈkæktaɪ] (= Kaktus – Kakteen / Kaktusse) • *fungus* [ˈfʌŋgəs] – *fungi* [ˈfʌŋgiː] / *funguses* (= Pilz – Pilze) • *syllabus* [ˈsɪləbəs] – *syllabuses* / *syllabi* [ˈsɪləbaɪ] (= Lehrplan – Lehrpläne) • *curriculum* [kəˈrɪkjələm] – *curricula* [kəˈrɪkjələ] / *curriculums* (= Curriculum – Curricula) • *referendum* [refəˈrendəm] – *referendums* / *referenda* [-də] (= Referendum – Referenden / Referenda)
Nur regelmäßig: *census* [ˈsensəs], *chorus* [ˈkɔːrəs], *circus* [ˈsɜːkəs], *virus* [ˈvaɪrəs]

Idioms

Idioms sollte man nur in kleinen Dosen (= *in small doses*) gebrauchen. Es ist kein guter Stil, einen Text mit *idioms* zu spicken (= *to pepper a text with idioms*). Trotzdem bieten wir Ihnen mit der folgenden Zusammenstellung ein Konzentrat solcher Redensarten, vor allem zum Thema Tiere und Pflanzen – nur für Lernzwecke und um Ihnen zu zeigen, dass man im Englischen fast jeden Gedanken durch ein *idiom* ausdrücken kann.

Wenn mich jemand fragt: *How are things at your end?* (= Wie geht's denn bei euch so?), dann sage ich manchmal: ***Everything in the garden is rosy.*** Damit meine ich: *Everything's going well, couldn't be better* (= alles bestens, könnte gar nicht besser sein).

Sometimes people try to ***lead me up the garden path*** (= mir ein X für ein U vorzumachen). Es gibt ja so manchen ***wolf in sheep's clothing*** (= Wolf im Schafspelz) – ***it's the law of the jungle*** (= das Gesetz des Dschungels) *out there*, ***it's dog eat dog*** (= fressen oder gefressen werden).

I've heard people say ***it's a dog's life*** (= ein Hundeleben), aber damit können sie nicht unseren Hund gemeint haben (= *they can't have meant our dog*). *To him*, ***life is all roses***. *He's* ***as happy as a clam at high tide*** (= so glücklich wie eine Venusmuschel bei Flut).

I don't know if you're one of those courageous (= mutig) *people who* ***swim against the tide*** (= die gegen den Strom schwimmen). *I'm afraid I'm* ***too chicken*** (= zu feige) *for that. When someone is needed to* ***bell the cat*** (= der Katze die Schelle umzuhängen), *I'm the first to* ***chicken out*** (= der erste, der kneift). *I'm not the kind who goes into* ***the lion's den*** (= in die Höhle des Löwen) *to* ***take the bull by the horns*** (= um den Stier bei den Hörnern zu packen). (*A mixed metaphor, I know.*)

I'm ***as meek as a lamb*** (= sanft wie ein Lamm), ***as quiet as a mouse*** (= still wie eine Maus), *and inclined* (= neige dazu) *to* ***let sleeping dogs lie*** (= schlafende Hunde nicht zu wecken). *I'm not a* ***bull in a china shop*** (= Elefant im Porzellanladen).

But I'm ***an eager beaver*** (= „eifriger Biber", Arbeitstier) *who does* ***the donkey work*** (= uninteressante Routinearbeit) *for others. It's always, "Harry do this, Harry do that." I have a feeling they're* ***making a monkey out of me*** (= die machen mich zum Affen). *In the evening I often say, "I've had* ***a pig of a day*** (= einen Misttag)."

I think it's time to ***move on to pastures new*** (= mich nach neuen Weidegründen umzusehen), *to* ***turn over a new leaf*** (= ein neues Blatt aufzuschlagen). *My friends say,* ***"A bird in the hand is worth two in the bush."*** *What they mean, of course, is that I might* ***jump from the frying pan into the fire*** (= von der Bratpfanne ins Feuer). *The question is: Shall or shan't I* ***take the plunge*** (= den Sprung wagen)? *I'm* ***caught between the devil and the deep blue sea***.

Science
Wissenschaft

16

1 **Physics**
   Physik

2 **Chemistry**
   Chemie

3 **Medicine**
   Medizin

4 **Mathematics**
   Mathematik

5 **Numbers**
   Zahlen

6 **Measures and weights**
   Maße und Gewichte

Zur Aussprache längerer Wörter

Physics
Physik

→ 16.2 Chemistry, 17.3 Electricity and electronics

The content of physics is the concern of physicists, its effect the concern of all humanity. (*Friedrich Dürrenmatt, Swiss dramatist, 1921–90*)

physics ['fɪzɪks]	(die) **Physik**
theoretical [θɪəˈretɪkl] physics	(die) theoretische Physik
particle ['pɑːtɪkl] physics	(die) Elementarteilchenphysik
solid-state [sɒlɪdˈsteɪt] physics	(die) Festkörperphysik
nuclear ['njuːkliə] physics	(die) Kernphysik
astrophysics [æstrəʊˈfɪzɪks]	(die) Astrophysik
physicist ['fɪzɪsɪst]	**Physiker(in)**
physical (laws) [fɪzɪkl ('lɔːz)]	**physikalisch**(e Gesetze)
basic research [beɪsɪk rɪˈsɜːtʃ]	(die) **Grundlagenforschung**
mechanics [mɪˈkæniks]	(die) **Mechanik**
statics [æ] – **dynamics** [daɪˈnæmɪks]	(die) **Statik** – **(die) Dynamik**
thermodynamics [θɜːməʊdaɪˈnæmɪks]	(die) **Thermodynamik**
optics ['ɒptɪks]	(die) **Optik**
acoustics [əˈkuːstɪks]	(die) **Akustik**
Acoustics is a science ['saɪəns].	Die Akustik ist eine Wissenschaft.
The acoustics (= acoustic properties) of this hall are excellent.	Die Akustik (= akustischen Eigen- schaften) dieses Saales ist (sind) ausgezeichnet.

Wissenschaftsnamen auf *-ics* werden als Singular konstruiert (→ S. 83): *Physics / Mechanics / Statics / Thermodynamics / Electronics / Optics is not taught at this college.* (= Physik / Mechanik / Statik / Thermodynamik / Elektronik / Optik wird an dieser Hochschule nicht gelehrt.)

theory ['θɪəri] – **theorist** ['θɪərɪst]	**Theorie – Theoretiker(in)**
Einstein's theory of relativity	Einsteins Relativitätstheorie
experiment [ɪkˈsperɪmənt]	**Experiment; Versuch**
conduct / do an experiment	einen Versuch durchführen / machen
experimental [ɪksperɪˈmentl]	**experimentell; Experimental-**
experimental results [rɪˈzʌlts]	Versuchsergebnisse
verify something experimentally	etwas experimentell beweisen
atom ['ætəm] – **atomic** [əˈtɒmɪk]	**Atom – Atom-**
atomic weight [weɪt]	Atomgewicht
the properties of the atomic nucleus	die Eigenschaften des Atomkerns
matter and energy ['enədʒi]	**Materie und Energie**
an **electric** [ɪˈlektrɪk] current	ein **elektrischer** Strom
an electric(al) charge [tʃɑːdʒ]	eine elektrische Ladung
electrically charged [tʃɑːdʒd]	elektrisch geladen
(semi- / super)**conductor** [kənˈdʌktə]	(Halb- / Supra-)**Leiter**
magnetism ['mægnətɪzm]	**Magnetismus**
a **magnetic** [mægˈnetɪk] **field**	ein **Magnetfeld**

an **electric(al)** [ɪˈlektrɪk(l)] **field**	ein elektrisches Feld
a **gravitational** [grævɪˈteɪʃnəl] **field**	ein Gravitationsfeld
heat [hiːt]	**Wärme**
convert [kənˈvɜːt] heat into work	Wärme in Arbeit umwandeln
power [ˈpaʊə]	**Energie; Kraft; Leistung**
Newton's **laws of motion** [ˈməʊʃn]	Newtons Bewegungsgesetze
the **moment of inertia** [ɪˈnɜːʃə]	das Trägheitsmoment
angular / linear [ˈlɪniə] **velocity** [vəˈlɒsəti]	Winkel- / Lineargeschwindigkeit
acceleration – deceleration	Beschleunigung – Verlangsamung
at twice the **speed / velocity** [vəˈlɒsəti] of light	mit zweifacher **Lichtgeschwindigkeit**
an object [ˈɒbdʒɪkt] **at rest**	ein **ruhender** Körper
the **force** acting on an object	die auf einen Körper einwirkende **Kraft**
centrifugal [sentrɪˈfjuːgl] force	Zentrifugalkraft; Fliehkraft
the **mass** [mæs] of a body / an object	die **Masse** eines Körpers
solid [ˈsɒlɪd]	**fest; Festkörper / fester Körper**
liquid [ˈlɪkwɪd]	**flüssig; Flüssigkeit**
a solid / liquid substance [ˈsʌbstəns]	ein fester / flüssiger Stoff
a **gaseous** [ˈgæsiəs] substance	eine **gasförmige** Substanz
vapour [ˈveɪpə] **– evaporate** [iˈvæpəreɪt]	**Dampf – verdampfen**
fluid [ˈfluːɪd]	**fließend; Fluid**
fluid mechanics [mɪˈkænɪks]	Strömungslehre; Strömungsmechanik
fluid pressure [ˈpreʃə]	hydraulischer Druck
Liquids and gases are fluids.	Flüssigkeiten und Gase sind Fluide.
volume [ˈvɒljuːm]	**Volumen; (Raum-)Inhalt**
electron [ɪˈlektrɒn]	**Elektron; Elektronen-**
the electron arrangement of an atom [ˈætəm]	die Elektronenkonfiguration eines Atoms
electronic [ɪlekˈtrɒnɪk]	**elektronisch; Elektronen-**
electronics [ɪlekˈtrɒnɪks]	(die) **Elektronik**
proton [ˈprəʊtɒn] **– neutron** [ˈnjuː-]	**Proton – Neutron**
photon [ˈfəʊtɒn]	**Photon**
quark [kwɑːk]	**Quark** (= Elementarteilchen)
quantum [ˈkwɒntəm] **– quanta** [-tə]	**Quant – Quanten**
quantum mechanics / theory	Quantenmechanik / -theorie
quantum jump / leap	Quantensprung
vacuum [ˈvækjuəm]	**Vakuum**
wave(length) [ˈweɪv(leŋθ)]	**Welle(nlänge)**
frequency [ˈfriːkwənsi]	**Frequenz**
spectrum [ˈspektrəm] **– spectra** [-trə]	**Spektrum – Spektren**
measure [ˈmeʒə] a current	einen Strom **messen**
resistance [rɪˈzɪstəns]	**Widerstand**
density [ˈdensəti]	**Dichte**
specific **gravity** [spəsɪfɪk ˈgrævəti]	spezifisches **Gewicht**
the centre of gravity	der Schwerpunkt
(un)stable **equilibrium** [iːkwɪˈlɪbriəm]	stabiles / labiles **Gleichgewicht**
random error [rændəm ˈerə]	**Zufallsfehler**
systemic [sɪˈstiːmɪk] **error**	**systematischer Fehler**

Chemistry
Chemie

→ 16.1 Physics

There's nothing colder than chemistry. (*Anita Loos, US novelist, 1888–1981*)

chemistry ['kemɪstri] — (die) **Chemie**
organic / inorganic chemistry — (die) organische / anorganische Chemie

analytical [ænə'lɪtɪkl] chemistry — (die) analytische Chemie
physical ['fɪzɪkl] chemistry — (die) physikalische Chemie
biochemistry [baɪəʊ'kemɪstri] — (die) Biochemie
radiochemistry [reɪdiəʊ'kemɪstri] — (die) Radio- / Strahlenchemie
the chemistry of carbon ['kɑːbən] — die chemischen Eigenschaften des Kohlenstoffs

chemist ['kemɪst] — **Chemiker(in)**
pharmaceutical chemist — Arzneimittelchemiker(in)
the **pharmaceutical** [fɑːmə'suːtɪkl] industry — die **pharmazeutische** Industrie / Pharmaindustrie
chemical ['kemɪkl] — **chemisch; Chemikalie**
a chemical reaction [ri'ækʃn] — eine chemische Reaktion
chemical processes ['prəʊsesɪz] — chemische Prozesse / Vorgänge
a chemical laboratory [lə'bɒrətri] — ein chemisches Labor(atorium)
chemical research [rɪ'sɜːtʃ] — (die) chemische Forschung
chemical bond(ing) — chemische Bindung
the chemical industry ['ɪndəstri] — die chemische Industrie
chemical engineering [endʒɪ'nɪərɪŋ] — Chemietechnik; Chemieingenieur-wesen

chemical engineer [endʒɪ'nɪə] — Chemieingenieur(in); Chemotechniker(in)

the use [juːs] of toxic chemicals — der Einsatz giftiger Chemikalien
a precise **science** ['saɪəns] — eine exakte **Wissenschaft**
scientific [saɪən'tɪfɪk] instruments — **wissenschaftliche** Instrumente
laboratory [lə'bɒrətri] / **lab** [læb] — **Laboratorium** / **Labor**
lab(oratory) assistant [ə'sɪstənt] / technician [tek'nɪʃn] — Laborant(in)
(electron) microscope ['maɪkrəskəʊp] — **(Elektronen-)Mikroskop**
microscopic [maɪkrə'skɒpɪk] — **mikroskopisch (klein)**
pipette [pɪ'pet] – **burette** [bju'ret] — **Pipette – Bürette**
observation [ɒbzə'veɪʃn] — **Beobachtung**
analysis [ə'næləsɪs] *Pl.* -lyses [-ləsiːz] — **Analyse; Untersuchung**
analyse ['ænəlaɪz] a sample — eine Probe **untersuchen**
the **composition** of a substance — die **Zusammensetzung** eines Stoffes
cancer-causing substances ['sʌbstənsɪz] — **krebserregende / krebserzeugende** Stoffe
the chemical **properties** of an element ['elɪmənt] — die chemischen **Eigenschaften** eines Elements
a chemical **compound** ['kɒmpaʊnd] — eine chemische **Verbindung**

form a compound	eine Verbindung eingehen
mixture [ˈmɪkstʃə]	**Gemenge; Gemisch**
solution [səˈluːʃn]	**Lösung**
a concentrated [ˈkɒnsntreɪtɪd] solution	eine konzentrierte Lösung
a dilute [daɪˈluːt] solution	eine verdünnte Lösung
a saturated [ˈsætʃəreɪtɪd] solution	eine gesättigte Lösung
(water-)**soluble** [ˈsɒljʊbl]	(wasser)**löslich**
dissolve [dɪˈzɒlv]	**(sich) auflösen; (sich) zersetzen**
crystals [ˈkrɪstlz] dissolved in water	in Wasser aufgelöste Kristalle
Acetone [ˈæsətəʊn] is used as a **solvent** [ˈsɒlvənt].	Aceton wird als **Lösungsmittel** verwendet.
component [kəmˈpəʊnənt]	**Bestandteil**
(a hydrocarbon) **derivative** [dɪˈrɪvətɪv]	(ein Kohlenwasserstoff-)**Derivat**
formula [ˈfɔːmjʊlə] Pl. -las / -lae [-liː]	**Formel**
symbol [ˈsɪmbl]	**Symbol**
O is the symbol for oxygen [ˈɒksɪdʒən].	O ist das Symbol für Sauerstoff.
classification of the elements	**Anordnung** der Elemente
the **periodic table** [pɪərɪɒdɪk ˈteɪbl]	das **Periodensystem**
acid [ˈæsɪd] – **base** [beɪs]	**Säure – Base**
acids and bases [ˈbeɪsɪz]	Säuren und Basen
the arrangement of **atoms** [ˈætəmz]	die Anordnung der **Atome**
atomic weight [weɪt]	**Atomgewicht**
atomic [əˈtɒmɪk] number	Kernladungszahl; Ordnungszahl
molecule [ˈmɒlɪkjuːl]	**Molekül**
the **molecular** [məˈlekjʊlə] **structure**	die **Molekularstruktur**
radioactive **isotopes** [ˈaɪsətəʊps]	radioaktive **Isotope**
hydrogen [ˈhaɪdrədʒən]	**Wasserstoff**
hydrocarbons [haɪdrəʊˈkɑːbənz]	**Kohlenwasserstoffe**
carbohydrates [kɑːbəʊˈhaɪdreɪts]	**Kohle(n)hydrate**
alcohol [ˈælkəhɒl]	**Alkohol**
combustion [kəmˈbʌstʃn]	**Verbrennung**
combustible [kəmˈbʌstəbl]	brennbar
corrosion [kəˈrəʊʒn] – **corrode** [kəˈrəʊd]	**Korrosion – korrodieren**
oxidation – **reduction** [rɪˈdʌkʃn]	**Oxidation – Reduktion**
boiling point [ˈbɔɪlɪŋ pɔɪnt]	**Siedepunkt; Kochpunkt**
Oxygen boils at –183 degC [dɪgriːz ˈselsiəs].	Die Siedetemperatur des Sauerstoffs liegt bei –183°C.
catalyst [ˈkætəlɪst]	**Katalysator**
act as a catalyst	als Katalysator wirken
synthesis [ˈsɪnθəsɪs] Pl. -eses [-əsiːz]	**Synthese**
synthesize [ˈsɪnθəsaɪz] organic compounds	organische Verbindungen **synthetisch herstellen**
synthetic fibres [sɪnθetɪk ˈfaɪbəz]	**Chemiefasern**
electrolysis [ɪlekˈtrɒləsɪs] Pl. -lyses [-ləsiːz]	**Elektrolyse**
electrode [ɪˈlektrəʊd]	**Elektrode**
electron tube [ɪˈlektrɒn tjuːb]	**Elektronenröhre**
anode [ˈænəʊd] – **cathode** [ˈkæθəʊd]	**Anode – Kathode**
ion [ˈaɪən]	**Ion**

Medicine
Medizin

→ 4 Health care, 1.2 Parts of the body

The desire to take medicine is perhaps the greatest feature which distinguishes man from animals. (*Sir William Osler, Canadian physician, 1849–1919*)

internal medicine [ɪntɜːnl 'medsn]	(die) **innere Medizin**
the internal organs ['ɔːgənz]	die inneren Organe
occupational [ɒkjuˈpeɪʃənl] medicine	(die) Arbeitsmedizin
forensic [fəˈrensɪk] medicine	(die) Rechtsmedizin
internist ['ɪntɜːnɪst] *AE*	**Internist(in); Facharzt / -ärztin für innere Krankheiten**
nonmedical practitioner	**Heilpraktiker(in)**
the healing professions [prəˈfeʃnz]	**die Heilberufe**
cardiology [kɑːdiˈɒlədʒi]	(die) **Kardiologie**
dermatology [dɜːməˈtɒlədʒi]	(die) **Dermatologie**
gynaecology [gaɪnəˈkɒlədʒi]	(die) **Gynäkologie / Frauenheilkunde**
neurology [njuˈrɒlədʒi]	(die) **Neurologie**
ophthalmology [ɒfθælˈmɒlədʒi]	(die) **Augenheilkunde**
pathology [pəˈθɒlədʒi]	(die) **Pathologie**
radiology [reɪdiˈɒlədʒi]	(die) **Radiologie / Strahlenkunde**
rheumatology [ruːməˈtɒlədʒi]	(die) **Rheumatologie**
urology [juˈrɒlədʒi]	(die) **Urologie**

☞ Die vorstehenden -*ologies* werden jeweils auf der -*ol*-Silbe betont (→ S. 252): *cardi'ology, neu'rology* etc. – Die Namen der betreffenden Fachärzte (= *specialists*) lauten jeweils auf -*ologist: urologist* (– Urologe/in) etc.

obstetrics [əbˈstetrɪks]	**Geburtshilfe**
obstetric ward [əbstetrɪk 'wɔːd]	Entbindungsstation
midwife ['mɪdwaɪf] / obstetric nurse	Hebamme
obstetrician [ɒbstəˈtrɪʃn]	(ärztl.) Geburtshelfer(in)
paediatrics [piːdiˈætrɪks]	(die) **Pädiatrie / Kinderheilkunde**
paediatric (ward / surgery)	Kinder(station / -chirurgie)
orthopaedic [ɔːθəˈpiːdɪk] **surgery**	(die) **Orthopädie**
endoscopy [enˈdɒskəpi] – **endoscopic**	**Endoskopie – endoskopisch**
nursing ['nɜːsɪŋ]	(die) **Krankenpflege**
clinic ['klɪnɪk]	**(Poli-)Klinik; Klinikum**
clinical ['klɪnɪkl]	klinisch
during / in clinical trials ['traɪəlz]	bei / in der klinischen Erprobung
diagnose ['daɪəgnəʊz] an illness	eine Krankheit **diagnostizieren**
She was diagnosed with breast cancer.	Bei ihr wurde Brustkrebs festgestellt.
diagnosis [daɪəgˈnəʊsɪs] *Pl.* -ses [-siːz]	Diagnose
diagnostic [daɪəgˈnɒstɪk]	diagnostisch
blood sample ['blʌd sɑːmpl] / **test**	**Blutprobe / -untersuchung**
blood vessel / clot / bank	Blutgefäß / -gerinnsel / -bank
a **CAT scan** ['kæt skæn] / **CT scan**	eine **Computertomografie / CT**

Malpractice suits [mæl'præktɪs suːts] sind Prozesse, die – besonders in den USA – wegen ärztlicher Kunstfehler geführt werden und oft zu Schadenersatzzahlungen in Millionenhöhe führen. Diese Entwicklung hatte einen starken Anstieg der *medical costs* [kɒsts] (= Ausgaben für medizinische Leistungen) zur Folge, da die Ärzte ihre Honorare erhöhten (= *increased their fees*), um sich gegen die erhöhten Risiken versichern zu können.

thorax ['θɔːræks] *Pl.* thoraxes / thoraces ['θɔːrəsiːz]	**Thorax; Brustkorb / -kasten**
gastric ['gæstrɪk]	**gastrisch; Magen-**
gastric / stomach ['stʌmək] disorders	Magenleiden / -krankheiten
the gastrointestinal tract	der Magen-Darm-Trakt / -Kanal
pancreas ['pæŋkriəs]	**Pankreas; Bauchspeicheldrüse**
the large / small **intestine** [ɪn'testɪn]	der Dick- / Dünn**darm**
colon ['kəʊlən] *Pl.* colons / cola	**Colon; Grimmdarm**
rectum ['rektəm] – **rectal** ['rektl]	**Rektum / Mastdarm – rektal**
the **urinary** ['jʊərɪnəri] **tract**	die **Harnwege**
bone marrow ['bəʊn mærəʊ]	**Knochenmark**
the **spinal column** [spaɪnl 'kɒləm]	die **Wirbelsäule**
the **central nervous system**	das **Zentralnervensystem**
the **immune** system [ɪ'mjuːn sɪstəm]	das **Immunsystem**
immunodeficiency / immune deficiency [dɪ'fɪʃnsi]	**Immunschwäche**
(body) **fluid** ['fluːɪd] / **tissue** ['tɪʃuː]	(Körper-)**Flüssigkeit / Gewebe**
gland – **glandular** ['glændjʊlə]	**Drüse – Drüsen-**
lymph [lɪmf] node / gland [glænd]	Lymphknoten / -drüse
rheumatic [ruˈmætɪk]	**rheumatisch; Rheumakranke(r)**
rheumatic fever [rumætɪk ˈfiːvə]	Gelenkrheumatismus
arthritis [ɑːˈθraɪtɪs]	**Arthritis; Gelenkentzündung**
asthma ['æsmə]	**Asthma**
asthmatic [æsˈmætɪk]	asthmatisch; Asthmatiker(in)
an **occupational** disease [dɪˈziːz]	eine **Berufskrankheit**
pulmonary ['pʌlmənəri] diseases	**Lungenkrankheiten**
He died of a pulmonary embolism.	Er starb an einer Lungenembolie.
She died of **kidney** failure ['feɪljə].	Sie starb an **Nierenversagen.**
dialysis [daɪˈæləsɪs] *Pl.* -lyses [-ləsiːz]	**Dialyse; Blutwäsche**
perform a **transplant** ['trænsplɑːnt]	eine **Transplantation** durchführen
organ donor ['dəʊnə]	**Organspender(in)**
organ recipient [rɪˈsɪpiənt]	Organempfänger(in)
skin grafting ['skɪn grɑːftɪŋ]	**Hauttransplantation / -übertragung**
radiotherapy / **radiation therapy** ['θerəpi]	(die) **Strahlentherapie**
general / plastic **surgery** ['sɜːdʒəri]	(die) allgemeine / plastische **Chirurgie**
open-heart surgery [əʊpnhɑːt 'sɜːdʒəri]	(die) Offenherzchirurgie
hygiene ['haɪdʒiːn] – **hygienic** [haɪˈdʒiːnɪk]	(die) **Hygiene – hygienisch**
public-health [pʌblɪkˈhelθ] **officer**	**Amtsarzt / -ärztin**
public-health department [dɪˈpɑːtmənt]	Gesundheitsamt

Mathematics
Mathematik

→ 16.5 Numbers, 9.2 Subjects and skills

E = mc² (Energy equals mass times the speed of light squared.)
(*Albert Einstein, German-born US physicist, 1879–1955*)

mathematics [mæθə'mætɪks]	(die) **Mathematik**
maths [mæθs] *BE* / *AE* math [mæθ]	Mathe(matik)
write a math(s) test (– wrote – written)	eine Mathearbeit schreiben
arithmetic [ə'rɪθmətɪk]	(die) **Arithmetik**; (das) **Rechnen**
arithmetic(al) [ærɪθ'metɪk(l)]	**arithmetisch**
an arithmetical operation [ɒpə'reɪʃn]	eine Rechenoperation
solve an arithmetical problem	eine Rechenaufgabe lösen
geometry [dʒi'ɒmətri]	(die) **Geometrie**
geometric(al) [dʒi:ə'metrɪk(l)]	**geometrisch**
a geometric figure ['fɪgə]	eine geometrische Figur
geometric(al) progression [prə'greʃn]	geometrische Progression
trigonometry [trɪgə'nɒmətri]	(die) **Trigonometrie**
algebra ['ældʒɪbrə]	(die) **Algebra**
differential / integral **calculus**	Differenzial- / Integralrechnung
probability calculus ['kælkjuləs]	Wahrscheinlichkeitsrechnung
set theory ['set θɪəri]	(die) **Mengenlehre**
count [kaʊnt]	**zählen**
The child can count (up) to eight now.	Das Kind kann jetzt bis acht zählen.
reckon ['rekən] / **work out**	**ausrechnen**
reckon up some figures	einige Zahlen zusammenrechnen
sum [sʌm]	**Rechenaufgabe**
do sums (– did – done)	rechnen
He's good / bad at sums.	Er kann gut / schlecht rechnen.
You got all the sums right.	Du hast alles richtig gerechnet.
do / solve **problems** ['prɒbləmz]	**Textaufgaben** bearbeiten / lösen
calculate ['kælkjuleɪt]	**(be- / er- / aus)rechnen**
calculate the area of a square	die Fläche eines Quadrats berechnen
calculate it to two places	es auf zwei Stellen nach dem Komma ausrechnen
calculation [kælkju'leɪʃn]	**(Be-)Rechnung**
perform [pə'fɔːm] calculations	(Be-)Rechnungen durchführen
compute [kəm'pjuːt]	**(be- / er)rechnen**
compute / calculate a distance ['dɪstəns]	eine Entfernung berechnen
compute the square root [skweə 'ruːt] of a number	die Quadratwurzel einer Zahl errechnen
the **fundamental operations**	die **Grundrechenarten**
add [æd] – **subtract** [səb'trækt]	**addieren – subtrahieren**
add numbers together / up	Zahlen zusammenrechnen / aufaddieren
addition [ə'dɪʃn] – **subtraction**	**Addition – Subtraktion**
multiply ['mʌltɪplaɪ] – **divide** [dɪ'vaɪd]	**multiplizieren – dividieren**

multiplication – division [dɪ'vɪʒn]   Multiplikation – Division
memorize the multiplication tables   das Einmaleins auswendig lernen

---

55 + 44 = 99: *If you add 55 and / to 44, you get 99.*
55 plus [plʌs] *44 is / equals* ['i:kwəlz] *99. / 55 and 44 is / are / make(s) 99.*
99 – 44 = 55: *If you subtract 44 from 99, you get 55.*
99 minus ['maɪnəs] *44 leaves* [li:vz] *55. / 44 from 99 is 55.*
11 x 6 = 66: *If you multiply 11 by 6, you get 66.*
11 multiplied ['mʌltɪplaɪd] *by 6 is 66. / 11 times 6 is 66.*
66 ÷ 11 = 6: *If you divide 66 by 11, you get 6.*
66 divided [dɪ'vaɪdɪd] *by 11 is 6. / 66 over 11 is 6.*

---

a **function** ['fʌŋkʃn]   eine (mathematische) **Funktion**
a **quantity** ['kwɒntəti]   eine (mathematische) **Größe**
finite ['faɪnaɪt] – **infinite** ['ɪnfɪnət]   **endlich – unendlich**
constant ['kɒnstənt] – **variable**   **Konstante – Variable**
['væriəbl]
prime number [praɪm 'nʌmbə]   **Primzahl**
integer ['ɪntɪdʒə] / **whole number**   **ganze Zahl**
square [skweə]   **Quadrat; quadratisch; Quadrat-**
two square metres ['mi:təz]   zwei Quadratmeter
144 is the square of 12   144 ist das Quadrat von 12
12^2 (= 12 squared) is 144   12 hoch 2 ist 144
cube [kju:b]   **dritte Potenz**
2^3 (= 2 cubed / the third power of 2)   2 hoch 3 / die 3. Potenz von 2
power ['paʊə]   **Potenz**
2 to the power of 4 is 16   2 hoch 4 ist 16
logarithm ['lɒgərɪðm] / **log** [lɒg]   **Logarithmus**
decimal / vulgar **fraction** ['frækʃn]   Dezimal- / gemeiner **Bruch**
quotient ['kwəʊʃnt]   **Quotient**
numerator – denominator [-'nɒm-]   Zähler – Nenner
seek a common [ɒ] denominator   einen gemeinsamen Nenner suchen
equal ['i:kwəl]   **gleich**
equation [ɪ'kweɪʒn]   **Gleichung**
an equation with two unknowns   eine Gleichung mit zwei Unbekannten
circle ['sɜ:kl]   **Kreis**
the centre of a circle   der Mittelpunkt eines Kreises
circular ['sɜ:kjələ]   **kreisförmig; Kreis-**
diameter [daɪ'æmɪtə]   **Durchmesser**
circumference [sə'kʌmfrəns]   **(Kreis-)Umfang**
the ratio ['reɪʃiəʊ] of the circumference   das Verhältnis des Umfangs zum
to the diameter   Durchmesser
tangent ['tændʒənt]   **Tangente; Tangens**
rectangle ['rektæŋgl] – **rectangular**   **Rechteck – rechteckig**
triangle ['traɪæŋgl] – **triangular**   **Dreieck – dreieckig**
a triangular [traɪ'æŋgjʊlə] pyramid   eine dreiseitige Pyramide
quadrangle ['kwɒdræŋgl]   **Viereck**
quadrangular [kwɒ'dræŋgjʊlə]   **viereckig**
an **angle** ['æŋgl] of 90 degrees   ein **Winkel** von 90 Grad
the **base** [beɪs] of a pyramid ['pɪrəmɪd]   die **Grundfläche** einer Pyramide

Numbers
Zahlen

→ 16.4 Mathematics

This is the third time; I hope good luck lies in odd numbers ...
There is divinity in odd numbers, either in nativity, chance or death.
(*William Shakespeare, English dramatist and poet, 1564–1616*)

even [ˈiːvn] / **odd** [ɒd] numbers   **gerade** / **ungerade** Zahlen

Null
4 – 4 = 0: *Four minus four is* **zero** [ˈzɪərəʊ] / BE auch **nought** [nɔːt].
3.06: three point **zero** / BE auch **nought** *six*
There are three **zeros** / BE auch **noughts** *in 1,000.*
The temperature was ten degrees [dɪˈɡriːz] *below* **zero**. (= 10° unter null)
My phone / room / account [əˈkaʊnt] *number is 7030* (= *seven* **oh** *three* **oh**).
zero *growth* [ɡrəʊθ] (= Nullwachstum)
Our chances are **nil** / **zero**. (= Unsere Chancen sind gleich null.)
Leeds United won 3-0 (= *three* **nil**). (= Leeds hat 3:0 gewonnen.)
The Chicago White Sox won 3-0 (= *three* **nothing** / **zip**).
(Tennis:) *15-0* (= *fifteen* **love**), *30-0* (= *thirty* **love**), *40-0* (= *forty* **love**).

one book – twenty-one books	ein Buch – einundzwanzig Bücher
two / fifty-two books	zwei / zweiundfünfzig Bücher
(forty-)**three** books	drei(undvierzig) Bücher
four – fourteen – forty	vier – vierzehn – vierzig
five – fifteen – fifty	fünf – fünfzehn – fünfzig
six – sixteen – sixty	sechs – sechzehn – sechzig
seven – seventeen – seventy	sieben – siebzehn – siebzig
eight – eighteen – eighty	acht – achtzehn – achtzig
nine – nineteen – ninety	neun – neunzehn – neunzig
nine hundred and four / *AE auch* nine hundred four	neunhundertvier

Numbers over 100 (= **Zahlen über 100**)
100 = one / a hundred [ˈhʌndrəd]
144 = one / a hundred and forty-four / AE auch *one hundred forty-four*
555 = five hundred and fifty-five / AE auch *five hundred fifty-five*
1,000 = one / a thousand [ˈθaʊznd]
1,888 = one thousand eight hundred and eighty-eight (AE auch ohne *and*)
3,000 = three thousand
100,000 = one / a hundred thousand
159,000 = one hundred and fifty-nine thousand (AE auch ohne *and*)
1,000,000 = a / one million [ˈmɪljən]
5,000,000 = five million
2,000,000,000 = two billion [ˈbɪljən] / BE auch *two thousand million*

Aussprachehinweise

Bei den Zahlen *thirteen* bis *nineteen* muss die *-teen*-Silbe deutlich, in der Regel betont gesprochen werden, da es sonst leicht zu Verwechslungen mit den *-ty*-Zahlen (*thirty, forty* etc.) kommt.
Bei den Ordnungszahlen *twentieth, thirtieth, fortieth* etc. ist das *-tieth* als [-tiəθ] zu sprechen: ['twentiəθ], ['θɜːtiəθ], ['fɔːtiəθ].

the **first** / thirty-first day	der **erste** / einunddreißigste Tag
the **second** day	der **zweite** Tag
the **third** / forty-third row [rəʊ]	die **dritte** / dreiundvierzigste Reihe

Die Ordnungszahlen (= *ordinal* ['ɔːdɪnl] *numbers*) als Ziffern

1st [fɜːst]	*4th* [fɔːθ]	*16th*
2nd / AE auch *2d* ['sekənd]	*5th* [fɪfθ]	*27th*
3rd / AE auch *3d* [θɜːd]	*6th* [sɪksθ]	*38th* etc.

the **fourth** row [rəʊ]	die **vierte** Reihe
the **fifth** anniversary [ænɪ'vɜːsəri]	der **fünfte** Jahrestag
George VI = George the **Sixth**	Georg VI. = Georg der **Sechste**
This is the **eighth** [eɪtθ] time.	Dies ist das **achte** Mal.
in (the) **ninth** [naɪnθ] grade *AE*	in der **neunten** Klasse
the **thirtieth** ['θɜːtiəθ] of May	der **dreißigste** Mai
her **seventieth** ['sevntiəθ] birthday	ihr **siebzigster** Geburtstag

Fractions ['frækʃnz] (= Brüche)

$^1/_2$ = *a half / one half* • $^3/_2$ = *three halves* • $1^1/_2$ = *one and a half*
$^1/_3$ = *a third / one third* • $^2/_3$ = *two thirds* • $2^1/_3$ = *two and a third*
$^1/_4$ = *a / one quarter / one fourth* • $^3/_4$ = *three quarters / fourths*
$^4/_5$ = *four fifths* • $3^3/_5$ = *three and three fifths* • $^{145}/_{360}$ = *145 over 360*

Decimals ['desɪmlz] (= Dezimalzahlen)

Dem deutschen Komma entspricht im Englischen ein Punkt:
2.684 = two point six eight four (dt. = 2,684)
0.259 = zero point two five nine / BE auch *(nought) point two five nine*

once [wʌns]	**einmal**
Once / One times five is five.	Einmal fünf ist fünf.
twice [twaɪs]	**zweimal**
Twice / Two times five is ten.	Zwei mal fünf ist zehn.
Three times five is fifteen.	**Drei mal** fünf ist fünfzehn.
Four times three is twelve.	**Vier mal** drei ist zwölf.
Six times eight is forty-eight.	**Sechs mal** acht ist achtundvierzig.

Jahreszahlen

1066 = ten sixty-six
1997 = nineteen (hundred and) ninety-seven
1900 = nineteen hundred
1905 = nineteen oh five / nineteen hundred and five
2005 = two thousand (and) five / twenty oh five
2012 = two thousand (and) twelve / twenty twelve

Measures and weights
Maße und Gewichte

Give a fool an inch and he'll take a mile. (*Proverb*)

In Großbritannien werden alltägliche Dinge wie Körpergröße, Entfernungen und Körpergewicht oft noch in den traditionellen Maßeinheiten *foot* [fʊt], *inch* [ɪntʃ], *mile* und *stone* angegeben. In Handel, Technik und Wissenschaft dagegen hat sich das metrische System, das die Kinder auch in der Schule lernen, bereits weitgehend durchgesetzt. In den USA werden metrische Maßeinheiten sehr viel seltener benutzt.

1 **inch** [ɪntʃ] is equal to 2.54 centimetres ['sentɪmiːtəz].	1 **Zoll** entspricht 2,54 Zentimetern.
a gap less than three inches ['ɪnʃɪz] wide	ein Spalt, der weniger als drei Zoll breit ist
a three-inch gap	ein drei Zoll breiter Spalt
a three-inch file	eine ca. acht Zentimeter dicke Akte
She didn't give / yield [jiːld] an inch.	Sie gab keinen Fingerbreit nach.
foot [fʊt] *Pl.* feet [fiːt]	**Fuß** (= 30,48 cm)
One foot is about a third of a metre ['miːtə].	Ein Fuß ist ungefähr ein Drittelmeter.
The tree has grown [grəʊn] a few feet.	Der Baum ist ein paar Fuß gewachsen.
We're flying ['flaɪɪŋ] at 30,000 feet now.	Wir fliegen jetzt in einer Höhe von 10 000 Metern.
a large room – 25 feet by 15	ein großes Zimmer – 7,60 mal 4,60 m
He's six feet / foot two inches tall.	Er ist 1,88 m groß.
a six-foot man	ein Mann, der über eins achtzig groß ist / war
He's 1.88 (= one point eight eight) **metres** tall.	Er ist 1,88 Meter groß.

Inch, foot, yard, mile und ihre metrischen Entsprechungen

	1 inch / in	=	2.54 centimetres / cm	
12 inches / in(s)	=	1 foot / ft	=	30.48 centimetres / cm
3 feet / ft	=	1 yard / yd	=	0.914 metre / m
1760 yards / yd(s)	=	1 mile / m	=	1.609 kilometres / km

A **yard** [jɑːd] is slightly less than a metre.	Ein **Yard** ist etwas weniger als ein Meter.
a few hundred yards from where I live	ein paar hundert Meter von meiner Wohnung entfernt
One **mile** is 1760 yards.	Eine **Meile** hat 1760 Yard.
It's ten miles to Hatfield.	Nach Hatfield sind es zehn Meilen.
a four-mile jog	ein Dauerlauf über vier Meilen
an area of ten square miles	ein Gebiet von zehn Quadratmeilen
There's a speed limit of 50 **kilometres** ['kɪləmiːtəz] per hour (kph).	Es gilt ein Tempolimit von 50 Stunden**kilometern** (km/h).

Beachten Sie den Gebrauch der Pluralform bei Maßen über 1:
2.54 centimetres (= 2,54 Zentimeter) • *two inches* (= zwei Zoll) •
36 kilos (= 36 Kilo) • *five litres* (= fünf Liter)
Bei Maßen unter null kann der Singular oder Plural stehen:
0.914 metre(s) (= 0,914 Meter) • *0.454 kilogram(s)* (= 0,454 Kilogramm)
Stone steht in der Regel im Singular; die Pluralform gilt als nicht so korrekt:
I weigh about ten stone / (weniger korrekt:) *stones.*

One **pound** is equal to 0.454 kilogram(s) ['kɪləgræm(z)].	Ein **Pfund** ist gleich 0,454 Kilogramm.
Half a pound of Cheddar, please.	Bitte ein halbes Pfund Cheddar.
There are 16 **ounces** ['aʊnsɪz] in a pound.	Ein Pfund hat 16 **Unzen.**
The baby weighs 7 lb(s) [paʊnd(z)] 6 oz ['aʊnsɪz].	Das Baby wiegt 3,4 Kilo.
I weigh about ten **stone.** *BE*	Ich wiege ungefähr 63 Kilo.
I weigh about 139 lbs [paʊndz]. *AE*	Ich wiege ungefähr 63 Kilo.
The police found 1,200 **kilos** ['kiːləʊz] of cocaine [kəʊ'keɪn].	Die Polizei fand 1200 **Kilo** Kokain.
The Irish consumed [kən'sjuːmd] 12.7 **kilograms** ['kɪləgræmz] of chocolate per person last year.	Die Iren haben im vorigen Jahr pro Person 12,7 **kg** Schokolade konsumiert.

Ounce, pound, stone und ihre metrischen Entsprechungen

		1 ounce / oz	=	*28.35 grams / g*
16 ounces / oz(s)	=	*1 pound / lb*	=	*0.454 kilogram / kg*
14 pounds / lb(s)	=	*1 stone / st*	=	*6.356 kilograms / kg*

one **pint** [paɪnt]	(*BE* = 0,568 / *AE* = 0,473 Liter)
a pint of milk / beer	(*etwa*) ein halber Liter Milch / Bier
I just had a couple of pints.	Ich habe nur ein paar Bier getrunken.
one **gallon** ['gælən]	(*BE* = 4,546 / *AE* = 3,785 Liter)
ten gallons of petrol *BE* / *AE* gas	45 *BE* / *AE* 38 Liter Benzin

Gallon ['gælən] – *litre* ['liːtə] bei Benzin
In Großbritannien wird Benzin heute in *litres* verkauft, in den USA nach wie vor in *gallons*.

Zur Aussprache längerer Wörter

Für das allgemeine Englisch gilt: Kürzere Wörter werden häufiger gebraucht als längere. So ist also die Gebrauchshäufigkeit von einsilbigen größer als die von zweisilbigen, die von zweisilbigen größer als die von dreisilbigen usw. Im wissenschaftlichen Sprachgebrauch kommen längere Wörter wesentlich häufiger vor als in der Allgemeinsprache. Doch je länger ein Wort, desto größer die Gefahr, dass man nicht die richtige Silbe betont.
Üben Sie die Aussprache der folgenden, nach Silben und Betonung geordneten Wörter, indem Sie besonders auf die richtige Betonung achten.

2 Silben, Betonung auf der 1. Silbe
anode cathode atom carbon constant figure fraction function
structure liquid moment organ problem solid system crystal
solvent physics substance

2 Silben, Betonung auf der 2. Silbe
burette pipette compute dilute degree disease dissolve
unknown divide perform subtract immune precise

3 Silben, Betonung auf der 1. Silbe
algebra nuclear circular energy industry chemistry rectangle
triangle diagnose memorize analyse concentrate microscope
molecule synthesis element isotope oxygen therapy vacuum

3 Silben, Betonung auf der 2. Silbe
arrangement department addition combustion corrosion division
profession progression reaction reduction solution subtraction
assistant circumference technician component electrode electron
malpractice intestine magnetic mechanics obstetrics

4 Silben, Betonung auf der 1. Silbe
embolism magnetism logarithm centimetre numerator variable

4 Silben, Betonung auf der 2. Silbe
deficiency endoscopy geometry neurology pathology radiology
urology analysis dialysis diameter practitioner arithmetic experiment
quadrangular rectangular molecular derivative

4 Silben, Betonung auf der 3. Silbe
engineering calculation composition diagnosis fundamental
hydrocarbons carbohydrates scientific geometric mathematics
radioactive electronic paediatrics orthopaedic obstetrician

5 Silben, Betonung auf der 3. Silbe
analytical arithmetical geometrical theoretical cardiology dermatology
gynaecology electrolysis equilibrium

Technology
Technik

1 **Materials, tools, machines**
Werkstoffe, Werkzeuge, Maschinen

2 **Manufacturing**
Fabrikproduktion

3 **Electricity and electronics**
Elektrizität und Elektronik

4 **Containers**
Behälter

At the cutting edge

Materials, tools, machines
Werkstoffe, Werkzeuge, Maschinen

Technological progress has merely provided us with more efficient means for going backwards. (*Aldous Huxley, English writer, 1894–1963*)

technology [tek'nɒlədʒi]	(die) **Technik / Technologie**
science ['saɪəns] and technology	Wissenschaft und Technik
the advantages of laser ['leɪzə] technology	die Vorteile der Lasertechnik
materials [mə'tɪəriəlz] technology	(die) Werkstoffkunde
high technology / high tech [haɪ 'tek]	(die) **Spitzen- / Hochtechnologie**
We have hi(gh)-tech equipment [ɪ'kwɪpmənt].	Wir haben eine High-Tech-Ausstattung.
technological [teknə'lɒdʒɪkl]	**technisch; technologisch**
technical ['teknɪkl] (innovations)	**technisch**(e Neuerungen)
engineering [endʒɪ'nɪərɪŋ]	(angewandte) **Technik; Ingenieurwesen**
engineering progress	technischer Fortschritt
material [mə'tɪəriəl]	**Material; Werkstoff**
properties ['prɒpətiz] of materials	Materialeigenschaften
work a material	ein Material bearbeiten
This material is easily machined [mə'ʃiːnd].	Dieses Material lässt sich leicht (maschinell) bearbeiten.
metal ['metl]	**Metall(-)**
The collapse [kə'læps] of the bridge was due to metal fatigue [fə'tiːg].	Der Einsturz der Brücke war auf Metallermüdung zurückzuführen.
the components [kəm'pəʊnənts] of an **alloy** ['ælɔɪ]	die Bestandteile einer **Legierung**
(high-speed) **steel** [stiːl]	(Schnellarbeits-)**Stahl**
a steel sheet [ʃiːt]	ein Stahlblech
wood [wʊd] – **wooden** ['wʊdn]	**Holz – Holz- / hölzern**
hardwood – softwood ['sɒftwʊd]	Hartholz – Weichholz
plywood ['plaɪwʊd]	Sperrholz
timber *BE* / *AE* **lumber** ['lʌmbə]	**(Nutz-)Holz; Bauholz**

Nutzholz auf dem Stamm ist auch AE *timber* ['tɪmbə]; nach der Bearbeitung nennt man es AE *lumber*. Beispiel: *timber species* ['spiː.ʃiːz] *unsuitable* [ʌn'suːtəbl] *for lumber* (= Baumarten, die sich nicht als Bauholz eignen).

chipboard *Keine Pluralform möglich!*	**Spanplatte(n)**
doors made of chipboard ['tʃɪpbɔːd]	aus Spanplatten gefertigte Türen
glass [glɑːs]	**Glas(-)**
ceramic [sə'ræmɪk]	**Keramik(-); keramisch**
plastic ['plæstɪk]	**Plastik(-); Kunststoff-**
rubber ['rʌbə]	**Gummi(-); Kautschuk**
Rubber is a highly elastic [ɪ'læstɪk] material.	Gummi ist ein äußerst elastisches Material.

made of | (gemacht / hergestellt) aus
It's made of glass / plastic / steel. | Es ist aus Glas / Kunststoff / Stahl.
semiconductor [semikən'dʌktə] | **Halbleiter**
silicon (chip) ['sɪlɪkən] | **Silicium**(chip)
elasticity [i:læ'stɪsəti] | **Elastizität**
strength [streŋθ] | (*z.B. Bruch-*)**Festigkeit**
ductility [dʌk'tɪləti] | **Dehnbarkeit; Duktilität**
heat / corrosion **resistance** [rɪ'zɪstəns] | Hitze- / Korrosions**beständigkeit**
conductivity [kɒndʌk'tɪvəti] | **Leitfähigkeit** / -vermögen
brittle ['brɪtl] | **spröde**
This material is extremely brittle. | Dieses Material ist äußerst brüchig / spröde.

a **tool** [tu:l] – my **tools** | ein **Werkzeug** – mein(e) **Werkzeug(e)**
hammer and chisel ['tʃɪzl] | **Hammer und Meißel**
nail [neɪl] | **Nagel**
screw(driver) ['skru:(draɪvə)] | **Schraube(nzieher)**
thread [θred] | **(Schrauben-)Gewinde**
nut and bolt [bəʊlt] | **Mutter und Bolzen / Schraube**
spanner *BE* / *AE* **wrench** [rentʃ] | **Schraubenschlüssel**
lever ['li:və] | **Hebel**
file [faɪl] | **Feile; feilen**
drill [drɪl] | **Bohrer; Bohrmaschine; bohren**
pneumatic [nju'mætɪk] drill | Pressluftbohrer
vice [vaɪs] *BE* / *AE* **vise** [vaɪs] | **Schraubstock**
a pair of **scissors** ['sɪzəz] / **pliers** ['plaɪəz] | eine **Schere** / **Zange**
Where are my scissors / pliers? | Wo ist meine Schere / Zange?
a pair of **pincers** ['pɪnsəz] | eine **Kneif-** / **Beißzange**
Have you got any pincers? | Hast du eine Kneifzange?
saw [sɔ:] (– sawed – sawn*) | **sägen**
handsaw – hacksaw | Fuchsschwanz – Bügelsäge
circular saw [sɜ:kjʊlə 'sɔ:] | Kreissäge
plane [pleɪn] | **Hobel; hobeln**
planing machine / planer | Hobelmaschine
machine [mə'ʃi:n] | **Maschine**
metalworking machine | Metallbearbeitungsmaschine
woodworking machine | Holzbearbeitungsmaschine
sewing machine ['səʊɪŋ məʃi:n] | Nähmaschine
printing machine ['prɪntɪŋ məʃi:n] | Druckmaschine
grinding machine / grinder ['graɪndə] | Schleifmaschine
machine component [kəm'pəʊnənt] | Maschinenteil
machine tool [mə'ʃi:n tu:l] | Werkzeugmaschine
machinery *Als Singular konstruiert!* | **Maschinen**
earth-moving machinery [mə'ʃi:nəri] | Erdbewegungsmaschinen
equipment *Als Singular konstruiert!* | **Ausrüstung; Geräte; Maschinen**
the construction of machinery and equipment [ɪ'kwɪpmənt] | der Bau von Maschinen und Anlagen
device [dɪ'vaɪs] | **Vorrichtung; Gerät**
The crank is a motion-transmitting device. | Die Kurbel ist eine Vorrichtung zur Bewegungsübertragung.
mechanism ['mekənɪzm] | **Mechanismus**

lathe [leɪð]	Drehbank / -maschine
(electric) **motor** [ˈməʊtə]	(Elektro-)**Motor**
(internal-combustion) **engine** [ˈendʒɪn]	(Verbrennungs-)**Motor**
four-stroke engine	Viertaktmotor
steam engine [ˈstiːm endʒɪn]	Dampfmaschine / -lokomotive
carburettor [kɑːbəˈretə] *BE / AE* **carburetor**	**Vergaser**
cylinder [ˈsɪlɪndə]	**Zylinder**
piston [ˈpɪstən]	**Kolben**
gear [gɪə] – **gears**	**Zahnrad – Getriebe;** (*Auto*) **Gang – Gänge**
gearbox [ˈgɪəbɒks]	Getriebe(gehäuse)
gear-cutting machine	Zahnradfräsmaschine
drive in first gear (– drove – driven)	im ersten Gang fahren
change (into third) gear	(in den dritten Gang) schalten
(drive) **shaft** [ʃɑːft]	(Antriebs-)**Welle**
crankshaft – camshaft	Kurbelwelle – Nockenwelle
connecting rod [kəˈnektɪŋ rɒd]	**Pleuelstange**
flywheel [ˈflaɪwiːl]	**Schwungrad**
torque [tɔːk]	**Drehmoment**
(ball) **bearing(s)** [(bɔːl) ˈbeərɪŋ(z)]	(Kugel-)**Lager**
spring [sprɪŋ]	**Feder**
(safety) **valve** [vælv]	(Sicherheits-)**Ventil**
washer [ˈwɒʃə]	**Unterleg- / Dichtungsscheibe**
brake [breɪk]	**Bremse; bremsen**
apply [əˈplaɪ] / put on the brakes	die Bremse betätigen
I had to brake hard / sharply.	Ich musste scharf bremsen.
clutch (pedal) [ˈklʌtʃ (pedl)]	**Kupplung**(spedal)
patent [ˈpætnt] applied for / pending	(zum) **Patent** angemeldet

Earth-moving equipment.

Manufacturing
Fabrikproduktion

… the throb and whine of machinery, the clash of metal, the unceasing motion of the assembly lines, the ebb and flow of workers changing shifts, the hiss of airbrakes and the growl of diesel engines from wagons delivering raw materials at one gate, taking away finished goods at the other.
(*David Lodge, English novelist, born in 1935*)

manufacture [mænju'fæktʃə]	**herstellen; fertigen; Herstellung**
manufacture a wide range of products	eine Vielzahl von Produkten herstellen
manufactured goods / products	Industrieerzeugnisse
manufacturing method ['meθəd]	Fabrikationsmethode / -weise
manufacturing / production facilities	Fertigungs- / Produktionsanlagen
plan manufacturing processes	Herstellungsprozesse / -abläufe planen
manufacturing engineer [endʒɪ'nɪə]	Betriebsingenieur(in)
the manufacture of children's clothing	die Fabrikation von Kinderkleidung
manufacturer [mænju'fæktʃərə]	**Hersteller**
the leading car manufacturers	die führenden Automobilhersteller
send it back to the manufacturers	es an die Herstellerfirma zurückschicken
fabricate ['fæbrɪkeɪt]	**herstellen**
The wooden parts used to be fabricated piece by piece.	Die Holzteile wurden früher einzeln hergestellt.
the fabrication of consumer goods	die Herstellung von Konsumgütern

Fabricate / fabrication können *manufacture / manufacturing* ersetzen, kommen aber weniger häufig vor. Außerdem haben *fabricate / fabrication* auch eine übertragene Bedeutung, nämlich „fälschen / Fälschung": *fabricate banknotes* (= Banknoten fälschen), *the fabrication of works of art* (= die Fälschung von Kunstwerken).

make (– made – made)	**machen; erzeugen; herstellen**
We make / manufacture toys.	Wir stellen Spielwaren her.
made in Germany	in Deutschland hergestellt
produce [prə'dju:s]	**herstellen; produzieren**
steel produced in the USA	in den USA hergestellter Stahl
a mass-produced article ['ɑːtɪkl]	ein Massenartikel
finished products [fɪnɪʃt 'prɒdʌkts]	Fertigerzeugnisse
production [prə'dʌkʃn]	**Produktion; Herstellung; Fertigung**
mass production [mæs prə'dʌkʃn]	Massenherstellung / -fertigung
production line [prə'dʌkʃn laɪn]	Fertigungsstraße; Fließband
processing ['prəʊsesɪŋ]	**Bearbeitung; Veredelung**
a paper-processing plant [plɑːnt]	ein Papierverarbeitungsbetrieb
assemble [ə'sembl]	**montieren**
assembly [ə'sembli] (plant)	**Montage**(werk)
assembly shop [ə'sembli ʃɒp]	Montagehalle
assembly line [ə'sembli laɪn]	Montageband; Fließband
computer-controlled assembly	computergesteuerte Montage

maintenance ['meɪntənəns]	**Wartung; Instandhaltung**
factory ['fæktri]	**Fabrik**
factory workers / hands	Fabrikarbeiter(innen)
(manufacturing) **plant** [plɑːnt]	**Werk; Betrieb; Maschinen**
Opel's Eisenach plant	das Opel-Werk in Eisenach
outdated [aʊt'deɪtɪd] plants	veraltete Anlagen
manage ['mænɪdʒ] a plant	ein Werk / einen Betrieb leiten
plant / works manager ['mænɪdʒə]	Betriebsleiter(in)
invest [ɪn'vest] millions in plant	Millionen in Maschinen investieren
(a cement [sə'ment]) **works** *Pl.* works	(ein Zement-)**Werk**
(work)shop [('wɜːk)ʃɒp]	**Werkstatt; Betrieb; Werk**
a repair shop [rɪ'peə ʃɒp]	eine Reparaturwerkstatt
an engineering [endʒɪ'nɪərɪŋ] shop	ein Maschinenbaubetrieb
on the shop floor [ʃɒp 'flɔː]	im Betrieb; in der Produktion
the workers on the shop floor	die einfachen Arbeiter(innen)
the car / automotive **industry**	die Automobil**industrie**
the processing industries ['ɪndəstriz]	die verarbeitende Industrie
industrial [ɪn'dʌstriəl] development	die **industrielle** Entwicklung
industrial robot [ɪndʌstriəl 'rəʊbɒt]	Industrieroboter
output ['aʊtpʊt]	**(Produktions-)Leistung**
output per worker hour	Ausstoß pro Arbeitsstunde
boost [buːst] output (by) 5 per cent	die Produktionsleistung um 5 Prozent steigern
efficiency [ɪ'fɪʃnsi]	**Leistung(sfähigkeit); Wirkungsgrad**
thermal ['θɜːml] efficiency	Wärmewirkungsgrad
performance [pə'fɔːməns]	(*Maschine*) **Leistung**
increased **productivity** [prɒdʌk'tɪvəti]	erhöhte **Produktivität**
mechanization [mekənaɪ'zeɪʃn]	**Mechanisierung**
automation [ɔːtə'meɪʃn]	**Automatisierung; Automation**
an **automated** production process	ein **automatisierter** Produktionsablauf
automatic [ɔːtə'mætɪk] regulation	**automatische** Regelung / Einstellung
perform [pə'fɔːm] an operation automatically	einen Arbeitsgang automatisch ausführen
computerize [kəm'pjuːtəraɪz] a process	einen Arbeitsablauf **computerisieren**
cost(s) [kɒst(s)]	**Kosten**
cut labour costs ['leɪbə kɒsts]	die Lohnkosten senken
lower ['ləʊə] the cost per unit ['juːnɪt]	die Stückkosten senken
conveyor belt [kən'veɪə belt]	**Förderband**
interchangeable [ɪntə'tʃeɪndʒəbl] **parts**	**auswechselbare Teile**
mechanic [mɪ'kænɪk]	**Mechaniker(in)**
fitter ['fɪtə]	**Monteur; (Maschinen-)Schlosser**
(machine) **operator** ['ɒpəreɪtə]	**(Maschinen-)Bediener(in)**

Bei der Fertigungssteuerung (= *in production management*) wird heute zunehmend *JIT* (= *just-in-time*) praktiziert: Die Zulieferer (= *suppliers* [sə'plaɪəz]) der Automobilindustrie z.B. liefern die Teile (= *components* [kəm'pəʊnənts]) exakt zu dem Zeitpunkt an (= *supply / deliver*), wo sie für die Montage (= *assembly* [ə'sembli]) benötigt werden.

Electricity and electronics
Elektrizität und Elektronik

→ 16.1 Physics, 18.7 Computers

Why sir, there is every possibility that you will soon be able to tax it!
*(English scientist and electricity pioneer Michael Faraday, 1791–1867,
to Prime Minister Gladstone, when asked whether electricity was useful)*

electricity [ɪlek'trɪsəti]	(die) **Elektrizität**; (elektrischer) **Strom**
electricity company ['kʌmpəni]	Elektrizitätsgesellschaft
(electricity) meter ['miːtə]	(Strom-)Zähler
an **electric(al)** [ɪ'lektrɪk(l)] shock	ein **elektrischer** Schlag / Stromschlag
electrical engineering [endʒɪ'nɪərɪŋ]	(die) Elektrotechnik
electrical engineer [endʒɪ'nɪə]	Elektroingenieur(in)
electrician [ɪlek'trɪʃn]	**Elektriker(in)**
generate ['dʒenəreɪt] electricity	Elektrizität / Strom **erzeugen**
generating station	Kraftwerk; Elektrizitätswerk
generator ['dʒenəreɪtə]	**Generator**; *(Auto AE)* **Lichtmaschine**
dynamo ['daɪnəməʊ]	**Dynamo**; *(Auto BE)* **Lichtmaschine**
battery ['bætəri]	**Batterie**
accumulator [ə'kjuːmjəleɪtə] *BE / AE* **storage cell**	**Akku(mulator)**
capacitor [kə'pæsɪtə] / **condenser**	**Kondensator**
spark [spɑːk]	**Funke**
spark plug / *BE auch* sparking plug	Zündkerze
an electrostatic [ɪlektrə'stætɪk] **charge**	eine elektrostatische **Aufladung**
put a battery on charge [tʃɑːdʒ] *BE*	eine Batterie aufladen
(re)charge the battery ['bætəri]	die Batterie (wieder) aufladen
direct current [daɪrekt 'kʌrənt] / **DC**	**Gleichstrom**
alternating ['ɔːltəneɪtɪŋ] **current** / **AC**	**Wechselstrom**
the current flowing through a device	der Strom, der durch ein Gerät fließt
alternator ['ɔːltəneɪtə]	**Wechselstromgenerator**
220 **volts** [vəʊlts]	220 **Volt**
voltage ['vəʊltɪdʒ]	**(Volt- / Netz-)Spannung**
high voltage / high tension ['tenʃn]	Hochspannung
high-voltage / high-tension line	Hochspannungsleitung
a 100-**watt** [wɒt] light bulb	eine 100-**Watt**-Glühbirne
ampere ['æmpeə] / **amp** [æmp]	**Ampere**
a 30-amp fuse [fjuːz]	eine 30-Ampere-Sicherung
amperage ['æmpərɪdʒ]	**Stromstärke**
three-phase power ['paʊə]	**Dreiphasenstrom; Drehstrom**
converter [kən'vɜːtə]	**Umformer**
transformer [træns'fɔːmə]	**Transformator**
coil [kɔɪl]	**Spule**
the **peak load** ['piːk ləʊd]	die **Spitzenbelastung**
electricity supply / *BE auch* **mains**	**Stromnetz**
switch the electricity off at the mains	den Strom am Hauptschalter abschalten

cable ['keɪbl]	Kabel; Leitung
flex [fleks] *BE* / *AE* **cord** [kɔːd]	(Anschluss-)Kabel / Schnur; Litze
extension lead [liːd] *BE* / *AE* **cord**	Verlängerungsschnur
the **live wire** [laɪv 'waɪə]	die **Strom führende Ader**; die **Phase**
earth [ɜːθ] *BE* / *AE* **ground** [graʊnd]	Erde; Erdung; Masse
The appliance [ə'plaɪəns] wasn't properly earthed *BE* / *AE* grounded.	Das Gerät war nicht richtig geerdet.
circuit ['sɜːkɪt]	Stromkreis; Schaltkreis
circuit breaker ['sɜːkɪt breɪkə]	Leistungsschalter; Unterbrecher
short circuit [ʃɔːt 'sɜːkɪt]	Kurzschluss
fuse [fjuːz] (box)	**Sicherung**(skasten)
The fuse has blown [bləʊn].	Die Sicherung ist raus(geflogen).
outlet ['aʊtlet]	Steckdose; (Strom-)**Verbrauchsstelle**
socket ['sɒkɪt] / *BE auch* **power point**	Steckdose
plug [plʌg]	Stecker
plug it in	den Stecker in die Steckdose stecken
Where do you plug in the speakers?	Wo schließt man die Lautsprecher an?
It can't work. It isn't plugged [plʌgd] in.	Es kann nicht funktionieren. Es ist ja nicht angeschlossen.
unplug [ʌn'plʌg] the TV	den Stecker des Fernsehers rausziehen
adaptor [ə'dæptə]	**Adapter; Zwischenstecker**
on – off	*(an elektr. Geräten)* **an – aus**
switch [swɪtʃ]	**Schalter; schalten**
flick a switch	einen Schalter an- / ausknipsen
switch / turn the TV on / off	den Fernseher ein- / ausschalten
switch / turn the lights on / off	das Licht an- / ausmachen
turn off the supply [sə'plaɪ] / power	den Strom **abschalten**
light bulb ['laɪt bʌlb]	*(elektr. Leuchtkörper:)* **Birne**
incandescent [ɪnkæn'desnt] **lamp**	Glüh(faden)lampe
fluorescent [flɔː'resnt] **lamp**	Leuchtstofflampe
energy ['enədʒi] **saving lamp**	Energiesparlampe
insulate – insulation [ɪnsjuˈleɪʃn]	isolieren – Isolierung
insulating tape ['ɪnsjuleɪtɪŋ teɪp]	Isolierband
He was **electrocuted** [ɪ'lektrəkjuːtɪd].	Er erhielt einen tödlichen Stromschlag.

 Silicon Valley [sɪlɪkən 'væli] (= „das Silicium-Tal") heißt die *region* ['riːdʒən] *south of San Francisco*, in der die amerikanische *computer and electronics industry* [ɪlek'trɒnɪks ɪndəstri] konzentriert ist.

electronic data ['deɪtə] processing	elektronische Datenverarbeitung; EDV
electronic devices [ɪlektrɒnɪk dɪ'vaɪsɪz]	elektronische Geräte
microelectronics *Mit Singularverb!*	(die) Mikroelektronik
microchip ['maɪkrəʊtʃɪp]	(Mikro-)Chip
microprocessor ['maɪkrəʊprəʊsesə]	Mikroprozessor
transistor [træn'zɪstə]	Transistor; Transistorradio
amplify ['æmplɪfaɪ] – **amplifier**	verstärken – Verstärker
digital ['dɪdʒɪtl]	digital; Digital-
digitize ['dɪdʒɪtaɪz] – **digitization**	digitalisieren – Digitalisierung

Containers
Behälter

→ S. 59

You can't tell what's in a package by its cover. (*Proverb*)

container [kən'teɪnə]
Behälter; (*genormter*) **Container**
The box contains spare parts.
Die Kiste / Der Karton / Kasten enthält Ersatzteile.

receptacle [rɪ'septəkl]
Behälter; Gefäß
pack [pæk]
(ein)packen
Have you packed (your bags)?
Hast du (deine Koffer) gepackt?
Aren't you going to pack a sweater?
Willst du keinen Pullover einpacken?
put it in a cardboard box (– put – put)
es in einen Pappkarton **tun** / **packen**
a **packet** of biscuits ['bɪskɪts] *BE* / *AE*
eine **Packung** Kekse
   a **package** of cookies
packaging ['pækɪdʒɪŋ] (material)
Verpackung(smaterial)
a **carton** ['kɑːtn] of milk
eine **Tüte** Milch
a carton of yoghurt ['jɒgət]
ein Becher Joghurt
chest [tʃest]
(große Holz-)**Kiste; Truhe**
a **case** [keɪs] of wine
eine **Kiste** Wein
a **crate** [kreɪt] of beer
ein **Kasten** Bier
a **sack** [sæk] of potatoes
ein **Sack** Kartoffeln
backpack / *BE auch* **rucksack**
Rucksack
   ['rʌksæk]

handbag *BE* / *AE* **purse** [pɜːs]
Handtasche
carrier bag *BE* / *AE* **shopping bag**
Tragetasche
attaché case [ə'tæʃeɪ keɪs]
Diplomatenkoffer
briefcase ['briːfkeɪs]
Aktentasche
file [faɪl]
Aktenordner
(file) folder ['fəʊldə]
Aktendeckel
file a letter (away)
einen Brief ablegen
envelope ['envələʊp]
(Brief-)Umschlag
(coffee / tea) **pot** [pɒt]
(Kaffee- / Tee-)**Kanne**
The pot was full to the brim.
Der Topf war randvoll.
Is the US a melting pot ['meltɪŋ pɒt]?
Sind die USA ein Schmelztiegel?
bucket ['bʌkɪt] / *bes. AE auch* **pail**
Eimer
pour [pɔː] water into the bucket
Wasser in den Eimer gießen / schütten
can [kæn]
Kanne; Büchse; Dose
a can / *BE auch* tin of beans [biːnz]
eine Büchse / Dose Bohnen (→ S. 59)
petrol ['petrəl] can *BE* / *AE* gas can
Benzinkanister
oilcan ['ɔɪlkæn]
Ölkanne
(fuel / petrol / oil) **tank** [tæŋk]
(Treibstoff- / Benzin- / Öl-)**Tank**
fill up the tank
den Tank voll machen
barrel ['bærəl]
Fass; Tonne
a barrel of beer [bɪə]
ein Fass Bier
Sherry is stored in oak **casks** [kɑːsks].
Sherry wird in Eichen**fässern** gelagert.
thermos flask / **thermos bottle**
Thermosflasche
vase [vɑːz]
Vase

At the cutting edge

Never before in history has innovation offered promise of so much to so many in so short a time. (*Bill Gates, co-founder of Microsoft, born in 1955*)

Viele von uns bemühen sich, *state of the art* (= auf der Höhe der Zeit) zu sein, zum Beispiel indem wir das neueste *smartphone* kaufen. Wirklich faszinierend (= *fascinating*) finden wir *cutting-edge research projects* (= hochinnovative Forschungsprojekte) wie den *Large Hadron Collider* – *LHC* (= Großer Hadronen-Speicherring), den größten *particle accelerator* (= Teilchenbeschleuniger) der Welt.

Operational (= in Betrieb) seit 2008, musste der LHC zunächst zahlreiche *test runs* (= Probeläufe) bestehen. Im Juli 2012 erfolgte der *breakthrough* (= Durchbruch), als Wissenschaftler die Existenz des *Higgs boson* (= Higgs-Teilchen) bewiesen, das mitunter auch *God particle* genannt wird. Die Ergebnisse dieses Experiments wurden in einer *landmark study* (= bahnbrechende Studie) veröffentlicht, deren Autorenliste sich über 19 Seiten erstreckt und *contains roughly 6,000 names (difficult to cite in a footnote, you can imagine!)*.

Der LHC gehört zu einer Reihe von *large-scale projects of internationally collaborative research* (= groß angelegte Forschungsprojekte in internationaler Zusammenarbeit). Ein weiteres ist *ITER*, der *International Thermonuclear Experimental Reactor* (= Internationaler Thermonuklearer Experimentalreaktor), der *most advanced nuclear fusion reactor* (= fortschrittlichste Fusionsreaktor) der Welt, der in Frankreich gebaut wird.

ITER soll den *commercial use* (= kommerzielle Nutzung) der Kernfusion ermöglichen. Zur Zeit aber müssen Wissenschaftler noch einige wichtige *operational issues* (= den Betrieb betreffende Fragen) klären, so etwa die, aus welchem Material die Reaktorwand bestehen muss *to withstand intense neutron bombardment* (= um intensivem Neutronenbeschuss standzuhalten. *R&D* / *Research and Development Departments* (= F&E / Forschungs-und Entwicklungs-Abteilungen) und *research consortiums* überall in der Welt bemühen sich, *cutting edge* zu sein – sei es mit innovativen *solar-powered devices* (= solar betriebene Geräte), *pliable medical sensors* (= biegsame medizinische Sensoren) oder *carbon nanotubes* (= Kohlenstoffnanoröhren). *A particular concern in *current research* (= in der aktuellen Forschung) *is sustainability* (= Nachhaltigkeit).

In Portugal will ein früherer Microsoft-Manager das Beste an moderner Technologie (= *the best of modern technology*) in einer *smart city* (= intelligente Stadt) vereinen. *A multitude of *sensors* controlled by an Urban OS (= operating system) will be *facilitating public transport and infrastructure* in an entire city* (= Eine Vielzahl von Sensoren, kontrolliert von einem städtischen Computerbetriebssystem, werden öffentlichen Verkehr und Infrastruktur einer ganzen Stadt vereinfachen.) *Who knows what the future holds?* (= Wer weiß, was die Zukunft bereithält?)

Information and communications
Information und Kommunikation

1   **Reference sources**
    Nachschlagemöglichkeiten

2   **Books and publishing**
    Bücher und Verlagswesen

3   **The press**
    Die Presse

4   **Radio and television**
    Rundfunk und Fernsehen

5   **The postal service**
    Der Postdienst

6   **Telephone and fax**
    Telefon und Fax

7   **Computers**
    Computer

Going portable

Reference sources
Nachschlagemöglichkeiten

→ 18.7 Computers

Information networks straddle the world. Nothing remains concealed. But the sheer volume of information dissolves the information. We are unable to take it all in. (*Günter Grass, German writer, born in 1927*)

a **reference** ['refrəns] book / work	ein **Nachschlage**buch / -werk
dictionary ['dɪkʃənəri]	**Wörterbuch**
I'll look it up in the dictionary.	Ich werde es im Wörterbuch nachschlagen.
thesaurus [θɪ'sɔːrəs]	**Thesaurus; Wörterbuch sinn-verwandter Wörter**
encyclopedia [ɪnsaɪklə'piːdiə]	**Enzyklopädie; (Konversations-) Lexikon**
an entry in an encyclopedia	ein Eintrag in einem Lexikon
supplement ['sʌpləmənt]	(*Lexikon*) **Nachtragsband**
online encyclopedia [ɪnsaɪklə'piːdiə]	**Online-Enzyklopädie**
He checked the definition [defə'nɪʃn] on Wikipedia™.	Er schaute die Definition bei Wikipedia™ nach.
google ['guːgl] something	etwas **mit Google suchen**
run an **online search** [sɜːtʃ]	eine **Internet-Suche** durchführen
glossary ['glɒsəri]	**Glossar; Wörterverzeichnis**
gazetteer [gæzə'tɪə]	**alphabetisches Ortsverzeichnis**
index ['ɪndeks]	**Register; Index**
almanac ['ɔːlmənæk]	**Almanach**
manual ['mænjuəl] / **handbook**	**Handbuch**
consult [kən'sʌlt] the manual	im Handbuch nachsehen
yearbook ['jɪəbʊk]	**Jahrbuch**
catalogue ['kætəlɒg]	**Katalog**
atlas ['ætləs] – atlases ['ætləsɪz]	**Atlas** – Atlanten
bibliography [bɪbli'ɒgrəfi]	**Bibliografie; Schriftenverzeichnis**
directory [də'rektəri]	**Adressbuch**
telephone ['telɪfəʊn] directory	Telefonbuch
library ['laɪbrəri]	**Bibliothek; Bücherei**
borrow a book from the library	ein Buch aus der Bibliothek entleihen
public library [pʌblɪk 'laɪbrəri]	öffentliche Bibliothek
reference library ['refrəns laɪbrəri]	Präsenzbibliothek
audiovisual [ɔːdiəʊ'vɪʒuəl] library	Mediothek
librarian [laɪ'breəriən]	**Bibliothekar(in)**
photocopy ['fəʊtəʊkɒpi]	**Fotokopie; fotokopieren**
study the specialist literature ['lɪtrətʃə]	die Fachliteratur **studieren**
browse [braʊz] through a book	in einem Buch **blättern**
search [sɜːtʃ] for a particular name	einen bestimmten Namen **suchen**
scan / skim (through) a text	einen Text **überfliegen**
record [rɪ'kɔːd] something	etwas (schriftlich oder auf Daten-träger) **aufzeichnen** / **festhalten**

information [ɪnfəˈmeɪʃn] *Kein Plural!* — Information(en)
try to find a piece of information — eine Information suchen
information retrieval [rɪˈtriːvl] — Informations- / Datenabruf
a computerized information system — ein computerisiertes Informations-
system

the information (super)highway — die Datenautobahn
cyberspace [ˈsaɪbəspeɪs] / **virtual** — **virtuelle Realität**
reality [vɜːtʃuəl riˈæləti]
online [ˈɒnlaɪn] services — **Online**-Dienste
the **Internet** [ˈɪntənet] / the **Web** — das **Internet**
download text from the Internet — Text aus dem Internet kopieren /
herunterladen / downloaden

e-mail [ˈiː meɪl] (= **electronic mail**) — **E-Mail** (= **elektronische Post**)
an e-mail (message [ˈmesɪdʒ]) — eine E-Mail
E-mail us your questions. — Senden Sie uns Ihre Fragen per
E-Mail.

CD-ROM [siːdiːˈrɒm] — **CD-ROM**
A 24-volume [ˈvɒljʊm] encyclopedia — Eine 24-bändige Enzyklopädie passt
fits on a single CD-ROM. — auf eine einzige CD-ROM.
full-text **search** [sɜːtʃ] — Volltext**suche**
run a search (– ran – run) — einen Suchlauf durchführen / machen
search engine [ˈsɜːtʃ enʒɪn] — Suchmaschine
search term [ˈsɜːtʃ tɜːm] — Suchbegriff
keyword [ˈkiːwɜːd] — **Suchwort; Stichwort**
multimedia [mʌltiˈmiːdiə] — **Multimedia**
interactive [ɪntərˈæktɪv] — **interaktiv**
transmit **data** [trænzmɪt ˈdeɪtə] — **Daten** übertragen
The data are / is interesting [ˈɪntrəstɪŋ]. — Die Daten sind interessant.
database [ˈdeɪtəbeɪs] — Datenbestand; Datenbank
data bank [ˈdeɪtə bæŋk] — Datenbank

Virtual reality.

Books and publishing
Bücher und Verlagswesen

→ 11.7 Literature

When I get a little money, I buy books; and if any is left, I buy food and clothes. (*Erasmus of Rotterdam, Dutch humanist scholar, 1466–1536*)

book [bʊk]	**Buch**
nonfiction [nɒnˈfɪkʃn] books	Sachbücher
bookseller – bookstall [ˈbʊkstɔːl]	Buchhändler(in) – Bücherstand
book club [ˈbʊk klʌb]	Buchklub; Buchgemeinschaft
secondhand / **antiquarian** books	**antiquarische** Bücher
secondhand / antiquarian bookshop	Antiquariat

Ein *antiquarian* [ˌæntɪˈkweəriən] *book* ist kostbarer als ein *secondhand book* und ein *antiquarian bookshop* ist teurer als ein *secondhand bookshop*.

the **cover** [ˈkʌvə] of a book	der **Einband** eines Buches
a **hardback** *BE* / *AE* **hardcover** (book)	ein **Buch mit festem Einband**
the hardback / hardcover edition	die gebundene Ausgabe
paperback [ˈpeɪpəbæk]	**Taschenbuch(-)**
a paperback edition [ɪˈdɪʃn]	eine Taschenbuchausgabe
the **binding** [ˈbaɪndɪŋ]	der **Einband**; die **Bindung**
(bound [baʊnd] in) **cloth** [klɒθ]	(in) **Leinen** (gebunden)
the **(dust) jacket** [(ˈdʌst) dʒækɪt]	der **Schutzumschlag**
the **blurb** [blɜːb]	der **Klappentext** / **Waschzettel**
the **title page** [ˈtaɪtl peɪdʒ]	die **Titelseite**
foreword / **preface** [ˈprefəs]	**Vorwort**

Ein *preface* stammt vom Autor; ein *foreword* ist von jemand anders verfasst.

introduction [ˌɪntrəˈdʌkʃn]	**Einleitung**
(table of) **contents** [ˈkɒntents]	**Inhalt**(sverzeichnis)
page [peɪdʒ]	(Buch-)**Seite**
chapter [ˈtʃæptə]	**Kapitel**
footnote [ˈfʊtnəʊt]	**Fußnote**
the lists in the **appendix** [əˈpendɪks]	die Listen im **Anhang**
author [ˈɔːθə] – **reader** [ˈriːdə]	**Autor(in)** – **Leser(in)**
pen name [ˈpen neɪm]	**Schriftstellername; Pseudonym**
translate [trænsˈleɪt]	**übersetzen; übertragen**
a **translation** [trænsˈleɪʃn] into Danish	eine **Übersetzung** ins Dänische
a translation from the Danish [ˈdeɪnɪʃ]	eine Übersetzung aus dem Dänischen
translator [trænsˈleɪtə]	**Übersetzer(in)**

ISBN (= International Standard [ˈstændəd] *Book Number):* International eingeführtes Identifikationsmerkmal für jedes Buch. Zum Beispiel in 978-3-19-202657-7 steht 978 für das Präfix, 3 für deutschsprachig, 19 für Hueber Verlag, 202657 für den Titel *Große Lerngrammatik Englisch* und 7 als Prüfziffer.

adapt [ə'dæpt] – **adaptation**	**bearbeiten** – **Bearbeitung**
TV adaptation of a novel ['nɒvl]	Fernsehbearbeitung eines Romans
abridge [ə'brɪdʒ] – **abridgment**	**kürzen** – **Kürzung**
an (un)abridged version ['vɜːʃn]	eine (un)gekürzte Fassung
copyright ['kɒpiraɪt]	**Copyright; Urheberrecht**
royalties ['rɔɪəltiz]	**Autorenhonorar(e)**
publish ['pʌblɪʃ]	**veröffentlichen; publizieren; verlegen**
publishing house / firm / company	Verlag
one of the leading textbook publishers	einer der führenden Lehrbuchverlage

The book came out / was published ['pʌblɪʃt] *last May.* (= Das Buch ist im vergangenen Mai erschienen.) • *bring a book out* (= ein Buch herausbringen) • *launch a book* (= ein Buch auf den Markt bringen)

manuscript ['mænjuː-] – **typescript**	**Manuskript** – **Typoskript**
edit ['edɪt] a manuscript	ein Manuskript **lektorieren / redigieren**
editor ['edɪtə]	**Lektor(in); Redakteur(in)**
editorial [edɪ'tɔːriəl] **department**	**Lektorat**
edition [ɪ'dɪʃn]	**Ausgabe; Auflage**
the first edition of a book	die Erstausgabe eines Buches
typeset a book (– typeset – typeset)	ein Buch **setzen**
typesetter / **compositor** [kəm'pɒ-]	**(Schrift-)Setzer(in)**
read the proofs [pruːfs]	**Korrektur lesen**
the page proofs ['peɪdʒ pruːfs]	der Umbruch
proofreader ['pruːfriːdə]	**Korrektor(in)**
printer's error ['erə]	**Satzfehler**
misprint ['mɪsprɪnt]	**Druckfehler**
print [prɪnt]	**drucken; Druck**
printed on acid-free ['æsɪd friː] paper	auf säurefreiem Papier gedruckt
large / clear print	großer / deutlicher Druck
books in print	lieferbare Bücher
The book is out of print.	Das Buch ist vergriffen.
a print run of 5,000 copies	eine (Druck-)Auflage von 5000
the **printer(s)** ['prɪntə(z)]	die **Druckerei**
The book has gone [ɒ] to the printer(s).	Das Buch ist in Druck gegangen.
pub(lication) date [pʌb(lɪ'keɪʃn)]	**Erscheinungstermin**
a **copy** ['kɒpi] of the book	ein **Exemplar** des Buches
advance copy [əd'vɑːns kɒpi]	Vorausexemplar
the **Frankfurt Book Fair**	die **Frankfurter Buchmesse**
bestseller [best'selə]	**Bestseller**
a best-selling author ['ɔːθə]	ein(e) Bestseller(autor/in)

A good read (= eine spannende Lektüre) kann *exhilarating* [ɪg'zɪləreɪtɪŋ] (= anregend), *harrowing* (= erschütternd) oder *terrifying* (= furchterregend) sein. Andere gängige Adjektive sind *gripping* (= packend) und *riveting* ['rɪvɪtɪŋ] (= fesselnd). Ein sehr spannendes Buch ist a *page turner*, ja es ist *unputdownable*.

The press
Die Presse

How many beautiful trees gave their lives that today's
scandal should, without delay, reach a million readers!
(*Edwin Way Teale, US naturalist and writer, 1899–1980*)

the (mass) **media** ['miːdiə] are / is …	die (Massen-)**Medien** sind …
a media event [ɪ'vent]	ein Medienereignis
freedom ['friːdəm] of the **press**	**Presse**freiheit
press censorship ['sensəʃɪp]	(die) Pressezensur
hold a press conference ['kɒnfərəns]	eine Pressekonferenz geben
journalism ['dʒɜːnəlɪzm] – **journalist**	**Journalismus – Journalist(in)**
an **item** / a **news item** ['njuːz aɪtəm]	eine **Nachricht**
news agency ['njuːz eɪdʒənsi]	Nachrichtenagentur

Fleet Street – die Londoner Straße, wo früher die meisten *national newspapers*
ihre *headquarters* (= Zentralen) hatten – wird immer noch zur Bezeichnung
der britischen Presse verwendet: *a Fleet Street reporter* (= *a reporter working for
a British paper*). Seit den 80er-Jahren ist das östlich der *Tower Bridge* gelegene
Wapping ['wɒpɪŋ] das neue *centre of the UK newspaper industry.*

a national **(news)paper** [('njuːs)peɪpə]	eine überregionale **Zeitung**
a local ['ləʊkl] (news)paper	eine Lokalzeitung
morning / evening paper	Morgen- / Abendzeitung
news(paper)man / -woman	Reporter / Reporterin
newsagent *BE* / *AE* newsdealer	Zeitungshändler(in)
newsvendor ['njuːzvendə] *BE*	Zeitungsverkäufer(in)
newsstand ['njuːzstænd]	Zeitungskiosk; Zeitungsstand
a **daily** ['deɪli] (paper)	eine **Tageszeitung**
a **weekly** ['wiːkli]	eine **Wochenzeitung** / **-zeitschrift**
magazine [mægə'ziːn]	**Magazin; Zeitschrift**
women's ['wɪmɪnz] magazine	Frauenzeitschrift
newsmagazine ['njuːzmægəziːn]	Nachrichtenmagazin
periodical [pɪəri'ɒdɪkl]	**Zeitschrift**
a monthly / satirical periodical	eine Monats- / satirische Zeitschrift
a **technical journal** ['dʒɜːnl]	eine **Fachzeitschrift**

Der Boulevardpresse (= *popular press* / *tabloid* ['tæblɔɪd] *press*) steht die
seriöse Presse (= *quality* ['kwɒləti] *press* / *serious press*) gegenüber. Die
kleinformatigen Boulevardzeitungen sind *tabloids,* während man groß-
formatige Qualitätszeitungen wie die britische *Financial Times* und die
amerikanische *Washington Post* als *broadsheets* ['brɔːdʃiːts] bezeichnet. Die
Sensationspresse (= *sensational press*) nennt man abschätzig (= *disparagingly* [dɪ'spærɪdʒɪŋli]) im BE *the gutter press* und im AE *the yellow press.*
Hier arbeiten *irresponsible* [ɪrɪ'spɒnsəbl] (= verantwortungslose) *journalists,*
die *muckraking* (= „Mistharken", also Sensationsmache) betreiben und für
pikante (= *spicy*) Informationen (= *information*) hohe Summen zahlen

18

3

(*chequebook journalism* = Scheckbuchjournalismus). Skandalblätter (= *scandal* ['skændl] *sheets*) haben riesige Auflagen (= *huge* [hju:dʒ] *circulations*).

story ['stɔːri]	Bericht; Meldung; Story
carry a story	eine Meldung bringen
the reporter who wrote the story	der Reporter, der den Artikel schrieb
cover ['kʌvə] a story	über ein Ereignis berichten
report [rɪ'pɔːt]	**berichten; melden; Bericht; Meldung**
Heavy fighting is reported from X.	Aus X werden schwere Kämpfe gemeldet.
according [ə'kɔːdɪŋ] to news reports	Presseberichten zufolge
a report on child prostitution	eine Reportage über Kinderprostitution
a **feature** ['fiːtʃə] on the Mafia ['mæfiə]	ein **Dokumentarbericht** über die Mafia
bulletin ['bʊlətɪn]	**Meldung; Nachricht; Bulletin**
announce [ə'naʊns]	**bekannt geben; verlautbaren**
He announced his resignation.	Er kündigte seinen Rücktritt an.
cover ['kʌvə]	(*Magazin*) **Titelseite**
cover story / lead [liːd] story	Titelgeschichte
the **front page** [frʌnt 'peɪdʒ]	die **Titelseite** (*einer Zeitung*)
The divorce made front-page news.	Die Scheidung machte Schlagzeilen.
sports / business ['bɪznəs] **section**	Sport- / Wirtschafts**teil**
Sunday **supplement** ['sʌpləmənt]	Sonntags**beilage**
(international) **edition** [ɪ'dɪʃn]	(internationale) **Ausgabe**
editor ['edɪtə] (in chief [tʃiːf])	(Chef-)**Redakteur(in)**
city editor *AE* / *BE* local news editor	Lokalredakteur(in)
City editor *BE* / *AE* financial editor	Wirtschaftsredakteur(in)
letters to the editor	Leserbriefe
editorial [edɪ'tɔːriəl] / **leader**	**Leitartikel**
lead [liːd] with a story (– led – led)	eine Story **groß herausstellen**
column ['kɒləm]	(*Zeitung*) **Spalte, Kolumne**
agony ['ægəni] *BE* / *AE* advice column	Ratgeber(spalte)
gossip ['gɒsɪp] column	Klatschspalte
columnist ['kɒləmnɪst]	**Kolumnist(in)**
a TIME **contributor** [kən'trɪbjʊtə]	ein(e) TIME-**Mitarbeiter(in)**
correspondent [kɒrə'spɒndənt]	**Korrespondent(in)**
copy ['kɒpi]	**Text(e); Artikel; Stoff**
The war [wɔː] made good copy.	Der Krieg ließ sich gut verkaufen.
heading ['hedɪŋ]	**Überschrift**
headline ['hedlaɪn]	**Schlagzeile**
hit the headlines (– hit – hit)	Schlagzeilen machen
the **caption** ['kæpʃn] read …	die **Bildunterschrift** lautete …
deadline ['dedlaɪn]	(*Manuskriptabgabe*) **(letzter) Termin**
a **circulation** [sɜːkju'leɪʃn] of 3 million	eine **Auflage** von 3 Millionen
subscribe [səb'skraɪb] to a newspaper	eine Zeitung **im Abonnement beziehen**
subscriber – **subscription**	**Abonnent(in)** – **Abonnement**
take out a subscription to a paper	eine Zeitung abonnieren
spokesman ['spəʊks-] / **-woman**	**(Presse-)Sprecher** / **Sprecherin**

Radio and television
Rundfunk und Fernsehen

→ 18.3 The press, 11.5 Theatre and cinema

I find television very educational. Every time someone
switches it on I go into another room and read a good book.
(*Groucho Marx, US comedian, 1890–1977*)

radio ['reɪdiəʊ]	**Rundfunk(-); Radio(-); Hörfunk**
listen ['lɪsn] to the radio	Radio hören
I heard [hɜːd] it on the radio.	Das habe ich im Radio gehört.
radio set ['reɪdiəʊ set]	Rundfunk- / Radiogerät
television ['telɪvɪʒn] / **TV** [tiː'viː]	(das) **Fernsehen; Fernseh-; Fernseher**
What's on (the) television tonight?	Was ist heute Abend im Fernsehen?
watch [wɒtʃ] television / TV	fernsehen
cable ['keɪbl] television	(das) Kabelfernsehen
commercial [kə'mɜːʃl] television	(das) Privatfernsehen
broadcast (– broadcast – broadcast)	**senden; übertragen; ausstrahlen**
broadcast ['brɔːdkɑːst] a soccer match	ein Fußballspiel (im Fernsehen / Rundfunk) übertragen
The ceremony was broadcast live [laɪv].	Die Feier wurde direkt übertragen.
live broadcast [laɪv 'brɔːdkɑːst]	Direktübertragung; Livesendung
broadcasting corporation [kɔːpə'reɪʃn]	Rundfunkanstalt
televise / **telecast** (– telecast – telecast)	**im Fernsehen senden / übertragen**
the telecast of the concert	die (Fernseh-)Übertragung des Konzerts
network ['netwɜːk] / **station**	(*Rundfunk / Fernsehen*) **Sender**
The show was broadcast on 50 television networks.	Die Show wurde von 50 Fernsehsendern übertragen.
channel ['tʃænl]	**(Fernseh-)Kanal**
channel-hop *BE* / *AE* channel-surf	zwischen den Programmen hin und her schalten
zap [zæp] – **zapping**	**zappen** (= *channel-hop*) – **Zappen**
tune in to a German station	einen deutschen Sender **einstellen**
go on / off the **air** [eə]	die Sendung(en) beginnen / beenden
The programme (was) aired last Monday.	Das Programm wurde vorigen Montag gesendet / ausgestrahlt.
many hours of **airtime**	viele Stunden **Sendezeit**

Als *couch potatoes* bezeichnet man Leute, die körperliche Bewegung
(= *physical exercise*) meiden bzw. ihre Freizeit (= *leisure* ['leʒə] *time*)
überwiegend mit Fernsehen (= *watching television*) verbringen. Für den
Fernsehapparat selbst (= *the television set / the TV set / the television /
the telly*) gibt es vielsagende (= *telltale*) Bezeichnungen wie *boob tube*
['buːb tjuːb] (= „Dummenröhre") oder *idiot* ['ɪdiət] *box*. Unverzichtbarer
(= *indispensable*) Bestandteil der Programmplanung (= *programming*)
sind seichte (= *shallow*), sentimentale (= *sentimental*), melodramatische
(= *melodramatic*) „Seifenopern" (= *soap operas / soaps*) wie *Dallas* und

Dynasty, die man auch *cotton candy for the mind* (= Zuckerwatte für den Geist) genannt hat.

(radio / TV) **programme** ['prəʊgræm]	(Rundfunk- / Fernseh-)**Sendung**
news programme *BE* / *AE* newscast	Nachrichtensendung
sports programme *BE* / *AE* sportscast	Sportsendung
documentary [dɒkju'mentri]	**Dokumentarfilm**
docudrama ['dɒkjudrɑːmə]	**Dokumentarspiel**
a **commercial** [kə'mɜːʃl]	ein **Werbespot**
television play / **teleplay**	**Fernsehspiel**
television film / **telefilm**	**Fernsehfilm**
a popular TV **series** ['sɪəriːz] *Pl.* series	eine beliebte Fernseh**serie**
renewed for another **season**	um eine weitere **Staffel** verlängert
sitcom / **situation comedy**	(amüsante) **Familienserie**
quiz show ['kwɪz ʃəʊ]	**Quizsendung**
chat show *BE* / *AE* talk show	Talkshow
chat / talk show host [həʊst]	Talkmaster(in)
call-in (programme)	**Anrufsendung**
candid camera [kændɪd 'kæmərə]	**versteckte Kamera**
edutainment / **infotainment**	(Unterhaltung, die bildet / informiert)
episode ['epɪsəʊd]	**Folge** (einer Fernsehserie)
repeat [rɪ'piːt] / **rerun** ['riːrʌn]	**Wiederholung**
interview ['ɪntəvjuː] – **interviewer**	Interview – Interviewer(in)
announcer [ə'naʊnsə]	Ansager(in); Sprecher(in)
newscaster / *BE auch* **newsreader**	Nachrichtensprecher(in)
presenter [prɪ'zentə] *BE* / *AE* **anchor** ['æŋkə] / **anchorman** / **-woman**	Moderator(in)
a show anchored by Dan Fox	eine von Dan Fox moderierte Sendung
commentator ['kɒmənteɪtə]	**Kommentator(in)**
sports commentator	Sportreporter(in)
disc jockey ['dɪsk dʒɒki]	**Diskjockey**
weatherman / **-woman** / **-person**	**Wettermann** / **-frau**
producer [prə'djuːsə]	**Produzent(in)**
sponsor ['spɒnsə]	**Sponsor(in)**
listener ['lɪsnə]	(Rundfunk-)**Hörer(in)**
Thanks for listening ['lɪsnɪŋ].	Danke fürs Zuhören.
viewer ['vjuːə]	(Fernseh-)**Zuschauer(in)**
prime time ['praɪm taɪm]	**Hauptsendezeit; Haupteinschaltzeit**
high / low **ratings** ['reɪtɪŋz]	hohe / niedrige **Einschaltquoten**
The series has done well in the ratings.	Die Serie hat gute Einschaltquoten.
clock radio / **radio alarm** [ə'lɑːm]	**Radiowecker**
ghetto blaster / *AE auch* **boom box**	(**Lärm erzeugender Radiorekorder**)
tape recorder ['teɪp rɪkɔːdə]	**Tonbandgerät**
cassette recorder [kə'set rɪkɔːdə]	Kassettenrekorder
video ['vɪdiəʊ]	**Video(-)**; *BE* **Videorekorder**
videocassette [vɪdiəʊkə'set]	Videokassette
video(cassette) recorder / VCR	Videorekorder
DVD [diːviː'diː] **(player)**	**DVD(-Player** / **-Abspielgerät)**
microphone ['maɪkrəfəʊn] / **mike**	**Mikrofon**
good / poor **reception** [rɪ'sepʃn]	guter / schlechter **Empfang**

The postal service
Der Postdienst

Britain remains the only country in the world not to be named on its stamps –
the monarch's head is considered sufficient national identification.
(*Adapted, from Encyclopedia of Britain, by Bamber Gascoigne, born in 1935*)

post [pəʊst]	**Post**
take a letter to the post	einen Brief auf die Post bringen
My letter was ten days in the post.	Mein Brief war zehn Tage unterwegs.
We'll send it by post.	Wir schicken es mit der Post.
by the same post	mit gleicher Post
inland post *BE* / *AE* domestic [də'mestɪk] mail	Inlandspost
post *BE* / *AE* mail a letter	einen Brief auf die Post geben
by return [rɪ'tɜːn] (of post)	postwendend
We posted *BE* / *AE* mailed the parcel yesterday.	Wir haben das Paket gestern abge- schickt.
post office ['pəʊst ɒfɪs]	**Post(filiale / -amt)**
the Post Office	die Post (*als Einrichtung*)
post-office box / POB / PO box	Postfach
the **Postmaster General** ['dʒenrəl]	der / die **Postminister(in)**
postal rates / charges ['tʃɑːdʒɪz]	**Post**gebühren
postal worker / employee [ɪm'plɔiː]	Postbeschäftigte(r) / -mitarbeiter(in)
postal order ['pəʊstl ɔːdə] *BE*	Postanweisung
postal vote ['pəʊstl vəʊt]	Briefwahl; briefl. Stimmabgabe

Für Postzusteller(in) / Briefträger(in) / Postfrau etc. gibt es eine Reihe von
Entsprechungen: BE *postman / postwoman,* AE *mailman / mail carrier / letter
carrier / postman.*

mail [meɪl]	**Post(-)**
Has the mail / *BE auch* post come yet?	Ist die Post schon da?
mail train / plane ['meɪl treɪn / pleɪn]	Postzug / -flugzeug
surface mail ['sɜːfɪs meɪl]	auf dem Land- / Seeweg beförderte Post
mailing list ['meɪlɪŋ lɪst]	Adressenliste

In den USA versteht man unter *first-class mail* Briefe (= *letters*) und
Postkarten (= *postcards / postal cards*); *second-class mail* sind Zeitungen
(= *newspapers*) etc.; *third-class mail* sind Bücher (= *books*) etc.; *fourth-class
mail* ist Paketpost (= *parcel post*). Im UK bedeutet *first class* bevorzugte
Beförderung: *first-class letters* sind normalerweise nur einen Tag unterwegs,
second-class post bis zu drei Tagen. *Swiftair* gewährleistet bevorzugte
Luftpostbeförderung vom UK ins Ausland (= *overseas*); *Express* [ɪk'spres]
Mail, Priority [praɪ'ɒrəti] *Mail* und *Special Handling* bieten bevorzugte
Beförderung in den USA.

aerogramme ['eərəʊɡræm] / *BE auch* **airletter**	**Aerogramm** (= Luftpostleichtbrief)

parcel ['pɑːsl]	**Paket**
pack / unpack a parcel	ein Paket / Päckchen packen / auspacken
a bulky ['bʌlki] parcel	ein sperriges Paket
The items will be shipped by parcel post.	Die Artikel werden per Paketpost versandt.
parcel bomb ['pɑːsl bɒm]	Paketbombe
small packet ['pækɪt] *BE* / *AE* **small parcel**	**Päckchen**
printed matter ['prɪntɪd mætə]	**Drucksache(n)**
an item ['aɪtəm] of printed matter	eine Drucksache

Postkarten sind im BE immer *postcards,* im AE entweder *postcards* (= kommerziell hergestellte Post- bzw. Ansichtskarten) oder *postal cards* (= von der Post verkaufte Postkarten mit aufgedruckter Briefmarke).

deliver [dɪ'lɪvə] – **delivery** [dɪ'lɪvəri]	**zustellen – Zustellung**
millions of pieces ['piːsɪz] of undelivered mail	Millionen nicht zugestellter Post- sendungen
If undelivered, please return [rɪ'tɜːn] to sender.	Falls unzustellbar, bitte zurück an Absender.
special delivery [speʃl dɪ'lɪvəri]	Eilzustellung
cash *BE* / *AE* collect [kə'lekt] on delivery (COD)	per Nachnahme
send something COD	etwas per Nachnahme schicken
send a letter **recorded delivery** *BE* / *AE* by **certified** ['sɜːtɪfaɪd] **mail**	einen **Brief per Einschreiben** (*unversichert*) schicken
by **registered** ['redʒɪstəd] **post** *BE* / *AE* **mail**	**per Einschreiben** (*versichert*)
by *BE* / *AE* via ['vaɪə] **airmail**	mit / per **Luftpost**
We'll send it (by / via) airmail.	Wir schicken es per Luftpost.
poste restante [pəʊst 'restɒnt] *BE* / *AE* **general delivery**	**postlagernd**
Freepost ['friːpəʊst] *BE*	**Werbeantwort; Gebühr zahlt Empfänger**
international reply coupon ['kuːpɒn]	**internationaler Antwortschein**

Ein Briefkasten auf der Straße ist im BE *postbox, letterbox* oder (veraltet) *pillar box* ['pɪlə bɒks], im AE *mailbox.* Ein privater Briefkasten ist im BE *letterbox,* im AE *mailbox.*

please **forward** ['fɔːwəd]	bitte **nachsenden**
forwarding address ['fɔːwədɪŋ ədres]	Nachsendeanschrift
date as **postmark** ['pəʊstmɑːk]	Datum des **Poststempels**
The letter was postmarked "Leeds".	Der Brief war in Leeds abgestempelt.
postage ['pəʊstɪdʒ]	**Porto**
What's the postage on this letter?	Was kostet dieser Brief an Porto?
(postage) stamp [stæmp]	**Briefmarke**
the **postcode** *BE* / *AE* **zip code**	die **Postleitzahl**
shipment tracking ['trækɪŋ]	**Sendungsverfolgung**

Telephone and fax
Telefon und Fax

Well, if I called the wrong number, why did you answer the phone?
(*James Thurber, US writer and cartoonist, 1894–1961*)

(tele)phone [(ˈtelɪ)fəʊn]
Our phone is out of order.
You're wanted on the phone.
answer [ˈɑːnsə] the phone
pick up the phone
during a (tele)phone conversation
telephone charges [ˈtelɪfəʊn tʃɑːdʒɪz]
cordless [ˈkɔːdləs] phone
mobile (phone) *BE* / *AE* cell phone
We (tele)phoned the doctor.
We (tele)phoned for a doctor.
call [kɔːl]
I called her (up) at the office.
Can I call you back?
Thank you / Thanks for calling.
make a phone call (– made – made)
local call [ˈləʊkl ˈkɔːl]
long-distance call / *AE auch* toll call
the **caller** [ˈkɔːlə] / **calling party**
ring (– rang – rung) *BE* / *AE* call
I'll ring you tonight.
I rang her up in London.
Give me a ring sometime.
ring off *BE* / *AE* hang up
buzz [bʌz]
I'll give you a buzz when it comes.
(tele)phone number [ˈnʌmbə]
You can call me on *BE* / *AE* at this
  number.
You've got the / a wrong number.
toll-free [ˈtəʊl friː] number
an ex-directory [eksdəˈrektəri] *BE* /
  AE unlisted number

Telefon(-); Fernsprech-
Unser Telefon ist gestört.
Sie werden am Telefon verlangt.
ans Telefon / an den Apparat gehen
den Hörer abnehmen
während eines Telefongesprächs
Telefongebühren
schnurloses Telefon
Funk- / Mobiltelefon; Handy
Wir riefen den Arzt an.
Wir telefonierten nach einem Arzt.
anrufen; Anruf; Telefonat
Ich habe sie im Büro angerufen.
Kann ich Sie zurückrufen?
Vielen Dank für Ihren Anruf.
ein Telefongespräch führen
Ortsgespräch
Ferngespräch
der / die **Anrufer(in)**
anrufen
Ich rufe dich heute Abend an.
Ich habe sie in London angerufen.
Rufe mich doch mal an.
einhängen; auflegen
summen; Summen
Ich ruf dich an, wenn es kommt.
Telefonnummer
Sie können mich unter dieser
  Nummer anrufen.
Sie sind falsch verbunden.
(gebührenfrei anrufbare Nummer)
eine Nummer, die nicht im Telefon-
  buch steht

☞ ***How to say phone numbers*** (= **Wie man Telefonnummern spricht**)
From Germany, the code for the UK is 0044 (double oh, double four).
Within the UK, the code for central London is 0171 (oh one seven one).
Our phone number is 385 1300 (three eight five, one three double oh).
Our fax number is 734 6117 (seven three four, six one one seven).

phone book / **telephone directory**
Yellow Pages [jeləʊ ˈpeɪdʒɪz]
directory enquiries [ɪnˈkwaɪəriz] *BE* /
  AE **directory assistance** [əˈsɪstəns]

Telefonbuch
Gelbe Seiten; Branchentelefonbuch
(die) **Telefonauskunft**

subscriber [səb'skraɪbə]	(Telefon-)**Kunde** / **Kundin**
the (dialling *BE* / *AE* area) **code** [kəʊd]	die **Vorwahl**(nummer)
dial ['daɪəl] a number	eine Nummer **wählen**
dialling *BE* / *AE* dial tone [təʊn]	Freizeichen; Wählton; Rufton
The number's **engaged** *BE* / *AE* **busy**.	Die Nummer ist **besetzt**.

Phrases used on the phone (= **Am Telefon benutzte Redensarten**)
Who's this? (= Wer ist da?) • *Is that Mrs King?* (= Ist da Frau King?) •
Speaking. (= Am Apparat.) • *Can I speak to Pat, please?* (= Kann ich bitte
Pat sprechen?) • *Hold on, I'll connect you.* (= Moment, ich verbinde Sie.) •
One moment, please. (= Einen Augenblick bitte.) • *This is Jill Fox (speaking).*
(= Hier ist / spricht Jill Fox.) • *Can you speak a bit louder, please?* (= Kön-
nen Sie bitte ein bisschen lauter sprechen?) • *We've been disconnected.*
(= Wir sind getrennt worden.)

a bad **connection** [kə'nekʃn] / **line**	eine schlechte **Verbindung** / **Leitung**
tap a telephone **line** [laɪn]	eine Telefon**leitung** anzapfen
have a new line installed [ɪn'stɔːld]	einen Neuanschluss einrichten lassen
Will you please hold the line.	Bleiben Sie bitte am Apparat.
hot line ['hɒt laɪn]	**Servicetelefon; tel. Beratungsdienst**
extension [ɪk'stenʃn]	**Nebenstelle; Apparat**
I'm on extension 244.	Ich habe Apparat 244.
receiver [rɪ'siːvə]	**(Telefon-)Hörer**
replace [rɪ'pleɪs] the receiver	(den Hörer) auflegen
answering machine / *BE auch*	**Anrufbeantworter**
answerphone	
call box *BE* / **(tele)phone box** *BE* /	**Telefonzelle**
AE **(tele)phone booth** [buːð]	
pay phone / *AE auch* **pay station**	**Münz-** / **Kartentelefon**
phonecard ['fəʊnkɑːd]	**Telefonkarte**
operator ['ɒpəreɪtə]	**Vermittlung**
a call through the operator	ein handvermitteltes Gespräch
switchboard ['swɪtʃbɔːd]	**(Telefon-)Zentrale** / **Vermittlung**
send an **SMS (message)** / a **text**	eine SMS senden
Please text me.	Bitte schicke mir eine SMS.
multimedia message (MMS)	**Multimedia-Nachricht (MMS)**
roaming ['rəʊmɪŋ]	**Roaming**

Beachten Sie den Unterschied zwischen *hang on* (= warten / dran bleiben)
und *hang up* (= einhängen / auflegen): *Hang on a minute.* (= Augenblick
bitte.) *He had the cheek to hang up on me.* (= Er besaß die Frechheit,
einfach aufzulegen.)

fax [fæks]	**(Tele-)Fax; faxen**
Didn't you get my fax?	Hast du denn mein Fax nicht
	erhalten?
Could you send it by fax?	Könnten Sie es per Fax senden?
I'll give you my fax number.	Ich gebe Ihnen meine Faxnummer.
We'll fax you our offer today.	Wir faxen Ihnen heute unser Angebot.
We'll fax it through to you.	Wir faxen es Ihnen durch.
fax machine	(Tele-)Faxgerät

Computers
Computer

→ 18.1 Reference sources

To err is human but to really foul things up requires a computer.
(*Anonymous, in Farmers' Almanac for 1978*)

computer [kəmˈpjuːtə]	**Computer; Rechner**
personal [ˈpɜːsnəl] computer / PC	Personalcomputer / PC
computer-aided instruction [ɪnˈstrʌkʃn]	computergestützter Unterricht
computer game [geɪm]	Computerspiel
computer literacy [ˈlɪtrəsi]	Computerkenntnisse / -verstand
computer-literate [ˈlɪtrət] kids	Kinder mit Computerverstand
computer science [ˈsaɪəns]	(die) Informatik
notebook / laptop	**Notebook / Laptop**
desktop computer	**Schreibtisch-PC / -Computer**
use a **word processor** [ˈprəʊsesə]	eine **Textverarbeitung** benutzen
a word-processing program	ein Textverarbeitungsprogramm
enter **data** [ˈdeɪtə] into the computer	**Daten** in den Computer eingeben
data processing (system)	Datenverarbeitung(sanlage); EDV
data exchange [ɪksˈtʃeɪndʒ]	Datenaustausch
data transfer [ˈtrænsfɜː]	Datenübertragung / -transfer
data retrieval [rɪˈtriːvl]	Datenwiedergewinnung
data protection [prəˈtekʃn] (act)	Datenschutz(gesetz)
program [ˈprəʊgræm]	**Programm(-); programmieren**
programmer [ˈprəʊgræmə]	**Programmierer(in)**
programming [ˈprəʊgræmɪŋ]	**Programmieren; Programmierung**
software package [ˈsɒftweə pækɪdʒ]	**Software**paket; **Programm**paket
bundled [ˈbʌndld] software	Gratissoftware
bug [bʌg]	**Programmfehler; Macke**
debug [diːˈbʌg] a program	ein Programm von Fehlern befreien
correct a **flaw** [flɔː]	einen **Fehler** beheben
crash [kræʃ]	**abstürzen; Absturz**
operating system [ˈsɪstəm] / OS	Betriebssystem / BS

Aussprache ins Deutsche übernommener Computerwörter
configuration [kənfɪgjəˈreɪʃn] • *cursor* [ˈkɜːsə] • *display* [dɪˈspleɪ] • *excel* [ɪkˈsel] • *hacker* [ˈhækə] • *hardware* [ˈhɑːdweə] • *hypertext* [ˈhaɪpətekst] • *icon* [ˈaɪkɒn] • *interactive* [ɪntərˈæktɪv] • *joystick* [ˈdʒɔɪstɪk] • *laptop* [ˈlæptɒp] • *macro* [ˈmækrəʊ] • *modem* [ˈməʊdem] • *monitor* [ˈmɒnɪtə] • *parameter* [pəˈræmɪtə] • *software* [ˈsɒftweə]

workstation [ˈwɜːksteɪʃn]	**Bildschirmarbeitsplatz**
online – offline	**verbunden – nicht verbunden**
(loud)speaker [(laʊd)ˈspiːkə]	**Lautsprecher**
wireless headphones [ˈhedfəʊnz]	**kabellose Kopfhörer**
keyboard [ˈkiːbɔːd]	**Tastatur**
VDU (= visual [ˈvɪʒuəl] display unit)	**Bildschirm(gerät); Monitor**

(VDU) **screen** [skriːn] — Bildschirm
change the text on screen — den Text am Bildschirm ändern
LCD (= liquid-crystal [ˈkrɪstl] display) — **Flüssigkristallanzeige**
(ink-jet / laser [ˈleɪzə]) **printer** — (Tintenstrahl- / Laser-)**Drucker**
thermal [ˈθɜːml] printer — Thermoprinter
printout [ˈprɪntaʊt] — **Ausdruck**
interface [ˈɪntəfeɪs] — **Schnittstelle**
a USB **port** [juː es ˈbiː pɔːt] — ein USB-**Anschluss**
drive [draɪv] — **Laufwerk**
CD / DVD / Blu-ray™ drive — CD- / DVD- / Blu-ray™-Laufwerk
Blu-ray Disc™ [bluː reɪ ˈdɪsk] — **Blu-ray Disc™**
high-definition [defəˈnɪʃn] (**HD**) — **Hochauflösung**
boot (up) [buːt] / **start up** — **hochfahren; starten**
power up [ˈpaʊə] – **power down** — **an- / einschalten – ab- / ausschalten**
shut down / **off** — **abschalten**
load [ləʊd] — **laden; Lade-**
download a file from the Net — eine Datei aus dem Netz herunterladen
a download [ˈdaʊnləʊd] — eine heruntergeladene Datei
upload [ʌpˈləʊd] — hochladen
install [ɪnˈstɔːl] — **installieren**
installation [ɪnstəˈleɪʃn] — **Installation**
log on [lɒg ˈɒn] – **log off** [lɒg ˈɒf] — **sich anmelden – sich abmelden**
log-on [ˈlɒg ɒn] — Anmeldung; Anmelde-
log-off [ˈlɒg ɒf] — Abmeldung; Abmelde-
I/O (= input [ˈɪnpʊt] – output) — **Eingabe – Ausgabe**
(sub)directory [(sʌb)daɪˈrektəri] — **(Unter-)Verzeichnis**
file [faɪl] — **Datei(-)**
create [kriˈeɪt] a file — eine Datei anlegen / erstellen
open / close a file — eine Datei öffnen / schließen
file management [ˈmænɪdʒmənt] — Dateiverwaltung
file compression [kəmˈpreʃn] — Dateikomprimierung
access [ˈækses] to the Net — **Zugang** zum Internet
access data [ˈdeɪtə] — auf Daten zugreifen
exit [ˈeksɪt] a program — ein Programm **verlassen**
format [ˈfɔːmæt] — **formatieren; Format**
scroll [skrəʊl] (**up** / **down**) — **(zurück- / vor)scrollen**
highlight [ˈhaɪlaɪt] — **hervorheben; markieren**
edit [ˈedɪt] — **editieren; bearbeiten**
search and replace [rɪˈpleɪs] — **suchen und ersetzen**
copy [ˈkɒpi] — **kopieren; Kopie**
delete [dɪˈliːt] / **erase** [ɪˈreɪz] — **löschen**
drag and drop — **„ziehen und fallen lassen"** (Transport von Text- / Bildteilen mit der Maus)
save [seɪv] — **sichern; schützen; (ab)speichern**
store [stɔː] – **storage** [ˈstɔːrɪdʒ] — **speichern – Speicher-**
data stored on the hard disk — auf der Festplatte gespeicherte Daten
storage capacity [kəˈpæsəti] — Speicherkapazität
memory [ˈmeməri] — **(Arbeits-)Speicher**
memory expansion [ɪkˈspænʃn] — Speichererweiterung

buffer ['bʌfə]   Puffer(speicher); Zwischenablage
backup (copy) ['bækʌp]   Sicherungskopie

 Ein Akronym (= aus Anfangsbuchstaben gebildetes Wort) aus der Früh-
zeit des Computers: *GIGO* ['gaɪgəʊ] (= *garbage* ['gɑːbɪdʒ] *in, garbage out*)
(= Gibt man Unsinn ein, kommt Unsinn raus.)

menu control [kən'trəʊl]   Menüsteuerung
command [kə'mɑːnd] (line / menu)   Befehl(szeile / -smenü)
pop-up menu ['menjuː]   Pop-up-Menü; Balkenmenü
toggle ['tɒgl]   Zweistellungsschalter
tool bar ['tuːl bɑː]   Symbolleiste
dialog box ['daɪəlɒg bɒks]   Dialogfeld
mode [məʊd]   Modus; Betriebsart
default [dɪ'fɔːlt] (option / setting)   Standard(einstellung); Voreinstellung
click on the Search button   die Schaltfläche Suchen **anklicken**
double-click on an icon ['aɪkɒn]   auf ein Bildsymbol doppelklicken
shift key ['ʃɪft kiː]   Umschalttaste
function key ['fʌŋkʃn kiː]   Funktionstaste
arrow key ['ærəʊ kiː]   Pfeiltaste; Cursortaste
press / hit the return key [rɪ'tɜːn kiː]   die Eingabetaste drücken
control [kən'trəʊl] / **Ctrl**   Steuerung / Strg
press / hit **Enter** ['entə]   Eingabe drücken
execute ['eksɪkjuːt]   ausführen
character ['kærəktə]   Zeichen
proportional font [fɒnt] / **spacing**   Proportionalschrift
hard hyphen ['haɪfn]   geschützter Bindestrich
soft [sɒft] hyphen   bedingter Trennstrich
paragraph ['pærəgrɑːf] **mark** / **sign**   Absatzmarke
backslash ['bækslæʃ]   Backslash; negativer Schrägstrich
spell checker ['spel tʃekə]   Rechtschreibhilfe
activate ['æktɪveɪt] the spell checker   die Rechtschreibhilfe aktivieren
message ['mesɪdʒ]   Mitteilung; Meldung; Nachricht(en-)
machine-readable [məʃiːn 'riːdəbl]   maschinenlesbar
OCR (= optical character recognition)   optische Zeichenerkennung
optical ['ɒptɪkl] **scanner**   optischer Scanner
bar code ['bɑː kəʊd]   Strichcode; Streifencode; Balkencode
voice recognition [rekəg'nɪʃn]   Spracherkennung
update [ʌp'deɪt]   aktualisieren
an updated version of the software   eine aktualisierte Fassung der Software
upgrade ['ʌpgreɪd]   verbesserte Version
upgrade [ʌp'greɪd] the software   die Software auf den neuesten Stand
                                                                  bringen

technical support [teknɪkl sə'pɔːt]   technische Unterstützung
user ['juːzə]   Anwender(in); Benutzer(in)
user interface ['ɪntəfeɪs]   Benutzeroberfläche, -schnittstelle
user-friendly ['juːzə frendli]   benutzerfreundlich
telecommuting ['telikəmjuːtɪŋ]   Tele(heim)arbeit
telecommuter ['telikəmjuːtə]   Tele(heim)arbeiter(in)
books on demand [dɪ'mɑːnd]   auf Bestellung (elektronisch) produ-
                                                                  zierte Bücher

electronic [elek'trɒnɪk] **publishing**	elektronisches Publizieren
network ['netwɜːk]	Netz(werk)
terminal ['tɜːmɪnəl]	Terminal; Dateneingabestation
modem ['məʊdem]	Modem
wireless / Wi-Fi™ ['waɪfaɪ] Internet access	kabelloser / WLAN-Internetzugang
ethernet cable ['iːθənet keɪbl]	Ethernet-Kabel
leased line [liːst 'laɪn]	Standleitung
host [həʊst]	Host (= Zentralrechnersystem)
node [nəʊd]	Knoten(punkt)
data link ['deɪtə lɪŋk]	Datenverbindung
data capture ['deɪtə kæptʃə]	Datenerfassung
compress [kəm'pres] a file	eine Datei **komprimieren**
encode [ɪn'kəʊd] – **decode** [diː'kəʊd]	kodieren – dekodieren
encrypt [ɪn'krɪpt] – **decrypt** [diː'krɪpt]	verschlüsseln – entschlüsseln
cache [kæʃ]	Cache; temporärer Zwischenspeicher
clipboard ['klɪpbɔːd]	Zwischenablage
algorithm ['ælgərɪðm]	Algorithmus
blank [blæŋk]	Leerzeichen
activate ['æktɪveɪt]	aktivieren; einschalten
deactivate [diː'æktɪveɪt]	deaktivieren; ausschalten; abschalten
path [pɑːθ]	Pfad
dial-up ['daɪəl ʌp]	Einwahl
provider [prə'vaɪdə]	Betreiber; Anbieter (eines Zugangs zum Internet)
online service provider	Online-Dienst
flat rate [flæt 'reɪt]	Pauschaltarif (zum Surfen im Internet)
the **Web** (= the **World Wide Web**)	das **Netz**
search [sɜːtʃ] the Web / Internet / Net	das Netz / Internet durchsuchen
companies ['kʌmpəniz] on the Web	im Netz / Internet vertretene Firmen
web browser ['web braʊzə]	(Programm zum Verwalten, Finden und Ansehen von Internet-Dateien)
website ['websaɪt]	Website
visit ['vɪzɪt] a website	eine Website besuchen
design [dɪ'zaɪn] the website of a company	den Internetauftritt einer Firma gestalten
webpage ['webpeɪdʒ]	Webseite
webpage designer [dɪ'zaɪnə]	Webpage-Designer(in)
web-enabled [ɪn'eɪbəld] / Internet-enabled (mobile phone)	internetfähig(es Handy / Mobiltelefon)
on the **Internet** ['ɪntənet]	im **Internet**
homepage ['həʊmpeɪdʒ]	Start- / Ausgangsseite im WWW
site [saɪt]	Site (= „Standort" einer Firma etc. im Internet)
hit [hɪt]	Zugriff (auf eine Internet-Seite)
browse [braʊz]	browsen; surfen
browse / surf the Internet	im Internet surfen
link [lɪŋk]	(interaktiver Verweis auf andere Informationen in demselben oder einem anderen Dokument)

hyperlink ['haɪpəlɪŋk]	(Verbindung von einer Internetseite zu einer anderen)
country code ['kʌntri kəʊd]	**Länderkennung** (z.B. .de für Deutschland)
domain [dəʊ'meɪn]	**Domain; Domäne**
@ (= at [æt])	(in E-Mail-Adressen) bei
the @ sign [ðɪ 'æt saɪn]	das at-Zeichen; der Klammeraffe
.edu ['edjʊ]	(in Internetadressen) US-amerik. Bildungseinrichtung
e-mail ['i: meɪl] – **snail mail** ['sneɪl meɪl]	**E-Mail – herkömmliche Post**
mail server ['meɪl sɜːvə]	(Rechner, über den der E-Mail-Verkehr abgewickelt wird)
mailbox ['meɪlbɒks]	elektronischer Briefkasten
voice mail ['vɔɪs meɪl]	Voicemail
attachment [ə'tætʃmənt]	(E-Mail-)**Anlage**
smiley ['smaɪli]	**Smiley** (= „Lächeln"-Symbol)
emoticon [ɪ'məʊtɪkɒn]	**Emoticon** (= Symbol, das die Stimmungslage illustriert)
spam [spæm]	**unerwünschte Reklame-E-Mails; Werbemüll**
spam somebody	jemand zuspammen
netiquette ['netɪket]	**Internet-Verhaltenskodex**
Internet café ['kæfeɪ] / **cybercafé** ['saɪbəkæfeɪ]	**Internetcafé**
chat [tʃæt]	**Chat** (= Konversation über das Internet); **chatten**
join a chat group ['tʃæt gruːp]	in einer Chat-Group mitmachen
Internet forum [ɪntənet 'fɔːrəm]	**Internetforum; Diskussionsforum**
thread [θred]	**Thread; Thema** (einer Forumsdiskussion)
posting ['pəʊstɪŋ]	**Posting; Beitrag** (in einem Thread)
user ['juːzə]	Benutzer(in); Mitglied eines Forums
off-topic [ɒf 'tɒpɪk]	**nicht zum Thema gehörig**
flame [fleɪm]	verbaler Angriff gegen eine(n) Benutzer(in)
adult check [ædʌlt 'tʃek]	(System zum Jugendschutz im Internet)
cookie ['kʊki]	**Cookie**
crack [kræk]	(den Kopierschutz) **knacken**
cracker ['krækə]	Cracker(in) (= jem., der illegal in ein Computersystem eindringt)
(computer) **virus** ['vaɪrəs]	(Computer-)**Virus**
the virus erases [ɪ'reɪzɪz] your hard disk / hard drive	der Virus löscht deine Festplatte
(anti)virus protection [prə'tekʃn]	Schutz gegen Viren
antivirus software ['sɒftweə]	Antivirenprogramm(e), -software
Trojan horse [trəʊdʒən 'hɔːs]	**Trojanisches Pferd**
worm [wɜːm]	**Wurm**
firewall ['faɪəwɔːl]	(Schutzmechanismus gegen Zugriffe aus dem Internet)
e-business ['i: bɪznəs]	**Internetgeschäfte; Internetfirma**

Mit dem Begriff *Web* (kurz für *World Wide Web*) sind in neuerer Zeit
eine Vielzahl von Zusammensetzungen gebildet worden. So werden
zum Beispiel mit einem *webcam* fotografische Aufnahmen in das Internet
eingespeist, *webcasts* sind (analog zu *broadcasts* und *telecasts*) Liveüber-
tragungen, die im Internet gesendet werden, und *weblogs* (häufiger
kurz *blogs* genannt) sind *websites*, in denen sogenannte *bloggers* regelmäßig tagebuchartige Beiträge zu bestimmten Themen ins Netz stellen.
Ein *webmaster* verwaltet (= *administers*) *a website*, und *web address* ist
eine andere Bezeichnung für das Akronym *URL* (= *uniform resource locator*).

e-commerce ['iː kɒmɜːs]	**elektronischer Handel**
m-commerce ['em kɒmɜːs]	elektronischer Handel über
	mobile Geräte
s-commerce ['es kɒmɜːs]	(durch Verschlüsselung sicherer
	E-Commerce)
secure server [sɪ'kjʊə 'sɜːvə]	**sicherer** (d.h. verschlüsselter) **Server**
online / Internet banking	**Online-Banking**
digital signature [dɪdʒɪtl 'sɪgnətʃə]	**digitale Unterschrift / Signatur**
password ['pɑːswɜːd]	**Passwort**
a **dot com** [dɒt 'kɒm] /	eine **Internetfirma**; ein
a **dot-com company**	**Internetunternehmen**
cyberfraud ['saɪbəfrɔːd]	(Betrug beim Einkaufen im Internet)
courseware ['kɔːsweə]	**Lernsoftware**
shareware ['ʃeəweə]	(kostenlose Testversion einer Software)
freeware ['friːweə]	(frei kopierbare Software)
multimedia [mʌlti'miːdiə]	**Multimedia**
media player ['miːdiə pleiə]	**Mediaplayer**
playlist ['pleɪlɪst]	**Wiedergabeliste; Musikfolge**
music visualization [vɪʒuəlaɪ'zeɪʃn]	**Audiovisualisierung**
shuffle ['ʃʌfl] songs	Lieder **mischen**
bookmark ['bʊkmɑːk]	**Lesezeichen**
ascending [ə'sendɪŋ] – **descending**	(*Tabelle*) **aufsteigend – absteigend**
[dɪ'sendɪŋ]	
simple **query** ['kwɪəri]	einfache **Abfrage**
advanced [əd'vɑːnst] query	erweiterte Abfrage
FAQ(s) (= frequently asked questions)	**häufig gestellte Fragen**

Computer und Internet werden oft als *disruptive innovations* (= disruptive / bahnbrechende / revolutionäre Neuerungen) betrachtet. Zunehmend (= *increasingly*)
wird das Internet zum weltweiten *open-sourcing* (= kostenlosen Bereitstellen) von
Wissen und Informationen (= *information*) genutzt, was wiederum zu *empower-
ment* (= Befähigung, Ermächtigung) von Millionen Menschen (= *millions of
people*) führt, die bislang nicht am menschlichen Fortschritt (= *human progress*)
teilhatten. Auch erlauben es uns Computer nun, die Herausforderungen (= *chal-
lenges*) von *big data* (= Datenmengen, die zu groß für konventionelle Datenverarbeitung sind) zu bewältigen, wodurch wir *groundbreaking new insights* gewinnen – ob *into the genome* ['dʒiːnəʊm] oder die *online shopping habits* (= Einkaufs-
gewohnheiten im Internet) *of hundreds of millions of people*. Sehr viel alltäglicher
(= *much more mundane*) sind die immer wieder neuen *lifehacks* (= praktischen
Tricks für den Alltag, oft durch Anpassung etablierter Technologien), *which will
enable us to manage our time and daily activities in a more efficient way*.

Going portable

battery life [bætəri 'laɪf]	Akkulaufzeit
charger ['tʃɑːdʒə]	Ladegerät
docking station ['dɒkɪŋ steɪʃn]	Dockingstation
external [ɪk'stɜːnl] **hard drive**	externe Festplatte
memory stick / USB flash drive	USB-Stick
tablet (computer) ['tæblət]	Tablet
stylus ['staɪləs]	Stift
digital painting [dɪdʒɪtl 'peɪntɪŋ]	digitales Malen
mobile operating system ['sɪstəm]	mobiles Betriebssystem
Tablets and smartphones are running on mobile operating systems such as Android™.	Tablets und Smartphones laufen mit mobilen Betriebssystemen wie Android™.
wireless technology [tek'nɒlədʒi]	Drahtlos- / Funktechnologie
SD (Secure Digital) Memory Card	SD-Speicherkarte
screen protector ['skriːn prətektə]	Displayschutzfolie
case [keɪs]	Gehäuse
voice control ['vɔɪs kəntrəʊl]	Sprachsteuerung
e-reader / e-book reader	E-Reader
electronic paper / e-paper	elektronisches Papier

A father-son chat

Dad   So why should I be buying you one of these **smartphones**, son? Your old phone seemed to be working just fine this morning.

Son   Fine for making calls, yes.

Dad   Sending texts too …

Son   Yes. But smartphones have **mobile broadband** (*Breitband-Internet*), which means I could use the Internet anywhere I go.

Dad   For free?

Son   Not for free. I would need a **data plan** (= *Datentarif*).

Dad   That as well? As if the phone itself wasn't expensive enough!

Son   Just think about how useful it would be, though! It'll have GPS too, so it will know where I am and will be able to show me how to get to places. It has a **portable media player** (= *tragbarer Mediaplayer*) too, like an iPod™ really. It's not for nothing they're calling smartphones the greatest invention of the 2000s.

Dad   Well, isn't that smart of you. – It doesn't seem to have a keyboard, does it?

Son   It has a **touchscreen** (= *Touchscreen, Berührungsbildschirm*), so you can press or even **swipe** (= *wischen*) buttons on the display. It's got a **virtual keyboard** (= *virtuelle Tastatur*) for writing too. And you can add all kinds of functions through **apps** (= *Apps, Softwareanwendungen*) which you can download, many of them for free.

Dad   Games?

Son   Among other things …

Dad   I thought so. Honestly, son, if I buy this smartphone for you, will I ever have your attention for more than thirty seconds again?

Son   Don't think so, Dad.

Dad   That was honest at least. All right, let's get you this miracle phone then.

Means of transport
Transportmittel

1 **Motor vehicles and road traffic**
  Kraftfahrzeuge und Straßenverkehr

2 **Rail transport**
  Beförderung mit der Eisenbahn

3 **Air transport**
  Beförderung mit dem Flugzeug

4 **Water transport**
  Beförderung auf dem Wasserweg

5 **Public transport**
  Öffentlicher Nahverkehr

Motor vehicles and road traffic
Kraftfahrzeuge und Straßenverkehr

Take most people, they're crazy about cars. They worry if they get a little scratch on them, and they're always talking about how many miles they get to a gallon, and if they get a brand-new car already they start thinking about trading it in for one that's even newer. (J.D. Salinger, US writer, 1919–2010)

(motor) vehicle [(məʊtə) ˈviːɪkl]	**(Kraft-)Fahrzeug**
an efficient **means of transport** [ˈtrænspɔːt] *BE* / *AE* **transportation**	ein effizientes **Transportmittel / Verkehrsmittel**
car / *AE auch* **auto(mobile)** [ˈɔːtəʊ]	**Auto**
I usually [ˈjuːʒəli] go by car.	Meistens fahre ich mit dem Wagen.
car rental [ˈrentl] – rental car	Autovermietung – Mietwagen
limo(usine) [ˈlɪməʊ / ˈlɪməziːn]	**Limousine**
stretch limo [ˈstretʃ lɪməʊ] *AE*	(verlängerte, luxuriöse Limousine)
lorry [ˈlɒri] *BE* / *AE* **truck** [trʌk]	**Lastwagen; Lkw; Laster**
lorry driver *BE* / *AE* truckdriver / trucker	Lkw-Fahrer(in); Fernfahrer(in)
van [væn]	(geschlossener) **Lieferwagen**
removal van *BE* / *AE* moving van	Möbelwagen
fire engine / *AE auch* **fire truck**	**Feuerwehrfahrzeug**
drive [draɪv] (– drove – driven)	**fahren** (*d.h. am Steuer sitzen*)
She drives very well.	Sie fährt sehr gut.
It's an hour's drive.	Mit dem Auto ist es eine Stunde.
drive-by shooting [ˈdraɪv baɪ ʃuːtɪŋ] *AE*	Schießen aus dem fahrenden Auto
driver [ˈdraɪvə]	**Fahrer(in)**
a **driving school** [ˈdraɪvɪŋ skuːl]	eine **Fahrschule**
run [rʌn] (– ran – run)	(*jemand / ein Fahrzeug*) **fahren**
Shall I run / drive you home?	Soll ich Sie nach Hause fahren?
cruise [kruːz] at 55 mph (= miles per hour)	mit einer Dauer- / Reisegeschwindig-keit von 90 km/h **fahren**
motorist [ˈməʊtərɪst]	**Autofahrer(in); Kraftfahrer(in)**
commute [kəˈmjuːt]	**pendeln**
I commute to X every day.	Ich fahre jeden Tag nach X zur Arbeit.
a two-hour commute [kəˈmjuːt]	eine zweistündige Fahrt zur Arbeit
commuter [kəˈmjuːtə]	Pendler(in)
hitchhike [ˈhɪtʃhaɪk]	**per Anhalter fahren; trampen**
hitchhiker [ˈhɪtʃhaɪkə]	Anhalter(in); Tramper(in)
Can you give me a **lift** / **ride**?	Können Sie mich mitnehmen?
We had a smooth [smuːð] ride.	Wir hatten eine ruhige Fahrt.

 Autobahnen sind im BE *motorways*; im AE heißen autobahnartige Straßen *superhighways, freeways, expressways* oder *interstates.* Auf amerikanischen *thruways* (= Schnellstraßen), *turnpikes* und anderen *toll roads* zahlt man für die Benutzung *a toll* [təʊl] (= eine Gebühr), die *at a tollgate or tollbooth* [ˈtəʊlbuːð] entrichtet wird. Hauptverkehrsstraßen (= *main roads*) heißen im AE allgemein *highways,* im BE auch *trunk roads* (= Fernstraßen). Deutsche Autobahnen nennt man meist auch englisch so – der Plural lautet *autobahns* (→ S. 157): *There's no speed limit on the autobahns.*

19 1

road [rəʊd]	Straße (als Verkehrsweg)
ship goods by road	Waren auf der Straße befördern
road safety ['seɪfti]	Verkehrssicherheit
road rage ['rəʊd reɪdʒ]	extrem aggressives Verhalten im Straßenverkehr
thoroughfare ['θʌrəfeə]	Durchgangs- / Durchfahrtsstraße
through traffic ['θruː træfɪk]	Durchgangsverkehr
side street ['saɪd striːt]	Nebenstraße
one-way street [wʌn weɪ 'striːt]	Einbahnstraße
cul-de-sac ['kʌl də sæk]	Sackgasse
bend / curve [kɜːv]	Kurve
There's a bend in the road.	Die Straße macht da eine Kurve.

Idioms mit *bend: He must be (a)round the bend.* (= Der muss ja verrückt sein.) • *This noise is driving / sending me (a)round the bend.* (= Dieser Lärm macht mich wahnsinnig.) • *Have you gone* [gɒn] *(a)round the bend?* (= Spinnst du?)

at / on the **corner** ['kɔːnə]	an der Ecke
stop at a **crossroads** ['krɒsrəʊdz]	an einer Kreuzung (an)halten
junction *BE* / *AE* **intersection**	(Straßen-)Kreuzung
roundabout *BE* / *AE* **traffic circle**	Kreisverkehr
traffic light(s) ['træfɪk laɪt(s)]	Verkehrsampel
stop at a red light	an einer roten Ampel halten
Turn right at the lights.	Biegen Sie an der Ampel rechts ab.
make a **U-turn** (– made – made)	wenden
lane [leɪn] – **bus lane**	(Fahr-)Spur – Busspur
the best / quickest **route** [ruːt] to X	der beste / schnellste Weg nach X
We came by a roundabout route.	Wir haben einen Umweg gemacht.
make a **detour** ['diːtʊə] (– made – made)	einen Umweg machen
diversion [daɪ'vɜːʃn] – **bypass**	Umleitung – Umgehungsstraße
pavement *BE* / *AE* **sidewalk**	Bürgersteig; Gehsteig
(pedestrian [pə'destriən]) **crossing**	(Fußgänger-)Überweg
zebra ['zebrə] crossing *BE* / *AE* crosswalk	Zebrastreifen; Fußgängerüberweg
heavy **traffic** ['træfɪk]	starker Verkehr
an obstruction [əb'strʌkʃn] to traffic	ein Verkehrshindernis
rush-hour ['rʌʃ aʊə] traffic	Berufsverkehr
stop-and-go traffic	stockender Verkehr
get snarled [snɑːld] up / stuck in traffic	im Verkehr stecken bleiben
traffic jams during rush hours	Staus während der Hauptverkehrszeiten
congested [kən'dʒestɪd] roads	verstopfte Straßen
increasing traffic congestion	immer mehr Staus auf den Straßen
tailbacks on the motorway *BE*	Staus auf der Autobahn
backups on the expressway *AE*	Staus auf der Autobahn
Traffic regularly backs up here.	Hier kommt es regelmäßig zu Staus.
bumper to bumper ['bʌmpə]	Stoßstange an Stoßstange
gridlock ['grɪdlɒk] *AE*	Verkehrsinfarkt; Verkehrskollaps
service area ['sɜːvɪs eəriə] *BE*	(Autobahn-)Raststätte

transport café ['kæfeɪ] *BE* / *AE*
  truck stop — Fernfahrerlokal, -raststätte

petrol ['petrəl] *BE* / *AE* **gas station** — Tankstelle

a **breakdown** ['breɪkdaʊn] — eine **Panne**

My car's at the **garage** ['gærɑːʒ]. — Mein Auto ist in der **Werkstatt.**

a spare **tyre** ['taɪə] / wheel — ein Ersatz**reifen** / -rad

check the tyre pressure ['preʃə] — den Reifendruck prüfen

burst tyre / flat tyre / blowout — geplatzter Reifen; Reifenpanne

change [tʃeɪndʒ] a tyre / the oil — einen Reifen / das Öl **wechseln**

Can you **fix** it? — Können Sie es **reparieren?**

I've just had my car **serviced** ['sɜːvɪst]. — Mein Auto war gerade zur Inspektion.

Das Schild *TOWAWAY ZONE* ['təʊəweɪ zəʊn] (= Abschleppzone) warnt Sie in den USA, dass Ihr Fahrzeug abgeschleppt wird (= *gets towed* [təʊd] *away*), wenn es falsch geparkt ist (= *illegally* [ɪˈliːgəli] *parked*).

You can't **park** here. — Hier können Sie nicht **parken.**

a parked [pɑːkt] car — ein parkendes Auto

a no parking sign — ein Parkverbotsschild

find a parking space (– found – found) — eine Parklücke finden

parking meter ['miːtə] — Parkuhr

parking attendant [ə'tendənt] — Parkwächter(in)

parking ticket ['tɪkɪt] — Strafzettel (für Falschparken)

parking fine [faɪn] — Geldbuße für Falschparken

car park *BE* / *AE* **parking lot** — **Parkplatz**

multi-storey (car park) *BE* / *AE* parking garage — Parkhaus

traffic cop ['træfɪk kɒp] *AE* — **Verkehrspolizist(in)**

traffic violation [vaɪə'leɪʃn] — **Verkehrsverstoß / -delikt**

driving licence ['laɪsns] *BE* / *AE*
  driver's license — **Führerschein**

car / vehicle **documents** ['dɒkjumənts] — Auto- / Fahrzeug**papiere**

I was fined for **speeding**. — Ich bekam einen Bußgeldbescheid wegen **zu schnellen Fahrens.**

He **ran a stop sign** [saɪn]. *AE* — Er **überfuhr ein Stoppschild.**

reckless driving [rekləs 'draɪvɪŋ] — **rücksichtsloses Fahren**

drink-driving *BE* / *AE* **drunk driving** — **Trunkenheit am Steuer**

road / **traffic accident** ['æksɪdənt] — **Verkehrsunfall**

road / traffic fatalities [fə'tælətiz] — Verkehrstote

motorcycle ['məʊtəsaɪkl] / **motorbike** — **Motorrad**

ride a motorcycle / motorbike
  (– rode – ridden) — Motorrad fahren

He got on / off his motorbike. — Er stieg aufs / vom Motorrad.

motorcyclist / **motorcycle rider** — **Motorradfahrer(in)**

moped ['məʊped] — **Moped**

bicycle ['baɪsɪkl] / **bike** / **cycle** ['saɪkl] — **Fahrrad**

go by bike / bicycle / cycle — mit dem Fahrrad fahren

go for a bike / bicycle / cycle ride — eine Radtour machen

They jumped on their cycles and rode away. — Sie sprangen auf ihre Fahrräder und fuhren davon.

bike path ['baɪk pɑːθ] — **Fahrradweg; Radweg**

Rail transport
Beförderung mit der Eisenbahn

One broken rail will wreck a train. (*Proverb*)

rail [reɪl]	**Schiene(n-); (Eisen-)Bahn(-)**
rail strike ['reɪl straɪk]	Eisenbahnerstreik
London's rail terminals ['tɜ:mɪnlz]	die Londoner (Fern-)Bahnhöfe
railway *BE* / *AE* **railroad**	**Eisenbahn**
railway *BE* / *AE* railroad line	(Eisen-)Bahnlinie / -strecke
the rail(way) workers	die Eisenbahner
nationalize ['næʃnəlaɪz] the railways	die Eisenbahnen verstaatlichen
privatize ['praɪvətaɪz] the railways	die Eisenbahnen privatisieren
an important railway junction	ein wichtiger Eisenbahnknotenpunkt
The train (was) **derailed** on a curve.	Der Zug **entgleiste** in einer Kurve.

Amtrak ['æmtræk], die staatlich subventionierte (= *government-subsidized* ['sʌbsɪdaɪzd]) Eisenbahngesellschaft der USA, ist für die Personenbeförderung auf der Schiene (= *by rail*) zuständig: *go by* / *take Amtrak* (= mit Amtrak / mit der Eisenbahn fahren).

train [treɪn]	**Zug**
go / travel by train	mit dem Zug / der Bahn fahren
catch a train (– caught [ɔ:] – caught)	einen Zug nehmen / schaffen
We missed our train.	Wir haben unseren Zug verpasst.
When's the next train to / for Hull?	Wann geht der nächste Zug nach Hull?
goods train *BE* / *AE* freight [eɪ] train	Güterzug
local (train) ['ləʊkl]	Nahverkehrszug; Regionalbahn
express (train) [ɪk'spres]	Schnellzug
high-speed train [haɪ spi:d 'treɪn]	Hochgeschwindigkeitszug
a through train ['θru: treɪn]	ein durchgehender Zug
train service ['sɜ:vɪs]	**Zugverbindung**
a direct ['daɪrekt] service	eine Direktverbindung
intercity services to York	Intercity-Verbindungen nach York
The service for Poole departs [dɪ'pɑ:ts] from platform 1.	Der Zug nach Poole fährt von Bahnsteig 1 (ab).
No services will operate ['ɒpəreɪt] between A and B.	Zwischen A und B werden keine Züge verkehren.
a **shuttle** (service) ['ʃʌtl]	**Pendelverkehr**
railway **carriage** ['kærɪdʒ] *BE* / *AE* railroad **car**	Eisenbahn**wagen**
sleeping car / sleeper	Schlafwagen
dining car / *AE auch* diner / *BE auch* restaurant ['restrɒnt] car	Speisewagen
buffet (car) ['bʊfeɪ]	Büfettwagen; (*Dt. Bahn*) Bistro
(non-)smoker ['sməʊkə]	**(Nicht-)Raucher(wagen** / **-abteil)**
engine ['endʒɪn] / **loco(motive)**	**Lokomotive**
electric locomotive [ləʊkə'məʊtɪv]	Elektrolok(omotive)
steam / diesel locomotive	Dampf- / Diesellok(omotive)

engine driver *BE* / *AE* **engineer**	Lok(omotiv)führer(in)
(first-class) **compartment** [kəm'pɑːt-]	(Erster-Klasse-)**Abteil**
reserve [rɪ'zɜːv] a **seat**	einen **Platz** reservieren
This seat is taken / occupied.	Dieser Platz ist besetzt.
guard [gɑːd] *BE* / *AE* **conductor**	**Zugbegleiter(in); Schaffner(in)**
station / *AE auch* **depot** ['depəʊ]	**Bahnhof**
mainline station	Fernbahnhof
call at a station	an einem Bahnhof halten
terminus ['tɜːmɪnəs]	**Endstation**
platform 3 *BE* / *AE* **track** 3	**Bahnsteig** 3; **Gleis** 3
Keep off the tracks.	Betreten der Gleise verboten.
waiting room ['weɪtɪŋ rʊm]	**Wartesaal**
luggage trolley *BE* / *AE* **baggage cart**	**Kofferkuli**
Where can I check in my **luggage**?	Wo kann ich mein **Gepäck** aufgeben?
the left-luggage (office) *BE* / *AE* checkroom	die Gepäckaufbewahrung
the lost-property (office) *BE* / *AE* lost-and-found (office)	das Fundbüro
fare (increase / *AE auch* hike)	**Fahrpreis**(erhöhung)
ticket (office)	**Fahrkarte**(nschalter)
return ticket *BE* / *AE* round-trip ticket	Rückfahrkarte
Two first-class singles to Hull, please.	Bitte zweimal erste Klasse einfach nach Hull.
cheap day return [rɪ'tɜːn] *BE*	verbilligte Tagesrückfahrkarte
get on a train / **board** [bɔːd] a train	in einen Zug **einsteigen**
get off (a train) (– got – got)	(aus einem Zug) **aussteigen**
a train **journey** / *AE auch* train **ride**	eine Bahn**fahrt**
outward / return journey ['dʒɜːni]	Hin- / Rückreise
the journey there and back / the round trip	die Hin- und Rückfahrt
journey time / travel time	Fahrzeit
a comfortable ['kʌmftəbl] **ride**	eine bequeme **Fahrt**
a 10-ride ticket *AE*	eine Zehnerkarte
change [tʃeɪndʒ] at Rugby	in Rugby **umsteigen**
Where do I change for Cologne?	Wo muss ich nach Köln umsteigen?
make / miss a **connection** [kə'nekʃn]	einen **Anschluss** schaffen / verpassen
a **stopover** in Chicago [ʃɪ'kɑːgəʊ]	ein **Zwischenaufenthalt** in Chicago
departure [dɪ'pɑːtʃə] – **arrival**	**Abfahrt** – **Ankunft**
timetable *BE* / *AE* **schedule**	**Fahrplan; Kursbuch**
The train was on **schedule** ['ʃedjuːl].	Der Zug war **pünktlich.**
The train is behind schedule.	Der Zug hat Verspätung.
The train is **scheduled** to arrive at 6.35.	Der Zug soll fahrplanmäßig um 6.35 Uhr ankommen.
The trains usually run **on time**.	Meistens fahren die Züge **pünktlich.**
Many trains are running **late** today.	Viele Züge haben heute Verspätung.
cut **travel time** in half	die **Fahrzeit** auf die Hälfte verkürzen
travel **off peak** [ɒf 'piːk]	**außerhalb der Stoßzeiten** reisen
What time do we **get to** York?	Wann **kommen** wir in York **an?**
passenger ['pæsɪndʒə]	**Fahrgast; Reisende(r); Passagier**

Air transport
Beförderung mit dem Flugzeug

'Tis better to bear the ills we have than fly to others we know not of. (*Proverb, based on a quotation from Skakespeare's* Hamlet)

fly [flaɪ] (– flew [fluː] – flown [fləʊn])	**fliegen**
fly economy [ɪˈkɒnəmi] / *AE* fly coach	in der Touristenklasse fliegen
He's afraid of flying.	Er hat Angst vor dem Fliegen.
ideal [aɪˈdɪəl] flying weather	ideales Flugwetter
The flying / flight time is six hours.	Die Flugzeit beträgt sechs Stunden.
frequent flyer [friːkwənt ˈflaɪə]	**Vielflieger(in)**
travel / go by **air** / **plane**	mit dem **Flugzeug** reisen / fliegen
ship / send goods by air	Waren auf dem Luftweg versenden
the latest increase [ˈɪŋkriːs] in air fares	die letzte Erhöhung der Flugpreise
aircraft [ˈeəkrɑːft] *Plural ohne -s!*	**Flugzeug(e)**
This aircraft is very fast.	Dieses Flugzeug ist sehr schnell.
These aircraft are very fast.	Diese Flugzeuge sind sehr schnell.
a supersonic [suːpəˈsɒnɪk] aircraft	ein Überschallflugzeug
plane / **airplane** *AE* / *BE* **aeroplane**	**Flugzeug**
He died [daɪd] in a plane crash.	Er kam bei einem Flugzeugabsturz ums Leben.
airliner [ˈeəlaɪnə]	**Verkehrsflugzeug, -maschine**
jet [dʒet]	**Düsenflugzeug, -maschine**
jet lag [ˈdʒet læg]	Jetlag
jumbo (jet) [ˈdʒʌmbəʊ]	(Boeing 747 Großraumflugzeug)
jetliner [ˈdʒetlaɪnə]	Düsenverkehrsflugzeug
airline [ˈeəlaɪn]	**Fluggesellschaft; (Flug-)Linie**
an airline ticket in his name	ein Flugschein auf seinen Namen
airport [ˈeəpɔːt]	**Flughafen**
Shall I meet you at the airport?	Soll ich dich am Flughafen abholen?
The city is served by two airports.	Die Stadt hat zwei Flughäfen.
heliport [ˈhelipɔːt]	**Hubschrauberlandeplatz**
terminal [ˈtɜːmɪnl]	(Abfertigungsgebäude am Flughafen)
timetable / **flight schedule** [ˈʃedjuːl]	**Flugplan**
arrival(s) [əˈraɪvl(z)] – **departure(s)**	**Ankunft – Abflug**
arrival / departure lounge [laʊndʒ]	Ankunfts- / Abflughalle
Scheduled arrival time is 16:05 (sixteen oh five), but the flight will be delayed.	Die flugplanmäßige Ankunftszeit ist 16.05 Uhr, aber der Flug wird verspätet eintreffen.
cancel [ˈkænsl]	**streichen; stornieren; ausfallen lassen**
Flight 452 has been cancelled.	Flug 452 fällt aus.
cancel a reservation [rezəˈveɪʃn]	eine Reservierung rückgängig machen
destination [destɪˈneɪʃn]	**Zielflughafen; Reiseziel**
domestic **flight** [dəmestɪk ˈflaɪt]	Inland**flug**
direct flight [daɪrekt ˈflaɪt]	Direktverbindung mit Zwischenlandung
nonstop flight [nɒnstɒp ˈflaɪt]	Flug ohne Zwischenlandung
I want to book a seat on the 9 o'clock flight to Chicago.	Ich möchte einen Platz für den 9-Uhr-Flug nach Chicago buchen.
security [sɪˈkjʊərəti] **search** / **check**	**Sicherheitskontrolle**

Da erfahrungsgemäß ein bestimmter Prozentsatz von Fluggästen (= *passengers*) mit bestätigter Reservierung (= *a confirmed reservation*) zum Abflug nicht erscheint (= *don't show up* – man nennt sie deshalb *no-shows*), überbuchen (= *overbook*) die *airlines* routinemäßig (= *routinely* [ru:'ti:nli]) ihre Flüge. Stellen sich alle Fluggäste entgegen der Statistik zum Abflug ein, so ist die *airline* gezwungen, überzählige *passengers* zurückzulassen – in der *airline*-Sprache: *to bump them.*

check-in counter ['tʃekin kaʊntə] | (Fluggast-)**Abfertigungsschalter**
What time do we have to check in? | Um welche Zeit müssen wir am Abfertigungsschalter sein?

upgrade ['ʌpgreɪd] | **Höherstufung** (z.B. von *economy class* zur *business* ['bɪznəs] *class*)

Your flight leaves from **gate** 4. | Ihr Flug geht von **Flugsteig** 4 (ab).
an **unaccompanied minor** ['maɪnə] | ein **unbegleitetes Kind**
carry-on bag – carry-on baggage | **Bordtasche – Kabinengepäck**
one piece of hand baggage / luggage | ein Stück Handgepäck
boarding pass / **card** | **Einsteigekarte; Bordkarte**
standby ['stændbaɪ] (passenger) | Fluggast / Passagier auf Warteliste
charter ['tʃɑ:tə] flight / plane | **Charter**flug / -maschine
go charter (– went – gone [gɒn]) | einen Charterflug nehmen
charter a helicopter ['helɪkɒptə] | einen Hubschrauber chartern
scheduled ['ʃedjuːld] flight | Linienflug / -maschine
Please fasten ['fɑːsn] your **seatbelt**. | Bitte schnallen Sie sich an.
oxygen mask ['ɒksɪdʒən mɑːsk] | **Sauerstoffmaske**
life jacket ['laɪf dʒækɪt] / **life vest** | **Schwimmweste**
overhead ['əʊvəhed] **rack** / **locker** | **über dem Sitz befindliches Gepäckfach**

Seatbelts must be fastened and all your luggage must be stowed [stəʊd] in the overhead compartments or under the seat in front of you. | Die Sitzgurte müssen angelegt sein und Ihr gesamtes Gepäck muss in den Gepäckfächern über Ihnen oder unter dem Sitz vor Ihnen verstaut sein.

cockpit ['kɒkpɪt] | **Cockpit; Pilotenkabine**
Captain Fox and his **crew** [kruː] | Flugkapitän Fox und die **Besatzung**
the ground crew ['graʊnd kruː] | das Bodenpersonal
pilot ['paɪlət] | **Pilot(in); Flugzeugführer(in)**
runway ['rʌnweɪ] | **Start- / Landebahn**
shortly after **takeoff** ['teɪkɒf] | kurz nach dem **Start**
cruising altitude ['kruːzɪŋ æltitjuːd] | **Reiseflughöhe**

Flugbegleiter(innen) (= *flight attendants* ['flaɪt ətendənts]) heißen auch *stewardesses* / *stewards* oder (nur weibl.) *(air) hostesses* ['həʊstəsɪz].

The air(-traffic) **controllers** [kən'trəʊləz] are on strike. | Die **Fluglotsen** streiken.
hijack ['haɪdʒæk] / **skyjack** a plane | ein Flugzeug **entführen**
a hijacking / skyjacking | eine Flugzeugentführung
the hijackers / skyjackers | die Flugzeugentführer
air freight ['eə freɪt] / **air cargo** | **Luftfracht**
We'll airfreight it (out) to you today. | Wir schicken es Ihnen heute per Luftfracht.

Water transport
Beförderung auf dem Wasserweg

Land was created to provide a place for steamers to visit.
(*Brooks Atkinson, US critic and essayist, 1894–1984*)

go to **sea** (– went – gone [gɒn])	zur See gehen
in heavy seas [hevi 'si:z]	bei schwerer See
in international [ɪntə'næʃnəl] **waters**	in internationalen **Gewässern**
in Libyan territorial [terə'tɔːriəl] waters	in den libyschen Hoheitsgewässern
ship [ʃɪp]	**Schiff; verschiffen**
The captain ['kæptən] goes down with his ship / vessel.	Der Kapitän geht mit seinem Schiff unter.
I had the books shipped over from the US.	Ich ließ mir die Bücher aus den USA schicken.
shipping ['ʃɪpɪŋ]	(die) **Schifffahrt; Schiffe**
closed [kləʊzd] to shipping	für die Schifffahrt gesperrt
They were **shipwrecked** ['ʃɪprekt].	Sie erlitten Schiffbruch.
shipyard ['ʃɪpjɑːd] (workers)	**Werft**(arbeiter)
a 23-**vessel** ['vesl] armada [ɑː'mɑːdə]	eine Armada / Flotte von 23 **Schiffen**
boat [bəʊt]	**Boot; Schiff; Fähre**
the boat train to Dover ['dəʊvə]	der Zug zur Fähre in Dover
canoe [kə'nuː]	**Kanu (fahren); Paddelboot; paddeln**
on board the **ferry** ['feri]	an Bord der **Fähre**

Kinds of watercraft (= **Arten von Wasserfahrzeugen**)

ocean liner ['əʊʃn laɪnə] (= Ozeandampfer) • *passenger liner* (= Passagier-schiff) • *steamship* (= Dampfschiff) • *steamer* (= Dampfer) • *cargo ship* / *freighter* (= Frachtschiff / Frachter) • *merchant* ['mɜːtʃənt] *ship* (= Handels-schiff) • *container ship* (= Containerschiff) • *oil tanker* (= Öltanker) • *supertanker* (= Supertanker) • *fishing trawler* ['trɔːlə] (= Fischkutter) • *whaler* ['weɪlə] (= Walfänger) • *paddle steamer* (= Raddampfer) • *tug (boat)* (= Schlepper) • *lifeboat* (= Rettungsboot) • *motorboat* (= Motor-boot) • *yacht* [jɒt] (= Jacht) • *sailing boat* BE / AE *sailboat* (= Segelboot) • *rowing* [əʊ] *boat* BE / AE *rowboat* (= Ruderboot) • *raft* [rɑːft] (= Floß)

sail [seɪl]	**Segel**
They went sailing.	Sie gingen segeln.
Our ship sails tomorrow.	Unser Schiff läuft morgen aus.
sail under a flag of convenience	unter einer Billigflagge fahren
sailing / yachting ['jɒtɪŋ]	**Segeln; Segel-**
go on a **cruise** [kruːz] (– went – gone)	eine **Kreuzfahrt** machen
voyage ['vɔɪdʒ]	**(See-)Reise**
the Titanic on its / her maiden voyage	die Titanic auf ihrer Jungfernfahrt

Schiffe sind *it* oder *she: The Titanic* [tai'tænɪk] */ It / She sank within three hours, and of its / her 2206 passengers* ['pæsɪndʒəz] *only 703 were saved.* (= Die Titanic sank innerhalb von drei Stunden, und von ihren 2206 Passagieren wurden nur 703 gerettet.)

passage ['pæsɪdʒ]	**Überfahrt**
book a passage to America	eine Schiffsreise nach Amerika buchen
passengers travelling steerage	**Passagiere**, die im Zwischendeck reisen
stowaway ['stəʊəweɪ]	**blinder Passagier**
embark [ɪm'bɑːk]	**sich einschiffen**
disembark [dɪsɪm'bɑːk]	von Bord gehen
aboard [ə'bɔːd] / **on board** (the) ship	**an Bord** des Schiffes
go / come **ashore** [ə'ʃɔː]	**an Land** gehen / kommen
run **aground** [ə'graʊnd] (– ran – run)	**auf Grund** laufen; stranden
capsize [kæp'saɪz]	**kentern**
The ferry capsized and sank.	Die Fähre kenterte und sank.
The Titanic **struck** / **hit** an iceberg.	Die Titanic **stieß gegen** / **rammte** einen Eisberg.
No ship is **unsinkable**.	Kein Schiff ist **unsinkbar**.
change **course** [tʃeɪndʒ 'kɔːs]	den **Kurs** ändern
on course – off course	auf Kurs – vom Kurs abgekommen
bow [baʊ] – **stern** [stɜːn]	**Bug – Heck**
port [pɔːt] – **starboard** ['stɑːbəd]	**Backbord – Steuerbord**
the port where the ship **docked** [dɒkt]	der Hafen, in dem das Schiff **anlegte**
anchor ['æŋkə]	**Anker; (ver)ankern**
ride / lie at anchor	vor Anker liegen

"Nautical" idioms (= „nautische" Idioms)

I was between the devil and the deep blue sea. (= Ich war in einer argen Zwickmühle.) • *Frankly, I'm all at sea.* (= Offen gesagt, ich blicke nicht mehr durch.) • *There are plenty more fish in the sea.* (= Auch andere Mütter haben schöne Töchter.) • *We're all in the same boat.* (= Wir sitzen doch alle im gleichen Boot.) • *Economically, we've missed the boat.* (= Wirtschaftlich haben wir den Anschluss verpasst.) • *You don't want to rock the boat, do you?* (= Du willst dich doch nicht quer legen, oder?) • *When my ship comes home …* (= Wenn ich mein Glück gemacht habe …) • *She accused* [ə'kjuːzd] *me of sailing under false* [fɔːls] *colours.* (= Sie warf mir vor, unter falscher Flagge zu segeln.) • *It's time for you to nail your colours* ['kʌləz] *to the mast* [mɑːst]. (= Es wird Zeit, dass du Farbe bekennst.)

sailor ['seɪlə]	**Seemann; Matrose**
I'm afraid I'm not a good sailor.	Leider bin ich nicht seefest.
captain ['kæptən] / **skipper** ['skɪpə]	**Kapitän**
radio operator ['reɪdiəʊ ɒpəreɪtə]	**Funker**
crew [kruː]	**Mannschaft; Besatzung**
All **hands** on deck!	Alle Mann an Deck!
pilot ['paɪlət]	**Lotse**
shipowner ['ʃɪpəʊnə]	**Schiffseigner(in); Reeder**
pirate ['paɪrət] – **piracy** ['paɪrəsi]	**Pirat – Piraterie**
seasick ['siːsɪk] – **seasickness**	**seekrank – Seekrankheit**
lighthouse ['laɪthaʊs]	**Leuchtturm**
navigable ['nævɪgəbl] waterways	**schiffbare / befahrbare** Wasserstraßen
lock [lɒk]	**Schleuse**
nautical miles [nɔːtɪkl 'maɪlz]	**Seemeilen**

Public transport
Öffentlicher Nahverkehr

Commuter – one who spends his life / In riding to and from his wife; /
A man who shaves and takes a train, / And then rides back to shave again.
(*E.B. White, US journalist and writer, 1899–1985*)

the **underground** *BE* / *AE* **subway**	die **U-Bahn**
underground *BE* / *AE* subway station	U-Bahnhof
ride the subway (– rode – ridden) *AE*	mit der U-Bahn fahren
the **tube** [tjuːb]	die **U-Bahn** (*in London*)
Where's the nearest tube? *BE*	Wo ist der nächste U-Bahnhof?
Buses are slower than tubes. *BE*	Busse sind langsamer als U-Bahnen.
the **metro** ['metrəʊ]	die **U-Bahn** (*z.B. in Washington, DC*)
a half-hour **journey** [ɜː] *BE* / *AE* **ride**	eine halbstündige **Fahrt**
The S-Bahn is useful for longer journeys / rides / runs.	Die S-Bahn ist gut für längere Fahrten.
Children age 4 and under ride free. *AE*	Kinder bis zu 4 Jahren fahren frei.
subway riders ['sʌbweɪ raɪdəz] *AE*	**U-Bahnfahrer; U-Bahnfahrgäste**
the **elevated railroad** / the **el** [el]	die **Hochbahn** (*z.B. in Chicago*)
a train **bound** for Watford ['wɒtfəd]	ein Zug nach Watford

Dem britischen *public transport* ['trænspɔːt] sowie den überwiegend im AE gebräuchlichen Bezeichnungen *public transportation, public transit* ['trænsɪt], *mass transportation* und *mass transit* entsprechen im Deutschen die Begriffe öffentlicher (Personen-)Nahverkehr bzw. öffentliche Verkehrsmittel.
Entsprechend: *use public transport* BE / AE *ride public transportation* (= öffentliche Verkehrsmittel benutzen), *an efficient* [ɪ'fɪʃnt] *public transport(ation) system* / *mass transit system* (= ein leistungsfähiges System von öffentlichen Verkehrsmitteln).
Means of transport(ation) kann Einzahl oder Mehrzahl sein: *a means of transport(ation)* (= ein Verkehrsmittel) – *these means of transport(ation)* (= diese Verkehrsmittel).

tram [træm] *BE* / *AE* **streetcar**	**Straßenbahn**
cable car ['keɪbl kɑː]	(seilgezogene Straßenbahn in San Francisco)
monorail ['mɒnəʊreɪl]	**Einschienenbahn**
I travel to work by **bus** [bʌs].	Ich fahre mit dem **Bus** zur Arbeit.
double-decker (bus) [dʌbl'dekə]	Doppeldecker(bus)
The buses run every five minutes.	Die Busse verkehren alle fünf Minuten.
the number 6 bus route ['bʌs ruːt]	die Buslinie 6
bus stop ['bʌs stɒp]	**Bushaltestelle**
request stop [rɪ'kwest stɒp]	**Bedarfshaltestelle**
trolley(bus) ['trɒli(bʌs)]	**Oberleitungs(omni)bus; Obus**
minibus ['mɪnibʌs]	**Kleinbus**
coach [kəʊtʃ] *BE*	**Reisebus**

Leute, die regelmäßig mit öffentlichen Verkehrsmitteln zur Arbeit fahren
(= *who commute* [kə'mjuːt] *to work by public transport*), nennt man auch
straphangers (= Leute, die sich am Halteriemen in Bus oder Bahn festhalten).

hail a **cab** / **taxi** ['tæksi]	ein **Taxi** heran- / herbeiwinken
a taxi ride / journey ['tæksi raɪd / dʒɜːni]	eine Taxifahrt
taxi rank *BE* / *AE* taxi stand	Taxistand
turn the **meter** ['miːtə] on / off	das **Taxameter** / die **Uhr** ein- / ausschalten
a $2 **surcharge** ['sɜːtʃɑːdʒ]	ein **Zuschlag** / **Aufschlag** von 2 Dollar
tip the driver ['draɪvə]	dem Fahrer **ein Trinkgeld geben**
short-trip / short-distance **ticket**	Kurzstrecken**karte**
ticket machine ['tɪkɪt məʃiːn]	Fahrkartenautomat
a **transfer** ['trænsfɜː] *AE*	ein **Umsteigefahrschein**
In London, **fares** are graduated ['grædʒueɪtɪd] according to zones.	In London sind die **Fahrpreise** nach Zonen gestaffelt.
The conductor [kən'dʌktə] collects the fares.	Der Schaffner / Die Schaffnerin kassiert das Fahrgeld.
a flat fare ['flæt feə]	ein Einheits- / Pauschalfahrpreis
a fare increase / *AE auch* fare hike	eine Fahrpreiserhöhung
fare dodging ['dɒdʒɪŋ]	Schwarzfahren
Fare dodgers face a stiff fine.	Schwarzfahrern droht eine hohe Geldstrafe.
One Day **Travelcard** ['trævlkɑːd]	(verbilligte Tageskarte in London)

Tokens ['təʊkənz] sind als Fahrausweis dienende Metallmarken, die man
an einer *token booth* kauft und beim Betreten des Bahnsteigs (= *platform*)
oder des Busses (= *bus*) in ein Drehkreuz (= *turnstile*) steckt.

Some useful expressions (= **Nützliche Redensarten**)

How do I get to X, please?	Wie komme ich bitte nach X?
Which platform for Victoria [vɪk'tɔːriə]?	Von welchem Bahnsteig geht es nach Victoria?
Follow the signs [saɪnz] for Circle Line.	Folgen Sie den Schildern zur Circle-Linie.
Take the Central Line eastbound ['iːstbaʊnd].	Fahren Sie mit der Central-Linie in Richtung Osten.
Does this train go to …?	Fährt dieser Zug nach …?
The train goes via Charing Cross.	Der Zug fährt über Charing Cross.
Where do I change / transfer for …?	Wo muss ich nach … umsteigen?
What bus / train do I take for …?	Welcher Bus / Zug fährt nach …?
When / Where do I have to get off?	Wann / Wo muss ich aussteigen?
It's six stops to Victoria.	Nach Victoria sind es sechs Stationen.
You can get there on Line 1.	Da kommen Sie mit der Linie 1 hin.
Train terminates ['tɜːmɪneɪts] here.	(Der) Zug endet hier.
The escalator is out of service.	Die Rolltreppe ist außer Betrieb.
Mind [maɪnd] the gap!	Beachten Sie den Spalt (zwischen Bahnsteig und Zug)!
There is no service between London Euston and Camden.	Zwischen London Euston und Camden besteht kein Zugverkehr.

The economy
Die Wirtschaft

1   **Economic theory and policy**
    Wirtschaftstheorie und -politik

2   **Business**
    Das Geschäftsleben

3   **Money and finance**
    Geld und Finanzwesen

4   **Advertising**
    Werbung

5   **Insurance**
    Versicherung

6   **Real estate**
    Immobilien

7   **Occupations and job titles**
    Berufe und Funktionsbezeichnungen

8   **In the office**
    Im Büro

9   **Labour relations**
    Beziehungen zwischen den Tarifpartnern

Economic theory and policy
Wirtschaftstheorie und -politik

The truth is, we are all caught in a great economic system which is heartless.
(*Woodrow Wilson, US president, 1856–1924*)

economic(ally) [iːkəˈnɒmɪk(li)]	**wirtschaftlich; ökonomisch**
economic system [ˈsɪstəm]	Wirtschaftssystem
economic performance [pəˈfɔːməns]	(die) Wirtschaftsleistung
economic policy [ˈpɒləsi]	(die) Wirtschaftspolitik
raise economic growth [grəʊθ]	das Wirtschaftswachstum steigern
a slow economic recovery [rɪˈkʌvəri]	eine langsame Erholung der Wirtschaft
Is it **economically** viable [ˈvaɪəbl]?	Ist es **wirtschaftlich** sinnvoll?
economist [ɪˈkɒnəmɪst]	**Volkswirt(schaftler)(in); Wirtschaftswissenschaftler(in)**
the (national) **economy** [ɪˈkɒnəmi]	die (Volks-)**Wirtschaft**
command [kəˈmɑːnd] economy	Kommandowirtschaft
(centrally [ˈsentrəli]) planned economy	(zentrale) Planwirtschaft
(social) market economy	(soziale) Marktwirtschaft
black economy [ɪˈkɒnəmi]	Schattenwirtschaft

Economic ist „wirtschaftlich = mit der Wirtschaft zusammenhängend";
economical ist „wirtschaftlich = sparsam". – *The economy* ist die Wirtschaft
(eines Landes); *economy* (ohne Artikel) ist Sparsamkeit / Wirtschaftlichkeit.
Economics ist (die) Wirtschaftswissenschaft / Volkswirtschaftslehre.

goods and services	**Waren und Dienstleistungen**
the exchange [ɪksˈtʃeɪndʒ] of goods	der Warenaustausch / -verkehr
investment [-ˈvest-] / capital goods	Investitionsgüter
the **service** sector [ˈsektə]	der **Dienstleistungs**bereich / -sektor
supply and demand [dɪˈmɑːnd]	**Angebot und Nachfrage**
market forces [ˈfɔːsɪz]	(die) **Marktkräfte**
market share [ʃeə]	Marktanteil
in the global [ˈgləʊbl] **marketplace**	auf dem **Weltmarkt**
free / unfair **competition** [kɒmpəˈtɪʃn]	freier / unlauterer **Wettbewerb**
(government) **regulation** [regjuˈleɪʃn]	(staatliche) **Regulierung / Kontrolle**
deregulation [diːregjuˈleɪʃn]	**Aufhebung staatlicher Kontrollen**
factors of **production** [prəˈdʌkʃn]	**Produktionsfaktoren**
production costs [kɒsts]	(die) Produktionskosten
private property [praɪvət ˈprɒpəti]	**Privat**eigentum
private ownership of the means of production	Privateigentum an den Produktionsmitteln
the private sector [praɪvət ˈsektə]	die Privatwirtschaft
(state) **enterprise** [ˈentəpraɪz]	(Staats-)**Unternehmen**
free enterprise [friː ˈentəpraɪz]	freies Unternehmertum
entrepreneur [ɒntrəprəˈnɜː]	**Unternehmer(in)**
business **profits** [bɪznəs ˈprɒfɪts]	(die) Unternehmer**gewinne**
maximize [ˈmæksɪmaɪz] profits	die Gewinne maximieren
accumulate [əˈkjuːmjəleɪt] **capital**	**Kapital** bilden

prosperity [prɒ'sperəti]	**Wohlstand**
wealth [welθ]	**Reichtum; Vermögen**
create [kri'eɪt] wealth	Vermögen bilden
the national wealth	das Volksvermögen
aggregate ['ægrɪgət] (income / cost)	**Gesamt**(einkommen / -kosten)
gross [grəʊs] **national product** / **GNP**	**Bruttosozialprodukt**
balance of trade [bæləns əv 'treɪd]	**Handelsbilanz**
balance of payments ['peɪmənts]	Zahlungsbilanz
a balanced **budget** ['bʌdʒɪt]	ein ausgeglichener **(Staats-)Haushalt**
the budget deficit ['defəsɪt]	das Haushaltsdefizit
budget cuts / freeze	Haushaltskürzungen / -stopp
fill budget holes / fill budget(ary) gaps / plug budget deficits	Haushaltslöcher stopfen
deficit spending [defəsɪt 'spendɪŋ]	**Defizitfinanzierung**
the national **debt** [det]	die Staats**schuld** / **-verschuldung**
austerity measures [ɔː'sterəti meʒəz]	**Sparmaßnahmen**
austerity programme ['prəʊgræm]	Sparprogramm
austerity package / austerity budget	Sparpaket
rationing ['ræʃnɪŋ]	**Rationierung**
cut / reduce **subsidies** ['sʌbsədiz]	**Subventionen** abbauen
eliminate [ɪ'lɪmɪneɪt] **trade barriers**	**Handelsschranken** beseitigen
cut **interest rates** ['ɪntrəst reɪts]	die **Zinsen** senken
push up interest rates	die Zinsen in die Höhe treiben
increase **productivity** [prɒdʌk'tɪvəti]	die **Produktivität** erhöhen
the **standard of living** / **living standard** ['stændəd]	der **Lebensstandard**
the **cost of living** [kɒst əv 'lɪvɪŋ]	die **Lebenshaltungskosten**
cost increases ['ɪŋkriːsɪz]	Kostensteigerungen
purchasing ['pɜːtʃəsɪŋ] **power** / **buying power**	**(die) Kaufkraft**
consumer prices [kən'sjuːmə praɪsɪz]	**(die) Verbraucher**preise
consumption [kən'sʌmpʃn]	**(der) Verbrauch** / **Konsum**
(in)stability [(ɪn)stə'bɪləti]	**(In-)Stabilität**
the ups and downs of the **business cycle** ['bɪznəs saɪkl]	das Auf und Ab der **Konjunktur**
wait for the **upturn** ['ʌptɜːn]	auf den **Aufschwung** warten
a **downturn** in the economy	ein **Rückgang** der Konjunktur
recession [rɪ'seʃn]	**Rezession; Konjunkturrückgang**
the (Great) **Depression** [dɪ'preʃn]	die **Weltwirtschaftskrise** (*ab 1929*)
inflation [ɪn'fleɪʃn] – **deflation**	**Inflation – Deflation**
the inflation rate	die Inflationsrate
creeping / galloping ['gæləpɪŋ] inflation	schleichende / galoppierende Inflation
double-digit ['dʌbl dɪdʒɪt] inflation	eine zweistellige Inflationsrate
stimulus ['stɪmjʊləs] **package**	**Konjunkturpaket**
exponential growth [grəʊθ]	**exponentielles Wachstum**
projections [prə'dʒekʃnz]	**Prognosen**

Business
Das Geschäftsleben

→ 12.7 Shopping, 20.3 Money and finance

The business of America is business. (*Calvin Coolidge, US president, 1872–1933*)

business ['bɪznəs]	(das) **Geschäft; Geschäfts-**
Business is good / brisk / booming.	Die Geschäfte gehen gut.
Business is bad / slack / quiet.	Die Geschäfte laufen schlecht.
We do a lot of business with them.	Wir haben viel mit ihnen zu tun.
Are you here on business?	Sind Sie geschäftlich hier?
a business appointment [ə'pɔɪntmənt]	ein geschäftlicher Termin
a thriving ['θraɪvɪŋ] export business	ein florierendes Exportunternehmen
She's in the textile ['tekstaɪl] business.	Sie ist in der Textilbranche.
business acumen ['ækjəmən]	**Geschäftssinn**
businessman / **-woman** / **-people**	**Geschäftsmann** / **-frau** / **-leute**
in our **line** of business ['bɪznəs]	in unserer **Branche**
our spring line	unsere Frühjahrskollektion
a successful [sək'sesfl] line	ein gut gehender (Waren-)Artikel
commerce ['kɒmɜːs]	**Handel(sverkehr)**
chamber ['tʃeɪmbə] of commerce	(Industrie- und) Handelskammer
U.S. Department of Commerce	Handelsministerium der USA
U.S. Commerce Secretary	Handelsminister(in) der USA
commercial [kə'mɜːʃl]	**kaufmännisch; kommerziell; Handels-**
commercial English ['ɪŋglɪʃ]	Handelsenglisch
trade [treɪd]	**Handel; Gewerbe**
the furniture ['fɜːnɪtʃə] trade	die Möbelbranche
sell to the trade (– sold – sold)	an Wiederverkäufer verkaufen
trade show / trade fair	(Handels-)Messe; Ausstellung
merchant ['mɜːtʃənt]	**Kaufmann** / **-frau**
arms merchant / arms dealer	Waffenhändler(in)
(quality) **merchandise** / **goods**	(Qualitäts-)**Ware**
deal in something (– dealt [e] – dealt)	mit etwas **handeln**
companies ['kʌmpəniz] we've been dealing with for years	Firmen, mit denen wir seit Jahren Geschäfte machen
It's a deal.	Abgemacht.
partnership ['pɑːtnəʃɪp]	**Personen- / Personalgesellschaft**
owner / **proprietor** [prə'praɪətə]	**Besitzer(in); Eigentümer(in)**
shopkeeper ['ʃɒpkiːpə]	**Ladenbesitzer(in)**
company ['kʌmpəni]	**Gesellschaft; Firma; Unternehmen**
a troubled ['trʌbld] company	ein in Schwierigkeiten geratenes Unternehmen
multinational (company / corporation)	multinationaler Konzern; Multi
non-profitmaking *BE* / *AE* nonprofit company	gemeinnützige Gesellschaft
(un)limited **liability** [laɪə'bɪləti]	(un)beschränkte **Haftung**

 Die Abkürzung *plc* / *PLC* nach britischen Firmennamen bedeutet, dass es sich um eine *public limited company* handelt, d.h. eine Gesellschaft, die ungefähr einer Aktiengesellschaft entspricht; der Zusatz *Ltd* (= *limited*) deutet auf eine GmbH-ähnliche Gesellschaftsform. – *Inc.* [ɪŋk] (= *incorporated* [ɪn'kɔːpəreɪtɪd]) nach amerikanischen Namen bezeichnet eine *corporation*, also eine (als juristische Person eingetragene) (Kapital-)Gesellschaft.

General Motors and other **corporate** giants ['dʒaɪənts]	General Motors und andere Riesenkonzerne
their corporate ['kɔːpərət] culture	ihre Unternehmenskultur
outsourcing ['aʊtsɔːsɪŋ]	**Auslagerung / -gliederung** (von Unternehmensaktivitäten)
industrialist [ɪn'dʌstriəlɪst]	**Industrielle(r)**
shareholder / stockholder	**Aktionär(in)**
shareholder value ['væljuː]	Wertsteigerung für Aktionäre
director [də'rektə]	**Direktor(in)**
the **board** [bɔːd] **of directors**	der **Vorstand**
chairman of the board	Vorstandsvorsitzende(r); *AE auch* Aufsichtsratsvorsitzende(r)
manager ['mænɪdʒə]	**Leiter(in)**
data-processing manager	Leiter(in) der EDV-Abteilung
sales manager / *AE auch* vice president of sales	Verkaufs- / Vertriebsdirektor(in)
middle **management** ['mænɪdʒmənt]	mittleres **Management**
a hands-on management style	ein zupackender Führungsstil
executive [ɪg'zekjətɪv]	**leitende(r) Angestellte(r); Manager(in)**
several top-flight executives	mehrere Spitzenmanager

Der *president* einer amerikanischen *corporation* (= Kapitalgesellschaft) entspricht etwa einem Vorstandsvorsitzenden oder Generaldirektor; *vice presidents* [vaɪs 'prezɪdənts] sind Vorstandsmitglieder oder Direktor(inn)en, je nach Größe der Gesellschaft aber auch nur Abteilungsleiter(innen). Ein *vice president of marketing* entspricht etwa einem Marketingdirektor, ein *sales vice president* einem Vertriebsleiter und ein *vice president for human resources* ist ein Personaldirektor. *The CEO / chief executive officer* ist im AE Chef(in) / Vorstandsvorsitzende(r) eines Großkonzerns: *He was appointed* [ə'pɔɪntɪd] *CEO.* (= Er wurde zum Vorstandsvorsitzenden berufen.)

sell (– sold – sold)	**verkaufen**
hard / soft [sɒft] sell	harte / weiche Verkaufsmethoden
a hard-sell campaign [kæm'peɪn]	eine aggressive Werbekampagne
sale [seɪl]	**Verkauf; Vertrieb**
boost sales [buːst 'seɪlz]	die Umsätze in die Höhe treiben
the latest sales figures ['seɪlz fɪgəz]	die neusten Verkaufs- / Absatzzahlen
a drop / fall / decline [dɪ'klaɪn] in sales	ein Umsatzrückgang
a slump [slʌmp] in sales	ein dramatischer Umsatzrückgang
Sales have dropped / fallen / declined.	Die Umsätze sind zurückgegangen.
Sales have plummeted ['plʌmɪtɪd] / slumped.	Die Umsätze sind stark / dramatisch zurückgegangen.
Earnings ['ɜːnɪŋz] have jumped.	Die **Erträge** sind sprunghaft angestiegen.

seller – buyer ['baɪə]
This line is a big seller / a winner.
salesman – saleswoman
travelling salesman
our sales force ['seɪlz fɔːs]
salesmanship ['seɪlzmənʃɪp]
representative [reprɪ'zentətɪv]
sales rep(resentative) ['seɪlz rep]
a **prospect**(ive customer) ['prɒspekt]
a **commission** [kə'mɪʃn] of 25 per cent
They paid millions of dollars in
  kickbacks.
wholesale ['həʊlseɪl] – **retail** ['riːteɪl]
wholesaler – retailer ['riːteɪlə]
distribute [dɪ'strɪbjuːt] goods
our distributors [dɪ'strɪbjʊtəz] abroad
sole distribution [dɪstrɪ'bjuːʃn]
distribution agreement [ə'griːmənt]
under the terms of the **contract** ['kɒn-]
buy [baɪ] (– bought [ɔː] – bought)
buyout ['baɪaʊt]

turnover ['tɜːnəʊvə]
turn over 1.5 billion ['bɪljən]
Volume ['vɒljuːm] is down / up
  9 per cent.
make a **profit** ['prɒ-] (– made – made)
high / low profit margins ['mɑːdʒɪnz]
issue a profit warning
profitable ['prɒfɪtəbl]
profitability [prɒfɪtə'bɪləti]
break even ['iːvn] (– broke – broken)
in the black / **red**
lose [luːz] (– lost [lɒst] – lost)
loss [lɒs]
suffer huge [hjuːdʒ] losses
They face big losses.
haggle ['hægl] over the best **price**
list price ['lɪst praɪs]
purchase price ['pɜːtʃəs praɪs]
retail price ['riːteɪl praɪs]
cut prices (– cut – cut)
slash prices / costs [kɒsts]
price tag ['praɪs tæg]
The price tag is going up.
overpriced ['əʊvəpraɪst] goods
They **priced** [praɪst] themselves out
  of the market.
overcharge [əʊvə'tʃɑːdʒ] someone
discount ['dɪskaʊnt]
at a discount of 25 per cent [pə 'sent]

Verkäufer(in) – Käufer(in)
Dieser Artikel ist ein Renner.
Verkäufer – Verkäuferin
(Handels- / Reise-)Vertreter
unser Vertreterstab / Außendienst
die Kunst des Verkaufens
Vertreter(in); Repräsentant(in)
(Handels-)Vertreter(in)
ein(e) **potenzielle(r) Kunde / Kundin**
eine **Provision** von 25 Prozent
Sie zahlten **Schmiergelder / illegale
  Provisionen** in Millionenhöhe.
Großhandel(s-) – Einzelhandel(s-)
Großhändler – Einzelhändler
Waren **vertreiben / ausliefern**
unsere Vertriebspartner im Ausland
Alleinvertretung / -vertrieb
Vertriebsvereinbarung
gemäß den **Vertrags**bestimmungen
(an- / ein)kaufen
Firmenkauf (durch Erwerb einer
  Mehrheit von Anteilen)
(der) **Umsatz**
1,5 Milliarden umsetzen
Der **Umsatz** ist um 9 Prozent
  gesunken / gestiegen.
Gewinn erzielen
große / kleine Gewinnspannen
eine Gewinnwarnung ausgeben
Gewinn bringend; rentabel
Rentabilität
kostendeckend arbeiten
in den schwarzen / roten Zahlen
verlieren
Verlust
enorme Verluste erleiden
Es drohen ihnen große Verluste.
um den besten **Preis** feilschen
Listen- / Katalogpreis
Einkaufspreis
Einzelhandels- / Ladenpreis
die Preise senken
die Preise / Kosten drastisch senken
Preisschild
Die Kosten steigen.
zu teure / überteuerte Ware(n)
Sie waren durch überhöhte Preise
  nicht mehr wettbewerbsfähig.
jemand **zu viel abverlangen**
Discount-; Diskont-
mit einem Rabatt von 25 Prozent

a **me-too** product ['prɒdʌkt] | ein der Konkurrenz nachempfundenes Produkt ohne Originalität

fierce [fɪəs] / sharp / keen **competition** | heftige / scharfe **Konkurrenz**

cut-throat competition [kɒmpə'tɪʃn] | Verdrängungswettbewerb

drive a **competitor** [kəm'petɪtə] out of business | einen **Konkurrenten** / **Mitanbieter** vom Markt verdrängen

go into **liquidation** [lɪkwɪ'deɪʃn] | in **Liquidation** gehen

bid for something (– bid – bid) | ein Angebot für etwas abgeben

takeover (bid) ['teɪkəʊvə] | **Übernahme**(angebot)

acquisition [ækwɪ'zɪʃn] | **Neuerwerbung; Übernahme**

merger ['mɜːdʒə] | **Fusion**

offer ['ɒfə] | **Angebot; anbieten**

showroom ['ʃəʊruːm] | **Ausstellungsraum**

We're **in the market for** a couple ['kʌpl] of new PCs. | Wir **wollen** eine Reihe von neuen PCs **kaufen**.

place an **order** with a firm | (einen) **Auftrag** an eine Firma erteilen

fill / fulfil / execute an order | einen Auftrag ausführen

the execution [eksɪ'kjuːʃn] of an order | die Ausführung eines Auftrags

Can you **supply** these items ['aɪtəmz]? | Können Sie diese Artikel **liefern**?

supplier [sə'plaɪə] | **Lieferant**

deliver [dɪ'lɪvə] from stock | vom Lager **(aus)liefern**

the **delivery** [dɪ'lɪvəri] of goods | die **Lieferung** von Waren

ship / **forward** / **dispatch** something | etwas **versenden**

shipment / **consignment** [kən'saɪn-] | **(Waren-)Sendung; Lieferung**

shipping documents ['dɒkjumənts] | **Versandpapiere / -dokumente**

packing list ['pækɪŋ lɪst] | **Packliste**

stock [stɒk] | **Lager**

The model is in stock / out of stock. | Das Modell ist (nicht) vorrätig.

Our stocks are running low. | Unsere Vorräte gehen zur Neige.

while stocks last | solange der Vorrat reicht

warehouse ['weəhaʊs] | **Lagerhaus; (Waren-)Lager**

inventory ['ɪnvəntri] | **Inventar; Lager- / Warenbestand**

guarantee [gærən'tiː] | **garantieren (für); Garantie(schein)**

a two-year guarantee / warranty [ɒ] | eine zweijährige Garantie

It isn't covered by the guarantee. | Das fällt nicht unter die Garantie.

franchise ['fræntʃaɪz] | **(eine) Lizenz / Konzession (erteilen)**

a chain of franchise restaurants ['restrɒnts] | eine Kette von Restaurants, die in Franchise-Form geführt werden

import ['ɪmpɔːt] – **export** ['ekspɔːt] | **Import – Export**

import [ɪm'pɔːt] / export something | etwas importieren / exportieren

Spätestens seit Hilmar Kopper, der seinerzeitige Vorstandssprecher (= *chief executive*) der Deutschen Bank, im Zusammenhang mit den durch den Konkurs (= *bankruptcy*) der Schneider-Gruppe entstandenen Riesenverlusten (= *huge losses*) von *peanuts* (= einem lächerlichen Betrag) sprach, kennt in Deutschland jeder wirtschaftlich Interessierte das Wort. Statt *peanuts* hätte man auf Englisch auch *chicken feed* oder *small potatoes* sagen können.

Money and finance
Geld und Finanzwesen

→ 6.9 Taxation, 20.2 Business, 20.1 Economic theory and policy

Money is a good servant but a bad master. (*Proverb*)

(make a lot of) **money** [ˈmʌni]	(viel) **Geld** (verdienen)
a large / small amount of money	ein großer / kleiner Geldbetrag
Money is tight [taɪt].	Das Geld ist knapp.
I haven't got any **cash** [kæʃ] on me.	Ich habe kein (**Bar-)Geld** bei mir.
five thousand dollars in cash	5000 Dollar in bar
Are you paying (in) cash?	Zahlen Sie bar?
I'm rather short of cash.	Ich bin ziemlich knapp bei Kasse.
cash payment [ˈkæʃ peɪmənt]	Barzahlung
cash register [ˈkæʃ redʒɪstə]	**(Registrier- / Laden-)Kasse**
cash machine / *BE auch* **cash dispenser** / *AE auch* **ATM** (= automated-teller machine)	**Geldautomat**

☞ **Beachten Sie die Einzahl- und Mehrzahlformen bei Geldbeträgen**
*We've got £60 (= sixty **pounds**) in the bank.* (= Wir haben 60 Pfund auf der Bank.) • *They bid half a million **dollars**.* (= Sie boten eine halbe Million Dollar.) • *That's eleven **euros** thirty.* (= Das macht dann elf Euro dreißig.) • *He had only **20 cents** in his pocket.* (= Er hatte nur 20 Cent in der Tasche.) • *a 20-**euro** note* BE / AE *bill* (= ein 20-Euro-Schein) • *a 50-**pound** note / 50-**dollar** bill* (= eine 50-Pfund-Note / 50-Dollar-Note).
Genaue Geldbeträge stehen mit Einzahlverb: *50,000 pounds / dollars **is** a lot of money.* (= 50 000 Pfund / Dollar sind viel Geld.) • *Five million dollars **doesn't** mean much to her.* (= Fünf Millionen Dollar bedeuten ihr nicht viel.)
Unbestimmte Summen stehen mit Mehrzahlverb: *There **are** millions of dollars involved.* (= Es geht um Millionen Dollar.)

How much did he **charge** for the job?	Was hat er für die Arbeit **berechnet**?
You can charge it to my account.	Belasten Sie es meinem Konto.
bank charges [ˈbæŋk tʃɑːdʒɪz]	Bankspesen / -gebühren
cost [kɒst] (– cost – cost)	**kosten**
It costs / cost £500.	Es kostet / kostete 500 Pfund.
They cost 60p [sɪksti ˈpiː] each.	Sie koste(te)n 60 Pence das Stück.
change a 100-euro note	einen Hunderteuroschein **wechseln**
Have you got change for a pound?	Können Sie mir ein Pfund wechseln?

Names of US coins (= **Namen amerikanischer Münzen**)
1¢ = one cent = a penny	25¢ = twenty-five cents = a quarter
5¢ = five cents = a nickel	50¢ = fifty cents = a half dollar
10¢ = ten cents = a dime	

pay [peɪ] (– paid [peɪd] – paid)	**(be)zahlen**
pay for goods	Waren bezahlen

pay the cabdriver	den Taxifahrer bezahlen
pay a bill	eine Rechnung bezahlen
She's paid (off) all her debts [dets].	Sie hat alle ihre Schulden bezahlt.
pay by cheque / by credit card	mit Scheck / Kreditkarte bezahlen
pay / settle an account [ə'kaʊnt]	ein Konto ausgleichen; eine Rechnung begleichen
payment / **settlement** of an outstanding invoice	**Bezahlung** / **Ausgleich** einer offenstehenden Rechnung
wallet ['wɒlɪt] / AE auch **billfold**	**Brieftasche**
purse [pɜːs] BE / AE **change purse**	**Portemonnaie; Geldbeutel**

Dollars sind umgangssprachlich *bucks*; *pounds* sind *quid: I owe her two hundred bucks / quid.* (= Ich schulde ihr zweihundert Dollar / Pfund.)

spend money (on) (– spent – spent)	Geld **ausgeben** (für)
expenditure(s) [ɪk'spendɪtʃə(z)]	**Ausgaben; Aufwendungen**
overheads BE / AE **overhead**	**Gemeinkosten**
lend money to someone (– lent – lent)	jemand Geld **leihen**
borrow money from someone	(sich) Geld von jemand **borgen**
grant [grɑːnt] / repay a **loan**	einen **Kredit** gewähren / zurückzahlen
lease [liːs] a car	einen Wagen **leasen**
save money ['mʌni]	Geld **sparen**
encourage [ɪn'kʌrɪdʒ] saving	die Spartätigkeit fördern
the savings rate ['seɪvɪŋz reɪt]	die Sparquote
invoice ['ɪnvɔɪs]	**(Waren-)Rechnung; Faktura**
foot [fʊt] the **bill**	die **Rechnung** bezahlen / begleichen
open an **account** [ə'kaʊnt] with a bank	bei einer Bank ein **Konto** eröffnen
deposit [dɪ'pɒzɪt] money in an account	Geld auf ein Konto einzahlen
transfer [-'fɜː] money to an account	Geld auf ein Konto überweisen
pay money into an account	Geld auf ein Konto einzahlen
current account BE / AE checking account	Girokonto
savings account BE / AE thrift account	Sparkonto
deposit account / AE auch time deposit	Festgeldkonto
bank (sorting) code [kəʊd]	**Bankleitzahl**
bank **deposits** [dɪ'pɒzɪts]	Bank**einlagen**
withdraw (– withdrew – withdrawn)	(*Geld*) **abheben**
make a withdrawal [wɪð'drɔːəl]	Geld abheben
I'd like to **take out** £100 (= a / one hundred pounds) in cash.	Ich möchte 100 Pfund in bar **abheben.**
savings bank ['seɪvɪŋz bæŋk]	**Sparkasse**
building society BE / AE **savings and loan association**	**Bausparkasse**
building loan ['bɪldɪŋ ləʊn]	**Baudarlehen**
overdraft ['əʊvədrɑːft]	**(Konto-)Überziehung**

Thrift institutions / *thrifts* [θrɪfts] ist in den USA eine kollektive Bezeichnung für *savings banks* und *savings and loan associations* [əsəʊsi'eɪʃnz].

the **high street banks** BE	die **Großbanken**
banker – **bank manager** ['mænɪdʒə]	**Bank(i)er** – **Zweigstellenleiter(in)**

the **central bank** [sentrəl 'bæŋk]	die **Zentralbank**
cut / reduce **key** [kiː] **interest rates**	die **Leitzinsen** senken
the **Fed(eral Reserve Board)**	der amerikanische **Zentralbankrat**
treasurer ['treʒərə]	**Schatzmeister(in); Leiter(in) der**
	Finanzabteilung; Kassenwart
the city treasurer	der Stadtkämmerer
the **Treasury** ['treʒəri] (Department)	das **Finanzministerium**
Treasury Secretary ['sekrətri] *AE*	Finanzminister(in)
monetary ['mʌnɪtri] policy	(die) **Geld(markt)-** / **Währungspolitik**
monetary union [mʌnɪtri 'juːnɪən]	(die) Währungsunion
fiscal policy [fɪskl 'pɒləsi]	(die) **Finanzpolitik**
the peso was **devalued** by 50%	der Peso wurde um 50% **abgewertet**
a 10% devaluation [diːvæljuˈeɪʃn]	eine zehnprozentige Abwertung
exchange rates [ɪksˈtʃeɪndʒ reɪts]	**Wechsel-** / **Devisenkurse**
foreign exchange [fɒrən ɪksˈtʃeɪndʒ]	Devisen
the foreign-exchange markets	die Devisenbörsen
create a common **currency** ['kʌrənsi]	eine gemeinsame **Währung** schaffen
invest – investor – investment	**investieren – Investor(in) –**
	Investition
invest millions in a project ['prɒdʒekt]	Millionen in ein(em) Projekt investieren
a highly lucrative ['luːkrə-] investment	eine höchst lukrative Geldanlage
our **financial** [faɪˈnænʃl] position	unsere **finanzielle** Lage
They can't meet their financial	Sie können ihren finanziellen
obligations [ɒblɪˈgeɪʃnz].	Verpflichtungen nicht nachkommen.
their financial strength / power	ihre Finanzkraft
the financial markets	die Finanzmärkte
the previous ['priːvɪəs] financial year	das vorangegangene Geschäftsjahr
finance [faɪˈnæns] a project	ein Projekt **finanzieren**
become **insolvent** [ɪnˈsɒlvənt]	**zahlungsunfähig** werden
stave off / avert [əˈvɜːt] **insolvency**	die **Zahlungsunfähigkeit** abwenden
pay for something by **instalments**	etwas in **Raten** bezahlen
The first instalment is due in May.	Die erste Rate ist im Mai fällig.
assets and liabilities [laɪəˈbɪlətiz]	**Aktiva und Passiva**
per capita [pə ˈkæpɪtə] **income**	Pro-Kopf-**Einkommen**
disposable [dɪˈspəʊzəbl] income	verfügbares Einkommen
the **stock exchange** ['stɒk ɪkstʃeɪndʒ]	die **Börse**
commodity [kəˈmɒdəti] exchange	Warenbörse
stocks [stɒks]	**Aktien**
bonds [bɒndz]	**festverzinsliche Wertpapiere**
securities / **stocks and bonds**	**Wertpapiere**
unit trust *BE* / *AE* **mutual fund**	**Investmentfonds**
hedge fund ['hedʒ fʌnd]	**Hedgefonds**
speculator ['spekjuleɪtə]	**Spekulant(in)**
bull [ʊ] **market – bear** [eə] **market**	(*Börse*) **Hausse – Baisse**
dividend ['dɪvɪdend]	**Dividende; Gewinnanteil**
maximum **returns** [rɪˈtɜːnz]	maximale **Erträge**
derivatives [dɪˈrɪvətɪvz]	**Derivate**
broker ['brəʊkə]	(*z.B. Börsen-*)**Makler(in)**
portfolio [pɔːtˈfəʊliəʊ] **manager**	**Effektenverwalter(in)**
fund [fʌnd] **manager**	**Fondsverwalter(in)**
stock-market crash [kræʃ]	**Zusammenbruch des Aktienmarktes**

Advertising
Werbung

Doing business without advertising is like winking at a girl in the dark: you know what you are doing, but nobody else does.
(*E.W. Howe, US editor and writer, 1853–1937*)

advertising ['ædvətaɪzɪŋ]	(die) **Werbung; Reklame**
make advertising more efficient	(die) Werbung wirksamer gestalten
deceptive [dɪ'septɪv] advertising	irreführende Werbung
the advertising industry ['ɪndəstri]	die Werbeindustrie / -branche
advertising agency ['eɪdʒənsi]	Werbeagentur
advertising department [dɪ'pɑːtmənt]	Werbeabteilung
advertising manager ['mænɪdʒə]	Werbeleiter(in)
advertising concept ['kɒnsept]	Werbekonzeption
advertising campaign [kæm'peɪn] / drive	Werbekampagne / -feldzug
advertising medium ['miːdiəm]	Werbemittel; Werbeträger
advertising rates [reɪts]	Anzeigentarif(e) / -preise
advertising slogan ['sləʊɡən]	Werbeslogan
advertise ['ædvətaɪz] a product	für ein Produkt **Reklame machen**
advertiser ['ædvətaɪzə]	**Inserent(in)**
They're big advertisers.	Sie haben einen großen Werbeetat.
advertisement [əd'vɜːtɪsmənt] / **ad** [æd] / *BE auch* **advert** ['ædvɜːt]	**(Werbe-)Anzeige; Werbespot; Reklame**
It isn't a good advertisement for us.	Das ist keine gute Reklame für uns.
place ad(vertisement)s	Anzeigen schalten
an ad series ['æd sɪəriːz]	eine Anzeigenserie
classified ad(vertisement) ['klæsɪfaɪd]	Kleinanzeige

 Madison Avenue [mædɪsn 'ævənjuː]: Straße in New York City, in der viele Werbeagenturen (= *advertising agencies*) ihre Büros (= *offices*) haben – von daher ein Symbol für amerikanische Werbepraktiken (= *advertising practices*) und für Werbung (= *advertising*) schlechthin: *the latest buzzword on Madison Avenue* (= das neueste Schlagwort in der amerikanischen Werbeindustrie).

the **clients** ['klaɪənts] of an agency	die **Kunden** einer (Werbe-)Agentur
account [ə'kaʊnt]	**Kunde(netat)** (einer Werbeagentur)
account executive [ɪɡ'zekjʊ-] / manager	Kundenberater(in) / -betreuer(in)
estimate ['estɪmət]	**Kosten(vor)anschlag**
art director ['ɑːt dərektə]	**Artdirector; künstlerische(r) Leiter(in)**
copywriter ['kɒpiraɪtə]	**(Werbe-)Texter(in)**
copy ['kɒpi]	(ein / der) **Werbetext**
He writes good copy.	Er schreibt gute Werbetexte.
creative(ly) [kri'eɪtɪv(li)]	**kreativ; schöpferisch; gestaltend**
marketing ['mɑːkɪtɪŋ]	**Marketing(-)**
direct ['daɪrekt] marketing	Direktmarketing; Direktwerbung
telemarketing ['telimɑːkɪtɪŋ]	(Verkauf / Werbung per Telefon)
market-oriented ['ɔːrientɪd]	**marktorientiert**

market research [rɪ'sɜ:tʃ]	(die) **Marktforschung**
promotion [prə'məʊʃn]	**Verkaufsförderung**
sales promotion ['seɪlz prəməʊʃn]	Verkaufs- / Absatzförderung
promotional materials [mə'tɪəriəlz]	**Werbe**material / -unterlagen
promote [prə'məʊt] a product	ein Produkt **bewerben**
plug [plʌg] a product	für ein Erzeugnis **die Werbetrommel rühren**
USP [ju: es 'pi:] (= unique [ju:'ni:k] selling proposition)	einzigartiges verkaufsförderndes Merkmal; Alleinstellungsmerkmal
publicity [pʌb'lɪsəti]	**Publicity; Werbung**
launch [lɔ:ntʃ] a publicity campaign	eine Werbekampagne starten
a publicity tour [pʌb'lɪsəti tʊə]	eine Werbereise / -tour
Public relations [pʌblɪk rɪ'leɪʃnz] is very important.	(Die) **Öffentlichkeitsarbeit** ist sehr wichtig.
They hired a public relations expert to revamp [ri:'væmp] their image.	Sie holten sich einen PR-Fachmann, der ihr Image aufpolieren sollte.
It's a PR (= public relations) disaster.	Es ist eine PR-Katastrophe.
hype [haɪp]	**(Reklame-)Rummel; Publicity**
introduce a product with a lot of hype	ein Produkt mit großem Reklame-rummel einführen
media hype ['mi:diə haɪp]	Medienrummel
our corporate **identity** [aɪ'dentəti]	die **Identity** unseres Unternehmens
our corporate **image** ['ɪmɪdʒ]	unser Firmen-**Image**
logo ['ləʊgəʊ]	(*Firmen-*)**Signet** / **Logo**
goodwill [gʊd'wɪl]	**Goodwill; ideeller Firmenwert**
brand loyalty ['lɔɪəlti] (of consumers)	**Markentreue** (der Verbraucher)
press kit ['pres kɪt]	**Pressemappe** (*mit Infomaterial*)
photo opportunity [ɒpə'tju:nəti]	**Fototermin**
commercials [kə'mɜ:ʃlz]	(*Fernsehen* / *Radio*) **Werbespots**
product placement ['prɒdʌkt pleɪsmənt]	**Schleichwerbung**
brochure ['brəʊʃə]	**Werbeschrift; Prospekt**
leaflet ['li:flət]	**Werbezettel; Prospekt**
flyer ['flaɪə] / **handbill**	**Handzettel**
direct mail [daɪrekt 'meɪl]	**Infopost; Postwurfsendungen**
junk mail ['dʒʌŋk meɪl]	(*abfällig*) **Reklamesendungen**
hoarding ['hɔ:dɪŋ] *BE* / *AE* **billboard**	**Reklame- / Plakatwand**
bus / subway **card** *AE*	Bus- / U-Bahn**plakat**
display [dɪ'spleɪ]	**Display**
shopwindow display	Schaufensterauslage
distribute **coupons** ['ku:pɒnz]	**(Werbe-)Gutscheine** verteilen
giveaway ['gɪvəweɪ]	**Werbegeschenk**
response rate [rɪ'spɒns reɪt]	**Rücklauf**
positive ['pɒzətɪv] / negative **feedback**	positives / negatives **Echo**
target group / **target audience** ['ɔ:diəns]	**Zielgruppe**
test market ['test mɑ:kɪt]	**Testmarkt**
age group ['eɪdʒ gru:p]	**Altersgruppe**

Insurance
Versicherung

I detest life-insurance agents. They always argue that I shall some day die, which is not so. (*Stephen Leacock, Canadian humorist, 1869–1944*)

insurance [ɪnˈʃʊərəns] *Kein Plural!*	**Versicherung**
take out / buy insurance / an insurance policy	eine Versicherung abschließen
make an insurance claim	einen Versicherungsanspruch geltend machen
I've got private health insurance.	Ich bin privat krankenversichert.

Insurance wird in der Bedeutung Versicherung nicht mit dem unbestimmten Artikel *a(n)* und nicht im Plural gebraucht! Eine Versicherung ist je nach Bedeutung *an insurance policy / a policy* oder *an insurance company.*

insurance rates [reɪts]	(die) Versicherungstarife
life insurance / *BE auch* life assurance	Lebensversicherung
accident [ˈæksɪdənt] insurance	Unfallversicherung
disability [dɪsəˈbɪləti] insurance	Invaliditätsversicherung
fire insurance [ˈfaɪər ɪnʃʊərəns]	Feuerversicherung
household (contents) insurance	Hausratversicherung
motor / car / automobile insurance	Kfz- / Kraftfahrt- / Autoversicherung
comprehensive insurance	Vollkaskoversicherung
third party, fire and theft *BE*	Teilkasko(versicherung)
third-party insurance / policy *BE*	(*Kfz*) Haftpflichtversicherung
liability [laɪəˈbɪləti] insurance	(*allg.*) Haftpflichtversicherung
insurance policy [ˈpɒləsi]	Versicherung(spolice / -schein)
insurance agent / salesman / -woman	Versicherungsvertreter(in)
insure [ɪnˈʃʊə] against a risk	**sich** gegen ein Risiko **versichern**
Are we insured against theft [θeft]?	Sind wir gegen Diebstahl versichert?
the insured (person / party)	die versicherte Person
policyholder [ˈpɒləsihəʊldə]	**Versicherungsnehmer(in)**
insurer [ɪnˈʃʊərə] / **underwriter**	**Versicherer**
cover [ˈkʌvə] / **coverage** [ˈkʌvərɪdʒ]	**Versicherungsschutz**
Do we have adequate cover(age)?	Sind wir ausreichend versichert?
provide [prəˈvaɪd] cover(age)	Versicherungsschutz gewähren
cover note [ˈkʌvə nəʊt]	Deckungskarte / -zusage
fill out / *BE auch* fill in / complete a **form**	ein **Formular** ausfüllen
under the **terms** of the policy	gemäß den Versicherungs- bedingungen
annual **premium** [ˈpriːmiəm]	Jahres**prämie**; jährlicher **Beitrag**
settle / **adjust** [əˈdʒʌst] a claim	einen Schaden / Anspruch **regulieren**
settlement / **adjustment** of a claim	**Regulierung** eines Schadens
damage [ˈdæmɪdʒ] caused by an act of God	durch höhere Gewalt verursachte **Schäden**
pay **damages** [ˈdæmɪdʒɪz]	**Schadenersatz** leisten

Real estate
Immobilien

→ 5.1 Flats and houses, 7.1 Housing shortage, 11.6 Architecture

This was one of my prayers: for a parcel of land not so very large, which should have a garden and a spring of ever-flowing water near the house, and a bit of woodland as well as these. (*Horace, Roman poet, 65–8 BC*)

property ['prɒpəti] *BE* / *AE* **real estate** ['rɪəl ɪsteɪt] / *AE* **real property**	Immobilien; Grundstücke
invest money in property / real estate	Geld in Immobilien anlegen
He's in property / real estate.	Er ist im Immobiliengeschäft.
the property / real-estate market	der Immobilien- / Grundstücksmarkt
property / real-estate prices	(die) Grundstücks- / Immobilienpreise
property / real-estate speculator	Grundstücksspekulant(in)
property / real-estate management	Grundstücksverwaltung
property owner ['prɒpəti əunə]	Grundstückseigentümer(in)
Private property. Keep off / out.	Privatgrundstück. Betreten verboten.
estate agent *BE* / *AE* **real estate agent** / *AE* **realtor** ['rɪəltə]	**Immobilien- / Grundstücks- makler(in)**
plot / **parcel of land**	**Stück Land; Grundstück; Parzelle**
This plot (of land) is for sale.	Dieses Grundstück ist zu verkaufen.
a building plot ['bɪldɪŋ plɒt]	ein Baugrundstück
a **piece of land** [piːs əv 'lænd]	ein **Stück Land**
a vacant ['veɪkənt] **lot**	ein unbebautes **Grundstück**
the **site** for the new school	das **Gelände** für die neue Schule
a developed [dɪ'veləpt] site / property	ein erschlossenes Grundstück
an undeveloped **tract** of land	ein unerschlossenes **Gelände**
a 40,000-acre ['eɪkə] tract	ein Gebiet von 40 000 Morgen; 40 000 Morgen Land
a **strip** of land [lænd]	ein **schmaler Streifen** (Land)
land / **property register** ['redʒɪstə]	**Grundbuch**
have a property on **leasehold** ['liːs-]	ein Grundstück in **Pacht** haben
have the **freehold** of a house	(zeitlich unbegrenztes) **Eigentums- recht** an einem Haus haben
let *BE* / *AE* **rent** a house to someone	ein Haus an jemand **vermieten**
rent a house from someone	ein Haus von jemand mieten
house to let *BE* / *AE* house for rent	Haus zu vermieten
building regulations *BE* / *AE* **building code**	**Bauordnung**
planning permission *BE* / *AE* **building permit** ['pɜːmɪt]	**Baugenehmigung**
notary (public) ['nəutəri ('pʌblɪk)]	**Notar(in)**
abstract ['æbstrækt] **of title**	**Eigentumsnachweis**
title deed ['taɪtl diːd]	**Eigentumsurkunde**
mortgage ['mɔːgɪdʒ]	**Hypothek; Grundschuld**
take out a mortgage (– took – taken)	eine Hypothek aufnehmen
high mortgage rates	hohe Hypothekenzinsen
mortgage a house	ein Haus mit einer Hypothek belasten

Occupations and job titles
Berufe und Funktionsbezeichnungen

Hier nicht aufgeführte Berufe sind in den betreffenden Sachkapiteln zu finden.

Work is much more fun than fun. (Noël Coward, English playwright, 1899–1973)

vocation [vəʊˈkeɪʃn]
His real vocation was composer,
   not conductor.
family, home and **job**

Berufung
Seine eigentliche Berufung war das
   Komponieren, nicht das Dirigieren.
Familie, Haushalt und **Beruf**

Beruf
What does she do (for a living)? (= Was macht sie beruflich?) • *He's a
butcher* [ˈbʊtʃə] *by trade.* (= Er ist Fleischer von Beruf.) • *Occupation*
[ɒkjuˈpeɪʃn]: *Housewife* (= Beruf: Hausfrau)
Professional people sind Angehörige der freien bzw. hoch qualifizierter
oder besonders hoch angesehener Berufe, also etwa der *legal* [ˈliːgl],
medical [ˈmedɪkl], *or teaching professions.* Entsprechend: *She's a lawyer*
[ˈlɔːjə] *by profession.* (= Von Beruf ist sie Rechtsanwältin.)

work as an **au pair** [əʊ ˈpeə]
work **freelance** [ˈfriːlɑːns]
freelance(r) [ˈfriːlɑːns(ə)]
as a freelance writer
a **self-employed** photographer [-ˈtɒg-]
the self-employed [self ɪmˈplɔɪd]
the **boss** [bɒs]
foreman [ˈfɔːmən] *Pl.* -men
head [hed] (of a department)
**head(master / -mistress) / head
   teacher** *BE / AE* **principal** [ˈprɪnsəpl]
(school)master – (school)mistress
   (*veraltet*)

als **Au-pair-Mädchen** arbeiten
freiberuflich tätig sein
Freiberufler(in)
als freie(r) Schriftsteller(in)
ein(e) **selb(st)ständige(r)** Fotograf(in)
die Selb(st)ständigen
der **Chef** / die **Chefin**
Vorarbeiter; (Werk-)Meister
Leiter(in) (einer Abteilung)
(*Schule*) **Direktor(in) / Leiter(in)**

Lehrer – Lehrerin

Lehrer(in) kann auch *instructor* [ɪnˈstrʌktə] sein:
driving instructor (= Fahrlehrer/in) • *riding instructor* (= Reitlehrer/in) •
swimming instructor (= Schwimmlehrer/in) • *ski* [skiː] / *skiing instructor*
(= Skilehrer/in) • *flight / flying instructor* (= Fluglehrer/in)

chief of police [tʃiːf əv pəˈliːs] *AE*
chief administrative [-ˈmɪnɪs-] officer
the **chair**(man) [ˈtʃeə(mən)]
the chair(woman) [ˈtʃeə(wʊmən)]
the chair(person) [ˈtʃeə(pɜːsn)]
She chairs the committee [kəˈmɪti].
She was elected chair(woman).
labourer [ˈleɪbərə]
unskilled **worker** [ʌnskɪld ˈwɜːkə]
semiskilled worker [semɪskɪld ˈwɜːkə]

Polizei**chef(in)** / -**präsident(in)**
Verwaltungschef(in)
der **Vorsitzende**
die Vorsitzende
der / die Vorsitzende
Sie ist Vorsitzende des Ausschusses.
Sie wurde zur Vorsitzenden gewählt.
(Hilfs-)Arbeiter(in)
ungelernte(r) **Arbeiter(in)**
angelernte(r) Arbeiter(in)

skilled worker [skɪld 'wɜ:kə]	Facharbeiter(in)
blue-collar [blu: 'kɒlə] worker	Arbeiter(in)
white-collar worker	Angestellte(r)
office worker ['ɒfɪs wɜ:kə]	Büroangestellte(r)
social worker ['səʊʃl wɜ:kə]	Sozialarbeiter(in)
apprentice [ə'prentɪs]	**Lehrling; Auszubildende(r)**
trainee [treɪ'ni:]	**in der Ausbildung Stehende(r)**
lecturer BE / AE **assistant professor**	(etwa) **Lehrbeauftragte(r)**

☞ **Artikelgebrauch**

Nicht einmalige Berufe / Funktionen stehen mit dem Artikel a(n):
He's a professor of sociology at the University of California. (Die University of California hat mehr als einen Lehrstuhl für Soziologie.)
Funktionen, die es nur einmal gibt, stehen ohne Artikel oder mit the:
She's professor of sociology at the University of Akron. (Die Universität Akron hat nur einen Lehrstuhl für Soziologie.)
He's the city manager of Hartford, Connecticut. (= Er ist Stadtdirektor von Hartford, Connecticut.)

caretaker BE / AE **janitor** ['dʒænɪtə]	**Hausmeister(in)**
miner ['maɪnə] – **miners**	**Bergmann – Bergleute**
docker BE / **longshoreman** Pl. -men	**Hafen- / Dockarbeiter; Schauermann**
fisherman ['fɪʃəmən] Pl. -men	**Fischer; Angler**
hunter / huntsman ['hʌntsmən]	**Jäger**
forest warden ['wɔ:dn] BE /	**Förster(in)**
AE **forest ranger** ['reɪndʒə]	
workman / tradesman ['treɪdzmən]	**Handwerker**
craftsman ['krɑːfts-] / **craftswoman**	**Kunsthandwerker(in)**

Traditionelle Handwerksberufe (deutsch jeweils auch weiblich)
baker (= Bäcker) • shoemaker (= Schuhmacher) • bricklayer (= Maurer) •
butcher ['bʊtʃə] (= Fleischer / Metzger) • cabinetmaker (= Kunst- / Möbeltischler) • carpenter (= Zimmermann / Bautischler) • chimney sweep
(= Schornsteinfeger) • clockmaker / watchmaker (= Uhrmacher) • joiner
(= Tischler / Schreiner) • decorator ['dekəreɪtə] (BE = Maler und Tapezierer) •
dressmaker (= Damenschneider) • tailor (= Herrenschneider) • plumber
['plʌmə] (= Klempner / Installateur)

accountant [ə'kaʊntənt] / **book-keeper**	**Buchhalter(in)**
chartered accountant BE / AE certified ['sɜ:tɪfaɪd] public accountant	Wirtschaftsprüfer(in)
teller / cashier [kæ'ʃɪə]	(Bank) **Kassierer(in)**

Consultant [kən'sʌltənt] **ist Berater(in) für ein spezielles Fachgebiet**
management consultant (= Unternehmensberater/in) • political consultant
(= politische/r Berater/in) • technical consultant (= technische/r Berater/in) •
pension scheme [ski:m] consultant (= Rentenberater/in)

shorthand typist [ʃɔ:thænd 'taɪpɪst]	**Stenotypistin**
secretary ['sekrətri]	**Sekretär(in)**
personal assistant [ə'sɪstənt] / **PA** *BE*	*(etwa)* **Chefsekretärin / Assistentin**
office management assistant	**Fachkauffrau / -kaufmann für Büromanagement**
girl / man Friday [gɜ:l 'fraɪdeɪ] *BE*	**„Mädchen für alles"** *(im Büro)*
telephonist [tə'lefənɪst] *BE / AE*	**Telefonist(in)**
switchboard operator	

Employee [ɪm'plɔɪi:] = **Angestellte(r) / Mitarbeiter(in)**
bank employee (= Bankangestellte/r) • *civil service employee* (= Angestellte/r im öffentlichen Dienst) • *a male employee* (= ein Mitarbeiter) • *a female employee* (= eine Mitarbeiterin) • *a former employee* (= ein früherer Mitarbeiter / eine frühere Mitarbeiterin)

shop assistant ['ʃɒp əsɪstənt] *BE*	**Verkäufer(in)** *(in Laden, Kaufhaus etc.)*
(street) **vendor** ['vendə]	(Straßen-)**Verkäufer(in)**
icecream vendor	Eisverkäufer(in)

Clerk **hat oft eine ähnliche Bedeutung wie** *employee*
bank clerk ['bæŋk klɑ:k] (= Bankangestellte/r) • *booking clerk* BE / AE *reservation and ticketing clerk* (= jemand, der Fahrkarten verkauft oder Reservierungen vornimmt) • *checkout clerk* (= Kassierer/in im Supermarkt) • *desk clerk* (AE = Dame / Herr an der Hotelrezeption) • *filing clerk* (= jemand, der in der Ablage / im Archiv arbeitet) • *office clerk* (= Büroangestellte/r) • *postal clerk* (= Schalterangestellte/r bei der Post) • *salesclerk* (AE = Verkäufer/in) • *supermarket clerk* (= Supermarktangestellte/r)

civil servant [sɪvl 'sɜ:vənt] / *AE auch* **government employee**	*(etwa)* **Beamter / Beamtin**
civil engineer [sɪvl endʒɪ'nɪə]	**Bauingenieur(in)**
inventor [ɪn'ventə]	**Erfinder(in)**
(aircraft) **designer** [dɪ'zaɪnə]	(Flugzeug-)**Konstrukteur(in)**
fashion designer	Modeschöpfer(in)
model ['mɒdl]	**Mannequin; Fotomodell**

Attendants [ə'tendənts] **sind Männer oder Frauen, die an öffentlichen Orten aufpassen oder Dienstleistungen erbringen**
swimming-pool attendant (= Bademeister/in) • *car-park attendant* BE / AE *parking attendant* (= Parkwächter/in) • *lavatory* ['lævətri] *attendant* (= Toilettenmann / -frau) • *museum* [mju'zɪəm] *attendant* (= Museumswärter/in)

housewife / *AE auch* **homemaker**	**Hausfrau**
househusband / *AE auch* homemaker	Hausmann
housekeeper ['haʊski:pə]	**Haushälterin; Wirtschafterin**
cleaner ['kli:nə]	**Raumpfleger(in); Reinigungskraft**
maid [meɪd]	**Dienstmädchen**
chambermaid ['tʃeɪmbəmeɪd]	Zimmermädchen *(im Hotel)*
chauffeur ['ʃəʊfə]	**Chauffeur(in)**
gardener ['gɑ:dnə]	**Gärtner(in)**

In the office
Im Büro

→ 18.5 The postal service, 18.6 Telephone and fax, 18.7 Computers

(Boss to department head:) How many people work in your office? –
(Department head:) About half of them, sir.
(*Gyles Brandreth, English author and broadcaster, born in 1948*)

office ['ɒfɪs]	Büro; (*Anwalt*) **Kanzlei**
open-plan office	Großraumbüro
office manager ['mænɪdʒə]	Bürovorsteher(in) / -leiter(in)
office hours ['aʊəz]	Dienst- / Arbeitsstunden
after office hours	nach Dienstschluss
office block *BE* / *AE* office building	Bürogebäude
superior [suˈpɪərɪə] / *AE auch* **super-visor** ['suːpəvaɪzə]	**Vorgesetzte(r)**
my **colleagues** ['kɒliːgz] / **coworkers**	meine **Kolleg(inn)en**
her **subordinates** [səˈbɔːdɪnəts]	ihre **Untergebenen** / **Mitarbeiter(innen)**
the **receptionist** [rɪˈsepʃənɪst]	die **Dame** / der **Herr am Empfang**
arrange an **appointment** [əˈpɔɪntmənt]	einen **Termin** vereinbaren
I've an appointment to see Mr Fox.	Ich habe einen Termin bei Herrn Fox.
A Mr Dole to **see** you.	Ein Herr Dole möchte Sie sprechen.
meet with someone (– met – met)	mit jemand **eine Unterredung haben**
hold a **meeting** (– held – held)	eine **Sitzung** / **Besprechung** abhalten
She's going to a meeting.	Sie ist auf dem Weg zu einer Besprechung.
She's still in **conference** ['kɒnfrəns].	Sie ist noch in einer **Besprechung.**
conference room	Konferenzzimmer
business card ['bɪznəs kɑːd]	**Visiten-** / **Geschäftskarte**
business lunch ['bɪznəs lʌntʃ]	**Arbeitsessen**
luncheon voucher ['lʌntʃən vaʊtʃə] *BE*	**Essen(s)marke**
desk [desk]	**Schreibtisch**
desk lamp	Schreibtischlampe
a desk job	eine Bürotätigkeit
draft [drɑːft] a letter	einen Brief **entwerfen**
a draft letter	ein Briefentwurf
type [taɪp] a letter	einen Brief (auf dem PC etc.) **schreiben** / **tippen**
a typed [taɪpt] letter	ein maschine(n)geschriebener Brief
Could you type this right away?	Könnten Sie dies direkt schreiben?
You don't need to type it out again.	Sie brauchen es nicht noch einmal zu schreiben.
How long will it take to type up / out the contract ['kɒntrækt]?	Wie lange wird es dauern, den Vertrag zu tippen?
You just need to type in your password.	Du brauchst nur dein Passwort einzutippen.

typing error ['erə] / typo ['taɪpəʊ]	Tippfehler
typing paper ['taɪpɪŋ peɪpə]	Schreibmaschinenpapier
typing pool ['taɪpɪŋ puːl]	Schreibzentrale; zentraler Schreib- dienst
typewriter ['taɪpraɪtə]	Schreibmaschine
dictate [dɪk'teɪt] letters to a secretary	einer Sekretärin Briefe **diktieren**
dictated by X and signed in his / her absence ['æbsəns]	nach Diktat verreist
dictating machine [dɪk'teɪtɪŋ məʃiːn]	Diktiergerät
take **dictation** (– took – taken)	ein **Diktat** aufnehmen
take something down in **shorthand**	etwas **stenografieren**
Get me the Smith **file**, please.	Bringen Sie mir bitte die **Akte** Smith.
These things can be filed (away).	Diese Sachen können in die Ablage.
photocopier / **Xerox™ machine**	Fotokopierer
photocopy / **xerox™** ['zɪərɒks]	Fotokopie; fotokopieren
I have some copying / xeroxing to do.	Ich muss noch einiges fotokopieren.
a xeroxed copy of the document	eine Fotokopie des Dokuments
copy paper ['kɒpi peɪpə]	Kopierpapier
take on extra work (– took – taken)	zusätzliche Arbeit **übernehmen**
I'm afraid I'm **busy** ['bɪzi] right now.	Im Moment bin ich leider **beschäftigt.**
(office) **stationery** ['steɪʃənri]	Büromaterial; (Firmen-)**Briefpapier**
paper clip ['peɪpə klɪp]	Büroklammer
clipboard ['klɪpbɔːd]	Klemmbrett; Manuskripthalter
staple ['steɪpl] – **stapler** ['steɪplə]	Heftklammer – Heftmaschine
staple papers together	Papiere zusammenheften
(hole) **punch** [pʌntʃ]	Locher
notepad ['nəʊtpæd] – **notebook**	Notizblock – Notizbuch
ring binder ['rɪŋ baɪndə]	Ringbuch
card index [kɑː 'ɪndeks]	Kartei
notice board *BE* / *AE* **bulletin board**	Anschlagtafel; schwarzes Brett
drawing pin *BE* / *AE* **thumbtack**	Reißzwecke; Reißnagel
write [raɪt] (– wrote – written)	schreiben
writing paper ['raɪtɪŋ peɪpə]	Schreibpapier, Briefpapier
pencil ['pensl]	Bleistift
pencil sharpener ['ʃɑːpnə]	Bleistift(an)spitzer
propelling *BE* / *AE* mechanical pencil	Drehbleistift; Druckbleistift
ballpoint (pen) / *BE auch* biro ['baɪrəʊ]	Kugelschreiber
refill ['riːfɪl]	(Kugelschreiber- / Bleistift-)**Mine**
felt tip (pen) / **felt pen** ['felt pen]	Filzstift; Filzschreiber
marker (pen) ['mɑːkə]	Markierstift
fountain pen ['faʊntən pen]	Füll(feder)halter; Füller
written in **ink** [ɪŋk]	mit **Tinte** geschrieben
(ink) **cartridge** ['kɑːtrɪdʒ]	(Tinten-)**Patrone**
rubber *BE* / *AE* **eraser** [ɪ'reɪzə]	Radiergummi
Sellotape™ *BE* / *AE* **Scotch tape™**	Tesafilm™; Klebefilm

Etwas mit Bleistift / Kugelschreiber / etc. schreiben ist *write something in pencil / ballpoint / etc. Pencilled notes* sind mit Bleistift geschriebene Notizen; *pencil something in* heißt etwas nicht endgültig notieren: *We can pencil it in for Monday.* (= Wir können es ja erst mal für Montag vormerken.)

Labour relations
Beziehungen zwischen den Tarifpartnern

→ 6.10 Social security, 7.2 Unemployment

It is one of the characteristics of a free and democratic modern nation that it have free and independent labor unions. (*Franklin D. Roosevelt, US president, 1882–1945*)

labour [ˈleɪbə]	**Arbeit; die Arbeiterschaft**
labour unrest [ʌnˈrest]	Unruhe in der Arbeit(nehm)erschaft
organized / unionized [ˈjuːniənaɪzd] labour	gewerkschaftlich organisierte Arbeitnehmer(innen)
the **work force** [ˈwɜːk fɔːs]	die **Belegschaft**
10% of the industry's [ˈɪndəstriz] work force	10% der in dem Industriezweig Beschäftigten

Labour relations bezeichnet die Beziehungen zwischen der Unternehmensleitung (= *management*) und den Mitarbeitern (= *employees* [ɪmˈplɔiːz]), zwischen Arbeitgebern (= *employers*) und Gewerkschaften (= *unions*):
The company was losing [ˈluːzɪŋ] *money, and labour relations were poor.*
(= Das Unternehmen machte Verlust und die Beziehungen zwischen Betriebsleitung und Belegschaft waren schlecht.)

trade union *BE* / *AE* **labor union**	**Gewerkschaft**
enrol *BE* / *AE* enroll in a union	in eine Gewerkschaft eintreten
belong to a union [ˈjuːniən]	einer Gewerkschaft angehören; gewerkschaftlich organisiert sein
union member [ˈjuːniən membə]	Gewerkschaftsmitglied
nonunion workers [ˈnɒnjuːniən wɜːkəz]	nicht gewerkschaftlich organisierte Arbeiter(innen)
the union leadership [ˈliːdəʃɪp]	die Gewerkschaftsführung
(trade *BE* / *AE* labor) **unionist**	**Gewerkschaft(l)er(in)**
federation of trade / labor unions	Gewerkschafts**bund**
TUC / **Trades Union Congress**	(britischer Gewerkschaftsbund)

Häufig in den Schlagzeilen (= *headlines*) der US-Presse war und ist die *Teamsters Union,* die mächtigste Einzelgewerkschaft der USA, die Lkw-Fahrer (= *teamsters*) und Arbeiter zahlreicher anderer Industrien repräsentiert. Korruption (= *corruption* [kəˈrʌpʃn]) und Verbindungen zu Verbrecherorganisationen (= *organized crime*) gehören bei dieser Gewerkschaft zur Tradition, und zahlreiche Funktionäre kamen ins Gefängnis (= *went to prison*), u.a. der berüchtigte (= *notorious*) James R. Hoffa, der die Gewerkschaft vom Gefängnis aus leitete und – nach vorzeitiger Freilassung 1971 unter Präsident Nixon – 1975 unter mysteriösen Umständen verschwand.

strike (– struck – struck)	**streiken**
striking workers	streikende Arbeiter(innen)
take strike action against a company	eine Firma bestreiken
The miners are on strike.	Die Bergarbeiter streiken.
The strike has paralysed ['pærəlaɪzd] public transport.	Der Streik hat den öffentlichen Nahverkehr lahm gelegt.
There's a strike on at this plant.	Dieser Betrieb wird bestreikt.
a strike-bound company ['kʌmpəni]	ein bestreiktes Unternehmen
a strike in the public sector ['sektə]	ein Streik im öffentlichen Dienst
an unofficial / wildcat strike	ein wilder Streik
a sympathy ['sɪmpəθi] strike	ein Sympathiestreik
stage warning ['wɔːnɪŋ] strikes	Warnstreiks organisieren / durchführen
call a (general ['dʒenrəl]) strike	einen (General-)Streik ausrufen
call off a strike	einen Streik abblasen / beenden
head off a strike	einen Streik abwenden
settle a strike	einen Streik beilegen
strikebreaker ['straɪkbreɪkə]	**Streikbrecher(in)**
the result of the **ballot** ['bælət]	das Ergebnis der **Urabstimmung**

Arbeitskämpfe sind allgemein *industrial disputes* [dɪ'spjuːts] oder *labour disputes.* Kommt es zum Streik, so heißt das im BE gern offiziell-beschönigend *industrial action: CLOSED DUE TO INDUSTRIAL ACTION* (= Wegen Streiks geschlossen.) Im AE gibt es den Euphemismus (= beschönigenden Ausdruck) *job action: a job action among 2,300 workers at a GM plant* (= ein Streik von 2300 Arbeitern in einem Werk von General Motors). In den Streik / Ausstand treten wird auch durch *walk out* ausgedrückt: *Thousands of workers have walked out* (= sind in den Streik / Ausstand getreten). *A fast-spreading walkout* (= ein schnell um sich greifender Streik). Wo (z.B. bei *public employees* = Beschäftigten im öffentlichen Dienst) Streiks verboten sind, hilft man sich mit einem *sickout*, d.h. einem organisierten Fernbleiben von der Arbeit.

work to rule [ruːl]	**Dienst nach Vorschrift (machen)**
a **go-slow** BE / AE **slowdown**	ein **Bummelstreik**
stop work / **down tools** [tuːlz]	die **Arbeit niederlegen**
disrupt [dɪs'rʌpt] holiday travel	den Urlaubsreiseverkehr **empfindlich stören**
lock out [lɒk 'aʊt] – **lockout** ['lɒkaʊt]	**aussperren – Aussperrung**
lock out thousands of workers	tausende von Arbeitern aussperren
the workers affected [ə'fektɪd] by the lockout	die von der Aussperrung betroffenen Arbeiter
showdown ['ʃaʊdaʊn]	**Auseinandersetzung; Kraftprobe**

Picketing nennt man das Aufstellen von Streikposten, *a picketer* ist ein Streikposten und *cross(ing) (the) picket line(s)* heißt, dass man sich als Streikbrecher betätigt.

minimum **wage** [mɪnɪməm 'weɪdʒ]	**Mindestlohn**
demand [dɪ'mɑːnd] wage increases	Lohnerhöhungen fordern
a higher hourly ['aʊəli] wage	ein höherer Stundenlohn
an increase in **piecework pay**	eine Erhöhung des **Akkordlohns**
fringe benefits ['frɪndʒ benɪfɪts]	zusätzlich (zu Lohn / Gehalt) gewährte Leistungen
bonus ['bəʊnəs]	**Bonus; Zulage; Prämie**
a Christmas ['krɪsməs] bonus	eine Weihnachtsgratifikation
a reduction in **working hours**	eine Verkürzung der **Arbeitszeit**
work **overtime** ['əʊvətaɪm]	**Überstunden** machen
overtime rates / pay	Überstundentarife / -lohn
paid holidays BE / AE **vacations**	**bezahlter Urlaub**
improved **working conditions**	verbesserte **Arbeitsbedingungen**
job security [sɪ'kjʊərəti]	**Sicherung des Arbeitsplatzes**
equal opportunity / -**ities**	**Chancengleichheit**
promotion [prə'məʊʃn]	**Beförderung**
employment contract ['kɒntrækt]	**Arbeits- / Dienstvertrag**
violate ['vaɪəleɪt] rights	Rechte **verletzen**
industrial tribunal [traɪ'bjuːnl] BE	(etwa) **Arbeitsgericht**
workers' **grievances** ['griːvnsɪz]	**Beschwerden / Klagen** der Arbeiter
a **grievance procedure** [prə'siːdʒə]	ein **Schlichtungsverfahren**

Kollektive Tarifverhandlungen zwischen Arbeitgeber- und Gewerkschafts-seite nennt man generell *collective bargaining*; im konkreten Einzelfall spricht man auch von *pay / wage negotiations* / AE auch *labor negotiations*. Dem deutschen Tarifvertrag entsprechen Bezeichnungen wie *collective bargaining agreement* oder *pay / wage* / AE auch *labor agreement*.

negotiate [nɪ'gəʊʃieɪt] / **bargain** ['bɑːgən] with the unions	mit den Gewerkschaften **verhandeln**
negotiate a pay agreement [ə'griːmənt]	einen Tarifvertrag aushandeln
their negotiators [nɪ'gəʊʃieɪtəz]	ihre Verhandlungsführer
mediate ['miːdieɪt] (in) a dispute	in einem Streit **vermitteln**
mediator ['miːdieɪtə]	Vermittler(in); Schlichter(in)
arbitrate ['ɑːbɪtreɪt] – **arbitrator**	**schlichten** – **Schlichter(in)**
arbitration [ɑːbɪ'treɪʃn]	Schlichtung
settle a dispute [dɪ'spjuːt]	einen Streit **beilegen**
pay / wage settlement ['setlmənt]	Tarifabschluss
return [rɪ'tɜːn] to / **go back** to work	die Arbeit **wieder aufnehmen**
layoffs ['leɪɒfs]	(vorübergehende) **Entlassungen**
short-time work	**Kurzarbeit**
They're on short time [ʃɔːt 'taɪm].	Sie machen Kurzarbeit.

Das „Freisetzen", also Entlassen von Arbeitskräften (= *workers*) wird gern beschönigend umschrieben durch Ausdrucksweisen wie *making redundant* [rɪ'dʌndənt] (*She's been made redundant.*) oder *downsizing* ['daʊnsaizɪŋ] (= Verschlanken). Direkter wären: *dismiss* [dɪs'mɪs] (= entlassen), *fire* (= feuern), *sack* (= rausschmeißen), *give someone notice* ['nəʊtɪs] (= jemand kündigen). – *Lay off* hieß ursprünglich „vorübergehend entlassen", meint aber heute in der Regel das endgültige Aus. (Vgl. S. 126–127.)

Anhang

- **Englische Kurzgrammatik**

- **ABC der Sprachgebrauchsprobleme**

- **Register Englisch**

- **Register Deutsch**

Englische Kurzgrammatik

Geometry is to sculpture what grammar is to the art of the writer.
(*Guillaume Apollinaire, French poet, 1880–1918*)

Nomen: Pluralbildung

Durch Anhängen von -s = [z]:	cars dogs	Autos Hunde	balls paths	Bälle Pfade
Durch Anhängen von -s = [s]:	streets roofs	Straßen Dächer	books months	Bücher Monate
Nach Zischlauten: -es = [ɪz]:	buses boxes	Busse Kästen	churches pages	Kirchen Seiten
-f(e) wird oft zu -ves:	leaf wife wolf	leaves wives wolves	Blatt Ehefrau Wolf	Blätter Ehefrauen Wölfe
-y wird nach Konsonant zu -ies:	baby copy	babies copies	Baby Kopie	Babys Kopien
	Nicht aber bei Namen: Kennedy – the Kennedys			
Unregelmäßig:	man [mæn] woman ['wʊmən] foot [fʊt] goose [guːs] tooth [tuːθ] mouse [maʊs] child [tʃaɪld] crisis ['kraɪsɪs]	**men** [men] **women** ['wɪmɪn] **feet** [fiːt] **geese** [giːs] **teeth** [tiːθ] **mice** [maɪs] **children** ['tʃɪldrən] **crises** ['kraɪsiːz]	Mann Frau Fuß Gans Zahn Maus Kind Krise	Männer Frauen Füße Gänse Zähne Mäuse Kinder Krisen
Pluralform identisch mit Singularform:	aircraft crossroads	Flugzeug/e Kreuzung/en	series sheep	Serie/n Schaf/e

Nomen: Singular oder Plural

Stets **Singular**:	this information **is** the furniture **is** her knowledge **is** this news **comes** the United States **is** the Netherlands **is** the United Nations **is**	diese Informationen **sind** die Möbel **sind** ihre Kenntnisse **sind** diese Nachrichten **kommen** die Vereinigten Staaten **sind** die Niederlande **sind** die Vereinten Nationen **sind**

Stets **Plural**:	the police **are**	die Polizei **ist**
	these trousers / pants / shorts **are**	diese Hose **ist**
	my glasses **are**	meine Brille **ist**
	my pyjamas **are**	mein Schlafanzug **ist**
	his ashes **are**	seine Asche **ist**
	the contents **are**	der Inhalt **ist**
	these stairs **are**	diese Treppe **ist**

Genus: Besonderheiten

Je nachdem, ob das **Geschlecht bekannt oder unbekannt** ist:	The **baby** has lost **his/her/its** rattle.	Das Baby hat **seine** Klapper verloren.
Personifizierung (he/she) oder Nichtpersonifizierung (it) von **Tieren**:	The **cat** scratches but the old lady loves **her / him / it**.	Die Katze kratzt, aber die alte Dame liebt **sie**.
Sachen heute nur noch selten personifiziert:	The **Titanic** sank on **its/ her** maiden voyage.	Die Titanic sank auf **ihrer** Jungfernfahrt.
Bezug auf **geschlechtsneutrale Pronomen**:	**Everyone** did **their** job.	Jeder machte **seine** Arbeit.
	Someone has lost **their** key.	Jemand hat **seinen** Schlüssel verloren.
	No one wants to revenge **themselves**.	Niemand will **sich** rächen.

Genitiv

Unterschied zwischen **Singular (-'s)** und **Plural (-s')** beachten:	the **boy's** room	das Zimmer des Jungen
	the **boys'** room	das Zimmer der Jungen
Bei **nicht** auf -s endendem **Plural** dagegen stets -'s:	the **child's** room	das Zimmer des Kindes
	the **children's** room	das Zimmer der Kinder
Namen auf -s haben im Genitiv -'s oder -s':	Mrs **Collins's/Collins'** house	Frau Collins' Haus
	Aussprache in beiden Fällen meist: [ˈkɒlɪnzɪz]	

Apostroph stets am **letzten** **Element**:	the Duke of **Kent's** car	der Wagen des Herzogs von Kent
	my parents-in-**law's** house	das Haus meiner Schwiegereltern
	someone **else's** umbrella	der Schirm von jemand anderem
Genitiv häufig mit **of**-Konstruktion austauschbar:	the **boss's** daughter = the daughter **of the boss**	
	the **book's** success = the success **of the book**	
	Die Wahl erfolgt aufgrund von Wohlklang oder beabsichtigter Betonung:	
	Betonung auf name:	the **woman's** name
	Betonung auf woman:	the name **of the woman**
	Genitiv unmöglich:	the name **of the woman** in the red dress
Alleinstehender Genitiv:	Your plan is better than **Tim's**.	Dein Plan ist besser als der von Tim.
	We met at **Sarah's**.	Wir trafen uns bei Sarah.
	It's near **St Paul's**.	Es ist in der Nähe des St.-Pauls-Doms.
	Genitiv und endungslose Form gleich richtig:	
	They're friends of **Bill('s)**.	Sie sind Freunde von Bill.
	I'm a patient of **Dr Brown('s)**.	Ich bin eine Patientin von Herrn Dr. Brown.
Genitiv in **Zeitangaben**:	It's ten **minutes'** walk.	Es sind zehn Minuten zu Fuß.
	It's an **hour's** drive.	Es ist eine einstündige Fahrt.
	Aber auch: It's **a ten-minute** walk.	
	It's **a one-hour** drive.	

Bestimmter Artikel (*the*)

Aussprache [ðə] vor gesprochenem **Konsonant**:	the [ðə] book	the [ðə] USA
	the [ðə] hotel	the [ðə] one-eyed man
Aussprache [ðɪ] vor gesprochenem **Vokal**:	the [ðɪ] answer	the [ðɪ] honour
	the [ðɪ] egg	the [ðɪ] MP
Verwendung des Artikels **seltener** als im Deutschen, d. h. nur bei **besonderer Spezifizierung**:	She's not afraid of **death**.	Sie hat keine Angst vor dem Tod.
	The death of her dog upset her.	Der Tod ihres Hundes erschütterte sie.

Institutionen, Weltanschau-ungen etc. meist **ohne** the, außer bei **besonderer Spezifizierung**:	parliament	das Parlament
	congress	der Kongress
	socialism	der Sozialismus
	democracy	die Demokratie
	religion	die Religion
	freedom	die Freiheit
	Aber:	
	the European Parliament	das Europäische Parlament
	the US Congress	der amerikanische Kongress
	the socialism of the future	der Sozialismus der Zukunft
	the democracy they wanted	die Demokratie, die sie sich wünschten
	the Christian religion	die christliche Religion
	the freedom of the press	die Freiheit der Presse
Ländernamen stehen ohne the:	in Switzerland	in der Schweiz
	in Turkey	in der Türkei
	invade Iraq	in den Irak einmarschieren
	greetings from sunny Italy	Grüße aus dem sonnigen Italien
	Ausnahmen mit the: the United States, the Netherlands, the Czech [tʃek] Republic	
Wochentage, Monatsnamen, Jahreszeiten und night **ohne** the, außer bei Spezifizierung:	on **Monday**	on **the Monday** following the concert
	Spring is a wonderful time.	**The spring** of that year was extremely warm.
	at **night**	abends/nachts
	on **the night** of May 6	am Abend des 6. Mai
Fügungen ohne the:	go by car/train	mit dem Auto/Zug fahren
	the kids at/in school	die Kinder in der Schule
	go to kindergarten/school	in den Kindergarten / in die Schule gehen
	She's at church / in prison.	Sie ist in der Kirche / im Gefängnis.
	Most people know about it.	Die meisten Leute wissen davon.
	at first sight	auf den ersten Blick
	out of practice	aus der Übung
	lose interest	das Interesse verlieren

GR

The vor Komparativen:	the sooner, the better	je eher, desto besser
	The more you practise, the better you play.	Je mehr man übt, desto besser spielt man.
	That makes it all the harder.	Das macht es umso schwieriger.

Stellung von the bei all, most, half, twice, double, quite:	shut all the windows	die Fenster alle schließen
	most of the time	den größten Teil der Zeit
	half the children	die Hälfte der Kinder
	at twice/double the speed	mit zweifacher/doppelter Geschwindigkeit
	quite the wrong thing	genau das Falsche

Unbestimmter Artikel (*a/an*)

A vor gesprochenem Konsonant, an vor gesprochenem Vokal:	a number	eine Zahl
	a woman	eine Frau
	a one-way street	eine Einbahnstraße
	a US soldier	ein US-Soldat
	Aber: an honest man	ein ehrlicher Mann

Gebrauch von a(n) bei nicht einmaligen Berufen, Funktionen etc.:	She's an architect.	Sie ist Architektin.
	He's a US citizen.	Er ist amerikanischer Staatsbürger.
	He's a Roman Catholic.	Er ist Katholik.

Bei einmaligen Funktionen jedoch ohne a(n):	He was elected mayor in 2002.	Er wurde 2002 zum Bürgermeister gewählt.
	As president you don't have many friends.	Als Präsident hat man nicht viele Freunde.

A(n) bei hundred/thousand etc. und in der Bedeutung „pro":	a hundred years	hundert Jahre
	about a thousand visitors	etwa tausend Besucher
	a hundred thousand	hunderttausend
	50 miles an hour	50 Meilen in der Stunde
	once a week	einmal in der Woche

Nicht zählbare Begriffe ohne a(n):	It's good advice.	Es ist ein guter Rat.
	That's interesting information.	Das ist eine interessante Information
	She brought good news.	Sie brachte eine gute Nachricht.
	It pays to take out insurance.	Es lohnt sich, eine Versicherung abzuschließen.

Anders als im Deutschen mit Artikel:	have **a** birthday	Geburtstag haben
	have **a** fever	Fieber haben
	have **a** headache	Kopfschmerzen haben
	come to **an** end	zu Ende gehen
	be in **a** hurry	in Eile sein
	in **a** loud voice	mit lauter Stimme
	without **a** break	ohne Unterbrechung
	for **a** change	zur Abwechslung
Besonderheiten der Stellung von **a(n)**:	That's **rather a** lot.	Das ist ziemlich viel.
	It was **quite an** achievement.	Es war eine ziemliche Leistung.
	She's **such a** nice girl.	Sie ist so ein nettes Mädchen.
	What a fool I was!	Was für ein Idiot ich doch war!

Personalpronomen

	Subjektform	Objektform
Singular	I — ich you — du/Sie he — er she — sie it — es/er/sie	me — mich/mir you — dich/Sie/dir/Ihnen him — ihn/ihm her — sie/ihr it — es/ihn/sie/ihm/ihr
Plural	we — wir you — ihr/Sie they — sie	us — uns you — euch/Sie/Ihnen them — sie/ihnen
One (= man) als neutrale Form des Personalpronomens:	That's something **one** often hears. **One** must have a style of **one's** own. **One** must learn to control **oneself**.	So etwas hört man oft. Man muss einen eigenen Stil haben. Man muss lernen, sich zu beherrschen.
Besonderer Gebrauch der Objektform:	It's **me**. "Who said that?" – "**Me**." if I were **him** He's younger than **her**.	Ich bin's. „Wer hat das gesagt?" – „Ich." wenn ich er wäre Er ist jünger als sie.

It als bedeutungsleeres Strukturwort:	Who is **it**?	Wer ist da?
	if **it** hadn't been for you	wenn du nicht gewesen wärest
	The car has had **it**.	Das Auto ist im Eimer.
	The old man is still very much with **it**.	Der Alte ist immer noch schwer auf Zack.
Entsprechungen für dt. „sie":	I don't know who **you** mean.	Ich weiß nicht, wen **Sie** meinen.
	I mean **you**, not your sister.	Ich meine **Sie**, nicht Ihre Schwester.
	She loves him and he loves **her**.	**Sie** liebt ihn und er liebt **sie**.
	It (the turkey) tasted awful.	**Sie** (die Pute) schmeckte furchtbar.
	He pulled a gun and aimed **it** at me.	Er zog eine Pistole heraus und richtete **sie** auf mich.
	They lost their jobs.	**Sie** verloren ihren Arbeitsplatz.
	She picked some berries and ate **them**.	**Sie** pflückte einige Beeren ab und aß **sie**.

Pronomen auf *-self/-selves*

Rückbezüglicher Gebrauch:	I consider **myself** an expert.	Ich betrachte **mich** als Experten.
	Make **yourself** comfortable.	Machen Sie es **sich** bequem.
	He introduced **himself**.	Er stellte **sich** vor.
	She regards **herself** as an innocent victim.	Sie sieht **sich** als unschuldiges Opfer.
	The baby might hurt **itself**.	Das Baby könnte **sich** wehtun.
	We have to protect **ourselves**.	Wir müssen **uns** schützen.
	Enjoy **yourselves**.	Amüsiert **euch** schön.
	They call **themselves** idealists.	Sie nennen **sich** Idealisten.
Wichtiger Unterschied:	They love **themselves**.	Sie lieben sich (d. h. sich selbst).
	They love **each other** / **one another**.	Sie lieben sich (d. h. einander).

Betonender Gebrauch:	I spoke to the president **myself**.	Ich sprach **selbst** mit dem Präsidenten.
	I spoke to the president **himself**.	Ich sprach mit dem Präsidenten **selbst**.
	She ate the chocolate **herself**.	Sie aß die Schokolade **selbst**.
	She **herself** ate the chocolate.	Sie **selbst** aß die Schokolade.
	You **yourself** are not to blame.	Dich **selbst** trifft keine Schuld.
	He has a dog nearly as big as **himself**.	Er hat einen Hund, der fast so groß wie **er selbst** ist.

Possessivpronomen

Begleitende (d.h. vor einem Nomen stehende) **Possessivpronomen:**	Singular	**my** work	meine Arbeit
		your work	deine/Ihre Arbeit
		his work	seine Arbeit
		her work	ihre Arbeit
		its work	seine/ihre Arbeit
	Plural	**our** work	unsere Arbeit
		your work	eure/Ihre Arbeit
		their work	ihre Arbeit
	Neutrale Form	One must do **one's** work.	Man muss seine Arbeit machen.
Vom Deutschen abweichender Gebrauch bei Körperteilen, Kleidungsstücken etc.:	She opened **her** eyes.		Sie öffnete **die** Augen.
	He had **his** hands in **his** pockets.		Er hatte **die** Hände in **den** Taschen.
	She saved **his** life.		Sie rettete ihm **das** Leben.
Allein stehende Possessivpronomen:	His room is below **mine**.		Sein Zimmer ist unter meinem.
	She's a friend of **mine**.		Sie ist eine Freundin von mir.
	The choice is **yours**.		Die Wahl liegt bei dir/Ihnen/euch.
	The decision is **his/hers**.		Die Entscheidung liegt bei ihm/ihr.
	It's a speciality of **ours**.		Es ist eine Spezialität von uns.
	The house is still **theirs**.		Das Haus gehört immer noch ihnen.
	Theirs is a difficult relationship.		Ihre ist eine schwierige Beziehung.

Fragepronomen

Who fragt nach **Personen**.	**Who**'s that woman?	Wer ist die Frau da?
	I don't know **who** she is.	Ich weiß nicht, wer sie ist.
	Who do you mean?	Wen meinen Sie?
	I don't know **who** you mean.	Ich weiß nicht, wen Sie meinen.
	Who's the parcel for?	Für wen ist das Paket?
	I don't know **who** the parcel is for.	Ich weiß nicht, für wen das Paket ist.
Whose fragt nach dem **Besitzer**.	**Whose** are these gloves?	Wem gehören diese Handschuhe?
	Whose fault is it?	Wessen Schuld ist es?
What fragt aus einer **nicht näher bezeichneten Menge**.	**What** happened then?	Was passierte dann?
	What do you do?	Was machen Sie beruflich?
	What does she look like?	Wie sieht sie aus?
	What size are you?	Welche Größe haben Sie?
Which wählt aus einer **genannten oder gedachten Menge** aus.	**Which** diet is the best?	Welche Diät ist die beste?
	Which of them is the best?	Welche von ihnen ist die beste?
	Which is the best diet?	Welches ist die beste Diät?

Relativpronomen und Relativsätze

Who steht als Relativpronomen mit Bezug auf **Personen(gruppen)** und personifizierte Tiere.	I have an uncle **who is a lawyer**.	Ich habe einen Onkel, der Anwalt ist.
	the dog **who loved too much**	der Hund, der zu sehr liebte
Das Relativpronomen **whom** ist als **Objektform** von who fast nur in der **Schriftsprache** gebräuchlich.	She married a man **(who[m]) she didn't love**.	Sie heiratete einen Mann, den sie nicht liebte.
	They had six children, two of **whom** died in infancy.	Sie hatten sechs Kinder, von denen zwei im frühen Kindesalter starben.
Whose steht als Relativpronomen mit Bezug auf **Personen** oder **Sachen**.	children **whose parents are dead**	Kinder, deren Eltern tot sind
	a car **whose engine runs fine**	ein Auto, dessen Motor gut läuft

Which steht als Relativpronomen mit Bezug auf **Nicht-Personen** und nicht personifizierte Tiere.	ideas **which look good on paper** the dogs **which roam the streets**	Ideen, die auf dem Papier gut aussehen die Hunde, die in den Straßen herumstreunen
Which kann sich auch auf **Sätze** beziehen.	He has money, **which is a good thing**.	Er hat Geld, was ein Vorteil ist.
That steht als Relativpronomen mit Bezug auf **Sachen** und – seltener – **Personen**.	the plane **that takes off at 9.30** companies **that offer this service** the dearest friend **(that) I have ever had**	die Maschine, die um 9.30 Uhr abfliegt Firmen, die diesen Service anbieten der liebste Freund, den ich je hatte
Ein in **Objektposition** stehendes Relativpronomen wird in **bestimmenden Relativsätzen** häufig **weggelassen**.	the books (which) **he wanted to buy** a person (whom/that) **you can trust**	die Bücher, die er kaufen wollte ein Mensch, dem man trauen kann

Demonstrativpronomen

This (Plural: **these**) weist auf **näher Liegendes**, **that** (Plural: **those**) auf **ferner Liegendes**.	**this** boy here **that** boy over there **These** are my socks. **Those** were the days.	dieser Junge hier dieser Junge da drüben Dies sind meine Socken. Das waren noch Zeiten.
This und **that** werden auch **adverbial** gebraucht.	It's about **this** thick. He isn't **that** good.	Es ist ungefähr so dick. So gut ist er nun auch wieder nicht.

Indefinite Pronomen

Some steht in **bejahten Aussagesätzen**.	I've got **some** photos.	Ich habe einige Fotos.
Some steht auch in **Fragesätzen**, auf die man eine **bejahende Antwort** erwartet oder die als **Einladung** gemeint sind.	Can I have **some** salt, please? Would you like **some- thing** to drink?	Kann ich bitte etwas Salz haben? Möchtest du was zu trinken?

Any steht in **echten Fragesätzen** und **verneinten Aussagesätzen** sowie häufig in **if**-Sätzen.	Is there **any** news? I don't know **any- body** round here. if you have **any** doubts	Gibt es Neues? Ich kenne hier niemand. falls Sie Zweifel haben
In **bejahten Aussagesätzen** be- deutet any „jede(r/s) x-beliebige".	**Any** child knows that.	Das weiß doch jedes Kind.
Every bedeutet „jede(r/s) allgemein", **each** dagegen „jede(r/s) aus einer beschränkten Anzahl".	**Every** child needs love. **Each** child in the group gets a card.	Jedes Kind braucht Liebe. Jedes Kind in der Gruppe erhält eine Karte.

Steigerung und Vergleich

Kürzere Adjektive werden mit **-(e)r / -(e)st** gesteigert.	cheap – cheap**er** – cheap**est** fine – fin**er** – fin**est** early – earl**ier** – earl**iest**	billig – billiger – billigste fein – feiner – feinste früh – früher – frühste
Längere Adjektive werden mit **more/most** gesteigert.	modern – **more** modern – **most** modern attractive – **more** attrac- tive – **most** attractive	modern – moderner – modernste attraktiv – attraktiver – attraktivste
Beachten Sie den Unterschied:	**the most** convincing answer **a most** convincing answer	die überzeugendste Antwort eine höchst überzeu- gende Antwort
Unregelmäßige Steigerung:	bad – worse – worst good – better – best little – less – least much/many – more – most	schlimm – schlimmer – schlimmste gut – besser – beste wenig – weniger – wenigste viel/viele – mehr – meiste
Typische **Vergleichs- konstruktionen:**	cold**er than** **less** cold **than** **(not) as** cold **as** **the** cold**est** night **of** the year	kälter als weniger kalt als (nicht) so kalt wie die kälteste Nacht des Jahres

Stützwort *one*

Will man ein zählbares Nomen nicht wiederholen, so ersetzt man es durch das Stützwort **one** (im Plural: **ones**).	The last exercise was easy but this is a hard **one**. Secondhand cars are cheaper than new **ones**.	Die letzte Übung war leicht, aber dies ist eine schwierige. Gebrauchtwagen sind billiger als neue.

Mit *-ly* abgeleitete Adverbien

Adjektive werden durch Anhängen von **-ly** zu **Adverbien**.	slow – slow**ly** surprising – surprising**ly**	langsam – langsam überraschend – überraschend(erweise)
Die -ly-Form steht, wenn das Wort sich nicht auf ein (Pro-) Nomen bezieht, sondern auf ein Verb, Adjektiv, Adverb oder einen (Teil-)Satz.	He's a **slow** worker. He works **slowly**. It's **unpleasant**. It's **unpleasantly** hot. Time passed **extremely slowly**.	Er ist ein langsamer Arbeiter. Er arbeitet langsam. Es ist unangenehm. Es ist unangenehm heiß. Die Zeit verging äußerst langsam.
Das Adverb zu **good** ist **well**.	She did a **good** job. She did it very **well**.	Sie hat gute Arbeit geleistet. Sie hat es sehr gut gemacht.
Hardly hat eine von **hard** abweichende Bedeutung.	He works **hard**. I **hardly** know her.	Er arbeitet schwer. Ich kenne sie kaum.

Verb: *Simple Present Tense*

Die -**s**-Form des Verbs steht nach **he/she/it** oder einem Wort, das durch he/she/it ersetzt werden kann.	He/She **knows** about it. The solution **satisfies** both parties. He **has** an ulcer. **Does** she live here?	Er/Sie weiß davon. Die Lösung befriedigt beide Parteien. Er hat ein Magengeschwür. Wohnt sie hier?
Alle anderen Formen sind identisch mit dem **Infinitiv**.	I/you/we/they **know** about it.	Ich weiß davon. / Sie/ wir/sie wissen davon.

Verb: *Simple Past Tense*

Die Vergangenheitsform wird bei **regelmäßigen Verben** durch Anhängen von **-(e)d** gebildet. (Zur Vergangenheitsform der **unregelmäßigen Verben** → S. 336–337)	play play**ed** ask ask**ed** act act**ed** guide guid**ed** hurry hurr**ied** stop stop**ped** travel travel**(l)ed**	[pleɪd] [ɑːskt] [ˈæktɪd] [ˈgaɪdɪd] [ˈhʌrɪd] [stɒpt] [ˈtrævəld]
Besteht eine ausdrückliche oder gedachte Zuordnung zu einem Zeitpunkt oder Zeitraum der Vergangenheit („**Datierung**"), so muss das **Past Tense** (statt des im Deutschen oft möglichen Perfekts) stehen.	He **arrived** yester- day. When **did** you send it off? **Did** Brahms also write an opera?	Er ist gestern ange-kommen. Wann hast du es abgeschickt? Hat Brahms auch eine Oper geschrieben?

Verb: *Simple Present Perfect*

Das Simple Present Perfect wird aus **have/ has (!)** + **-ed**-Partizip (→ S. 334) gebildet.	I **have seen** the new model. They **have disappeared**.	Ich habe das neue Modell gesehen. Sie sind verschwunden.
Gebrauch für **abgeschlossene Handlungen**:	I **have shut** all the windows. She **has published** a new book.	Ich habe alle Fenster zugemacht. Sie hat ein neues Buch herausgebracht.
Bei „Datierung" hingegen steht das **Past Tense**	She **published** a new book last year.	Sie hat voriges Jahr ein neues Buch heraus-gebracht.
Gebrauch für **in die Gegenwart reichende Hand-lungen**:	We **have been** married (for) six years. We **have lived** here since 1995.	Wir sind sechs Jahre verheiratet. Wir wohnen seit 1995 hier.
„seit" = **since** mit Bezug auf **Zeitpunkt**:	**since** two o'clock	seit zwei Uhr
„seit" = **for** mit Bezug auf **Zeitraum**:	**for** two hours	seit zwei Stunden

Verb: *Simple Past Perfect*

Das Simple Past Perfect wird aus **had (!)** + **-ed**-Partizip (→ S. 334) gebildet.	I **had borrowed** it.	Ich hatte es mir geliehen.
	She **had** already **left**.	Sie war bereits abgereist.
	I wish you **hadn't done** that.	Ich wünschte, du hättest das nicht getan.

Verb: Verlaufsform

Bildung der Verlaufsform / Progressive Form aus einer Form von **be** + **-ing**-Partizip:	He **is sleeping**.	Er schläft (gerade).
	It **was raining**.	Es regnete (gerade).
	Look, it **has been snowing**.	Schau mal, es hat geschneit.
	They **had been waiting** for hours.	Sie hatten (bereits) stundenlang gewartet.
	This possibility **is being** discussed.	Diese Möglichkeit wird (zurzeit) diskutiert.
Durch den Gebrauch der **Verlaufsform** betont man den **Verlauf einer Handlung** zu einem bestimmten Zeitpunkt bzw. innerhalb eines bestimmten Zeitraums, während die **einfache Form** zum Ausdruck von **Tatsachenfeststellungen** und sich **wiederholenden Vorgängen** dient.	What **are** you **reading?**	Was liest du gerade?
	I often **read** poetry.	Ich lese oft Lyrik.
	Is she still **working** for Scott & Trimble?	Arbeitet sie immer noch bei Scott & Trimble?
	She **works** for a car rental firm.	Sie arbeitet bei einer Mietwagenfirma.
	Were you **dreaming?**	Hast du geträumt?
	Did you **dream** that?	Hast du das geträumt?
	How long **have** you **been waiting?**	Wie lange **wartest** du schon?
	Why **have** you **waited** so long?	Warum hast du so lange gewartet?

Verb: Futur

Im Englischen lässt sich die Zukünftigkeit von Handlungen oder Ereignissen auf unterschiedliche Weise ausdrücken:

Durch **will** / **'ll** („neutrale" Zukunft):	The boy **will be** five next February.	Der Junge wird nächsten Februar fünf.
	When **will** I **see** you again?	Wann sehe ich dich wieder?
	I'm sure we**'ll meet** again.	Ich bin sicher, dass wir uns wiedersehen.

Durch **be going to** (Betonung von **Absicht** oder **Gewissheit**):	I'm not **going to argue** with you. We**'re going to be** very busy.	Ich will mich nicht mit dir streiten. Wir werden sehr viel zu tun haben.
Durch die **Verlaufsform**, meist mit Zeitbestimmung der Zukunft (betont, dass etwas **geplant** ist):	They**'re getting married** in May. What **are** you **doing** on Sunday?	Sie heiraten im Mai. Was macht ihr am Sonntag?
Durch **will + be + -ing** (für **fest vorgesehene Handlungen, höfliche Fragen** nach jemandes Plänen und für Handlungen, die zu einem bestimmten Zukunftszeitpunkt **gerade ablaufen** werden):	We**'ll be staying** at the King's Hotel. What time **will** you **be arriving**, sir? At this time tomorrow we'**ll be sunbathing** in Florida.	Wir werden im King's Hotel wohnen Um welche Zeit werden Sie ankommen? Morgen um diese Zeit werden wir in Florida sonnenbaden.
Durch das **Simple Present Tense** (für „**fahrplanmäßig**" festgesetzte Zukunftshandlungen):	The show **begins** at eight. He **retires** next year.	Die Vorstellung beginnt um acht. Er geht nächstes Jahr in Rente.

Bedingungssätze

Grundtyp 1 (if-Satz Present Tense, Hauptsatz will + Infinitiv):	If we **get** tickets, we **will go**.	Wenn wir Karten bekommen, werden wir gehen.
Grundtyp 2 (if-Satz Past Tense, Hauptsatz would + Infinitiv):	If we **got** tickets, we **would go**.	Wenn wir Karten bekämen, würden wir gehen.
Grundtyp 3 (if-Satz Past Perfect, Hauptsatz would have + -ed-Partizip):	If we **had got(ten)** tickets, we **would have gone**.	Wenn wir Karten bekommen hätten, wären wir gegangen.
Übliche Kurzformen:	If we get tickets, we'll go. If we got tickets, we'd go. If we'd got(ten) tickets, we would've gone.	

Indirekte Rede und Frage

Steht das **Berichtsverb** (said, asked etc.) in der **Vergangenheit**, so **rückt** das Verb in der indirekten Rede bzw. Frage gegenüber der direkten um eine Zeitstufe **in die Vergangenheit**.	"I **like** him." She said (that) she **liked** him.	Sie sagte, dass er ihr gefiele.
	"I**'m** married." He told her (that) he **was** married.	Er sagte ihr, dass er verheiratet sei.
	"**Will** you come?" He asked if I **would** come.	Er fragte, ob ich kommen würde.
Indirekte Aufforderung:	"Hurry up!" She told him to hurry up.	Sie sagte ihm, er solle sich beeilen.
	"Please don't go away." She asked him not to go away.	Sie bat ihn, nicht wegzugehen.

Verb: Passiv

Das Passiv wird aus einer Form von **be + -ed-Partizip** (→ S. 334) gebildet. Der im Aktiv genannte Verursacher der Handlung (Subjekt) wird im Passiv gelegentlich mit **by** angeschlossen.	Our teachers **recommend** the book. The book **is recommended** by our teachers.	Unsere Lehrern empfehlen das Buch. Das Buch wird von unseren Lehrern empfohlen.
	Someone **has stolen** my bike. My bike **has been stolen**.	Man hat mir mein Fahrrad gestohlen. Mein Fahrrad ist gestohlen (worden).
	We **can solve** that problem. That problem **can be solved**.	Wir können dieses Problem lösen. Das Problem kann gelöst werden.
	The FBI **is investigating** the case. The case **is being investigated** (by the FBI).	Der/Das FBI untersucht den Fall. Der Fall wird (zurzeit) (vom FBI) untersucht.
Passiver Infinitiv:	That was **to be expected**. That remains **to be seen**.	Das war zu erwarten. Das bleibt abzuwarten.

Englische Kurzgrammatik 333

Verb: *-ing*-Form

Gebrauch als **Subjekt, Prädikativum, Objekt:**	**Reading** broadens the mind. My favourite pastime is **reading**. I prefer **reading** to **watching** TV.	Lesen erweitert den Horizont. Meine Lieblingsbeschäftigung ist Lesen. Ich ziehe (das) Lesen dem Fernsehen vor.
Gebrauch **nach Präpositionen:**	I'm looking forward to **seeing** you. He insisted on **paying** the bill.	Ich freue mich darauf, dich zu sehen. Er bestand darauf, die Rechnung zu bezahlen.
Gebrauch nach **Kettenverben, Kettennomen** etc.:	I enjoy **reading**. It's no use **hoping** for better times. I had difficulty **understanding** him. She's busy **packing** her bags.	Ich lese gern. Es hat keinen Zweck, auf bessere Zeiten zu hoffen. Ich hatte Schwierigkeiten, ihn zu verstehen. Sie ist damit beschäftigt, ihre Koffer zu packen.
Gebrauch **mit eigenem Sinnsubjekt:**	I can't imagine her **doing** that. I'm sorry I kept you **waiting**.	Ich kann mir nicht vorstellen, dass sie das tut. Es tut mir Leid, dass ich Sie habe warten lassen.
Gebrauch zur **Satzverkürzung:**	Who's the man **standing** next to the president? He was shot while **walking** his dog.	Wer ist der Mann, der neben dem Präsidenten steht? Er wurde erschossen, als er mit seinem Hund spazieren ging.

Verb: *-ed*-Partizip

Das -ed-Partizip wird bei regelmäßigen Verben wie das Simple Past (→ S. 330) gebildet.
Zur Form des -ed-Partizips bei unregelmäßigen Verben → S. 336–337.

Typische Fügungen mit dem -ed-Partizip:	an **escaped** prisoner She had the letter **translated**. I want this blouse **dry-cleaned**.	ein entflohener Gefangener Sie ließ den Brief übersetzen. Ich möchte diese Bluse reinigen lassen.

(Zum -ed-Partizip in Perfekt- und Passivformen → S. 330, 331, 333)	the data **supplied** by you	die von Ihnen gelieferten Daten
	Impressed by his eloquence, she hired him.	Von seinem Redetalent beeindruckt, stellte sie ihn ein.
Beachten Sie den Unterschied:	We had **made** a copy.	Wir hatten eine Kopie gemacht.
	We had a copy **made**.	Wir ließen eine Kopie anfertigen.

Verben mit *to*-Objekt

Bei describe, dictate, explain, introduce, report, suggest kann ein zweites Objekt **nicht ohne to** stehen.	She described the man **to the police**.	Sie beschrieb den Mann der Polizei.
	He explained the method **to me**.	Er erklärte mir die Methode.
	She introduced me **to her friend**.	Sie stellte mich ihrer Freundin vor.
	He suggested this solution **to us**.	Er schlug uns diese Lösung vor.

Bildung von Frage und Verneinung

Bei **Vollverben** werden **Frage** und **Verneinung** mit Hilfe von **do/does/did** gebildet.	**Do you know** him?	Kennst du ihn?
	Does he come often?	Kommt er oft?
	Where **did you get** it?	Wo hast du es bekommen?
	I **don't need** it.	Ich brauche es nicht.
	She **doesn't work**.	Sie arbeitet nicht.
	They **didn't want** it.	Sie wollten es nicht.
	Don't you like it?	Gefällt es dir denn nicht?
Ist ein **Fragewort Subjekt** oder Teil des Subjekts, wird die Frageform **nicht mit do** gebildet.	Who **wants** a pizza?	Wer möchte eine Pizza?
	Which picture **looks** better?	Welches Bild sieht besser aus?
	Aber:	
	Who **doesn't want** it?	Wer will es nicht?
Bei Formen von **be** sowie bei den **Modalverben** can, could, must, should, will, would etc. wird **nicht mit do** umschrieben.	Is(n't) that true?	Stimmt das (denn nicht)?
	Can you help us?	Kannst du uns helfen?
	He wouldn't do such a thing.	Er würde so etwas nicht tun.
	Shouldn't we wait?	Sollten wir nicht warten?

Englische Kurzgrammatik 335

Ausnahme sind Imperative mit **be**:	**Don't be** so stubborn.	Sei doch nicht so stur.

Außer in Kombination mit got und in anderen Perfektkonstruktionen wird **have** heute in **Frage** und **Verneinung** meist mit **do** umschrieben.	**Do they have** any children?	Haben sie Kinder?
	What time **do you have** to leave?	Um welche Zeit müsst ihr weg?
	We **don't have** a freezer.	Wir haben keine Tiefkühltruhe.
	We **didn't have** to wait.	Wir brauchten nicht zu warten.

Frageanhängsel

Die im Englischen variablen Question Tags entsprechen deutschen Frageanhängseln wie „nicht wahr?" und „oder?".

Vorne bejaht, hinten verneint:	You **know** him, **don't you?**	Sie kennen ihn doch, nicht wahr?
	She's coming to the meeting, **isn't she?**	Sie kommt doch zu der Sitzung, nicht wahr?
	We **could** take a taxi, **couldn't we?**	Wir könnten doch ein Taxi nehmen, oder?
Vorne verneint, hinten bejaht:	You **don't** want that happening, **do you?**	Du willst doch nicht, dass das passiert, oder?
	They **didn't** see you, **did they?**	Man hat dich doch nicht gesehen, oder?

Unregelmäßige Verben

Angegebene Formen: Infinitiv, Past Tense, -ed-Partizip.
* = Auch die regelmäßige Form (auf -ed) ist gebräuchlich.

beat, beat, beaten	bring, brought, brought
become, became, become	build, built, built
begin, began, begun	burn, burnt*, burnt*
bet, bet*, bet*	burst, burst, burst
bid, bid, bid	buy, bought, bought
bind, bound, bound	catch, caught, caught,
bite, bit, bitten	choose, chose, chosen
bleed, bled, bled	come, came, come
blow, blew, blown	cost, cost, cost
break, broke, broken	creep, crept, crept

cut, cut, cut
deal, dealt [e], dealt [e]
dig, dug, dug
do, did, done [ʌ]
draw, drew, drawn
dream, dreamt* [e], dreamt* [e]
drink, drank, drunk
drive, drove, driven [ɪ]
eat, ate, eaten
fall, fell, fallen
feed, fed, fed
feel, felt, felt
fight, fought, fought
find, found, found
flee, fled, fled
fly, flew, flown
forbid, forbade, forbidden
forget, forgot, forgotten
forgive, forgave, forgiven
freeze, froze, frozen
get, got, got (AE auch gotten)
give, gave, given
go, went, gone [ɒ]
grow, grew, grown
hang, hung*, hung*
hear, heard [ɜː], heard [ɜː]
hide, hid, hidden / hid
hit, hit, hit
hold, held, held
hurt, hurt, hurt
keep, kept, kept
know, knew, known
lay, laid, laid
lead, led, led
lean, leant* [e], leant* [e]
learn, learnt*, learnt*
leave, left, left
lend, lent, lent
let, let, let
lie, lay, lain
light, lit*, lit*
lose, lost, lost
make, made, made
mean, meant [e], meant [e]
meet, met, met

pay, paid, paid
put, put, put
read, read [e], read [e]
ride, rode, ridden
ring, rang, rung
rise, rose, risen [ɪ]
run, ran, run
say, said [e], said [e]
see, saw, seen
seek, sought, sought
sell, sold, sold
send, sent, sent
set, set, set
shake, shook, shaken
shoot, shot, shot
show, showed, shown
shrink, shrank, shrunk
shut, shut, shut
sing, sang, sung
sink, sank, sunk
sit, sat, sat
sleep, slept, slept
smell, smelt*, smelt*
speak, spoke, spoken
spell, spelt*, spelt*
spend, spent, spent
split, split, split
spread, spread, spread
stand, stood, stood
steal, stole, stolen
strike, struck, struck
swear, swore, sworn
sweep, swept, swept
swim, swam, swum
take, took, taken
teach, taught, taught
tell, told, told
think, thought, thought
throw, threw, thrown
understand, understood, -stood
wake, woke*, woken*
wear, wore, worn
weep, wept, wept
win, won, won
write, wrote, written

Schreibunterschiede AE – BE

AE *or* / BE *our*	
AE *behavior*	BE *behaviour*
AE *color*	BE *colour*
AE *favor*	BE *favour*
AE *favorite*	BE *favourite*
AE *flavor*	BE *flavour*
AE *harbor*	BE *harbour*
AE *honor*	BE *honour*
AE *honorable*	BE *honourable*
AE *labor*	BE *labour*
AE *laborer*	BE *labourer*
AE *misdemeanor*	BE *misdemeanour*
AE *neighbor*	BE *neighbour*
AE *tumor*	BE *tumour*
AE *vapor*	BE *vapour*

AE *er* / BE *re*	
AE *center*	BE *centre*
AE *centimeter*	BE *centimetre*
AE *fiber*	BE *fibre*
AE *kilometer*	BE *kilometre*
AE *liter*	BE *litre*
AE *meter*	BE *metre*
AE *theater*	BE *theatre*

AE *l* / BE *ll*	
AE *canceled*	BE *cancelled*
AE *canceling*	BE *cancelling*
AE *counselor*	BE *counsellor*
AE *dialed*	BE *dialled*
AE *dialing*	BE *dialling*
AE *disheveled*	BE *dishevelled*
AE *jeweler*	BE *jeweller*
AE *modeled*	BE *modelled*
AE *quarreled*	BE *quarrelled*
AE *teetotaler*	BE *teetotaller*
AE *traveled*	BE *travelled*
AE *traveler*	BE *traveller*
AE *traveling*	BE *travelling*

AE *ll* / BE *l*	
AE *enroll*	BE *enrol*
AE *fulfill*	BE *fulfil*
AE *installment*	BE *instalment*

AE *s* / BE *c*	
AE *defense*	BE *defence*
AE *license*	BE *licence*[1]
AE *offense*	BE *offence*

AE *log* / BE *logue*	
AE *catalog*	BE *catalogue*
AE *dialog*	BE *dialogue*

AE *k* / BE *c*	
AE *disk*	BE *disc*
AE *skeptic*	BE *sceptic*
AE *skeptical*	BE *sceptical*
AE *skepticism*	BE *scepticism*

AE *e* / BE *ae*	
AE *anesthesia*	BE *anaesthesia*
AE *anesthetic*	BE *anaesthetic*
AE *anesthetist*	BE *anaesthetist*
AE *archeological*	BE *archaeological*
AE *archeologist*	BE *archaeologist*
AE *archeology*	BE *archaeology*
AE *Cesarean*	BE *Caesarean*
AE *feces*	BE *faeces*
AE *gynecologist*	BE *gynaecologist*
AE *gynecology*	BE *gynaecology*
AE *hemorrhoids*	BE *haemorrhoids*
AE *orthopedist*	BE *orthopaedist*
AE *orthopedic*	BE *orthopaedic*
AE *pediatrician*	BE *paediatrician*
AE *pediatric(s)*	BE *paediatric(s)*
AE *toxemia*	BE *toxaemia*

Verschiedene	
AE *check*	BE *cheque*[2]
AE *donut*	BE *doughnut*
AE *draft*	BE *draught*
AE *gray*	BE *grey*
AE *maneuver*	BE *manoeuvre*
AE *paralyze*	BE *paralyse*
AE *percent*	BE *per cent*
AE *program*	BE *programme*[3]
AE *story*	BE *storey*
AE *tire*	BE *tyre*

[1] Dieser Unterschied gilt nur beim Nomen; das Verb wird auch im BE meist mit *s* geschrieben.

[2] BE *cheque* nur in der Bedeutung *Scheck*.

[3] Im Zusammenhang mit Computerprogrammen ist auch im BE die AE-Schreibung *program* üblich.

Ausspracheunterschiede AE – BE

1. AE mit [r] – BE ohne [r]:

car	AE [kɑ:r]	BE [kɑ:]
word	AE [wɜ:rd]	BE [wɜ:d]

2. AE [æ] – BE [ɑ:]:

chance	AE [tʃæns]	BE [tʃɑ:ns]
half	AE [hæf]	BE [hɑ:f]

3. AE [ɑ:] – BE [ɒ]:

job	AE [dʒɑ:b]	BE [dʒɒb]
not	AE [nɑ:t]	BE [nɒt]

4. AE [u:] – BE [ju:]:

new	AE [nu:]	BE [nju:]
tune	AE [tu:n]	BE [tju:n]

5. AE [d] – BE [t]:

city	AE ['sɪdi]	BE ['sɪti]
matter	AE ['mædər]	BE ['mætə]

Nach *n* verschwindet das *t* im AE mitunter ganz:

twenty	AE ['tweni]	BE ['twenti]
center / centre	AE ['senər]	BE ['sentə]

6. Kein „Verschlucken" schwach betonter Silben im AE:

secretary	AE ['sekrəteri]	BE ['sekrətri]
temporary	AE ['tempəreri]	BE ['temprəri]

7. Einzelfälle abweichender Aussprache:

advertisement	AE [ædvər'taɪzmənt]	BE [əd'vɜ:tɪsmənt]
clerk	AE [klɜ:rk]	BE [klɑ:k]
derby	AE ['dɜ:rbi]	BE ['dɑ:bi]
garage	AE [gə'rɑ:ʒ]	BE ['gærɑ:ʒ]
laboratory	AE ['læbrətɔ:ri]	BE [lə'bɒrətri]
leisure	AE ['li:ʒər]	BE ['leʒə]
lever	AE ['levər]	BE ['li:və]
neither	AE ['ni:ðər]	BE ['naɪðə]
schedule	AE ['skedʒu:l]	BE ['ʃedju:l]
tomato	AE [tə'meɪdou]	BE [tə'mɑ:təʊ]
vase	AE [veɪs]	BE [vɑ:z]
z	AE [zi:]	BE [zed]

ABC der Sprachgebrauchsprobleme

English is among the easiest languages to speak badly, but the most difficult to use well. *(C. L. Wrenn, English philologist, 1895–1969)*

Able – capable

Beide Adjektive haben die Grundbedeutung „fähig", unterscheiden sich aber wesentlich in der Art, wie ein nachfolgendes Verb angeschlossen wird. Auf *able* folgt ein *to*-Infinitiv, auf *capable* die Konstruktion *of + -ing*-Form:

I am **able to make** you a special offer.	Ich bin in der Lage, Ihnen ein besonderes Angebot zu machen.
He's **capable of making** people laugh.	Er schafft es, die Leute zum Lachen zu bringen.

Able ist das schlichtere, wesentlich häufigere Wort, *capable* das gewähltere, förmlichere. Eine inhaltliche Unterscheidung ist weniger von der Bedeutung als von den Umständen des Gebrauchs her möglich. Es gibt Fälle, wo nur *able* oder *capable* möglich ist, und Fälle, die (bei leichten Unterschieden in der Bedeutung oder Stilebene) beide Ausdrucksweisen erlauben:

(Normal:) Will you be **able to come** to our party? (Kaum vorstellbar:) ~~Will you be capable of coming to our party?~~	Wirst du zu unserer Party kommen können? ~~Werden Sie es vermögen, zu unserer Party zu kommen?~~
(Normal:) Would you be **able to kill** a person? (Seltener, aber ebenfalls möglich:) Would you be **capable of** killing a person?	Würdest du einen Menschen töten können? Wärest du imstande, einen Menschen zu töten?
(Normal:) Were you **able to access** the Internet? (Die Alternative mit *capable* ist hier nicht vorstellbar.)	Konntest du ins Internet?

In den folgenden drei Sätzen ist die gewählte Form jeweils die einzig natürliche:

He is never quite **able to say** what he means.	Es gelingt ihm nie ganz, zu sagen, was er meint.
She is quite **capable of saying** no to him.	Sie ist durchaus imstande, Nein zu ihm zu sagen.
He is quite **capable of telling** you the most outrageous lies.	Er bringt es durchaus fertig, einem die unverschämtesten Lügen aufzutischen.

In den folgenden Fällen sind jeweils beide Ausdrucksweisen denkbar:

Are you **able to stand** / Are you **capable of standing** on your feet for an entire shift?	Können Sie eine ganze Schicht lang auf den Beinen stehen?
She is **able to explain** / She is **capable of explaining** difficult concepts in simple terms.	Sie hat die Fähigkeit, schwierige Konzepte in einfachen Worten zu erklären.
Nobody seems to be **able to explain** / **capable of explaining** this enormous budget gap.	Niemand scheint imstande zu sein, diese enorme Finanzierungslücke zu erklären.
In his present state he is not **able to make** / not **capable of making** these decisions himself.	In seiner gegenwärtigen Verfassung ist er nicht in der Lage, diese Entscheidungen selbst zu treffen.
A dog is **able to tell** / **capable of telling** a red object from a black one.	Ein Hund kann einen roten Gegenstand von einem schwarzen unterscheiden.
Donkeys are **able to carry** / are **capable of carrying** half their own weight.	Esel können die Hälfte ihres Eigengewichts tragen.

Advice

Advice ist in der Bedeutung „Rat" nicht zählbar, weshalb man das Wort nicht mit *a(n)* (*a good advice*) kombinieren oder im Plural (*advices*) gebrauchen kann:

That was **good advice**.	Das war ein guter Rat.
He had **some good advice** for me.	Er hatte einen guten Rat für mich.
We always appreciate **advice**.	Für Ratschläge sind wir immer dankbar.
He gave me three **pieces of advice**.	Er gab mir drei Ratschläge.
Let me give you a **word of advice**.	Ich will Ihnen einen Rat geben.

„Aktuell"

Actual heißt nicht „aktuell", sondern „tatsächlich", „eigentlich":

The movie is based on **actual** events.	Der Film beruht auf tatsächlichen Ereignissen.
We had to wait a long time beforehand, but the **actual** ceremony was very short.	Wir mussten vorher lange warten, aber die eigentliche Feier war sehr kurz.

Für das deutsche „aktuell" bieten sich im Englischen vor allem *current* und *topical* an.
Current bezeichnet das gerade Ablaufende (*the current year*), zur Zeit Bestehende (*the current crisis*), jetzt Gültige (*the magazine's current issue*).
Topical betont den Bezug zum Hier und Heute (*a topical novel*), dass nämlich etwas im Augenblick gerade – und möglicherweise nur vorübergehend – von Interesse ist (*a highly topical issue* = ein hochaktuelles Thema).

In the **current** situation higher public spending would be the best solution.	In der aktuellen Lage wären höhere Staatsausgaben die beste Lösung.
The **current** edition contains interviews with two prominent scientists.	Die aktuelle Ausgabe enthält Interviews mit zwei prominenten Wissenschaftlern.
Most people are interested in **topical** / **current** events such as Mars landings, terrorist attacks, or natural disasters.	Die meisten Leute interessieren sich für aktuelle Ereignisse wie Marslandungen, Terroranschläge oder Naturkatastrophen.
The magazine covers issues of **topical** interest.	Das Magazin behandelt Themen von aktuellem Interesse.

Already – yet

In Aussagesätzen kann „schon / bereits" durch *already*, nicht aber durch *yet* ausgedrückt werden:

| She **already** knows how to read. | Sie kann schon / bereits lesen. |
| The shipment has **already** arrived. | Die Sendung ist bereits angekommen. |

In Fragesätzen fragt *yet* sachlich, ob das Erwartete bereits eingetreten ist, während *already* ein unerwartet frühes Eintreten der Handlung unterstellt:

Does he have a girlfriend **yet**?	Hat er schon eine Freundin? (Das wäre normal für sein Alter.)
Does he **already** have a girlfriend?	Hat er schon eine Freundin? (Das wäre früh für sein Alter.)
Has the post been here **yet**?	Ist die Post schon da gewesen?
Are you **already** in the mood for Christmas?	Bist du denn schon in Weihnachtsstimmung?

„Als"

Als Entsprechungen für „als" sind zu unterscheiden:
when in „Zeit"-Nebensätzen,
if in der Bedeutung „falls",
as zur Einleitung einer näheren Erläuterung,
than nach Steigerungsformen (wie *better*, *easier*, *more modern* etc.).

When the rain stopped we went for a walk.	Als der Regen aufhörte, machten wir einen Spaziergang.
If the rain ever stops, we'll take some pictures.	Wenn der Regen je aufhört, machen wir ein paar Bilder.
As your teacher, I expect you to give your all.	Als euer Lehrer erwarte ich, dass ihr alles gebt.
I regard him **as** a friend.	Ich betrachte ihn als Freund.
The film was better **than** the book.	Der Film war besser als das Buch.

Anführungszeichen

Anführungszeichen (*quotation marks* / *quotes*) stehen im Englischen stets oben; anders als im Deutschen platziert man das Komma am Ende einer wörtlichen Rede innerhalb der Anführungszeichen:

"I didn't go anyway," she said.	„Ich bin sowieso nicht gegangen", sagte sie.

„Bis"

Die Wahl der Präposition vor einem Ausdruck wie *next Friday* hängt von der Bedeutung ab:
till / *until next Friday* = die ganze Zeit bis zum nächsten Freitag
by next Friday = nicht später als nächsten Freitag

I can't wait **till** / **until** next Friday.	Ich kann nicht bis nächsten Freitag warten.
The results will be in **by** next Friday.	Die Ergebnisse werden bis nächsten Freitag vorliegen.

Drive – go

In der Bedeutung „nicht selbstlenkend" ist „fahren" = *go*:

We're **going** on holiday next week.	Wir fahren nächste Woche in Urlaub.
We're **going** to Switzerland this year.	Wir fahren dieses Jahr in die Schweiz.
Why don't you **go** by train?	Warum fahrt ihr nicht mit dem Zug?
Shall we **go** by car or walk?	Wollen wir fahren oder zu Fuß gehen?

In der Bedeutung „selbstlenkend" ist „fahren" = *drive*; *drive* heißt auch allgemein „Auto fahren":

She **drives** a convertible.	Sie fährt ein Kabrio.
He's learning to **drive**.	Er lernt Auto fahren.
We **drove** all night.	Wir fuhren die ganze Nacht.
I **drove** her to the station.	Ich fuhr sie zum Bahnhof.
Shall we **drive** or go by train?	Sollen wir mit dem Auto oder mit dem Zug fahren?
Which is cheaper – flying or **driving**?	Was ist billiger – fliegen oder mit dem Auto fahren?

Experience

Im Deutschen „macht" man eine Erfahrung, im Englischen „hat" man sie:

I've **had** the same experience.	Ich habe dieselbe Erfahrung gemacht.
That was one of the most painful experiences I've **had** in a long time.	Das war eine der schmerzlichsten Erfahrungen, die ich je gemacht habe.

Explain

Nach *explain* wird das Personenobjekt stets mit *to* konstruiert und in der Regel nachgestellt:

She **explained** the game **to the boys**.	Sie erklärte den Jungen das Spiel.
She **explained** it **to them**.	Sie erklärte es ihnen.

Also nicht ~~Can you explain me this?~~, sondern *Can you explain this to me?*

„Ganz"

Beim Suchen nach einer Entsprechung für „ganz" trifft man leicht daneben (= *one easily misses the mark*):

She read the **whole** book online.	Sie las das ganze Buch online.
She's eaten **all** the biscuits.	Sie hat die ganzen Kekse gegessen.
The **whole** thing was a rip-off.	Das Ganze war eine Abzocke.
On the whole, we're not making much progress.	Im Ganzen machen wir keine großen Fortschritte.
He lost **all** his money gambling.	Er verlor sein ganzes Geld durch Spielen.
By and large, I'm not a lazy person.	Im großen Ganzen bin ich kein fauler Mensch.
She's **all** / **quite** alone now.	Sie ist jetzt ganz allein.
He did it **all** by himself.	Er hat es ganz allein gemacht.
You're **quite** right.	Du hast ganz recht.
Are you **totally** crazy / mad?	Bist du denn ganz verrückt?
It's **quite** a lovely little picture.	Es ist ein ganz reizendes kleines Bild.

Good / bad at

Im Englischen ist man *good / bad at something*, nicht *in*:

I'm **good at** spelling but **bad at** grammar.	Ich bin gut in Rechtschreibung, aber schlecht in Grammatik.
English people are **good at** queuing.	Engländer sind gut im Schlangestehen.
I'm **bad at** expressing emotions.	Ich bin schlecht darin, Gefühle auszudrücken.

Großschreibung von Namensadjektiven

Von Namen abgeleitete Adjektive werden, im Gegensatz zum Deutschen, großgeschrieben:

a **German** car	ein deutsches Auto
an **Austrian** wine	ein österreichischer Wein
a **British** bank	eine britische Bank
an **American** company	ein amerikanisches Unternehmen

„Haben"

Ein häufig anzutreffender Germanismus ist der Gebrauch von *have* mit Studienfächern. Es heißt aber richtig:

Did you **do** Spanish at school?	Hast du Spanisch in der Schule gehabt?
I **did** some French at school.	Ein bisschen Französisch habe ich in der Schule gehabt.

Headline – heading – title

Mitunter wird der Titel einer Geschichte irrtümlich als *headline* oder *heading* bezeichnet. Richtig ist aber:

What does the **title** of the story refer to?	Worauf verweist der Titel der Geschichte?

Headline ist dagegen die „Schlagzeile" in einer Zeitung:

A tabloid ran the story under the **headline**, "End of the World Postponed".	Ein Boulevardblatt brachte die Geschichte unter der Überschrift: „Weltuntergang verschoben".

Heading ist die Überschrift eines Textes, Abschnitts, Kapitels etc.:

The **heading** of chapter 20.4 is "Advertising". These points are summarized under the **heading** (of) "Social Effects".	Die Überschrift von Kapitel 20.4 ist „Werbung". Diese Punkte sind unter der Überschrift / in der Rubrik „Soziale Auswirkungen" zu- sammengefasst.

„Heute Morgen / Nachmittag" etc.

„Heute Morgen" ist nicht ~~today morning~~, sondern *this morning*. Entsprechend *this afternoon* (= heute Nachmittag) und *this evening* (= heute Abend). „Morgen früh" ist *tomorrow morning*.

Homework

Auf Deutsch macht man seine Hausaufgaben, auf Englisch *you do your home-work*:

Have you **done** your homework yet?	Hast du schon deine Hausaufgaben gemacht?

Human – humane

Human und *humane* müssen unterschieden werden:
human ['hju:mən] = den Menschen betreffend, zum Menschen gehörend, für ihn charakteristisch
humane [hju'meɪn] = menschenfreundlich, human

Poverty is a violation of **human** rights.	Armut ist eine Verletzung der Menschenrechte.
Children are being used as **human** shields.	Kinder werden als menschliche Schutzschilde benutzt.
The crash was caused by **human** error.	Der Absturz ist auf menschliches Versagen zurückzuführen.
We need to stand together and help our fellow **human beings**.	Wir müssen zusammenstehen und unseren Mitmenschen helfen.

We need to find a **humane** solution to this problem.	Wir müssen für dieses Problem eine humane Lösung finden.
We are committed to the **humane** treatment of animals in our care.	Wir haben uns zu einer humanen Behandlung der uns anvertrauten Tiere verpflichtet.
Prisoners must be treated **humanely**.	Gefangene müssen menschenwürdig / menschlich / human behandelt werden.

Information

Information ist nicht zählbar (*an information*) und hat keine Pluralform (*informations*). Beachten Sie die stattdessen möglichen Konstruktionen:

I found this **information** online.	Ich fand diese Information / Informationen im Internet.
That's an interesting **piece of information**.	Das ist eine interessante Information.

Island – isle

Das übliche Wort für „Insel" ist *island*. *Isle* ist heute nur noch als Teil von Namen und in literarischen Texten gebräuchlich. „Auf einer Insel" ist normalerweise *on an island*; bei großen Inseln sagt man auch *in* (*in / on the island of Crete* = auf der Insel Kreta).

Carisbrooke Castle is one of the main tourist attractions in the **Isle** of Wight.	Die Burg Carisbrooke ist eine der Haupttouristenattraktionen auf der Insel Wight.
We recently spent a short holiday on the **island** of Jersey in the British Channel **Islands**.	Vor Kurzem haben wir einen kleinen Urlaub auf der Insel Jersey auf den britischen Kanalinseln verbracht.
I live on a small **island** off the Scottish west coast.	Ich lebe auf einer kleinen Insel vor der schottischen Westküste.
Wild boars have been extinct in the British **Isles** since the 17th century.	Wildschweine sind auf den Britischen Inseln seit dem 17. Jahrhundert ausgestorben.

Komma

Betrachten Sie die Kommasetzung nicht als ein unwichtiges Thema! Falsch gesetzte Kommas stören im Englischen extrem. Und damit gleich der erste Rat: *When in doubt(,) leave it out.* (= Setzen Sie im Zweifel kein Komma.)

Zwingend ist das Komma eigentlich nur bei Aufzählungen und vor und nach wörtlicher Rede:

You need sugar, flour, eggs, butter**(,)** and vanilla.	Du brauchst Zucker, Mehl, Eier, Butter und Vanille.
The queen said, "Good evening, Mr Bond."	Die Königin sagte: „Guten Abend, Herr Bond."
"Good evening, Mr Bond," said the queen / the queen said.	„Guten Abend, Herr Bond", sagte die Königin.

Anders als im Deutschen setzt man kein Komma vor nachgestellten Nebensätzen:

Don't talk to him_when he's busy.	Sprich ihn nicht an, wenn er beschäftigt ist.
He said_(that) he knew nothing about it.	Er sagte, er wisse nichts davon.
I know_what I know_if you know_what I mean. (*Edie Brickell*)	Ich weiß, was ich weiß, wenn Sie wissen, was ich meine.

„Konnte"

Could ist keine sichere Entsprechung für „konnte"! Man kann zwar sagen:

I **could** swim when I was five.	Ich konnte mit fünf schon schwimmen.

In dem folgenden Satz hingegen kann man „konnte" nicht durch *could* ausdrücken:
Wir konnten heute ein bisschen im Pazifik schwimmen.

Die Entsprechung für „konnte" ist hier zwingend *was / were able to*:

> We **were able to** swim in the Pacific Ocean for a bit today.

Betrachten Sie noch die folgenden Beispiele, um vielleicht selbst auf die Regel zu kommen:

500 years ago the king **could** just order your head to be chopped off.	Vor 500 Jahren konnte der König einfach bestimmen, dass einem der Kopf abgeschlagen wurde.
Yesterday the king **was able to** leave his bed for the first time.	Gestern konnte der König zum ersten Mal das Bett verlassen.
Before his illness he **could** outrun any of his children.	Vor seiner Krankheit konnte er schneller laufen als jedes seiner Kinder.
The burglar **was able to** escape.	Der Einbrecher konnte entkommen.

Die Beispiele zeigen uns, dass *could* in der Bedeutung „konnte" immer dann möglich ist, wenn es sich um eine Fähigkeit im Allgemeinen handelt; geht es um Fähigkeit in einem bestimmten Einzelfall, so muss „konnte" durch *was / were able to* ausgedrückt werden.
Besteht die Gefahr, dass *could* als „könnte" missverstanden wird, so sollte man es auf jeden Fall durch *was / were able to* ersetzen.

„Lassen"

Deutsche Formulierungen mit „lassen" haben im Englischen viele Entsprechungen, die man in guten Wörterbüchern nachschlagen kann.
Wichtig ist, dass man Folgendes versteht: Das deutsche „lassen" kann sowohl „zulassen" als auch „veranlassen" bedeuten. Diese beiden Grundbedeutungen des einen deutschen Verbs werden im Englischen durch verschiedene Verben ausgedrückt:

She **let** the class out early. She **allowed** the class **to** use their smartphones.	Sie ließ die Klasse früher gehen. Sie ließ die Klasse ihre Smartphones benutzen.
She **had** the class write an essay. She **made** the class stand up.	Sie ließ die Klasse einen Aufsatz schreiben. Sie ließ die Klasse aufstehen.

Less – fewer

Less gebraucht man bei nichtzählbaren Wörtern, *fewer* bei zählbaren:

less work – **fewer** jobs	weniger Arbeit – weniger Arbeitsplätze
less money – **fewer** friends	weniger Geld – weniger Freunde
less time – **fewer** visits	weniger Zeit – weniger Besuche

„Letzte"

The last bezeichnet das Letzte, nach dem nichts mehr kommt; „letzte" in der Bedeutung „neueste" ist dagegen *latest*:

When is the **last** train to Egham, please?	Wann bitte geht der letzte Zug nach Egham?
According to the **latest** reports, two aftershocks have occurred so far.	Nach den letzten Meldungen kam es bisher zu zwei Nachbeben.

Mean

Durch die Interferenz des Deutschen wird bei *mean* mitunter die Umschreibung mit *do* unterlassen: ~~What means "edge"?~~ Richtig muss es heißen:

What **does "edge" mean**?	Was bedeutet „edge"?

Wichtig ist auch die Fügung *mean + by*:

What do you **mean by** "perfect"?	Was meinen Sie mit „perfekt"?

Mistake

Aus der Erfahrung heraus, dass dem deutschen „machen" im Englischen mitunter *do* entspricht (*do one's homework = seine Hausaufgaben machen*), sagen Lernende manchmal ~~do a mistake~~. Es heißt aber *make a mistake*:

A lot of people **made** the same mistake.	Viele Leute haben den gleichen / denselben Fehler gemacht.

Moment

„Im Moment" ist *at the moment*:

I'm into Swedish crime novels **at the moment**.	Im Moment stehe ich auf schwedische Kriminalromane.

„Müssen"

Wegen der lautlichen Nähe zum Deutschen neigen Lernende dazu, den Gebrauch von *must* überzustrapazieren. Soll eine objektiv (etwa durch Regeln, Vorschriften, Umstände) gegebene Verpflichtung ausgedrückt werden, so ist in der Gegenwartsform *have to* angebracht, nicht *must*:

When I'm at the office I often **have to** skip lunch.	Wenn ich im Büro bin, muss ich das Mittagessen oft ausfallen lassen.
All students **have to** take a written exam.	Alle Studierenden müssen eine schriftliche Prüfung machen.
At what time do you **have to** be there?	Um welche Zeit musst du dort sein?

Mit *must* hingegen drückt man etwas aus, das man selbst oder eine andere am Gespräch beteiligte Person subjektiv als notwendig empfindet:

You **must** eat more fruits and veggies.	Du musst mehr Obst und Gemüse essen.
It is indeed a big problem and we **must** do something about it.	Es ist in der Tat ein großes Problem, und wir müssen etwas dagegen tun.
Must you really contradict me every time I say something?	Musst du mir wirklich jedes Mal widersprechen, wenn ich etwas sage?

„Nächste"

Das entfernungsmäßig Nächste ist *the nearest*; das in der Reihenfolge als Nächstes Kommende ist *the next*:

The **nearest** tube station is Covent Garden.	Der nächst(gelegen)e U-Bahnhof ist Covent Garden.
The **next** train is in 20 minutes.	Der nächste Zug geht in 20 Minuten.

Near

Durch die Interferenz des Deutschen hört man von Lernenden häufig ~~in the near of~~. Diesen Ausdruck gibt es im Englischen nicht, sondern man sagt:

The hotel is **near** the airport.	Das Hotel ist in der Nähe des Flughafens.
Banchory is a small town **near** Aberdeen.	Banchory ist eine kleine Stadt in der Nähe von Aberdeen.

„Neueste"

In der Bedeutung „zeitlich letzte und damit aktuellste" ist „neueste" = *latest*; in der Bedeutung „erst seit sehr kurzer Zeit vorhanden", ist „neueste" = *newest*.

Have you heard the **latest** (news)?	Weißt du schon das Neueste?
The XX5 is the **latest** model in the series.	Das XX5 ist das neueste Modell in der Serie.
Canada's **newest** coin glows in the dark.	Kanadas neueste Münze leuchtet im Dunkeln.
Liz Bartlett is the **newest** member of our club.	Liz Bartlett ist das neueste Mitglied unseres Vereins.

Pay (for)

Eine Sache oder Leistung bezahlen ist *pay for*, nicht einfach *pay*:

You only **pay for** what you order.	Man bezahlt nur, was man bestellt hat.
Are you sure you **paid for** it?	Bist du sicher, dass du es bezahlt hast?
Have the tickets been **paid for**?	Sind die Karten bezahlt (worden)?

In allen anderen Fällen dagegen ohne *for*:

Has the bill / fee / rent been **paid**?	Ist die Rechnung / Gebühr / Miete bezahlt (worden)?
Did you **pay** the electrician?	Hast du den Elektriker bezahlt?

People

Auf *people* (= Leute / Volk) folgt immer ein Pluralverb (also *are*, *were*, *have*, *do*, *know* etc.; nicht *is*, *was*, *has*, *does*, *knows* etc.):

These **people know** what they want.	Diese Leute wissen, was sie wollen.
People don't know much about him.	Die Leute wissen nicht viel über ihn.
The American **people have** made their choice.	Das amerikanische Volk hat seine Wahl getroffen.

In der Bedeutung „Volk" kann *people* auch den *-s*-Plural bilden:

the **peoples** of East Asia	die Völker Ostasiens
the English-speaking **peoples**	die englischsprachigen Völker

Von der Bedeutung hängt es auch ab, ob *people* mit dem unbestimmten Artikel gebraucht werden kann oder nicht:

They're **industrious people**.	Sie sind fleißige Leute / Menschen.
They're **an industrious people**.	Sie sind ein fleißiges Volk.

Reason – cause

Reason for zielt auf den logischen Grund, die Erklärung, während *cause of* auf das (oft physische) Ereignis deutet, das etwas verursacht. Die beiden Ausdrücke sind manchmal austauschbar, haben dann aber eine unterschiedliche Bedeutung:

What was the **reason for** this delay?	Was war der Grund für diese Verzögerung?
What was the **cause of** this delay?	Was war die Ursache dieser Verzögerung?

| Am I the **reason for** the smile on your face? The icy road was the **cause of** the accident. | Bin ich der Grund für das Lächeln auf deinem Gesicht? Ursache des Unfalls war die vereiste Straße. |

Rechtschreibprobleme

Häufig falsch geschrieben werden:

accommodation = Unterkunft: Doppel-m!
address = Adresse: Doppel-d!
be = sein, *bee* = Biene: nicht verwechseln!
British, English, American, German etc.: Namensadjektive großschreiben!
cannot = kann nicht: nicht getrennt schreiben!
committee = Komitee: Doppel-*m*, Doppel-*t*!
describe – description = beschreiben – Beschreibung: nicht *dis*-!
don't, doesn't, didn't: richtige Position des Apostrophs beachten!
environment = Umwelt: -*n*- in -*viron*- beachten!
four – fourteen – forty: forty ohne u!
I = ich: immer großschreiben!
interesting = interessant: nicht *intr*-!
it's = *it is*, *its* = sein / ihr: nicht verwechseln!
live music: nicht *life*!
Mr, Mrs, Dr: vor Namen niemals ausschreiben!
parliament = Parlament: *i* nicht vergessen!
piece = Stück, *peace* = Frieden: nicht verwechseln!
Plurale auf -s, z. B. *cars* = Autos: kein Apostroph!
said = sagte: nicht mit *y*!
weather = Wetter, *whether* = ob: nicht verwechseln!
you're = *you are*, *your* = dein / euer / Ihr: nicht verwechseln!

-s-Form des Verbs

Beachten Sie diese optische Hilfe für das Setzen bzw. Nichtsetzen der -s-Endung (S. → 329):

| The **necklace looks** pretty. The **necklaces look** pretty. | Die Kette sieht hübsch aus. Die Ketten sehen hübsch aus. |

Das -s ist entweder am Verb (*looks*) oder am Nomen (*necklaces*).

Die folgenden Kombinationen sind also nicht möglich:

| The ~~necklace look~~ pretty. The ~~necklaces looks~~ pretty. |

„Sagen"

Say lässt sich nicht mit einem Personenobjekt kombinieren. In solchen Fällen ist stets *tell* das Verb der Wahl:

You'll have to **tell** your father.	Du wirst es deinem Vater sagen müssen.
He **told** me something extremely important.	Er sagte mir etwas äußerst Wichtiges.

Say hingegen steht häufig bei direkter oder indirekter Rede. Der Adressat des Gesagten wird gegebenenfalls mit *to* eingeleitet:

She **said** (to me), "I don't trust you."	Sie sagte (zu mir): „Ich traue dir nicht."
She **said** she didn't trust me.	Sie sagte, sie traue mir nicht.
I don't remember what she **said** to me.	Ich erinnere mich nicht, was sie zu mir gesagt hat.

Short(ly) – brief(ly)

Sowohl *short* als auch *brief* bedeutet „kurz". Beim Gebrauch ist Folgendes zu beachten.

Oft sind *short* und *brief* austauschbar:

The rebels surrendered after a **short** / **brief** struggle.	Nach kurzem Kampf ergaben sich die Rebellen.
Make your speech as **short** / **brief** as you can.	Mach deine Rede so kurz, wie du kannst.

In Bezug auf lineare Ausdehnung ist nur *short* möglich:

I covered the **short** distance in seconds.	Ich legte die kurze Strecke in Sekunden zurück.
Which is the **shortest** route?	Welches ist die kürzeste Strecke?

Von *short* lässt sich kein gleichbedeutendes Adverb auf *-ly* ableiten, denn *shortly* heißt „in Kürze", „bald". Das Adverb der Wahl ist dann *briefly*:

He mentioned that **briefly**.	Er erwähnte das kurz.
She **briefly** summarized what she had read so far.	Sie fasste kurz zusammen, was sie bisher gelesen hatte.

Your order should arrive **shortly**.	Ihre Bestellung müsste in Kürze eintreffen.
We will **shortly** start planning for next year.	Wir werden in Kürze mit den Planungen für das kommende Jahr beginnen.

„Sollen"

Englische Entsprechungen für „sollen":

Shall nur bei Vorschlägen (*Shall I ...?*) oder in biblischen Geboten (*You shall not ...*); in den meisten anderen Fällen liegt man mit *be* (*supposed*) *to* richtig:

Shall I explain it to you?	Soll ich es dir erklären?
You **shall** not steal.	Du sollst nicht stehlen.
We**'re supposed to** read 100 pages for tomorrow.	Wir sollen bis morgen 100 Seiten lesen.
The project **is to** be completed by 15 November.	Das Projekt soll bis zum 15. November abgeschlossen sein.

Their – they're – there

Fast zu banal, um hier aufgenommen zu werden, aber doch ein so hartnäckiges, hochfrequentes Rechtschreibproblem, dass wir ihm ein paar Zeilen gönnen wollen.

they're = they are = sie sind
their = (besitzanzeigendes Fürwort:) ihr
there = dort

In dem folgenden Beispiel haben wir *their*, *they're* und *there* in einem Satz:

Marion and Patrick are hiking in the Highlands. **They're** in **their** element **there**.	Marion und Patrick wandern in den Highlands. Dort sind sie in ihrem Element.

„Thema"

Subject ist die allgemeinste und am wenigsten spezifische Entsprechung. *Topic* bezeichnet eher ein aktuelles, vielleicht kontroverses Thema von allgemeinem Interesse.
Mit *theme* spricht man einen Leitgedanken, ein Leitmotiv an. Auch das Hauptthema, die mehrfach wiederkehrende Melodie in einem Musikstück ist *the theme*:

The **subject** is too complex to be treated adequately in a short article.	Das Thema ist zu komplex, um in einem kurzen Artikel angemessen behandelt zu werden.
It's an interesting **subject** / **topic** for essays, discussions, and debates.	Es ist ein interessantes Thema für Aufsätze, Diskussionen und Debatten.
What's the **subject** / **topic** of the paper?	Was ist das Thema der Klausur / des Referats?
High housing prices are a perennial **topic** at dinner parties.	Die hohen Immobilienpreise sind ein ständig wiederkehrendes Thema bei Abendgesellschaften.

The death of the American dream is a dominant **theme** in the work of this novelist.	Der Tod des amerikanischen Traums ist ein beherrschendes Thema im Werk dieses Erzählers.
The band was playing the **theme** from Star Trek.	Die Kapelle spielte das Thema aus Star Trek.

„Treffen"

Das deutsche Allerweltswort „treffen" hat im Englischen verschiedene Entsprechungen:

A spectator was **hit** by a golf ball.	Ein Zuschauer wurde von einem Golfball getroffen.
The plane was **struck** by lightning.	Das Flugzeug wurde vom Blitz getroffen.
We **met** for lunch in the cafeteria.	Wir trafen uns zum Mittagessen in der Cafeteria.
I **ran into** her in the street.	Ich traf sie zufällig auf der Straße.
You've **made** the right choice.	Sie haben die richtige Wahl getroffen.
The experience has **affected** her deeply.	Dieses Erlebnis hat sie tief getroffen.
The doctor *is* in no way *to blame*.	Den Arzt trifft keinerlei Schuld.

Verlaufsform

Bei der Bildung der Verlaufsform dürfen Sie die Form von *be* (*am, is, are, was, were* etc.) nicht vergessen:

They **are staying** at a hotel in Kensington.	Sie wohnen in einem Hotel in Kensington.
I **was reading** a novel last night and came across this quote.	Ich las gestern in einem Roman, und da stieß ich auf diese Stelle.
I have **been trying** to reach you for the past few days.	Ich versuche seit Tagen, dich zu erreichen.

Very – (very) much

Very ist in der Bedeutung „sehr" auf den Gebrauch bei Adjektiven und Adverbien beschränkt. Mit Bezug auf Verben steht nicht *very*, sondern *much* oder (häufiger) *very much*:

She's **very** choosy.	Sie ist sehr wählerisch.
She was **very** hurt.	Sie war sehr verletzt.
She was **very** obliging.	Sie war sehr zuvorkommend.
The menu changes **very** frequently.	Die Speisekarte wechselt sehr oft.
His economic policy has been **much** criticized.	Seine Wirtschaftspolitik ist sehr kritisiert worden.
I admire her **very much**.	Ich bewundere sie sehr.

Visit

Die nach dem Nomen *visit* das „Ziel" des Besuchs bezeichnende Präposition ist *to*:

The minister is currently on a **visit to** India. The president paid a **visit to** the hospital.	Der Minister besucht zur Zeit Indien. Der Präsident stattete dem Krankenhaus einen Besuch ab.

Welcome

Beachten Sie die Präposition *to* nach *welcome* sowie die Fügung *welcome home*:

Welcome to London. **Welcome to** my blog. You're **welcome to** use my bike.	Willkommen in London! Willkommen auf meinem Blog! Du kannst gerne mein Fahrrad benutzen.
Welcome home – I missed you.	Willkommen zu Hause – du hast mir gefehlt!

When – if

When meint „Zeit"; *if* meint „Bedingung":

Will you be home **when** we arrive? Can we still get food **if** we arrive late?	Wirst du zu Hause sein, wenn wir ankommen? Können wir noch etwas zu essen bekommen, wenn / falls wir verspätet ankommen?

While – during

Dem deutschen „während" kann im Englischen *while* oder *during* entsprechen. *While* leitet einen verbalen Ausdruck ein (z. B. *while they were running*); *during* hingegen bezieht sich auf ein Nomen / Substantiv (*during the race*):

They came **while** we were sleeping. They came **during** the night.	Sie kamen, während wir schliefen. Sie kamen während der Nacht.

Register Englisch

Zahlen, Wochentage, Monatsnamen, Personennamen und Ländernamen sowie die nachstehend aufgelisteten Wörter sind in diesem Register normalerweise nicht berücksichtigt – es sei denn, sie sind Teil einer Kollokation oder vom Sprachgebrauch her besonders zu beachten.

a(n)	didn't	into	ourselves	too
about	do	is	out	up
after	does(n't)	it	over	us
again	don't	its	people	US(A)
all	down	itself	she	very
also	England	just	so	was
am	English	man	some	we
American	first	many	somebody	well
and	for	me	someone	were
are	from	more	something	what
as	got	most	such	when
at	had	much	than	where
be	has	must	that	which
because	have	my	the	who
been	he	myself	their	why
before	her	no	them	will
between	here	not	themselves	with
Britain	herself	now	then	without
British	him	of	there	woman
but	himself	on	these	won't
by	his	one	they	would(n't)
can('t)	how	only	this	yes
cannot	I	or	those	you
couldn('t)	if	other	through	yourself
did	in	our	to	yourselves

A

a few 27, 168, 171, 176, 250
à la carte 63
A level(s) 152
a lot 173, 196, 201
a lot of 226, 227, 298, 302, 306
abandon 51, 219
abbreviation 94
abdomen 13
abduction 131
abhor 29
ability 113, 156
ability test 144
able 340
abnormal 143
aboard 292
abolitionist 98
Aborigines 139
abort 206
abortion 37, 104, 136
abortion movement 98
abortive putsch 108
about 35, 134
above freezing 227
above zero 227
abrasions 72

abridge 267
abridged 267
abridgment 267
abroad 52, 300
abs 84, 94
absence 313
absent 155
absentee voting 104
absolute monarchy 99
absolutely 27
absolution 163
absolutism 99, 141
abstain 103
abstention 103
abstract 146, 169
abstract of title 308
abuse 36, 51, 128, 142
AC 259
academic 146, 156
academy 149
Academy Award 176
acceleration 241
accelerator 262
access 277, 279
access data 277
accessible 73

accessories 66, 171, 172
accident 14, 71, 73, 286
accident insurance 307
accommodation 125
accommodation(s) 191
accompany 173
accomplice 33
accord 117
according to 156, 269, 294
account 146, 205, 302, 303, 305
account executive 305
account manager 305
account number 248
accountant 114, 310
accounting 114
accumulate 296
accumulator 259
accuse of 180, 292
accuse sb. of 107
ace 197
acetone 243

-ache 76
ache 78
achieve 36, 117, 153
achieve aims 142
achievement 30
achievement test 144, 152
aching 78
acid 128, 129, 237, 243
acid-free paper 267
acid rain 226
acorn 235
acoustic 240
acoustics 240
acquaintance 34
acquainted 34
acquisition 301
acre 308
acronym 94
across 216
act 23, 36, 103, 108, 114, 176, 276
act a part 176
act as 243
act of God 307
act on 241
act out 155
acting 176

action 98, 119, 176, 315
activate 278, 279
active 142
active citizenship 98
activism 98
activist 98, 107, 232
activities 108, 199
activity 83, 107, 127, 198
actor 176
actress 176
acts of 107
acumen 298
ad 94, 305
AD 94
adapt 175, 267
adaptation 139, 267
adaptor 260
add 202, 246, 247
add together/up 246
addict 128, 129
addicted to 128, 201
addiction 128
addictive 128
addition 246
additive-free 82
address 11, 273
adequate 307
ADHD 94
adherent 158
adjust 172, 307
adjustment 307
administer 72
administration 105
administrative 309
admit 21
adolescence 18
adolescent 18
adopt 51
adoption 51
adore 28
adorned with 169
ads 124
adult 19, 37
adult check 280
adult education 149
adult education centre 149
adult education classes 149
adultery 49
advance 119
advance copy 267
advanced 20, 152, 262
advanced query 281
advanced technical college 148
advantage 197, 254
advert 94, 305
advertise 305
advertisement 305
advertiser 305
advertising 305

advertising agency 305
advertising department 305
advertising industry 305
advertising manager 305
advice 234, 341
advice column 269
adviser 105
aerobics 83
aerogramme 272
aeroplane 289
aesthetics 166
AFAIK 94
affair 49, 83
affairs 116
affected by 315
affection 29, 34
affiliation 11
affirmative action 98
afflicted with 73
affliction 68
afford 58
affordable 86, 124
afraid 92, 127, 173, 191, 292, 313
afraid of 40, 289
afraid of/to 30
Africa 214, 215
African 214
African-American(s) 135
after-sales service 193
aftereffects 230
afterlife 42
afternoon 228
afternoon! 60
aftershave 38, 39
aftershock 229
against 30, 92, 107, 108, 109, 112, 118, 131, 133, 134, 163, 196, 217, 307, 315
against the tide 238
age 10, 15, 19, 20, 21, 40, 141, 164, 206, 211, 212, 293
age v. 52
Age Concern 21
age group 306
ag(e)ing 20
agency 106, 112, 127, 139, 188, 268, 305
agent 24, 93, 124, 188, 307, 308
aggregate 297
aggression 119
aggressive 24
aggressor 119
agitated 24
agitation 107

agitator 107
agnostic 164
agnosticism 164
ago 56, 74
agony column 269
agree 121
agreement 34, 117, 300, 316
agricultural 220
agriculture 220
aground 292
aid 72, 117
aide 101
aids 25, 26, 154
AIDS 37, 70, 94
ailment 68
aim 142
air 103, 270, 289
air a room 93
air base 119
air cargo 290
air con 94
air conditioner 90
air-conditioning 26
air controllers 290
air fare 289
air force 118
air freight 290
air hostess 290
air pollution 225
air raid 119
air-raid shelter 119
air traffic 290
air transport 289
aircraft 18, 289
aircraft designer 311
aired 270
airfield 119
airfreight sth. 290
airletter 272
airline 289, 290
airline ticket 289
airliner 289
airmail 273
airplane 289
airport 289
airsickness 68
airtime 270
aisle 178
aka 94
alarm 90, 271
alarm clock 90
album 171
alcohol 128, 129, 243
alcoholic 129, 200
Alcoholics Anonymous 129
alcoholism 129
ale 57, 200
alga(e) 237
algebra 246
algorithm 279
alimony 49
all-powerful 99

Allah 160
allergic 70
allergy 70
alleviate 130
alliance 116
allied 116
allowance 51, 114, 115
allowed 232
alloy 212, 254
ally 116
almanac 264
almighty 160
almost 16, 74, 78
almsgiving 158
along 33
aloud 154
Alps 218
already – yet 342
Alsatian 232
altar 163
alter 77
alternating current 259
alternator 259
altitude 290
aluminium 212
aluminum 212
always 26, 34, 64, 133, 156, 201, 213
Alzheimer's 21, 68, 74
amateur 195
amazed 30
ambassador 116, 121
ambition 23
ambitious 208
ambulance 72
amen 163
amendment 103, 114
America 214, 230
American 214
American cheese 54
American football 196
American plan 191
American West 201
Americas 214
amino acid 237
ammunition 119
amoeba(e) 237
among 20, 27, 34, 121, 130, 315
amount of money 302
amp 259
amperage 259
ampere 259
amphetamines 129
amplifier 260
amplify 260
Amtrak 287
amusement park 187

anaesthesia 81
anaesthetic 81
anaesthetist 81
anal 37
analyse 165, 210, 242
analysis 142, 143, 146, 156, 165, 242
analytical 242
ancestor 46
anchor 217, 271, 292
anchored by 271
anchorman 271
anchorwoman 271
ancient 164, 165, 169
ancient(s) 141
ancient cultures 138
ancient history 140
ancient world 141
anecdote 179
angel 50, 162
anger 144
angle 247
Anglican 159
anglophobia 134
angry 30
angular 241
animal 17, 25, 71, 96, 232
animal feed 221
animal kingdom 232
animal rights 232
animal welfare 232
animosity 35
ankle 72
anniversary 49, 184, 249
announce 269
announcer 271
annoyed 30
annual 236, 307
anode 243
anointing 40
anonymous 129
anorak 64
another 200, 271
answer 91, 122, 156, 164
answer the phone 274
answering machine 275
answerphone 275
ant 234
Antarctic 214
anthology 179
anthropological 138
anthropologist 138
anthropology 138
anthroposophy 164
anti-choice 98
anti-Semite 135

anti-Semitic 135
anti-Semitism 135
antiabortion 98
antiapartheid 98
antifeminism 98
antigovernment 107
antinuclear 98
antipathy 35
antiquarian 194, 266
antiquarian bookshop 266
antique shop 194
antiques 199
antiquity 141
antivirus 280
antiwar 98, 105
anus 13, 14
anxiety 144
any 23, 46, 77, 191, 195, 232, 255, 302
apartheid 135
apartment 86, 88, 124
apartment building 86
apartment house 87
ape 233
aperture 172
app 94, 282
appalling 130
apparent 127
appeal 19, 109, 111
appeal to 29
appealing 22
appearance 15, 16, 166
appeasement 117
appendectomy 81
appendicitis 70, 81
appendix 69, 266
appetite 27, 76
applause 176
apple 27, 56
apple juice 57
appliance 90, 260
application 189
applied 143
applied for 256
apply 77, 191
apply for 117, 189
apply make-up 39
apply paint 168
apply the brakes 256
appoint 106, 299
appointment 75, 106, 298, 312
appreciate 186
apprentice 310
approach 20
approaching 26
apron 66
aptitude 152
aptitude test 144, 152
Arab 134

arable land 220
arbitrate 316
arbitration 316
arbitrator 316
arch 178
archaeological 138
archaeology 138
archbishop 163
architect 177
architect's client 177
architectural 177
architecture 177, 178
archives 140
Arctic 214
area 97, 117, 197, 206, 215, 218, 219, 223, 224, 229, 246, 250, 285
area code 275
argument 165
aristocracy 99
arithmetic 151, 246
arithmetic(al) 246
arithmetical problem 246
arm 12, 13, 40, 71
armada 291
armchair 90
armed 117, 132
armed forces 118
arms control 118
arms dealer 298
arms merchant 298
arm wrestling 84
army 118, 119, 159
aroma 27
around 37, 51, 91, 97, 188, 204, 211
around here 232
around the bend 285
arousal 36
arouse 36
arrange 198, 312
arrangement 168, 173, 243
arrest 112, 131
arrest warrant 112
arrival 189, 288, 289
arrival lounge 289
arrival time 289
arrivals board 189
arrive 44, 288
arrow key 278
arse 208
arson 131
arsonist 131
art 83, 100, 138, 141, 150, 167, 169, 170, 212, 257
art academy 149
art college 149
art dealer 194
art deco 177
art director 305
art gallery 169

art nouveau 169, 177
artefact 139
artery 14
arthritis 245
article 26, 66, 257, 264
artificial 207, 220
artillery 119
artist 48, 61, 131, 168, 170
artistic 198
Arts 149
arts 153
artwork 170
Aryan 135
asap 94
as follows 176
as if 26
as the crow flies 233
ascend to heaven 162
ascending 281
ash 229
ash (tree) 235
ashamed 32
ashcan 91
ashes 41
ashore 292
ashtray 201
Asia 214, 215
Asian 214, 215
ask a question 281
ask for the moon 205
asleep 40
asparagus 55, 220
ass 208, 233
assailant 131
assassinate 108
assassination 108
assault 132
assemble 257
assembly 117, 257, 258
assembly line 257
assembly shop 257
assess 156
assessment 114, 152, 156
assets 304
assign homework 154
assignment 154
assistance 115, 130, 274
assistant 193, 242, 311
assistant professor 310
associate 33
association 96, 124, 303
Association football 196
assume 110

A

assumption 146
assurance 307
asteroid belt 205
asthma 68, 245
asthmatic 245
astonished 30
astrologer 164
astrological 138
astrology 138, 164
astronaut 206
astronomy 205
astrophysics 240
asylum 134
asylum seeker 112, 134
at a speed of 204
at all 27
at anchor 292
at break 182
at first 228
at home 27, 51, 113
at last 27
at least 92
at peace 40
at rest 40, 241
at school 154
at sea 292
at the bottom 155, 197
at the corner 285
at the docks 217
at the moment 82, 126, 127, 191, 199
at the office 274
at the seaside 216
at the top 155
at your end 238
atheism 164
atheist 10, 160, 164
athlete's foot 70
athletics 83, 196
Atlantic Ocean 216
atlas 264
ATM 302
atmosphere 180, 205
atom 240, 241
atomic 240
atom(ic) bomb 119
atomic nucleus 240
atomic number 243
atomic weight 240, 243
atoms 243
atrocities 133
attaché case 261
attached house 87
attachment 280
attack 24, 68, 108, 119, 120, 132, 134, 135
attacker 131
attend 162, 175, 186

attend a course 150
attend a school 148
attendant 63, 286, 290, 311
attending 80
attic 88
attic room 88
attitude 28, 142
attorney 109, 110
attraction(s) 187
attractive 15, 24, 36
attractiveness 15
au pair 309
audible 26
audience 176, 306
audio 26
audiovisual 264
audiovisual aids 154
audit 114
aunt 47, 51, 185
austerity 297
austerity measures 297
austerity programme 297
Australia 214
Australian 74, 214
author 180, 266, 267
authoritarian 99
auto(mobile) 284
auto racing 195
autobahn 284
autobiographical 179
autobiography 179
autofocus 172
autograph 199
automated 258
automated-teller 302
automatic 171
automatic regulation 258
automatically 258
automation 258
automobile insurance 307
automotive industry 258
autopsy 41
available 77
available-light 171
avalanche 229
avarice 32
average 227
avert 304
award 176, 197
aware 121
awareness 225
away 182, 286
away from 86, 97
away victory 196
axiom 146
axis 204

B
BA 149, 153
B&B 192
baby 13, 15, 17, 30, 39, 50, 51, 81, 133, 251
baby boom 17
baby boomers 17
baby carriage 17
baby-minder 17
baby-sitter 17
babyish 44
bachelor 48
Bachelor of Arts 149, 153
Bachelor of Science 153
bachelor's degree 149, 153
bacillus 237
back 78, 90, 91, 188, 316
back (n.) 13, 14, 72, 75, 78, 83
back door 88
back garden 88, 219
back passage 14
back up 285
backyard 88, 94, 219
back yard 88, 94, 219
backache 76, 78
backbencher 102
backhand 197
backpack 261
backpacking 199
backside 14, 208
backslash 278
backup 278
backups 285
backwoods 219
backwoodsman 219
backyard 88
bacon 55, 192
bacon and eggs 60
bacterium 237
bad 28, 31, 69, 298
bad – good 23
bad / good at 344
bad at sums 246
bad blood 35
bad connection 275
bad line 275
bad nerves 14
badly 72, 153
badly groomed 16
badminton 197
bag 61, 190, 193, 261, 290
baggage 190, 290
baggage cart 190, 288
baggage insurance 190
baggage room 190
baggy 84

bags 190, 261
baguette 54
bail 111
bake 58
baked 56
baked potatoes 56
baker 310
balance 104
balance of payments 297
balance of trade 297
balanced budget 297
balcony 88
bald(ing) 16
ball 17, 186
ball bearing(s) 256
ballad 180
ballet 174
ballot 104, 315
ballots 104
ballpark 195
ballpoint 313
Baltic Sea 216
banana 56
band 174, 187
Band-Aid™ 72
bang 205
bank 216, 226, 244, 265, 302, 303, 304
bank charges 302
bank clerk 311
bank code 303
bank deposits 303
bank employee 311
bank heist 132
bank holiday 182
bank manager 303
bank raid 132
bank robbery 132
bank sorting code 303
banker 303
banking 281
banknote 257
bankruptcy 301
banns 48
baptism 50
Baptist 159
baptize 163
Bar 110
bar 61, 63, 174, 196, 201, 278
bar code 278
bar of chocolate 55
bar of soap 38
barbecue 59
barber 39
bargain 193
bargain with 316
bargaining 111, 316
bark 236
barkeeper 63
barmaid 63, 201
barman 63, 201
barn 88, 222

baroque 169, 177
barrel 261
barriers 117, 297
barrister 110
bartender 63, 201
base 119, 243
base of a pyramid 247
baseball 195, 197
baseball cap 66
baseline 197
basement 88
basic 130, 165
basic research 240
basket 91, 193
basketball 197
basketry 198
bass 173
bath 38, 51, 90, 191
bath mat 91
bathe 51
bathing suit 65
bathrobe 65
bathroom 87, 92
bathroom cabinet 90
bathroom scale(s) 90
bathtub 90
battalion 119
batter 133
battered wife 133
battery 172, 259
battery life 282
battle 119
battlefield 119, 236
battleship 119
Bauhaus 157, 177
bay 216
BBM™ 202
BC 94
be a gem and 212
be absent 155
be accused of 180
be afraid 127, 173, 191, 292, 313
be afraid of 289
be allowed to 232
be bad at 246
be cancelled 289
be charged with 110
be delayed 289
be derailed 287
be descended from 233
be drowned 229
be due to 254
be entitled to 114, 115
be equal to 250, 251
be fined for 286
be good at 246
be good company 185
be in for 228
be in pain 78

be inclined to 238
be into sth. 83, 84, 128, 199
be lucky to 197
be lukewarm on 105
be my guest 186
be offside 197
be on a committee 103
be on painkillers 81
be on short time 316
be on social security 115
be on strike 290, 315
be on the pill 77
be on welfare 115
be passionate about 198
be prejudiced 134
be required to 226
be scheduled to 288
be set in 176
be shot at 132
be sick 76
be supposed to 82, 83
be surplused 126
beach 216, 219
bean 222
beans 55, 59
bear 17
bear (n.) 233
bear (v.) 29
bear market 304
bear sb. a grudge 35
bearing 15
bearing(s) 256
beast 232
beat 58, 93, 133, 174
beat time 174
beat up 133
beaten 19
beautiful 15, 16, 166, 218
beauty contest 187
beaver 238
become 70, 73, 159
become addicted 128
become fossilized 211
become insolvent 304
become petrified 211
bed 36, 60, 74, 89, 93
bed and breakfast 191, 192
bedroom 87, 88
bedside table 89
bedsit(ter) 86
bedtime story 51
bee 24, 234
beech (tree) 235

beef 55, 58
beekeeping 198, 199
beer 57, 200, 251, 261
beer mat 199
beetle 234
beets 221
before taxes 113
behave 22, 23, 91
behaved 156
behaviour 22, 24, 31, 35, 142, 143, 144, 195
behaviour pattern 145
behavioural 143
behaviourism 143
beheading 43
behind 14, 69, 125, 208
behind schedule 288
being 9, 161, 164
Belgium 215
belief 158, 164
believe 158, 164
believe in 161, 164
believe in God 160
believer 139, 164
bell 84, 91
bell the cat 238
belong 84
belong to 314
below 14
below freezing 227
below zero 227, 248
belt 66, 205, 219, 223, 258
bench 84
bench press 84
bend 52, 285
bender 129
benefit 115, 124, 127
benefit(s) 126
benefits 316
benevolent 23
benign 69
bereaved 42
bereavement 42
Bermuda shorts 65
Bermudas 65
berries 56
beside table 90
best 13, 32, 70, 172, 285, 300
best man 48
best-selling 267
bestseller 267
better 34, 61, 64, 91, 155
better world 40
between jobs 127
between shows 127
beverage 57
beyond 223
Bible 31, 160, 205

bibliography 264
bicycle 18, 286
bid 302
bid for 301
biennial 236
big 52, 193, 305
big bang 205
Big Dipper 205
big game 233
big issue 125
big losses 300
big seller 300
Big Wheel 187
bigamist 49
bigamy 49
bike 18, 94, 286
bike path 286
bikini 65
bill 62, 102, 103, 104, 302, 303
bill for 193
billboard 306
billfold 303
billion 230, 300
bin 56, 91
bind 133
binder 313
binding 266
binge 129
biochemistry 242
biodegradable 56
bioengineering 56
bioethics 56
biofuel 56, 226
biographer 179
biographical 179
biography 179
biological 138
biology 150
bioweapons 56
birch (tree) 235
bird 18, 233
bird flu 69
bird of prey 233
bird's nest 233
birdwatching 199
biro 313
birth 10, 50, 74, 99, 158
birth control 37
birth-control movement 98
birthday 10, 184
biscuit 54
biscuits 261
bisexual 98
bishop 48, 163
bistro 61
bit 12, 54, 227, 275
bitch 232
bite 78, 101, 234
bite the dust 43
biting cold 227
bitter 27, 200, 201
black 64, 96

B

black(s) 135
black community 135
black currants 56
black economy 296
Black Forest 219
black hole 205
black magic 164
black nationalism 98
black power 98
black sheep 222
black tea 57
black-and-white 171
black-tie 64
blackberries 56
blackboard 155
blackmail 131
blackmailer 131
bladder 14
blank 279
blanket 89
blaster 271
blazer 64
bleed 72, 78
blender 59
blessed 41
blighted 224
blind 12, 26, 74
blind(s) 91
blind drunk 129
blindness 74
bloated 16
bloc 116
block 87, 170, 178, 312
block legislation 103
block of flats 86
blockhouse 87
blond(e) 16
blood 13, 14, 35, 69
blood bank 244
blood clot 244
blood donor 14
blood poisoning 69
blood pressure 69, 77
blood sample 244
blood test 244
blood vessel 244
bloodless 108
bloody 32
bloom 236
blossom 236
blotto 129
blouse 16, 64
blow 39, 129
blow (blown) 260
blow coke 129
blow-dry 38
blow up 172
blow-up 172
blowout 286
blue 15, 205, 292
blue-collar worker 310
blue jeans 65

blue tit 233
blueberries 56
blueprint 177
Blu-ray Disc™ 277
Blu-ray™ drive 277
blurb 266
boar 55
board 106, 155, 189, 191, 223, 291, 292, 299, 304, 313
board a train 288
board and lodging 191
board game 18
board of directors 299
Board of Trade 298
boarding card 290
boarding pass 290
boarding school 148
boat 291, 292
boat train 291
boat trip 188
boater 65
bodily harm 131
body 12, 13, 39, 40, 166, 171, 204, 241
body fluid 245
body tissue 245
bodybuilding 83, 84
bodyweight exercise 84
bog 218
boil 58, 243
boil (n.) 69
boiled egg 54
boiled eggs 192
boiled potatoes 56
boiler 91
boiler suit 66
boiling point 243
bold 24
bolt 255
bolt (v.) 222
bomb 119, 273
bomb attack 134
bombardment 262
bombing 119
bon appetit! 60
bond(ing) 242
bonds 304
bone 13, 14
bone marrow 245
bonnie 216
bonus 316
boob tube 270
book 18, 29, 32, 199, 264, 266, 272, 278
book (v.) 61, 188, 191, 292
book a seat 289
book club 266
book fair 267
bookcase 89

booked 191
booking 188
booking clerk 311
bookkeeper 310
bookkeeping 114
bookmark 281
books in print 267
bookseller 266
bookshelf 89
bookshop 37, 193, 194
bookstall 266
bookstore 193
bookworm 234
boom 17
boom box 271
booming 298
boondocks 215
boost 299
boost output 258
booster 207
boot (up) 277
booth 26, 275, 294
boots 65
booze 129, 200
boozed 129
boozer 129, 200
border 116
border clash 116
boring 24
born 10, 81, 208
borough 96, 97
borrow 264, 303
boson 262
boss 30, 58, 309
botanic(al) garden 236
botany 236
both 102, 153
both … and 97, 105
bottle 38, 57, 59, 129, 226, 261
bottle bank 226
bottle-feed 50
bottom 14, 87, 155, 197, 208
bottom set 156
bottoms up! 200
bouncing powder 129
bound 266
bound for 293
boundary 204, 223
bow 292
bow tie 66
bowdlerize 180
bowel movement 13
bowels 13, 14, 76
bowl 59
bowler (hat) 65
box 38, 125, 260, 261, 270, 271, 272, 273, 275, 278
box of cigars 201

box office 175
boxer shorts 65
boxers 65
boxing 196, 197
Boxing Day 183
boy 15, 18, 31, 130
boycott 107
boyfriend 34
boyish 44
bra 65
braces 66, 79
brain 12
brain tumour 12, 81
brake 256
bran 54, 82
branch 145, 159, 166, 236
brand 194
brand loyalty 306
brass 24, 212
brass band 174
brass tacks 212
brat 18
brave 24
bravery 31
brawl 133
BRB 94
bread 54, 56, 58, 60, 82
break 71, 113, 182
break (broke) 12
break (broken) 12
break a record 195
break even 300
break-in 132
break out 74, 133
break out in 70
break up 49
breakdown 14, 286
breaker 260
breakfast 60, 191, 192
breaking and entering 132
breakthrough 117, 262
breast 14
breast(s) 13
breast cancer 69, 244
breast-feed 50
breast milk 13
breath 76, 78
breathe 76
breathing 83
breeding 221
breeze 228
bribery 131
brick 178
bricklayer 310
bride 48, 186
bridegroom 48
bridesmaid 48
bridge 79, 177, 254
brief 42, 155

brief(ly) 353
briefcase 261
briefs 65
brigade 119
bright 16
brightness 172
brim 261
bring (brought) 189
bring a suit 109
bring down 82, 126
bring out 267
bring up 51, 52
brisk 298
Britain 156
British Isles 217
brittle 255
broad(-shouldered) 15
broad-minded 23
broadband 282
broadcast 270
broadcasting corporation 270
broadsheet 268
brochure 188, 306
broil 59
broke (break) 12
broken 30
broken (break) 12
broker 304
bronchitis 70
bronze 169, 212
Bronze Age 212
bronze bust 169
brook 217
broom 92, 93
broth 55
brothel 37
brother 46
brother-in-law 46
brown 87
brown bear 233
brown bread 54
brownstone 87
browse 264, 279
browser 279
bruise 72
bruised 72
brunch 60
brunette 16
brush 38, 93, 168
brush one's teeth 78
Brussels sprouts 55
BSc 153
BSE 221
bucket 43, 261
bucks 303
bud 38, 39, 236
Buddha 160
Buddhism 158
Buddhist 158
buddy 33
budgerigar 233
budget 104, 297
budget cuts 297

budget deficit 297
budget freeze 297
budget hole 297
budgetary 297
budgie 233
buff 199
buffer 278
buffet 63
buffet (car) 287
bug 68, 234, 276
bugger 50
build 177
builder 177
building 33, 73, 87, 134, 177, 178, 224, 312
building blocks 18
building code 308
building contractor 178
building loan 303
building materials 177
building permit 308
building plan 177
building plot 308
building regulations 308
building site 177
building society 303
building work 177
built 15
built-in 89
bulb 236, 259, 260
bulky 273
bull 22, 91, 238
bull in a china shop 238
bull market 304
bulletin 269
bulletin board 313
bully 19
bum 208
bump sb. 290
bump sb. off 43
bumper 285
bun 54
bundled software 276
bungalow 87
burden 232
bureau 89, 106, 227
bureau de change 190
burette 242
burglar 132
burglarize 132
burglary 132
burgle 132
burial 41
burly 15
burn 225
burning 43
burns 71
burnt 52

burst tyre 286
bury 24, 41, 229
bus 71, 132, 293, 294
bus card 306
bus lane 285
bus route 293
bus stop 293
busboy 63
bush 233
bushes 219
business 26, 182, 280, 298, 301
business acumen 298
business card 312
business class 290
business college 148
business cycle 297
business executive 136
business lunch 312
business profits 296
business school 148
business section 269
business suit 64
business tax 114
businessman 136, 298
businesspeople 298
businesswoman 298
busker 187
busking 187
bust 14, 169
busy 24, 97, 275, 313
butcher 309, 310
butter 54, 60
buttercup 235
butterfly 199, 234
butterscotch 55
buttocks 13, 14
button 66, 171, 172, 278
buxom 15
buy 193, 300
buy (bought) 194
buy a pig in a poke 222
buy insurance 307
buy the farm 43
buyer 300
buying power 297
buyout 300
buzz 274
buzzword 98, 305
BVD's™ 65
by air 289
by airmail 273
by birth 158
by bus 293
by certified mail 273
by cheque 303
by credit card 303
by mail order 193

by plane 289
by post 272, 273
by profession 309
by rail 287
by registered post 273
by return 272
by road 285
by the same post 272
by the time 44
by trade 309
by-election 102
bypass 285
bystander 132

C
cab 294
cabbage 55
cabdriver 303
cabin 87
cabinet 89, 90, 105
cabinet meeting 105
cabinet minister 121
cabinet reshuffle 105
cabinetmaker 310
cable 260, 279
cable car 293
cable television 270
cache 279
cactus 236, 237
cadaver 40
Caesarean 50, 81
café 61, 286
cafeteria 61
cage 234
cake 54, 58
calculate 246
calculate to two places 246
calculation 246
calculus 246
call 13, 77, 83, 160, 192, 193, 274, 275
call a strike 107, 315
call an election 104
call at 288
call back 274
call box 275
call for 72
call girl 37
call-in (programme) 271
call off a strike 315
call on 185
call sb. up 274
called 158, 232
caller 274
calling party 274
calm 24, 26
Calvinism 159
camera 171, 172, 271
camera body 171
camera store 194

camp 40, 133
campaign 101, 104, 299, 305, 306
campus 149
camshaft 256
can (n.) 90, 261
can (v., n.) 59
can of beans 261
can opener 59
canal 217
canary 233
cancel 188, 191, 206, 289
cancellation 190
Cancer 214
cancer 40, 42, 69, 74, 244
cancer-causing 242
candid camera 271
candidate 101, 104
candy 55, 129, 171
cannabis 129
canned 59
canoe 291
canteen 60, 61
canvas 168
canyon 218
cap 37, 66, 171
capable of 340
capacitor 259
capacity 277
cape 216
Cape of Good Hope 216
capital 296
capital-gains tax 114
capital goods 296
capital punishment 111
capitalism 99
capitalist 99
capsize 292
capsule 206
captain 118, 182, 196, 290, 291, 292
caption 269
capture 120, 279
car 26, 28, 71, 193, 284, 286, 287
car industry 258
car insurance 307
car manufacturers 257
car park 286
car-park attendant 311
car rental 284
caravan 87
carbohydrates 243
carbon 242
carbon dioxide 226
carbon nanotube 262
carbonated 57
carburetor 256

carburettor 256
carcass 40
card 114, 153, 172, 189, 190, 197, 272, 281, 290, 306, 312
card index 313
cardboard box 125, 261
cardigan 64
cardinal 163
cardio training 84
cardiology 244
cards 17, 199
care 43, 51, 81, 115
care for 28, 62
career 131
careful 23
careless 23
caretaker 310
cargo 290
cargo ship 291
carnal knowledge 36
carnation 236
carnival 184
carpenter 310
carpet 92, 93
carpet(ing) 91
carport 88
carriage 17, 287
carrier 272
carrier bag 261
carry 196
carry a story 269
carry-on bag(gage) 290
carry out 145
carryall 190
carryout 61
carsick 68
cart 190, 193, 222, 288
carte du jour 63
carton 201, 261
cartoon 170
cartridge 313
carve 169
carving 169
case 44, 109, 111, 190, 201, 261, 282
case history 80
case of wine 261
case study 144, 146
cash 190, 193, 281, 302, 303
cash dispenser 302
cash in one's chips 43
cash machine 302
cash on delivery 273
cash payment 302
cash register 302
cashier 192, 310
cashier's desk 192
casino 187
cask 261

cassette recorder 271
cast 176
cast in bronze 169
cast their ballots 104
castle 86
casual 64
casuals 65
casualties 120
casualty 72, 81
cat 70, 232
CAT scan 244
catalogue 193, 264
catalyst 243
catch 233
catch (a) cold 69, 74
catch (caught) 29
catch a glimpse of 26
catch a train 287
catch at a straw 222
catechism 163
cathedral 162
cathode 243
Catholic 159
Catholicism 84, 158, 159
cattle 220, 221
cattle breeding 221
caught 56, 238
cauliflower 55
causality 165
cause 32, 69, 130, 146, 166, 184, 189, 230, 351
cause (v.) 229
cause a nuisance 131
cause damage 307
caused by 14, 78, 230
cave 218
CD 212
CD drive 277
CD player 26
CD-ROM 29, 265
CD-ROM drive 277
cease-fire 117
ceiling 89
celebrate 48, 184, 185
celebration 184
celestial 204
cell 40, 237, 259
cell division 237
cell phone 274
cellar 88
Celsius 228
cement works 258
cemetery 41
censorship 268
census 145, 237
cent 110, 193, 300
cent(s) 302
centimetre 250
central 274
central bank 304

central city 224
central heating 91
Central Intelligence Agency 106
central London 224
central nervous system 245
centralized 112
centrally 91
centrally planned 296
centre 80, 97, 100, 158, 204, 223, 247, 268
centre of gravity 241
centre-left 100
centrifugal 241
cents 302
CEO 299
ceramic 254
cereals 55, 60, 192
ceremony 48, 153, 184, 270
certain 21
certificate 40, 48, 50, 77, 152, 153
certificate of 190
certified mail 273
certified public accountant 310
cesspit 88
cesspool 88
CFCs 225
chain 301
chain-smoker 201
chair 43, 90, 309
chair (v.) 106, 309
chairman 309
chairman of the board 299
chairperson 309
chairwoman 309
chalk 155
chalk cliffs 218
chalk drawing 170
challenge 195
challenged 73
challenger 195
chamber 43, 102
chamber music 173
chamber of commerce 280, 281, 298
chamber orchestra 173
chambermaid 311
chamois 93
champagne 200
champion 195, 197
championship 195
chancel 178
chancellor 105, 121
chances 248
change 50, 100, 145, 171, 190, 226, 302

change a tyre 286
change at/for 288
change course 292
change for 294
change gear 256
change into 190
change of climate 228
change of life 20
change purse 303
change sth. 277
Channel 217
channel 217, 270
channel-hop 270
channel-surf 270
Channel Tunnel 189
chaplain 80, 163
chapter 266
character 32, 176, 278
character part 176
character recognition 278
charge 62, 110, 114, 259, 302
charge(d) 240
charge nurse 81
charged with 110
charger 282
charges 111, 272, 274, 302
charitable 114
charity 21, 24, 32
charlie 129
charm 23, 44
charming 23
charter 290
charter flight 290
charter plane 290
chartered accountant 310
chat 280
chat group 280
chat show 271
chat show host 271
chauffeur 311
chauvinism 134, 136
chauvinist 136
cheap 194
cheap day return 288
cheat 32, 152
check 62, 193, 264, 280
check in 192, 290
check-in counter 290
check one's bags 190
check out 84, 192
check sth. in 288
check the pressure 286
checker 278
checking account 303
checkout 192

checkout clerk 311
checkroom 61, 288
checkroom attendant 63
checkup 77
Cheddar 251
cheek 275
cheeky 24
cheer 57
cheerful 24
cheers! 186, 200
cheese 54, 172
chef 63
chemical 220, 242
chemical engineer 242
chemical enginee-ring 242
chemical properties 242
chemist 194, 242
chemistry 150, 242
cheque 190, 303
chequebook journa-lism 269
cherry 56
cherry tree 236
chess 195, 198
chest 13, 14, 76, 261
chest of drawers 89
chest training 84
chestnut 56
chestnut (tree) 235
chestnuts 235
chew 201
chick 18
chicken 55, 58
chicken adj. 238
chicken and egg 222
chicken feed 301
chicken out 238
chickenpox 69
chickens 221
chief 198, 269
chief administrative officer 309
chief cook 63
chief executive 301
chief executive officer 299
chief of police 309
chief of staff 105
chief resident 80
child 246
child(ren) 17, 19, 50, 51
child abuse 17, 51
child labour 17, 130
child prostitution 269
childhood 17
childminder 17
children 18, 49, 130, 133
children's 257

children's wear 17
chilly 227
chimney 88
chimney sweep 310
chimp 233
chimpanzee 233
china 91
china shop 22, 91, 238
chip 255
chip shop 61
chipboard 254
chippy 61
chips 56, 61
chiropractor 70
chisel 255
chocaholic 129
chocolate 55, 251
choir 173
cholesterol 82
choose 62, 104
chop 58
chord 174
chore 92
chores 51
chorus 173, 180, 237
Christ 160, 161
christen 163
christening 50
Christian 101, 162
Christian(s) 158
Christian name 10
Christianity 158
Christmas 183
Christmas bonus 316
Christmas Day 183
Christmas Eve 183
chronic 68
chronicle 140
chronicler 140
chronological 138
chronology 138
chuckle 30
chum 33
church 41, 48, 96, 159, 162, 178
church choir 173
Church of England 41, 159
church wedding 48
churchyard 41
CIA 106
CID 112
cigar 201
cigarette 201
cigarette case 201
cigarette machine 201
cinema 175, 198
circle 247, 285, 294
circle (v.) 206
circuit 260
circuit breaker 260
circuit training 84
circular 204, 247

circular saw 255
circulation 14, 269
circumcision 163
circumference 247
circumstances 111
circus 187, 237
CIS 96
citizen 21, 33, 108
citizenship 98
City 97
city 25, 96, 97, 223, 224, 289
city boundaries 223
city centre 97, 223
city council 223
city dweller 223
city editor 269
City editor 269
city limits 223
city manager 310
city planning 223
city treasurer 304
civic education 142
civics 142
civil disobedience 107
civil engineer 311
civil rights 98, 106, 107
civil rights activist 98, 107
civil rights move-ment 107
civil servant 20, 311
civil service em-ployee 311
civil wedding 48
civilian 120
civilization 215
civilized 22, 24
claim 116, 135, 229, 307
clam 238
clash 35, 116
class 33, 156, 272, 288
class (v.) 138
class register 155
class reunion 185
classical 141, 173, 198
classification 243
classified ad 305
classless 145
classroom 155
claustrophobia 134
claw 233
clay 169
clean 91, 92, 93, 129, 155
clean (v.) 58
Clean Air Act 103
clean out 92
clean up 92
cleaner 92, 201, 311

C

cleaners 39
cleaning 92
cleaning agent 93
cleaning cloth 93
cleaning lady 92
cleaning rag 93
cleaning utensil 93
cleanliness 38
cleansing 135
cleansing cream 39
clear 31, 267
clear away 93
clear day 227
clear up 228
clearance 189, 194
clearing 219
clearly 25, 155
cleft palate 74
clergy 122, 136, 163
clergyman 136, 163
clergywoman 163
clerk 311
clever 23, 24
click 278
client 62, 177, 305
cliff 218
cliffhanger 179
climate 226, 227, 228
climate change 226
climate disaster 230
climax 36, 180
clinic 78, 244
clinical 143, 244
clinical trials 244
clip 313
clipboard 279, 313
clitoris 36
cloakroom 61
cloakroom attendant 63
clock 90, 91, 198
clock radio 271
clockmaker 310
clone 222
close 155
close (adj.) 34, 227
close (v.) 40
close a file 277
closed 291, 315
closet 89
close-up 172
clot 244
cloth 93, 266
clothes 64, 65, 77
clothes brush 93
clothes store 194
clothesaholic 129
clothing 64, 66, 196, 257
cloud 228
cloud over 228
cloudless 228
cloudy 228
clover 236

clown 187
cloze test 152
club 18, 21, 33, 185
club sandwich 54
club soda 57
clubfoot 74
cluster bomb 119
clutch 256
cm 250
co-op 86
coach 197, 289, 293
coalition 100
coast 215, 216, 234
coast(line) 216
coaster 187
coat 64, 93
cobweb 234
cocaine 128, 129, 251
coccus 237
cockney 217
cockpit 290
cockroach 234
cocoa 57
COD 273
code 113, 145, 237, 274, 275, 278, 280, 303, 308
coffee 27, 56, 57, 60, 62, 192
coffee bar 61
coffee grinder 58
coffee mill 58
coffee plantation 220
coffee shop 61, 192
coffee table 89
coffeemaker 59
coffeepot 59, 261
coffin 41
coil 37, 259
coin 199, 302
coitus 36
coitus interruptus 37
coke 129
coked (up) 129
cola 57
cold 69, 74, 77, 78, 227
cold as charity 24
cold front 227
coleslaw 56
collaboration 186
collaborative 262
collage 170
collapse 68, 254
collapsible 89, 90
collapsible bag 190
colleague 33, 312
collect 113, 199, 206, 294
collect on delivery 273
collective bargaining 316

collective bargaining agreement 316
college 148, 149, 240
college for further adult education 149
collide 71
collider 44
collision 71
colloquial 44
cologne 38, 39
colon 245
Colonial 177
Colorado beetle 234
colour 73, 135, 180
colour prints 171
colour slide 172
coloured(s) 135
colouring book 18
colouring set 18
colours 292
column 178, 245, 269
columnist 269
com 281
comb 39
combat 112, 131
combine 166
combine harvester 222
combustible 243
combustion 243, 256
come 25, 215, 272
come ashore 292
come by a route 285
come down to 208
come down with 69, 74
come from 46
come home 292
come into flower 235
come of age 19
come out 36, 227, 267
come out in 70
come to power 100
come to see 47
come true 208
comedy 179, 271
comet 204
comfortable 288
comic 179
comic(s) 18
comic relief 179
command 118, 278
command economy 296
command module 207
commander 118
commander-in-chief 118

commandments 160
Commandments 162
commentator 271
commerce 298
Commerce (Department) 298
Commerce Secretary 298
commercial 207, 262, 298
commercial (n.) 271
commercial art 170
commercial artist 170
commercial college 148
commercial English 298
commercial school 148
commercial television 270
commercials 306
commission 300
commission (on) 106
commit 42, 49
commit a crime 110
committee 102, 103, 105, 133, 309
commodity exchange 304
common 68, 100, 124, 186, 304
common denominator 247
common soldier 118
common-law 48
Commons 102, 103
commonwealth 96
commune 98
communication 35
communications 263
communications satellite 207
Communion 163
communiqué 117
communism 99
communist 101
community 96, 116, 135
community charge 114
community work 96
commute 284, 294
commuter 284
companion 33
companionship 34
company 13, 34, 86, 118, 185, 193, 226, 259, 267, 279, 281, 298, 314, 315
comparative 143
compartment 201, 288, 290

compassionate 23
competition 177, 195, 296, 301
competitor 33, 301
complaint 68
complete 79, 113
complete a form 307
completely 23
complexion 16
component 243, 255
components 254, 258
compose a tweet 202
composer 173, 309
composition 151, 168, 173, 210, 242
compositor 267
compound 242, 243
comprehension 151
comprehensive insurance 307
comprehensive school 148
compress 172, 279
compression 172, 277
comprise 102
compromise 117
compulsory 150
compulsory deposit 226
compulsory subject 150
compute 246
computer 194, 276
computer-aided 276
computer-controlled 257
computer game 276
computer industry 260
computer literacy 276
computer-literate 276
computer science 150, 276
computer virus 280
computerize 258
computerized 265
comrade 33
con artist 132
con man 132
conceited 24
concentrate 225
concentrated 243
concentration camp 133
concept 165, 305
conception 37
concern 21
concert 174, 270
concerto 174
concierge 192

conclusion 146
concrete 169, 178
concussion 71
condenser 259
condition 13, 68, 72, 74, 143
conditioned 143
conditioner 39
conditioning 143
conditions 224, 316
condo(minium) 86
condom 37
conduct 145, 174
conduct an experiment 240
conductivity 255
conductor 174, 240, 288, 294, 309
cone 235
confederation 96
conference 117, 268
conference room 312
confession 163
confidence 104
confidence man 132
confidence trickster 132
configuration 276
confined to 74
confirmation 163
confirmed 290
conflict 31, 35, 116, 117, 142
congenital 73
congested 285
congestion 285
congregation 163
congress 102, 314
Congress 104
Congressman 102
Congresswoman 102
conifer 235
coniferous 235
connect 275
connecting rod 256
connection 129, 275, 288
connection(s) 35
conquest 156
conscience 31
conscious 82, 143
conscription 118
conscripts 118
conservative 23, 100
Conservative 101
conservatory 88
considerate 22
consideration 35
consignment 301
consist of 102
consistent 165
consommé 55
conspiracy 107, 108

conspirator 107
constant 247
constellation 205
constipation 69
constituency 103
constitution 103
constitutional 99
construct 124, 177
construction 124, 177, 178, 255
construction industry 177
construction time 178
construction work 177
consulate 189
consulate general 189
consult 264
consultant 80, 114, 127, 310
consume 251
consumer goods 257
consumer prices 297
consumption 70, 297
contact 35, 202
contain 261
container 261
container ship 291
contemporary 140
contempt 35
content 180, 202
contented 22
contents 266, 307
contest 187, 195
contested 49
Continent 214
continent 214
Continental 214
continental 60, 214, 228
continental breakfast 192
continental drift 210
continental shelf 210
continued education 149
continuing education 149
continuous 156
contraception 37
contract 300, 312, 316
contract (v.) 68, 70, 74
contractor 178
contralto 173
contribute 226
contribution 114
contributor 269
control 37, 74, 82, 118, 124, 189, 207, 225, 229, 278, 282

controlled by 262
controller 290
convalescent home 21
convenience 291
convenience food 54
convention 101, 104
conversation 35, 274
convert 158
converter 259
conveyor belt 258
convict 111
convincing 176
convincingly 176
cook 63
cookbook 58
cooker 59, 90
cookery book 58
cookie 24, 54, 280
cookies 261
cooking 58, 198
cool 227
cool as a cucumber 24
coop 222
cooperate 34
cooperation 34
cooperative 22, 86, 124
cop 208, 286
copper 212
copperplate print 170
cops and robbers 17
copy 267, 269, 277, 278, 305, 313
copy down 155
copy off from 152
copy paper 313
copying 313
copyright 267
copywriter 305
cord 260
cordless phone 274
cords 65
corduroys 65
core 84, 210
core subject 150, 152
Corinthian column 178
corkscrew 59
corn 55, 70, 221
corn poppy 236
corner 285
cornflakes 55, 60
cornflower 235
coronary 69
corporal punishment 19
corporate 299
corporate culture 299
corporate identity 306
corporate image 306

C

corporation 113, 270, 298, 299
corporation tax 114
corps 119
corpse 40
correct 36, 122
correct a flaw 276
correspondence course 149
correspondent 269
corridor 88
corrode 243
corrosion 243, 255
corrupt 23
corruption 32, 107, 314
corset 65
cosmetics 39, 194
cosmology 205
cosmonaut 206
cosmos 204
cost 297, 302
cost(s) 258
cost increases 297
cost of living 297
cost per unit 258
costs 115, 245, 296, 300
costume 176
costume jewellery 213
cot 17
cottage 87
cottage cheese 54
cotton 39, 221
cotton bud 39
cotton buds 38
cotton candy 271
cotton wool 39
couch 89, 90
couch potatoes 270
cough 69, 201
council 114, 117, 163
council flat 86, 124
council house 86
council housing 86, 124
council tax 114
counsel 109, 110
counsellor 48, 105, 144
count 246
count (up) to 246
countdown 206
counter 61, 193, 290
counterculture 98
counterfeiter 131
counterfeiting 131
counterintelligence 118
counteroffensive 119
counterrevolution 108

country 19, 46, 96, 116, 117, 119, 142, 188, 215, 218
country code 280
countryside 218
county 97, 112
coup 108
couple 48, 51
couple of 251, 301
coupon 273, 306
courage 23
courageous 24, 238
courageously 23
course 62, 149, 150, 195, 292
courseware 281
court 19, 109, 111, 114, 195, 197
court proceedings 109
court shoes 65
court-martial 120
courteous 23
courtesy 10, 35
courtyard 88
cousin 47
cover 269, 307
cover (n.) 266
cover a story 269
cover charge 62
cover note 307
cover story 269
coverage 307
covered 115
covered by 301
covered with 219
cow 158, 221
coward 24
cowardly 24
coworker 312
cowshed 222
crack 128, 280
cracked soil 230
cracker 54, 280
cradle 17
craft shop 194
crafts 198
craftsman 310
craftswoman 310
cram for an exam 152
cramp 70
crank 255
crankshaft 256
crash 42, 71, 276, 289, 304
crash helmet 66
crash into 71
crate 261
crater 205
crave (for) 29
craven 24
craving 29
crayons 18
crazed 131

cream 38, 39, 54, 74
cream soda 57
create 304
create a file 277
create an event 202
create wealth 297
creation account 205
creative(ly) 305
creativity 144
creator 160
crèche 17
credit card 303
credit(s) 152
Creed 163
creeping inflation 297
cremate 41
cremation 41
crematorium 41
crematory 41
Crescent 230
crew 290, 292
crew cut 16
crib 17
crib off from 152
cricket 197
cricket ground 195
cricket pitch 195
crime 36, 110, 120, 131, 314
crime rate 131
crimes against humanity 133
criminal 36, 120, 131
criminal case 109
criminal investigation department 112
criminal offence 131
criminals 33
criminological 138
criminology 138
cripple 73
crippled by 73
crisis 117, 124
critic 176
critical 72
critically 71
critically acclaimed 176
criticism 140, 141, 179
criticize 29
critique 164
crockery 91
crocodile 234
crocodile tears 234
croissant 60
croissants 192
crook 32
crop 221, 230
crop a photo 172
crop dusting 221
crop failure 221, 230
crop rotation 221

crop yields 221
cross 158, 196, 217
cross (adj.) 30
cross-examine 110
cross the border 116
cross the picket line 315
crossbar 196
crossing 27, 285
crossroads 285
crosswalk 285
crossword puzzle 199
crotchet 174
crow 233
crowd 33
crown 79
crown court 109
crown jewels 213
crown prince 121
crown princess 121
crucifixion 43
cruelty 96
cruelty to animals 232
cruise 284, 291
cruising altitude 290
crumb 92
Crusade 141
Crusader 141
crust 210
cry 30, 136, 234
crystal 277
crystals 210, 243
CT scan 244
Ctrl 278
cube 129, 247
cubed 247
cubism 169
cubists 169
cucumber 24, 56
cufflinks 66
cuisine 58, 63
CUL8R 94
cul-de-sac 285
cultivate 220
cultivated 235
cultural 36, 138, 139
cultural facilities 224
cultural heritage 138
cultural history 140
culture 98, 134, 138, 142, 158, 299
cum 88
cummerbund 66
cunning 24
cup 57, 59, 196, 197
cup that cheers 57
cupboard 89
curb 115
curd 192
cure 70, 129
curly 16
currant 54
currants 56

currency 304
current 217, 240, 259, 262
current account 303
curriculum 150, 151, 237
curry 55, 63
cursor 276
curtain 91
curtains 91
curve 285, 287
cushion 89
custody 49, 112
custom 138
customer 193, 300
customer service 193
customs 189
customs clearance 189
customs duty 114, 189
cut 12, 16
cut costs 258
cut diamond 213
cut flowers 235
cut in half 288
cut interest rates 297, 304
cut prices 300
cut subsidies 297
cut taxes 113
cut-throat competition 301
cute 15, 16
cuts 115, 124, 130, 297
cuts and bruises 72
cutting 212
cutting edge 262
CV 94
cybercafé 280
cyberfraud 281
cyberspace 265
cycle 286, 297
cyclical 126
cycling 199
cyclone 229
cylinder 256

D

dad(dy) 50
daff 235
daffodil 235
daily 77
daily (paper) 268
dairy cattle 221
dairy farming 220
daisy 235
damage 230
damage(s) 307
damages 109
Dame 121
damn 146
dance 173, 174, 185, 187

dance band 174
dance floor 174
dance studio 174
dancer 48, 174
dancing 174, 187
dandelion 235
Danish 266
dark 16
dark-haired 16
darkish 44
darling 50
dash 195
dashing 15
data 10, 140, 146, 265, 276, 277
data bank 265
data capture 279
data exchange 276
data link 279
data plan 282
data processing 260, 276
data-processing manager 299
data protection (act) 276
database 265
date 56, 267
date (v.) 185
date as postmark 273
date of birth 10
dating 211
daughter 46, 48
daughter-in-law 46
day 19, 24, 74, 128, 219, 284
day-care center 17
day centre 21
day nursery 17
day of sickness 68
day off 182
day trip 188
day tripper 188
DC 259
deactivate 279
dead 40, 120, 132
dead body 40
Dead Sea 215
deadline 269
deadly 32
deadly sin 32, 162
deaf 26, 74
deaf and dumb 26
deaf-and-dumb 74
deaf-mute 26, 74
deaf-muteness 74
deafness 74
deal 27, 298
deal in 298
deal with 298
dealer 128, 129, 194, 298
dear 121
dear departed 42

death 40, 130, 133, 184, 197
death camp 40, 133
death certificate 40
death penalty 43, 111
death toll 230
deathbed 40
deaths 128
debate 102
debate over 111
debt 297, 303
debug 276
decaffeinated 57
decay 79
deceased 40
deceleration 241
decency 32, 35
decent 22, 32, 125
deceptive 305
decide 58, 202
decide (on) 62
decide on 101
deciduous 235
decimal fraction 247
decimals 249
decipher 140
decision 105, 114
decision-making 142, 145
deck 292
deck chair 90
declare 189
declare war on 119
decline 21, 299
declining years 21
decode 279
decorator 310
decrepit 21
decrypt 279
deductible 114
deed 31, 308
deep 69, 292
deep breath 76
deep structure 180
deeply 158
deer 233
deerstalker 66
defamation 133
default 278
defeat 120
defecate 14
defect 73
defence 106, 110, 111, 118, 196
defence minister 106
defence policy 100
defence secretary 106
defence spending 118
defend 118
defendant 111
defender 196
deficiency 74, 245

deficit 297
deficit spending 297
define 165
definition 165, 264
deflation 297
deforestation 225
deg(rees) 214
degC 243
degree 148, 149, 153
degrees 247, 248
deity 160
delay 189
delayed 289
delegate 96, 104
delete 277
deli(catessen) 61, 194
delicious 27
delinquent 19
deliver 258, 273, 301
deliver a speech 103
delivery 50, 273, 301
deluge 228
demand 278, 296, 316
dementia 74
demise 40
democracy 99
democrat 101
democratic 99, 101
Democratic 101, 102
democratically 97
Democrats 101
demographic 145
demolish 224
demonstration 107
den 238
denims 65
denomination 158, 159
denominational school 159
denominator 247
denounce 107
dense 219
density 241
dental 78
dental floss 38, 79
dental surgeon 78
dentist 78
denture(s) 79
deny 160
deodorant 39
depart 287
depart from 151
departed 42
department 105, 112, 114, 116, 149, 245, 267, 298, 304, 305, 309
Department of Commerce 298
Department of Defense 118

D

Department of the Interior 106
department store 193
departure 189, 288, 289
departure lounge 289
departures board 189
depend on 202
dependence 128
dependency 128
dependent on 130, 230
depict 168
deployment 120
depose 108
deposit 191, 193, 210, 226, 303
deposit account 303
depot 288
depreciation 114
depressed 28
depression 297
deprivation 130
deprived 97, 130
depth of field 172
deputy 102
derail 287
derby 65
deregulation 296
derivative 243
derivatives 304
dermatology 244
descended from 233
descending 281
descent 46
describe 133
desert 218, 225
deserve 34, 52
design 156, 170, 177, 279
designer 279, 311
desire 29
desired 29
desk 89, 192, 312
desk clerk 311
desk job 312
desk lamp 312
desktop computer 276
despair 30, 130
desperately 130
despise 30
despite 225
dessert 62
destination 188, 289
destitute 130
destroy 120, 225, 230
destroyer 120
destruction 119, 120
detain 112
detective 112

detective novel 179
detective story 179
détente 117
detention 112
detention center 19
detergent 93
deteriorate 127
deterrence 118
deterrent 118
detest 29
detour 285
detox 129
detoxification 129
deuce 197
devaluation 304
devalue 304
devastate 230
devastating 229, 230
devastation 230
develop 70, 74, 165, 166
developed site 308
developer 178
developing country 117
development 179, 224, 226, 258, 262
development aid 117
developmental 143
deviant behaviour 145
deviation 144
device 37, 180, 255, 259, 260, 262
devil 162, 238, 292
devoid of 23
devote 198
dew 287
diagnose 244
diagnosis 244
diagnostic 244
dial a number 275
dial tone 275
dial-up 279
dialectical 166
dialling code 275
dialling tone 275
dialog box 278
dialogue 35, 155
dialysis 245
diameter 247
diamond 212, 213
diaper 50
diaphragm 37
diarrhoea 69
diary 179
dictate 313
dictating machine 313
dictation 151, 313
dictator 99
dictatorship 99
dictionary 264
die 14, 71, 102, 112, 289

die (of/from) 40
die of 12, 42, 69, 71, 72, 129, 130, 230, 245
diesel engine 26
diesel locomotive 287
diet 82
difference 208
different 166, 223
differential calculus 246
difficulty 27
digit 297
digital 172, 260, 282
digital signature 260
digitization 260
digitize 260
dignitary 121
dilute 243
dime 302
diminished responsibility 111
diner 61, 287
ding an sich 166
dining car 61, 287
dining room 87, 88
dining table 89
dinner 60, 186
dinner jacket 64
dioxide 226
diploma 152, 153
diplomacy 116
diplomat 20, 116
diplomatic 116
diplomatic relations 116
dipso 129
direct current 259
direct flight 289
direct mail 306
direct marketing 305
direct service 287
directed by 176
direction(s) 180
directly 168
director 41, 176, 299, 305
directory 264, 274, 277
directory assistance 274
directory enquiries 274
dirty 16
dirty dishes 93
disability 73, 74, 144, 307
disabled 73
disadvantaged 130
disagreement 34
disarmament 117
disaster 225, 229, 230, 306
disastrous 230

disc jockey 271
disco dancing 187
disconnect 275
discontented 22, 23
discount 300
discretion 62
discrimination 21, 98, 135, 136
discussion 35
disease 21, 37, 68, 74, 221, 230, 245
disembark 292
disguised 127
dish 59, 62
dish liquid 93
dish mop 93
dish towel 93
dishes 92, 93
dishevelled 16
dishonest 22
dishonesty 32
dishwasher 63, 90
disk 277, 280
diskette 277
dislike 29
dislikes 28
dislocate 72
dismantle 115
dismiss 126, 316
disobedience 32
disorder 68, 73, 144, 245
disparagingly 268
dispatch 301
dispenser 302
disperse 107
display 276, 277, 306
disposable 304
disposable camera 171
disposal 226
dispute 116, 315, 316
disrespect 35
disrespectful 234
disrupt 315
dissertation 153
dissident 107
dissolve 104, 243
distance 204, 246
distance learning 149
distinguished 21
distribute 300, 306
distribution 300
distributor 300
district 96
district attorney 110
disturb 192
disturbed 28, 144
diversion 285
diversity 138
divide 215, 246, 247
divided 105
divided by 247

divided into 97, 156
dividend 304
divine 161
diving 196
divinity 160, 161
division 119, 214, 237, 247
divorce 48, 49, 269
divorced 11, 49
DIY 94, 199
DNA 237
do 62, 63
do a course 150
do a dictation 151
do a drawing 168
do a lot of reading 199
do a problem 246
do a sport 195
do an evening class 149
do an experiment 240
do away with 43
do badly 153
do business 298
do chores 51
do crossword puzzles 199
do dope 128
do drugs 19, 128
do for a living 309
do good 31, 83
do ill 52
do-it-yourself 199
do-it-yourselfer 199
do one's doctorate 153
do one's military service 118
do one's round 80
do one's shopping 193
do revision 156
do sb. in 43
do sums 246
do the beds 93
do the chores 92
do the dishes 59, 92
do the drying 93
do the washing 39, 93
do well 271
do with sth. 228
dock 292
docker 310
docking manoeuvre 206
docking station 282
docks 217
doctor 14, 72, 75, 77, 80, 81, 115, 274
doctor's certificate 77
doctor's degree 153

doctor's office 75
doctor's surgery 75
doctoral thesis 153
doctorate 153
doctrine 162
docudrama 271
document 140, 142, 313
documentary 271
documents 286, 301
doddering 21
doddery 21
dodger 294
dodging 113, 294
dog 25, 30, 232
doghouse 88
dogma 162
dole 127
dole money 127
doll 17
doll carriage 17
dollar(s) 302
dollars 300, 303
dollhouse 17
dolphin 234
domain 280
dome 178
domestic flight 289
domestic policy 100
domestic post 272
domestic waste 226
done 59
donkey 233
donkey work 238
donor 14, 245
door 88, 91, 222, 254
doorbell 91
doormat 91
doorway 88
dope 128, 129
dope dealer 129
dope peddler 129
dope pusher 129
doper 129
Doric column 178
dormitory 125
dormitory town 215
dose 129
dot com 281
double 201, 274
double (room) 191
double bed 89
double-breasted 64
double-click 278
double-decker 54, 293
double-digit inflation 297
double fault 197
doubles 197
doubt 164
doubting Thomas 164
dough 55

doughnut 54
dove 100, 233
dovish 100
down below 14
down payment 193
down the hatch! 200
down tools 315
Down's syndrome 74
downers 128
Downing Street 105
download 265, 277
downpour 228
downs 297
downsizing 126, 316
downtown 97, 224, 229
downtown area 97, 224
downturn 127, 297
Dr 75, 122
draft 118
draft a letter 312
draft letter 312
draftees 118
drag and drop 277
drama 179
drapes 91
draught 200
draught beer 200
draughtsman 168
draughtswoman 168
draw 168, 197
draw (drew) 91
draw on 146
draw up 188
drawer 92
drawers 89
drawing 168, 170
drawing board 223
drawing pin 313
dread 52
dreadful 179, 227
dream 144, 208
dream man 44
dreaming 144
dress 48, 64
dress(ed) 16
dress a wound 72
dress the salad 58
dressed 64, 77
dresser 16
dressing 56, 72
dressing gown 65
dressmaker 310
dressmaking 198
drill 79, 255
drink 28, 57, 62, 129, 136, 200, 201
drink a toast to 186
drink-driving 286
drinker 129, 200
drinking 200
drinking chocolate 57

drinking spree 129
drinking water 57
drinks 192
drip 81
drive 44, 256, 277, 280, 284
drive n. 277, 282
drive a car 110
drive-by shooting 284
drive-in 61
drive out of business 301
drive sb. round the bend 285
drive – go 343
drive shaft 256
driver 129, 284, 288, 294
driver's license 286
driving 286
driving instructor 154, 309
driving licence 286
driving school 284
drizzle 228
drop 230, 277, 299
drop bombs 119
drop dead 40
drop out 19
drought 229
drown 42, 229
drug 19, 37, 77, 128, 129
drug abuse 128
drug addict 128
drug dealer 128
drug pusher 128
drug-related 128
drug seller 129
drug squad 128
drug trade 128
drug trafficker 128
drug user 129
drugged 128, 129
drugs 194
drugstore 194
drunk 129, 200
drunk driving 286
drunkard 129
drunken 52
dry 62, 63, 228
dry (up) 93
dry-clean 39
dry cleaners 39
dryer 90
dub a film 175
duchess 121
duck 55, 58, 106, 233
duck(s) 232
ductility 255
due 215, 304
due to 130, 254, 315
duke 121

E

dull 228
dull ache 78
dull pain 76
dumb 26
dumb bells 84
dummy 17
dump 86, 226
dumping 226
dumpling 55
dunes 219
duotone 170
duplex (house) 87
during 34, 74, 133, 141, 274, 285
during trials 244
during – while 356
dust 43, 93
dust jacket 266
dust to dust 41
dustbin 91
duster 93
dusting 221
dustpan 93
duty 80, 114, 189
duty-free 189
duvet 89
DVD (player) 271
DVD drive 277
dweller 223
dying 40
dynamics 145, 146, 240
dynamo 259
dysentery 69
dyslexia 74

E
e-business 280
e-commerce 281
e-mail 265, 280
e-mail address 11
e-paper 282
each 74, 104, 156, 302
each other 33
eager beaver 238
ear 12, 26, 74
ear, nose, and throat specialist 75
earache 76, 78
eardrum 12
early 19, 158, 233
early cultures 138
earn 113
earnings 299
Earth 204
earth 160, 204, 207, 209, 210, 260
earth-moving 255
earth to earth 41
earthed 260
earthenware 91
earthquake 211, 229, 230
easily 68, 76

easily machined 254
east 116, 214
East Asian 215
eastbound 294
Easter 182
Easter Monday 182
Easter Sunday 182
easterly 228
eastern 96, 116, 215
Eastern Europe(an) 215
easy 91, 172
easy chair 90
easygoing 23
eat 25, 31, 59, 222
eat out 61
eat your tea 60
eatery 61
Ebola fever 70
ec 150
ecclesiastical 140
ECG 77
eclectic 166
eclipse 204
ecofriendly 225
ecological 138, 225
ecology 138
economic 117, 134
economic activity 127
economic growth 296
economic history 140
economic policy 100, 296
economic system 296
economic theory 296
economic(ally) 296
economical 296
economically 130, 292, 296
economics 150, 153, 296
economist 296
economy 127, 289, 295, 296, 297
economy class 290
ecosystem 139
ecstasy 129
edge 130
edit 267, 277
editing 172
edition 266, 267, 269
editor 267
editor (in chief) 269
editorial 269
editorial department 267
.edu 280
educate 51
educated 208

education 36, 51, 142, 147, 148, 149, 150, 152
educational 143, 148, 224
educational scene 153
edutainment 271
Edwardian 177
eel 55
eel pie 62
effect 29, 166, 225
efficiency 258
efficient 22, 111, 284, 293, 305
effort 86
egg 27, 54, 60, 82, 222
eggs 56, 192, 221
eighth note 174
ejaculation 36
EKG 77
el 293
elastic 254
elasticity 255
Elastoplast™ 72
elbow 12, 70
elderly 20, 21, 115
elect 97, 104, 112, 309
elected 99
election 101, 104, 224
election campaign 104
Election Day 183
election platform 101
elective 150
electoral 142
electric(al) 241
electric chair 43
electric(al) charge 240
electric current 240
electric kettle 90
electric locomotive 287
electric motor 256
electric razor 38
electric(al) shock 259
electric socket 90
electrical 90
electrical engineer 259
electrical engineering 259
electrically 240
electrician 259
electricity 259
electricity company 259
electricity mains 259
electricity meter 259
electricity supply 259

electrocute(d) 260
electrocution 43
electrode 243
electrolysis 243
electron 241
electron microscope 242
electron tube 243
electronic 241, 260
electronic data processing 260
electronic mail 265
electronic paper 282
electronic publishing 279
electronics 240, 241, 259
electronics industry 260
electronics shop 194
electrostatic charge 259
element 82, 242, 243
elementary school 148
elephant(s) 232
elevated railroad 293
elevator 88
eliminate 297
elliptical 204
embargo 117
embark 292
embassy 116, 189
embezzlement 131
embolism 245
embroidery 198
emerald 213
emergency 72
emergency doctor 72
emergency room 72, 81
emergency shelter 125
emigrate 159
emigration 230
emissions 226
emoticon 280
emotion 28, 144
emotional 28
emotional upsets 76
emotionally 28
emperor 105
empire 96
empirical 145, 165
empirical study 146
employ 127
employee 126, 272, 311, 314, 315
employer 314
employment 114, 127
employment agency 127

employment contract 316
employment exchange 127
empress 105
empty 13, 208
empty (v.) 91
enable 104
enabled 279
enact 103
enact legislation 104
encode 279
encourage 303
encrypt 279
encyclopedia 264, 265
end 156, 215, 238
end moraine 211
endangered 226
endearment 50
ending 180
endoscopic 244
endoscopy 244
enemy 35, 119
energy 21, 226, 240
energy saving lamp 260
enforce the law 109
enforcement 111, 112
Eng. Lit. 152
engage in sth. 198
engaged 48, 275
engagement 48
engine 26, 207, 256, 265, 284, 287
engine driver 288
engineer 154, 242, 257, 259, 288, 311
engineering 145, 222, 242, 254, 259
engineering geology 210
engineering shop 258
English 158
English breakfast 60, 192
English Channel 217
engrave 170
engraver 170
engraving 170
enjoy 28, 29, 60, 199
enlarge 172
enlargement 117, 172
enlightened 160
Enlightenment 141
enlightenment 164
enormous 189
enough 83
enquiries 274
enrol(l) in 149, 314
enter 132
enter data into 276
enterprise 296
entertain 186

entertaining 186
entertainments 187
enthusiastic 176
entire 262
entitle to 114
entitled to 115
entitlement mentality 115
entrance hall 87
entrée 63
entrepreneur 296
entry 132, 264
envelope 261
environment 145, 225
environmental 225
environmental pollution 225
environmental protection 106
environmentalism 225
environmentalist 225
environmentally friendly 225
envoy 116
envy 30, 32
enzyme 237
epic 179
epicentre 229
epilepsy 74
episode 271
epistemology 165
epitaph 41
epoch 141, 211
equal 247
equal opportunity 316
equal to 250, 251
equality 98, 135, 136
equalizer 197
equals 247
equation 247
equator 205, 214
equilibrium 241
equipment 26, 171, 222, 254, 255
era 211
erase 277, 280
eraser 313
erect 36
erection 36
erosion 211
erotic 36
error 241, 267, 312
eruption 211, 229
escalate 117
escalator 294
escape 109
esoteric 164
essay 146, 156, 179
essay on 151
essential 82
established 159
estate 86, 308

estate agent 124, 308
estimate 305
estimate at 230
estimated 230
estuary 217
Estuary English 217
etc. 89
etcher 170
etching 170
ethernet cable 279
ethical 31
ethics 166
ethnic 134
ethnic cleansing 135
ethnological 138
ethnology 138
EU 117
euphemism 37
euro 190, 302
Europe 116, 214, 215, 230
European 96, 214, 215
European plan 192
European Union 96, 117
Europhobia 134
euthanasia 42
evangelical 159
evaporate 241
evasion 113
eve 183
even 300
even numbers 248
even-tempered 23
even though 82
evening 27, 227
evening classes 149
evening dress 64
evening gown 64
evening paper 268
event 140, 195, 196, 202, 268
ever-ready case 172
evergreen 236
every 17, 74, 83, 185, 187, 284
every five minutes 293
everyone 29, 136, 155
everything 158
evict 125
eviction 125
evidence 111, 146
evil 31, 166
evolution 139, 210
evolutionary 139
ex-directory 274
ex-husband 49
exam 94, 152, 156
examination 41, 152
examine 77
example 146, 153

excel 276
Excellency 121
excellent 63, 176, 196, 240
excess (v.) 126
exchange 127, 139, 190, 276, 296
exchange rate 190, 304
exchequer 121
excitable 23
excursion 188, 206
excuse me 112, 122
execute 43, 278, 301
execution 43, 301
executive 136, 299, 301
executive officer 299
exegesis 162
exempt 114
exercise 83, 84, 270
exercise power 142
exhaust fumes 226
exhibit 169
exhibition 168, 169
exhibitionism 37
exhibitionist 37
exhilarating 267
existence 160, 164
existentialism 166
existentialist 166
exit a program 277
expansion 277
expect 185
expectancy 20, 130
expectant 50
expecting 50
expenditure(s) 303
expensive 89, 191, 213
experience 165, 344
experienced 20, 22, 75
experiment 240
experimental 232, 240, 262
experimentally 240
expert 306
expire 189
explain 165, 344
exploit 23
exploration 206
exponential 297
export 301
export business 298
exposure 72
exposure (speed) 172
exposure meter 172
express (train) 287
Express Mail 272
expression 294
expressionism 169, 180

E

F

expressionist 169
expressionists 169
expressway 284, 285
extension 275
extension lead 260
exterminate 133
extermination 133
external 282
extortion 131
extra time 196
extra work 313
extract 79
extramarital 36, 49
extreme 100, 134
extremely 130, 153, 255
extremism 134
extremist 100
eye 12, 13, 15, 16, 25, 29
eye opener 129
eye shadow 39
eye specialist 75
eyebrow pencil 39
eyes 40, 158

F

fabricate 257
fabrication 257
facade 178
face 12, 16, 39, 212
face (v.) 111, 125, 215, 294, 300
facebook™ v. 202
face powder 39
face resistance 119
facilitate 262
facilities 148, 224, 257
facsimile 170
factor 296
factory 258
factory farming 220
factory hands 258
factory workers 258
faeces 13, 14
Fahrenheit 228
fail an exam 152
failed putsch 108
failure 69, 84, 206, 230, 245
failure(s) 221
faint 146
fair 22
fair (n.) 187, 267, 298
fair weather 227
fairly 24, 124, 227
fairy tale 18, 179
faith 32
faithful 32, 49
faithfulness 31, 32
fall 126, 140, 299
fall (fell) 58
fall asleep 40
fall behind 125

fall in love 34
fall into poverty 130
falling star 204
fallow 220
falls 217
false 23, 292
falsification 165
falsify 165
family 33, 46, 51, 130, 138, 309
family doctor 75
family name 10
family planning 37, 98
family reunion 185
family tree 46
family way 50
famine 230
famous 169, 176
famous for 187
fan 90, 195
fancy 28, 29
fantasy novel 179
FAQ(s) 281
far 105
Far East 214
fare 289, 294
fare dodger 294
fare dodging 294
fare hike 288, 294
fare increase 288, 294
farewell parade 184
farm 82, 220, 221
farm hand 220
farm products 220
farmer 56, 59, 219, 220, 221
farmhouse 87, 220
farming 56, 220, 222
farmland 219
farmworker 220
farsighted 25
fascinate 29
fascinating 262
fascism 99
fascist 99
fashion designer 311
fashion shop 194
fashion show 187
fashioned from 169
fast 90, 289
fast (v.) 82
fast food 54
fast lens 172
fast-spreading 315
fasten seatbelt 290
fat 16, 55, 82
fat farm 82
fatalities 230, 286
father 46, 74
Father 160
Father Almighty 160
father-in-law 46

fatigue 254
fatten 221
fatwa 163
faucet 90
fault 32, 197, 210
faultless 32
favour 104, 109
favourite 63, 150, 195, 198
fax 274, 275
fax machine 275
fax number 274, 275
fax sth. (through) 275
FBI 106
fear 28, 160
fears 30
feast 184
feather 233
feature film 175
feature on 269
featuring 175
Fed(eral Reserve) 304
federal 99, 114
Federal Bureau of Investigation 106
federal government 105
Federal Republic 99
federation 99, 314
fee 245
feeble 21
feebleness 21
feed 301
feed (n.) 221
feedback 306
feel 27, 28, 52, 78
feel (felt) 28
feel like 28, 185
feel pain 78
feel sick 76
feeling 28, 144
feet 12, 250
fellow 15, 33
felony 110
felt pen 313
felt tip 313
female 11, 14
female employee 311
feminism 98
feminist 136
fence 88
fern 236
Ferris wheel 187
ferry 291, 292
fertile 219, 220
fertilization 220
fertilize 220
fertilizer 220
festival 184
festive 184
festivity 184
fever 68, 76

few 27, 168, 171, 174, 176, 250
fewer – less 348
fiancé(e) 48
fibre 82
FICA tax 114
fiction 179
field 83, 142, 146, 172, 195, 196, 205, 219, 220, 221, 241
field hospital 80
fields 219
fieldwork 138
fierce 301
fight 32, 131, 133
fight a war 108
fighter 120
fighting 120, 269
fighting dog 232
figure 15, 140, 141, 168, 169, 246
figure skating 196
figures 246, 299
figurine 169
file 113, 250, 255, 261, 277, 279, 313
file a letter 261
file a suit 109
file away 261, 313
file folder 261
file for divorce 49
file management 277
filibuster 103
filing clerk 311
fill 79, 297
fill an order 301
fill in a form 307
fill out a form 307
fill up 261
filling 79
film 171, 175, 176
film festival 184
film star 175
filmgoer 175
filter 171, 201
filter-tipped 201
final 74, 173, 180
final exam 152
finals 152
finance 101, 302, 304
financial 304
financial editor 269
financial markets 304
financial power 304
financial strength 304
financial year 304
financing 101
find 13, 127, 155, 193, 265, 286
find (found) 109, 126
finder 172
fine 25, 199, 233, 294

fine (n.) 111, 286
fine (v.) 132, 286
fine arts 150
fine day 227
finger 12, 13
fingernail 12
finish 155
finish off 155
finish sb. off 43
finished products 257
finite 247
Finn 153
fir 235
fir cone 235
fire 52, 58, 71, 230, 235
fire (v.) 126
fire disaster 230
fire engine 284
fire insurance 307
fire sb. 316
fire truck 284
fire(place) 88
firearm 132
firebomb 134
firefighter 136
fireman 136
firewall 280
firing squad 40, 43
firm 193, 267, 301
first aid 72
first class 288
first-class letters 272
first-class mail 272
first-degree murder 110
first edition 267
first floor 87
first half 196
first name 10
first night 175
first offender 112
first performance 175
first-person narrator 179
First World War 236
fiscal policy 304
fish 29, 55, 58, 63, 200, 292
fish farming 220
fish(es) 233
fisherman 310
fishing 199
fishing trawler 291
fishpond 216
fit 83, 91, 265
fit a bridge 79
fitness 83
fitted 89
fitted carpet 91
fitter 258
fittings 89
fix 128, 129, 286
fizzy 57

flag of convenience 291
flame 280
Flanders poppy 236
flannel 38
flash 171
flash drive 282
flash of lightning 228
flash shot 171
flashback 180
flask 261
flat 88, 124, 174
flat (n.) 86
flat fare 294
flat hunting 124
flat rate 279
flat sharing 124
flat tyre 286
flatmate 124
flats 87
flatshare 124
flavour 27
flaw 276
flea(bite) 234
Fleet Street 268
flex 260
flexible 22
flexion 84
flick a switch 260
flight 188, 206, 289, 290
flight attendant 290
flight instructor 309
flight schedule 289
flight time 289
flip-flops 65
flit 208
flock 221
Flood 229
flood 229
flood-prone 229
flooded 229
floor 87, 89, 91, 92, 174
floor lamp 90
floor polish 93
floor show 187
flop 175, 176
floppy (disk) 277
flora 236
florist 194
floss 38, 79
flour 54
flow 216, 259
flower 235
flower arranging 198
flu 69, 94
fluid 241, 245
fluid mechanics 241
fluid pressure 241
flunk an exam 152
fluorescent lamp 260
flush the toilet 90
fly 30, 52, 233, 234, 250, 289

fly a kite 18
fly-by 206
fly coach 289
flyer 289, 306
flying 289
flying instructor 309
flying time 289
flying weather 289
flywheel 256
focal length 171
focus 172
fodder 221
foe 34
fog 228
foggy 228
foldaway 89
folder 261
folding bed 89
folding chair 90
folding table 89
folk 20
folk art 138
folk music 138
folk song 138
folk tale 138, 179
folklore 138
folks 46
follow 62, 176, 294
follow a hobby 199
follow a policy 100
fond of 28
font 278
food 56, 63
food poisoning 69, 74
food(s) 54, 82
fool 52
foolish 23
foolishly 23
foot 12, 13, 70, 78
foot (feet) 250
foot the bill 303
football 196, 197
football ground 195
football hooligan 131
football pitch 195
footnote 266
footwear 65
for example 153
for sale 308
for years 298
force 112, 241, 300, 314
force(s) 118, 146
forces 116, 117, 119, 296
forecast 227
foreground 172
forehand 197
foreign 134
foreign affairs 116, 142
foreign aid 117
foreign exchange 304

foreign-exchange markets 304
foreign language 150
foreign-language teaching 154
foreign minister 106, 116
foreign ministry 116
Foreign Office 106, 116
foreign policy 100, 116, 142
foreign secretary 106, 116
foreigner 28, 30, 35, 134
foreman 309
forename 10
forensic medicine 244
forest 219, 225, 235
forest fire 230
forest ranger 310
forest warden 310
foreword 266
forger 131
forget 77
forget-me-not 236
fork 59
form 83, 99, 115, 148, 166, 180
form a compound 243
form a government 105
format 277
formation 210
former 49, 96, 116
former employee 311
formerly 96
forms of address 121
formula 243
fortitude 32
fortuneteller 164
fortunetelling 164
forum 280
forward 90, 103
forward (v.) 273, 301
forwarding address 273
fossil 211
fossil fuels 226
fossilize(d) 211
foster 51
foul 227
foul (v.) 197
foundation subject 150
fountain pen 313
four-stroke engine 256
fourth-class mail 272
fox 24, 233
fraction 247, 249

F

G

fracture 71
fragrance 27
fragrant 236
frail 21
frame 172
framework 146
franchise 301
frank(furter) 55
frankly 292
fratricide 42
fraud 131
freak 82, 129
freak out 128
free 113, 293
free (v.) 111
free competition 296
free enterprise 296
free kick 197
free of tax 113
free-range eggs 82, 221
free-range hens 221
free trade 117
free weights 84
freedom 158, 321
freedom of the press 268
freehold 308
freelance 309
freelancer 309
Freepost 273
freeware 281
freeway 284
freeze 227, 297
freezer 90
freezing 227
freight 290
freight train 287
freighter 291
French fried potatoes 56
French fries 56, 61
French Revolution 141
French windows 88
frequency 241
frequent flyer 289
frequently 281
fresh 59, 192, 235
fresh-baked 56
fresh breeze 228
fresh-brewed 56
fresh-caught 56
fresh fruit 62
fresh-ground 27
fresh-laid eggs 56
fresh-picked 56
fresh-squeezed 56
freshly 56
Freudian (slip) 144
Friday 311
fridge 90, 94
fried eggs 54, 58, 192
fried potatoes 56

friend 23, 34
friendliness 35
friendly 225
friendly (n.) 196
friendship 34
frieze 169
frigid 37
frigidity 37
fringe 175
fringe benefits 316
frizzy 16
frog 234
front 227
front door 88
front garden 88, 219
front page 269
front-page news 269
front passage 14
front stalls 175
front yard 88, 219
frontbencher 102
fronted 87
frontier 116
frost 227
fruit 56, 60, 62
fruit juice 57, 60
fruit salad 56
fruitcake 54
fry 58
frying pan 58, 59, 238
ft 250
fuchsia 236
fuddy-duddy 21
fuel 207, 226
fuel tank 261
fulfil an order 301
full 236, 261
full-blown 70
full board 191
full-cream 54
full of 29
full-text search 265
fully 56
fully automatic 171
fully booked 191
fumes 226
function 247
function key 278
fund 101, 115, 116, 304
fund manager 304
fundamental operations 246
fundamentalism 163
funeral 41
funeral director 41
funeral home 41
funeral service 41
funfair 187
fungus 230, 236, 237
fur 232
fur coat 64
furious 30

furnace 91
furniture 89, 298
furniture polish 93
further 127
further education 149
fuse 259
fuse (box) 260
fusion 262
fussy 23
future 52, 262
FYI 94

G

g 251
gag 133
gaga 21
gain 153
galactic 204
galaxy 204
gale 228
gallery 169, 187
gallon(s) 251
galloping inflation 297
gallstone 69
gambling casino 187
game 18, 55, 195, 199, 233, 276
game park 233
game reserve 233
gang 33, 43, 134
gangster 131
gap 250, 294, 297
garage 88, 286
garbage 225, 226, 278
garbage can 91
garbage container 91
garbage dump 226
garden 88, 219, 234, 236
garden city 223
garden path 238
garden plant 235
gardener 311
gardening 198, 199
garlic 55
garlicky 44
garnish 58
gas 27, 210, 226, 241, 251
gas can 261
gas chamber 43
gas station 286
gaseous 241
gassy 57
gastrectomy 81
gastric 245
gastritis 70
gastrointestinal 245
gate 88, 290
gatecrash 185
gateau 54

gaunt 15
gay 36, 98
gay marriage 49
gazetteer 264
GCSE(s) 152, 153
gear(s) 256
gear-cutting machine 256
gearbox 256
gem 212
gemeinschaft 157
gemstone 212
gemütlich(keit) 157
gender 136
gender-neutral 136
gender role 136
gene 237
genealogy 140
general 118, 189, 272
general anaesthetic 81
General Assembly 117
General Certificate 152
general delivery 273
general election 104
general practitioner 75
general staff 118
general strike 107, 315
general surgery 245
generate 202, 259
generating station 259
generation 20, 46
generator 259
generosity 31
generous 23
genetic code 237
genetic engineering 222
genitals 14
genocide 42, 133
genre 179
gentle breeze 228
gentleness 31
geochronology 210
geographical 214
geography 150, 210
geologic(al) 210
geologist 210
geology 210
geometric(al) 246
geometry 246
Georgian 177
geoscience 150
German 153
German measles 69
German shepherd 232
get 14, 113, 183, 247
get a pass 152
get a spanking 19

get acquainted 34
get along 33
get back 41
get beaten 19
get custody of 49
get divorced 49
get down to 212
get dressed 77
get engaged 48
get in touch 35, 202
get into trouble 19
get it at the sales 194
get married 48
get off 13, 129, 286, 294
get off a train 288
get old 20
get on 33, 286
get on (in years) 20
get on a train 288
get one's doctorate 153
get sb. sth. 313
get snarled up 285
get started 155
get sth. done 189
get sth. right 246
get stuck in traffic 285
get the pink slip 126
get the sack 126
get there 294
get to 288
get to a place 294
get to know 34
get together 185
get-together 185
get towed away 286
get up 129
get warmer 227
ghetto 223
ghetto blaster 271
ghost 160
giant 299
gift exchange 139
gift shop 194
gift-wrapped 193
gifted 51
giggle 30
GIGO 278
ginger ale 57
ginger beer 57
girdle 65
girl 15, 18, 19, 185
girl Friday 311
girlfriend 34
give 51, 184, 250, 275
give (gave) 60
give(n) 182
give … a cleaning 92
give … a good airing 93
give … a reading 103

give a party 185
give a presentation 156
give a speech 103
give an injection 77, 79
give birth 50
give homework 154
give lessons 154
give my regards 49
give notice 125
give offence 135
give oneself a shot 128
give out 155
give sb. a buzz 274
give sb. a lift 284
give sb. a ride 284
give sb. a ring 274
give sb. notice 316
give sb. the works 43
give the floor a scrub 92
give the sack 126
give trouble 75
giveaway 306
given name 10
glacier 211
glaciology 210
glad 88
glance 25
gland 14, 245
glandular 245
glass 57, 93, 178, 254, 255
glasses 25, 115
glimpse 26
global 228, 296
global warming 109, 226
globe 46
gloomy 24
glossary 264
glossy 171, 172
gloves 66
gluttony 32
gnat 234
GNP 297
go 19, 40, 61, 126, 294
go (= sagen) 84
go (went) 48, 56, 80
go – drive 343
go ashore 292
go away 182
go back to work 316
go blind 74
go by air 289
go by Amtrak 287
go by car 284
go by train 287
go charter 290
go co-op 86
go dancing 174
go down 70, 291

go downtown 224
go fishing 199
go for a jog 83
go for a walk 219
go hungry 130
go in for sports 195
go in for sth. 199
go into extra time 196
go into liquidation 301
go into politics 100, 142
go into town 223
go off the air 270
go on 230
go on a binge 129
go on a cruise 291
go on a hike 188
go on a spree 193
go on a tour of 188
go on an excursion 188
go on the air 270
go on the stage 176
go on to 155
go online 202
go organic 56
go out 60, 185, 200
go out with 185
go round the bend 285
go sailing 291
go sightseeing 189
go skiing 196
go-slow 315
go to bed with 36
go to church 162
go to college 149
go to prison 314
go to sea 291
go to the city 223
go to the movies 175
go to the polls 104
go to the printers 267
go to town 97
go to university 149, 152
go underground 107
go up 300
go up to town 223
go west 43
go with 63
goal 197
goalkeeper 196
goalless draw 197
goat cheese 54
god 23
God 164, 307
god/God 160
godchild 50
godfather 50
godmother 50

going to 39, 50, 127
gold 212
gold medal 212
golden 212
golden age 212
golden goal 197
golden wedding 48, 184, 212
golden years 21
goldfish 234
golf course 195
gone 40
gonorrhea 37
good 23, 28, 31, 51, 82, 83, 92, 93, 298
good afternoon 60
good and evil 166
good at sums 246, 344
good company 185
good-for-nothing 32
good for your health 82
Good Friday 182
good-looking 15, 208
good nerves 14
good read 267
good reception 271
good sailor 292
goodbye 122
goodness 31
goods 27, 257, 285, 296, 298, 300, 301, 302
goods train 287
goodwill 306
goofed 129
google sth. 264
goose 55, 233
gooseberries 56
gospel 162
gossip column 269
Gothic 169, 177
Gothic novel 179
Gothic Revival 177
gout 70
govern 99
government 99, 100, 101, 105, 107, 151, 224, 296
government employee 311
government-provided 115
government-subsidized 287
governmental 105
governor 105
gown 64
GP 75
grade 148
grade school 148
grades 153

gradually 34
graduate 153
graduate from 149, 152
graduate school 149
graduated 294
graduation 153
grafting 245
grain 54
grain(s) 221
grammar school 148
grams 251
grandaunt 47
grandchildren 47
granddaughter 47
grandfather 47
grandfather clock 90
grandmother 24, 47
grandnephew 47
grandniece 47
grandparents 47
grandson 47
granduncle 47
grant 115, 146, 177
grant a loan 303
grant asylum 134
grape 56
grape juice 57
grapefruit 56
grapefruit juice 57
graphic 170
graphic art(s) 170
graphic artist 170
graphic design 170
graphic designer 170
grass 129
grass(es) 236
grassland 218
grassroots 101
gratuity 62
grave 17, 41
gravedigger 41
gravestone 41
graveyard 41
gravitation 205
gravitational 205, 241
gravity 205, 241
gravure 170
gravy 55
Gray Panthers 21
graze 220, 221
grazes 72
greasy spoon 61
great 29, 31, 230
great-aunt 47
Great Depression 297
great-grandfather 47
great-grandmother 47
great-grandparents 47
great-grandson 47
great-great-grand-father 47

great-nephew 47
great-niece 47
great tit 233
great-uncle 47
greatest 73
Greece 164
greed 32
greedy 32
Greek 158, 165
green 38, 220
Green 225
green belt 219, 223
green channel 189
green salad 56
green spaces 223
green tea 57
greengrocer 194
greenhouse 88, 222
greenhouse effect 225
greenish 44
grey 16
gridlock 101, 285
grievance 316
grievance procedure 316
grill 59
grilled 192
grillroom 61
grin 30
grind 58
grinder 58, 255
grinding machine 255
gripping 267
grizzly bear 233
grocer 194
grocery 194
groom 48, 186
groomed 16
gross 113
gross national product 297
ground 195, 206, 260
ground crew 290
ground floor 87
ground plan 177
groundbreaking 146
grounded 260
grounds 112
group 33, 34, 133, 134, 142, 145, 155, 225, 280, 306
group call 202
group dynamics 145
group therapy 144
grove 219
grow 221
grow (grown) 82, 250
grow old 20
grown-up 19, 51
grownup 19, 51

growth 145, 248, 297
grubby 16
grudge 35
guarantee 301
guard 288
guardian 51
guardianship 51
guerrilla 108
guerrilla fighter 120
guest 61, 186
guest of honour 186
guesthouse 191
guestroom 87
guffaw 30
guidance 48
guide 189
guide dog 26
guided tour of 188
guillotine 43
guilty 31, 110
guilty plea 111
guinea pig 233
gulf 216
gum(s) 78
gun 132
gun down 132
gunman 131
gutter 208
gutter press 268
guy 18, 24, 32, 50, 84
guzzler 129
gym 83, 84, 94, 195
gymnastic 83
gymnastics 83
gynaecologist 75
gynaecology 244
gypsy 135

H

habit 129
habitual 131
hacker 276
hacking 280
hacksaw 255
had rather 175
haddock 55
Hadron 44
haemorrhoids 70
haggard 15
haggle 300
hail a cab 294
hair 12, 16, 39
hair conditioner 39
hairbrush 38
haircut 38
hairdo 16
hairdresser 39, 194
hairdryer 39
hairstyle 16
half 196, 201, 249, 288
half a 251, 302
half board 191

half-brother 46
half dollar 302
half-hour 293
half note 174
half-sister 46
half tone 174
halftone 170
halibut 55
hall 87, 240
hall porter 192
halves 249
ham 55, 192
hamburger 194
hamburger place 61
hammer 255
hamster 233
hand 12, 13, 27, 38, 39, 220, 233
hand baggage 290
hand in 155
hand luggage 290
hand out 155
hand puppet 17
handbag 261
handball court 195
handbill 306
handbook 264
handgun 132
handicap 73
handicapped 73
handkerchief 39
handle 27
handling 272
hands 292
hands-on 299
handsaw 255
handsome 15
hang-gliding 199
hang on 275
hang up 274
hang up (on) 275
hanging 40, 43
hangnail 70
hangover 129, 200
hanky 39
happen 71
happy 183, 184, 238
harassment 36, 136
harbour 217
hard 16, 26, 256
hard-boiled 58
hard disk 277, 280
hard drinks 200
hard drive 280, 282
hard drug 128
hard hyphen 278
hard of hearing 26
hard porn 37
hard sell 299
hard-sell campaign 299
hard stuff 129
hardback 266
hardcover 266
hardest hit 230

hardware 276
hardwood 254
hardy 235
hare 55
harm 131
harmony 174
harrowing 267
harsh 146
harvest 31, 59, 221
harvester 222
hash 128, 129
hashish 128, 129
hat 64, 65
hatch 200
hate 29
hatred 29, 134, 135
hatter 24
have 62
have a baby 50
have a bath etc. 38
have a birthday 184
have a break 182
have a checkup 77
have a date 185
have a drink 200, 201
have a fever 76
have a game 195
have a get-together 185
have a hangover 200
have a lie-in 60
have a look at 25
have a medical 80
have a nice trip 188
have a pain 78
have a party 185
have a ride 187, 284
have a sauna 83
have a smoke 201
have a talk 35
have a tooth out 79
have a word 122
have an affair 49
have an operation 81
have an X-ray 77
have breakfast 60
have liftoff 206
have lunch 60
have sex 36
have sth. done 275, 286
have surgery 81
have the brass to 212
have the cheek to 275
have the freehold of 308
have time off 182
have to 121, 127, 156, 189
have trouble -ing 75
haven 113
hawk 100

hawkish 100
hay 129, 221, 222
hay fever 68
haystack 221, 222
hazard 82
hazardous 226
haze 228
hazelnut 56
hazy 228
HD 277
he language 136
head 12, 13, 78, 88, 96, 159
head for 208
head injuries 71
head of department 309
head of government 105
head of state 105
head off a strike 315
head-on 71
head teacher 309
headache 78
headache(s) 76
header 196
headgear 65
heading 155, 269, 345
headline 269, 345
headlines 314
headmaster 309
headmistress 309
headphones 276
headquarters 268
headscarf 66
headwaiter 63
healing 244
health 21, 68, 82, 115, 200
health! 186
health care 115
health-care reform 115
health-conscious 82
health education 150
health farm 82
health food 54
health food(s) 82
health food shop 82
health freak 82
health hazard 82
health insurance 115, 307
health insurance company 115
health resort 82
healthy 82
hear 26, 52, 58, 122
hear (heard) 270
hearing 26, 73
hearing aid 26
heart 13, 68, 83, 154
heart attack 68

heart condition 13, 68
heart failure 69
heart surgery 81
heart trouble 69
heat 29, 91, 227, 241
heat resistance 255
heat wave 227
heath 219
heather 219
heating 91
heatstroke 68
heaven 40, 52, 160, 162
heavily 196, 228
heavy fighting 120, 269
heavy metal 212
heavy resistance 119
heavy seas 291
heavy traffic 285
hedge 219
hedge fund 304
heels 65
heesh 129
hegemony 139
height 11
heist 132
helicopter 290
heliport 289
hell 162
hello! 60
helmet 66, 196
help 13, 30, 125, 130, 225
help the police 112
helping 63
hemisphere 214
hen 221
henhouse 222
herb 236
herb(al) tea 57
herb(al) tea(s) 82
herbs 55
herd 221
here's looking at you! 186
here's to … 186
here's to you! 186, 200
hereditary 74
hereditary informa-tion 237
heritage 138
hermeneutics 166
hernia 69
hero 176, 208
heroin 128, 129
herring 55
heterosexual 36
hi! 60
hi(gh)-tech 254
hiding 19
Higgs boson 262

high 69, 128, 130, 148, 218, 225, 300
high birth 99
high-definition 277
high heels 65
high in fibre 82
high jump 196
high ratings 271
high relief 169
high-rise 87
high school 148, 152
high school diploma 152
high school graduate 153
high-speed steel 254
high-speed train 287
High Street 224
high street banks 303
high-tar 201
high tech 254
high technology 254
high tension 259
high tide 217, 238
high treason 108
high voltage 259
higher 316
higher education 148
highland(s) 218
highlight 277
highly 28, 112, 128, 254, 304
highway 265, 284
hijack 132, 290
hijacker 290
hijacking 290
hike 188, 288, 294
hiker 188
hiking 199
hills 218
hilly 218
Hindu 158, 160
Hinduism 158
hippie 98
hire 127
hire puchase 194
hire sb. 306
historian 140
historic 140
historical 140, 146
historical geology 210
historical novel 179
history 29, 80, 140, 141, 150, 152, 169, 179, 230
history of the earth 210
hit 19, 51, 71, 196, 229, 230
hit (n.) 176, 279
hit a key 278

hit an iceberg 292
hit Enter 278
hit the bottle 129
hit the hay 222
hit the headlines 269
hit the needle 129
hitchhike 284
hitchhiker 284
HIV positive 70
hoarding 306
hobby 168, 198, 199
hockey 197
hog 221
hoghouse 221
hold 262
hold a diploma 153
hold a meeting 312
hold a press confer-
  ence 268
hold a record 195
hold an election 102,
  104
hold on 275
hold one's liquor 200
hold prejudices 134
hold the line 275
hold your breath 76
holdall 190
holder 201
holdup 132
hole 205, 297
hole punch 313
holiday 58, 188, 216
holiday(s) 182
holiday travel 315
holidays 316
hollow-eyed 16
Holocaust 133
Holy Communion
  163
Holy Ghost 160
Holy Spirit 160
Holy Trinity 160
home 19, 20, 21, 27,
  85, 113, 125, 132,
  134, 184, 284,
  292, 309
home cooking 58
home ec 150
home economics
  150
home match 196
Home Office 106
home visit 77
homeless 86, 125
homeless shelter 125
homelessness 125
homely 16, 52
homemaker 311
homepage 279
hometown 97
homework 154,
  155, 156, 346
homework assign-
  ments 154

homicide 110, 131
homicide squad 110
homily 162
homophobia 134
homosexual 36
homosexuality 36
honest 22, 23, 24
honesty 32
honey 192
honeymoon 48
honour 122, 186
Honourable 121
honours 152
hoodlum 131
hooker 37
hook(e)y 19
hooligan 131
hoover 93
hope 30, 32, 121,
  216, 227
hopelessness 130
hopes 30
horn 238
horoscope 164
horrific 230
hors d'oeuvres 63
horse 17, 136, 221,
  222, 280
horse chestnut 235
horse-riding 199
horseradish 56
hospice 40
hospitable 192
hospital 72, 78, 80,
  224
hospitality 186
hospitalization 80
hospitalized 80
host 186, 271, 279
hostage taking 131
hostel 18, 125, 134,
  191
hostess 63, 186, 290
hostile 35
hostility 35, 134
hot 63, 192, 215,
  219, 227
hot chocolate 57
hot dog 55
hot line 275
hot spring 217
hotel 63, 188, 191
hound(s) 232
hour 90, 172, 250,
  270, 284, 291, 293
hour's drive 284
hourly wage 316
hours 75, 189, 312,
  316
hours of trading 103
House 102
house 51, 86, 92,
  125, 132, 178,
  267, 308
house (v.) 86

house call 77
House of Commons
  102
House of Lords 102,
  121
House of Represen-
  tatives 102, 104
house to let 308
house trailer 87
houseboat 87
housebreaker 132
household contents
  307
household insurance
  307
household waste 226
househusband 311
housekeeper 311
houseman 80
housewarming 185
housewife 309, 311
housework 92
housing 86, 124
housing benefit 115,
  124
housing construc-
  tion 124
housing estate 86
housing shortage
  124
hovel 87
how much 193
HP 194
hrs 192
huge 199, 269,
  300, 301
human 33, 346
human(s) 138
human agency 139
human being 9
human mind 143
human resources 299
human rights 98,
  142
human rights record
  142
humane 346
humanity 133, 160
humble 24
humid 227
humidity 227
humorous 170
humour 23
humpback 74
hunchback 74
hundreds of 229
hunger 130
hungry 130
hunt 232
hunter 310
hunting 124, 199
hunting dog 232
huntsman 310
hurricane 229
hurt 12, 28, 71, 78

husband 24, 49, 217
husky 15
hustler 37
hut 87
hydrocarbon 243
hydrocarbons 243
hydrogen 207, 243
hydrogen bomb 119
hygiene 38, 245
hygienic 245
hype 306
hyperlink 280
hypertext 276
hyphen 278
hypocrite 32
hypothesis 146
hysterectomy 81

I

ice age 211
ice cream 54
ice skates 18
ice-skating 196, 199
iceberg 217, 292
icecream vendor 311
icon 276, 278
icy 44
icy cold 227
ID card 189
idea 29, 100, 105,
  140, 165, 166
ideal 31, 289
idealism 166
idealist 166
idealistic 166
identify 146
identity 306
identity card 189
idiom 13, 24
idiot box 270
i.e. 94
if – when 356
ill 42, 52, 81, 144
ill-treat 51
illegal 19, 134
illegally 132, 286
illegitimate 49
illicit 114
illiteracy 130
illness 42, 68, 244
illustration 170
I'm afraid 127, 313
image 172, 306
image editing 172
image review 171
imagemaker 101
imagery 180
IMF 116
imitation gems 212
immature 22
immaturely 23
immediately 28
immigrant 134
immigration 103,
  134

immoral 31
immorality 31
immortal 41
immune deficiency 245
immune system 245
immunodeficiency 245
IMO 94
impact area 206
impair 73
impaired 73
impairment 73
impatient 22
impeccable 146
impending 230
impolite 22
impoliteness 35
import 301
important 100, 142, 182, 287, 306
impose 117
impotence 37
impotent 37
impoverished 130
impression 79
impressionism 169
impressionist 169
improve 83, 84, 127, 224
improved 316
impudence 35
in(s) 250
in bloom 236
in blossom 236
in bud 236
in cash 302, 303
in church 162
in conference 312
in favour of 104
in focus 172
in front of 290
in honour of 186
in-laws 47
in power 100
in print 267
in recess 103
in sb.'s favour 109
in session 103
in stock 301
in the bank 302
in the black 300
in the boondocks 215
in the country 218
in the fields 219
in the market for 301
in the red 300
in the sticks 215
in the world 215
in time 174
in town 223
in tune 173
inability 73
inaudible 26

Inc. 127, 299
incandescent lamp 260
incest 139
inch(es) 250
incident 135
incineration 226
incline 52
inclined to 238
include 156, 198
included 62
inclusive of 113
income 113, 114, 124, 297, 304
income tax 113
income tax return 113
inconsiderate 22
incorporated 299
increase 25, 51, 124, 125, 221, 245, 288, 294, 297, 316
increase in 289
increase taxes 113
increased 118, 258
increasing 285
incumbent 104
indecent 22, 32
Independence Day 182
independent 96, 101
index 264, 313
index fossil 211
indifference 34
indifferent 34
indigestion 69
indispensable 270
indulge (in) 199
industrial 119, 223
industrial action 315
industrial dispute 315
Industrial Revo-lution 141
industrial robot 258
industrial tribunal 316
industrial waste 226
industrialist 299
industrializing 117
industrious 23
industry 175, 177, 242, 268, 305, 314
inefficient 22, 24
inertia 241
inexperienced 22
infancy 17
infant 17
infant mortality 130
infanticide 42
infantry 119
infection 12
infectious 68
infidel 163
infidelity 49
infinite 247

infirm 21
infirmity 21
inflation 297
inflation rate 297
inflexible 22
inflict 43
influence 101, 128, 142, 145
influential 146
information 118, 188, 237, 263, 265, 268, 346
information highway 265
information retrieval 265
information system 265
infotainment 271
infrastructure 262
inhibited 22
inject 128
injection 43, 77, 79
injure 12, 71
injured 71
injuries 41, 68, 71
injustice 32
ink 170, 313
ink cartridge 313
ink-jet printer 277
inland post 272
Inland Revenue 113
inland sea 216
inlay 79
inlays 169
inn 191
inner city 97
innocence 32
innocent 32, 110, 133
inoperable 81
inorganic chemistry 242
inpatient 80
input 277
inquiries 112
insanity 110
inscription 140
insect 234
insecticide 220
insert 172
insincere 22
insolvency 304
insolvent 304
insomnia 70
instability 297
install 275, 277
installation 277
installment plan 194
instalment 194
instalments 304
instant Zen 129
institute 149
institution 138, 142, 162, 303

instruction 150, 154, 276
instruction material 154
instructor 154, 309
instrument 173
insulate 260
insulating tape 260
insulation 260
insult 234
insurance 114, 115, 126, 190, 307
insurance agent 307
insurance claim 307
insurance company 307
insurance policy 307
insurance rates 307
insure against 307
insured 307
insured party 307
insurer 307
insurrection 107
intake 82
integer 247
integral calculus 246
integrated degree programme 149
integrity 32
intellectual 29
intelligence 118, 143
intelligence quotient 143
intelligence test 144
intend 19
intense 262
intensive care unit 81
interactive 265, 276
interchangeable 171, 258
intercity service 287
intercourse 36, 37
interest 29, 35, 140, 198
interest rates 297, 304
interested 29
interesting 24, 29, 83, 265
interface 277, 278
Interior 106
interior 210
intermediary 117
internal 244
internal-combustion engine 256
internal medicine 244
Internal Revenue Service 113
international 142, 184, 266, 269
international affairs 116

International Monetary Fund 116
international relations 116
international reply coupon 273
international waters 291
Internet 265, 279
Internet banking 281
Internet café 280
Internet-enabled 279
Internet forum 280
internist 244
interpret 180
interpretation 146, 166, 180
interruptus 37
intersection 285
interstate 284
interval 227
intervention 117, 161
interview 144, 271
interviewer 271
intestine 245
intestines 13
intimate 34, 36
into 80, 83, 196, 199
into drugs 128
intolerant 22, 23
intoxicated 200
intrauterine 37
introduce 306
introduction 266
inundate 229
invade 119
invalid 73
invasion 119
inventor 311
inventory 301
invest 113, 304, 307
invest in 258
investigation 112, 146
investment 304
investment goods 296
investor 304
invisible 25
invite 186
invoice 303
involved 146
I/O 277
ion 243
IQ 143
Ireland 215, 230
Irish 215, 216, 230, 251
iron 93, 212
iron ore 212
irony 180
irresponsible 22, 268
irresponsibly 23
irrigate 220

irrigation 220
IRS 113
ISBN 266
-ish 44
Islam 158
Islamic 158
Islamophobia 134
island 188, 217, 346
isle 346
Isle of 217
isometric 84
isotopes 243
Israel 163
issue 105, 115, 117, 125, 165, 225, 300
issue a visa 189
it's a deal 298
itching 70
item 190, 268, 273, 301
item of 89
item of printed matter 273
itinerary 188
IUD 37
Ivorian 234
ivory 169
Ivory Coast 234

J

jabber 129
jacket 64, 65, 266, 290
jacuzzi™ 83
jail 111
jam 60, 192, 285
jam-packed 219
jammies 65
janitor 310
jar 38, 59
jaundice 69
jaw 78
jealous 30
jealousy 30
jeans 65
jersey 64
Jesus 158, 162, 164
Jesus Christ 160
jet 79, 277, 289
jet lag 289
jetliner 289
Jew 133, 158, 159, 162
jewel(s) 213
jeweller 194
jewellery 213
Jewish 158, 160
jigsaw 18
jihad 163
jingoism 134
JIT 258
Job 24
job 30, 114, 126, 127, 136, 186, 302, 309, 312

job action 315
job-creating scheme 127
job-creation 127
job security 316
job sharing 127
job shedding 126
job title 309
jobcentre 127
jobhunter 127
jobless 126
jobless rate 126
joblessness 126
jockey 271
Jockey™ shorts 65
jog 83, 250
jogging 83, 199
jogging suit 64
john 39, 90
join 33, 118, 280
join the underground 107
joiner 310
joint 14, 129
joke 28, 63
journal 268
journalism 268, 269
journalist 268
journey 121, 188, 288, 293
journey time 288
joy 16, 28, 31, 144
joy powder 129
joyride 19
joyriding 129, 132
joystick 276
jubilee 184
Judaism 158
judge 109, 122
jug 59
Jugendstil 169
juice 56, 57, 129, 192
jumbo (jet) 289
jump 30, 238, 241, 286, 299
jump out of 58
jumper 64
jumping 196
jumpsuit 66
junction 285, 287
June bug 234
jungle 219, 238
junior high 148
junk 129, 206
junk art 169
junk artist 169
junk food 54
junk mail 306
junker 129
junkie 129
junta 108
Jupiter 204
jury 109
just 312
just (= gerecht) 32

just-in-time 258
just now 89
just then 184
justice 32, 131
juvenile 19
juvenile court 19
juvenile offender 112

K

Kaddish 41
keef 129
keen 199, 301
keen on 29
keep 13
keep … open 26
keep as 232
keep company 34
keep doing sth. 19
keep in contact 35
keep off 288, 308
keep out 308
keep sb. company 185
keep the commandments 160
keep the pot boiling 58
keep waiting 30
keep warm 74
kennel 88
kettle 58, 59, 90
key 174, 192, 278
key interest rates 304
keyboard 276, 282
keyword 265
kg 251
kick 19, 196, 197
kick the bucket 43
kick the habit 129
kickbacks 300
kid 19, 50, 60
kidnapper 131
kidney 13
kidney failure 245
kidney stoney 69
kill 30, 42, 132, 229, 230
killed in action 119
killed in battle 119
killer 131
killer dog 232
kilogram(s) 251
kilometre 250
kilos 251
kilt 65
kin 46
kind (n.) 61, 86, 87
kindergarten 148
kind(li)ness 35
kindness 31
kinds 179, 180, 194
kinds of 291
king 105, 108
king of beasts 232
kingdom 232, 235

kinship 138
kipper 55
kiss 12
kit 306
kitchen 25, 58, 87, 92, 130
kitchen cabinet 89
kitchen clock 90
kitchen-cum- 88
kitchen cupboard 89
kitchen sink 90
kitchen table 89
kite 18
kitten 233
Kleenex™ 39
km 215, 250
knee 12
knickers 65
knife 59
knighthood 121
knitting 198
knock down 71
knock off 43
knock over 71
knock sb. off 43
know 31, 34, 164
knowledge 36, 165
Koran 163
kosher 163
kph 250
Krishna 160

L
lab 242
lab assistant 242
lab technician 242
labor agreement 316
Labor Day 182
labor negotiations 316
labor union 314
labor unionist 314
laboratory 242
Labour 100, 101, 103
labour 50, 130, 314
labour costs 258
labour dispute 315
labour exchange 127
labour market 127
labour relations 314
labourer 309
lack 154
lack of 111
lad 18
lady 18
Lady 121
ladybird 234
ladybug 234
lag 289
lager 200
lager lout 131
lake 216, 217
Lake Constance 216
lamb 24, 55, 238
lame 73

lame-duck 106
lament(ed) 42
lamp 90, 260, 312
lampshade 90
land 96, 220, 308
land register 308
lander 206
landfill 226
landing 88, 206
landlord 15
landmark 262
landowners 108
landscape 168, 218
landslide 229
lane 285
language 136, 150, 154
laptop 276
larceny 132
lard 55
larder 88
large 69, 97, 168, 217, 219, 224, 229, 302
large intestine 245
large print 267
large-scale 262
laryngitis 70
laser 254
laser printer 277
lass 18
last 13, 80, 251, 267, 270
last – latest 349
last (v.) 301
last name 10
last night 76
last straw 222
Last Supper 163
last will 43
last year 149, 152, 153
late 31, 42, 288
lately 84
later 228
latest 124, 289, 299, 305
latest – last 349
lathe 256
Latin America 214
latitude 214
laugh 30
launch 206
launch a book 267
launch a campaign 306
launch an offensive 119
launcher 206
launching pad 206
launching site 206
launchpad 206
launder 93
laund(e)rette 39
laundromat™ 39

laundry 39, 93
laundry detergent 93
lav 90
lava 229
lavatory 39, 90
lavatory attendant 311
lavatory brush 93
lavatory paper 39
law 32, 103, 109, 142, 163
law and order 109
law enforcement 111, 112
law(s) of 165
law of the jungle 238
lawn 88
laws of motion 241
lawsuit 109
lawyer 110, 309
lay (laid) 91
lay a wreath 41
lay off 126, 316
lay to rest 41
layer 225, 229
layoffs 316
lazy 23
lb(s) 251
LCD 277
lead 136, 212, 238, 260
lead-free 212
lead story 269
lead with a story 269
leader 33, 100, 102, 108, 269
leadership 33, 314
leading 221, 257, 267
leaf 236, 238
leaflet 306
league 197
league champion 197
lean 15
lean back 78
lean-to 222
leap 241
learn 154
learn by heart 154
learner 154
learning 149
learning disability 144
learning disorder 73
learning psychology 143
lease 303
leased line 279
leasehold 308
least 52
leave 69, 115, 182, 192

leave (left) 73, 80, 188
leave from 290
leaves (v.) 247
lecturer 310
LED 94
left 12, 98, 100, 175, 196
left-lugagge 288
left-luggage locker 190
left-luggage office 190
left wing 100
leftist 100
leg 12, 13, 15, 70, 71, 233
legal holiday 182
legal proceedings 109
legal profession 309
legalization 128
legend 179
legibly 155
legislation 103, 104
legislature 102
legitimate 49
leisure 181, 198
leisure activity 198
leisure time 270
lemon 27, 56
lemon curd 192
lemonade 57
lend 303
length 13, 171
lengthy 44
lenient 111
lens 171
lens cap 171
lesbian 36, 98
less 153, 250
less than 250
less – fewer 348
lesson(s) 154, 156
lessons 173
let 93, 104, 308
let a house 308
let sb. go 127
let sb. have it 43
let us 160
let's 155, 200, 212, 227
lethal 43
letter 31, 261, 272, 312, 313
letter carrier 272
letter of referral 75
letterbox 273
letterpress 170
letters to the editor 269
lettuce 56
level 82, 130
lever 255
levy 114

L

LGBT movement 98
liabilities 304
liability 298
liability insurance 307
liar 32
lib(eration) 98
libber 98
libel 133
Liberal Democrats 101
liberation 98
librarian 264
library 264
libretto 173
licence 110, 286
license 286
licensed 191
lichen 237
lie 52, 77, 89, 238
lie at anchor 292
lie buried 41
lie-in 60
life 20, 48
life assurance 307
life expectancy 20, 130
life forms 237
life insurance 307
life jacket 290
life support system 207
life vest 290
lifeboat 291
lift 88, 117, 284
liftoff 206
light 25, 90, 204, 241, 285
light a cigarette 201
light breeze 228
light bulb 259, 260
light fiction 179
light metal 212
light music 173
light rain 228
light speed 204
light up 201
light years 204
lighter 201
lighthouse 25, 292
lightly 15
lightning 228, 230
like (prep.) 22, 28, 52, 91, 200, 222, 227
like (v.) 28, 30, 34, 62, 63, 192, 193
like a status 202
like (to) 28
like to 19, 62, 171, 190, 303
likes 28
liking 28
lily 235
lily of the valley 235
lime (tree) 235

limerick 180
limestone 169
limit 134, 208, 250, 284
limitations 146
limited 299
limited liability 298
limited to 176
limits 223
limo(usine) 284
linden 235
line 100, 170, 192, 257, 259, 275, 287, 294, 298, 300
line of business 298
linear 241
liner 291
linguistic 136, 165
link 202, 279
linocut 170
lion 24, 232, 233
lion's den 238
lip 12
lipstick 39
liqueur 200
liquid 93, 241
liquid-crystal display 277
liquidate 42, 133
liquidation 301
liquor 129, 200
list 62, 266, 272, 301
list price 300
listen 26, 30
listen to 173, 198, 199
listen to the radio 270
listener 271
listening compre-hension 151
Lit. 152
literacy 276
literary 179, 180, 198
literary criticism 179
literary history 179
literate 276
literature 167, 179, 264
lithograph 170
lithographer 170
lithography 170
litre(s) 91, 251
little 15, 26, 52, 86, 129, 155
little one 50
live 13, 26, 46, 86, 87, 97, 125, 214, 218, 224
live (adj.) 270
live band 187
live broadcast 270
live off sb. 188
live on sth. 188

live to a ripe old age 20
live up to 31
live wire 260
liver 13
liver sausage 55
liverwurst 55
lives 229
livestock 221
livestock feed 221
livid 30
living 82, 130, 309
living conditions 224
living room 87, 88, 93, 215
living space 124
living standard 297
living thing 231
living wage 130
load 171, 259, 277
load of 208
loaded 129
Loafers™ 65
loan 303
loathe 29
lobby 192
lobbyist 104
lobster 55
local (train) 287
local anaesthetic 81
local call 274
local colour 180
local history 140
local news editor 269
local paper 268
local taxes 114
loch 216
lock 292
lock out 315
lock the stable door 222
locker 190, 290
lockout 315
locks 16
loco(motive) 287
locust plague 230
lodging 191
lodgings 86
loft 87, 88
log(arithm) 247
log cabin 87
log off 277
log-off 277
log on 277
log-on 277
logic 165
logical 165
logjam 101
logo 306
Londoner 219
long 24, 42, 192, 217
long (adv.) 86
long for 29, 34
long johns 65

long jump 196
long-distance call 274
long-sleeved 64
long-term 126, 143
longer 28, 127, 164
longevity 21
longitude 214
longshoreman 15, 310
longsighted 25
loo 39, 90
look 23, 24, 25, 91
look after 21
look at 30, 90, 91, 155, 208
look for 25, 65, 111, 124, 127, 193, 222
look fresh 235
look sth. up 264
looking 16
loop 37
loose 78
Lord 40, 41, 121, 122, 160
Lord (God) 160
Lord's Prayer 163
Lord's Supper 163
Lords 102, 121
lorry 284
lorry driver 284
lose 195, 300, 314
lose (lost) 34, 104, 109
lose contact 35
lose one's life 230
lose one's temper 22
lose the beat 174
lose weight 76
loss 300, 301
lost-and-found 288
lost-property 288
lot 19, 35, 64, 79, 83, 136, 154, 173, 196, 201, 286
lot of 185, 186, 199, 226, 227, 298, 302, 306
lotion 39
loud 26
louder 26, 155, 275
loudly 26
loudness 26
loudspeaker 276
lough 216
lounge 87, 192, 289
lounge suit 64
louse 234
lout 131
love 25, 28, 29, 31, 34, 36, 174, 197, 218, 248
love affair 49
love to 28
loved one 42

lovely 15
lover 49
low 69, 130, 205, 219, 300, 301
low-cal food 54
low-cost 124
low-fat 54
low-grade 68
low in fat 82
low income 115
low-income 124
low-paid 114
low ratings 271
low relief 169
low-tar 201
low tide 217
lower (v.) 258
lower chamber 102
lower class 33
lower jaw 78
lower taxes 113
lowland(s) 218
loyalty 306
LSD 128, 129
Ltd 299
lucky 197
lucky star(s) 208
lucrative 304
luggage 190, 288, 290
luggage insurance 190
luggage trolley 190, 288
lukewarm 105
lullaby 51
lumbago 70
lumber 254
lunar eclipse 204
lunar landing 206
lunar module 206
lunch 312
lunch club 21
lunch counter 61
lunch(eon) 60
luncheon voucher 312
luncheonette 61
lung activity 83
lung cancer 69
lung specialist 75
lung(s) 13
lush 129
lust 32
Lutheran 159
Luther(an)ism 159
lymph gland 245
lymph node 245
lynch 42
lyric poet(ry) 179
lyrics 173

M

m 250
m-commerce 281

MA 153
ma(ma) 50
mac 64
macaroni 55
machine 201, 255, 275, 302, 313
machine (v.) 254
machine operator 258
machine-readable 278
machine tool 255
machinery 220, 255
machines 254
macho 136
mackintosh 64
macro 276
mad as a hatter 24
mad cow disease 221
madam 62
made in 257
made of 254, 255
Madison Avenue 305
Mafia 269
magazine 37, 268
magic 164
magistrates' court 109
magnetic field 205, 240
magnetism 240
maid 311
maiden name 10
maiden voyage 291
mail 265, 272, 273, 280, 306
mail a letter 272
mail carrier 272
mail order 193
mail-order catalogue 193
mail-order company 193
mail-order firm 193
mail server 280
mail train 272
mailbox 273, 280
mailing list 272
mailman 272
main 87, 187
main road 284
Main Street 224
mainline station 288
mainly 221
mains 259
maintained school 148
maintenance 258
maisonette 86
maître d' 62
maître d'(hôtel) 63
maize 55, 221
major 104, 115, 159, 174, 229

major key 174
majority 102, 105
make 24, 52, 74, 233, 257
make(s) 247
make a bed 89
make a call 274
make a claim 307
make a connection 288
make a detour 285
make a drawing 168
make a landing 206
make a monkey out of 238
make a motion 103
make a profit 300
make a reservation 191
make a save 196
make a speech 103
make a U-turn 285
make a withdrawal 303
make an ass of 233
make enemies 35
make good copy 269
make love 36
make money 302
make news 269
make notes 155
make redundant 126, 316
make sb. do sth. 136
make sb.'s acquaintance 34
make sure 77, 155, 156
make the beds 93
make up 96
make-up 39
maker 160
male 11, 14, 136
male chauvinism 136
male chauvinist 136
male employee 311
male pill 37
malevolent 23
malicious gossip 133
malignant 69
mall 193
malnutrition 130
malpractice suit 245
mamma 50
mammal 232
man-above position 36
man and beast 232
man Friday 311
man language 136
manage a plant 258
management 258, 277, 299, 308, 311, 314

management consultant 310
management style 299
manager 62, 196, 299, 303, 304, 305, 310, 312
manger 222
maniac 36
manicure 39
manned 206
manoeuvre 206
manor (house) 87
mansion 87
manslaughter 110, 131
manual 264
manufacture 257
manufactured goods 257
manufacturer 257
manufacturing 257
manufacturing engineer 257
manufacturing plant 258
manure 220
manuscript 267
many happy returns 184
map 210, 224, 227
maple (tree) 235
marble 169
marble inlay 169
marble statue 169
marbles 18
marching orders 126
margarine 55
margin 300
marguerite 235
marijuana 129
marine geology 210
marital 36
marital status 11
maritime 228
mark 278
marked by 184
marker 313
market 117, 124, 127, 300, 301, 304, 306, 308
market economy 296
market forces 296
market-oriented 306
market research 306
market share 296
marketing 299, 305
marketplace 296
marks 153
marmalade 59, 60, 192
marriage 48, 49, 98
marriage counselling 144

M

married 11
married couple 48
married to 48
marrow 245
marry 48
Mars 204
marsh 218
mashed potatoes 56
mask 196, 290
masked 132
masochism 37
masonry 178
mass 41, 162, 241
mass destruction 119
mass media 268
mass-produced 257
mass production 257
mass transit 293
mass transportation 293
massacre 133
massage 38, 83
mast 292
mastectomy 81
master 23
master builder 177
Master of Arts 153
Master of Science 153
master's degree 153
masturbate 37
masturbation 37
mat 91, 199
match 195, 196, 197, 270
match (v.) 65
match point 197
matchbox 199
mate 33
material 27, 92, 154, 177, 226, 255, 261
material(s) 254
materialism 166
materialist 164, 166
materialistic 166
materials 306
materials technology 254
maternity allowance 115
maternity leave 115
maternity ward 80
math 150
math(s) 246
math(s) test 246
mathematics 145, 150, 246
maths 150, 156
matinée 175
matriarchal 139
matriarchy 136
matricide 42
matrimony 48

matronly 15
matt 172
matter 140, 166, 168, 273
matter and energy 240
mattress 89
mature 20, 22
maturity 20
maximize 296
maximum 304
may 41, 185
May bug 234
May Day 182
MD 94, 153
Me Inc. 127
Me plc 127
me-too product 301
meal 60, 62, 191
meals on wheels 21
mean 84, 160, 302, 349
mean to 28
means 103
means of production 296
means of transport 283, 284
means of transport(ation) 293
measles 69
measure (v.) 241
measures 250, 297
measuring cup 59
measuring spoon 59
meat 55, 56
meatball 55
mechanic 258
mechanical pencil 313
mechanics 240, 241
mechanism 255
mechanization 258
medal 212
media 101, 202, 268
media event 268
media hype 306
media player 281, 282
mediate 117, 316
mediator 117, 316
Medicaid 115
medical 80, 112, 224, 262
medical care 115
medical costs 245
medical history 80
medical insurance 115
medical profession 309
medical school 149
medical ward 80
Medicare 115
medication 77

medicine 77, 138, 193, 206, 244
medieval 140
meditation 164
Mediterranean 215, 216
medium 59, 305
meek as a lamb 24, 238
meet 215
meet (met) 86
meet (n.) 195
meet obligations 304
meet up with 185
meet with sb. 312
meeting 103, 105, 116, 312
mega- 44
megapixels 172
mega-rich 44
megastar 44
melodramatic 270
melody 173
melting pot 261
meltwater 211
member 33, 100, 102, 104, 121, 122, 136, 145, 159, 314
membership 33, 84, 100, 117
memorize 247
memory 143, 277
memory card 172, 282
memory stick 282
men's jobs 136
meningitis 70, 74
menopause 20
mental 73
mental deficiency 74
mental disorder 73, 144
mental illness 68
mentality 115
mentally challenged 73
mentally disabled 73
mentally disturbed 144
mentally handicap-ped 73
mentally ill 144
mentally retarded 51, 73, 144
mention n. 202
menu 62, 278
menu control 278
merchandise 298
merchant 298
merchant ship 291
Mercury 204
mercury 212
merger 301
meritocracy 99

merry 183
merry-go-round 187
mess 93
message 192, 265, 275, 278
messaging service 202
messenger 160
Messiah 158, 160
Met Office 227
met sb. at 289
metal 212, 254
metal fatigue 254
metalwork 198
metalworking machine 255
metaphor 180
metaphorically 180
metaphysical 164, 166
metaphysics 166
meteor 204
meteorite 204
meter 172, 259, 286, 294
methadone 128
method 37, 43, 146, 170, 257
Methodist 159
methodology 146
metre 180, 195, 247, 250
metro 293
metropolis 224
metropolitan 112
metropolitan area 97, 224
mice 232
microbe 237
microbiology 237
microchip 260
microelectronics 260
microgravity 207
microorganism 237
microphone 271
microprocessor 260
microscope 242
microscopic 242
microwave 59
mid-life crisis 20
middle 234
middle age 20
middle-aged 21
Middle Ages 141
middle class 33
middle-class 33
middle ear 12
Middle East 116, 214, 215
Middle Eastern 215
middle management 299
middle name 10
middle-of-the-road 100

middle school 148
Middle West 214
midfield player 196
midfielder 196
midge 234
Midlands 215
midst 41
midtown 97
Midwest 214
Midwestern 214
midwife 50, 244
might 92, 117
migraine 68
migration 139
migratory bird 233
mike 271
mild 68, 200, 227
mildew 237
mile 216, 223, 233, 250, 292
miles per hour 284
military 118
military junta 108
military service 118
milk 54, 56, 59, 192, 251, 261
milk a cow 221
milkaholic 129
milkshake 57
Milky Way 204
mill 58
millennium 229
million(s) 126, 230, 258, 300, 302, 304
millions of 273
mince 58
minced meat 58
mincemeat 58
mind 77, 83, 143, 166, 271
mind-altering 128
mind the gap 294
mine (pron.) 34, 46, 47
miner 310
mineral resources 210
mineral water 57
mineralogy 210
minerals 210
miners 315
minibus 293
minim 174
minimum wage 130, 316
minister 86, 106, 116, 121, 163
minister of defence 106, 118
minister of state 106
ministry 106, 116
ministry of defence 118
minor 19, 109, 174, 229, 290

minor key 174
minority 102, 134
minus 247, 248
minute 189, 275, 293
minutes 103
mirror 91
miscarriage 50
misdemeanour 110
miser 13
misery 130
misleading 145
misogyny 136
misprint 267
Miss 122
miss a connection 288
miss a train 287
miss the boat 292
missile 119, 207
missile attack 119
missing 89, 213
mission 116, 206
mission control 207
missionary 36
mist 228
mistake 349
mistress 49
mitigating 111
mixed doubles 197
mixed salad 56
mixture 243
MMS 275
mob 42
mobile 282
mobile broadband 282
mobile home 87
mobile phone 274, 279
mobster 131
mod cons 94
mode 278
model 18, 146, 194, 301, 311
modelled in clay 169
modem 276, 279
moderate 100, 228
modern 148, 150, 179
modern art 169
modern history 140
module 206, 207
moisturizing cream 39
molecular 243
molecule 243
mom(my) 50
moment 26, 28, 30, 76, 82, 126, 127, 191, 275, 349
moment of inertia 241
monarch 96, 99, 159
monarchy 99

monastery 163
monetary 116
monetary policy 304
Monetary Union 117
monetary union 304
money 32, 127, 302, 303, 308, 314
mongrel 232
monitor 276
monk 163
monkey 233, 238
monologue 176
monorail 293
monotheism 161
monotone 170
monthly 115, 268
months 13
mood 28
moon 204, 205
moonlight v. 208
moonlight flit 208
moonshine 208
moor 219
moorland 219
mop 93
mop up 92
moped 286
moppet 50
moraine 211
moral 31, 166
morality 31
morally 31
morals 31
more than 219
morning 80, 83, 227
morning-after pill 37
morning call 192
morning paper 268
morning sickness 50
mortal 41, 122
mortal sin 162
mortality 130
mortar 178
mortgage 308
mortgage rates 308
mosaic 169
moselle 200
Moselle 217
mosque 162
mosquito 234
moss 236
most 52
mostly 228
motel 191
moth 199, 234
mother 46, 50, 51
mother-in-law 46
mothers and fathers 17
motion 103, 241
motion picture 175
motion-transmitting 255
motions 13, 14
motivate 154

motivation 144, 154
motor 256
motor insurance 307
motor racing 195
motor vehicle 284
motorbike 286
motorboat 291
motorcycle 286
motorcyclist 286
motorist 284
motorway 284, 285
mould 237
Mount 162, 218
mount photos 171
mount the lens 171
Mount Vesuvius 229
mountain(s) 97, 218
mountain climbing 199
mountain range 218
mountaineering 199
mountainous 215
mourn 42
mourning 42
mouse 24, 233, 238
mouse (mice) 232
mouth 12, 13, 76, 217
mouth-to-mouth 72
mouthwash 38
move 97, 215
move into 184
move on 238
movement 13, 98, 101, 107, 141, 169
movie(s) 175
movie buff 199
movie star 175
movie theater 175
moviegoer 175
moving 30
moving van 284
mow 88, 222
mower 222
MP 102, 121
mph 284
Mr 75, 121, 122
Mrs 75, 121, 122
Mrs Mop(p) 92
Ms 75, 122, 127
MSc 153
muckraking 268
muddy 44
muesli 60
mug 132
mugger 131
mugging 132
muggy 227
Muhammad 160
mulberry (tree) 235
mule 24
multi-storey 286
multicellular 237
multicultural 10
multimedia 265, 281

multimedia
message 275
multinational 298
multiple-choice test
152
multiplication 247
multiplication tables
247
multiplied by 247
multiply 246, 247
multipurpose 88
multistage 207
multitude of 262
mum(my) 50
municipal 224
municipality 97
murder 110, 131
murderer 131
muscle 14, 78, 83
muscles 74
muscular 15
museum 169, 177,
187
museum attendant
311
mushroom 55, 236
mushrooms 192
music 138, 150, 155,
173, 198, 199
music shop 194
music visualization
281
musical 173
musician 173
Muslim 158, 162
mustard 55
mutton 55
mutual 33
mutual fund 304
muzak 173
my Lord 122
myself 38, 126

N

nail 12, 255, 292
nail polish 39
nail scissors 39
nail varnish 39
nailbrush 38
naked 25
name 10, 62, 289,
302
nanny 17
nanotube 262
napkin 39
nappy 50
narc(o) 129
narcotic 128
narcotics agent 129
narcotics squad 128
nark 129
narrative 179
narrator 179
narrow 217
narrow-minded 23

narrowly 104
nation 96, 116, 117,
215
nation state 142
national 297
National Curriculum
150, 152
national debt 297
national economy
296
National Gallery 169
National Health
doctor 115
National Health
Service 115
National Insurance
114
national paper 268
national park 219
national wealth 297
nationalism 98, 134
nationalist 134
nationality 11
nationalize 287
Native-American 138
native city 223
NATO 94, 118
natural 40, 226, 229
natural disaster 229
natural gas 210
naturalism 180
nature 166
nature reserve 219
naughty 52
nausea 68
nautical 292
nautical mile 292
nave 178
navigable 292
navy 118
nazis 99
nazism 99
near 350
nearest 293
nearsighted 25
nebula 204
neck 12, 13, 74
neck and neck 101
necklace 212, 213
necktie 66
née 10
need 12, 17, 23, 27,
52, 64, 79, 83,
92, 152, 154
need to 156, 208,
312
needle 128, 129,
222
needlework 198
needs 130
needy 130
negative 113, 172,
306
negative reinforce-
ment 143

neglect 51
negotiate 117, 316
negotiations 111,
117, 316
negotiator 316
Negro 135
neighbour 23, 34,
214
neighbourhood 26,
34, 97, 224
neighbourhood
watch group 133
neighbouring 119
neither ... nor 204
neoclassical 169, 177
neoclassicism 169
neoclassicists 169
neofascist 99
neo-Gothic 177
neo-Nazi 99
nephew 47
nephrectomy 81
Neptune 204
nerve 13
nerve(s) 14
nervous 14, 245
nest 233
net 113, 115
Net 277, 279
net curtain 91
netiquette 280
network 270, 279
neuritis 70
neurology 244
neurosis 144
neurotic 144
neutron 241, 262
never 18, 31, 49, 52,
64, 86, 232
new 24, 64, 172, 177
New Age 164
new-laid eggs 56
New Left 98
New Testament 162
new town 223
New World 159,
214
New Year's Day 182
New Year's Eve 182
New Year's party 185
newborn 17
newish 44
newly industrializing
117
newlyweds 48
news 269
news agency 268
news item 268
news programme
101, 271
news report 269
newsagent 194, 268
newscast 271
newscaster 271
newsdealer 194, 268

newsmagazine 268
newspaper 268,
269, 272
newspaper industry
268
news(paper)man 268
news(paper)woman
268
newsreader 271
newsstand 268
newsvendor 268
next 10, 47, 104,
155, 156, 185,
287
next (one) 155
next of kin 46
next time 155, 185
NGO 105
NHS 115
NI contributions 114
Niagara Falls 217
NIC 117
nice 97, 124, 183,
188, 227
nice and 44, 227
nickel 302
nickname 10, 92
nicotine 201
niece 47, 185
night 76, 132, 175
night clothes 65
night school 149
nightclub 187
nightdress 65
nightgown 65
nightie 65
nightingale 233
nightmare 144
nights 187
nightshirt 65
nightspot 187
nightstand 89
nihilism 164
nihilist 164
nil 248
nimby 94
nippy 227
No 10 (Downing St)
105
no longer 127, 164
no one 25
no parking 286
no-shows 290
no smoking 201
nobility 99
nobody 25
node 245, 279
noise 26, 285
noise pollution 225
noiseless 26
noisy 26
nominate 101
nomination 101
nonaggression pact
118

nonaligned 116
non-Aryan 135
non-Christian 10
none 32
nonfiction 266
non-governmental 105
nonmedical practitioner 244
nonprofit company 298
non-profitmaking 298
nonproliferation 117
nonreligious 164
nonreturnable 226
non-smoker 201
non-smoking 201
nonstop flight 289
nontaxable 114
nonunion workers 314
nonviolence 107
noodles 55
norm 145
normalization 116
north 214, 215
North Africa 119
north of Watford 215
North Pole 215
North-South divide 215
northerly 228
northern 215, 218
Northern Ireland 215
Northern Irish 215
northwest 215
nose 12, 13, 27, 39, 75, 76
nose candy 129
notary (public) 308
note 36, 77, 174, 302, 307
note down 155
notebook 276, 313
notepad 313
notes 155, 313
nothing 26, 32, 189, 248
notice 25
notice board 313
notice to quit 125
noticeable 25
notified 46
notorious 187, 314
nought 248, 249
nouvelle cuisine 63
nova 204
novel 175, 179, 267
novelist 180
novella 179
NP 94
nuclear 117, 119, 226
nuclear fusion 262
nuclear physics 240

nuclear weapons 119
nucleus 240
nude 168
nude painting 168
nuisance 131
number 40, 128, 156, 243, 246, 274, 275
number 6 bus 293
numbers 248
numerator 247
nun 163
nurse 77, 81, 244
nursery 17
nursery school 148
nursing 244
nursing-care insurance 115
nursing home 21
nursing officer 81
nut 56
nut and bolt 255
nut(s) 54
nutcracker 59
nutrients 82
nutrition 130
nutty 54
nylons 66

o

oak 235
oak cask 261
oat bran 82
oatmeal 55, 82
oats 54
obedience 32, 107
obit 42
obituary 42
object 204, 241
objectionable 31
objective 30, 146
obligations 304
o.b.o. 94
obscene 32
observation 242
observatory 205
observe 25
obstetric nurse 244
obstetric ward 244
obstetrician 244
obstetrics 244
obstruction 285
obstruction of justice 131
obtain 112
obviously 72, 78
occasion 184
occasional poem 180
occasionally 82
occult 164
occupation 20, 119, 136, 309
occupation forces 119
occupational 144, 244, 245

occupied 215, 288
occupy a country 119
occur 71
ocean 216, 226
ocean-floor spreading 210
ocean liner 291
o'clock 90, 289
OCR 278
OD 129
odd numbers 248
odour 27
off 13, 182, 193, 216
off – on 260
off course 292
off-off-Broadway 175
off peak 288
off the air 270
off-topic 280
offence 110, 131, 135
offender 36, 112, 131
offensive 18, 119
offer 34, 191, 194, 275, 301
office 48, 75, 106, 115, 116, 124, 175, 188, 190, 224, 227, 272, 274, 288, 305, 312, 313
office block 312
office building 312
office clerk 311
office hours 75, 312
office management 311
office manager 312
office worker 310
officer 15, 81, 111, 118, 245, 299, 309
official 86
offline 276
offset 170
offside 197
often 35, 130, 186, 187, 230, 232
oh 248, 249, 274, 289
OHP 155
oil 55, 210, 286
oil(s) 168
oil painting 168
oil slick 226
oil spill 226
oil tank 261
oil tanker 291
oilcan 261
ointment 70, 77
old 19, 20, 21, 29, 74, 185, 196, 198, 199, 224
old age 15, 20, 40
old-age home 21
old-age pension 115
old-age pensioner 20

old Europe 214
old folk 20
old folk's home 20
old lady 50
old man 50
old people's home 21
Old Testament 133, 162
Old World 214
older 20
oligarchy 99
olive 56
olive oil 55
omelette 54
omnipotent 161
omnipresent 161
omniscient 161
on – off 260
on a binge 129
on a drip 81
on bail 111
on board 291
on board ship 292
on business 182, 298
on campus 149
on course 292
on deck 292
on draught 200
on drugs 128
on duty 80
on hire purchase 194
on leasehold 308
on line 1 294
on low incomes 115
on offer 194
on prescription 77
on probation 111
on remand 111
on schedule 288
on short time 126, 316
on sick leave 182
on strike 290, 315
on tap 200
on the air 270
on the corner 285
on the dole 127
on the installment plan 194
on the Internet 279
on the National Health 115
on the needle 128
on the outskirts 224
on the phone 275
on the radio 270
on the rocks 49
on the shop floor 258
on (the) television 270
on the town 223
on time 288
on trial 109

on vacation 182
once 83
once a week 144
once again 155
once in a blue moon 205
one for the road 200
one-way street 285
onion 56
online 171, 202, 264, 265, 276, 279
online banking 281
online search 264
only 191, 291, 302
onset 20, 50
ontology 165
ooze 70
open 14, 26, 155
open a file 277
open an account 303
open fire(place) 88
open-heart surgery 245
open-plan office 312
open sandwich 54
Open University 149
opener 59, 129
opening ceremony 184
opening hours 189
opera 173, 270
operable 81
operate 287
operate on 81
operating room 81
operating system 262, 276, 282
operating theatre 81
operation 24, 81, 246, 258
operational 262
operations 177, 246
operator 258, 275, 277, 292, 311
ophthalmologist 75
ophthalmology 244
opinion 84, 142, 145
opinion poll 101, 142
opponent 35, 44
opportunity 96, 306, 316
opposite 36
opposition 102
oppression 136
optical character recognition 278
optical scanner 278
optics 240
optimism 30
optimistic 18, 24, 30
option 278
optional subject 150
oral 140

oral exam 152
orange 56
orange juice 56, 192
orange squash 57
orbit 204, 207
orbit (v.) 207
orchard 219
orchestra 173
orchid 236
order 62, 93, 109, 138, 192, 193, 272, 274, 301
orders 126
ordinal numbers 249
ordinary 122
ore 212
organ 244
organ donor 245
organ recipient 245
organ transplant 81
organic 56, 243
organic chemistry 242
organic food(s) 82
organically grown 82
organism 237
organization 21, 105, 116, 142
organizational 118
organize 186
organized crime 314
organized labour 314
orgasm 36
oriented 306
origin 204
original 170
original sin 162
originate 36
orphan 51
orphanage 51
Orthodox 158, 159
orthopaedic specialist 75
orthopaedic surgeon 75
orthopaedic surgery 244
orthopaedist 75
OS 262, 276
Oscar 176
other 234, 299
ought to 110, 182
ounce(s) 251
oust 108
out- 44
out of 74
out of a job 126
out of breath 76, 78
out-of-court 109
out-of-doors 168
out of focus 172
out of order 274
out of print 267
out of service 294
out of stock 301

out of the fire 235
out of this world 208
out of town 223
out of tune 173
out of work 126
out on the town 223
outdated 258
outdoor 199
outdoors 125
outdoorsy 44
outer space 204, 206
outgoing 24
outgunned 44
outhouse 88
outlet 90, 260
outlook 227
outnumbered 44
outpatient 80
output 258, 277
outraise 44
outside 33, 88, 215
outskirts 224
outsourcing 299
outspend 44
outstanding invoice 303
outward 15
outward journey 288
outwitted 44
oval 16
ovary 14
oven 59
over the counter 193
over the moon 205
overall(s) 66
overbook 290
overcast 228
overcharge 300
overcoat 64
overdose 40, 129
overdraft 303
overexposed 171
overexposure 172
overfertilization 226
overhead(s) 303
overhead locker 290
overhead projector 155
overhead rack 290
overhear 35
overpriced 300
overseas 272
overthrow 106, 107
overtime 316
overtime pay 316
overtime rates 316
overture 174
overweight 15
owe 303
owing to 230
owl 233
own 18, 31, 58, 83, 136, 166, 184
own goal 197

owner 298, 308
owner-occupied flat 86
ownership 296
ox 221
ox-eye daisy 235
oxfords 65
oxidation 243
oxygen 243
oxygen mask 290
oyster 55
oz(s) 251
ozone layer 225

P
PA 311
pa(pa) 50
Pacific Ocean 216
pacifier 17
pacifism 98
pack 38, 261, 273
pack sth. 261
pack(et) 201
package 114, 126, 261, 276, 297
package holiday 188
package tour 188
packaging 226
packaging (material) 261
packet 261, 273
packing list 301
pact 118
pad 206
padded 196
paddle steamer 291
paediatric 244
paediatrician 75
paediatrics 244
page 155, 266, 269, 274
page proofs 267
page turner 267
paid 13
paid holidays 316
paid vacations 316
pail 18, 261
pain 13, 25, 27, 78
pain(s) 76
painkillers 81
pain-killing 77
painful 14, 70
paint 168
paint(s) 18
painter 168, 169
painting 168, 169, 198, 282
pair 39, 65, 155, 208
pair of 255
pajamas 65
pal 33, 49
palace 87, 188
palate 74
pale 16

pale ale 200
paleontology 210
palimony 49
pallid 16
palm (tree) 235
palpitations 69
pan 58, 59
Panama Canal 217
pancake 54, 56
pancreas 245
panel 226
panther 21
panties 65
pantry 88
pants 49, 65
pantsuit 64
pantyhose 65
paper 25, 38, 39,
153, 201, 267, 268,
269, 312, 313
paper(s) 313
paper clip 313
paper on 151
paperback 266
papers 126
parable 162
parachute 119
parachuting 199
parade 184
paragraph 155
paragraph mark 278
paralyse 315
paralysed 74
paralysis 74
parameter 276
paraplegia 74
parasite 234
paratrooper 119
parboil 58
parcel 272, 273
parcel bomb 273
parcel of land 308
parcel post 272, 273
parent(s) 51
parenthood 37
parents 24, 49, 50,
86
parents-in-law 46
parish 97, 163
parish council 163
parish register 140
park 219, 224, 233
park (v.) 286
parka 64
parked 286
parking 286
parking attendant
286, 311
parking fine 286
parking garage 286
parking lot 286
parking meter 286
parking space 286
parking ticket 286
Parkinson's 68

parliament 102, 104
parliamentary 99
parody 179
parquet (floor) 91
parricide 42
parrot 233
parsley 55
part 12, 14, 87, 155,
176, 257, 258
part of 96
part-time 127
partial 79
particle 262
particle accelerator
262
particle physics 240
particular 264
partisan 120
partisan warfare 120
partner 33, 49, 117
partnership 33, 298
parts 261
party 18, 99, 100,
101, 104, 105, 134,
185, 274, 307
party convention 104
party leader 100
party line 100
party-political 101
partying 185
pass 152, 290
pass an exam 152
pass away 14, 40
pass water 14, 75
passage 14, 292
passenger 33, 288,
290, 291, 292
passenger liner 291
passion 199
passionate 198
passive euthanasia
42
passive resistance
107
passive smoking 201
passport 189
passport control 189
password 281, 312
past her prime 20
past it 21
past paper 151
pasta 55
pastime 198, 199
pastor 163
pastries 54
pastry cook 63
pasture 220, 238
pâté 55
patent pending 256
path 279
pathology 143, 244
patience 31
patient 22, 24, 75, 81
patio 88
patriarchal 139

patriarchy 136
patricide 42
patron 61
patronize 61
pattern 142, 145, 180
pavement 224, 285
pay 113, 300, 303,
316
pay (paid) 13
pay a deposit 193
pay a visit 185
pay agreement 316
pay alimony 49
pay as you earn 113
pay cash 302
pay damages 307
pay duty 189
pay duty on 114
pay (for) 302, 351
pay for 304
pay negotiations 316
pay off 303
pay phone 275
pay settlement 316
pay station 275
PAYE 113
payload 207
pay(ment) 126
payment 193, 194,
302, 303
payments 297
payroll tax 113
PC 73, 276, 301
PE 150
peace 29, 31, 40
peace accord 117
peace movement 98
peace plan 117
peaceful 27
peacekeeping force
117
peach 56
peacock 24
peak 36, 218, 288
peak load 259
peak oil 226
peaked cap 66
peanut 56
peanuts 301
pear 56
pearl 213
peas 55
peasant 108, 220
pebble 219
pedal 256
peddler 129
pedestrian crossing
285
pedicure 39
peel 58
peeping Tom 132
peer 121
peer group 145
peerage 121
pen 313

pen-and-ink 170
pen name 266
penalty 43, 111
penalty area 197
penalty kick 197
penalty shootout 197
pencil 39, 313
pencil sharpener 313
pencil sth. in 313
pencilled 313
pending 256
penguin 233
peninsula 217
penis 14, 36
penny 302
penny dreadful 179
pension 115
pension fund 115
pension scheme 115
pension scheme
consultant 310
pensionable 20
pensioner 20
pent-up 144
Pentagon 118
penthouse 86, 87
people (= Volk) 99,
138
people(s) 351
peoples 138
pepper 55
pepper v. 238
per 258, 284
per capita 304
per cent 110, 193,
219, 258, 300
per hour 250, 258
per person 251
per second 172
perceive 25
perception 25, 143
perfect 168
perfect pitch 174
perform 13, 41, 42,
153
perform a transplant
245
perform an opera-
tion 258
perform calculations
246
performance 175,
258, 296
performance art
169
performance artist
169
perfume 27, 39
period 76, 84, 141,
155, 211, 227, 229
periodic table 243
periodical 268
periphery 224
perish 40
perjury 109, 131

P

permanent 127
permission 177, 308
permit 308
permitting 227
persecution 107, 134
Persian Gulf 216
person 40, 70, 136, 158, 251, 307
personal 10, 38
personal assistant 311
personal computer 276
personality 22, 140, 143
perspective 168
persuasive 146
pessimism 30
pessimistic 24, 30
pest(s) 234
pesticide 220
pesticides 221
pet 232
petrified 211
petrify 211
petrol 226, 251
petrol can 261
petrol station 286
petrol tank 261
petrology 210
petticoat 65
petting 36
pharmaceutical 242
pharmacy 194
PhD 153
pheasant 55
philanderer 49
Philharmonic 174
philological 138
philology 138
philosopher 165
philosophical 165
philosophize 165
philosophy 150, 154, 165, 166
phlebitis 70
phobia 134
phone 91, 186, 274, 279
phone book 274
phone booth 275
phone box 275
phone call 274
phone conversation 274
phone for 72, 274
phone number 248, 274
phonecard 199, 275
phoney 127
photo(graph) 171, 172, 202
photo opportunity 306
photocopier 313

photocopy 264, 313
photograph 171
photographer 171, 309
photographic 171
photographic shop 194
photography 171, 199
photon 241
photoshop v. 172
physical 21, 73, 80, 83, 240, 242
physical education 150
physical exercise 270
physically challenged 73
physically handi- capped 73
physician 75, 80
physicist 240
physics 150, 240
physiotherapy 83
pianist 173
piano 173
pick 13
pick up 68
pick up a car 208
pick up the phone 274
picket line 315
picketer 315
picketing 315
pickles 29
pickpocket 132
pickpocketing 132
picture 32, 168, 169, 171, 172, 175
picture book 18
pie 62
pie in the sky 208
piece 190, 197, 213, 257
piece of 89, 155
piece of baggage 290
piece of information 265
piece of land 308
piece of music 173
pieces of mail 273
piecework pay 316
piercing 78
pig 136, 221, 222, 233
pig of a 238
pigpen 221
pigs 221
pigsty 221
pigtails 16
piles 70
pill 37, 77, 129
pillar 158, 178
pillar box 273

pillow 89
pills 82
pilot 290, 292
pimp 132
pimping 131
pin 313
pincers 255
pine (tree) 235
pineapple 56
pineapple juice 57
pink slip 126
pinstripe suit 64
pint 201
pint(s) 251
pipe 201
pipe cleaner 201
pipette 242
piracy 292
pirate 292
PISA shock 153
pissed 129
piston 256
pitch 174, 195
pitcher 59
pitiless 23
pixels 172
pizza 55
pizzeria 61
Pj's 65
place 63, 86, 149, 176, 191, 195
place an ad 305
place an order 301
place into orbit 207
place of birth 10
place of residence 10
place to live 125
placement 306
placement test 152
places 246
plagiarism 180
plagiarize 180
plague 230
plaice 55
plain 16, 23, 216, 218
plain cooking 58
plan 117, 118, 119, 177, 185, 192, 194
plan a process 257
plane 132, 255, 289, 290
plane crash 289
planer 255
planet 204
planing machine 255
plank 24
planned 296
planned city 223
planned parenthood 37, 98
planners 177
planning 37, 177, 223, 224
planning permission 177, 308

planning stage 177
plant 88, 221, 235, 257, 258, 315
plant kingdom 235
plant manager 258
plant seeds 221
plantation 220
plaque 79
plaster 72
plaster figure 169
plastered 129
plastic 254, 255
plastic surgery 245
plat du jour 63
plate 59, 170
plate tectonics 210
plateau 218
platform 101, 202, 287, 288, 294
platoon 118
play 17, 72, 174, 176, 197, 213, 271
play (n.) 176
play (against) sb. 92
play a game 195
play a part 176
play cards 199
play the piano 173
play truant 19
player 26, 196, 271, 281, 282
playgroup 17
playlist 281
playmate 33
playwright 176
plc 127, 298
plea 111
plea bargaining 111
pleasant 22, 121
please 27, 62, 77, 78, 90, 155, 172, 191, 192, 201, 251, 273, 275, 288, 290, 294, 313
please forward 273
pleated skirt 65
plentiful 233
plenty 156, 292
pliable 262
pliers 255
plot 107, 155, 176, 180
plot of land 308
plough 222
plow 222
plug 259, 260, 297
plug a product 306
plug in 260
plugged in 260
plum 56
plumber 310
plummet 299
plump 15, 16
plunge 238
plus 247

plywood 254
pneumatic drill 255
pneumonia 69
PO box 272
poacher 132
poaching 131
POB 272
pocket 302
pocket money 51
poem 180
poet 179, 180
Poet Laureate 180
poetic 180
poetry 179, 180
pogrom 133
point 90, 197, 243, 248, 249, 250, 260
point of view 180
poison 42, 129
poisoning 69
poke 202, 222
Poland 119
polar bear 233
pole 205, 215
police 27, 109, 111, 112, 251, 309
police agency 112
police department 112
police force 111
police officer 111
police state 99
police station 112
policeman 15
policies 100
policy 32, 100, 116, 117, 142, 296, 304, 307
policyholder 307
polio 73
polish 39, 93
polite 22
politeness 35
political 99, 100, 115, 117, 138, 142, 146
political consultant 310
political correctness 73
political science 142
political scientist 142
political unrest 107
political violence 107
politically 100, 142
politician 23, 100
politics 83, 100, 142
poll 101, 142
poll tax 114
polls 104
pollutants 225
pollution 225
polo shirt 64
polytheism 161
polyunsaturated 82

pond 216
ponytail 16
pool 88, 216, 311, 313
poor 14, 130, 145, 173, 314
poor health 21
poor nutrition 130
poor reception 271
poor soils 220
poorly trained 154
pop 50, 57
pop art 169
pop artist 169
pop culture 98
pop off 43
pop song 173
pop-up menu 278
pope 163
poplar 235
poppy 235
Poppy Day 236
popular 195, 198, 199, 271
popular press 268
populated 97
population 138, 141, 145, 224, 230
populous 97
porch 88
pork 55, 58
porn 37
pornographic 37
pornography 32
porridge 55, 192
port 217, 277, 292
portable 282
porter 192, 288
portfolio manager 304
portion 63, 216
portly 15
portrait 168
portrait bust 169
position 36, 304
positive 70, 306
positive discrimination 98
positive reinforcement 143
positivism 166
positivist 166
possess 132
possession 132
possible 83, 100
post 272, 273
post a letter 272
post office 272
post-office box 272
post-war 176
postage 273
postage stamp 273
postal card 272, 273
postal clerk 311
postal order 272

postal rates 272
postal service 272
postal worker 272
postbox 273
postcard 199, 272, 273
postcode 273
poste restante 273
poster 156, 170
postgraduate 149
posting 280
postman 272
postmark 273
postmarked 273
Postmaster General 272
postmodern 177
postmortem 41
postwoman 272
pot 58, 59, 129, 261
pot plant 235
potato(es) 56, 58, 230, 261, 270, 301
potato bug 234
potato chips 56
potato pancake 56
potato salad 56
potency 37
potted 88
pottery 198
potty 50
poultry 55, 221
pound(s) 251, 302
pounds 303
pour 261
pour with rain 228
poverty 20, 130
poverty trap 130
POW 120
powder 39, 93, 129
power 98, 100, 102, 108, 142, 247, 259, 260, 297, 304
power breakfast 60
power down 277
power point 90, 260
power up 277
powerful 99
PR disaster 306
practice 162
practices 305
practise 42
practitioner 75, 244
pragmatic 166
pragmatism 166
pragmatist 166
prairie 218
praise 146
pram 17
prawns 55
pray 28
pray to God 160
prayer 163
pre-shave 39
preach 162

preacher 162
practically 248
precariat 130
precious metal 212
precious stone 212, 213
precipitation 228
precise 242
predictable 142
predominant 159
prefab(ricated) 87
prefabricated 178
preface 266
prefer 29, 36, 200
prefix 44
pregnancy 37, 50
pregnant 37, 50
prehistoric 138, 140
prehistory 140
prejudice 30, 134
prejudiced 30, 134
premature 50
Premier League 197
premiere 175
premium 307
prep(aratory) school 148
prepare 113, 114
prepare for an exam 152
preparer 114
Presbyterian 159
prescription 77
present 121
presentation 156
presenter 271
preservation 226
president 34, 73, 103, 105, 108, 118, 121, 186, 299
presidential 99
press 84, 93, 268
press a key 278
press conference 268
press kit 306
press-up 83
pressing problem 125
pressure 69, 77, 241, 286
pressure cooker 59
pressure group 142
pretended 127
pretty (= hübsch) 15, 216
pretty (= ziemlich) 24
prevention 96, 131, 232
previous 48, 304
prey 233
prez 94
price 113, 114, 193, 297, 300, 308
price oneself out of the market 300

price tag 300
prick 78
pride 30, 32, 98
priest 99, 163
priesthood 99
primary 140
primary (election) 104
primary school 148
prime 20
prime minister 86, 106
prime number 247
prime time 271
primitive art 138
primitive peoples 138
prince 48, 121, 149
princess 121
principal 160, 309
principle 31, 166
print 170, 171, 267
print run 267
printed matter 273
printer 277
printer(s) 267
printer's error 267
printing 170
printing block 170
printing machine 255
printing process 170
printmaking 170
printout 277
Priority Mail 272
prison 111, 314
prisoner of war 120
private 184, 307
private eye 208
private ownership 296
private part(s) 14
private property 296, 308
private sector 124, 296
privates 14
privatize 287
pro 94
pro-choice 98
probability 246
probably 160, 227
probation 111
probation officer 111
probe 206, 207
problem 18, 52, 123, 125, 136, 165, 225, 246
problem drinker 200
problem solving 143
procedure 316
proceedings 109
process 142, 145, 146, 170, 210, 242, 257, 258

processing 257, 260, 276
processing industries 258
procession 41
processor 276
produce 176, 257
produce (n.) 220
producer 271
product 56, 257, 297, 301, 305, 306
product placement 306
production 176, 257, 296
production costs 296
production line 257
production management 258
production process 258
productivity 258, 297
products 220, 257
profession 244, 309
professional 15, 195, 309
professor 21, 122, 149, 310
profiling 135
profit 296, 300
profit margin 300
profit warning 300
profitability 300
profitable 27, 300
profusely 72
program 276, 277
programme 19, 101, 124, 127, 154, 206, 270, 271
programmer 276
programming 270, 276
progress 254
progression 246
progressive 23
prohibited 187
project 262, 304
projections 297
projector 155
promise the moon 205
promote 118, 124, 306
promotion 306, 316
promotional 306
prompting 155
prone 229
pronounce 160
proofreader 267
proofs 267
propelling pencil 313
properly 260

properties 240, 242, 254
property 114, 288, 296, 308
property developer 178
property management 308
property register 308
property tax 114
prophet 160
proportion 113
proportional font 278
proposal 48, 146
propose 103
propose to 48
proposition 306
proprietor 298
props 176
propulsion system 207
prose 179
prosecute 109, 131
prosecuting attorney 109
prosecuting counsel 109
prosecution 109, 110, 111, 112
prosecutor 110
prospect 300
prospective 300
prosperity 297
prostate 14
prostitute 37
prostitution 37, 130, 131, 269
protect 52, 225
protection 106, 225, 226, 276, 280
protector 282
protein 237
protest 98, 107, 225
protest rally 107
Protestant 159
Protestantism 159
protester 105, 107
proton 241
protozoa(ns) 237
proud 24, 30
prove 24, 110
proverb 52, 89
provide 82, 115, 118, 124, 125, 307
provider 279
province 96, 97
provincial 223
proving ground 206
prudence 32
psalm 162
pseudo 127
psychiatrist 75, 143, 144

psychiatry 143
psychoanalysis 143
psychoanalyst 143, 144
psychological 143
psychological test 144
psychologist 143
psychology 143, 150
psychopath 143
psychopathic 143
psychopathology 143
psychosis 144
psychotherapist 75, 143, 144
psychotherapy 143
pub 191, 201
pub date 267
puberty 18
public 124, 131, 184, 211
public assistance 115, 130
public employees 315
public-health department 245
public-health officer 245
public holiday 182
public library 264
public limited company 298
public opinion 142, 145
public relations 306
public school 148
public sector 315
public transit 293
public transport 262, 294, 315
public transport/ transportation 293
publication date 267
publicity 306
publicity campaign 306
publish 267
publisher 267
publishing 266, 279
publishing firm 267
publishing house 267
pull 91, 205
pull back 91
pull down 91
pull out 79
pull out of the fire 235
pull-in 61
pullover 64
pulmonary 245
pulp fiction 179
pulp novel 179

pulsar 204
pumps 65
pun 180
punch 313
Punch-and-Judy show 187
punishment 19, 111
pup(py) 232
pupil 152
puppet 17
puppet show 187
purchase 194
purchase price 300
purchasing power 297
pure 164
Puritan 159
purse 261, 303
purse snatcher 132
purse snatching 132
pursue a hobby 199
pursue a policy 117
pursuits 198
pus 70
push 207
push up interest rates 297
push-up 83
pushchair 17
pusher 128, 129
put 13, 156
put back 90
put down 107
put forward 90, 103
put in 261
put into orbit 207
put on 59, 64, 173
put on/off 90
put on charge 259
put on the brakes 256
put on weight 76
put photos in 171
put the cart 222
put the kids to bed 60
put up a fight 133
put up for 51
put up with 29
putsch 108
puzzle 18, 199
pyjamas 65
pyramid 247

Q
Q-tip™ 39
quadrangle 247
quadrangular 247
quake 211, 229
qualifications 152
qualify 197
quality 31, 298
quality press 268
quantity 59, 247
quantum 241

quantum jump 241
quantum leap 241
quantum mechanics 241
quark 241
quarrel 35
quarter 302
quarter(s) 249
quarter note 174
quarters 86
quartet 174
quasar 204
quaver 174
queen 87, 105, 184
Queen's Speech 103
query 281
question 31, 109, 122, 166, 265, 281
questioning 112
queue 192
quick 61, 72, 154
quick temper 22
quickest 285
quid 303
quiet 26, 155, 298
quinine water 57
quit 125
quite 93
quiz show 271
quotient 143, 247

R
rabbi 163
rabbit 55
rabies 68
race 33, 135, 138, 187, 195
race discrimination 135
race hatred 135
race relations 135
racial 135
racial equality 98, 135
racial hatred 135
racial segregation 107
racing 195
racing car 196
racing driver 196
racism 134, 135
racist 135
rack 290
racket 197
racketeer 131
radiant 16
radiation 68, 207, 225
radiation therapy 245
radiator 91
radical 100, 134
radio 26, 270, 271
radio alarm 271
radio operator 292
radio programme 271

radio set 270
radioactive 226, 243
radiocarbon dating 211
radiochemistry 242
radiology 244
radiotherapy 245
radish 56
raft 291
rag 93
rage 285
raid 119, 132
rail 287
rail line 287
rail strike 287
rail terminal 287
rail transport 287
rail(way) worker 287
railroad 18, 287, 293
railroad car 287
railway 18, 287
railway carriage 287
railway junction 287
rain 226, 228
rain forest 219
raincoat 64
rainy 228
rainy day 228
raise 13, 51, 121, 221, 296
raise livestock 221
raise taxes 113
raisin 54
raisins 56
rally 105, 107
Ramadan 163
rampage 133
ranch 220
random 241
random sample 145
range 218
range of 257
rangefinder 172
ranger 310
rank 294
rap 28
rape 37, 131
rapid 120
rapist 37, 131
rare 59
rascal 50
rash 70, 74
raspberries 56
rat 27, 233
rate 126, 130, 131, 279, 297, 303, 306
rate of exchange 190
rates 272, 297, 304, 305, 307, 308, 316
rather 24, 175, 227, 302
ratify 103
ratings 271
ratio 247
rational 165

rationalism 164, 166
rationalist 166
rationalistic 166
rationing 297
ravine 218
ravioli 55
raw data 146
raw materials 226
ray 77
razor 38
RE 150
re-entry 206
re-establish 116
reach 11, 20, 36
reach a compromise 117
reach a decision 105
reach an agreement 117
reach for 208
reaction 242
reactor 262
read 29, 154, 155
read *n.* 267
read music 173
read the proofs 267
reader 266
reading 103, 151, 199
reading comprehension 151
real 13, 309
real estate 114, 308
real estate agent 124, 308
real gem 212
real property 308
realism 166, 169, 180
realist 166, 169
realistic 166
realists 169
reality 166, 265
really 13, 28
realtor 308
rear 51, 221
reason 164, 351
reasoning 143, 165
rebellion 108
receive 121
receive an Oscar 176
receive into 159
receiver 275
recently 74
receptacle 261
reception 186, 192, 271
reception desk 192
receptionist 75, 312
recess 103
recession 297
recharge 259
recipient 245
reciprocity 139
reckless driving 286
reckon 246

R

reckon up 246
reclining 168
recognition 29, 116, 278
recognize 73
recommend 62
record 59, 142, 195
record (v.) 264
recorded delivery 273
recorder 271
records 140
recovery 296
recovery room 81
recreation 181, 198
recruitment consultant 127
rectal 245
rectangle 247
rectangular 247
rector 163
rectum 245
recycle 226
recycling 226
red 92, 111
red card 197
red carpet 91
Red Crescent 230
Red Cross 230
red-letter day 184
red light 285
red wine 200
redcap 288
reddish-brown 87
redhead 16
reduce 117, 226, 297
reduce taxes 113
reducing pills 82
reduction 114, 243, 316
reduction in charges 111
redundancy 126
redundancy package 126
redundancy pay 126
redundant 126, 316
refer 75
referee 197
reference 264
reference book 264
reference library 264
referendum 104, 237
referral 75
refill 313
reflex 143
reflex camera 171
reform 101, 104, 115
Reformation 141
Reformed 159
refrain 180
refreshments 194
refrigerator 90
refugee 134
refund 114

refuse 225, 226
refuse tip 226
regards 49
Regency 177
regicide 42
regimen 82
regiment 118
region 97, 215, 219, 260
regional 97
regional office 106
register 140, 155, 302, 308
register office 48
registered post 273
registrar 80
registry office 48
regular 76
regular (n.) 61
regularly 162, 285
regulation 258, 296
regulations 308
rehire 127
rehouse 125
reinforced concrete 178
relation(s) 46
relations 33, 36, 116, 135, 142, 145, 306, 314
relationship 33
relationships 145
relative 46
relativity 205, 240
relax 83
relaxation 198, 199
relaxed 24
relay race 195
release 110, 111, 112, 172
reliability 144, 146
reliable 22
relief 169, 179, 230
religion 11, 158, 159
religious 11, 158, 162
religious education 150
religious instruction 150
remain 24, 32
remains 41, 211
remand 111, 112
remark 13, 135
remedy 77
remember 132, 202
Remembrance Day 236
Remembrance Sunday 236
remote 97
removal van 284
remove 79, 171
remover 39
Renaissance 141, 169, 177

rendezvous 206
renew 189, 271
renewable 226
renewal 224
rent 124, 125, 208
rent a house 308
rent boy 37
rent control 124
rent increase 124
rent subsidy 115
rental 284
rental car 284
repair 198
repair shop 258
repay 303
repeat (n.) 271
repeat after 155
repeat offender 112
replace 79, 275, 277
reply 273
report 156, 227, 269
report (card) 153
reporter 268, 269
represent 103
representative 99, 145, 300
Representatives 102, 104
repressed 144
reproduction 169
reps 84
reptile 234
republic 99
Republican 101
Republicans 101
request 61
request stop 293
requiem mass 41
require 191
required 226
rerun 271
rescue team 230
rescue work 230
research 140, 143, 145, 146, 237, 240, 242, 262, 306
research facilities 224
research institute 149
research into 140
research project 262
reservation 61, 191, 289, 290
reservation clerk 311
reserve 62, 219, 233, 288, 304
reserved 24
reservoir 216
reshuffle 105
residence 10, 86, 87
resident 80
residential 97
residents 223
resign 106
resignation 106, 269

resistance 107, 119, 241, 255
resisting arrest 131
resolution 117, 172
resort 82, 189
resources 210, 226, 299
respect 33, 35
respectful 24
respectfully 121
respiratory 68
response 143
response rate 306
responsibility 111
responsible 22
rest 40, 41, 241
rest day 84
rest home 21
rest in peace 41
rest period 84
restaurant 61, 97, 301
restaurant car 287
restrict 134
restructuring 126
result 30, 240, 315
Resurrection 162
resuscitate 72
resuscitation 72
retail 300
retail price 114, 193, 300
retailer 300
retarded 51, 73, 144
retire 20
retired 20
retiree 20
retirement 20
retirement pension 115
retrain 127
retraining 127
retreat 119
retrieval 265, 276
retrorocket 207
return 113, 114, 155, 272, 273, 278, 288
return journey 288
return ticket 288
return to work 316
returnable 226
returns 184, 304
reunion 185
revamp 306
revelation 161
Revenue 113
revere 158
Reverend 122
reverse discrimination 98
review 156, 171, 176
revise 156
revision 156
revolt 108

revolution 98, 108, 141
revolutionary 108
revolve 204
revolving door 88
rewarding 198
rhetorical 180
rheumatic 245
rheumatic fever 245
rheumatism 70
rheumatology 244
Rhine 216, 217
rhubarb 56
rhyme 180
rhyme scheme 180
rhythm 37, 174
RI 150
rib 13, 234
rice 54, 221
rich 219
Richter scale 211
ride 187, 284, 286, 288, 293, 294
ride at anchor 292
ride free 293
ride public transportation 293
ride the subway 293
rider 286, 293
riding 73, 199
riding instructor 309
Riesling 62
right 31, 134, 136, 196, 285
right away 312
Right Honourable 121
right now 127, 313
right of asylum 134
right-to-life 98
right wing 100
right-wing 134
rightist 100, 134
rights 98, 106, 107, 142, 316
ring 48
ring (up) 274
ring binder 313
ring off 274
ring the bell 91
ringleader 108
rinse 78, 93
riot 133
rioter 133
RIP 41, 94
ripped 84
rise 126
rise (risen) 110
rise from 40
rise in rebellion 108
rise in rents 124
rise in revolt 108
rise to 230
rising 131
risk 307

ritual 139
rivalry 96
river 43, 215, 216, 217, 229
riverside 216
riveting 267
roach 234
road 200, 224, 284, 285
road accident 286
road rage 285
road safety 285
road traffic 284
roaming 275
roast 58
robber 40, 131, 132
robbery 131, 132
robot 258
rock(s) 49, 210
rock samples 206
rock the boat 292
rocket 119, 206, 207
rocket engine 207
rocking chair 90
rocking horse 17
rococo 169
rod 52, 256
rogue state 96
role 96, 136
roll 38, 54, 60
roll out 91
roll-up 201
roll-your-own 201
rolled oats 55
roller coaster 187
roller skates 18
roller-skating 196, 199
rolling 218
rolling paper 201
rolls 192
Roman 156
Roman Catholic 159
Roman Catholicism 158, 159
Romanesque 169, 177
romantic 180
romanticism 180
roof 88
room 87, 188, 191, 215
room service 192
roommate 124
root 236, 246
root beer 57
root treatment 79
rose 27, 235, 236
rosy 238
rosy-cheeked 15
rotate 204
rotation 221
rotten 27
rough 125, 213, 215
rough diamond 212

roughage 82
round 16, 91, 188, 204
round (n.) 80
round the bend 285
round the world 188
round trip 288
round-trip ticket 288
roundabout 187, 285
roundabout route 285
route 285, 293
routinely 290
row 175, 230
row house 87
rowboat 291
rowing boat 291
royalties 267
RSVP 94
Rt Hon 121
rub down 38
rub in 39
rub off 155
rubber 254, 313
rubber boots 65
rubbish 225
rubbish bin 91
ruby 213
rucksack 261
rudder 52
ruddy 16
rude 23
rudeness 35
rug 91
rugby 197
rule 212, 315
ruler 23
ruling party 100
rummy 129
rumpled 16
run 101, 104, 195, 212, 267, 284, 293
run (n.) 293
run a race 195
run a search 264, 265
run a stop sign 286
run a temperature 68
run aground 292
run away 19
run down 71
run-down 224
run for office 104
run late 288
run low 301
run on sth. 282
run on time 288
run out of 62, 106
run over 71
run sb. home 284
runner 15
runner-up 195
running 83, 196
running event 196
runny 12, 44

runoff 104
runway 290
rupture(d) 69
rural 219
rush 29
rush-hour traffic 285
rush hours 285
rye 54, 221
rye bread 54

S

S
s-commerce 281
Sabbath 163
sabotage 107
sack 126, 261
sack sb. 316
sacrament 163
sacred 158
sadism 37
safety 285
safety net 115
safety valve 256
sail 291, 292
sailboat 291
sailing 199, 291
sailing boat 291
sailor 52, 223, 292
saint 162
salad 56, 58, 194
salad bar 63
salad bowl 59
salary tax 114
sale 194, 308
sale(s) 194, 299
sales 193, 299
sales figures 299
sales force 300
sales manager 299
sales promotion 306
sales rep 300
sales tax 114
sales vice president 299
salesclerk 311
salesman 300, 307
salesmanship 300
salesperson 193
saleswoman 300, 307
salmon 55, 62
salon 83
saloon 201
salt 55
salty 27
Salvation Army 159
same 33, 272, 292
same-sex 98
sample 145, 244
samples 206
sanctions 117
sand dunes 219
sandals 65
sandbox 18
sandpit 18
sandstone 87

sandwich 54, 192, 194
sandwich bar 61
sandy 219
sanitary napkin 39
sanitary towel 39
Sanka™ 57
sapphire 213
sash window 88
sassy 24
SAT 152
SAT™ 152
satellite 204, 207
satellite city 223
satellite town 223
satire 179
satirical 179, 268
saturated 243
saturation 172
Saturn 204
sauce 44, 55, 129
saucepan 59, 92
saucer 59
sauna 38, 83
sausage 55, 192
save 193, 277, 291, 303
save (n.) 196
saving 260, 303
savings account 303
savings and loan 303
savings bank 303
savings rate 303
saw 255
say 26, 274
say after 155
say cheese 172
scale 174, 211
scales 90
scampi 55
scan 77, 244, 264
scandal 101
scandal sheet 269
scanner 278
scar 69
scarcely 26
scarf 66
scarlet fever 68
scatter 46
scattered 228
ScD 153
scenario 44
scene 72, 101, 153, 176
scenery 176, 218
scenic 218
scent 27
sceptic 166
sceptical 166
scepticism 164, 166
sceptics 164
schedule 288
scheduled 289, 290
scheduled to 288

scheme 115, 126, 127, 180, 310
schizophrenia 144
schizophrenic 144
scholar 140
scholarly 146
scholastic 166
Scholastic Aptitude Test 152
school 19, 26, 148, 149, 152, 154, 159, 174, 182, 284
schoolboy 18
school choir 173
schoolgirl 18
schoolmaster 52, 309
schoolmate 33
schoolmistress 309
sciatica 70
science 137, 142, 150, 153, 239, 240, 242, 254, 276
science fiction 179
scientific 165, 242
scissors 39, 255
scold 51
scone 54
score 153, 197
Scotch 201
Scotch tape™ 313
Scotland Yard 112
scour 92
scrambled eggs 54, 192
screen 170, 175, 277
screen protector 282
screenplay 175
screw(driver) 255
script 175
scroll down/up 277
scrub 92
scruffy 16
scruple 32
scuba-diving 199
sculpt 169
sculptor 169
sculptural 169
sculpture 168, 169
sculptured 169
SD Memory Card 282
sea 27, 28, 41, 213, 215, 216, 292
sea(s) 291
seabed 216
seafloor 216
seafloor spreading 210
seafood 55
seal 234
search 166, 265, 277, 278, 279, 289
search engine 265

search for 264
search term 265
seasick 292
seasickness 68, 292
seaside 216
seaside resort 189
season 271
seasonal 126
seasoning 55
seat 14, 103, 175, 288, 289, 290
seatbelt 290
seaview 191
second 172
second-class mail 272
second-class post 272
second-degree burns 71
second-degree murder 110
second half 196
secondary education 152
secondary modern 148
secondary school 148
secondhand 194
secondhand books 266
secondhand book-shop 194, 266
secret 116
secretarial 149
secretary 24, 106, 116, 212, 311, 313
secretary-general 117
secretary of defense 106, 118
secretary of state 106, 116, 118
secretary of state for 106
section 50, 81, 201
sector 124, 296, 315
secure 282
secure server 281
securities 304
security 114, 115, 316
security check 289
Security Council 117
sedimentation 210
sediments 210
see 25, 30, 62, 122, 128, 144, 312
see (seen) 232
see a lawyer 110
see action 119
seed(s) 221
seeds 221
seek 125, 247
seeker 112, 134

seem 35, 105, 227
seesaw 18
segregation 107, 135
seismology 210
seize power 108
self 166
self-actualization 144
self-assured 23
self-confident 23
self-conscious 23
self-control 31
self-employed 127, 309
self-employment 127
self-esteem 84
self-instruction 154
self-portrait 168
self-realization 144
self-service 61
selfish 22
sell 193, 213, 298, 299
seller 129, 300
selling 306
Sellotape™ 313
seltzer 57
semen 36
semibreve 174
semiconductor 240, 255
semidetached 87
seminal 146
seminary 149
semiotics 139
semiprecious 213
semiskilled 309
senate 102
Senate 102, 103, 104
senator 102, 103
send back 257
send by air 289
send off 197
send sb. round the bend 285
send sb. up the river 43
send sth. by airmail 273
send sth. by fax 275
send sth. by post 272
send sth. COD 273
sender 273
senile 21
senile dementia 74
senility 21
senior 100
senior citizen 21
senior consultant 80
senior high school 148
senior nurse 81
senior nursing officer 81
senior registrar 80

sensation(s) 25
sensational press 268
sense(s) 25
sensible 23
sensibly 23
sensitive 23, 78
sensor 172, 262
sentence 12, 111
sentimental 30, 270
separate(d) 49
separation 49
separation of powers 102
series 104, 271, 305
serious 37, 68, 73, 74, 109
serious drinker 200
serious press 268
seriously 71
sermon 162
Sermon on the Mount 162
servant 20, 311
serve 96, 104, 186, 192
serve an ace 197
served by 289
server 280, 281
service 21, 41, 113, 115, 118, 162, 192, 193, 272, 287, 294
service (v.) 286
service (charge) 62
service area 285
service module 207
service provider 279
service sector 296
services 130, 296
serving 63
session 102, 103
set 38, 176, 197, 270
set a record 195
set a wage 130
set homework 154
set in the silver sea 213
set of dentures 79
set piece 197
set point 197
set the alarm 90
set the aperture to 172
set the speed 172
set theory 246
settee 90
setting 138, 180, 278
settle 224, 303
settle a claim 307
settle a conflict 117
settle a dispute 316
settle a quarrel 35
settle a strike 315
settlement 109, 303, 307
sever 116

several 89, 103, 213, 230, 299
severance pay 126
severe 227
sewing 198
sewing machine 255
sex 11, 23, 36, 136
sex discrimination 136
sex education 150
sex roles 136
sex(ual) equality 136
sexism 136
sexist 134, 136
sexist language 136
sexual 36, 136
sexual harassment 36, 136
sexuality 36
sexually 36
sexy 36
shabby 16
shack 87
shade 91
shadow 39
shadow cabinet 105
shaft 256
shall 59, 86, 160, 173
shall I 284, 289
shallow 270
shammy 93
shampoo 38, 39
shandy 200
shanty 87
shantytown 125
shapely 15
share 171, 202, 296
share a flat 124
shareholder 299
shareholder value 299
shareware 281
sharia (law) 163
shark 234
sharp 172, 174, 233, 301
sharp increase 125
sharp pain 76
sharpener 313
sharply 256
shave 38
shaver 38
shaver outlet 90
shaver point 90
shaving cream 38
shed 88, 222
shed v. 146, 234, 236
shedding 126
sheep 221, 222
sheep's milk cheese 54
sheep's clothing 238
sheesh 129
sheet 89, 254, 269

shelf 89, 210
shellfish 55
shelter 86, 119, 125
shepherd 221, 232
sheriff 112
shift key 278
shine 93, 208
shining 16
ship 119, 217, 291, 292
ship (v.) 273, 285, 291, 301
ship by air 289
shipment 301
shipment tracking 273
shipowner 292
shipping 291
shipping documents 301
shipwrecked 291
shipyard 291
shirt 16, 38, 64, 92, 93
shit 129
Shiva 160
shock 72, 153, 259
shoe shop 194, 224
shoe store 224
shoemaker 310
shoes 65, 93
shoeshine 38
shoot 128, 129, 132
shoot (shot) 232
shoot and kill 132
shoot and wound 132
shoot dead 40, 132
shooting 284
shooting gallery 187
shooting star 204
shootout 197
shop 22, 56, 192, 193, 194, 224, 257, 258
shop assistant 311
shop floor 258
shopkeeper 298
shoplifting 132
shopping 193
shopping bag 193, 261
shopping basket 193
shopping cart 193
shopping centre 193
shopping mall 193
shopping spree 193
shopping trolley 193
shopwindow display 306
shore 216, 217
short 15, 155
short circuit 260
short-distance ticket 294

short of 302
short of breath 76
short-order cook 63
short short story 179
short-sleeved 64
short story 179
short-term 143
short time 126, 316
short-time work 316
short-trip ticket 294
shortage 86, 124
shortbread 54
shorthand 313
shorthand typist 311
short(ly) 353
shortly 290
shorts 65
shortsighted 25
shot 128, 171
shot at 132
shotgun wedding 48
should 32, 74, 113
shoulder 12, 72, 78
shout 107
shovel 18
show 127, 165, 175, 187, 270, 271, 298
show the red card 197
show up 290
showbiz 94
showdown 315
shower 38, 90
showers 228
showing 101
showroom 301
shrimps 55
shrink 144
shrubs 219
shrug 12
shuffle songs 281
shut 155
shut down 277
shut off 277
shutter 172
shutter speed 172
shutters 88
shuttle 206
shuttle diplomacy 116
shuttle service 287
sick 14, 40, 76
sick leave 182
sick note 77
sickness 50, 68
sickness benefit 115
sickout 315
side 21, 78, 196
side dish 62
side order 62
side street 285
sideboard 89
sideline 197
sideshow 187
sidewalk 224, 285

S

sieve 58
sight 25
sightseeing 189
sightseeing tour 189
sign 117, 278, 280,
    286, 294, 313
signature 281
silage 222
silent 26
silently 154
silicon (chip) 255
Silicon Valley 260
silo 222
silver 212
silver jubilee 184
silver wedding 48,
    184
simple 237, 281
simplify 113
sin 31, 32, 162
since 144
sincere 22
sinful 31
sing 173
singer 173
singing 173
singing lessons 173
singing voice 173
single 11, 265
single (n.) 288
single (room) 191
single-breasted 64
single-celled 237
Single European
    Market 117
single-lens 171
single parent 51
singles 197
sink 90
sink (sank) 217, 291,
    292
sir 61, 62, 121, 122
Sir 121
sister 46, 74, 81
sister-in-law 46
sit an exam 152
sit-in 107
sit on/in 90
sit on a committee
    103
sit still 27
sit-ups 84
sitcom 271
site 177, 206, 226,
    279, 308
sitter 17
sitting 168
sitting room 87
situated 216
situation 127, 222
situation comedy
    271
sixth form 148
sixth form college
    148

skateboard 18
skates 18
skating 196
skeleton 14, 89, 178
ski instructor 309
skiing 196, 199
skiing instructor 309
skill 150
skilled worker 310
skillet 59
skim (through) sth.
    264
skim(med) 54
skin 13, 14, 39, 69,
    77, 135
skin-diving 199
skin grafting 245
skinhead 134
skinny 15
skins 56
skipper 292
skirt 16, 65
skol! 200
skull 12
sky 208, 228
skydiving 199
skyjack 290
skyjacker 131, 290
skyjacking 131, 290
skype™ 202
skyscraper 87
slack 298
slacks 65
slander 133
slash prices 300
slaughter 133
sled 18
sledge 18
sleep 125
sleep around 37
sleep it off 129
sleep rough 125
sleep with 36
sleeper 287
sleeping car 287
sleeping dogs 238
sleeplessness 70
sleeveless 64
slender 15
slice 58
sliced 58
slick 226
slide 172
sliding door 88
slight 32, 70
slightly 15, 172, 250
slim 15
slimming pills 82
slip 65, 126, 144
slip-on shoes 65
slip-ons 65
slippers 65
slit dress 64
slogan 107, 305
sloth 32

slow 83, 90, 154, 296
slowdown 315
slower 293
slowly 25
SLR 171
slum 223
slump 299
slush-fund scandal
    101
smack 13, 19
small 17, 63, 302
small game 233
small intestine 245
small packet 273
small parcel 273
small potatoes 301
small town 214, 223
smallpox 69, 190
smart 15, 16, 262
smart casual 64
smartphone 262
smash hit 176
smell 25, 27
smile 30
smile please 172
smiley 280
smog 228
smoke 128, 201
smoked salmon 55,
    62
smoker 201, 287
smoker's cough 201
smoking 31, 82,
    200, 201
smoking area 201
smooth 27, 284
SMS (message) 275
smuggler 132
smuggling 131
snack 61
snack bar 61
snail 234
snail mail 280
snake 211, 234
snap(shot) 171
snarled up 285
snatch 132
snatcher 132
sneakers 65
sneeze 69
sniff 128
snifter 129
snooker 197
snow 129, 228
snowed (in/up) 129
so far 105
So-and-so 223
so-called 138
soap 38, 93
soap opera 270
soaps 270
sober 200
soccer 196
soccer hooligan 131
soccer match 270

social 98, 123, 145
social anthropology
    138
social conflict 142
social engineering
    145
social history 140
social insurance 115
social life 138
social market econ-
    omy 296
social media 202
social order 93, 138
social problem 125
social safety net 115
social sciences 137
social security 114,
    115
social security office
    115
social services 130
social structure 138
social studies 150
social system 138
social welfare office
    115
social welfare system
    115
social worker 310
socialism 99
socialist 101
socialization 145
socializing 185
socially 97
society 10, 96, 138,
    145, 303
society for 232
sociological 145,
    146
sociologist 145
sociology 145, 310
socket 90, 260
socks 66
soda (pop) 57
sofa 90
sofa bed 89
soft 27, 206, 233
soft-boiled 58
soft drink 57
soft drinks 200
soft drug 128
soft hyphen 278
soft-land 206
soft porn 37
soft sell 299
software 276, 278,
    280
software package
    276
softwood 254
soil 220, 230
soil pollution 225
solar eclipse 204
solar panel 226
solar power 226

solar system 204
solar-powered 262
solarium 83
soldier 15, 24, 41, 118
sole 55, 300
solicitor 110
solid 241
solid-state physics 240
solidarity 34, 114
soliloquy 176
soluble 243
solution 117, 243
solve a problem 246
solvent 243
solving 143
some 19
something 27, 29
sometime 274
sometimes 52, 103, 174, 219
somewhere 21
son 19, 42, 46
Son 160
son-in-law 46
sonata 174
song 138, 173, 223
songbird 233
sonnet 180
soon 52
sophisticated 22
soprano 173
sorcerer 164
sorcery 164
sore throat 12, 69, 75
sorts 198
soul 41
sound 26
sound (adj.) 178
sound bite 101
soundproof 26
soup 27, 31, 55
soup bowl 59
soup du jour 62, 63
soup kitchen 130
soup of the day 62
soupspoon 59
sour 27
sour cream 54
source 129, 140, 166, 264
souse 129
south 214, 215, 216
South Africa 215
south of 260
South Pole 215
southerly 228
southern 215, 216
southern Africa 215
southwest 215
sovereign 116
sovereignty 116
sow 236

sozzled 129
spa 82, 83
space 124, 166, 190, 204, 206, 223, 226, 286
space age 206
space exploration 206
space probe 206, 207
space shuttle 206
space station 206, 207
space travel 206
spacecraft 206
spaceflight 206, 207
spaceship 206
spacesuit 206
spacing 278
spaghetti 55
spam 280
spanking 19
spanner 255
spare 52
spare parts 261
spare room 87
spare time 198
spare tyre 286
spark 259
spark plug 259
sparking plug 259
sparkling water 57
sparkling wine 200
sparrow 233
sparsely 97
speak 26, 73
speak clearly 155
speak in public 211
speak louder 155, 275
speak to 275
speak up 155
speaker 102, 276
speakers 260
speaking 275
special adviser 105
special delivery 273
special education 51
special envoy 116
Special Handling 272
special offer 194
special school 148
specialist 75
specialist department 112
specialist literature 264
spécialité de la maison 63
specialize in 37, 81
species 226, 254
specific gravity 241
specs 94
spectrum 241
speculation 146

speculator 304, 308
speech 103
speech defect 73
speed 129, 171, 172, 204, 241
speed limit 250, 284
speed reading 151
speeding 286
spell 227
spell checker 278
spend 19, 64, 199, 303
spending 118, 297
spent (spend) 18
sperm 36
spice 55
spicy 268
spider 234
spiderweb 234
spiel 157
spill 92, 226
spin doctor 101
spina bifida 74
spinach 55
spinal column 245
spinning 198
spire 178
spirit 31, 160
spirit of the age 141
spit 201
splash 129
spoil 51, 52
spoil(t) 27
spoilt 18
spokesman 269
spokeswoman 269
sponge 38, 93, 237
sponsor 271
spoon 59, 61
sport(s) 195
sport coat 64
sporting event 195
sports 196, 199
sports car 44
sports commentator 271
sports festival 184
sports jacket 64
sports programme 271
sports section 269
sports shop 194
sportscast 271
sportsground 195
sportsman 195
sportsmanlike 195
sportswoman 195
spouse 49
sprain 72
spread 158, 225, 315
spreading 210
spree 129, 193
spring 217, 256, 298
spring chicken 20
spy 120

sq km 215
squad 40, 43, 110, 128, 196
square 246, 247
square metre 247
square miles 250
square of 247
square root 246
squared 247
squash 57, 72, 197
squat 83, 125
squatter 125
squirrel 233
St 162
st 251
stab 133
stab to death 133
stabbing 76
stability 84, 297
stable 88, 142, 222
stable (adj.) 241
stadium 195
staff 105
staffed 91
stage 176, 177
stage a sit-in 107
stage a strike 315
stage direction(s) 180
stain 92
stainless steel 212
stairs 87
stake 43
stalls 175
stamp 273
stamps 199
stand 26, 29, 52, 101, 104, 294
standard 31, 171, 266
Standard Assessment Task 152
standard deviation 144
standard lamp 90
standard of living 130, 297
standardized 144
standby 290
standing 168
stanza 180
staple 313
staple together 313
stapler 313
star 175, 204
star v. 202
starboard 292
starring 175
start 155, 182
start a family 46, 51
start up 277
starter 62
starvation 42, 130
starve 42, 130
starve to death 130

state 27, 96, 97, 99, 105, 106, 107, 115, 116, 118, 142
State Department 105, 116
state enterprise 296
state of the art 262
state school 148, 150
state-subsidized 124
state trooper 112
state visit 116
statesman 116
statesmanship 116
statics 240
station 112, 132, 206, 212, 259, 270, 275, 286, 288, 293
stationer 194
stationery 194, 313
statistics 145
statue 169
statuette 169
status 11, 202
statute 104
stave off 304
stay 28, 48, 74, 188, 228
stay at 188, 192
stay at/in 191
stay fit 83
stay in time 174
stays 65
steady 27, 34
steak 59
steakhouse 61
stealing 132
steam 106
steam engine 256
steam locomotive 287
steam room 83
steamer 291
steamship 291
steel 212, 254, 255, 257
steel skeleton 178
steeple 178
steerage 292
stem 236
stem cell 237
step down 106
stepbrother 46
stepchildren 46
stepdaughter 46
stepfather 46
stepmother 46
stepparents 46
steppe 218
stepsister 46
stepson 46
stereotypes 134
stereotyping 136
sterilization 37
sterling 190
stern 292

stetson 65
stew 55, 58
steward 63, 290
stewardess 290
stick 282
stick to 151
sticks 215
stickup 132
sticky 44
stiff (n.) 40
stiff fine 294
still 27, 109, 111, 127, 128, 149, 175, 178, 230
still life 168
still water 57
stimulate 83
stimulus 143, 237
stimulus package 297
stingy 23
stink 27
stir 58
stir up 134
stock 46, 221, 301
stock(s) 301
stock exchange 304
stock-market crash 304
stockholder 299
stockings 66
stocks 304
stocks and bonds 304
stocky 15
stomach 13, 19, 69, 245
stomach trouble 75
stomach upset 69, 76
stomachache 76, 78
stone 69, 178, 212, 213, 250
stone(s) 251
stone carving 169
stone-cold sober 200
stoned 129
stoning 43
stool 90
stools 13, 14
stooped 15
stop 19, 61, 88, 285, 286, 293, 294
stop-and-go 285
stop sign 286
stop work 315
stopover 288
storage 277
storage capacity 277
storage cell 259
store 82, 172, 193, 194, 224, 277
store (v.) 261

storey 87
stork 233
storm 228
story 51, 155, 179, 269
stout 15, 200
stove 59, 90
stow 290
stowaway 292
straight 16, 153
straighten up 93
strain 72
strained 116
strait 216
strangle 133
straphangers 294
strapping 15
stratum 210
straw 221, 222
straw boater 65
strawberries 56
stream 217
street 68, 107, 125, 224, 285
street children 130
street vendor 311
streetcar 293
strength 255, 304
strengthen 83, 101
stretch 12
stretch limo 284
stretcher 72
strict 51
strike 107, 120, 189, 287, 290, 315
strike (v.) 71, 90, 217
strike action 315
strike an iceberg 292
strike-bound 315
strikebreaker 315
striker 196
strikers 107
striking workers 315
string of pearls 213
string quartet 174
strip of land 308
strips 18
stroke 68, 74, 168, 256
stroller 17
strong 24, 196, 233
strong on 146
strong showing 101
structural 126, 178, 210
structurally sound 178
structure 138, 145, 180, 243
struggle 131
stubborn 24
stucco 178
stuck in traffic 285

student 20, 122, 152, 153, 154
student activism 98
student nurse 81
student protest 98
studies 150, 156
studio 86, 168, 174
studio couch 89
study 144, 149, 154, 264
study (n.) 87
study the ads 124
stuff 128, 129, 222
stuffed animal 17
stupid 23, 24
stuttering 74
style 169, 177, 299
stylish 16
stylus 282
subconscious 144
subcontinent 214
subdirectory 277
subject 150, 152, 154, 172, 354
subject (matter) 168
subjective 30
submarine 119
submit 113
subordinate 312
subplot 180
subscribe to 269
subscriber 269, 275
subscription 269
subsidies 297
subsidized 124, 287
subsidy 115
subsistence level 130
substance 128, 241, 242
substitute 196
subtitles 175
subtract 246, 247
subtraction 246
suburbs 224
subway 293
subway card 306
subway riders 293
subway station 293
subzero 227
succeed 106
success 35
successful 197, 298
successor 106
such as 28, 144, 225
sudden death 197
suddenly 126
sue 109
Suez Canal 217
suffer 68, 71
suffer from 21, 72, 73, 74, 76
suffer losses 300
sufferer 70
suffering 130

suffix 44
suffocate 71
suffocation 71
sugar 59, 129
sugar beets 221
sugar plantation 220
suicide 42
suicide attack 120
suicide strike 120
suit 16, 64, 66, 109, 245
suitable 37, 101
suitcase 190
sultry 227
sum(s) 246
summarize 155
summary 155
summer 185
summer holidays 182
summer vacation 182
summit 218
summit meeting 116
Sun 204
sun 204, 227
sun-hungry 219
sunbathing 83
Sunday school 149
Sunday supplement 269
sunflower 235
sunlamp 83
sunny 227
sunny-side up 58
sunset years 21
sunshine 227
sunshine pill 129
sunstroke 68
suntan 39
super- 44
Super Large Hadron Collider 44
super-excited 44
superconductor 240
superhighway 265, 284
superintendent 112
superior 312
superior to 135
superiority 136
supermarket 194
supermarket clerk 311
supernova 204
supersonic 289
superstition 164
superstitious 164
supertanker 291
supervisor 312
supper 60, 163
supplement 191, 264, 269
supplier 301
suppliers 258
supplies 119

supply 258, 259, 260, 296, 301
support 33, 34, 136, 207, 278
supporter 34
suppose 68
supposed to 82, 83
suppress 108
supreme being 161
supreme court 111, 114
surcharge 114, 294
sure 32, 77, 155
surf the Internet 279
surface 168
surface mail 272
surgeon 75, 78, 81
surgery 75, 81, 244, 245
surgery hours 75
surgical centre 80
surgical ward 80
surname 10
surplus (v.) 126
surprise 30
surprise ending 180
surprised 30
surrealism 169
surrealist 169
surrealists 169
surrender 120
surrounded by 88
surrounding 218
survey 145, 210
survive 69, 230
survivor 72
suspect 112
suspenders 66
suspense 180
sustainability 262
sustainable 226
swallow 233
swamp 218
swan 233
swear (swore) 32
sweater 64, 261
sweatshirt 64
sweep 92, 310
sweet 13, 27, 57, 62
sweets 55, 194
swelling 70
Swiftair 272
swim 28, 217, 238
swimming 82, 196, 197
swimming instructor 309
swimming pool 88
swimming-pool attendant 311
swimsuit 65
swimwear 65
swindler 132
swine 32
swine flu 69

swing 18
swing voter 104
swipe 282
Swiss cheese 54
Swiss Confederation 96
switch 260
switch off 259
switch on/off 260
switchboard 275
switchboard operator 311
swivel chair 90
swollen 14, 70
syllabus 151, 237
symbol 139, 158, 243
symbolic 96
symbolic(ally) 39
symbolize 139
sympathetic 22
sympathy 34
symphony 173
symptom 68, 129
synagogue 162
syndrome 74
synthesis 146, 243
synthesize 243
synthetic fibres 243
synthetic gems 212
syphilis 37
system 99, 115, 138, 142, 204, 207, 245, 265, 276, 293, 296
systemic 241

T

T-shirt 64, 84
table 61, 62, 89, 243
table a motion 103
table d'hôte 63
table of contents 266
tablecloth 89, 92
tablet 282
tabloid 268
taboo 139
tackle 134
tacks 212
tact 35
tactful 23
tactfully 23
tactfulness 35
tactless 23
tactlessness 35
tag 300
tag sb. 202
tail 13
tailback 285
tailcoat 64
tailor 310
tails 64
take 62, 72, 81, 189, 294, 312
take (taken) 80
take a bath 38

take a break 182
take a breath 76
take a bus 294
take a course 150
take A levels 152
take a liking to 28
take a snap(shot) 171
take a trip 188
take a vote on 104
take after 51
take Amtrak 287
take an evening class 149
take an exam 152
take an impression 79
take away 41, 61
take back 226
take care of 43
take dictation 313
take drugs 19, 128
take into care 51
take into custody 112
take lessons 154, 173
take medication 77
take notes 155
take notice of 25
take off 64
take off (clothes) 77
take office 106
take on 313
take out 79, 155, 303
take out a mortgage 308
take out a subscrip-tion 269
take out insurance 307
take pictures 171
take place 48, 176, 195
take prisoner 120
take proceedings 109
take sb. to court 109
take sb.'s blood pressure 77
take sth. down 313
take sth. to 272
take strike action 315
take the plunge 238
take time off 182
take to the streets 107
take up 86, 93, 199
take up a hobby 199
takeaway 61
taken 288
takeoff 290
takeout 61
takeover (bid) 301
tale 18, 138, 179
talent 23
talk 35
talk about 185
talk show 271

talk show host 271
tall 15, 250
Talmud 163
tame 232
tangent 247
tank 91, 119, 261
tanker 291
tanning salon 83
tap 90, 200
tap a phone line 275
tap dancer 174
tap dancing 174
tap water 57
tape 260, 313
tape recorder 271
tapeworm 234
tar 201
target 119
target audience 306
target group 306
tart 54
tartar 79
task 29, 152
taste 25, 27, 57
tavern 201
tax 113, 114
tax breaks 113
tax code 113
tax consultant 114
tax cut 113
tax dodging 113
tax evasion 113
tax-exempt 114
tax-free 113, 114
tax haven 113
tax increase 113
tax reduction 114
tax refund 114
tax return 114
taxable 114
taxation 113
taxes 113
taxi 71, 294
taxi rank 294
taxi ride 294
taxi stand 294
taxman 113
taxpayer 113
TB 69
TBD 94
tea 57, 60, 129, 192
tea pot 261
tea towel 93
tea trolley 89
tea wagon 89
teach 154
teach (taught) 240
teacher 20, 24, 34,
   154, 309
teacher training
   college 149
teachers college 149
teaching 309
team 196, 230
team captain 196

teamster 314
Teamsters Union 314
teapot 59
tearoom 61
tears 234
teaspoon 59
teaspoonfuls 59
tech 254
technical 254
technical college 148
technical consultant
   310
technical journal 268
technical support
   278
technician 242
technological 254
technology 150,
   253, 254, 262
tectonics 210
teddy bear 17
teen(age) mother 19
teen(ager) 19
teenage 19
teenager 16
teeth 12, 38, 78, 79
teetotaller 200
telecast 270
telecommuter 278
telecommuting 278
telefilm 271
telemarketing 306
telephone 90, 91,
   274
telephone booth 275
telephone box 275
telephone charges
   274
telephone directory
   264, 274
telephone for 274
telephone line 275
telephone number
   274
telephonist 311
telephoto lens 171
teleplay 271
televise 270
television 270
television film 271
television network
   270
television play 271
television set 270
tell 13, 136
tell (told) 109
tell off 51
tell the truth 52
teller 302, 310
telling-off 51
telltale 270
telly 94, 270
temp 127
temper 22, 28
temperance 32

temperate 228
temperature 68, 76,
   225, 227, 248
temple 163
temporary 79, 125
Ten Command-
   ments 162
ten-gallon hat 65
ten-ride ticket 288
tenant 125
tenement 87
tennis 197, 198
tennis coach 197
tennis court 195, 197
tennis elbow 70
tenor 173
tense 24
tension 34, 259
tensions 117
tent 87
term 104, 156, 265
term of office 106
terminal 42, 81, 279,
   287, 289
terminal moraine
   211
terminal ward 81
terminally ill 42, 81
terminate 294
terminus 288
terms 33, 50, 165,
   196, 197, 300, 307
terrace 88
terrace(d) house 87
terrain 215
terrible 63, 93
terrible twos 51
terrifying 267
territorial 116
territorial waters
   215, 291
territory 215
terrorism 108, 112
terrorist 108
terrorist acts 108
test 152, 154, 155,
   244, 246
test market 306
test run 262
test(ing) 144
testament 43
Testament 133, 139,
   162
testing ground 206
text 154, 155, 180,
   265, 277
textbook 154, 267
textile 298
textual 141
textual criticism 140
Thames 217
thank 208
thank you 75
thank you for 274
thanks 274

thanks for 271
thanks very much
   122
Thanksgiving 183
that'll do 155
that's why 35
thatched 87
theatre 81, 97, 175,
   224
theatre sister 81
theft 25, 132, 307
theme 176, 354
theme on 151
theme park 187
theocracy 99
theological 149
theology 162
theoretical 240
theorist 240
theory 139, 165,
   205, 240, 241,
   246, 296
theory of evolution
   139
theory of relativity
   240
therapist 144
therapy 144, 245
there and back 188,
   288
thermal efficiency
   258
thermal printer 277
thermodynamics
   240
thermometer 227
thermonuclear 262
thermos bottle 261
thermos flask 261
thesaurus 264
thesis 153
thick 219, 229
thick as two planks
   24
thicket(s) 219
thickset 15
thief 71, 132
thin 15
thing 24, 40, 90
thing-in-itself 166
think 62, 165, 182
think of 46
thinker 165
thinking 143, 165
thinning 16
third party 307
third power of 247
Third World 214
third(s) 249
third-class mail 272
thirst 25
thistle 235
thorax 245
thorn 52
thorough 92

thoroughfare 285
thoroughly 78
though 73
thought 165
thoughtlessness 35
thousands 126
thousands of 315
thrashing 19
thread 255, 280
threat 126
threaten 109
three Rs 151
three-four time 174
three-phase 259
three-piece suit 64
thresh 222
thresher 222
thrift account 303
thrift institution 303
thrifts 303
thriller 176, 179
thriving 298
throat 12, 69, 75
thrombosis 69
through 219
through traffic 285
through train 287
throughout 165
throw 91, 134
throw a party 185
throw up 76
throwing 196
throwing up 68
thrush 233
thrust 207
thruster 206
thruway 284
thug 131, 133
thumbtack 313
thump 19
thunder 228
thunderstorm 228
tick 234
tick bite 234
ticker-tape parade
   184
ticket 175, 286, 288,
   289, 294
ticket machine 294
ticket office 288
ticketing clerk 311
tidal wave 229
tide 217, 238
tidy up 93
tie 66
tiebreak 197
ties 116
tiger 233
tight 65, 129
tight money 302
tightrope 217
tights 65
timber 254
time 92, 166, 174,
   196, 198

time deposit 303
time of day 97
time of year 227
time off 182
time zone 214
times 76, 82, 247,
   249
timeline 202
timetable 288, 289
timid 24
tin 212
tin of beans 261
tip 13, 62, 189, 226,
   313
tip (v.) 189, 294
tipped 201
tipsy 129
tiramisu 62
tired 28
tissue 39, 245
tissues 38
tit 233
title 121, 308, 345
title deed 308
title page 266
to follow 62
to go 61
to go with 63
to let 308
to take away 61
to the power of 247
to your health! 186
toad 234
toadstool 236
toast 59, 60, 186,
   192
toaster 59, 90
tobacco 201
tobacconist 201
today 10, 151, 155,
   189, 193, 227,
   288, 290
today's 18
toddler 17
toe 12
toe (v.) 100
toffee 55
toggle 278
toilet 39, 90
toilet brush 93
toilet paper 38, 39
toilet tissue 39
toilet training 50
toiletries 194
token 294
token booth 294
tolerant 22
tolerate 29
toll 230, 284
toll call 274
toll-free number
   274
toll road 284
tollbooth 284
tollgate 284

tom(cat) 232
tomato 27, 56
tomato salad 56
tomatoes 192
tomb 41
tomorrow 97, 154,
   175, 227, 291
tomorrow('s) 156
tone 26, 174, 275
tongue 12, 13, 78
tonic (water) 57
tonight 60, 83, 175,
   185, 186, 270, 274
tonsillectomy 81
tonsillitis 70
tool bar 278
tool(s) 255
tools 254, 315
toolshed 88
tooth 12, 13, 27, 78,
   79
toothache 78
toothbrush 38
toothpaste 38, 194
toothpick 38
top 64, 155, 218
top-flight 299
top hat 65
top marks 153
top set 156
topcoat 64
topic 354
topography 211
topper 65
Torah 163
Tories 101
tornado 229
torque 256
torrential 228
tortoise 234
tossed salad 56
total 215
totalitarianism 99
totally 74, 230
totem 139
totemism 139
touch 25, 27, 35, 78
touching 30
touchscreen 282
tough 24
tough cookie 24
tour 188, 189, 306
tour guide 189
tour operator 188
tourism 188
tourist 188
tourist attraction 187
tourist information
   office 188
tournament 195
tow away 286
towards 28, 35, 100,
   117, 134
towaway zone 286
towel 38, 39, 93

towel down 38
tower 178
tower block 87, 178
town 97, 120, 185,
   214, 223
town council 223
town planning 223
townsman 223
townspeople 223
townswoman 223
toxaemia 69
toxic 242
toxic waste 226
toy car 17
toy shop 194
toy train set 17
toy(s) 17
track 196, 288
track and field 83,
   196
track and field meet
   195
track event 196
tracking 273
tracking station 206
tract 245, 308
tractor 222
trade 117, 128, 297,
   298, 309
trade barriers 117, 297
trade fair 298
trade school 148
trade show 298
trade tax 114
trade union 314
trade unionist 314
Trades Union
   Congress 314
tradesman 310
trading 103
trading partner 117
tradition 140
traditionally 36
traffic 285
traffic accident 286
traffic circle 285
traffic congestion
   285
traffic cop 286
traffic jam 285
traffic light 285
traffic violation 286
trafficker 128
trafficking 128
tragedy 179
tragic 179
trailer 87
train 25, 28, 29,
   272, 287, 288,
   291, 293, 294
train journey 288
train ride 288
train service 287
train(ed) 154
trained 114

trainee 310
trainers 65
training 50, 127, 149, 154
training programme 154
trajectory 206
tram 293
transcendent 164
transept 178
transfer 114, 276, 294, 303
transfer for 294
transformer 259
transgender 98
transistor 260
transit 293
translate 266
translation 266
translator 266
transmit 37, 255, 265
transparency 172
transplant 13, 81, 245
transport 283, 284, 287, 289, 291, 293, 294, 315
transport café 61, 286
transportation 284, 293
trap 130
trash 225
trauma 81
trauma center 81
travel 28, 29, 188, 206, 223, 288, 293, 315
travel agency 188
travel agent 188
travel brochure 188
travel by air 289
travel by train 287
travel steerage 292
travel time 288
Travelcard 294
travellers cheque 190
travelling salesman 300
trawler 291
tray 59
treadmill 84
treason 108
treasurer 304
Treasury Department 304
Treasury Secretary 304
treat 70, 72
treatment 78, 79, 80
treaty 103, 117
tree 46, 52, 219, 235, 236

tree trunk 236
treeless 219
trench coat 64
trendy 16
trespasser 131
trespassing 131
trial 109
trials 244
triangle 247
triangular 247
tribal 139
tribe 139
tribunal 316
tributary 217
trickster 132
tricycle 18
trigonometry 246
Trinity 160
trip 128, 129, 188, 189, 190
tripper 129
triumphal arch 178
Trojan horse 280
trolley 89, 190, 193, 288
trolley(bus) 293
trooper 112
troops 119
tropic of 214
tropical 68
tropical forest 225
tropics 214
trouble 19, 69, 75, 76
troubled 144, 298
troublemaker 32
trouser suit 64
trousers 64, 65, 93
trout 55, 56
truant 19
truck 284
truck stop 61, 286
truckdriver 284
trucker 284
true 166
trunk 236
trunk road 284
trunks 65
trust 18, 304
trustworthy 32
truth 13, 52, 166
truthfulness 31
try 103
try to 26, 42, 155
try to find 265
tsunami 229
tube 38, 243, 270, 293
tuberculosis 70
TUC 314
tuck in 89
Tudor 177
tug (boat) 291
tulip 236
tulip bulb 236

tumour 12, 69, 81
tuna 55
tune 173
tune in to 270
tunnel 189
turkey 55
Turkish bath 83
turn 155
turn cooler 227
turn grey 16
turn off 260, 294
turn on 294
turn on/off 90, 260
turn out of 125
turn over 238, 300
turn right 285
turn up/down 26
turnover 300
turnpike 284
turnstile 294
turtle 234
tuxedo 64
TV 270
TV programme 271
TV series 271
TV set 270
tweet 202
twice 77, 128, 241
twig 52, 236
twilight years 21
twin 50
twin(-bedded) 191
twin beds 89
twist 72
Twitter™ 202
two-piece suit 64
type (n.) 14, 200
type a letter 312
type in 312
type sth. out 312
type sth. up 312
type up / out 312
typed letter 312
types of 200
typescript 267
typeset 267
typesetter 267
typewriter 313
typhoid 68
typhoid vaccination 190
typhoon 229
typical 68
typing error 312
typing paper 312
typing pool 313
typist 311
typo 312
tyre 286
tyre pressure 286

U
U-turn 285
ugly 16, 166
ulcer 69, 78

ultrasound 77
umpire 197
UN 117
unable 73, 105
unabridged 267
unaccompanied minor 290
unattractive 16
unattractiveness 16
unbearable 78
unbelief 164
unbelieving 164
uncivilized 22
uncle 47
unconscious 70, 143, 144
unconsciousness 70
uncontested 49
uncooperative 22
undelivered 273
under 13, 229, 291, 293
under (terms) 307
under construction 178
under false colours 292
under his administration 105
under his command 118
under social security 115
under the influence 128
under the terms 300
underdog 195
underexposed 172
undergo an operation 81
undergo surgery 81
underground 293
underground (movement) 107
underground station 132, 293
underpants 65
undershirt 65
undershorts 65
underskirt 65
understand 19, 165
understanding 165
understatement 126
undertaker 41
underwear 65
underweight 15
underwriter 307
undeveloped 308
undress 64
unemployed 126
unemployment 126
unemployment benefit 127
unemployment benefit(s) 126

unenthused 146
unethical 31
unfair 22, 23
unfair competition
296
unfaithful 49
unfit 84
unfriendliness 35
unharmed 71
unhurt 71
uni 94
unicellular 237
uninhibited 22
union 36, 96, 101,
117, 314, 316
union member 314
unionist 314
unionized 314
unique 27, 306
unit 81, 118, 119,
258, 276
unit trust 304
United Nations 117
universe 160, 203,
204
university 149, 152,
310
university graduates
153
unjust 32
unkempt 16
unknown 41, 188
unknowns 247
unlawful entry 132
unleaded 212
unleaded petrol 226
unlicensed 132
unlimited 96, 298
unlisted 274
unmanned 206
unofficial 315
unpack 273
unpleasant 16, 22
unplug 260
unputdownable 267
unreliable 22
unrest 107, 314
unscathed 71, 230
unselfish 22
unselfishly 23
unsinkable 292
unskilled 309
unsophisticated 22
unsound 146
unstable 241
unsuitable 254
unsympathetic 22
until 110, 127
up to 193
upbringing 51
update(d) 278
upgrade 278, 290
upload 202, 277
upon 52
upper chamber 102

upper class 33
upper jaw 78
uppers 128, 129
upright 15, 32
uprising 108
ups and downs 297
upset stomach 69
upset(s) 76
uptown 97
upturn 127, 297
Uranus 204
urban 224
urban development
224
urban planning 224
urban renewal 224
urge 28
urinary tract 245
urinate 14
urine 14
urn 41
urologist 244
urology 244
USB flash drive 282
use (n.) 221, 242
use (v.) 79, 180, 186,
221, 243, 275,
276, 293
use drugs 129
use flash 171
use the needle 129
used to 156, 185,
257
useful 193, 293, 294
user 74, 129, 278
user-friendly 278
user-generated 202
user interface 278
USP 306
usually 168, 182,
284, 288
utensil 93
uterus 14
utility room 88

V
vacancy 191
vacant lot 308
vacation 182
vacations 316
vaccination 69, 190
vaccination card 190
vaccine 70
vacuum 241
vacuum (cleaner) 93
vacuum cleaner 90
vagina 14, 36
valid 189
validity 144
valley 235, 260
valleys 218
valuable 213
value 166, 299
value-added tax 113
valve 256

van 284
vandal 131
vandalism 131
vanilla 55
vapour 241
variable 146, 247
varicose veins 14,
70
varnish 39
vase 261
vasectomy 37, 81
vast 59, 229
VAT 113, 114
VCR 271
VDU 276
VDU screen 277
veal 55
veep 105
veg 94
vegetable(s) 55, 56
vegetables 58, 221
vegetarian 59, 82
vehicle 284, 286
vein 14, 70
velocity 241
velocity of light 241
vendor 125, 311
venereal 37
venetian blind 91
venison 55
venue 195
Venus 204
veranda 88
verification 165
verify 165, 240
vermicelli 55
vermin 234
verse 180
version 278
very (much) 355
vessel 244, 291
vest 64, 65, 290
Vesuvius 229
vet 94, 234
veteran 20
veto 103
via 294
via airmail 273
viable 101, 296
Viagra™ 37
vibrance 172
vicar 163
vice 31, 255
vice president 105
vice president for/of
299
victim 72, 131, 134,
229
Victorian 177
victory 120, 184, 196
victory parade 184
video 25, 32, 271
video call 202
video game 199
video recorder 271

video-sharing 202
videocassette 271
view 23, 25, 164, 180
viewer 271
viewfinder 172
vigilance 133
vigilance committee
133
vigilant 133
vigilante group 133
village 86, 96, 97
villain 176
vine 236
vineyard 219
vintage 200
violate 316
violation 142, 286
violence 19, 29, 107,
131, 133, 136
violent 22, 110, 133,
229
violent crime 131
violin 173
violin concerto 174
virtual keyboard
282
virtual reality 265
virtue 31, 32
virus 237, 280
virus protection 280
visa 189
vise 255
Vishnu 160
visible 25
visit 21, 57, 116,
185, 188, 356
visual 25, 73
visual aids 25
visual display unit
276
visualization 281
visually challenged
73
vitamin(s) 82
V-neck(ed) 64
vocation 309
vocational college
148
vocational school 148
vocational training
127, 154
voice 26, 173
voice control 282
voice mail 280
voice recognition
278
volcanic 211
volcano 211, 229
volcanology 210
volleyball 197
volt 259
voltage 259
volume 26, 241,
265, 300
voluntary 198

volunteer 21
vomit 14, 76
vomiting 68
vote 104, 272
vote of no confi-
    dence 104
vote on a bill 104
voter 104, 142
voting 104
voting behaviour 142
voucher 312
voyage 291
voyeur 132
vulgar fraction 247

W

waffle 54
wage 130, 316
wage agreement 316
wage increase 316
wage negotiations
    316
wage settlement 316
wage tax 114
wagon 89
waistcoat 64
wait 30, 38
wait for 297
waiter 62, 63, 154
waiting room 288
waitress 63
wake 192
wake-up call 192
walk 73, 136, 219
walk-in 89
walk out 315
walking 83
walking papers 126
walkout 315
walks 218
wall 71, 88, 140, 178
wall clock 90
wall-to-wall 91
wallet 303
walnut 56
waltz 174
waning 204
want 49, 59, 212
want sb. to 155, 195
want to 48, 51, 152,
    186, 190, 289, 292
wanted on the
    phone 274
Wapping 268
war 34, 97, 108,
    118, 119, 120,
    133, 236, 269
war crime 120
war criminal 120
ward 80, 244
ward doctor 81
ward sister 81
warden 310
wardrobe 65, 89
warehouse 301

warfare 120
warm 34, 74, 227
warm and humid
    227
warm front 227
warming 109, 226
warning 228, 229,
    300
warning strike 315
warrant 112
warranty 301
wash 38, 92
wash out 92
wash up 92
washbasin 90
washcloth 38
washer 256
washing 39, 93
washing machine 90
washing powder 93
washing-up liquid 93
wasp 234
waste(s) 56, 225,
    226
waste bin 91
waste disposal 226
waste incineration
    226
wastebasket 91
wasteland 218
wastepaper basket
    91
watch (n.) 212
watch (v.) 25, 83,
    187
watch group 133
watch television 270
watch TV 270
watchdog 232
watchmaker 310
water 14, 57, 75,
    136, 243, 261
water heater 90
water jet 79
water pollution 225
water-skiing 199
water-soluble 243
water transport 291
watercolour 168
watercraft 291
waterfall 217
waters 215, 291
waterways 292
watt 259
wave 227, 229, 241
wavelength 241
wax crayons 18
wax museum 187
waxing 204
waxworks 187
way 83, 136
ways and means 103
ways to help 125
weak 21, 24, 146
weakness 21

wealth 297
weapon 119
wear 16, 64, 213
wear the pants 49
weather 44, 227,
    228, 289
weather bureau 227
weather forecast
    227
weather map 227
weather permitting
    227
weather report 227
weather satellite 207
weathering 211
weatherman 271
weatherperson 271
weatherwoman 271
weaving 198
Web 279
web browser 279
web-enabled 279
webpage 279
webpage designer
    279
website 202, 279
wed 48
wedding 48, 184,
    212
wedding anniver-
    sary 49, 184
wedding dress 64
wedding feast 184
wedding gown 64
wedding ring 48
weed 129, 220
weed(s) 236
weed killer 220
week 50, 80, 83, 113,
    144, 182, 221
weekend 47, 182
weekend break 182
weekly 268
weep 30
weeping willow 235
weigh 251
weight 11, 76, 212,
    240, 243
weightlessness 207
weightlifting 84
weights 84, 250
welcome 356
welfare 115, 232
welfare cuts 115
welfare grant 115
welfare reform 115
welfare state 115
well attended 175
well behaved 156
well-built 15
well done 59
well groomed 16
well-known 205
well-produced 176
well trained 154

wellies 65
wellington boots 65
wellingtons 65
west 43, 158, 201,
    214
West Germany 214
westerly 228
western 214, 217
Western 165, 214
Western Europe 214
Western European
    214
western Germany
    214
westernization 139
westerns 201
wet 228
wetlands 218
whale 234
whaler 291
what … like? 227
what about 200
what is it about?
    176
what time 192
whatsapp™ 202
wheat 54, 221
wheel 187
wheelchair 74
wheelchair user 74
wheels 21
when – if 356
while 301
while – during 356
whip 58, 102
whipped cream 54,
    74
whirlpool 83
whirlwind 229
Whit Monday 182
Whit Sunday 182
white bread 54
white-collar worker
    310
white-haired 16
White House 105
white magic 164
white mice 232
white stuff 129
white-tie 64
white wine 200
Whitehall 105
Whitsun 182
whizz 129
whodunit 179
whole 27, 166, 208
whole-grain 54
whole milk 54
whole note 174
whole number 247
whole tone 174
whole-wheat 54
wholefood(s) 56, 82
wholemeal bread
    54, 82

wholesale 300
wholesaler 300
whooping cough 69
whore 37
whose turn 155
wide 250
wide-angle 171
wide range of 257
widely 220
widow 40, 49
widower 49
wife 48, 49, 133
Wi-Fi™ 279
wig 16
Wikipedia™ 264
wild 208, 232
wild boar 55
wild flower 235
wild plant 235
wildcat strike 315
wilderness 219
wildlife park 219
wildly 29
will (*n.*) 43
will and idea 165
willow 235
win 177, 195, 197
win (*n.*) 185, 197
win (won) 103, 104, 248
win an Oscar 176
wind 215, 228
wind power 226
window 88, 92, 178
window shade 91
windowsill 88
windsurfing 199
windy 228
wine 28, 62, 63, 200, 261
wine bar 61
wine list 62
wine steward 63
wine waiter 63
wing 100
winner 300
winter 196, 227
wipe 92
wipe off 155
wipe the floor with 92
wire 260
wireless 282
wireless head-phones 276
wireless Internet access 279
wiry 15
wisdom 31
wisdom tooth 79
wisely 23
wish 62, 183
witch 155, 164
witchcraft 164
withdraw 120, 303

withdrawal 37, 68, 129, 303
withholding tax 114
within 34, 223, 274, 291
withstand 262
witness 43, 109, 110
wolf 233, 238
womb 14, 41
women's jobs 136
women's lib(eration) 98
women's libber 98
women's magazine 268
women's rights 98
wonderful 168, 198, 223
wood 254
wood(s) 219
wood carving 169
wood engraving 170
woodcut 170
wooden 254, 257
woodpecker 233
woodshed 88
woodworking 198
woodworking machine 255
wool 39
Worcester(shire) sauce 55
word 32, 122
word-processing 276
word processor 276
words of a song 173
work 13, 63, 96, 114, 126, 127, 168, 177, 198, 217, 241, 260, 264, 277, 293, 294, 313, 315, 316
work a material 254
work as 309
work for 268
work force 314
work in groups 155
work in the fields 219
work of art 169, 257
work on sth. 84
work out 83, 246
work overtime 316
work to failure 84
work to rule 315
workaholic 129
worker 115, 127, 258, 272, 287, 291, 309
worker hour 258
workers 314, 315
working 126
working breakfast 60
working conditions 316

working hours 316
working mother 51
workman 310
workout 83
works 43, 258
works manager 258
workshop 258
workstation 276
world 40, 83, 97, 159, 164, 165, 188, 214, 215, 220
world champion 195
World Cup 196, 197
world of 208
world record 195
world war 119, 133, 236
World Wide Web 279
worm 233, 280
worries 77
worship 162
worst case scenario 44
worth 212, 233
worth a bean 222
worthless 32
wound 70, 72, 132
wounded 120
wrap 193
wrath 32
wreath 41
wrench 255
wrestling 84, 196, 197
wrinkle 16
write 151, 156, 175, 305, 313
write (written) 313
write (wrote) 269
write a test 246
write legibly 155
writer 180, 309
writing 151
writing desk 89
writing paper 313
written 140
written exam 152
written in verse 180
wrong 31
wrong number 274
wrong side of forty 21

X
X-ray 77
xenophobia 134
xenophobic 134
xerox™ 313
Xerox™ machine 313
xeroxed™ 313
xeroxing™ 313
XXX 94

Y
-y 44
yacht 291
yachting 196, 199, 291
yachtsman 196
yachtswoman 196
Yahweh 160
yard 88, 219, 250
yd(s) 250
year 13, 20, 21, 48, 56, 77, 86, 104, 111, 149, 152, 153, 298, 301, 304
yearbook 264
yeast 237
yellow 236
Yellow Pages 274
yellow press 268
yesterday 184, 272
yet 51, 111, 272
yet – already 342
yew 235
yield 250
yields 221
yoga 83
yoghurt 54, 261
young 15, 18, 19
young offender 112
youngster 18
Your Excellency 121
your good health! 200
your health! 186
Your Honour 122
yours 121
yourself 34
youth 17, 118, 133, 134
youth club 18
youth hostel 18, 191
youth movement 98

Z
zap 270
zapping 270
zebra crossing 285
Zen 129
zero 197, 227, 248, 249
zero growth 248
zinc 212
zip 66, 248
zip code 273
zipper 66
zone 214, 286, 294
zoo 94, 234
zoological garden 234
zoom 171

Z

Register Deutsch

Um Platz zu sparen, ist bei Wörtern wie *Politiker(in)*, *Rentner(in)*, *Student(in)* nur die männliche Form aufgeführt. Die weibliche Form ist nur dann genannt, wenn ihr im Englischen ein eigenes Wort entspricht (z. B. *headmistress = Direktorin*, *draughtswoman = Zeichnerin*).

A

Aal 55
Aalpastete 62
Abänderung 103
abbaubar 56
abbauen 117, 297
abbiegen 285
abblasen 315
abbrechen 19, 116, 206
Abbruch 206
abbürsten 93
abdrehen 90
Abdruck 79
Abend 27, 60, 83, 132, 175, 185, 186, 227, 270
Abendbrot 60
Abendessen 60
Abendkleid 64
abendländisch 165
Abendmahl 163
Abendschule 149
Abendzeitung 268
Aberglaube 164
abergläubisch 164
abfahren auf 199
Abfahrt 189, 288
Abfall 225
Abfallbeseitigung 226
Abfallentsorgung 226
Abfallstoffe 225, 226
Abfertigungsschalter 290
abfinden 29
Abfindung 126
Abflauen 127
Abflug 189, 289
Abflughalle 289
Abfrage 281
abfrottieren 38
abgeben 104, 113, 155
abgehen von 290
abgelegen 97
abgemacht 298
Abgeordnete 102, 104, 121
abgespannt 15
abgestempelt 273
abhalten 104, 312
Abhandlung 146
abhängig von 230

Abheben 206
abheben 303
abholen 289
Abitur 152
Abiturient 153
abkippen 226
abknallen 132
Abkommen 117
Abkürzung 94
abladen 22
Ablage 313
Ablagerung 211
ablaufen 189
Ableben 40
ablegen 64, 261
ableisten 118
Abmelde- 277
abmelden 277
Abmeldung 277
abmurksen 43
abnehmen 21, 64, 76, 171, 274
abnehmend 204
Abneigung 28, 35
abnorm 143
Abonnement 269
Abonnent 269
abonnieren 269
abräumen 93
Abreise 189
abreisen 192
abreißen 224
Abriss 146
abrubbeln 38
Abrüstungskonferenz 117
Absatz 155
Absatzförderung 306
Absatzmarke 278
Absatzzahlen 299
abschalten 259, 260, 277, 279
abschicken 272
Abschlachten 133
abschleppen 286
abschließen 153, 307
Abschluss 152, 153
Abschlussfeier 153
Abschlussprüfung 152
Abschneiden 101
abschneiden 153
Abschnitt 227
Abschreckung 118

abschreiben 152, 155
Abschreibung 114
Abschussbasis 206
Abschussrampe 206
Abschwung 127
Abseits 197
Absender 273
absetzbar 114
absetzen 108, 206
absichern 115
Absicht 299, 174
Absolution 163
Absolutismus 99, 141
Absolvent 153
abspeichern 277
Abspielgerät 271
abspülen 93
abstammen 233
Abstammung 46
abstauben 93
absteigen 286
absteigend 281
abstimmen 104
abstimmen über 104
Abstimmung 104
Abstinenzler 200
abstrakt 169
Absturz 42, 71, 276
abstürzen 71, 276
Abteil 288
Abteilung 80, 149, 262, 309
Abtragung 211
Abtreibung 37, 98, 104, 136
abtrocknen 38, 93
abwaschen 59, 92
abweichen 151
abweichend 145
abwenden 304, 315
abwerfen 236
abwerten 304
Abwertung 304
abwischen 155
abziehen 120
Abzug 171
Aceton 243
Achse 203
Achseln 12
Achtelnote 174
Achterbahn 187
Achtung 33, 35
Acker 219, 220

Ackerland 219, 220
Adapter 260
addieren 246
Addition 246
adeln 121
Adelsherrschaft 99
Ader 260
adoptieren 51
Adoption 51
Adoptivkind 51
Adressbuch 264
Adresse 11
Adressenliste 272
Aerobic 83
Aerogramm 272
Affäre 49
Affe 233, 238
Afrika 214, 215
afrikanisch 214
After 13
AG 299
Agentur 305
Aggression 119
Aggressor 119
Agitation 107
Agitator 107
Agnostiker 164
Agnostizismus 164
Ahnenforschung 140
Ahnentafel 140
Ahorn 235
Aids 37, 70
Akademie 149
Akademiker 153
akademisch 156
Akkord 174
Akkordlohn 316
Akku(mulator) 259
Akkulaufzeit 282
Akronym 94
Akt 168, 176
Akte 250, 313
Aktendeckel 261
Aktenordner 261
Aktentasche 261
Aktien 304
Aktiengesellschaft 299
Aktienmarkt 304
Aktionär 299
aktiv 98, 142
Aktiva 304
aktivieren 278, 279
Aktivität 108, 198, 199

Aktmalerei 168
aktualisieren 278
aktuell 16, 341
Akustik 240
Albtraum 144
Album 171
Alge 237
Algebra 246
Algorithmus 279
alias 94
Alkohol 200, 243
Alkoholabhängigkeit 129
alkoholfrei 57, 200
Alkoholiker 129, 200
Alkoholismus 129
Alkoholkrankheit 129
Alkoholmissbrauch 128
All 204, 206
Allah 160
alle 293
alle möglichen 198
Alleinerziehende 51
Alleinstellungsmerkmal 306
Alleinvertretung 300
Alleinvertrieb 300
Allergie 70
Allergiker 70
allergisch 70
allgegenwärtig 161
allgemein 245
Allgemeinmedizin 75
Allianz 116
alliiert 116
Alliierte 116
allmächtig 160, 161
Allmächtige 160
allmählich 34
allwissend 161
Almanach 264
Almosengeben 158
Alpen 218
als 342
Alsterwasser 200
alt 10, 138, 141, 164, 185, 199, 214
alt werden 20
Alt 173
Altar 162
Altarraum 178
Altbau 87, 224
alte Geschichte 140
Alte Welt 214
Altenheim 20
Alter 10, 15, 20, 52
älter 20
älter werden 20
ältere Leute 20
altern 52
Altern 20

Altersbestimmung 211
Altersgruppe 306
Altersheim 20
Altersrente 115
altersschwach 21
Altersschwäche 40
Altertum 141
Altes Testament 162
altgedient 20
Altglascontainer 226
Altklausur 151
Aluminium 212
Alzheimer(krankheit) 21, 68, 74
Amateur(-) 195
ambulant 80
Ambulanz 80
Ameise 234
amen 163
Amerika 195, 214, 292
amerikanisch 214
Aminosäure 237
Amöbe 237
Amokschütze 131
Ampel 285
Ampere 259
Amt 106
Amtsarzt 245
Amtsinhaber 104
Amtssitz 86
Amtszeit 104, 106
an 260
Analphabetentum 130
Analverkehr 37
Analyse 142, 146, 156, 165, 242
analysieren 165, 210
analytisch 156, 242
Ananas 56
Anästhesie 81
Anästhesist 81
Anästhetikum 81
Anbau 82
anbauen 220, 221
Anbauschuppen 222
anbeten 28
anbieten 34, 194, 301
Anbieter 279
anbringen 79
andauern 230
andere Geschlecht 36
ändern 277, 292
anders 223
Änderung 103
aneinander geraten 35
Anekdote 179
Anerkennung 29, 116
anfahren 71

Anfall 68
anfangen 155
anfassen 27
anfertigen 168
anfühlen 27
Anführer 33, 108
Angebot 194, 275, 296, 301
angehen gegen 134
angehören 314
Angeklagte 111
angelernt 309
Angeln 199
angeln 199
angenehm 227
angespannt 24
Angestellte 310, 311
angestrengt 26
angewandt 143, 145
angewiesen auf 130, 202
Angler 310
Anglikaner 159
anglikanisch 159
Anglistik 149
angreifen 119
Angreifer 131
Angriff 119, 132
Angst 134, 144
Angst haben 30, 40, 211, 289
ängstlich 14
anhalten 76, 285
Anhalter 284
Anhang 266
Anhänger 34, 158
anhören 35
Animosität 35
ankaufen 300
Anker 217, 292
ankern 292
Anklage 110, 111
Anklage(behörde) 109
Anklageerhebung 110
anklagen 107, 110
anklicken 278
anknipsen 260
ankochen 58
ankommen 288
ankündigen 269
Ankunft 189, 288, 289
Ankunftshalle 289
Ankunftszeit 289
Anlage 280
Anlagen 255, 258
Anlass 184
anlegen 277, 290, 292, 308
anliefern 258
Anliegen 21
anmachen 58, 90, 260

Anmelde- 277
anmelden 149, 189, 256, 277
Anmeldung 277
Anmerkung 36
Annahme 146
Anode 243
anonym 129
Anorak 64
Anordnung 168, 243
anorganisch 242
anormal 143
anpassen 172
Anpassung an 139
anpflanzen 221, 235
anprangern 107
anregen 83
anregend 267
Anreiz 154
Anrichte 89
anrichten 230
Anruf 274
Anrufbeantworter 275
anrufen 192, 274
Anrufer 274
Ansager 271
anschalten 277
anschauen 25, 84, 155, 189
anschießen 132
Anschlag 24
Anschlagtafel 313
anschließen 107, 260
Anschluss 277, 288, 292
Anschlusskabel 260
anschnallen 290
Anschrift 11
ansehen 25, 30, 175, 187
ansetzen 104
Ansichten 23
ansiedeln 224
anskypen 202
ansprechen 19
Anspruch 115, 116, 307
Anspruch haben auf 114
Anspruchsdenken 115
anspruchslos 22
anspruchsvoll 22
anständig 22, 32, 125
Anständigkeit 32, 35
anstecken 68
Ansteigen 124
ansteigen 299
anstößig 32
anstupsen 202
Antarktis 214
Anthologie 179

Anthropologe 138
Anthropologie 138
anthropologisch 138
Anthroposophie 164
antik 141, 165, 169
Antike 141
Antikriegs- 98
Antikriegsdemons-
tranten 107
Antikriegsdemons-
tration 107
Antipathie 35
Antiquariat 194, 266
antiquarisch 266
Antiquität 199
Antiquitätengeschäft
194
Antisemit 135
antisemitisch 135
Antisemitismus 135
Antivirenprogramm
280
Antivirensoftware
280
Antrag 48, 103, 189
Antrag stellen 103
antreten 106
Antriebssystem 207
Antriebswelle 256
antun 29
Antwortschein 273
Anus 13
Anwalt 110
Anwender 278
Anwendung 94,
282
Anzahlung 191, 193
anzapfen 275
Anzeichen 68
Anzeige 94, 305
Anzeigenpreise 305
Anzeigenserie 305
Anzeigentarif(e) 305
anziehen 64, 77
Anziehungskraft 205
Anzug 64
anzünden 201
Apfel 27, 56
Apfelsaft 57
Apfelsine 56
Apotheke 194
Apparat 171, 274,
275
Appetit 27, 60, 76
Applaus 176
Aquarell 168
Äquator 205, 214
Ära 211
Araber 134
Arbeit 13, 153, 155,
241, 293, 302,
313, 314, 315
arbeiten 155, 217,
219
arbeiten an 84

Arbeiter 258, 309,
310, 314, 315
Arbeiterschaft 314
Arbeitgeber 314
Arbeitnehmer 115,
314
Arbeitsamt 127
Arbeitsbedingungen
316
Arbeitsbeschaffungs-
127
Arbeitsessen 312
Arbeitsfrühstück 60
Arbeitsgang 258
Arbeitsgericht 316
Arbeitskampf 315
Arbeitskräfte 127,
316
arbeitslos 126
Arbeitslosengeld 126
Arbeitslosenhilfe 126
Arbeitslosenver-
sicherung 126
Arbeitslosenziffer 126
Arbeitslosigkeit 126
Arbeitsmarkt 127
Arbeitsmedizin 244
Arbeitsplatz 276
Arbeitsplatz verlieren
126
Arbeitsstunde 258
Arbeitsstunden 312
Arbeitssuche 127
Arbeitssuchende 127
Arbeitsvermittlung
127
Arbeitsvertrag 316
Arbeitszeit 316
Arbeitszimmer 87
Architekt 177
architektonisch 177
Architektur 177, 178
Archive 140
Ärger 19
ärgerlich 30
Argument 165
Argumentieren 165
Arier 135
arisch 135
Arithmetik 246
arithmetisch 246
Arktis 214
Arm 12, 71, 72
arm 130, 145
Armada 291
Armdrücken 84
Arme 130
Armee 118, 119
Ärmelkanal 217
ärmellos 64
Armut 130
Armutsfalle 130
Armutsgrenze 130
Aroma 27
Arrangement 173

Art 87, 115, 226
Artefakt 139
Artenschutz 226
Arterie 14
Arthritis 245
Artikel 26, 264, 269,
273, 298, 300, 301
Artillerie 119
Arznei 77
Arzneimittel 77
Arzneimittelchemiker
242
Arzt 14, 75, 77, 80,
274
ärztlich 77, 80
ärztlich versorgen 72
Arztpraxis 75
Asche 41
Aschenbecher 201
Asche(schicht) 229
asiatisch 214
Asien 214, 215
Ass 197
Assistentin 311
Assistenzarzt 80
Ast 236
Asteroidengürtel
205
Ästhetik 166
Asthma 245
Asthmaanfall 68
Asthmatiker 245
asthmatisch 245
Astrologe 164
Astrologie 164
Astronaut 206
Astronomie 205
Astrophysik 240
Asylantenwohnheim
134
Asylbewerber 112,
134
Asylrecht 134
Atelier 168
Atem 76, 78
Atemübungen 83
Atemwegserkran-
kung 68
Atheismus 164
Atheist 10, 160, 164
Atlantik 216
Atlas 264
atmen 76
Atmosphäre 180,
205
Atom 241, 243
Atom(-) 119, 240
Atombombe 119
Atomgewicht 240,
243
Atomkern 240
Atommüll 226
Atomwaffensperr-
vertrag 117
Attentat 108

Attest 77
Attraktion 187
attraktiv 15, 36
Attraktivität 15, 16
Ätzung 170
Audio- 26
Audiogeräte 26
Audiovisualisierung
281
audiovisuell 154
auf die Straße ge-
hen 107
auf Englisch 200
Auf und Ab 297
aufaddieren 246
aufdrehen 90
Aufenthalt 188
auferstehen 40
Auferstehung 162
auffahren 162
Aufführung 175
Aufgabe 29, 154, 198
aufgeben 154, 190,
288
Aufgebot 48
aufgedunsen 16
aufgeregt 24
aufgestaut 144
aufhaben 154
aufheben 117
aufheiternd 228
Aufheiterungen 227
aufhören 19
Aufklärung 141, 164
aufladen 259
Aufladung 259
Auflage 267, 269
auflegen 173, 274,
275
auflösen 104, 243
Auflösung 172
aufmachen 91
Aufnahme 171, 210
Aufnahmegegen-
stand 172
Aufnahmemotiv 172
Aufnahmen 171
Aufnahmeobjekt 172
aufnehmen 21, 62,
159, 308, 313
aufpolieren 306
Aufpreis 191
Aufputschmittel 128
aufräumen 93
aufrecht 15, 32
aufrichtig 22
aufrufen zu 107
Aufruhr 133
aufsammeln 206
Aufsatz 146, 151,
156
Aufschlag 191, 294
Aufschlagass 197
aufschlagen 155,
238

Aufschwung 127, 297
aufsetzen 64
Aufsichtsratsvor-
sitzende 299
aufspringen 286
Aufstand 107, 108, 133
aufsteigend 281
aufstellen 188, 195
aufsuchen 185
Auftrag 301
auftragen 39, 77, 168
Auftritt 176
Aufwendungen 303
aufwischen 92
aufzeichnen 141, 264
Aufzeichnungen 140
aufzeigen 146
aufziehen 52, 91, 221
Aufzug 88
Auge 12, 15, 16, 25, 158
Augenarzt 75
Augenblick 28, 275
Augenbrauenstift 39
Augenheilkunde 244
Au-pair-Mädchen 309
aus 260
aus Glas etc. 255
ausbilden 154
Ausbilder 154
Ausbildungs-
programm 154
Ausblick 25
ausbreiten 158, 225
Ausbruch 211, 229
Ausdruck 277
Auseinandersetzung 117, 133, 315
auseinandertreiben 107
ausfallen 188
ausfallen lassen 289
ausflippen 128
Ausflug 188
Ausflügler 188
ausfressen 52
ausführen 258, 278, 301
Ausführung 301
ausfüllen 113, 307
Ausgabe 266, 267, 269, 277
Ausgaben 303
ausgeben 64, 300, 303
ausgebucht 191
ausgeglichen 23, 297
ausgehen 62, 185
ausgeleiert 84

ausgemergelt 15
ausgepresst 56
ausgetrickst 44
ausgezehrt 15
ausgezeichnet 63, 240
Ausgleich 303
ausgleichen 104, 303
Ausgleichstreffer 197
Ausguss 90
aushalten 26, 29
aushandeln 117, 316
ausknipsen 260
auskommen 33
auskugeln 72
Auskunft 274
Ausland 272, 300
Ausländer 28, 30, 35, 134
ausländerfeindlich 134
Ausländerfeindlich-
keit 134
Ausländerhass 134
ausländisch 134
Auslandshilfe 117
auslaufen 291
Auslegung 162, 166, 180
ausliefern 300, 301
Auslöser 172
ausmachen 90, 260
ausnutzen 23
auspacken 273
Auspuffgase 226
ausrechnen 246
ausreichend 307
ausrenken 72
ausrollen 91
ausrotten 133
Ausrottung 133
ausrufen 315
Ausrüstung 255
Aussaat 221
aussäen 236
aussagen 109
ausschalten 260, 277, 279, 294
ausscheiden 14
ausschimpfen 51
ausschlafen 60, 129
Ausschlag 70, 74
ausschlagen 236
Ausschreitungen 133
Ausschuss 102, 103, 105, 106, 309
aussehen 235
Außendienst 300
Außenminister 106, 116
Außenministerium 105, 106, 116
Außenpolitik 100, 116, 142
Außenseiter 195

Außentoilette 88
außer Atem 78
außer Betrieb 294
äußere 15
außerehelich 36
außergerichtlich 109
außerhalb 88, 215
äußerst 254, 255
außerstande 73
Äußerung 135
aussetzen 51, 219
Aussicht 25
aussperren 315
Aussperrung 315
aussprechen 160
ausspülen 78
Ausstand 315
Ausstattung 89, 254
ausstehen 29, 34
aussteigen 288, 294
ausstellen 169, 189
Ausstellung 168, 169, 298
Ausstellungsraum 301
Ausstellungsstück 169
Aussterben 226
Ausstoß 226, 258
ausstrahlen 270
austeilen 155
Auster 55
Austragungsort 195
Australien 214
australisch 214
ausüben 142
Ausverkauf 194
Auswahl 145
auswählen 62, 104
auswandern 159
Auswanderung 230
auswärts essen 61
Auswärtssieg 196
auswechselbar 171, 258
auswechseln 171
Auswechselspieler 196
auswendig lernen 154, 247
Auszeichnung 152
ausziehen 64, 77
Auszubildende 310
Auto 71, 193, 284, 286
Autobahn 284, 285
Autobahnraststätte 285
Autobiografie 179
autobiografisch 179
Autofahren 110
Autofahrer 284
Autofokus 172
Autogramm 199
Automat 294

Automation 258
automatisch 258
automatisiert 258
Automatisierung 258
Automobilhersteller 257
Automobilindustrie 258
Autopapiere 286
Autopsie 41
Autor 180, 266
Autorenhonorar 267
Autorennsport 195
autoritär 99
Autovermietung 284
Autoversicherung 307
Axiom 146

B
Baby 13, 15, 17, 50, 51
Babysitter 17
Bach 217
Backbord 292
backen 58
Bäcker 310
Backofen 59
Backstein 178
Bad 38, 83, 92, 93, 191
Badeanzug 65
Badehose 65
Badekleidung 65
Badekurort 82
Bademantel 65
Badematte 91
Bademeister 311
baden 38, 51
Badeort 82
Badesandalen 65
Badewanne 90
Badezimmer 87
Badezimmerschrank 90
Badezimmerwaage 90
Baguette 54
Bahn 196, 204
Bahn(-) 287
bahnbrechend 262
Bahnfahrt 288
Bahnhof 287, 288
Bahnlinie 287
Bahnsteig 287, 288, 294
Bahre 17, 41
Baisse 304
Bakterie 237
Balg 18
Balkencode 278
Balkenmenü 278
Balkon 88
Ball 186
Ball spielen 17

Ballade 180
Ballaststoffe 82
ballaststoffreich 82
Ballett 174
Banane 56
Band 265
Bande 33, 43, 134
Bandwurm 234
Bank 302, 303
Bankangestellte 311
Bankdrücken 84
Bankeinlagen 303
Bank(i)er 303
Bankgebühren 302
Bankleitzahl 303
Banknote 257
Bankraub 132
Bankspesen 302
Baptist 159
Bar 201
bar 302, 303
Bär 233
Bardame 63, 201
bärenstark 15
Bargeld 302
Barkeeper 63
Barmann 201
Barock 169, 177
Barzahlung 193, 302
Base 243
Basis 101
Bass 173
Bastard 232
Basteln 198
Bataillon 119
Batterie 172, 259
Bau 255
Bau(-) 177, 178
Bauarbeiten 177
Bauch 13
Bauchmuskeln 84, 94
Bauchschmerzen 76, 78
Bauchspeicheldrüse 245
Baudarlehen 303
bauen 177
Bauen 177
Bauer 108, 219, 220, 234
Bäuerin 220
Bauernhaus 87, 220
Bauernhof 220
Baugenehmigung 177, 308
Baugrundstück 308
Bauherr 177
Bauholz 254
Bauindustrie 177
Bauingenieur 311
Bauklötze 18
baulich 178
Baum 219, 235, 236
Baumarten 254

Baumaßnahmen 177
Baumaterialien 177
Baumeister 177
baumlos 219
Baumstamm 236
Baumwolle 221
Bauordnung 308
Baupläne 177
Bausparkasse 303
Baustelle 177
Baustil 177
Baustoffe 177
Bausubstanz 178
Bautischler 310
Bauunternehmer 178
Bauunternehmung 178
Bauzeit 178
Bayern 106
Bazillus 68, 237
beachten 294
Beamte 20, 311
beantragen 117, 189
beantworten 156
bearbeiten 175, 254, 267, 277
Bearbeitung 173, 257, 267
Beatmung 72
Beben 211, 229
Becher 261
Bedarfshaltestelle 293
bedeckt 228
bedeuten 302
bedeutsam 100
bedienen 186
Bediener 258
Bedienung(sgeld) 62
bedingt 130, 143, 278
bedroht 226
bedrückt 24
bedürfen 52
Bedürfnis 28
Bedürftige 130
beeinflussen 142, 145
Beeinflussung 101
beeinträchtigen 73
Beeinträchtigung 73
beenden 315
Beerdigung 41
Beeren 56
befahrbar 292
befassen mit 198
Befehl 278
Befehlshaber 118
Befehlsmenü 278
Befehlszeile 278
befördern 118, 285
Beförderung 316
Befragte 145
befreien von 276
befreundet 34
Befürchtung 30

befürworten 136
begabt 51
Begabtenförderung 51
Begabung 156
begehbar 89
begehen 42, 49, 110, 184
Begehren 29
begehren 29
begeistert 176, 199
beginnen 235
begleichen 303
begleiten 173
begraben 41, 229
Begräbnis 41
Begrenzungen 146
Behälter 261
behandeln 70, 72
behandelnd 80
Behandlung 80
Behauptung 135
Behaviorismus 143
beheben 276
Behelfsunterkunft 125
Beherrschung 22
behindert 73
Behinderte 73
behindertengerecht 73
Behinderung 73, 74
Behörde 106
bei (= @) 280
beibringen 154
Beichte 163
beide 100, 101, 160
beiderseitig 33
Beifall 176
Beihilfe 115
Beilage 62
beilegen 35, 117, 315, 316
beim Arzt 14
Bein 12, 15, 70, 71, 76, 233
beinahe 16
Beisetzung 41
Beispiel für 146
beißen 78
Beißzange 255
Beitrag 307
beitragen 225, 226
beitreten 33, 118
bekannt 34, 205
bekannt geben 269
Bekannte 34
Bekanntschaft 34
bekehren 158
bekennen 36, 292
bekommen 74, 81, 183, 194
belasten 302, 308
Belästigung 36, 136
Belastungszeuge 109

Belege 140
Belegschaft 314
beleibt 15
Belgien 215
belgisch 116
Belichtungsmesser 172
Belichtung(szeit) 172
Belieben 62
beliebt 195, 198, 199, 271
Belletristik 179
bemannt 206
bemerken 25
Bemerkung 13
Bemühungen 86
benachrichtigen 46
benachteiligt 97, 130
benehmen 22
beneiden 30
benutzen 79, 186, 276, 293
Benutzer 278, 280
benutzerfreundlich 278
Benutzeroberfläche 278
Benutzerschnittstelle 278
Benzin 226, 251
Benzinkanister 261
Benzintank 261
beobachten 25
Beobachtung 242
bepflanzen 221
bequem 288
beraten 103
beraten über 102
Berater 105, 310
berechenbar 142
berechnen 246, 302
Berechnung 246
bereithalten 262
Bereitschaftstasche 172
bereitstellen 125
Berg 218
Bergarbeiter 315
Berggipfel 218
Bergheide 219
bergig 215
Bergleute 310
Bergmann 310
Bergpredigt 162
Bergregion 97
Bergsteigen 199
Bergungsarbeiten 230
Bergungskommando 230
Bericht 140, 269
berichten 141, 269
Berliner 54, 174
Bernstein 213
berüchtigt 187, 314

B

Beruf 20, 309
berufen 299
beruflich 127, 154, 309
berufsbildend 148
Berufsfachschule 148
Berufskrankheit 245
Berufsschule 148
berufstätig 51
Berufsverbrecher 131
Berufsverkehr 285
Berufung 111, 309
Berufung einlegen 111
Beruhigungsmittel 128
berühmt 169, 176, 187
berühren 27, 78
Berührung 27
Berührungsbildschirm 282
Besatzung 290, 292
Besatzungstruppen 119
beschäftigen 127
beschäftigt 313
Beschäftigte 126, 314, 315
Beschäftigung 127, 198
Beschäftigungssituation 127
Beschäftigungstherapie 144
beschämt 32
bescheiden 24
Bescheinigung 77
Beschleunigung 241
Beschluss 117
Beschneidung 163
beschränken 82, 176
beschränkt 298
beschuldigen 110, 180
beschützen 52
Beschwerden 69, 75, 316
Beschwichtigungspolitik 117
beschwipst 129
beseitigen 297
Besen 92, 93
besetzen 91, 119, 125
besetzt 215, 275, 288
besetztes Haus 125
Besetzung 119, 176
Besichtigungen 189
Besichtigungsfahrt 189
besiedelt 97
besitzen 13, 18
Besitzer 298
besondere 184

Besprechung 176, 312
bessern 127
Beständigkeit 255
Bestandteil 243, 254
bestätigen 290
Bestattung 41
Bestattungsinstitut 41
Bestattungsunternehmer 41
beste 285
Beste 31
Bestechlichkeit 32
Bestechung 131
bestehen 152, 294
Bestehen 184
bestehen aus 102
bestellen 62, 191, 192, 220
Bestellung 62, 278
besteuern 113
Bestie 232
bestimmt 264
Bestimmungen 300
Bestrafung 111
bestreiken 315
Bestseller 267
Bestsellerautor 267
Besuch 185, 188
besuchen 61, 148, 150, 185, 188, 279
besucht 175
betätigen 256
Betätigung 198
Betäubung 81
beten 28, 160
Beton 178
betrachten 91
betragen 289
betrauern 42
betreiben 199, 221
Betreiber 279
Betreten verboten 308
Betrieb 257, 258, 294, 315
Betriebsart 278
Betriebsingenieur 257
Betriebsleiter 258
Betriebssystem 262, 276, 282
betroffen sein 230
betroffen von 315
Betrug 131
betrügen 32
Betrüger 132
betrunken 129, 200
Betrunkene 52, 129, 200
Bett 60, 89, 217
Betten machen 93
Beugung 84
Beurteilung 156

Bevölkerungsgruppe 96
bevölkerungsreich 97
Bevölkerungswachstum 145
Bevölkerungszahl 230
Bevölkerungszahlen 141
bewaffnet 117, 132
Bewährung 111
Bewährungshelfer 111
bewässern 220
Bewässerung 220
bewegen 83
bewegend 28, 30
Bewegung 83, 98, 101, 270
Bewegungsgesetz 241
Bewegungsübertragung 255
Beweis 111
beweisen 240
Beweismaterial 146
bewerben 306
bewerten 156
bewirten 186
Bewirtschaftung 124
Bewohner 223
bewölken 228
bewölkt 228
bewundern 29
bewusst 121
Bewusste 143
bewusstlos 70
Bewusstlosigkeit 70
bewusstseinsverändernd 128
bezahlen 13, 114, 302, 303, 304, 351
bezahlt 316
Bezahlung 303
beziehen 86
Beziehung 36
Beziehungen 33, 35, 116, 135, 142, 145, 314
Bezirk 96, 97
Bezugsrahmen 146
bezweifeln 164
BH 65
Bibel 31, 160
Bibel 31, 160, 205
Bibliografie 264
Bibliothek 264
Bibliothekar 264
biegen 52
biegsam 262
Biene 24, 234
bienenfleißig 24
Bier 200, 261
Bierdeckel 199

Biersorten 200
bieten 63, 125, 191, 302
bieten lassen 29
Bigamie 49
Bigamist 49
Bild 168, 169, 172
Bildbearbeitung 172
Bildbetrachtung 171
bilden 51, 96, 105, 296, 297
bildende Kunst 150
Bilderbuch 18
Bilder(sprache) 180
Bildfrequenz 172
Bildhauer 169
Bildhauerei 168, 169
bildhauerisch 169
Bildhauerkunst 169
Bildmaterial 170
Bildnis 168
Bildschirm 276, 277
Bildschirmarbeitsplatz 276
Bildschirmgerät 276
Bildsymbol 278
Bildtafel 170
Bildung 51, 142, 154
Bildung von 210
Bildungseinrichtungen 148, 224
Bildungsszene 153
Bildungswesen 147
Bildunterschrift 269
Bildwerk 169
billig 194
Billigflagge 291
Binde 39
Bindestrich 278
Bindung 242, 266
Binnenklima 228
Binnenmarkt 117
Binnenmeer 216
Bio- 56
Bioanbau 56
Biobauer 56
Biochemie 242
Biogemüse 56
Biograf 179
Biografie 179
biografisch 179
Biokost 56, 82
Biokraftstoff 226
Bioladen 56, 82
Biologie 150
biologisch 56, 138
Biomilch 56
Biomüll 56
Biosprit 226
Biotonne 56
Birke 235
Birne 56, 260
bis 343
Bischof 48, 163

bisexuell 98
bisschen 12, 26, 129, 173, 275
Bistro 61, 287
bitte 155, 186
bitter 27
Blag 18
blamieren 233
Blase 13
blasen 39
Blaskapelle 174
Blatt 236, 238
blättern 264
blau 15
Blaubeeren 56
blauer Fleck 72
Blaumeise 233
Blei 212
Bleibe 125
bleiben 28, 32, 83, 228
bleich 16
bleifrei 212, 226
Bleistift 313
Bleistift(an)spitzer 313
Blende 172
Blick 23, 25
blicken 25, 208
blind 12
Blinddarm 69, 81
Blinddarment-
zündung 70
Blinddarmoperation 81
Blinde 26
Blindenhund 26
blinder Passagier 292
Blindheit 74
Blitz 228
blitzen 171, 228
Blitz(licht) 171
Blitzlichtaufnahme 171
Blitzschlag 230
blockfrei 116
Blockhaus 87
Blockhütte 87
blond 16
Blondine 16
bloßem Auge 25
blühen 235, 236
Blume 235
Blumengeschäft 194
Blumenkohl 55
Blumenstecken 198
Bluse 16, 64
Blut 13, 14, 69
Blutbank 244
Blutdruck 69, 77
Blüte 235, 236
bluten 72, 78
Bluterguss 72
Blutgefäß 244

Blutgerinnsel 244
Blutprobe 244
Blutspender 14
Blutsverwandtschaft 138
Blutuntersuchung 244
Blutvergiftung 69
Blutwäsche 245
Boden 87, 89, 220
Boden der Tat-
sachen 208
Bodenpersonal 290
Bodenschätze 210
Bodensee 216
Bodenstation 206
Bodenverschmut-
zung 225
Bogen 178
Bohnen 55, 261
bohnern 93
Bohnerwachs 93
bohren 79, 255
Bohrer 255
Bohrmaschine 255
Boiler 91
Bolzen 255
Bombardieren 119
Bombe 119
Bombenanschlag 134
Bonbon(s) 55
Bonus 316
Boot 291, 292
Bootsfahrt 188
Bord 89, 291, 292
Bordell 37
Bordkarte 290
Bordtasche 290
borgen 303
Borke 236
Börse 304
bösartig 69
böse 30, 31, 35, 166
Böse 31
böses Blut 35
boshaft 23
Botanik 236
botanisch 236
Bote 160
Botschaft 116, 189
Botschafter(in) 116, 121
Boulevardpresse 268
Boxen 196
Boykott 107
boykottieren 107
Brache 220
brachliegend 220
Branche 298
Branchentelefon-
buch 274
Brand 71, 230
Brandanschlag 134

Brandbombe 134
Brandkatastrophe 230
Brandsatz 134
Brandstifter 131
Brandstiftung 131
braten 58, 59
Braten 58
Bratensoße 55
Brathähnchen 58
Bratkartoffeln 56
Bratpfanne 59, 238
Brauch 162
Bräuche 138
brauchen 64, 83, 92, 312
Braunbär 233
Bräunungsstudio 83
Brause 57, 90
Braut 48
Bräutigam 48
Brautjungfer 48
Brautpaar 186
brav 31, 39
brechen 12, 71, 195
breit 250
breit(schultrig) 15
Breitband 282
Breite 214
Bremse 256
bremsen 256
Bremsrakete 207
brennbar 243
brennend 76, 125
Brennstoff 226
Brennweite 171
Brett 89, 313
Brettspiel 18
Brief 261, 272, 273, 312
Briefentwurf 312
Briefkasten 273, 280
Briefmarke 199, 273
Briefpapier 313
Brieftasche 303
Briefträger 272
Briefumschlag 261
Briefwahl 104, 272
Brigade 119
Brille 25, 94
bringen 13, 72, 81, 207, 272, 313
Brise 228
Britannien 156
britisch 96, 100, 213
Broiler 58
Brombeeren 56
Bronchitis 70
Bronze 169, 212
bronzen 212
Bronzezeit 212
Brot 54, 58, 60
Brötchen 54, 60, 192
browsen 279

Bruch 49, 69, 71, 210, 247, 249
Bruchbude 87
Bruchfestigkeit 255
brüchig 255
Brücke 79, 91, 177, 254
Bruder 46
Brühe 55
Brünette 16
Brust 13, 76
Brustamputation 81
Brüste 13
Brustkasten 245
Brustkorb 13, 245
Brustkrebs 69, 244
brutto 113
Brutto- 113
Bruttosozialprodukt 297
BS 276
BSE 221
Buch 114, 155, 199, 266, 267, 272
Buche 235
buchen 61, 188, 191, 289, 292
Bücherbord 89
Bücherbrett 89
Bücherei 264
Bücherregal 89
Bücherschrank 89
Bücherstand 266
Bücherwurm 234
Buchführung 114
Buchgemeinschaft 266
Buchhalter 310
Buchhaltung 114
Buchhändler 266
Buchillustrationen 170
Buchklub 266
Buchmesse 267
Buchprüfung 114
Büchse 241
Buchseite 266
Büchsenöffner 59
Bucht 216
Buckel 74
Bückling 55
Buddha 160
Buddhismus 158
Buddhist 158
buddhistisch 158
Büfett 63, 89
Büfettwagen 287
büffeln 152
Bug 292
bügeln 93
Bügelsäge 255
Bühne 176
Bühnenanweisungen 180
Bühnenbild 176

B

Bühnendekoration 176
Bulette 55
Bulletin 269
Bummelstreik 315
Bund 118
Bundes- 99
Bundeskanzler 105
Bundeskriminalamt 106
Bundesland 96, 97
Bundesregierung 105
Bundesrepublik 99
Bündnis 116
Bündnispartner 116
Bungalow 87
Buntstift 18
Bürette 242
Burg 86
Bürger 32, 108
Bürgergeld 113
Bürgerinitiative 101
Bürgerkunde 142
bürgerlich 33
Bürgerrechte 106, 107
Bürgerrechtler 98, 107
Bürgerrechtsbewegung 98, 107
Bürgersteig 224, 285
Büro 274, 305, 312
Büroangestellte 310, 311
Bürogebäude 312
Bürohochhaus 87
Büroklammer 313
Büroleiter 312
Büromanagement 311
Büromaterial 313
Bürotätigkeit 312
Bürovorsteher 312
Bursche 15, 24
Bürste 38, 93
bürsten 38, 93
Bürstenschnitt 16
Bus 71, 293, 294
Büsche 219
Bushaltestelle 293
Buslinie 293
Busplakat 306
Bußgeld 111
Bußgeldbescheid 286
Busspur 285
Büste 169
Butter 54
Butterblume 235

C
Café 61
Callgirl 37
Cardiotraining 84

Carport 88
CD-ROM 29, 265
CD-Spieler 26
Celsius 228
Cent 302
Champagner 200
Champignon 55, 236
Chance 248
Chancengleichheit 316
Chanson 173
Charakter 32
Charakterdarstellerin 176
Charakterrolle 176
charmant 23
Charme 23, 44
Charterflug 290
Chartermaschine 290
chartern 290
chatten 280
Chauffeur 311
Chauvi(nistenschwein) 136
Chauvinismus 134, 136
Chef 299, 309
Chefarzt 80
Chefredakteur 269
Chefsekretärin 311
Chemie 150, 242
Chemiefasern 243
Chemieingenieur 242
Chemieingenieurwesen 242
Chemietechnik 242
Chemikalie 242
Chemiker 242
chemisch 82, 242
Chemotechniker 242
Chester 54
Chip 260
Chiropraktiker 70
Chirurg 75, 81
Chirurgie 81, 245
chirurgisch 80
Cholesterin 82
Cholesterinspiegel 82
Chor 173, 178
Christ 158, 159, 162
Christenheit 158
Christentum 158
christlich 158
Christlich-Demokratisch 101
Christus 160, 161
Chronik 140, 202
chronisch 68
Chronist 140
City 224
Code 237
Coitus interruptus 37

Collage 170
Colon 245
Comic-Hefte 18
Computer 276
computergesteuert 257
computergestützt 276
computerisieren 258
computerisiert 265
Computerkenntnisse 276
Computerspiel 199, 276
Computertomografie 244
Computerverstand 276
Computervirus 280
Containerschiff 291
Copyright 267
Cordhose 65
Couchtisch 90
Cousin(e) 47
Cowboyhut 65
Creme 38, 39
Croissant 192
CT 244
Curriculum 151, 237
Curry 55, 63
Cursortaste 278

D
Dach 88
Dachboden 87, 88
Dachwohnung 87
Dachzimmer 88
dahingehen 40
dahinscheiden 14, 40
Damenbinde 39
Damenschneider 310
Dampf 241
Dampfbad 83
dämpfen 115
Dampfer 291
Dampflok 287
Dampflokomotive 256
Dampfmaschine 256
Dampfschiff 291
danach 62
Dänisch 266
dankbar 186, 198
dankbar sein 208
danke 271
daran denken 156
Darm 13
darüber 104
dastehen 126
Datei 277, 279
Datei- 277
Dateikomprimierung 277
Dateiverwaltung 277

Daten 140, 265, 276, 277
Datenabruf 265
Datenaustausch 276
Datenautobahn 265
Datenbank 265
Datenbestand 265
Dateneingabestation 279
Datenerfassung 279
Datenschutz(gesetz) 276
Datentarif 282
Datentransfer 276
Datenübertragung 276
Datenverarbeitung 260, 276
Datenverbindung 279
Datenwiedergewinnung 276
Dattel 56
Datum 273
Dauergeschwindigkeit 284
Dauerlauf 83, 250
dauern 189, 312
Dauerrede 103
davonfahren 286
dazugehören 84
deaktivieren 279
Debatte 102, 111
debattieren 102
Deck 292
Decke 89
Deckungskarte 307
Deckungszusage 307
definieren 165
Definition 165
Defizitfinanzierung 297
Deflation 297
Dehnbarkeit 255
dekodieren 279
Delegierte 96, 104
Delikt 110
Delphin 234
Demenz 74
demografisch 145
Demokraten 102
Demokratie 99
demokratisch 99
Demonstrant 107
Demonstration 107
demütig 24
Denken 143, 165
denken 165, 182
Denker 165
Denksportaufgabe 18
Deodorant 39
deprimiert 28
Derivat 243, 304
Dermatologie 244

Dessert 62
Detektiv 112
Detektivgeschichte 179
deutlich 25, 155, 267
deutsch 106, 116, 119, 153, 197, 215, 270
Deutsche 153
Deutschland 99, 257
Deutung 146
Devisen 304
Devisenbörse 304
Devisenkurse 304
Dezimalbruch 247
Dezimalzahlen 249
d. h. 94
Dia 172
Diagnose 244
diagnostisch 244
diagnostizieren 244
dialektisch 166
Dialog 35, 155
Dialogfeld 278
Dialyse 245
Diamant 213
Diät 82
Diätplan 82
dicht 219
Dichte 241
Dichter 180
dichterisch 180
Dichtung 179
Dichtungsscheibe 256
dick 16, 229, 250
Dickdarm 245
Dickicht 219
Dieb 71, 132
Diebstahl 25, 132, 307
Diele 87
dienen 96
Dienst 193, 315
Dienst habend 80
Dienstleistungen 21, 296
Dienstleistungs- bereich 296
Dienstleistungssektor 296
Dienstmädchen 311
Dienstschluss 312
Dienststelle 106
Dienststunden 312
Dienstvertrag 316
Diesellok 287
Dieselmotor 26
diesig 228
Differenzialrechnung 246
digital 260, 281
Digital- 260
digitale Kamera 172

digitales Malen 282
digitalisieren 260
Digitalisierung 260
Digitalkamera 172
Diktat 151, 313
Diktator 106
Diktatur 99
diktieren 313
Diktiergerät 313
Ding an sich 166
Diplom 153
Diplomat 20, 116
Diplomatenkoffer 261
Diplomatie 116
diplomatisch 116
Diplomvolkswirt 153
direkt 168, 312
direkt übertragen 270
Direktmarketing 305
Direktor 299, 309
Direktorin 309
Direktübertragung 270
Direktverbindung 287, 289
Direktwerbung 305
Dirigent 174
dirigieren 174
Dirigieren 309
Discount- 300
Diskette 277
Diskjockey 271
Disko 187
Diskont- 300
Diskriminierung 21, 136
Diskussion 35
Diskussionsforum 280
Displayschutzfolie 282
Dissertation 153
Dissident 107
Distel 235
diszipliniert 156
Dividende 304
dividieren 246
Division 119, 247
DNA 237
Dockarbeiter 310
Dogma 162
Doktorarbeit 153
Doktorwürde 153
Dokument 140, 301, 313
Dokumentarbericht 269
Dokumentarfilm 271
Dokumentarspiel 271
Dollar 302, 303
Dom 162
Domain 280

Domäne 280
donnern 228
Doppel- 191
Doppel 197
Doppelbett 89, 191
Doppeldecker 293
Doppelfehler 197
Doppelhaushälfte 87
doppelklicken 278
doppelt 201
Dorf 86, 96, 97
dorisch 178
Dorn 52
Dose 38, 261
Dosenöffner 59
Dosis 129
downloaden 265
Down-Syndrom 74
Dr. med. 94, 153
Dr. phil. 153
Drachen 18
Drachenfliegen 199
drahtig 15
Drahtlos- 282
Drahtseil 217
drall 15
Drama 176, 179, 213
Dramatiker 176
dran bleiben 275
dran sein 155
Drang 28
draußen 52
Dreckloch 86
Drehbank 256
Drehbleistift 313
Drehbuch 175
drehen 204
Drehkreuz 294
Drehmaschine 256
Drehmoment 256
Drehstrom 259
Drehstuhl 90
Drehtür 88
Dreieinigkeit 160
Dreieck 247
dreieckig 247
Dreifaltigkeit 160
dreinschauen 24
Dreiphasenstrom 259
Dreirad 18
dreiseitig 247
Dreivierteltakt 174
Dreizimmer- wohnung 88
dreschen 222
Drescher 222
dritte Potenz 247
Dritte Welt 214
drittgrößte 224
Droge 19, 128
Drogenabhängigkeit 128, 129
Drogeneinfluss 128
Drogenhandel 128

Drogenhändler 128
Drogenmissbrauch 128
Drogensucht 128
Drogensüchtige 128
Drogentote 128
drohen 109, 111, 125, 294, 300
drohend 126, 230
Drossel 233
Druck 241, 267
Druckauflage 267
Druckbleistift 313
drucken 267
drücken 84, 128, 278
drückend 227
Drucker 277
Druckerei 267
Druckfarbe 170
Druckfehler 267
Druckgrafik 170
Druckmaschine 255
Drucksache(n) 273
Druckstock 170
Druckverfahren 170
Drüse 14
Drüse(n-) 245
Dschihad 163
Dschungel 219, 238
duales Studium 149
Duft 27
duftend 236
Duktilität 255
dulden 29
duldsam 22
dumm 23, 24
dumpf 76, 78
Dünen 219
Dung 220
düngen 220
Dünger 220
Düngung 220
dunkel 16
dunkelhaarig 16
dünn 15
dünn besiedelt 97
Dünndarm 245
Dunst 228
dünsten 58
Dur 174
Durchblutung 14
Durchbruch 117, 262
Durcheinander 93
Durchfahrtsstraße 285
Durchfall 69
durchfallen 152
durchführen 13, 41, 77, 145, 240, 245, 246, 264, 265, 315
Durchgangsstraße 285

Durchgangsverkehr 285
durchgebraten 59
durchgehend 287
Durchmesser 247
durchrasseln 152
durchringen 105
Durchschnitts- 227
durchsuchen 279
Durchsuchungs-
  befehl 112
dürfen 185, 232
Dürre(periode) 229
Durst 25
Dusche 38, 90
duschen 38
Düsenflugzeug 289
Düsenmaschine 289
DVD(-Player) 271
Dynamik 240
Dynamo 259

E
Eau de Cologne 39
Ebbe 217
Ebene 216, 218
Ebola-Fieber 70
Echo 306
Ecke 285
Ecstasy 129
Edelmetall 212
Edelmut 31
Edelstahl 212
Edelstein 212, 213
editieren 277
EDV 260, 276, 299
Effektenverwalter
  304
effizient 111, 284
Ehe 48, 49, 98
eheähnlich 48
Eheberater 48
Eheberatung 144
Ehebruch 49
Ehefrau 49, 133
ehelich 36, 49
Ehemann 49
Ehepaar 48
eher 78
Ehering 48
Ehescheidung 48, 49
Eheschließung 48
Ehre 186
ehrenamtlich 198
Ehrengast 186
Ehrgeiz 23
ehrgeizig 208
ehrlich 22, 23, 32
Ehrlichkeit 32
Ei 27, 54, 60, 192
Eibe 235
Eiche 235
Eichel 235
Eichenfass 261
Eichhörnchen 233

Eidgenossenschaft
  96
Eier 82
Eierkuchen 54
Eierstock 14
Eifersucht 30
eifersüchtig 30
eigen 18, 166, 184
Eigengewichts-
  übung 84
Eigenschaft 31, 240
eigentlich 156, 309
Eigentor 197
Eigentümer 298, 308
Eigentumsnachweis
  308
Eigentumsrecht 308
Eigentumsurkunde
  308
Eigentumswohnung
  86
eignen als 254
Eignungsprüfung
  144
Eignungstest 144,
  152
Eiland 217
Eilzustellung 273
Eimer 261
Eimerchen 18
einäschern 41
Einäscherung 41
einäugig 171
Einbahnstraße 285
Einband 266
Einbauschrank 89
einbrechen 132
Einbrecher 132
einbringen 103
Einbruch 132
eindosen 59
einfach 172, 281,
  288
einfallen 119
einfarbig 170
Einfluss 146
einflussreich 146
einführen 306
Eingabe 277, 278
Eingabetaste 278
Eingang 88
Eingangshalle 87
eingeben 276
eingebildet 24
eingeschränkt 73
Eingeweide 76
eingravieren 170
Eingreifen 120, 161
einhängen 274, 275
Einheit 119
Einheitspreis 294
Einigung 117
einjährig 236
Einkäufe 193
Einkaufen 193

einkaufen 300
Einkaufsbummel 193
Einkaufskorb 193
Einkaufspreis 300
Einkaufstasche 193
Einkaufswagen 193
Einkaufszentrum 193
Einkommen 114,
  297, 304
Einkommensschwa-
  che 115, 124
Einkommen(steuer)
  113
Einkommensteuer-
  erklärung 113
einladen 186
einlegen 103, 171
Einleitung 266
Einliegerwohnung
  86
einlösen 190
einmachen 59
einmal 83, 249
Einmaleins 247
einmarschieren 119
einnehmen 77, 120
einpacken 193, 261
Einpeitscher 102
einreiben 39
einreichen 49
einreihig 64
Einreise 134
Einrichtung 138, 224
Einsatz 221, 242
einschalten 260,
  277, 279, 294
Einschaltquoten 271
einschätzen 156
Einschienenbahn
  293
einschiffen 292
einschlafen 40
einschlagen auf 133
einschließlich 113
einschränken 134
einschreiben 149
Einschreiben 273
Einsegnung 163
einsetzen 171, 172
Einsetzen 20, 50
einsperren 111
Einstand 197
einstechen auf 133
einstecken 89
Einsteigekarte 290
einsteigen 288
einstellen 127, 172,
  270
Einstellung 28, 142,
  258
Einstufungstest 152
Einsturz 254
einteilen 138, 156
Einteilung 214
eintippen 312

Eintopf 55
Eintrag 264
eintreten in 314
Einvernehmen 34
einverständlich 49
Einverständnis 34
Einwahl 279
Einwanderer 134
Einwanderung 134
Einwanderungs-
  gesetz 103
einwecken 59
Einwegflasche 226
Einwegkamera 171
Einweisung 80
einwirken 241
Einwirken 161
einzahlen 303
Einzel 197
Einzel- 191
Einzelhandel(s-) 300
Einzelhandelspreis
  114, 193, 300
Einzelhändler 300
Einzelkind 17
Einzeller 237
einzellig 237
Einzelzimmer 191
einziehen 113, 184
einzig 31, 265
Einzimmerwohnung
  86
Einzugsparty 185
Eisbär 233
Eisberg 217, 292
Eisen 212
Eisenbahn(-) 287
Eisenbahner 287
Eisenbahnerstreik
  287
Eisenbahnknoten-
  punkt 287
Eisenbahnlinie 287
Eisenbahnstrecke
  287
Eisenbahnwagen
  287
Eisenerz 212
eisern 212
eisig 44, 227
eiskalt 227
Eiskunstlauf 196
Eisverkäufer 311
Eiszeit 211
Eiter 70
eitern 70
Eiweiß(körper) 237
Ejakulation 36
EKG 77
Eklektiker 166
eklektisch 166
elastisch 254
Elastizität 255
Elefant 232, 238
elegant 16, 64

Elektriker 259
elektrisch 240, 241, 259
elektrischer Stuhl 43
Elektrizität 259
Elektrizitätsgesell- schaft 259
Elektrizitätswerk 259
Elektrode 243
Elektrogerät 90
Elektroingenieur 259
Elektrolok 287
Elektrolyse 243
Elektromotor 256
Elektron 241
Elektronen- 241, 242
Elektronenkonfigu- ration 241
Elektronenröhre 243
Elektronik 240, 241, 259
Elektronikgeschäft 194
elektronisch 241, 260, 265, 279, 280, 281
elektronisches Pa- pier 282
Elektrorasierer 38, 90
elektrostatisch 259
Elektrotechnik 259
Element 242, 243
Elementarteilchen- 240
Elend 130
Elfenbein 169
Elfmeterschießen 197
Ell(en)bogen 12
elliptisch 204
Eltern 24, 49, 50, 86
Elternschaft 37
E-Mail 265, 280
E-Mail-Adresse 11
Emanze 98
Embargo 117
Emoticon 280
Emotion 28
emotional 28
Empfang 186, 192, 271, 311, 312
Empfängnis 37
Empfängnis- verhütung 37
Empfangsdame 63
empfehlen 62
empfindlich 78
Empfindlichkeit 171
Empfindung 25
empirisch 145, 146, 165
emsig 24
Ende 155, 156
enden 294
endlich 27, 247
Endlosreden 103

Endmoräne 211
Endoskopie 244
endoskopisch 244
Endstation 288
Energie 21, 226, 240, 241
Energieträger 226
eng 34
Engel 162
England 159
Englandfeindlichkeit 134
englisch 59, 152, 168, 196, 218
Englischunterricht 154
engstirnig 23
Enkel 47
Enkelin 47
Enkelkinder 47
enorm 189, 300
Entbehrung 130
entbinden 81
Entbindung 50
Entbindungsstation 80, 244
Ente 55, 106, 232, 233
entfernen 39, 79
entfernt 216
Entfernung 204, 246
Entfernung einstellen 172
Entfernungsmesser 172
entführen 132, 290
Entführer 131
Entführung 131
entgegenkommend 22
entgehen 109
Entgiftung 129
entgleisen 287
enthalten 103, 261
entlassen 112, 126, 316
Entlassen 316
Entlassungen 316
Entlastungszeuge 110
entleihen 264
entscheiden 62, 101, 109
Entscheidung 105
Entscheidungs- prozess 145
Entscheidungs- prozesse 142
entschließen 202
entschlüsseln 279
entsetzlich 130, 230
entspannen 83, 198
entspannt 24
Entspannung 117, 198, 199

entsprechen 250
entsprechend 113, 156
Entstehung 204
Entwaldung 225
entwerfen 177, 312
entwickeln 165, 166
Entwicklung 179, 210, 226, 258
Entwicklungs- 139
Entwicklungshilfe 117
Entwicklungsland 117
Entwicklungspsy- chologie 143
entwöhnen 129
Entwöhnung 129
Entwurf 170, 177, 312
Entziffern 140
Entzug 129
Entzugserschei- nungen 68, 129
Entzündung 70
Enzyklopädie 264, 265
Enzym 237
Epik 179
Epilepsie 74
episch 179
Epistemologie 165
Epitaph 41
Epizentrum 229
Epoche 141, 211
Epos 179
Erb- 74
erbarmungslos 23
Erbe 138
Erbfaktor 237
Erbinformation 237
Erbkrankheit 74
erblich 74
erblinden 74
erbrechen 14
Erbrechen 68
Erbsen 55
Erbsünde 162
Erdatmosphäre 226
Erdball 46
Erdbeben 211, 229, 230
Erdbebenkunde 210
Erdbeeren 56
Erdbewegungs- maschinen 255
Erde 41, 160, 204, 205, 207, 210, 220, 230, 260
erden 260
Erderwärmung 226
Erdgasvorkommen 210
Erdgeschichte 210

Erdgeschoss 87
Erdinnere 210
Erdkern 210
Erdkruste 210
Erdkunde 150
Erdnuss 56
Erdrinde 210
erdrosseln 133
Erdrutsch 229
Erdteil 214
Erdung 260
Erdzeitalter 211
Ereignis 269
Erektion 36
erfahren adj. 22
Erfahrung 20, 165
erfahrungsmäßig 165
Erfahrungswissen 165
Erfinder 311
Erfolg 35, 176
erfolgreich 197
erfrieren 72
Erfrischungen 194
Ergebnis 30, 315
ergreifen 108
ergreifend 30
erhalten 197, 275
erhältlich 77
Erhängen 40, 43
erheben 108, 109, 114
erhöhen 51, 113, 221, 230, 245, 297
erhöht 68, 118, 258
Erhöhung 288, 289, 316
Erholung 181, 198, 296
erigiert 36
Erkältung 69, 77
erkennbar 25
erkennen 73
Erkenntnislehre 165
Erkenntnisse 146
erklären 119, 165
erkranken 69, 70
erkranken an 74
Erkrankung 68
erlassen 103, 104
erledigen 92
erleiden 14, 68, 71, 300
Erleuchtete 160
Erleuchtung 164
ermöglichen 104
ermorden 108, 133
Ermordung 108
Ernährung 82, 130
ernennen 106
Ernennung 106
erneuerbar 226
ernst 68
Ernte 221

Ernteausfall 230
Erntedank 183
Ernteerträge 221
ernten 221
erobern 120
Eroberung 156
eröffnen 303
Eröffnungsfeier 184
Erosion 211
erotisch 36
Erpresser 131
Erpressung 131
Erprobung 244
errechnen 246
erregbar 23
erregen 36
Erregung 36
erreichen 11, 20, 142, 193
erringen 103
Ersatz- 286
Ersatzrad 286
Ersatzreifen 286
Ersatzspieler 196
Ersatzteil 261
erscheinen 267
Erscheinung 15, 16, 166
Erscheinungstermin 267
erschießen 40, 132
Erschießen 40, 43
Erschießungskommando 43
erschlossen 308
erschütternd 267
Erschütterungen 76
erschwinglich 86, 124
ersetzen 79, 277
Erstattung 114
Erstaufführung 175
Erstausgabe 267
erste Hilfe 72
erstechen 133
erstellen 124, 277
ersticken 71
Ersticken 71
Ersttäter 112
erteilen 177, 301
Erträge 304
ertragen 29
ertränken 42
ertrinken 42, 229
erwachsen 19, 37
Erwachsene 19, 51
Erwachsenenbildung 149
Erwähnung 202
Erwärmung 226
erwarten 185
erweitert 185
erwerbslos 126
Erwerbslosigkeit 126

Erwerbsunfähigkeit 73
erwiesen 110
erwirken 112
erwünscht 29
erwürgen 133
Erzähl- 179
erzählend 179
Erzählliteratur 179
Erzählperspektive 180
Erzählung 179
Erzbischof 163
erzeugen 257, 259
Erzeugnis 220, 306
erziehen 51
Erziehung 51
erzielen 117, 197, 300
Esche 235
Esel 233
eskalieren 117
esoterisch 164
Essay 179
essen 13, 60
Essen 54, 60, 62, 186
Essen auf Rädern 21
Essen(s)marke 312
Essküche 88
Esstisch 90
Esszimmer 87
Etage 87
Etat 104, 305
Ethernet 279
Ethik 166
ethisch 31
ethnisch 135
Ethnologie 138
Ethnosoziologie 138
etwas 155, 250
euer Ehren 122
EU-Erweiterung 117
Eule 233
EU-Mitgliedschaft 117
Euro 190, 302
Europa 116, 214, 215
Europafeindlichkeit 134
europäisch 117, 214, 230
Europäische Union 96, 117
Euthanasie 42
evangelikal 159
evangelisch 159
Evangelium 162
Evolution 139
Evolutions- 139
Evolutionstheorie 139
EWU 117
exakt 242
Examen 94
Exegese 162
Exemplar 267

Exhibitionismus 37
Exhibitionist 37
Existenz 160, 164
Existenzialismus 166
Existenzialist 166
existenzialistisch 166
Existenzminimum 130
Exmann 49
Experiment 240
Experimental- 240
experimentell 240
exponentiell 297
Export 301
Export- 298
exportieren 301
Expressionismus 169, 180
extern 282
extra 62
extrem 128

F
Fabrik 258
Fabrikarbeiter 258
Fabrikation 257
Fabrikationsmethode 257
Fabrikationsweise 257
Fach 150, 154
Facharbeiter 310
Facharzt 80, 244
Fachbereich 149
Fächerkanon 151
Fachhochschule 148
Fachkauffrau für 311
Fachkaufmann für 311
Fachliteratur 264
Fach(ober)schule 148
Fachschule 149
Fachzeitschrift 268
Fadennudeln 55
fähig 22
Fähigkeiten 156
Fähre 291, 292
fahren 71, 97,185, 187, 224, 256, 284, 286, 287, 291, 293, 294, 343
Fahren 286
Fahrer 284, 294
Fahrgast 288
Fahrgeld 294
Fahrkarte 288
Fahrkartenautomat 294
Fahrkartenschalter 288
Fahrlehrer 154, 309
Fahrplan 288

fahrplanmäßig 288, 289
Fahrpreis 288, 294
Fahrpreiserhöhung 288, 294
Fahrrad 18, 94, 286
Fahrrad fahren 286
Fahrradweg 286
Fahrrinne 217
Fahrschule 284
Fahrspur 285
Fahrstuhl 88
Fahrt 188, 189, 284, 288, 293
Fahrzeit 288
Fahrzeug 284
Fahrzeugpapiere 286
fair 22
Fairness 195
Fäkaliengrube 88
Faksimile 170
Fakten 140
Faktura 303
Fakultät 149
Falken 100
Fallbeil 43
fallen 119, 230
fällig 304
falls 273
Fallschirm 119
Fallschirmjäger 119
Fallschirmspringen 199
Fallstudie 144, 146
falsch 23, 31, 292
falsch parken 286
falsch singen 173
falsch verbunden 274
fälschen 257
Fälscher 131
Fälschung 131, 257
Falsifikation 165
falsifizieren 165
Falten 16
Faltenrock 65
faltig 16
Familie 46, 130, 309
Familienname 10
Familienplanung 37, 98
Familienserie 271
Familienstand 11
Familienstrukturen 138
Familientreffen 185
Fan 199
fangfrisch 56
Fantasy-Roman 179
Farb- 171
Farbdia 172
Farbe 18, 73, 168
Farbe bekennen 292
Farm 221
Farmhaus 220

Farn(kraut) 236
Fasan 55
Faschismus 99
Faschist 99
faschistisch 99
Faser 82
Fass 200, 261
Fassade 178
Fassung 267, 278
fast 78
fast völlig 74
fasten 82
faszinieren 29
faszinierend 262
faul 23, 27
Favorit 195
Fax 274, 275
faxen 275
Faxgerät 275
Faxnummer 275
Fazit 146
FCKW 225
Feder 233, 256
Federball 197
Federbett 89
fegen 92
fehlen 89, 155, 213
Fehler 32, 73, 206, 241, 276
Fehlernährung 130
Fehlgeburt 50
Feier 184, 270
feierlich 184
Feierlichkeit 184
Feiern 184
Feiertag 182
feige 24, 238
Feile 255
feilen 255
feilschen 300
Feind 34, 35
feindlich 35, 119
feindselig 35
Feindseligkeit 35
Feinkostgeschäft 61
Feld 219, 220, 221
Feldforschung 138
Feldfrucht 221
Fell 232
Felswand 218
Feminist 136
feministisch 136
Fenster 88, 92, 178
Fensterbrett 88
Fensterladen 88
Fensterleder 93
Ferien 182
Fernbahnhof 287, 288
Ferne Osten 214
Fernfahrer 284, 314
Fernfahrerlokal 286
Fernfahrerraststätte 286
Ferngespräch 274

Fernkurs 149
Fernseh- 267, 270
Fernsehapparat 270
fernsehen 270
Fernsehen 94, 175, 270
Fernseher 94, 260, 270
Fernsehfilm 271
Fernsehkanal 270
Fernsehsender 270
Fernsehsendung 271
Fernsehserie 271
Fernsehspiel 271
Fernsehzuschauer 271
Fernsprech- 274
Fernstraße 284
Fernuniversität 149
fertig sein 155
Fertigbau- 178
fertigen 254, 257
Fertigerzeugnisse 257
Fertighaus 87
Fertigkeit 150
Fertignahrung 54
Fertigung 257
Fertigungsanlagen 257
Fertigungssteuerung 258
Fertigungsstraße 257
fesch 15
fesseln 133
fesselnd 267
fest 34, 241
Festessen 184
Festgeldkonto 303
festhalten 264
Festigkeit 255
Festival 184
Festkörper 241
Festkörperphysik 240
Festland(s)sockel 210
festlich 184
Festmahl 184
Festnahme 112
Festplatte 277, 280, 282
festsetzen 130
Festspiele 184
festverzinslich 304
Festwoche(n) 184
Fett 55
fettarm 82
fettarme Milch 54
Fettnäpfchen 13
Fettsäuren 82
Fetwa 163
feucht 227
Feuchtgebiete 218
Feuchtigkeit 227

Feuchtigkeitscreme 39
feuchtwarm 227
Feuer 52, 230, 235
feuern 126, 316
Feuerversicherung 307
Feuerwaffe 132
Feuerwehrfahrzeug 284
Feuerwehrleute 136
Feuerzeug 201
Fieber 68, 76
Figur 15, 246
Film 171, 175, 176
Filmfan 199
Filmfestspiele 184
Filmindustrie 175
Filmregisseur 176
Filmstar 175
Filter 171
Filterzigarette 201
Filzschreiber 313
Filzstift 313
Finanzamt 113
Finanzausschuss 103
Finanzchef 304
finanziell 304
finanzieren 304
Finanzierung 101
Finanzkraft 304
Finanzmärkte 304
Finanzminister 105, 304
Finanzministerium 304
Finanzpolitik 304
finden 193, 251, 286
Finger 12, 13
Fingerbreit 250
Fingernagel 12
Finne 153
Firma 226, 279, 298, 301, 315
Firmenbriefpapier 313
Firmenwert 306
Firmung 163
Fisch 55, 58, 233
Fisch(art) 234
Fischen 199
Fischer 310
Fischkutter 291
Fischteich 216
Fischzucht 220
fit bleiben 83
Fitnesscenter 94
Fitnessstudio 84
Fitnesstraining 83
Fix 128
fixen 128
Fläche 168, 215, 246
Flachland 218
Flachrelief 169
Flagge 292

Flanke 196
flanken 196
Flasche 38
Flaschenöffner 59
Flechte 237
Fleck 92
Flegel 18
Fleisch 55
Fleischer 309, 310
fleißig 23
flexibel 22
Fliege 66, 234
fliegen 52, 250, 289
Fliegen 289
Fliehkraft 241
Fließband 257
fließen 216, 259
fließend 241
Flipflops 65
Flitterwochen 48
Floh 234
Flohbiss 234
Flohstich 234
Flora 236
florierend 298
Floß 291
flott 15, 16
Flotte 291
Flug 188, 206, 289
Flugbahn 206
Flugbegleiter 290
Flügel 100
Fluggast 290
Fluggesellschaft 289
Flughafen 289
Flugkapitän 290
Fluglehrer 309
Fluglinie 289
Fluglotse 290
Flugplan 289
Flugplatz 119
Flugpreise 289
Flugschein 289
Flugsteig 290
Flugwetter 289
Flugzeit 289
Flugzeug 289, 290
Flugzeug entführen 132
Flugzeugabsturz 289
Flugzeugentführer 131, 290
Flugzeugentführung 131, 290
Flugzeugführer 290
Fluid 241
Flur 88
Fluss 215, 216, 229
Flussbett 217
flüssig 241
Flüssigkeit 39, 241, 245
Flüssigkristallanzeige 277
Flusstal 218

Flussufer 216
Flut 217, 229, 238
Flut- 229
Flutwelle 229
Föderation 99
Föhn 39
föhnen 38
Folge 271
folgen 294
folgendermaßen 176
Fondsverwalter 304
Förderband 258
fordern 229, 316
fördern 124, 303
Forelle 55, 56
Form 180
Format 277
formatieren 277
Formation 210
Formel 243
Formular 307
Forschung 145, 242
Forschungseinrich-
tungen 224
Forschungsfrage
146
Forschungsinstitut
149
Forschungsprojekt
262
Forschungsstipen-
dium 146
Forschungsvorha-
ben 146
Förster 310
Fortbildung 127
fortlaufend 156
Fortschritt 254
fortschrittlichste
262
fossil 226
Fossil 211
Foto 171, 172, 202
Foto- 171
Fotoapparat 171
Fotoausrüstung 171
fotogen 171
Fotogeschäft 194
Fotograf 171, 309
Fotografie 171
fotografieren 171, 199
fotografisch 171
Fotokopie 264, 313
fotokopieren 264,
313
Fotokopierer 313
Fotomodell 311
Fototermin 306
Foul 197
Foyer 192
Frachter 291
Frachtschiff 291
Frack 64
Frage 105, 166, 265
Fragen stellen 281

Fraktur 71
Frankfurter 267
Frankfurter
Würstchen 55
französisch 141
Fratz 50
Frau 15, 122
Frauen- 136
Frauenarzt 75
Frauenbewegung 98
Frauenfeindlichkeit
136
Frauenheilkunde 244
Frauenheld 49
Frauenrechte 98
Frauenrechtlerin 98
Frauenzeitschrift 268
Fräulein 122
frech 24
Frechheit 13, 275
frei 82, 296, 309
frei fahren 293
frei haben 182
frei laufend 221
frei nehmen 182
Freiberufler 309
freiberuflich 309
Freie 168
freie Hanteln 84
Freigabe 128
freigeben 51
Freigebigkeit 31
Freihandel(szone)
117
Freiheit 158, 268,
321
freilassen 110, 111
freisetzen 126
Freisetzen 316
Freistoß 197
Freitod 42
Freiwillige 21
Freizeichen 275
Freizeit 181, 198,
270
Freizeitbeschäfti-
gung 198
Freizeitkleidung 64
Freizeitpark 187
fremdenfeindlich 134
Fremdenfeindlich-
keit 134
Fremdenführer 189
Fremdenfurcht 134
Fremdenhass 134
Fremdenpension 191
Fremdsprache 150
Fremdsprachen-
unterricht 154
Frequenz 241
fressen 25
Freude 16, 28, 31,
144
Freund 23, 34, 185
Freundin 34, 185

Freundlichkeit 31, 35
Freundschaft 34
Freundschaftsspiel
196
Friede 31
Frieden 29, 41
Friedensabkommen
117
Friedensbewegung
98
Friedensplan 117
Friedenstruppen 117
Friedhof 41
frieren 227
Fries 169
frigide 37
Frigidität 37
Frikadelle 55
frisch 56, 59, 62,
227, 228, 235
frisch gemahlen 27
Frischmilch 59
Friseur 39, 194
Frisur 16
Fritten 61
Frittenbude 61
froh 88, 183
fröhlich 183
frönen 199
Frontalzusammen-
stoß 71
Frosch 234
Frost 227
fruchtbar 219, 220
Fruchtfolge 221
Fruchtsaft 57, 60
Fruchtwechsel 221
früh 1138
früher 19, 48, 49,
96, 257, 311
Frühjahrs- 298
Frühstück 60, 191,
192
frühstücken 60
Frühstücksbüfett 63
Frühstücksraum 192
Frühvorstellung 175
Fuchs 233
Fuchsie 236
Fuchsschwanz 255
fuchsteufelswild 30
fühlen 27, 28, 52,
84
führen 69, 108, 189,
193, 274
führend 100, 257,
267
Führer 33, 102, 189
Führerschein 110,
286
Führung 33, 188, 314
Führungsstil 299
füllen 79
Füller 313
Füll(feder)halter 313

füllig 15
Füllung 79
Fundamentalismus
163
Fundbüro 288
Funk- 282
Funke 259
Funker 292
Funktelefon 274
Funktion 247
funktionieren 260
Funktionsbezeich-
nung 309
Funktionsstörung 73
Funktionstaste 278
Furcht 28
furchtbar 93, 227
fürchten 30, 160
furchterregend 267
Furunkel 69
Fusion 301
Fusionsreaktor 262
Fuß 12, 72, 78, 250
Fußball 196
Fußballmeister 197
Fußballplatz 195
Fußballrowdy 131
Fußballspiel 270
Fußballweltmeister-
schaft 196
Fußbekleidung 65
Fußboden 92
Fußgängerüberweg
285
Fußmatte 91
Fußnote 266
Fußpilz 70
Futter 54
Futtertrog 222

G

Gabel 59
Gabentausch 139
galaktisch 204
Galaxie 204
Galaxis 204
Galerie 169
Gallenstein 69
galoppierend 297
Gang 62, 88, 256
Gangster 131
Ganove 131
Gans 55, 233
Gänseblümchen 235
ganz 156, 262, 344
Ganze 166
ganze Note 174
ganze Zahl 247
ganzer Ton 174
Garage 88
Garantie 301
garantieren 301
Garderobe 61
Garderobenfrau 63
Gardine 91

Garnelen 55
garnieren 58
Garten 88, 219, 236
Gartenarbeit 198, 199
Gartenpflanze 235
Gärtner 311
Gas 27, 241
gasförmig 241
Gaskammer 43
Gast 61, 62, 186
Gäste haben 60
Gästezimmer 87
gastfreundlich 192
Gastfreundschaft 186
Gastgeber(in) 186
Gasthaus 191
gastlich 192
gastrisch 245
Gatte 49
Gattin 49
GAU 44
Gaumenspalte 74
Gauner 32
gearbeitet 169
geb. 10
Gebäck 54
Gebärmutter 14
Gebäude 33, 73, 87, 134, 177, 178
geben 77
Gebet 163
gebeugt 15
Gebiet 97, 142, 146, 215, 229, 250, 308
gebildet 208
Gebirge 218
gebirgig 215
Gebirgszug 218
Gebiss 79
geboren 10, 208
Gebot 160, 162
gebrannt 52
Gebräuche 138
gebrauchen 180
gebräuchlich 186
Gebrauchsgrafik 170
Gebrauchsgrafiker 170
gebrechlich 21
Gebrechlichkeit 21
Gebühr 284
gebunden 266
Geburt 50, 74, 158
Geburtenkontrolle 37, 98
Geburtsdatum 10
Geburtsfehler 73
Geburtshelfer 244
Geburtshilfe 244
Geburtsort 10
Geburtsstadt 223
Geburtstag 10, 184, 249

Geburtstag haben 184
Geburtsurkunde 50
Geburtswehen 50
Gebüsch 219
Gedächtnis 143
Gedanke 29
Gedankengut 100
Gedärm 76
Gedeck 62
gedeihen 221
Gedicht(e) 154, 180
gedrungen 15
Geduld 31
geduldig 22, 24
geeignet 101
gefährden 82
Gefährte 33, 49
Gefährtin 33
Gefälle 215
gefallen 26, 29, 30, 44
gefangen nehmen 120
Gefangene 120
Gefängnis 111, 314
Gefäß 261
Gefecht 119
gefesselt an 74
Geflügel 55, 221
Geflügelkäfig 222
Geflügelzüchter 221
Gefrierpunkt 227
Gefrierschrank 90
Gefühl 25, 27, 28, 144
gegen 118, 196, 217
gegen den Strom 238
Gegend 26, 97, 215, 218, 219, 224
Gegenoffensive 119
gegenseitig 33
Gegenseitigkeit 139
Gegenspionage 118
Gegenstand 168
gegenständlich 169
gegenüber 35
Gegner 35, 44
gegossen 169
gegrillt 192
Gehacktes 58
gehauen 169
Gehäuse 171, 282
geheim 116
Geheimdienst 106, 118
gehemmt 22, 23
gehen 13, 14, 144, 155, 185, 186, 219, 287, 302
Gehirn 12
Gehirnerschütterung 71
Gehirntumor 12, 81

Gehör 26, 174
gehören zu 187
Gehorsam 32
Gehsteig 285
Geige 173
Geiselnahme 131
Geist 31, 83, 143, 160, 166, 271
Geistesgeschichte 140
geistesgestört 144
geisteskrank 144
Geisteskrankheit 68, 73
geistig 51, 73, 144
geistig behindert 73
geistig-seelisch 144
Geistliche 122, 136, 163
Geistlichkeit 163
Geiz 32
Geizhals 13
geizig 23
gekleidet 16, 64
gekocht 54, 192
gekürzt 267
geladen 240
gelähmt 74
Gelände 215, 308
gelangen zu 117
gelaunt 24
gelb 236
Gelbe Seiten 274
Gelbsucht 69
Geld 302, 303
Geld anlegen 308
Geldanlage 304
Geldautomat 302
Geldbetrag 302
Geldbeutel 303
Geldbuße 286
Geldgier 32
Geldpolitik 304
Geldstrafe 111, 132, 294
gelegen 216
Gelegenheitsgedicht 180
gelegentlich 82
gelehrt 146
Gelehrte 140
Gelenk 14
Gelenkentzündung 245
Gelenkrheumatismus 245
Geliebte 49
Geliebter 49
gelten als 110
geltend machen 307
Geltung verschaffen 109
gemacht aus 255
Gemälde 168
gemäß 300, 307

gemäßigt 100, 228
gemein 247
Gemeinde 97, 163
Gemeinderat 163
Gemeindeverwaltung 97
Gemeinkosten 303
gemeinnützig 96, 298
gemeinsam 100, 247, 304
Gemeinschaft 96
Gemeinschaftskunde 142
Gemeinschaftsleben 138
Gemenge 243
Gemetzel 133
Gemisch 243
gemischt 56, 197
Gemüse 55, 94, 221
Gen 237
Gendarm 17
Genealogie 140
Genehmigung 308
General 118
Generaldirektor 299
Generalkonsulat 189
Generalsekretär 117
Generalstab 118
Generalstreik 107, 315
Generation 20, 46
Generator 259
genetisch 237
Genick 12
genießen 28, 29
Genitalien 14
Gentechnik 222
genug 83
Geochronologie 210
geöffnet 189
Geografie 210
geografisch 214
Geologe 210
Geologie 210
geologisch 210
Geometrie 246
geometrisch 246
Geotektonik 210
Geowissenschaft 150
Gepäck 190, 288
Gepäckaufbewahrung 190, 288
Gepäckfach 290
Gepäckschließfach 190
Gepäckstück 190
Gepäckträger 288
Gepäckversicherung 190
gepflegt 16, 64
geplagt von 144
geplatzt 69, 286
gepolstert 196

gerade 15, 248
Gerät 255, 259, 260, 262, 270
geraten 35, 76, 130
Geräteschuppen 88, 222
Gerättauchen 199
Geräusch 26
geräuschlos 26
geräuschvoll 26
gerecht 22, 32
Gerechtigkeit 32
Gericht 59, 109
gerichtlich vorgehen 109
Gerichtsverfahren 109
gering 205
gern 13, 19, 28, 199
gern haben 28
gern tun 199
Geruch 27
Geruchssinn 25
gesamt 290
Gesamt- 297
Gesamtfläche 215
Gesamtschule 148
Gesandte 116
Gesang 173
Gesangstunden 173
Gesäß 13
gesättigt 243
Geschäft(e) 26, 27, 298
Geschäfte machen 298
geschäftlich 182, 298
Geschäfts- 298
Geschäftsführer 62, 102
Geschäftsjahr 304
Geschäftskarte 312
Geschäftsleben 298
Geschäftsleute 136
Geschäftsmann 298
Geschäftssinn 298
Geschäftsviertel 97
geschehen 31
gescheitert 49, 108
Geschenk 193
Geschenkladen 194
Geschichte 140, 150, 156, 169, 230
geschichtlich 140
Geschichtsforscher 140
Geschichtsforschung 140
Geschichtswissenschaft 140
geschieden 11
Geschirr 59, 92, 93
Geschirrspüler 63
Geschirrtuch 93

Geschlecht 11, 36, 136
Geschlechts- 36
Geschlechtsakt 36
Geschlechtskrankheit 37
geschlechtsneutral 136
Geschlechtsteile 14
Geschlechtsverkehr 36
geschliffen 213
geschlossen 315
Geschmack 27
Geschmackssinn 25
geschockt 211
Geschoss 87
geschützt 278
Geschwistermord 42
geschwollen 14, 70
Geschworene 109
Geschwulst 69
Geschwür 69
Gesellschaft 10, 34, 96, 138, 145, 185, 298, 299
Gesellschaft leisten 185
gesellschaftlich 98, 142, 145
Gesellschafts- 145
Gesellschaftsordnung 138
Gesetz 32, 103, 104, 109, 163, 165, 240
Gesetz des Dschungels 238
gesetzgebende Gewalt 102
gesetzlich 182
Gesicht 12, 16
Gesichtsfarbe 16
Gesichtspuder 39
Gesichtsschutz 196
gesinnt 35
gespannt 116
gesperrt 291
Gespräch 35, 144, 275
Gestalt 15
gestalten 156, 177, 279
gestaltend 305
Gestaltung 177
Gestank 27
Gestein(e) 210
Gesteinsprobe 206
gestört 28, 144, 274
gesund 68
Gesundheit 21, 82
Gesundheitsamt 245
gesundheitsbewusst 82
Gesundheitsfanatiker 82

Gesundheitsfarm 82
gesundheitsfördernd 82
Gesundheitsfürsorge 115
Gesundheitspflege 67
Getränke 57, 200
Getreide 54, 221
getrennt leben 49
Getriebe 256
Gettobewohner 223
Gewächshaus 88, 222
gewähren 134, 303, 307
Gewalt 107, 133, 136, 307
Gewaltakt 107
Gewaltanwendung 19
Gewaltenteilung 102
gewaltig 229
Gewaltkriminalität 110, 131
Gewaltlosigkeit 107
Gewalttat 107
gewalttätig 133
Gewalttätigkeit 29, 131, 133
Gewaltverbrechen 131
Gewaltverbrecher 131
Gewässer 291
Gewebe 245
Gewerbe 298
Gewerbeabfälle 226
Gewerbesteuer 114
Gewerkschaft 314, 316
Gewerkschaft(l)er 314
Gewerkschafts- 314
Gewerkschaftsbund 314
Gewerkschaftsmitglied 314
Gewicht 11, 76, 241, 250
Gewichtheben 84
Gewinde 255
Gewinn 296, 300
Gewinnanteil 304
Gewinn bringend 300
gewinnen 104, 177, 195, 197, 248
Gewinnspanne 300
Gewinnwarnung 300
Gewissen 31
Gewitter 228
Gewohnheitsverbrecher 131
gewöhnlich 122

Gewürz(e) 55
Gewürzgurke 29
Gewürzkräuter 55
Gezeiten 217
Gibraltar 216
Gicht 70
Gier 32
gieren 29
gießen 228, 261
giftig 242
Giftmüll 226
Giftpilz 236
Gipfel 218
Gipfeltreffen 116
Gipsfigur 169
Girokonto 303
glänzend 172
Glanzparade 196
Glas 59, 178, 254
Gläschen 200
glatt 16
Glatze 16
Glaube 32, 158
glauben 158, 160, 161, 164
Glaubensbekenntnis 163
Glaubensgemeinschaft 159
Glaubenszweifel 164
Glaziologie 210
gleich 247
Gleichberechtigung 98, 135, 136
gleicher Post 272
gleichgeschlechtlich 98
Gleichgewicht 241
gleichgültig 34
Gleichgültigkeit 34
Gleichnis 162
Gleichstrom 259
Gleichung 247
Gleis 288
Gletscher 211
global 228, 265
Glocke 91
Glossar 264
Glück 197
Glücksstern 208
Glückwunsch 184
Glühbirne 259
Glühfadenlampe 260
Glühlampe 260
GmbH 299
Gold 212
golden 212
goldene Hochzeit 48
Goldfisch 234
Goldhochzeit 184
Goldmedaille 212
Golf 216
Golfplatz 195
gönnen 35

Gonorrhöe 37
googeln 264
Gör(e) 18
Gosse 208
gotisch 169, 177
Gott 23, 160, 161, 164
Gottesdienst 162
Gottheit 160
Göttin 160
göttlich 161
Göttlichkeit 160, 161
Gouverneur 105
Grab 41
Grabinschrift 41
Grabmal 41
Grabstein 41
Grad 71, 153, 214, 247
Graduierung 153
Grafik 170
Grafikdesigner 170
Grafiker 170
grafisch 170
Grafschaft 97
Gras 236
grasen 220
Grasland 218
Gratissoftware 276
grau werden 16
Graubrot 54
Gräueltaten 133
Graveur 170
gravieren 170
Gravitation 205
Gravitationsfeld 241
Gravitationstheorie 205
greifen nach 208
Greifvogel 233
Grenze 116, 204
Grenzkonflikt 116
Grenzstreitigkeit 116
Griechenland 164
griechisch 160, 165
griechisch-orthodox 158
grillen 59
Grimmdarm 245
grinsen 30
Grippe 69, 94
Grislibär 233
grob 23
grober Unfug 131
Groll 35
Groschenheft 179
groß 11, 52, 69, 97, 168, 193, 217, 219, 229, 250, 267, 300, 302
groß (gewachsen) 15
Groß- 47
Großbanken 303
Großbritannien 102, 214

Größe 11, 247
Große Wagen 205
größer 229
Großhandel(s-) 300
Großhändler 300
großjährig 19
Großmutter 24
Großraum 97, 224
Großraumbüro 312
Großstadt 97
Großstädter 223
größte 73
größte Teil 198
Großwild 233
großziehen 51
großzügig 23
Großzügigkeit 31
grün 38, 56, 189, 220
Grund 112, 184, 292
Grundbedürfnisse 130
Grundbegriff 165
Grundbesitzer 108
Grundbuch 308
Grunderwerbsteuer 114
Grundfläche 247
Grundfreibetrag 114
Grundlagen-forschung 240
grundlegend 146
gründlich 78, 92
Grundlinie 197
Grundrechenarten 246
Grundregeln 151
Grundriss 177
Grundsatz 162, 166
Grundsatzpapier 142
Grundschuld 308
Grundschule 148
Grundsteuer 114
Grundstück(e) 308
Grundstückseigen-tümer 308
Grundstücksmakler 308
Grundstücksmarkt 308
Grundstückspreise 308
Grundstücksspeku-lant 178, 308
Grundstücks-verwaltung 308
Grüne 225
Grünflächen 223
Grüngürtel 219, 223
Gruppe 33, 99, 134, 156
Gruppenanruf 202
Gruppendynamik 145
Gruppentherapie 144

grüßen 49
gucken 91
Guerilla 108
Guerillakämpfer 108, 120
Guerillakrieg 108, 120
Guillotine 43
gültig 189
Gültigkeit 144
Gummi(-) 254
Gummistiefel 65
Gunsten 109
Gurke 24, 56
Gürtel 66
Guss 228
Gut 31
gut 23, 31, 166, 216, 271
gut ausgebildet 154
gut aussehend 15, 208
gut besucht 175
gut gehen 298
gut gehend 298
gut tun 83, 228
gutartig 69
Güte 31
gute Reise 188
Gutenachtgeschichte 51
Güterzug 287
gütig 23
Gutschein 306
Gutshaus 220
Gymnasium 148
Gynäkologe 75
Gynäkologie 244

H
Haar(e) 12, 16
Haarbürste 38
Haare schneiden 38
Haare waschen 39
Haartrockner 39
Haarwäsche 38
Haarwaschmittel 38
haben 200, 345
Habgier 32
habgierig 32
Habsucht 32
Hackfleisch 58
Hafen 217, 292
Hafenanlagen 217
Hafenarbeiter 15, 310
Hafenstadt 217
Hafer 54
Haferbrei 55, 82, 192
Haferflocken 55
Haferkleie 82
Haft 112
Haftbefehl 112
Haftpflichtver-sicherung 307

Haftung 298
Hai(fisch) 234
halb 251, 302
halb durch 59
Halbbruder 46
halbe Note 174
Halbedelstein 213
halber Ton 174
halbes Jahr 13
halbgar kochen 58
Halbinsel 217
Halbjahr 156
Halbkugel 214
Halbleiter 240, 255
Halbmond 230
Halbpension 191
Halbschuhe 65
Halbschwester 46
halbstündig 293
Halbtonbild 170
Halbzeit 196
Hälfte 219, 288
Halle 192
Hals 12, 75
Halskette 212
Halsschmerzen 12, 69, 75
Halstuch 66
halten 12, 103, 151, 160, 195, 232, 285, 288
Haltung 15, 28
Hammelfleisch 55
Hammer 255
Hämorriden 70
Hamster 233
Hand 12, 13, 233
Handarbeit 198
Handballplatz 195
Handbuch 264
Handel 281, 298
handeln 23, 31
handeln mit 298
handeln von 176
handelnde Person 176
Handels- 298
Handelsbilanz 297
Handelsenglisch 298
Handelshemmnisse 117
Handelskammer 298
Handelsminister 298
Handelsministerium 298
Handelspartner 117
Handelsschiff 291
Handelsschranken 117, 297
Handelsschule 148
Handelsverkehr 298
Handelsvertreter 300
Handfeger 93
Handfeuerwaffe 132

Handgepäck 290
Handlung 108, 155, 176, 180
Handpuppe 17
Handschuhe 66
Handtasche 261
Handtaschendieb 132
Handtaschenraub 132
Handtuch 38
handvermittelt 275
Handwerker 310
Handy 274, 279
Handzeichnung 170
Handzettel 306
Hanteln 84
Harmonie 174
Harn 13
Harnwege 245
hart 16, 24, 128, 200, 299
hart gekocht 58
harter Porno 37
Harzholz 254
Hasch(isch) 128
Hase 55
Haselnuss 56
Hass 29
hassen 29
hässlich 16
Hässliche 166
hauen 19, 51, 133
häufig 68, 281
Haupt- 187
Hauptgericht 63
Hauptinteressen 198
Hauptmann 118, 182
Hauptrichtung 159
Hauptrolle 175
hauptsächlich 221
Hauptschalter 259
Hauptschiff 178
Hauptschule 148
Hauptsendezeit 271
Hauptstraße 224
Hauptverkehrsstraße 284
Hauptverkehrszeiten 285
Haus 86, 87, 178, 308
Haus besetzen 125
Hausarbeit 51, 92
Hausarbeit(en) 154
Hausarzt 75
Hausaufgabe 155
Hausaufgabe(n) 154, 156
Hausbesetzer 125
Hausbesuch 77
Hausboot 87
Häuschen 87
Hausflur 87
Hausfrau 309, 311

Hausfriedensbruch 131
Haushalt 104, 297, 309
Haushälterin 311
Haushaltsarbeit 92
Haushaltsausschuss 103
Haushaltsdefizit 297
Haushaltskürzungen 297
Haushaltslöcher 297
Haushaltsplan 104
Haushaltsstopp 297
Hausmann 311
Hausmannskost 58
Hausmeister 310
Hausmüll 226
Hausratversicherung 307
Hausschuhe 65
Hausse 304
Haustier 232
Haustür 88
Hauswirtschaftslehre 150
Haut 13, 14, 69, 77
Hautfarbe 135
Hauttransplantation 245
Hebamme 50, 244
Hebel 255
Heck 292
Hecke 219
Hedgefonds 304
Heer 118
Hefe(n) 237
heftig 22, 76, 229, 301
Heftklammer 313
Heftmaschine 313
Heftpflaster 72
Hegemonie 139
hegen 134
Heide 219
Heidekraut 219
Heidemoor 219
Heilberufe 244
Heilbutt 55
heilen 129
heilig 158, 160, 162, 163
Heiligabend 183
Heilige 162
Heilige Geist 160
Heilmittel 70, 77
Heilpraktiker 244
Heilsarmee 159
Heim 86
Heimatforschung 140
Heimatgeschichte 140
Heimatstadt 97
Heimspiel 196

heimsuchen 230
Heimwerken 199
Heimwerker 94, 199
Heirat 48
heiraten 48
Heiratsantrag 48
Heiratsurkunde 48
heiß 215, 219, 227
heißen 10, 158, 160
Heißhunger 29
Heizkessel 91
Heizkörper 91
Held 176, 208
helfen 13, 125
Helligkeit 172
Hellraumschreiber 155
Helm 66, 196
Hemd 16, 38, 92, 93
Hemdbluse 64
Hemisphäre 214
Herannahen 20
Heranwachsende 18
heranwinken 294
herausbringen 267
Herausforderer 195
herausfordern 195
Herausforderung 195
herausgefordert 73
herauskommen 227
herausnehmen 155
herbeiwinken 294
Herd 59, 90
Hering 55
Herkunft 46
Hermeneutik 166
Hernie 69
Heroin 128, 129
heroinsüchtig 128
Herr 23, 41, 160
Herr Ober 62
Herrenhaus 87
Herrenschneider 310
herrlich 168, 198
Herr(n) 122
Herrscher 23
herstellen 255, 257
Hersteller 257
Herstellerfirma 257
Herstellung 257
Herstellungsablauf 257
Herstellungsprozess 257
herumreisen 188
heruntergekommen 224
herunterladen 265, 277
hervorheben 202, 277
Herz 13, 68
Herzaktivität 83
Herzanfall 68

Herzbeschwerden 69
Herzchirurgie 81
Herzinfarkt 68, 69
Herzjagen 69
Herzklopfen 69
herzkrank 13, 68
Herzkrankheit 68
herzlich 34, 184
Herzog(in) 121
Herzversagen 69
heterosexuell 36
Heterosexuelle 36
hetzen 29
Heu 221
Heuchler 32
Heuhaufen 222
Heuschnupfen 68
Heuschober 221
Heuschrecke 230
Heuschreckenplage 230
heute 155, 189, 193
heute Abend 60, 83, 175, 185, 186, 270
heute Morgen 227, 345
heutig 18
Hexe 155, 164
Hexenschuss 70
Hexerei 164
Hilfsarbeiter 309
Hilfskellner 63
Hilfsmittel 25, 154
Himbeeren 56
Himmel 52, 160, 162, 228
Himmelskörper 204
himmlisch 208
Hin- u. Rückfahrt 288
hin und zurück 188
Hindu(-) 158
Hinduismus 158
hinduistisch 158, 160
hinfällig 21
hingeben 199
hinkommen 294
hinlegen 77
hinnehmen 29
Hinreise 288
hinrichten 43
Hinrichtung 43
Hinrichtungsmethode 43
Hinscheiden 40
Hinterbänkler 102
Hinterbliebene 42
Hintergrund 138
Hinterhof 88
hinterlassen 69
Hintern 13, 14, 208
Hinterteil 13
Hintertür 88
Hinterwäldler 219
hinzufügen 202
Hiob 24

Hirnhautentzün-
dung 70, 74
Hirsch(e) 55, 233
Historiker 140
historisch 140, 179,
210
Hitze 29, 227, 255
Hitzewelle 227
Hitzschlag 68
HIV-positiv 70
HNO-Arzt 75
Hobby 168, 198, 199
Hobel 255
Hobelmaschine 255
hobeln 255
hoch 69, 201, 218,
225, 247, 271,
294, 308, 316
hoch gelobt 176
hoch nehmen 93
Hochauflösung 277
Hochbahn 293
Hochdruck 170
Hochebene 218
hochfahren 277
Hochgeschwindig-
keits- 287
Hochglanz- 171
hochhackig 65
Hochhaus 87, 178
hochinnovativ 262
hochladen 202, 277
Hochland 218
Hochmoor 219
Hochmut 32
hochnehmen 93
Hochrelief 169
Hochschulbildung
148
Hochschule 149, 240
Hochspannung 259
Hochsprung 196
höchst 304
Hochstapler 132
höchstes Wesen 161
Hochtechnologie
254
Hochverrat 108
Hochwasser- 229
hochwassergefähr-
det 229
Hochwürden 122
Hochzeit 48, 184,
212
Hochzeitskleid 48, 64
Hochzeitsmahl 184
Hochzeitsreise 48
Hochzeitstag 49, 184
Hocker 90
Hof 88
Hofdichter 180
hoffen 30
hoffentlich 30, 227
Hoffnung 30, 32,
216

Hoffnungslosigkeit
130
höflich 22, 23
Höflichkeit 10, 35
Hoheitsgebiet 215
Hoheitsgewässer
215, 291
Höhensonne 83
Höhepunkt 20, 36,
180
höhere Gewalt 307
höhere Schule 148
Höherstufung 290
hohes Gericht 122
hohläugig 16
Höhle 218
Höhle des Löwen
238
holen 69, 76
Hölle 162
Holz(-) 254
Holzarbeiten 198
Holzbearbeitungs-
maschine 255
hölzern 254
Holzhütte 87
Holzkiste 261
Holzschnitt 170
Holzschnitzerei 169
Holzschuppen 88
Holzteile 257
Homo-Ehe 49
Homosexualität 36
homosexuell 36
Homosexuelle 36
Honig 192
Honorar 245
hörbar 26
hören 26, 52, 173,
198, 199, 270
hören, dass 211
Hörer 271, 274, 275
Hörfunk 270
Hörgerät 26
Hörhilfe 26
Horn 238
Hörnchen 60
Horoskop 164
Hörverständnis 151
Hörverstehen 151
Hose 65, 93
Hosen anhaben 49
Hosenanzug 64
Hosenträger 66
Hospital 80
Hotel 63, 188, 191
Hotel garni 192
Hotelempfang 192
Hotelhalle 192
Hotelportier 192
Hotelzimmer 191
hübsch 15, 216
Hubschrauber 290
Hubschrauber-
landeplatz 289

Hüftgürtel 65
Hüfthalter 65
hügelig 218
Huhn 55, 221
Hühnchen 13
Hühner 82, 221
Hühnerauge 70
Hühnerstall 222
human 346
Hummer 55
Humor 23
Hund 25, 232
Hundehütte 88
hunderte 229
100-Meter-Lauf 195
Hündin 232
Hunger 130
Hungerhilfe 230
Hungerkatastrophe
230
Hungern 130
hungern 130
hungers 42
Hungersnot 230
hungrig 130
Hure 37
Hurrapatriotismus 134
Hurrikan 229
husten 69
Husten 69
Hut 64, 65
Hutmacher 24
Hütte 87
Hüttenkäse 54
hydraulisch 241
Hygiene 38, 245
hygienisch 245
Hypothek 308
Hypothekenzinsen
276, 308
Hypothese 146

I
Ich 166
Ich-AG 127
Ich-Erzähler 179
ideal 31, 289
Ideal 31
Idealismus 166
Idealist 166
idealistisch 166
Idee 165, 166
ideeller Firmenwert
306
Ideengeschichte 140
identifizieren 146
Idiom 292
illegal 134
Illustrationen 170
Imbiss 61
Imbissstube 61
Imkerei 198
Imkern 199
immer mehr 285
immergrün 236

Immobilien 308
Immobiliengeschäft
308
Immobilienmakler
124, 308
Immobilienmarkt
308
Immobilienpreise
308
Immunschwäche
245
Immunsystem 245
Imperium 96
Impfausweis 190
Impfpass 190
Impfstoff 70
Impfung 190
Impfzeugnis 190
Import 301
importieren 301
impotent 37
Impotenz 37
Impressionismus 169
inbegriffen 62
Index 264
indianisch 138
Indien 140
Industrie 242
Industrieanlagen 119
Industrieerzeugnisse
257
industriell 141, 258
Industrielle 299
Industrieroboter 258
Industriestadt 223
Industriezweig 314
Infanterie 119
Infarkt 69
Infekt(ion) 68
Infektionskrank-
heiten 68
Inflation 297
Inflationsrate 297
Infopost 306
Informatik 150, 276
Information 118,
268, 237, 265
Informations- 265
Infrastruktur 262
Infusion 81
Ingenieurgeologie
210
Ingenieurstudium 154
Ingenieurwesen 254
Inhalt 180, 241
Inhalt(e) 202
Inhalt(sverzeichnis)
266
Injektion 77, 79
Inland 113
Inlandflug 289
Inlandspost 272
Inlay 79
Innenministerium
106

Innenpolitik 100
Innenstadt 97, 224, 229
innere 244
innere Station 80
innerhalb 34, 223, 291
inoperabel 81
Inschrift 140
Insekt 234
Insektizid 220
Insel 188, 217
Inserent 305
Inspektion 286
Instabilität 297
Installateur 310
Installation 277
installieren 277
Instandhaltung 258
Institution 138, 142, 162
Instrument 242
inszenieren 176
Inszenierung 176
Intarsien 169
integer 32
Integralrechnung 246
Integrität 32
Intellektuelle 29
intelligent 262
Intelligenz 143
Intelligenzquotient 143
Intelligenztest 144
intensiv 262
Intensivstation 81
interaktiv 265
Intercity 287
interessant 24, 29, 265
Interesse 29, 140, 198
Interessengebiet 198
Interessenkonflikt 35
interessieren 29
Internat 148
international 116, 142, 184, 207, 269, 273, 291
Internet 171, 265, 277, 279
Internet- 281
Internetauftritt 279
Internetcafé 280
internetfähig 279
Internetfirma 280
Internetforum 280
Internetzugang 279
Interpretation 180
interpretieren 180
Intervention 117
Interview 271
Interviewer 271
intim 34, 36

Intrauterinpessar 37
invalide 73
Invalide 73
Invalidität 73
Invaliditätsversiche-rung 307
Invasion 119
Inventar 301
investieren 113, 258, 304
Investition 304
Investitionsgüter 296
Investmentfonds 304
Investor 304
Inzest 139
Ion 243
IQ 143
Ire 251
Iren 230
irgendwelche 77
irisch 216
Irland 230
Ironie 180
irreführend 145, 305
Ischias 70
Islam 158
Islamfeindlichkeit 134
islamisch 158
Islamophobie 134
Isolierband 260
isolieren 260
Isolierung 260
isometrisch 84
Isotop 243
Israel 163
IWF 116

J
Jacht 291
Jacke 64, 65
Jackett 64
Jagd 199
Jagdhund 232
jagen 232
Jäger 310
Jahr 251, 293
Jahrbuch 264
jahrelang 86
Jahresprämie 307
Jahrestag 184, 249
Jahreszeit 227
Jahrgang 200
jährlich 307
Jahrmarkt 187
Jahrtausendflut 229
Jahve 160
Jalousie 91
jäten 236
jenseits 223
Jesus (Christus) 160, 162
joggen 83
Joggen 199
Joghurt 54, 261

Johannisbeeren 56
Jokerzeichen 281
Journalismus 268
Journalist 268
Jubiläum 184
Jucken 70
Juckreiz 70
Judaismus 158
Jude 133, 158, 159, 162
Judentum 158
Jüdin 158
jüdisch 158, 160
Jugend 17, 18, 52
Jugend- 19
Jugendbewegung 98
Jugendgericht 19
Jugendherberge 18, 191
Jugendklub 18
jugendlich 112
Jugendliche 18, 134
Jugendstil 169, 177
Jugendstrafanstalt 19
Jugend(zeit) 18
jung 15, 18, 19, 74
Junge 130
junge Leute 18
jungenhaft 44
Junges 233
Jungfernfahrt 291
Junggeselle 48
Juni 221
Junta 108
Jupiter 204
Jury 109
Juwel 213
Juwelier 194
jwd 215

K
Kabel 260, 279
Kabelfernsehen 270
kabellos 276, 279
Kabine 26
Kabinengepäck 290
Kabinett 105
Kabinettsmitglied 121
Kabinettssitzung 105
Kabinettsumbildung 105
Kaddisch 41
Käfer 234
Kaffee 27, 56, 57, 60, 62, 192
Kaffeekanne 59, 261
Kaffeemaschine 59
Kaffeemühle 58
Kaffeeplantage 220
Käfig 234
Kaiser(in) 105
Kaiserschnitt 50, 81
Kakao 57
Kakerlake 234

Kaktus 236, 237
Kalbfleisch 55
Kalkstein 169
kalorienarm 54
kalt 227
Kälte 227
kälteempfindlich 78
Kaltluftfront 227
kaltmachen 43
Kalvinismus 159
Kamera 171, 172
Kamerad 33
Kameragehäuse 171
Kamerazubehör 171
Kamin 88
Kamm 39
kämmen 39
Kammer 102
Kammer- 173
Kampf 119, 120, 131, 133, 187, 195, 269
kämpfen 32, 133
Kampfhund 232
Kanal 217, 270
Kanaltunnel 189
Kanarienvogel 233
Kandidat 101, 104
kandidieren 101, 104
Kaninchen 55
Kanne 59, 261
Kantine 60, 61
Kanu 291
Kanzlei 312
Kap 216
Kapelle 174, 187
Kapital 296
Kapitalertrag(s)-steuer 114
Kapitalgesellschaft 299
Kapitalismus 99
Kapitalist 99
kapitalistisch 99
Kapitän 196, 291, 292
Kapitel 266
Kapitulation 120
kapitulieren 120
kaputt 30, 49
Kardinal 163
Kardiologie 244
Karfreitag 182
karg 220
Karies 79
Karikatur 170
karitativ 21
Karneval 184
Karte 175, 210, 224
Kartei 313
Karten spielen 17
Kartenspiel 199
Kartentelefon 275
Kartoffel 230
Kartoffelbrei 56
Kartoffelernte 230

Kartoffelkäfer 234
Kartoffeln 56, 58, 261
Kartoffelpuffer 56
Kartoffelsalat 56
Karton 261
Karussell 187
Käse 54
Kasino 187
Kasperletheater 187
Kasse 101, 115, 175, 192, 302
Kassenarzt 115
Kassenbrille 115
Kassenwart 304
Kassettenrekorder 271
kassieren 294
Kassierer 192, 310, 311
Kastanie 56, 235
Kasten 261
Katalog 264
Katalogpreis 300
Katalysator 243
Katastrophe 230, 306
Katastrophengebiet 229
Katechismus 163
Kater 129, 200, 232
Kathedrale 162
Kathode 243
Katholik 159
katholisch 158, 159
Katholizismus 158, 159
Kätzchen 233
Katze 70, 232
kauen 201
kaufen 193, 194, 300
Käufer 300
Kaufhaus 193
Kaufkraft 297
Kaufmann 298
kaufmännisch 298
kaum 26
Kausalgesetz 165
Kausalität 165
Kaution 111
Kautschuk 254
Kehle 12, 75
Kehlkopfent-
zündung 70
Keks 54, 261
Keller 88
Kellner 63, 154
Kellnerin 63
kennen lernen 34
kentern 292
Keramik(-) 254
keramisch 254
Kerl 32, 50
Kernfach 150
Kernkraft 98
Kernladungszahl 243

Kernphysik 240
Kernwaffen 119
Kessel 59, 90, 91
Kette 301
Kettenraucher 201
Keuchhusten 69
Kfz-Versicherung 307
kg 251
kichern 30
Kiefer 235
Kieselstrand 219
Kietz 97
Kilo 251
Kilogramm 251
Kind(er) 17, 46, 50, 51, 73, 290, 293
Kinder- 244
Kinderarbeit 17, 130
Kinderarzt 75
Kinderbekleidung 17
Kinderbett 17
Kinderchirurgie 244
Kindergarten 17, 148
Kinderheilkunde 244
Kinderkleidung 257
Kinderkrippe 17
Kinderlähmung 73
Kinderprostitution 130, 269
Kinderstation 244
Kinderstube 51
Kindertagesstätte 17
Kinderwagen 17
Kindesalter 17
Kindesmissbrauch 51
Kindesmisshandlung 17, 51
Kindesmord 42
Kindheit 17
Kino 175, 198
Kinofilm 175
Kinogänger 175
Kirche 48, 96, 159, 162
Kirchenarchitektur 178
Kirchenbuch 140
Kirchenchor 173
Kirchengemeinde 97, 163
Kirchengeschichte 140
Kirchhof 41
kirchliche Trauung 48
Kirchturm 178
Kirmes 187
Kirschbaum 236
Kirsche 56
Kissen 89
Kiste 201, 261
Kitzler 36
Klage 109
Klagen 316
Klammeraffe 280

klammern 222
Klamotten 64
Klang 26
Klappbett 89
Klappentext 266
Klappstuhl 90
Klappstulle 54
Klapptisch 90
Klaps 13
klar 227
Klasse 33, 148, 156, 249, 288
Klassenarbeit 153, 154, 156
Klassenbuch 155
klassenlos 145
Klassenstufe 148
Klassentreffen 185
Klassenzimmer 155
klassisch 173, 198
Klassizismus 169
klassizistisch 177
Klatschen 176
Klatschspalte 269
Klaustrophobie 134
Klausur 156
Klavier 173
Klebefilm 313
kleben 171
klebrig 44
Klee 236
Kleid 64
kleiden 16, 64
Kleiderschrank 89
Kleidung 16, 64, 196
Kleidungsstücke 66
Kleie 54
klein 15, 86, 300, 302
Kleinanzeige 305
Kleinbauern 220
Kleinbus 293
kleine Kinder 18
kleinere 229
Kleinkind 17
Kleinod 213
Kleinstadt 214, 223
Kleinstlebewesen 237
Klemmbrett 313
Klempner 310
Klerus 163
Klima 227, 228
Klimaanlage 26, 90, 94
Klimakatastrophe 230
Klimaveränderung 226, 228
Klimawandel 226
Klimawechsel 228
Klingel 91
klingeln 91
klingen 26
Klinik 80
Klinik(um) 244

klinisch 143, 244
Klischee 134
Klischeevorstellun-
gen 134
Klitoris 36
Klo 39, 90
klonen 222
klopfen 93
Kloß 55
Kloster 163
Klub 33, 185
klug 23
Klugheit 32
Klumpfuß 74
km/h 250, 284
knacken 280
knapp 104, 302
knapp bei Kasse 302
knapp werden 226
knauserig 23
Knaus-Ogino-
Methode 37
knebeln 133
kneifen 238
Kneifzange 255
Kneipe 94
Knie 12
Kniebeuge 83
Knoblauch 44, 55
Knochen 14
Knochenbruch 71
Knochenmark 245
Knödel 55
Knopf 66
Knospe 236
Knoten(punkt) 279, 287
Koalition 100
Koch 63
Kochbuch 58
kochen 58
Kochen 58, 198
Kochherd 59
Köchin 63
Kochpunkt 243
Kochtopf 59, 92
kodieren 279
koffeinfrei 57
Koffer 190, 261
Kofferkuli 190, 288
Kohl 55
Kohle(n)hydrat 243
Kohlendioxid 226
kohlensäurehaltig 57
Kohlenstoff 242
Kohlenstoffnano-
röhre 262
Kohlenwasserstoff(-) 243
Kohlmeise 233
Koitus 36
Kokain 128, 251
Kokke 237
Kolben 256
kollabieren 68

K

Kollege 33, 312
Kollegin 33
Kollektion 298
Kölnischwasser 38, 39
Kolumne 269
Kolumnist 269
Komet 204
Komfort 94
Komik 179
komisch 179
Komma 246
Kommando 118
Kommandokapsel 207
Kommandowirtschaft 296
kommen zu 71, 229
Kommentator 271
kommerziell 207, 262, 298
Kommission 106
Kommode 89
Kommunalwahlen 224
Kommunikation 263
Kommunion 163
Kommuniqué 117
Kommunismus 99
Kommunist 101
kommunistisch 101
Komödie 179
Kompanie 86, 118
Komplize 33
Komplizin 33
Komplott 107
Komponieren 309
Komponist 173
Komposition 168, 173
Kompression 172
komprimieren 172, 279
Komprimierung 172, 277
Kompromiss 117
Kondensator 259
konditionieren 143
Konditionierung 143
Konditor 63
Kondom 37
Konfektionshaus 194
Konferenzzimmer 312
Konfession 158, 159
Konfessionsschule 159
Konfettiparade 184
Konfirmation 163
Konflikt 31, 35, 117, 142
Konföderation 96
Kongress 102, 104

Kongressabgeordnete 102
König 105, 108, 232
Königin 87, 105, 184
Königsmord 42
Konjunktur 127, 297
konjunkturell 126
Konjunkturpaket 297
Konjunkturrückgang 297
Konkurrent 33, 301
Konkurrenz 301
Konkurs 301
konnte 347
könnte 155
konservativ 23
Konservative 100
konsistent 165
Konstante 247
Konstellation 205
konstitutionell 99
Konstrukteur 311
Konsulat 189
Konsum 297
Konsumgüter 257
konsumieren 251
Kontakt 35, 202
kontaktfreudig 24
Konterrevolution 108
Kontinent 214
kontinental 214
Kontinental- 228
Kontinentaldrift 210
Kontinentalverschiebung 210
Konto 302, 303
Kontoüberziehung 303
Kontrolle 74, 296
kontrollieren 74
kontrolliert von 262
Kontrollzentrum 207
Konversation 35
Konversationslexikon 264
konvertieren 158
Konzentrationslager 133
konzentrieren 225
konzentriert 243
Konzern 113, 298
Konzert 174, 270
Konzession 301
Kopf 12, 78, 88
Kopf an Kopf 101
Kopfball 196
Kopfbedeckung 65
Köpfen 43
Kopfhörer 276
Kopfkissen 89
Kopfsalat 56
Kopfschmerzen 76, 78
Kopfsteuer 114

Kopftuch 66
Kopfverletzungen 71
Kopie 277
kopieren 265, 277
Kopierpapier 313
Kopplungsmanöver 206
Koran 163
Korbflechten 198
korinthisch 178
Korkenzieher 59
Korn 221
Kornblume 235
Körner 221
Körper 166, 241
körperbehindert 73
körperlich 19, 21, 73, 83, 270
Körperpflege 38
Körperschaftssteuer 114
Körperteil 12
Körperverletzung 131
Korps 119
korpulent 15
Korrektor 267
Korrektur lesen 267
Korrekturtriebwerk 206
Korrespondent 269
Korridor 87, 88
korrodieren 243
Korrosion 243, 255
korrupt 23
Korruption 32, 314
Korsett 65
koscher 163
Kosewort 50
Kosmetika 39
Kosmetikartikel 194
Kosmologie 205
Kosmonaut 206
Kosmos 204
Kost 54, 82, 191
kostbar 213
kosten 193, 302
Kosten 258, 297, 300
Kosten dämpfen 115
Kostenanschlag 305
kostendeckend 300
Kostensteigerungen 297
köstlich 27
Kostüm 64, 176
Kot 13, 14
Kotelett 58
Krabben 55
Krach 26
Kraft 241
Kraftfahrer 284
Kraftfahrtversicherung 307
Kraftfahrzeug 284
kräftig 15, 233
Kraftprobe 315

Kraftwerk 259
Krähe 233
Kralle 233
Krampf 70
Krampfadern 14, 70
krank 42, 76, 144
Krankengeld 115
Krankengeschichte 80
Krankenhaus 72, 80, 224
Krankenhauspfarrer 80
Krankenkasse 115
Krankenpflege 244
Krankenpfleger 81
Krankensalbung 40
Krankenschein 77
Krankenschwester 81
krankenversichert 307
Krankenversicherung 115
Krankenwagen 72
krankgeschrieben 182
krankhaft 144
Krankheit 42, 68, 74, 230, 244
Kranz 41
Krater 205
kraus 16
Kraut 236
Kräuter- 236
Kräutertee 57, 82
kreativ 305
Kreativität 144
Krebs 40, 69, 214
krebserregend 242
krebserzeugend 242
Kredit 303
Kreditkarte 303
Kreidefelsen 218
Kreidezeichnung 170
Kreis 97, 155, 247
Kreis- 247
kreisen 204, 207
kreisförmig 204, 247
Kreislauf 14
Kreissäge 65, 255
Kreisumfang 247
Kreisverkehr 285
Krematorium 41
Kreuz 158
Kreuzfahrer 141
Kreuzfahrt 291
Kreuzigung 43
Kreuzritter 141
Kreuzung 285
Kreuzverhör 110
Kreuzworträtsel 199
Kreuzzüge 141
Kricket 195
Kriechtier 234

Krieg 97, 118, 119, 269
Krieg erklären 119
kriegen 19, 69
Kriegsgefangene 120
Kriegsgericht 120
Kriegsmarine 118
Kriegsverbrechen 120
Kriegsverbrecher 120
Kriegsveteran 20
Krimi 176, 179
Kriminalbeamte 112
Kriminalität 131
Kriminalkommissar 112
Kriminalpolizei 112
Kriminalroman 179
kriminell 131
Krippe 222
Krischna 160
Krise 20, 117
Kristall 210, 243
Kritik 29, 164, 176
Kritiker 176
kritisch 72
Krokodil 234
Krokodilstränen 234
Krone 79
Kronjuwelen 213
Kronprinz 121
Kronprinzessin 121
Krönung 20
Kröte 234
Krug 59
Krümel 92
krumm 13
Krüppel 73
Kubismus 169
Küche 58, 63, 87
Kuchen 54, 58
Küchenchef 63
Küchenschabe 234
Küchenschrank 89
Küchentisch 90
Küchenuhr 90
Kugellager 256
Kugelschreiber 313
Kuh 158, 221
kühl 24, 227
kühler 227
Kühlschrank 90, 94
kühn 24
kühnste Träume 208
Kuhstall 222
Kulissen 176
kultivieren 220
kultiviert 22
Kultur 138, 142, 158
kulturell 36, 138, 224
Kulturgeschichte 140
Kulturpflanze 235
Kummerbund 66

kümmern 21
Kumpel 33
Kunde 193, 275, 300, 305
Kundenberater 305
Kundenbetreuer 305
Kundenbetreuung 193
Kundendienst 193
kündigen 125, 316
Kunst 100, 141, 150, 166, 169, 170, 212
Kunstakademie 149
Künstdünger 220
Kunstfehler(prozess) 245
Kunstgalerie 169
Kunstgewerbeladen 194
Kunsthändler 194
Kunsthandwerk 198
Kunsthandwerker 310
Künstler 48, 61, 168, 170
künstlerisch 198
künstlich 207, 212
Kunstrichtung 169
Kunststil 169
Kunststoff 255
Kunststoff- 254
Kunsttischler 310
Kunstwerk 169, 257
Kupfer 212
kupfern 212
Kupferstich 170
Kuppel 178
Kupplung(spedal) 256
Kur 82
Kurbel 255
Kurbelwelle 256
kurieren 129
Kurort 82
Kurs 292
Kursbuch 288
Kurs(us) 149, 150
Kurve 285, 287
kurz 155
kurz nach 290
Kurzarbeit 126, 316
kurzärmelig 64
kürzen 267
Kurzgeschichte 179
kürzlich 74
Kurzschluss 260
kurzsichtig 25
Kurzstrecke 294
Kürzung 267
Kurzzeitgedächtnis 143
Küsse 94
küssen 12
Küste 216

L

labil 241
Labor 242
Laborant 242
Laboratorium 242
lächeln 30
lachen 30
Lachs 55
Lade- 277
Ladegerät 282
laden 277
Ladenbesitzer 298
Ladendiebstahl 132
Ladenkasse 302
Ladenpreis 300
Ladenschlussgesetz 103
Ladentisch 193
Ladung 240
Lage 304
Lager 40, 256, 301
Lagerbestand 301
Lagerhaus 301
lagern 261
Lagerstätte 211
lahm legen 315
lahme Ente 106
Lähmung 74
Laken 89
Lamm 24, 238
Lammfleisch 55
Lampe 90
Land 96, 100, 119, 188, 215, 218, 220, 292, 308
Landarbeiter 220
Landebahn 290
Landefähre 206
Landefahrzeug 206
landen 206
Länderkennung 280
Landezone 206
Landklima 228
Landkreis 97
ländlich 219
Landmaschinen 220
Landschaft 168, 218
landschaftlich 218
Landschildkröte 234
Landwirt 220
Landwirtschaft 220
landwirtschaftlich 220
Landwirtschafts- 220
lang 192, 217, 293
langärmelig 64
Länge 214
Langlebigkeit 21
langsam 25, 83, 154, 293, 296
Längsschiff 178
langweilig 24
Langzeitarbeitslose 126

Langzeitgedächtnis 143
Lappen 93
Laptop 276
Lärm 26
Lärmbelästigung 225
Lärmbelastung 225
Laserdrucker 277
Lasertechnik 254
lassen 12, 13, 168, 189, 192, 291, 348
lässig 23
lasst uns 160
Laster 31, 284
Lasttier 232
Lastwagen 284
Lateinamerika 100, 214
Latte 196
Laub 236
Laubbaum 235
Laubwald 235
Lauf 187, 195
Laufband 84
laufen 12, 44, 73, 175, 176, 195
Laufen 83, 196
Läufer 15, 91
Laufwerk 277
Laufwettbewerb 196
Laune 28
Laus 234
lauschen 26
laut 26
Laut 26
laut lesen 154
lauten auf 110
lauter sprechen 26, 155, 275
Lautsprecher 260, 276
Lautstärke 26
Lava 229
Lava(schicht) 229
Lawine 229
lax 23
Lazarett 80
leasen 303
leben 13, 26, 218
leben von 188
Lebendigkeit 172
Lebensbedingungen 224
Lebensbeschreibung 179
Lebenserwartung 20, 130
Lebensgefährte 49
Lebensgefährtin 48
Lebensgemeinschaft 48
Lebenshaltungs- kosten 297
Lebensjahre 74

Lebenslauf 94
Lebensmittelhändler 194
Lebensmittelver- giftung 69, 74
Lebensstandard 130, 297
Lebensversicherung 307
Leber 13
Leberwurst 55
Lebewesen 231, 237
ledig 11
leer 208
leeren 91
Leerzeichen 279
Legalisierung 128
Legasthenie 74
legen 38
Legende 179
legere Kleidung 64
legieren 212
Legierung 212, 254
Legislative 102
Legislaturperiode 104
Lehrbeauftragte 310
Lehrbuch 154, 267
Lehrbuch- 267
Lehre 162
Lehren 154
lehren 154, 165
Lehrer 20, 154, 309
Lehrerin 309
Lehrgang 150
Lehrling 310
Lehrmaterial 154
Lehrmeinung 162
Lehrplan 151, 237
Leib 12
Leibesübungen 150
Leiche 40
Leichenöffnung 41
Leichenzug 41
leicht 68, 70, 78, 228, 254
Leichtathletik 83, 196
Leichtathletikwett- bewerb 83
leichte Musik 173
Leichtmetall 212
Leid 130
Leiden 68, 75, 130
leiden an 21, 72, 73, 74, 76
leiden unter 73
Leidenschaft 198, 199
leider 92, 173, 191, 292, 313
leidtragend 42
leihen 303
Leinen 266
Leinwand 168, 175
leisest 32

leisten 34, 72, 185, 193
Leistung 30, 241, 258
Leistungen 316
leistungsfähig 293
Leistungsfähigkeit 258
Leistungsgruppe 156
Leistungsschalter 260
Leistungstest 144, 152
Leitartikel 269
leiten 258
Leiter 240, 299, 309
Leitfähigkeit 255
Leitfossil 211
Leitung 174, 259, 260, 275
Leitungswasser 57
Leitzinsen 304
Lektor 267
Lektorat 267
lektorieren 267
Lektüre 267
lernbehindert 73
Lernbehinderungen 144
lernen 154
Lernen 154
Lernende 154
Lernpsychologie 143
Lernschwester 81
lesbar 155
Lesbe 36
Lesbierin 36
lesbisch 36, 98
lesen 154, 199, 267
Leser 266
Leserbriefe 269
Leseverständnis 151
Leseverstehen 151
Lesezeichen 281
Lesung 103
letzte 13, 74, 180, 289, 349
letzte Ruhe 41
letzte Stelle 197
letzter Wille 43
Leuchtdiode 94
leuchtend 16
Leuchtstofflampe 260
Leuchtturm 25, 292
leugnen 160
Leute 18, 46, 185
Leutstoffröhre 260
Lexikon 264
Licht 25, 90, 260
lichten 16
Lichtgeschwindig- keit 204, 241
Lichtjahr 204

Lichtmaschine 259
lichtstark 172
Lichtstärke 171
Lichtung 219
Lidschatten 39
Liebe 25, 28, 31, 32, 34
lieben 28, 34, 218
lieber 29, 175, 200
Liebhaber 49
Lieblingsbeschäfti- gung 198
Lieblingsfach 150
Lied 173, 281
Lieferant 301
lieferbar 267
liefern 82, 118, 301
Lieferung 301
Lieferwagen 284
liegen 13, 52, 215, 217, 292
liegend 168
Liegestuhl 90
Liegestütz 83
Lift 88
Liga 197
Likör 200
Lilie 235
Limo(nade) 57
Limousine 284
Linde 235
lindern 130
Lineargeschwindig- keit 241
Linie 289, 294
Linienflug 290
Linienmaschine 290
Linke 98, 100
linker Flügel 100
links 196
Linksparteien 100
Linolschnitt 170
Lippe 12
Lippenstift 39
Liquidation 301
liquidieren 42, 133
Liste 266
Listenpreis 300
Liter 91, 251
literarisch 179, 198
Literatur 152, 179
Literaturgattung 179
Literaturgeschichte 179
Literaturkritik 179
Literaturwissen- schaft 179
Lithograf 170
Lithografie 170
Litze 260
Livesendung 270
Lizenz 301
Lkw 284
Lkw-Fahrer 284, 314
Lobbyist 104

loben 41
Loch 13, 205
Locher 313
Locken 16
lockig 16
Löffel 59
Logarithmus 247
Logik 165
Logis 191
logisch 165
Logo 306
Lohn 130
lohnend 27, 198
Lohnerhöhungen 316
Lohnkosten 258
Lohnsteuer 113, 114
Lohnsteuerkarte 114
Lokalkolorit 180
Lokalredakteur 269
Lokalzeitung 268
Lokführer 288
Lokomotive 287
Londoner 219, 287
löschen 277, 280
lose 78
lösen 199, 246
loskommen von 129
löslich 243
Lossprechung 163
Lösung 117, 243
Lösungsmittel 243
Lotse 292
Löwe 24, 232, 233
Löwenzahn 235
LSD 128
Lues 37
Luft holen 76
Luftangriff 119
lüften 93
Luftfeuchtigkeit 227
Luftfracht 290
Luftkrankheit 68
Luftlinie 233
Luftpost 273
Luftschlösser 208
Luftschutzbunker 119
Luftschutzkeller 119
Luftschutzraum 119
Luftverschmutzung 225
Luftwaffe 118
Luftwaffenstütz- punkt 119
Luftweg 289
Lügner 32
lukrativ 304
Lunge 83
Lungenarzt 75
Lungenembolie 245
Lungenentzündung 69
Lunge(nflügel) 13
Lungenkrankheiten 245

Lungenkrebs 69
Lutheraner 159
lutherisch 159
Luthertum 159
Lymphdrüse 245
Lymphknoten 245
lynchen 42
Lyrik 179
Lyriker 179

M
m 250
M.A. 153
machen 93, 155,
182, 188, 198,
257, 265, 285,
302, 309
Macho 136
Macht 100, 142
Macht ergreifen 108
Machtgier 32
Macke 276
Mädchen 15, 185
Mädchenname 10
Magazin 268
Magen 13, 19, 69
Magen- 245
Magen-Darm-Trakt
245
Magenbeschwerden
69, 75
Magengeschwür
69, 78
Magenkrankheiten
245
Magenkrebs 69
Magenleiden 245
Magenschleimhaut-
entzündung 70
Magenverstimmung
76
mager 15
Magie 164
Magister 153
Magnetfeld 205, 240
Magnetismus 240
Mähdrescher 222
mähen 88, 222
Mäher 222
mahlen 58
Mahlzeit 60, 62, 191
Mai 10
Maifeiertag 182
Maiglöckchen 235
Maikäfer 234
Mais 55, 221
Make-up 39
Makler 304, 308
Mal 185, 249
Malbuch 18
malen 168
Malen 168, 198
Maler 168, 310
Malerei 168
Malkasten 18

Manager 299
manche 135
manchmal 174
Mandat 103
Mandelentzündung
70
Mandeloperation 81
Mangel 86, 111, 130
Mangelernährung
130
mangeln an 23
Maniküre 39
Mann 15, 201, 217,
292
Mannequin 311
Männer- 136
männlich 11, 14, 136
Mannschaft 196, 292
Mannschaftskapitän
196
Mansarde 88
Manschettenknöpfe
66
Mantel 39, 64, 93
Manuskript 267
Manuskripthalter 313
Märchen 18, 179
Margarine 55
Margerite 235
Marienkäfer 234
Marine 118
Marionettenspiel 187
Marke 194
Markentreue 306
Marketing(-) 305
Marketingdirektor
299
markieren 202, 277
Markierstift 313
Markt 187
Marktanteil 296
Marktforschung 306
Marktkräfte 296
marktorientiert 306
Marktwirtschaft 296
Marmelade 60, 192
Marmor- 169
Mars 204
Maschine 254, 255
Maschinen 255, 258
Maschinenbau-
betrieb 258
maschine(n)ge-
schrieben 312
maschinenlesbar 278
Maschinenschlosser
258
Maschinenteil 255
Masern 69
maskiert 132
Masochismus 37
Maß 250
Massage 83
Massaker 133
Masse 241, 260

Massenartikel 257
Massenfertigung 257
Massenmedien 268
Massentierhaltung
220
Massenvernich-
tungswaffen 119
massieren 38, 83
Mäßigkeit 32
Maßstab 31
Mastdarm 245
mästen 221
Masturbation 37
masturbieren 37
Matchball 197
Materialeigen-
schaften 254
Materialismus 166
Materialist 164, 166
materialistisch 164,
166
Materie 166, 240
Mathe 150, 246
Mathe(matik) 156
Mathearbeit 246
Mathematik 145,
150, 246
Matheprüfung 156
Matinee 175
Matratze 89
Mätresse 49
matriarchal(isch)
139
Matriarchat 136
matronenhaft 15
Matrose 292
matt 21, 172
Matte 91
Mauer 71, 88, 178
Mauerwerk 178
Maul 12
Maulbeerbaum 235
Maultier 24
Maurer 310
Maus 24, 232, 233
maximal 304
maximieren 296
Mechanik 240, 241
Mechaniker 258
Mechanisierung 258
Mechanismus 255
Medien 25, 101,
268
Medienereignis 268
Medienrummel 306
Medikament(e) 77,
193, 194
Mediothek 264
Meditation 164
Medizin 77, 244
medizinisch 112, 115,
143, 149, 224
Meer 26, 28, 216,
226
Meerbusen 216

Meerenge 216
Meeresboden 216
Meeresfrüchte 55
Meeresgeologie 210
Meeresklima 228
Meerrettich 56
Meerschweinchen
233
Megapixel 172
Mehl 54
Mehltau(pilz) 237
mehrere 103, 213,
299
Mehrheit 102
Mehrstufenrakete
207
Mehrwegflasche 226
Mehrwertsteuer 113
mehrwertsteuerfrei
114
mehrzellig 237
Mehrzweckraum 88
Meile 216, 250
Meineid 109, 131
Meinung 142, 145
Meinungsumfrage
101, 142
Meinungsverschie-
denheit 34
Meise 233
Meißel 255
meißeln 169
meist 182
meisten 52
meistens 168, 284,
288
Meister 195, 309
Meisterschaft 195
melden 269
Meldung 269, 278
melken 221
Melodie 173
melodramatisch 270
Melone 65
Memme 24
Menge 33
Mengenlehre 246
Mensch 73, 158,
232, 233
Menschen 71, 133,
138, 229
Menschenaffe 233
Menschenmenge 33
Menschenrechte
142
Menschenrechts-
bewegung 98
Menschenrechts-
bilanz 142
Menschenrechts-
situation 142
Menschenrechts-
verletzungen 142
menschlich 33, 138,
143, 346

menschliches Tun 139
Menschlichkeit 160, 133
Menü 278
Menüsteuerung 278
Meritokratie 99
merklich 25
Merkur 204
Messbecher 59
Messe 162, 298
messen 77, 241
Messer 59
Messias 158, 160
Messing 24, 212
Messlöffel 59
Metall 212
Metall- 254
Metallarbeiten 198
Metallbearbeitungs maschine 255
Metallermüdung 254
Metapher 180
Metaphorik 180
metaphorisch 180
Metaphysik 166
metaphysisch 164, 166
Meteor 204
Meteorit 204
Meter 250, 251
Methadon 128
Methodik 146
Methodist 159
Methodisten- 159
methodistisch 159
Metropole 224
Metrum 180
Metzger 310
Meute 232
Miete 124
mieten 208, 308
Mieter 125
Mieterhöhung 124
Mietshaus 87
Mietskaserne 87
Mietwagen 208, 284
Mietzahlungen 125
Migräne 68
Migration 139
Mikrobe 237
Mikrobiologie 237
Mikrochip 260
Mikroelektronik 260
Mikrofon 271
Mikroorganismus 237
Mikroprozessor 260
Mikroskop 242
mikroskopisch 242
Mikrowelle(nherd) 59
Milch 54, 59, 192, 251, 261

Milchstraße 204
Milchvieh 221
Milchviehhaltung 220
mild 227
mild(ernd) 111
militant 100
Militär 118
Militärgericht 120
militärisch 118
Militärjunta 108
Milliarde 230, 300
Million 302
Millionen 126, 304
Millionenhöhe 300
Minderheit 102, 134
Minderjährige 19
Mindestlohn 130, 316
Mine 313
Mineralien 210
Mineralogie 210
Mineralwasser 57
Minijob 114
Minister 106
Ministerium 105, 106
Ministerpräsident 106
Minute 189, 293
mischen 281
Missbrauch 36, 128
Missernte 221, 230
misshandeln 51
misshandelt 133
Mission 116
Misstrauensvotum 104
Mist 220
Miststück 233
Mitanbieter 301
Mitarbeiter 269, 311, 312, 314
Mitarbeiterin 311
Mitbewohner 124
mitbringen 189
Mitbürger 33
mitfühlend 22, 23
Mitgefühl 34
Mitglied 33, 100, 145, 159
Mitgliedschaft 33, 84, 100, 117
Mitleid 23, 34
mitleidlos 23
mitmachen 280
mitnehmen 284
Mitreisende 33
mitspielen 176
Mittagessen 60
Mitte 100
Mitteilung 278
Mittel 77, 180
Mittelalter 141
mittelalterlich 140

Mittelfeldspieler 196
Mitte-Links- 100
Mittelklasse 33
mittellos 130
Mittelmeer 215, 216
Mittelohr- entzündung 12
Mittelpunkt 204, 247
Mittelschiff 178
Mittelsmann 117
Mittelsperson 117
mittlere 10, 299
mittlere Osten 215
mittlere Westen 214
Mitwirkende 176
Mixer 59
Möbel 89
Möbelbranche 298
Möbelpolitur 93
Möbelstück 89
Möbeltischler 310
Möbelwagen 284
mobil 282
Mobiltelefon 274, 279
möbliertes Zimmer 86
möchte, dass 155
Mode(n)schau 187
Modegeschäft 194
Modell 146, 194, 301
Modelleisenbahn 18
Modellflugzeug 18
modelliert 169
Modem 279
Moderator 271
moderieren 271
modern 169, 179
Modeschmuck 213
Modeschöpfer 311
modisch 16
Modus 278
mögen 28
möglich 100
Möglichkeit(en) 96, 125
Mohammed 160
Mohn(blume) 235
Molekül 243
Molekularstruktur 243
Moll 174
mollig 15
Moment 126, 199, 275, 313
Monarch 159
Monarchie 99
monatlich 115
Monatsblutung 76
Monatszeitschrift 268
Mönch 163
Mond 204, 206

Mondfinsternis 204
Mond(lande)fähre 206
Mondlandung 206
Mongolismus 74
Monolog 176
Monotheismus 161
Montag 10, 270
Montage 258
Montageband 257
Montagehalle 257
Montage(werk) 257
Monteur 258
montieren 257
Moor 218, 219
Moos 236
Moped 286
Moral(-) 31, 166
moralisch 31, 166
Moräne 211
Mord 110, 131
Mörder 131
Mordkommission 110
mordsaufgeregt 44
morgen 97, 175, 291
Morgen 227
Morgen (Land) 308
morgendlich 50
Morgenrock 65
Morgenzeitung 268
morgig 154, 156
Mörtel 178
Mosaik 169
Moschee 162
Mosel 217
Moselwein 200
Motel 191
Motiv 172
Motivation 144, 154
motivieren 154
Motor 256
Motorboot 291
Motorrad 286
Motorradfahrer 286
Motte 234
M. Sc. 153
Mücke 234
Mückenstich 234
müde 28
Müll 225, 226
Müllabladeplatz 226
Mülldeponie 226
Mülleimer 91
Müllkippe 226
Müllschaufel 93
Mülltonne 91
Müllverbrennung 226
Multi 298
multikulturell 10
Multimedia 265, 281
multinational 298
Multiplikation 247
multiplizieren 246

Mund 12, 13, 76
Munddusche 79
mündlich 140, 152
Mündung 217
Mundwasser 38
Mund-zu-Mund-
   Beatmung 72
Munition 119
Münze 199
Münztelefon 275
Murmeln 18
Museum 169
Museumswärter 311
Musical 173
Musik 155, 173, 198,
   199
Musik- 173
Musikalienhandlung
   194
musikalisch 173
Musikberieselung
   173
Musiker 173
Musikfolge 281
Musikinstrument 173
Musikladen 194
Musikstück 173
Musizieren 187
Muskel 14, 74
Muskeln 78
Muskelzerrung 72
muskulös 15, 84
Müsli 60
Muslim 158, 162
Muße 198
müssen 156, 189,
   213, 294, 349
Mussheirat 48
müsste 156
Mut 23
mutig 23, 24, 238
Mutter 17, 19, 46,
   51, 255
Muttermilch 13
Muttermord 42
Mutterschaftsgeld
   115
Mutterschaftsurlaub
   115
Mütze 66

N
nach Hause 284
Nachbar 23, 34,
   152, 214
Nachbarland 119
Nachbarschaft 34
Nachbeben 229
nachempfunden 301
nachfolgen 106
Nachfolger 106
Nachfrage 296
nachgeben 250
nachgehen 90
nachhaltig 226

Nachhaltigkeit 262
nachkommen 304
Nachkriegs- 176
nachlassen 21
Nachlassen 127
Nachmittag 228
Nachnahme 273
Nachname 10
Nachrede 133
Nachricht(en-) 192,
   268, 269, 278
Nachrichtenagentur
   268
Nachrichtendienst
   118
Nachrichtenmagazin
   268
Nachrichtensatellit
   207
Nachrichtensendung
   271
Nachrichtensprecher
   271
Nachruf 42
nachschauen 264
Nachschlage- 264
nachschlagen 51, 264
Nachschub 119
nachsehen 25, 264
Nachsendeanschrift
   273
nachsenden 273
nachsprechen 155
nächst(e) 10, 46,
   155, 287, 293,
   330
Nächste 34, 155
nächstes Mal 155
Nacht 76
Nachtfalter 199, 234
Nachthemd 65
Nachtigall 233
Nachtisch 62
Nachtklub 187
Nachtlokal 187
Nachtquartier 191
Nachtragsband 264
Nachttisch 90
Nachtwäsche 65
Nachwahl 102
Nachwirkungen 230
Nacken 74
Nadelarbeit 198
Nadelbaum 235
Nadelstreifenanzug
   64
Nadelwald 235
Nagel 12, 255
Nagelbürste 38
Nagellack 39
Nagelschere 39
Nahaufnahme 172
nahe 34
Nähe 211, 350
Nahe Osten 214, 215

nahe stehen 34
Nähen 198
nahen 26
Nähmaschine 255
Nährstoffe 82
Nahrung 54
Nahrungsmittel 54
Nahverkehr 292, 315
Nahverkehrszug 287
Name 10, 62, 289
Narbe 69
Narkose 81
Narkosearzt 81
Narkosemittel 81
Narr 52
Narzisse 235
Nase 12, 27, 39, 76
nass 228
Nation 96
Nationalgalerie 169
Nationalismus 134
nationalistisch 134
Nationalität 11
Nationalpark 219
Nationalstaat 142
Nationaltrainer 196
NATO 118
Naturalismus 180
Naturbursche 44
Naturell 22
Naturkatastrophe
   229
Naturkost 82
Naturkostladen 82
natürlich 40, 226
Naturschutzgebiet
   219
Naturwissenschaft
   150
naturwissenschaft-
   lich 165
nautisch 292
Nazi 99
Nazismus 99
neb(e)lig 228
Nebel 204, 228
Nebenfluss 217
Nebenhandlung 180
Nebenleistungen
   316
Nebenraum 88
Nebenstelle 275
Nebenstraße 285
Neffe 47
negativ 113, 134,
   143, 306
Negativ 172
nehmen 19, 62, 287
Neid 30, 32
Neige 301
neigen 52, 238
Neigung 28
Nelke 236
nennen 232
Nenner 247

neofaschistisch 99
Neonazi 99
Neptun 204
Nerv(en) 14
Nervenentzündung
   70
Nervenzusammen-
   bruch 14
nervös 14
Netto- 113
Netz 277, 279
Netzspannung 259
Netz(werk) 279
Neuanschluss 275
Neue Welt 159, 214
neuere Geschichte
   140
Neuerung 254
Neuerwerbung 301
Neues Testament
   162
neu(e)ste 124, 299,
   305, 350
Neugeborene 17
neugotisch 177
Neujahr 182
Neurologie 244
Neurose 144
Neurotiker 144
neurotisch 144
Neutron 241
Neutronenbeschuss
   262
Neuvermählte 48
Niagarafälle 217
Nichtangriffspakt 118
Nichtchrist 10
Nichte 47, 185
nichtehelich 49
Nichtraucher 201
Nichtregierungs-
   organisation 105
Nichtsnutz 32
nichtsnutzig 32
nichtswürdig 32
nie 52
Niederlage 120
niederlegen 315
niederschießen 132
Niederschlag 228
niederschlagen 107
Niederwild 233
niedlich 15, 16
Niednagel 70
niedrig 69, 130, 201,
   219, 271
Niere 13
Nierenstein 69
Nierentransplan-
   tation 13
Nierenversagen 245
Nieselregen 228
niesen 69
Nihilismus 164
Nihilist 164

nihilistisch 164
Nikotin 201
nikotinsüchtig 201
noch mal 155
Nockenwelle 256
nominieren 101
Nominierung 101
Nonne 163
Nord- 215
Nordafrika 119, 218
Nordamerika 214
Norden 215
nordirisch 215
Nordirland 215
nördlich 215, 228
Nordpol 215
Nord-Süd-Gefälle 215
nordwestlich 215
Normalisierung 116
Normen 145
Notar 308
Notarzt 72
Notaufnahme 72, 81
Note 174
Notebook 276
Noten 153, 173
Notfall 72
Notiz nehmen 25
Notizblock 313
Notizbuch 313
Notizen 313
Notizen machen 155
Notunterkunft 86, 125
Nova 204
Novelle 179
nüchtern 13, 200
Nudeln 55
null 197, 227, 248
Nullwachstum 248
Nummer 274, 275
nur 191, 312
Nuss 56
Nussknacker 59
Nutte 37
nutzergeneriert 202
Nutzholz 254
Nutzlast 207

O
Obdach 86
obdachlos 125
Obdachlose 86, 125
Obdachlosenheim 125
Obdachlosigkeit 125, 151
Obduktion 41
oben 155
Ober 62
Oberarzt 80
Oberhaupt 159
Oberhaus 102
Oberhemd 64

Oberkellner 63
Oberkiefer 78
Oberklasse 33
Oberkommandierende 118
Oberleitungsbus 293
Oberschwester 81
oberste 156
Oberteil 64
Obhut 51
Objekt 172
objektiv 30
Objektiv 171, 172
Objektivkappe 171
obligatorisch 150
Observatorium 205
Obst 56, 60, 62
Obst- u. Gemüsehändler 194
Obstgarten 219
Obstkuchen 54
Obstsalat 56
Obsttörtchen 54
obszön 32
Obus 293
obwohl 73, 82
Ochse 221
Ödland 218
Offenbarung 161
offene Wirbelsäule 74
Offenherzchirurgie 245
offensichtlich 72, 78
Offensive 119
offenstehend 303
öffentlich 142, 145, 148, 184, 264, 293, 315
öffentlich reden 211
öffentlicher Dienst 311
Öffentlichkeitsarbeit 306
Offizier 15, 118
öffnen 277
Öffnungszeiten 189
Offset(druck) 170
Off-Theater 175
Ohr 12, 26
Ohren 13
Ohrenschmerzen 76, 78
okkult 164
Ökobauer 56
ökologisch 82, 225
ökonomisch 296
Ökosystem 139
Öl 55, 168, 286
Ölfördermaximum 226
Ölgemälde 168
Oligarchie 99
Olive 56

Olivenöl 55
Ölkanne 261
Ölpest 226
Öltank 261
Öltanker 291
Ölteppich 226
Ölvorkommen 210
Omelett 54
Omnibus 293
onanieren 37
Onkel 47
Online-Banking 281
Online-Dienst 265, 279
Online-Enzyklopädie 264
Ontologie 165
Oper 173
operabel 81
Operation 24, 81
Operationssaal 81
Operationsschwester 81
operierbar 81
operieren 81
Opfer 72, 131, 229
Opposition 102
Oppositionsführer 102
Optik 240
Optimismus 30
optimistisch 18, 24, 30
optisch 278
Orangenmarmelade 60
Orangensaft 56, 192
Orchester 173
Orchidee 236
Ordnung 109
Ordnung schaffen 93
Ordnungszahl 243
Organ 244
Organempfänger 245
Organisation 21, 116, 142
organisch 242, 243
organisieren 315
organisiert 314
Organismus 237
Organspender 245
Organtransplantation 81
Orgasmus 36
Original- 170
Orkan 229
orthodox 158, 159
Orthopäde 75
Orthopädie 244
örtliche Betäubung 81
Ortsgespräch 274
Ost- 214, 215
ostasiatisch 215

Osten 214
Osterglocke 235
Ostermontag 182
Ostern 182
Ostersonntag 182
Osteuropa 215
osteuropäisch 96, 215
Ostküste 215
östlich 214, 215
Ostsee 216
Ostwind 228
Ouvertüre 174
oval 16
Overall 66
Oxidation 243
Ozean 216, 226
Ozeandampfer 291
Ozonschicht 225

P
paar 155, 171, 176, 250, 251
Paar 51
Pacht 308
Päckchen 273
packen 238, 261, 273
packend 267
Packliste 301
Packung 38, 201, 261
pädagogisch 143
Paddelboot 291
paddeln 291
Pädiatrie 244
Paket 272, 273, 297
Paketbombe 273
Paketpost 272, 273
Palast 87, 188
Palme 235
Panamakanal 217
Pankreas 245
Panne 286
Panzer 119
Papagei 233
Papier 267, 286, 313
Papierkorb 91
Papiertaschentuch 39
Papierverarbeitung 257
Pappel 235
Pappkarton 125, 261
Papst 163
Parade 184
Paralyse 74
Parasit 234
Pärchen 208
Parfüm 27, 39
parfümieren 27
Park 219, 224
Parka 64
parken 286

Parkett 175
Parkettfußboden 91
Parkhaus 286
Parkinsonkrankheit 68
Parklücke 286
Parkplatz 286
Parkuhr 286
Parkverbot 286
Parkwächter 286, 311
Parlament 102, 103, 104
parlamentarisch 99
parlamentarischer Geschäftsführer 102
Parlamentsabgeordnete 102
Parlamentssitz 103
Parodie 179
Parole 107
Partei 18, 100, 101, 105, 134
Parteibasis 101
Parteienfinanzierung 101
Parteienlandschaft 101
Parteiführer 100
Parteikonvent 104
Parteilinie 100
Parteimitglied(schaft) 100
Parteitag 101
Partie 195
Partisan 120
Partisanenkrieg 120
Partner 33, 49
Partnerarbeit 155
Partnerschaft 33
Party 185
Parzelle 308
Pass 189
Passagier 288, 290, 291, 292
Passagierschiff 291
passen 65, 265
passieren 176
passiv 107, 201
Passiva 304
Passkontrolle 189
Passwort 281, 312
Pastete 55
Pastor 122
Paten- 50
Patenkind 50
Patent 256
Pathologie 244
Patient 75, 80
patriarchal(isch) 139
Patriarchat 136
Patrone 313
pauken für 152

Pauschal- 294
Pauschalreise 188
Pauschaltarif 279
Pauschalurlaub 188
Pause 182
pausieren 103
Pazifik 216
Pazifismus 98
PC 276, 301
Pediküre 39
peinlich 32
Pellkartoffeln 56
Pelzmantel 64
Pendeldiplomatie 116
pendeln 284
Pendelverkehr 287
Pendler 284
Penis 14, 36
Pension 115, 191
pensioniert 20
Pensionsalter 20
per 265, 273, 275
Periode 76, 211
Periodensystem 243
Peripherie 224
Perle 213
Perlenkette 213
Persisch 216
Person 10, 168, 251, 307
Personalabbau 126
Personalausweis 189
Personalcomputer 276
Personaldirektor 299
Personalgesellschaft 298
Personengesellschaft 298
Persönlichkeit 22, 140, 143
Perspektive 168
perspektivisch 168
Perücke 16
Pessar 37
Pessimismus 30
pessimistisch 24, 30
Pestizid 220, 221
Petersilie 55
Petrologie 210
Petting 36
Pfad 279
Pfannen 59
Pfannkuchen 54
Pfarrer 122, 163
Pfau 24
Pfeffer 55
Pfeife 201
pfeifen 13
Pfeifenreiniger 201
Pfeiler 178
Pfeiltaste 278
Pferd 221
Pferderennen 187

Pferdeschwanz 16
Pferdestall 88, 222
Pfifferling 222
Pfingsten 182
Pfingstmontag 182
Pfingstsonntag 182
Pfirsich 56
Pflanze 221, 235
pflanzen 221, 235
Pflanzenkunde 236
Pflanzenreich 235
Pflanzung 220
Pflaster 72
Pflaume 56
Pflege 51
Pflegeeltern 51
Pflegeheim 21
Pfleger 81
Pflegespülung 39
Pflegeversicherung 115
Pflicht 92, 51
Pflichtfach 150
Pflug 222
Pfund 251, 302, 303
Pharmaindustrie 242
pharmazeutisch 242
Phase 260
Philharmoniker 174
Philosoph 165
Philosophie 150, 154, 165, 166
philosophieren 165
philosophisch 165
Phobie 134
Photon 241
Physik 150, 240
physikalisch 240, 242
Physiker 240
Physiotherapie 83
physisch 138
Pianist 173
pikant 268
pill 37
Pille 77
Pilot 290
Pilotenkabine 290
Pilz 56, 192, 230, 236, 237
pingelig 23
Pinguin 233
Pinnwand 202
Pinsel 168
Pinselstriche 168
Pipette 242
Pirat 292
Piraterie 292
Piste 196
Pixel 172
Pizza 55
Pizzeria 61
Plagiat 180
plagiieren 180
Plakat 170

Plakatwand 306
Plan 118, 177, 224
planen 119, 257
Planer 177
Planet 204
Plantage 220
Planung 177
Planungsstadium 177
Planwirtschaft 296
Plastik(-) 169, 254
plastisch 169, 245
Plateau 218
Plattentektonik 210
Plattform 101
Platz 175, 190, 288
Platz buchen 289
Platzverweis 197
Pleuelstange 256
Plombe 79
plombieren 79
plötzlich 126
Plumeau 89
Po 13
Pocken 69
Pockenimpfung 69
Pockenschutzimpfung 190
Poesie 180
poetisch 180
Pogrom 133
Pol 205
Polen 119, 159
polieren 93
Poliklinik 244
Politik 83, 100, 116, 117, 142
Politiker 23, 100
Politikwissenschaft 142
politisch 99, 100, 107, 115, 117, 138, 142
politisch korrekt 73
Politologe 142
Politologie 142
Polizei 19, 109, 111, 251
Polizeibeamte 111
Polizeibehörde 112
Polizeichef 309
Polizeigewahrsam 112
Polizeipräsident 309
Polizeirevier 112
Polizeistaat 99
Polizeiwache 112
Polizist 15, 111, 112
Polohemd 64
Polytheismus 161
Pommes 61
Pommes frites 56
Pommesbude 61
Population 138
Porno 37
Pornografie 32
Portemonnaie 303

Portier 192
Portion 63
Porto 273
Porträt 168
porträtieren 168
Porzellan 91
Porzellanladen 22,
91, 238
positiv 143, 306
Positivismus 166
Positivist 166
positivistisch 166
Post(-) 265, 272
Postamt 272
Postanweisung 272
Postbeschäftigte 272
Postdienst 272
Poster 170
Postfach 272
Postfiliale 272
Postflugzeug 272
Postfrau 272
Postgebühren 272
Postkarte 199, 272,
273
postlagernd 273
Postleitzahl 273
Postminister 272
Postmitarbeiter 272
Postsendungen 273
Poststempel 273
postwendend 272
Postwurfsendungen
306
Postzug 272
Postzusteller 272
Potenz 247
potenziell 300
Potenzmittel 37
PR 306
PR-Fachmann 306
PR-Katastrophe 306
Pragmatiker 166
pragmatisch 166
Pragmatismus 166
prähistorisch 138
prallen gegen 71
Prämie 316
Präsentation 156
Präsenzbibliothek
264
Präservativ 37
Präsident 73, 102,
103, 105, 106,
108, 118, 186
präsidentiell 99
predigen 162
Prediger 162
Predigt 162
Preis 113, 300
Preisschild 300
preiswert 124
Prekariat 130
Prellung 72
Premiere 175

Premierminister 86,
105, 106
Presbyterianer 159
presbyterianisch 159
Presse 268
Presseberichte 269
Pressefreiheit 268
Pressekonferenz 268
Pressemappe 306
Pressesprecher 269
Pressezensur 268
Pressluftbohrer 255
Priester 163
Primärquellen 140
primitiv 138
Primzahl 247
Prinz 48, 121
Prinzessin 121
Prinzip 31
privat 184, 307
Privatdetektiv 208
Privateigentum 296
Privatfernsehen 270
Privatgrundstück
308
privatisieren 287
Privatwirtschaft 296
pro 251
pro Sekunde 172
Probe 242
Probelauf 262
Problem 18, 52, 75,
125, 165
Produkt 257, 305,
306
Produktion 257, 258
Produktionsablauf
258
Produktionsanlagen
257
Produktionsfaktoren
296
Produktionskosten
296
Produktionsleistung
258
Produktionsmittel
296
Produktivität 258,
297
Produzent 271
produzieren 257
Professor 122, 149,
310
Profi(-) 94, 195
Profiling 135
Prognosen 297
Programm 19, 270,
276, 277
Programmfehler 276
programmieren 276
Programmierer 276
Programmierung
276
Programmpaket 276

Programmplanung
270
Progression 246
progressiv 23
Projekt 304
Pro-Kopf- 304
Promenaden-
mischung 232
promovieren 153
Prophet 160
Proportionalschrift
278
proppe(n)voll 219
Pros(i)t! 186
Prosa(-) 179
Prospekt 306
prost 200
Prostata 14
Prostituierte 37
Prostitution 37, 131
Protein 237
Protest 107, 225
Protestant 159
protestantisch 159
Protestantismus 159
Protestdemon-
stration 107
protestieren 107
Protestkundgebung
107
Prothese 79
Protokoll 103, 312
Proton 241
Protozoen 237
Provinz 96, 97, 223
Provinzstadt 223
Provision 300
provisorisch 79
Prozent 110, 193,
258, 300
Prozess 109, 242
prüfen 114, 286
Prüfung 94, 152,
156
Prüfungssemester
156
Prügel 19
Prügelei 133
prügeln 133
Psalm 162
Pseudonym 266
Psychiater 75, 143,
144
Psychiatrie 143
psychisch 144
Psychoanalyse 143
Psychoanalytiker 143
Psychologe 143
Psychologie 143
psychologisch 143,
144
Psychopath 143
psychopathisch 143
Psychopathologie
143

Psychose 144
Psychotherapeut 75
Psychotherapie 143
Pubertät 18
Publikum 176
publizieren 267
Publizieren 279
Puff 37
Puffer(speicher) 278
Pulli 64
Pullover 64, 261
Pulsar 204
pummelig 15
Pumps 65
pünktlich 76, 288
Puppe 17
Puppenspiel 187
Puppenstube 17
Puppenwagen 17
Puritaner 159
puritanisch 159
Pusteblume 235
Pute 55
Putsch 108
putzen 38, 39, 58,
78, 92, 93
Putzlappen 93
Puzzle(spiel) 18
Pyramide 247
Pyschotherapeut 143

Q
Quadrat 246, 247
Quadrat- 247, 250
quadratisch 247
Quadratmeter 247
Quadratwurzel 246
Qualifikation 152
qualifizieren 197
Qualitäts- 298
Quant(en) 241
Quanten- 241
Quantensprung 241
Quark 241
Quartier 86, 191
Quasar 204
Quatsch 208
Quecksilber 212
Quelle 140, 217
Querlatte 196
Querschiff 178
Quizsendung 271
Quotient 247

R
Rabatt 300
Rabbi(ner) 163
Rachen 75
Raddampfer 291
Rädelsführer 108
Räder 21
Radfahren 199
Radierer 170
Radiergummi 313
Radierung 170

Radieschen 56
radikal 100
Radikale 100
Radio 270
Radio hören 26
radioaktiv 225, 226, 243
Radiochemie 242
Radiogerät 270
Radiokarbon-
datierung 211
Radiologie 244
Radiowecker 271
Radlermaß 200
Radtour 286
Radweg 286
Rahmenplan 151
Rakete 119, 206, 207
Raketenabschuss-
basis 206
Raketenangriff 119
Raketentriebwerk 207
Ramadan 163
rammen 217, 292
Rand 130
Randale 133
randalieren 133
Randalierer 133
randvoll 261
Ranke 236
Rasen 88
Rasiercreme 38
rasieren 38
Rasse 33, 98, 135, 138
Rassendiskriminierung 135
Rassenhass 135
Rassentrennung 98, 107
Rassismus 134, 135
Rassist 135
rassistisch 135
Raster 170
Rasterbild 170
Raststätte 61, 285
Rat 223
Rate 194
Raten 304
Ratenzahlung 194
Ratgeber(spalte) 269
ratifizieren 103
rational 165
Rationalismus 164, 166
Rationalist 166
rationalistisch 166
Rationierung 297
Rätsel 18
Ratte 233
Raub 131
Räuber 40, 131, 132
Räuber und
Gendarm 17
Raubvogel 233

Rauch 201
rauchen 128, 201
Rauchen 31, 82, 200
Rauchen verboten 201
Raucher 201, 287
Raucherabteil 287
Raucherhusten 201
Räucherlachs 55, 62
Raucherwagen 287
Raum 87, 166, 206
Raumanzug 206
Raumfähre 206
Raumfahrt 206
Raumfahrtmedizin 206
Raumfahrtprogramm 206
Raumfahrzeug 206
Raumflug 206, 207
Raumforschung 206
Rauminhalt 241
Raumkapsel 206
Raumpfleger 311
Raumpflegerin 92
Raumschiff 206
Raumsonde 206
Raumstation 206, 207
Räumungsverkauf 194
raus! 134
Rausch 129
Rauschgift 128
Rauschgiftdezernat 128
Rauschgiftfahnder 129
Rauschgifthandel 128
Rauschgifthändler 128
rauschgiftsüchtig 128
Rauschmittel 128
rausgehen 92
rausschmeißen 126, 316
rausziehen 260
Reaktion 143, 242
Realismus 166, 169, 180
Realist 166
realistisch 166
Realität 265
Realschule 148
Rebellion 108
Rechenaufgabe 246
Rechenoperation 246
rechnen 246
Rechnen 151, 246
Rechnung 62, 193, 246, 303

Rechnungswesen 114
Recht 109, 142, 163
recht 31, 227
Recht auf 136
Rechte 100, 134, 316
Rechteck 247
rechteckig 247
rechter Flügel 100
rechts 196, 285
Rechtsanwalt 110, 309
rechtschaffen 32
Rechtschreibehilfe 278
rechtsextrem 100, 134
Rechtsextremismus 134
Rechtsextremist 100, 134
Rechtsmedizin 244
rechtsradikal 134
Rechtsradikale 100, 134
Rechtswesen 109
rechtswidrig 19
recyceln 226
Recycling 226
Recyclingpapier 226
Redakteur 267, 269
Rede 103
reden 13, 211
Redensart 275, 294
redigieren 267
redlich 32
Redlichkeit 32
Reduktion 243
reduzieren 226
Reeder 292
Referendum 104, 237
Reflex 143
Reform 104
Reformation 141
Reformhaus 82
reformiert 159
Reformkost 54, 82
Reformstau 101
Refrain 173, 180
Regal 89
Regalbrett 89
Regel 76, 212
regelmäßig 76, 162, 285
Regelung 258
Regen 226, 228
Regenguss 228
Regenmantel 64
Regentag 228
Regenwald 219
Regenwetter 228
Regie 176
regieren 99

Regierung 99, 100, 101, 105, 107
Regierungschef 105
Regierungspartei 100
Regierungssystem 99
Regierungsumbildung 105
Regimekritiker 107
Regiment 119
Region 97
regional 97
Regionalbahn 287
Regisseur 176
Register 264
Registrierkasse 302
regnerisch 228
regulieren 307
Regulierung 296, 307
Reh 55, 233
reichen 301
reichlich 233
Reichtum 297
reif 20, 22
Reife 20
Reifen 286
Reifendruck 286
Reifenpanne 286
Reihe 175, 249
Reihe von 104, 301
Reihenhaus 87
Reim 180
reimen 180
Reimschema 180
rein 31, 164
Reinfall 175, 176
reinigen 39
Reinigung 39
Reinigungscreme 39
Reinigungsfrau 92
Reinigungskraft 311
Reinigungsmittel 93
Reinigungsutensilien 93
Reinlichkeit 38
Reis 54
Reise 188, 221, 291
Reisebüro 188
Reisebus 293
Reiseflughöhe 290
Reiseführer 189
Reisegeschwindigkeit 284
Reiseleiter 189
Reisen 188
reisen 28, 29, 188, 288, 289, 292
Reisende 288
Reisepass 189
Reiseplan 188
Reiseprospekte 188
Reiseroute 188
Reiserücktritt(s)- 190

R

Reisescheck 190
Reisetasche 190
Reiseveranstalter 188
Reiseverkehr 315
Reiseziel 188, 289
Reißbrett 223
Reißer 176
Reißnagel 313
Reißverschluss 66
Reißzwecke 313
Reiten 199
Reitlehrer 309
Reitunfall 73
Reiz 143
reizen 29
reizend 15
Reklame 305
Reklamerummel 306
Reklamesendungen
306
Reklamewand 306
Rekord 195
rektal 245
Rektum 245
Relativitätstheorie
205, 240
Reliabilität 144
Relief 169
Religion 11, 158, 159
Religionsfreiheit 158
Religion(slehre) 150
Religionszugehörig-
keit 11
religiös 158, 162
Renaissance 141,
169
Rendezvous 206
Rennbahn 196
Rennen 187, 195
Renner 300
Rennfahrer 196
Rennsport 195
Rennstrecke 196
Rennwagen 196
rentabel 300
Rentabilität 300
Rente 115
Rentenalter 20
Rentenberater 310
Rentner 20
Reparaturwerkstatt
258
reparieren 198, 286
Reportage 269
Reporter 268, 269
Repräsentant 300
Repräsentantenhaus
102, 104
repräsentativ 145
Reproduktion 169
Reptil 234
Republik 99
Requisiten 176
reservieren 61, 62,
188, 191, 288

Reservierung 61,
188, 191, 289, 290
Residenz 86
Respektlosigkeit 35
respektvoll 24
Ressource 226
Restaurant 61, 301
retten 291
Rettungsboot 291
Rettungsmannschaft
230
Revier 112
Revision(sverfahren)
111
Revolte 108
revoltieren 108
Revolution 98, 108,
141
revolutionär 108
Revolutionär 108
Revolutionsführer
108
Rezept 77
rezeptfrei 193
Rezession 297
Reziprozität 139
Rhabarber 56
Rhein 216, 217
rhetorisch 180
Rheumakranke 245
rheumatisch 245
Rheuma(tismus) 70
Rheumatologie 244
Rhythmus 174
Richter 109, 122
Richter-Skala 211
richtig 31, 173
riechen 27
Riegel 55
Riesen- 301
Riesenerfolg 176
Riesenkonzern 299
Riesenrad 187
riesig 229, 269
Rinde 236
Rinder 220, 221
Rinderherde 221
Rinderwahnsinn 221
Rindfleisch 55
Rindvieh 221
Ringbuch 313
Ringen 196, 197
Rippe 13, 234
Risiko 307
rissig 230
Ritterstand 121
Ritual 139
Rivalität 96
Roaming 275
Rock 16, 65
Roggen 54, 221
Roggenbrot 54
Rohdaten 146
Rohdiamant 213
Rohstoffe 226

Rokoko 169
Rollbrett 18
-rolle 136
Rolle 38, 96, 155,
176
Rollladen 91
Rollo 91
Rollschuhe 18
Rollschuhlaufen
196, 199
Rollstuhl(fahrer) 74
Rolltreppe 294
Roma 135
Roman 175, 179,
267
Romanautor 180
romanisch 169, 177
Romanliteratur 179
Romantik 180
Romantiker 180
romantisch 180
Römer 156
röntgen 77
Röntgenaufnahme
77
Rose 27, 235, 236
Rosenkohl 55
rosig 16
Rosinen 56
Rosskastanie 235
rot 92, 111
rotbackig 15
rote Ampel 285
Rote Halbmond 230
rote Karte 197
Rote Kreuz 230
rote Zahlen 300
Röteln 69
Rothaarige 16
Rotwein 200
routinemäßig 290
Rowdy 131, 133
Rubin 213
Rückblende 180
Rücken 14, 75, 78
Rückenmuskulatur
83
Rückenschmerzen
76, 78
Rückenzerrung 72
Rückfahrkarte 288
Rückfalltäter 112
Rückgang 297, 299
rückgängig machen
188, 191, 289
Rückhand 197
Rücklauf 306
Rücknahme 226
Rückreise 288
Rucksack 261
Rucksackreisen 199
Rucksackwandern
199
Rücksicht 35
rücksichtslos 22, 286

Rücksichtslosigkeit
35
rücksichtsvoll 22
Rücktritt 106, 269
Rückzug 119
Ruder 52
Ruderboot 291
rufen 72
Rufton 275
Ruhe 13, 41, 155
Ruhe in Frieden 41
Ruhegehalt 115
ruhend 241
Ruhestand 20
Ruhetag 84
Ruhezeit 84
ruhig 24, 26
Ruhr 69
Rührei 54, 192
rühren 58
rührend 30
Rummel 306
Rumpfheben 84
rund 16
rund um die Uhr 91
Rundfahrt 188
Rundfunk 270
Rundfunkanstalt 270
Rundfunkgerät 270
Rundfunkhörer 271
Rundfunksendung
271
rundlich 15, 16
Rundreise 188
runter 193
runterkommen 208
runterlassen 91
runzlig 16
rupfen 13
Rüstungskontrolle
118
Rute 52

S
Saal 87, 240
Saat(gut) 221
Sabbat 163
Sabotage 107
Sabotageakt 107
Sabotagehandlung
107
sabotieren 107
Sachbücher 266
Sache 32, 140, 313
Sachschaden 230
Sack 261
Sackgasse 285
Sadismus 37
säen 221, 236
Saft 57, 58
Sage 179
sagen 51, 84, 155,
353
sägen 255
Sahne 54

Sahnebonbon 55
saisonbedingt 126
Sakko 64
Sakrament 163
Salat 56, 58
Salatsoße 56
Salbe 70, 77
Salz 55
salzig 27
Salzkartoffeln 56
Samen 221
Samenerguss 36
Samen(flüssigkeit) 36
sammeln 199
samstagabends 187
Sandalen 65
Sanddünen 219
Sandkasten 18
Sandstrand 219
sanft 24, 238
Sanftmut 31
Sänger 173
Saphir 213
Sarg 41
Satellit 204, 207
Satire 179
satirisch 179, 268
Sättigung 172
Saturn 204
Satz 84, 197
Satzball 197
Satzfehler 267
sauber machen 92
Sauberkeitserziehung 50
säubern 92
Säuberung(en) 135
sauer 27, 54, 226
Sauerstoff 243
Sauerstoffmaske 290
saufen 200
Säufer 129, 200
Sauftour 129
saugen 93
Säugetier 232
Säuglingssterblich- keit 130
Säule 158, 178
Sauna 38, 83
Säure 243
säurefrei 267
S-Bahn 293
Scanner 278
Schabe 234
schäbig 16
Schach 195, 198
Schachtel 38, 201
Schädel 12
Schaden 307
Schadenersatz 109, 307
Schädling 234
Schädlingsbekämp- fung 221

Schadstoff 225
Schaf 222
Schäfer 221
Schäferhund 232
schaffen 75, 169, 177, 287, 288, 304
Schaffner 288, 294
Schafherde 221
Schafhirte 221
Schafskäse 54
Schafspelz 238
Schal 66
Schale 59
schälen 58
schalldicht 26
schalten 256, 260, 305
Schalter 260, 288
Schalterangestellter 311
Schaltfläche 278
Schaltkreis 260
schämen 32
scharf 63, 172, 233, 301
scharf bremsen 256
Scharfeinstellung 172
Schärfentiefe 172
Scharia 163
Scharlach 68
Schattenkabinett 105
Schattenwirtschaft 296
schätzen auf 230
Schatzkanzler 105, 121
Schatzmeister 304
Schau 187
Schaubude 187
schauen 25
Schauer 228
Schauermann 310
Schauerroman 179
Schaufel 18
Schaufensterauslage 306
Schaukel 18
Schaukelpferd 17
Schaukelstuhl 90
Schaumwein 200
Schauplatz 180
Schauspieler 176
Schauspielerin 176
schauspielern 176
Scheck 303
Scheckbuchjourna- lismus 269
Scheibe 58
Scheide 14, 36
scheiden 49
Scheidendia- phragma 37
Scheidung 48, 49, 269

Schein 152, 302
scheinen 35, 105, 227
Scheinheilige 32
Scheinselb(st)ständ- igkeit 127
Scheiterhaufen 43
scheitern 49
Schellfisch 55
schelten 51
Schemel 90
schenken 184
Schere 255
scheu 24
scheuen 52
scheuern 92
Scheune 88, 222
Scheunendrescher 222
scheußlich 227
Schicht 210
Schichtenbruch 210
schick 15, 16
schicken 272, 273, 290
schicken lassen 291
Schiebefenster 88
Schiebetür 88
Schiedsrichter 197
Schiene(n-) 287
Schießbude 187
schießen 128, 132, 232
Schießstand 187
Schiff 119, 217, 291, 292
schiffbar 292
Schiffbruch 291
Schifffahrt 291
Schiffseigner 292
Schiffsreise 292
schikanieren 19
Schild 294
Schildkröte 234
Schimmel(pilz) 237
Schimpanse 233
schimpfen 51
Schinken 55, 192
Schirmmütze 66
Schiwa 160
schizophren 144
Schizophrene 144
Schizophrenie 144
Schlacht 119
Schlachtfeld 119, 236
Schlachtschiff 119
Schlafanzug 65
Schlafcouch 89
schlafende Hunde 238
Schlaflied 51
Schlaflosigkeit 70
Schlafsaal 125

Schlafstadt 215
Schlafwagen 287
Schlafzimmer 87
Schlag 13, 259
Schlaganfall 68, 74
Schläge 19
schlagen 19, 51, 58, 90, 133, 197
Schlager 173
Schläger 197
Schlägerei 133
Schlagsahne 54, 74
Schlagwort 98, 305
Schlagzeile 269, 314
schlammig 44
Schlange 192, 211, 234
schlank 15
Schlankheitskur 82
Schlankheitspillen 82
schlau 13, 24
schlecht 14, 21, 23, 31, 153, 271, 314
schlecht ausgebildet 154
schlecht laufen 298
schleichend 297
Schleichwerbung 306
Schleifen 212
Schleifmaschine 255
Schlepper 291
Schleuse 292
schlicht 23
schlichten 316
Schlichter 316
Schlichtungen 316
Schlichtungs- verfahren 316
schließen 277
schlimm 69
Schlingel 50
Schlips 66
Schlitten 18
Schlittschuhe 18
Schlittschuhlaufen 196, 199
Schloss 86
Schlosser 258
Schlucht 218
Schlüpfer 65
Schluss 180
Schlusschor 173
Schlüssel 192
Schlussfolgerung 146
schmal 15, 217
Schmarotzer 234
schmecken 27
Schmelztiegel 261
Schmelzwasser 211
Schmerz(en) 25, 27, 76, 78
-schmerzen 76

schmerzend 14, 70, 78
Schmerzmittel 77, 81
Schmetterling 199, 234
Schmiergelder 300
Schminke 39
schmoren 58
Schmuck 212, 213
Schmuckstein 212
Schmuckstück 213
schmuddelig 16
Schmuggel 131
Schmuggler 132
schmutzig 16, 93
Schnäppchen 193
Schnappschuss 171
Schnaps 129, 200
Schnecke 234
Schnee 228
schneiden 12
schneidend 227
Schneider 310
Schneidern 198
schneidig 15
schneien 228
schnell 120, 154, 289
Schnellgerichte 54
Schnellkochtopf 59
schnellste 285
Schnellstraße 284
Schnellzug 287
Schnittblumen 235
Schnittstelle 277, 278
Schnittwunden 72
schnitzen 169
Schnorcheltauchen 199
Schnuller 17
schnupfen 128
Schnupfen 69
Schnur 260
schnurlos 274
Schock 72, 153
Schöffe 109
Schokolade 55, 57, 251
Scholastiker 166
scholastisch 166
Scholle 55
schön 16, 25, 97, 183, 199, 216, 218, 227
Schöne 166
Schönheit 218
Schönheitswett-bewerb 187
schöpfen aus 146
Schöpfer 160
schöpferisch 305
Schöpfungsbericht 205
Schornstein 88

Schornsteinfeger 310
Schottenrock 65
schottisch 218
Schottland 219
Schrägstrich 278
Schrank 65, 89
Schraubenschlüssel 255
Schraube(nzieher) 255
Schraubstock 255
schrecklich 130
Schreibdienst 313
schreiben 155, 175, 246, 269, 305, 312, 313
Schreibmaschine 313
Schreibmaschinen-papier 312
Schreibpapier 313
Schreibtisch 90, 312
Schreibtisch-PC 276
Schreibtischlampe 312
Schreibwaren 194
Schreibwaren-geschäft 194
Schreibzentrale 313
schreien 30
Schreiner 310
schriftlich 140, 152
Schriftsetzer 267
Schriftsteller 180, 309
schrubben 92
Schub 207
Schublade 92
schüchtern 24
Schuhe 65
Schuhe putzen 38, 93
Schuhgeschäft 194
Schuhmacher 310
Schulaufsatz 151
Schulchor 173
Schuld 32, 110, 297
schulden 303
Schulden 303
Schuldgeständnis 111
schuldig 110
Schule 19, 154
Schüler 18, 153, 154
schulfrei 182
Schulkamerad 33
Schulmeister 52
Schulter 12, 78
Schultergelenk 72
Schundliteratur 179
Schundroman 179
Schuppen 222, 88
schüren 134
Schürfwunden 72
Schurke 176

Schurkenstaat 96
Schürze 66
Schürzenjäger 49
Schuss 128
Schüssel 59
Schusswaffen 132
schütten 261
Schutz 229, 280
schützen 277
Schutzimpfung 190
Schutzumschlag 266
schwach 21, 24, 228
Schwäche 21
Schwachsinn 74
Schwager 46, 47
Schwägerin 46
Schwalbe 233
Schwamm 38, 93, 237
Schwan 233
schwanger 37, 50
Schwangerschaft 37, 50
Schwangerschafts-abbruch 37, 98
schwänzen 19
schwärmen 28
schwarz 64, 96, 205
Schwarzarbeit 114
Schwarze 135
schwarze Brett 313
schwarze Kassen 101
schwarze Zahlen 300
Schwarzfahren 294
Schwarzfahrer 294
Schwarzgeldaffäre 101
Schwarzwald 219
Schwarzweiß- 171
Schwein 221
Schweinefleisch 55
Schweinegrippe 69
Schwein(ehund) 32
Schweineschmalz 55
Schweinestall 221
Schweizer Käse 54
schweizerisch 96
Schwellenland 117
Schwellung 70
schwer 13, 73, 120, 124, 269
schwer fallen 27
schwer verletzt 71
schwere See 291
Schwerelosigkeit 207
schwerhörig 26
Schwerhörigkeit 73
Schwerkraft 205
Schwermetall 212
Schwerpunkt 241
Schwerverletzte 81
Schwester 46, 77, 81
Schwieger- 46

Schwierigkeiten 75
Schwimmbad 88, 216
Schwimmbecken 216
schwimmen 28, 217
Schwimmen 82, 196
Schwimmlehrer 309
Schwimmweste 290
Schwindsucht 69
schwören 32
schwül 44, 227
schwul 36, 98
Schwule 36
Schwulenbewegung 98
Schwung verlieren 106
Schwungrad 256
scrollen 277
SD-Speicherkarte 282
Sedimentation 210
Sedimente 210
See 216, 291
Seebad 189
Seebestattung 41
Seeblick 191
seefest 292
Seehund 234
Seeklima 228
seekrank 292
Seekrankheit 68, 292
Seele 13, 41
Seeleute 52
seelisch 28, 76
Seemann 292
Seemeile 292
Seereise 291
Seezunge 55
Segel(-) 291
Segelboot 291
Segeln 196, 199, 291
segeln 292
segeln gehen 291
Segler(in) 196
sehbehindert 73
sehen 25, 182, 219, 232
Sehenswürdigkeiten 189
Sehkraft 73
sehnen 29, 34
sehr 29
Sehvermögen 25
seicht 270
Seife 38, 93
Seifenoper 270
seit 182
seit Jahren 13
Seite 78, 155, 266
Seitenlinie 197
Seitenschiff 178

Sekretär(in) 89, 311, 313
Sekt 200
Sekunde 172
Selbstachtung 84
Selbstbedienungs-restaurant 61
Selbstbefriedigung 37
Selbstbeherrschung 31
selbstbewusst 23
Selbstbildnis 168
selbstlos 22, 23
Selbstmord 42
Selbstmordanschlag 120
Selbstporträt 168
Selbstschutz 133
selb(st)ständig 127, 309
Selb(st)ständige 309
Selb(st)ständigkeit 127
selbstsüchtig 22
Selbsttötung 42
Selbstunterricht 154
Selbstverwirklichung 144
Selters(wasser) 57
Semester 156
Seminar 149
Semiotik 139
Senat 102, 103, 104
Senator 102, 103
senden 265, 270, 275
Sender 270
Sendezeit 270
Sendung 271, 301
Sendungsverfol-gung 273
Senf 55
senil 21
senile Demenz 74
Senilität 21
Senioren 21
senken 82, 113, 126, 258, 297, 300, 304
Sensationsmache 268
Sensationspresse 268
sensibel 23
Sensor 172, 262
sentimental 30, 270
Serie 271
Server 281
servieren 192
Sessel 90
Set 84
setzen 267
Setzer 267
Sex 23, 36

Sexismus 136
Sexist 136
sexistisch 134, 136
Sexual- 36
Sexualerziehung 36
Sexualität 36
Sexualkunde 150
Sexualtäter 36
Sexualverbrechen 36
Sexualverbrecher 36
sexuell 36, 136
Shampoo 39
Sherry 261
Show 270
Showgeschäft 94
sicher 281
Sicherheit 115
sicherheitshalber 77
Sicherheitskontrolle 289
Sicherheitsleistung 111
Sicherheitsrat 117
Sicherheitsventil 256
sicherlich 32
sichern 277
Sicherung 259
Sicherung(skasten) 260
Sicherungskopie 278
Sicht 25
sichtbar 25
Sichtvermerk 189
Sideboard 89
Sieb 58
sieben 58
sieden 58
Siedepunkt 243
Siedetemperatur 243
Sieg 120, 184, 185, 197
siegen 44
Siegesparade 184
Signet 306
Silage 222
Silber 212
Silberhochzeit 48, 184
silbern 184, 212
silberne Hochzeit 48
Silicium(chip) 255
Silo 222
Silvester 182
Silvesterparty 185
Sinfonie 173
singen 173
Singen 173
Singvogel 233
sinken 217, 291, 292, 300
Sinn 25
Sinneseindruck 25
sinnvoll 296
Sintflut 229

Sinti 135
Sitten 138
sittlich 31, 166
Sitz 103, 290
sitzen 27, 90, 175
sitzend 168
Sitzgurt 290
Sitzplatz 175
Sitzung 102, 103, 312
Sitzungsperiode 103
Skandalblatt 269
Skateboard 18
Skelett 14
Skeptiker 164, 166
skeptisch 166
Skeptizismus 164, 166
Ski laufen 196
Skifahren 196
Skilaufen 196, 199
Skilehrer 309
Skin(s) 134
Skonto 193
Skrupel 32
skulptieren 169
Skulptur 169
Slip 65
Slipper 65
Slogan 107
Slumbewohner 223
Smaragd 213
Smog 228
Smoking 64
SMS 275
Socken 66
Soda(wasser) 57
Sofa 90
Softwarepaket 276
sogenannt 138
Sohn 19, 46, 160
solange 301
solar betrieben 262
Solarkollektor 226
Solarmodul 226
Solarpanel 226
Solarzelle 226
Soldat 24, 41, 118
Solidarität 34
Solidaritätszuschlag 114
soll ich 173, 284
sollen 19, 160, 354
sollte 182
Sommer 185
Sommerferien 182
Sonate 174
Sonde 207
Sonderangebot 193, 194
Sonderbeauftragte 116
Sonderberater 105
Sondermüll 226
Sonderschule 148

Sonett 180
Sonne 204, 227
Sonnenbaden 83
Sonnenblume 235
Sonnenenergie 226
Sonnenfinsternis 204
sonnenhungrig 219
Sonnenkollektor 226
Sonnenöl 39
Sonnenschein 227
Sonnenstich 68
Sonnensystem 204
sonnig 227
Sonntagsbeilage 269
Sonntagsschule 149
Sopran 173
Sorgen 77
Sorgerecht 49
Soße 55
Souterrain 88
souverän 116
Souveränität 116
sowohl … als auch 97, 105
sozial 115, 125, 142, 145, 296
Sozial- 145
sozial benachteiligt 97
sozial Schwache 130
Sozialabbau 115, 130
Sozialabgaben 114
Sozialamt 115
Sozialarbeiter 310
soziale Netz 115
soziale Wohnungs-bau 86, 124
Sozialgeschichte 140
Sozialhilfe 115, 130
Sozialisation 145
Sozialisierung 145
Sozialismus 99
Sozialist 101
sozialistisch 101
Sozialkunde 150
Sozialleistungen 115
Sozialordnung 95
Sozialplan 126
Sozialreform 115
Sozialstaat 115
Sozialstruktur 138, 145
Sozialversicherung 115
Sozialwissenschaft 145
Sozialwissenschaften 137, 150
Sozialwohnung(en) 86, 124
Soziologe 145

Soziologie 145, 310
soziologisch 145
Spaghetti 55
Spalt 250, 294
Spalte 269
Spanien 118
spannend 267
Spanner 132
Spannung 34, 180, 259
Spannungen 117
Spanplatte(n) 254
sparen 52, 193, 303
Spargel 55, 220
Sparkasse 303
Sparkonto 303
Sparmaßnahmen 297
Sparpaket 297
Sparprogramm 297
Sparquote 303
sparsam 296
Sparsamkeit 296
Spartätigkeit 303
Spaßen 28
später 228
Spatz 233
spazieren gehen 219
Spazierengehen 83
Spaziergang 218
Specht 233
Speck 55, 60, 192
Speicher 87, 88
Speicher- 277
Speichererweiterung 277
Speicherkapazität 277
Speicherkarte 172
speichern 172, 277
Speiseeis 54
Speisekammer 88
Speisekarte 62
Speisepilz 55, 236
Speisewagen 61, 287
Spektrum 241
Spekulant 304, 308
Spekulation 146
Spende 114
Sperling 233
Sperma 36
Sperrholz 254
sperrig 273
spezialisiert 81
spezifisch 241
Spiegel 91
Spiegelei(er) 54, 58, 192
Spiegelreflexkamera 171
Spiel 195, 197
Spielbank 187
spielen 17, 155, 173, 176, 195, 197

Spielfeld 195
Spielfilm 175
Spielgruppe 17
Spielkamerad 33
Spielkasino 187
Spielwaren 257
Spielwarengeschäft 194
Spielzeug 17
Spielzeugauto 17
Spielzeugeisenbahn 17
Spinat 56
Spinne 234
Spinnen 198
Spinnwebe 234
Spion 120
Spionage 118
spionieren 120
Spirale 37
Spitzenbelastung 259
Spitzenmanager 299
Spitzentechnologie 254
Spitzname 10
Sponsor 271
Sport 150, 195, 199
Sportart 195, 196
Sportfest 184, 195
Sportgeschäft 194
Sportler 195
Sportlerin 195
sportlich 195
sportlich elegant 64
Sportplatz 195
Sportreporter 271
Sportsakko 64
Sportsendung 271
Sporttauchen 199
Sportteil 269
Spracherkennung 278
Sprachfehler 73
Sprachphilosophie 165
Sprachsteuerung 282
sprechen 26, 62, 73, 155, 275, 312
Sprecher 102, 269, 271
Sprecherin 269
Sprechstunde 75
Sprechstundenhilfe 75
Sprechzimmer 75
Sprengstoffanschlag 134
Sprichwort 52, 89
springen 30
Springen 196
Spritze 77, 79
Spritztour 19, 132
spröde 255

Sprudel 57
Sprühregen 228
Sprung wagen 238
spucken 201
Spülbecken 90
Spülbürste 93
Spule 259
Spüle 90
spülen 78, 90, 93
Spülmaschine 90
Spülmittel 93
Spülung 78
Spur 285
spüren 27, 78
Staat 96, 107, 116, 142, 215
Staatenbund 96
staatlich 296
Staats- 296
Staatsangehörigkeit 11
Staatsanwalt 109
Staatsanwaltschaft 109, 112
Staatsbesuch 116
Staatsbürgerkunde 142
Staatsbürgertum 98
Staatsgebiet 215
Staatshaushalt 297
Staatskirche 159
Staatskunst 116
Staatsmann 116
Staatsoberhaupt 105
Staatsschuld 297
Staatssekretär 106
Staatsstreich 108
Staatsunternehmen 296
Staatsverschuldung 297
Staatsvertrag 103, 117
stabil 142, 241
Stabilität 84, 297
Stabschef 105
Stachelbeeren 56
Stadion 195
Stadt 96, 97, 119, 185, 223, 224, 229, 230
Stadtbevölkerung 224
Stadtbewohner 223
Stadtbezirk 97
Stadtdirektor 310
Stadtentwicklung 224
Städter 223
Stadterneuerung 224
Stadtgebiet 97
Stadtgemeinde 97
Stadtgrenze 223
städtisch 224

Stadtkämmerer 304
Stadtplanung 223, 224
Stadtrand 224
Stadtrundfahrt 189
Stadtteil 96, 97
Stadtverwaltung 223, 224
Stadtzentrum 97, 223
Staffel 271
Staffellauf 195
staffeln 294
Stahl 212, 254, 255, 257
Stahlbeton 178
Stahlblech 254
Stahlskelettbauweise 178
Stahlstich 170
Stall 222
Stamm 139, 236
Stammbaum 46
Stammes- 139
Stammgast 61
stämmig 15
Stammzelle 237
Stammzell(en)forschung 237
Standard- 171
Standardabweichung 144
Standard(einstellung) 278
standardisiert 144
Standardsituation 197
Standesamt 48
standesamtlich 48
standhalten 262
ständig 133
Standleitung 279
Standuhr 90
Stange 201
stark 24, 72, 81, 119, 196, 228
stark adv. 156
starker Verkehr 285
Stärkung 83
Start 206
Startbahn 290
starten 119, 206, 277
Startrakete 207
Startrampe 206
Statik 240
Station 80, 294
Stationsarzt 81
Stationsschwester 81
statisch 178
Statistik(en) 145
stattfinden 48, 102
Statue 169
Statuette 169
Stau 285

Staub 41, 93
Staubsauger 90, 93
Staubtuch 93
Stausee 216
Steak 59
stechend 76, 78
Steckdose 90
stecken 13, 260
stecken bleiben 285
Stecker 260
Stecknadel 222
stehen 197
stehen (sich st.) 33
stehen zu 104
stehend 168
Stehlampe 90
Stehlen 132
steif 36
steigen 286, 299, 300
steigen lassen 18
steigern 258, 296
Stein 178
Steinigung 43
Steinplastik 169
Steinskulptur 169
Stelle 246
stellen 90, 103, 120, 172
Stellenabbau 126
stellvertretend 102
Stellvertreter 102
stempeln gehen 127
stenografieren 313
Stenotypistin 311
Steppe 218
Steppen 174
Stepptänzer 174
Sterbebett 40
Sterbehilfe 42
Sterbeklinik 40
sterben 14, 40, 42, 102, 112
sterben an 12, 69, 72, 129, 245
Sterben 40
sterbend 40
Sterbende 40
Sterbestation 81
Sterbeurkunde 40
sterblich 41
Sterbliche 122
stereotyp 134
Sterilisation 37
Stern 204
Sternbild 205
Sternschnuppe 204
Sternwarte 205
Steuer(n) 113
steuerbefreit 114
Steuerberater 114
Steuerbord 292
Steuererhöhung 113
Steuererklärung 113
Steuererstattung 114

steuerfrei 113, 114
Steuerhinterziehung 113
Steueroase 113
Steuerparadies 113
steuerpflichtig 114
Steuersenkung 113
Steuersenkungs-
gesetz 114
Steuersystem 113
Steuerung 278
Steuervergünsti-
gungen 113
Steuerzahler 113
Stich 78, 170
Stichprobe 145
Stichwahl 104
Stichwort 265
Sticken 198
Stief- 46
Stiel 236
Stier 238
Stift 282
still 52, 238
still lesen 154
stillen 50
stilles Wasser 57
Stillleben 168
Stimme 104
stimmen für 104
Stimmenthaltung 103
stimmig 165
Stimmlage 174
Stimmung 28
Stimulus 237
stockend 285
stocknüchtern 200
Stock(werk) 87
stinken 27
Stoff 27, 92, 128, 241, 242, 269
Stoffplan 151
Stofftier 17
stolz 24, 30
Stolz 30
stopfen 297
Stoppschild 286
Storch 233
stören 191
stornieren 191, 289
störrisch 24
Störung 73, 144
Story 269
stoßen auf 119
stoßen gegen 292
Stoßstange 285
Stoßzeiten 288
Stottern 74
strafbar 110
Strafe 111
Strafraum 197
strafrechtlich verfol-
gen 109
Strafsache 109

Strafstoß 197
Straftat 110, 131
Straftäter 19, 112, 131
Strafverfolgung 109
Strafzettel 286
strahlen 16
Strahlenchemie 242
strahlend 16
Strahlenkrankheit 68
Strahlenkunde 244
Strahlenschäden 68
Strahlentherapie 245
Strahlung 207
stramm 15
Strand 216
stranden 292
Straße 68, 216, 224, 285
Straßenanzug 64
Straßenbahn 293
Straßenkinder 130
Straßenkreuzung 285
Straßenmusikant 187
Straßenräuber 131
Straßenverkäufer 311
Straßenverkehr 284
Stratum 210
Sträucher 219
streichen 188, 289
Streichholzschachtel 199
Streichquartett 174
Streichung 115
Streifen 308
Streifencode 278
Streik 107, 189, 315
Streikbrecher 315
streiken 290, 315
Streikende 107
Streikposten 315
Streit 35, 117, 316
streiten 35
streitig 49
Streitigkeit 117
Streitkräfte 116, 118
streng 146, 227
streng erziehen 51
Streubombe 119
Strg 278
Strichcode 278
Stricher 37
Strichjunge 37
Stricken 198
Strickjacke 64
Stroh 221
Strohdach 87
Strohhalm 222
Strohhut 65
Strom 217, 240, 241, 259, 260
Strom führend 260

Ströme 228
Stromkreis 260
Stromnetz 259
Stromschlag 259, 260
Stromstärke 259
Strömung 217
Strömungslehre 241
Strömungsmechanik 241
Stromzähler 259
Strophe 180
Struktur 180, 241
strukturell 126
Strümpfe 65
Strumpfhose 65
Stuck 178
Stück 155, 176, 290, 302
Stück Land 308
Stück Seife 38
Stückeschreiber 176
Stückkosten 258
Student 20
Studienplatz 149
studieren 124, 149, 152, 154, 264
Studium 149, 153
Stuhl 90
Stuhl(gang) 13, 76
Stunde 90, 154, 155, 270, 289, 291
Stundenkilometer 250
Stundenlohn 316
Sturm 228
Stürmer 196
Sturmwarnung 228
Sturz 107
Sturzhelm 66
Stütze 178
subjektiv 30
Subkontinent 214
Substanz 241
subtrahieren 246
Subtraktion 246
Subventionen 297
Suchbegriff 265
Suche 264
Suche nach 166
suchen 25, 90, 111, 124, 125, 193, 247, 265, 277, 278
Sucher 172
Suchlauf 265
Suchmaschine 265
Sucht 128, 129
Süchtige 129
Suchwort 265
Süd- 215
Südafrika 215
Südamerika 214
Süden 215
Südküste 216
südlich 215, 216

Südpol 215
Südwesten 215
Südwind 228
Suezkanal 217
summen 274
Sumpf 218
Sünde 31, 162
sündhaft 31
sündig 31
Super-GAU 44
Supernova 204
Supertanker 291
Suppe 27, 55
Suppenküche 130
Suppenlöffel 59
Supraleiter 240
surfen 279
Surrealismus 169
süß 27, 57
Süßigkeiten 13, 55, 194
Süßschnabel 13
Symbol 139, 158, 243
symbolisch 139
symbolisieren 139
Symbolleiste 278
Sympathiestreik 315
sympathisch 22, 28
Symptom 68
Synagoge 162
synchronisieren 175
Synthese 146, 243
synthetisch 243
Syphilis 37
System 99, 142, 293
systemisch 241
Szene 176

T
Tabak 201
Tabakladen 201
Tablett 59
tabu 139
Tabu 139
tadellos 146
Tafel 55, 155, 170
Tag 182, 184, 227
Tagebuch 179
tagen 102, 103
Tageskarte 63, 294
Tageslichtprojektor 155
Tagesmenü 63
Tagesmutter 17
Tagesrückfahrkarte 288
Tagessuppe 62, 63
Tageszeit 97
Tageszeitung 268
täglich 77, 128
Taifun 229
Takt 35, 174
taktlos 23
Taktlosigkeit 35

Taktschlag 174
taktvoll 23
Tal 218
Talent 23
Talkmaster 271
Talkshow 271
Talmud 163
Tangens 247
Tangente 247
Tank 91, 261
Tankstelle 286
Tanne 235
Tannenzapfen 235
Tante 47, 51, 185
Tanz 173, 174, 187
Tanz- 174
Tanzabend 185
Tanzen 174
tanzen 174, 185, 187
tanzen gehen 174, 187
Tänzer(in) 48,174
Tanzfläche 174
Tanzkapelle 174
Tanzparty 185
Tanzschule 174
Tanzstudio 174
Tanzveranstaltung 185
Tapezierer 310
tapfer 24
Tapferkeit 31, 32
Tarif 316
Tarifabschluss 316
Tarifverhandlungen 316
Tarifvertrag 316
Tasche 190, 302
Taschenbuch(-) 266
Taschenbuch-
  ausgabe 266
Taschendieb 132
Taschendiebstahl 132
Taschengeld 51
Taschentuch 39
Tasse 59
Tastatur 276, 282
Tastsinn 25
Tat 31
tätig 98
tätig sein 309
Tätigkeit 198, 211
Tatverdächtige 112
Tau 228
taub 26, 74
Taube(n) 100, 233
Taubheit 74
taubstumm 26, 74
Taubstumme 74
Taubstummheit 74
Tauchen 196
Taufe 50
taufen 163
täuschen 152

tausende 126, 230, 315
Taxameter 294
Taxi 71, 294
Taxifahrer 303
Taxifahrt 294
Taxistand 294
Tbc 69
Technik 150, 254
technisch 254, 278
Technologie 254, 262, 282
technologisch 254
Teddybär 17
Tee 57, 60, 192
Teekanne 59, 261
Teelöffel 59
Teenager 16, 19
Teergehalt 201
Teewagen 89
Teich 216
Teig 55
Teigwaren 55
Teil 87, 216, 258
Teilchenbeschleu-
  niger 262
teilen 171, 202
Teilgebiet 145, 166
Teilkaskoversiche-
  rung 307
teilnehmen 119, 162, 186
Teilzeitarbeit 127
Telefax 275
Telefon(-) 91, 186, 274
Telefonat 274
Telefonauskunft 274
Telefonbuch 264, 274
Telefongebühren 274
Telefongespräch 274
Telefonhörer 275
telefonieren 274
Telefonist(in) 311
Telefonkarte 199, 275
Telefonkunde 275
Telefonleitung 275
Telefonnummer 274
Telefonzelle 275
Telefonzentrale 275
Tele(heim)arbeit 278
Tele(heim)arbeiter 278
Teleobjektiv 171
Teller 59
Tempel 163
Temperatur 68, 76, 225, 227
Tempolimit 250
Tennis 198
Tennisarm 70

Tennisellbogen 70
Tennisplatz 195, 197
Tennisschläger 197
Tennistrainer 197
Tenor 173
Teppich 92, 93
Teppich(boden) 91
Termin 75, 269, 298, 312
Terminal 279
Terrain 215
Terrasse 88
territorial 116
Territorium 215
Terroranschlag 108
Terrorismus 108
Terrorismusbekämp-
  fung 112
Terrorist 108
terroristisch 108
Tesafilm™ 313
Test 144
Testament 43, 162
Testmarkt 306
teuer 89, 191, 213, 300
Teufel 162, 238
Text 154, 155, 173, 180, 269, 277
Textaufgabe 246
Texter 305
Textilbranche 298
Textkritik 140
Textverarbeitung 276
Textverarbeitungs-
  programm 276
Theater 175, 176, 224
Theaterkasse 175
Theaterstück 176
Theaterviertel 97
Thema 115, 125, 165, 176, 354
Theokratie 99
Theologie 162
theologisch 149
Theoretiker 240
theoretisch 240
Theorie 146, 165, 240, 241
Therapeut 144
Thermalquelle 217
Thermodynamik 240
Thermometer 227
thermonuklear 262
Thermoprinter 277
Thermosflasche 261
Thesaurus 264
Thora 163
Thorax 245
Thronjubiläum 184
Thronrede 103
Thunfisch 55
tief 69, 76

Tiefdruck 170
Tiefenschärfe 172
Tiefenstruktur 180
Tiefkühltruhe 90
Tiefland 218
Tier 71, 232
Tierarzt 94, 234
Tierkadaver 40
Tierquälerei 232
Tierreich 232
Tierschutz 232
Tierschützer 232
Tierschutzverein 96,
232
Tiger 233
Tinte 170, 313
Tintenpartone 313
Tintenstrahldrucker
277
tippen 312
Tippfehler 312
Tisch 61, 62, 90
Tischdecke 90, 92
Tischler 310
Titelgeschichte 269
Titelseite 266, 269
Toast 59, 186
toasten 59
Toaster 59, 90
Tochter 46
Tod 40, 42
Todesanzeige 42
Todesfall 40
Todeslager 133
Todesopfer 229,
230
Todesspritze 43
Todesstrafe 111
Todestag 184
Todeszelle 40
tödlich 41
Todsünde 32, 162
Toilette 39, 61, 90
Toilettenartikel 194
Toilettenmann/-frau
311
Toilettenpapier 38,
39
tolerant 23
tolerieren 29
Tollwut 68
Tomate 27, 56, 192
Tomatensalat 56
Ton(-) 26, 169
Tonart 174
Tonbandgerät 271
Tonhöhe 174
Tonkrug 59
Tonlage 174
Tonleiter 174
Tonne 261
Topf 50, 59, 261
Töpfchen 50
Töpfe 59
Töpfern 198

Topfpflanze 88, 235
Topografie 211
Tor 88
töricht 23
torlos 197
Tornado 229
Torte 54
Torwart 196
tot 40
tot umfallen 40
total 176
totalitär 99
Tote 40, 120
Tote Meer 215
Totem 139
töten 42
Totengräber 41
Totenmesse 41
Totenschein 40
Totschlag 110, 131
Tötung 110
Tötungsdelikt 131
Tour 188
Tourist 188
Touristen- 187
Touristenklasse 289
Trabant 204
Trabantenstadt 223
Tracht Prügel 19
Tragbahre 72
tragbar 282
tragen 16, 64, 196,
213
Trägerrakete 206
Tragetasche 261
Trägheit 32
Trägheitsmoment
241
tragisch 179
Tragödie 179
trainieren 83
Training 83, 84
Traktor 222
trampen 284
Tramper 284
Transformator 259
Transistor 260
Transistorradio 260
Transplantation 245
Transportmittel 283
transsexuell 98
transzendent 164
Traubensaft 57
trauen 30, 48
Trauer 42
Trauerfall 42
Trauerfeier 41
trauern 42
Trauerweide 235
Trauerzug 41
Traum 144
Träumen 144
Trauring 48
Trauschein 48
Trauung 48, 184

Trauzeuge 48
treffen 86, 185, 355
Treffen 185
treiben 195
Treibhaus 88
Treibhauseffekt 225
Treibstoff 207
Treibstofftank 261
trennen 49, 275
Trennstrich 278
Trennung 49
Treppe 87
Treppenabsatz 88
treten 13, 19, 196,
315
treu 32, 49
Treue 31, 32
Triebverbrecher 36
Triebwerk 207
Trigonometrie 246
Trimester 156
trinken 28, 60, 186,
200, 201, 251
Trinken 200
Trinker 129, 200
Trinkgeld 62, 189,
294
Trinkspruch 186
Trinkwasser 57
Trip 128
Tripper 37
Triumphbogen 178
Trivialliteratur 179
trocken 62, 63, 228
Trockner 90
Trojanisches Pferd
280
Trommelfell 12
Tropen 214
Tropenkrankheiten
68
Tropenwald 225
Tropf 81
trotz 225
Trotzalter 51
trübe 228
trübsinnig 24
Truhe 261
Trunkenheit am
Steuer 286
Truppen 119
Truthahn 55
Tsunami 229
Tube 38
Tuberkulose 69
Tuch 93
Tugend 31, 32
Tulpe 236
Tulpenzwiebel 236
Tumor 69
tun 261
Tun 139
Tunichtgut 32
Tür 88, 254
türkisches Bad 83

Türklingel 91
Turm 178
Turmspitze 178
Turnen 83
Turnhalle 83, 195
Turnier 195
Turnschuhe 65
Turnübungen 83
Tusche 170
Tuschkasten 18
Tuschzeichnung 170
Tüte 61, 261
Typ 14, 24, 84
Typhus 68
Typhus(schutz)imp-
fung 190
typisch 68
Typoskript 267
tyrannisieren 19

U
U-Bahn 293
U-Bahnfahrer 293
U-Bahnfahrgäste 293
U-Bahnhof 132, 293
U-Bahnplakat 306
U-Boot 119
übel 76
Übelkeit 50, 68
über 134, 227, 294
überbelichtet 171
Überbelichtung 172
überbuchen 290
Überdosis 40, 129
Überdüngung 226
überfahren 71, 286
Überfahrt 27, 292
Überfall 119, 132
überfallen 119
überfliegen 26, 264
überflüssig 126
überfluten 229
übergeben 76
übergewichtig 15
Übergriff 135
überkronen 79
überleben 24, 69,
230
Überlebende 72
überlegen 135
Überlegenheit 136
Überlieferungen 140
übernachten 125
Übernachtung 191,
192
Übernahme 301
Übernahmeangebot
301
übernehmen 155,
313
überqueren 116, 217
überraschen 30
überraschend 180
überrascht 30
Überraschung 30

überregional 268
Überreste 41
Überschall- 289
Überschrift 155, 269
überschwemmen 229
Überschwemmung 229
übersetzen 266
Übersetzer 266
Übersetzung 266
Überstunden 316
überteuert 300
übertragen 37, 265, 266, 270
Übertragung 270
übertreten 158
Übertretung 110
Überweg 285
überweisen 75, 303
überwiegend 228
überzeugend 146
Überzeugung 142, 158, 164
Überziehung 303
Übung 83
Ufer 216
Uhr 90, 91, 198, 212, 294
Uhrmacher 310
Ultraschall- 77
um … herum 97
umbringen 30, 42, 43
Umbruch 267
Umfang 247
umfassen 102
Umfeld 145
Umformer 259
Umfrage 145
Umgang 33, 185
umgangssprachlich 44
umgeben 88
Umgebung 218
Umgehungsstraße 285
umkommen 40
umkreisen 204, 207
Umlaufbahn 204, 207
umlegen 43
Umleitung 285
umrühren 58
umrunden 206
ums Leben kommen 71
Umsatz 299, 300
Umsatzrückgang 299
Umschalttaste 278
Umschlag 261
umschulen 127
Umschulung 127
umsetzen 300
Umstände 111

umsteigen 288, 294
Umtausch 190
umtauschen 190
Umweg 285
Umwelt(-) 225
Umweltbewusstsein 225
umweltfreundlich 225
Umweltkatastrophe 225
Umweltorganisation 225
Umweltprobleme 225
Umweltschutz 225
Umweltschutz- behörde 106
Umweltschützer 225
Umweltthemen 225
Umweltverschmut- zung 225
Umzug 184
unabhängig 96
Unabhängige 101
Unabhängigkeit 182
unangenehm 16
unansehnlich 16, 52
unanständig 22, 32
unattraktiv 16
unaufrichtig 22
unbebaut 308
unbegeistert 146
unbegleitet 290
unbegrenzt 96
unbekannt 41, 188
Unbekannte 247
unbemannt 206
unbeschränkt 298
Unbeteiligte 132
unbewusst 144
Unbewusste 143
unblutig 108
unduldsam 22
uneben 215
unecht 212
unehrlich 22
Unehrlichkeit 32
Uneinigkeit 34
unendlich 247
Unentschieden 197
unerfahren 22
unerschlossen 308
unerträglich 78
unfähig 22
Unfähigkeit 73
unfair 22
Unfall 71
Unfallopfer 72
Unfallstation 81
Unfallstelle 72
Unfallversicherung 307
unflexibel 22
unfreundlich 227

Unfreundlichkeit 35
ungeduldig 22
ungefähr 233, 250, 251
ungehemmt 22
Ungehorsam 32, 107
ungekürzt 267
ungelernt 309
ungepflegt 16
ungerade 248
ungerecht 22, 32
Ungerechtigkeit 32
Ungeziefer 234
Unglaube 164
ungläubig 164
Ungläubige 163
Unglück 71
unheilbar 42, 81
unhöflich 22, 23
Unhöflichkeit 35
unhörbar 26
Uni 94
Union 96, 101, 117
Universität 149, 152
Universum 204
Unkeuschheit 32
Unkraut 220, 236
Unkrautvertilgungs- mittel 220
unkultiviert 22
unlauter 296
Unmäßigkeit 32
Unmoral 31
unmoralisch 31
UNO 117
unrecht 31
Unrecht 31
unreif 22, 23
Unruhe(n) 107, 314
Unruhestifter 32
unscharf 172
Unschuld 31
unschuldig 31, 110, 133
unsichtbar 25
unsinkbar 292
Unsinn 278
unsittlich 31, 32
Unsittlichkeit 31
unsolide 146
unsterblich 41
unsympathisch 22
unten 155, 216
unter 227
unterbelichtet 172
unterbewusst 144
Unterbrecher 260
Unterbrechung 182
unterbringen 86
unterdrücken 107, 108
unterdrückt 144
Unterdrückung 136
unteres Ende 87

Untergebene 312
untergehen 291
Untergeschoss 88
untergewichtig 15
Untergrund- 107
Untergrund- bewegung 107
Unterhalt 49
unterhalten 35, 185
Unterhaltung 35, 271
Unterhaus 102
Unterhauswahl 104
Unterhemd 65
Unterhose 65
Unterkiefer 78
Unterklasse 33
Unterkühlung 72
Unterkunft 86, 191
Unterlegscheibe 256
Unterleib 13
Untermiete 86
Unternehmen 296, 298, 314, 315
Unternehmens- berater 310
Unternehmens- kultur 299
Unternehmens- leitung 314
Unternehmer 296
Unternehmer- gewinne 296
Unternehmertum 296
Unterredung 35, 312
Unterricht 154, 276
unterrichten 51, 154
Unterrichtsfach 150
Unterrichtsstoff 156
Unterrichtsstunde 154
Unterrock 65
Unterschlagung 131
Unterschrift 281
unterste 156
unterstützen 34
Unterstützung 33, 34, 278
untersuchen 77, 242
Untersuchung 77, 80, 145, 146, 242
Untersuchungshaft 111, 112
Untertasse 59
untertauchen 107
unterteilen 97
Untertitel 175
Unterverzeichnis 277
Unterwäsche 65
unterzeichnen 117
unterziehen 80, 81, 152
untreu 49
Untreue 49
unverbleit 212

unverletzt 71
Unverschämtheit 35
unversehrt 230
unverzichtbar 270
unvorsichtig 23
Unwetter 228
Unze 251
unzüchtig 32
unzufrieden 22
Unzurechnungs-
fähigkeit 110
unzustellbar 273
unzuverlässig 22
Urabstimmung 315
Uranus 204
Uraufführung 175
Urchrist 158
Urenkel 47
Urgroß- 47
Urheberrecht 267
Urin 13
urinieren 13
Urknalltheorie 205
Urkunde 140, 308
Urlaub 182, 216, 316
Urlaubsort 189
Urlaubsreiseverkehr
315
Urne 41
Urologe 244
Urologie 244
Ursache 130, 166
Ursprungsdaten
146
Urteil 111
Ururgroßvater 47
Urwald 219
USA 116, 261
USB-Stick 282
use n. 262
Uterus 14

V
Vagina 14, 36
Vakuum 241
Validität 144
Vandalismus 131
Vanille 55
Variable 146, 247
Vase 261
Vasektomie 37
Vater 17, 46, 160
Vatermord 42
Vaterunser 163
V-Ausschnitt 64
Vegetarier 82
vegetarisch 59, 82
Vene 14, 70
Venenentzündung
70
Ventil 256
Ventilator 90
Venus 204
Venusmuschel 238
verabredet 185

Verabredung 185
verabscheuen 29
verachten 30
Verachtung 35
veraltet 258
Veranda 88
Verandatür 88
verändern 77
Veränderungen
100
verankern 292
Veranlagung 114
veranstalten 107,
145, 186
Veranstaltung 202
verantwortungsbe-
wusst 22
verantwortungslos
22, 23, 268
verarbeitend 258
verärgert 30
verarmt 130
Verband 72
verbessern 83, 224,
278
verbessert 316
verbesserte Version
278
verbilligt 288
verbinden 72, 166,
275
Verbindung 35, 242,
243, 275, 287
verblüfft 30
verboten 131, 187,
288, 308
Verbrauch 297
Verbraucher 306
Verbraucherpreise
297
Verbrauchsstelle
260
Verbrechen 110, 131,
133
Verbrechens-
bekämpfung 131
Verbrechensverhü-
tung 131
Verbrecher 131
Verbrecherbande
33
verbrennen 225
Verbrennung(en) 71,
243
Verbrennungsmotor
256
verbringen 18, 199
verbunden 276
Verbündete 116
Verdächtige 112
verdammen 146
verdammt 32
verdampfen 241
Verdauungsstörung
69

verderben 27, 52
Verdichtung 172
verdienen 34, 52,
113, 302
verdorben 27, 69
verdrängen 301
Verdrängungs-
wettbewerb 301
verdrehen 72
Verdunkelung 131
verdünnt 243
Veredelung 257
verehren 158
Verein 33
vereinbaren 312
Vereinbarung 300
vereinfachen 113,
262
Vereinigte Staaten
103
Vereinigung 36, 96
Vereinte Nationen
117
vereinzelt 228
vereist 44
Verfahren 109
Verfall 21, 79
verfassen 202
Verfasser 180
Verfassung 72, 83,
103
verfolgen 100, 109,
117
Verfolgte 134
Verfolgung 107
verfügbar 304
vergammelt 16
vergangen 267
Vergaser 256
Vergehen 110
vergessen 77
Vergewaltiger 37,
131
Vergewaltigung 37,
131
vergießen 234
vergiften 42
Vergiftung 42
Vergissmeinnicht
236
Vergleich 109
vergleichend 143
Vergnügungen
187
Vergnügungspark
187
vergriffen 267
Vergrößerung 171,
172
verhalten 22, 23
Verhalten 22, 31, 35,
142, 143, 144,
145, 195
Verhaltensforschung
143

Verhaltensmuster
142, 145
Verhaltensnormen
145
Verhaltenspsycho-
logie 143
Verhältnis 49, 247
verhandeln 117, 316
Verhandlungen 111,
117
Verhandlungsführer
316
verhängen 117
verhärmt 15
verheerend 229,
230
verheiratet 11, 48
verhindern 103
verhungern 42, 130,
230
Verhütungs-
methoden 37
Verifikation 165
verifizieren 165
verkalkt 21
Verkauf 194, 299
verkaufen 213, 298,
299, 308
Verkäufer 125, 193,
300, 311
Verkaufsdirektor 299
Verkaufsförderung
306
Verkaufszahlen 299
Verkehr 285
verkehren 61, 185,
287, 293
Verkehrsampel 285
Verkehrsamt 188
Verkehrsdelikt 286
Verkehrsflugzeug
289
Verkehrshindernis
285
Verkehrsinfarkt 285
Verkehrskollaps 285
Verkehrsmaschine 28
9
Verkehrsmittel 281,
293
Verkehrspolizist 286
Verkehrssicherheit
285
Verkehrssünder 112
Verkehrstote 286
Verkehrsunfall 286
verklagen 109
Verklappung 226
verkrüppelt 73
verkürzen 288
Verkürzung 316
Verlag 267
Verlagswesen 266
verlangen 191, 274
Verlangen 29

verlängern 189, 271
Verlängerung 196
Verlängerungs-
schnur 260
Verlangsamung 241
verlassen 188, 277
verlässlich 22
verlautbaren 269
verlegen 91, 267
verletzen 12, 28,
71, 316
Verletzte 72
Verletzung 41, 71, 81
Verleumdung 133
verlieben 34
verliebt 34
verlieren 35, 104,
109, 195, 300
verlobt 48
Verlobte 48
Verlobung 48
Verlust(e) 120, 300,
301, 314
vermerken 155
vermieten 308
vermindert 111
vermitteln 117, 316
Vermittler 117, 316
Vermittlung 275
Vermögen 297
Vermögensteuer 114
vernachlässigen 51
Vernehmung 112
vernichten 225, 230
Vernichtungslager
40
Vernunft 164
vernünftig 23
vernunftmäßig 165
veröffentlichen 117,
267
Verordnung 77
Verpackung 226
Verpackung(smate-
rial) 261
verpassen 287, 288,
292
Verpflegung 191
verpflichtet 226
Verpflichtungen 304
Verrat 108
verregnet 228
verreisen 182
verrenken 72
verringern 226
verrückt 24, 285
Vers 180
Versanddokumente
301
Versandhaus 193
Versandhauskatalog
193
Versandpapiere 301
verschieden 166
verschiffen 291

Verschlanken 126,
316
verschlechtern 127
verschlüsseln 279
Verschlusszeit 172
Verschmutzung 225
Verschuldung 297
verschütten 92
Verschwendung 226
verschwören 107
Verschwörer 107
Verschwörung 107,
108
Versdichtung 179
versenden 273, 289,
301
Versenkung 226
versessen 29
Verseuchung 225
Versform 180
Versicherer 307
versichern gegen
307
versichert 307
Versicherung 190,
307
Versicherungs-
anspruch 307
Versicherungs-
bedingungen 307
Versicherungs-
nehmer 307
Versicherungspolice
307
Versicherungsschein
307
Versicherungsschutz
307
Versicherungstarife
307
Versicherungs-
vertreter 307
Versmaß 180
Versorgungsteil 207
verspätet 289
Verspätung 189, 288
verstaatlichen 287
Verstand 143
Verständnis 165
verstärken 101, 260
Verstärker 260
Verstärkung 143
verstauchen 72
Verstauchung 72
verstauen 290
versteckte Kamera
271
verstehen 19, 33,
113, 165
versteinern 211
Versteinerung 211
Versteinerungskunde
210
verstimmt 173
verstopft 285

Verstopfung 69
verstorben 40, 42
Verstorbene 40
verstreut 46
Versuch 240
versuchen 26, 155
Versuchsergebnisse
20
Versuchsgelände 206
Versuchskaninchen
233
Versuchstiere 232
verteidigen 118
Verteidiger 110, 196
Verteidigung 110,
111, 118, 196
Verteidigungs-
ausgaben 118
Verteidigungs-
minister 106, 118
Verteidigungs-
ministerium 118
Verteidigungspolitik
100
verteilen 306
Vertrag 312
vertragen 29, 200
Vertragsbestimmun-
gen 300
Vertrauen 18
vertrauenswürdig 32
vertraulich 34
vertraut 34
vertreiben 300
vertreten 12, 72, 103
Vertreter 300
Vertreterstab 300
Vertrieb 299
Vertriebs- 299, 300
Vertriebsleiter 299
Vertriebspartner 300
vertrottelt 21
Veruntreuung 131
verurteilen 111
verursachen 14, 78,
229, 230, 307
Verwaltung 105, 308
Verwaltungschef 309
verwandt 46
Verwandte 46
Verwandtschaft 138
Verwarnungsgeld
111
verwenden 221, 243
Verwerfung 210
Verwestlichung 139
Verwitterung 211
verwöhnen 51, 52
Verwundete 120
verwuschelt 16
verwüsten 230
Verwüstungen 230
Verzeichnis 277
verziehen 51
Verzögerung 189

verzollen 189
verzweifeln 30
verzweifelt 30
Verzweiflung 30,
130
Vesuv 229
Veteran 20
Veto 103
Vetter 47
Viagra™ 37
Video(-) 25, 271
Videoanruf 202
Videokassette 271
Video-Plattform 202
Videorekorder 271
Vieh 221
Viehbestand 221
Viehfutter 221
Viehzucht 221
viel 199
Vielfalt 138
Vielflieger 289
vielsagend 270
Vielzahl 257, 262
Viereck 247
viereckig 247
Vierergruppe 155
Viertaktmotor 256
Viertel 97
Viertelnote 174
vierzehn Tage 185
Villa 87
Violinkonzert 174
virtuell 265, 282
Virus 237, 280
Visite 80
Visitenkarte 312
visuell 25
Visum 189
Vitamin 82
Vizepräsident 105
Vogel 233
Vogelbauer 234
Vogelbeobachtung
199
Vogelgrippe 69
Vogelnest 233
Volk 96, 138
Völker 138
Völkergemeinschaft
116
Völkerkunde 138
Völkermord 42, 133
Völkerrecht 142
Volksentscheid 104
Volksfest 184, 187
Volksgruppe 134
Volkshochschule 149
Volkshochschulkurs
149
Volkskunst 138
Volkslied 138
Volksmärchen 138
Volksmedizin 138
Volksmusik 138

Volksvermögen 297
Volkswirtschaft 296
Volkswirt(schaftler) 296
Volkswirtschaftslehre 296
Volkszählung 145
voll 97, 261
voll machen 261
vollautomatisch 171
Vollbild Aids 70
vollendet 168
völlig 74
Vollkaskoversicherung 307
vollkommen 23, 26, 230
Vollkornbrot 54, 82
Vollmilch 54
Vollnarkose 81
Vollpension 191
Volltextsuche 265
Vollversammlung 117
Vollwertkost 82
Vollzug 111
Volt 259
Volumen 241
vorangegangen 304
Vorarbeiter 309
Vorausexemplar 267
Vorbau 88
Vorbeiflug 206
vorbereiten 152, 153
vorbestellen 61
Vordach 88
Vordergrund 172
voreingenommen 30, 134
Voreinstellung 278
Vorfahr 46
Vorfall 135
vorführen 175
Vorgang 210, 242
Vorgarten 88
vorgehen 90, 109
Vorgehensweise 84
vorgerückt 20
Vorgeschichte 140
vorgeschichtlich 138, 140
Vorgesetzte 312
vorhaben 185
Vorhand 197
Vorhang 91
Vorherrschaft 139
vorherrschend 159
Vorhersage 227
vorig(e) 76, 152, 185, 251, 270
Vorkommen 210
Vorlage 102, 104
vorlesen 154
Vormarsch 119
vormerken 313

Vormund 51
Vormundschaft 51
Vorname 10
Vorort 224
Vorrat 301
vorrätig 301
Vorrichtung 255
vorsagen 155
Vorschrift 315
Vorschule 148
vorscrollen 277
vorsichtig 23
Vorsitz 106
Vorsitzende 309
Vorspeise 62
Vorspeisen 63
vorspielen 173
Vorstand 299
Vorstandsmitglied 299
Vorstandssprecher 301
Vorstandsvorsitzende 299
Vorsteherdrüse 14
vorstellen 90
Vorstellung 165, 175
Vorteil 254
vorübergehend 110
Vorurteil(e) 30, 134
Vorwahl(nummer) 104, 275
vorwerfen 292
Vorwort 266
vorzeitig 50
vorziehen 29
Voyeur 132
Vulkan 211, 229
Vulkanausbruch 211
Vulkanologie 210

W
Wache 112
Wachhund 232
Wachraum 81
wachsam 133
Wachsamkeit 133
wachsen 221, 250
Wachsfigurenkabinett 187
Wachsmalstift 18
Wachstation 81
Wachstum 297
wackeln 78
Waffel 54
Waffen 56
Waffenbesitz 132
Waffenhändler 298
Waffenstillstands- 117
Wagen 284, 303
Wagenburg 125
Wahl 101, 104
wählen 62, 99, 104, 275, 309

Wähler 104
Wählerverhalten 142
Wahlfach 150
Wahlkampf 104
Wahlkampffinanzierung 101
Wahlkreis 103
Wahlplattform 101
Wahlprogramm 101
Wählton 275
Wahnsinnspreis 13
wahr 166
während 141, 156, 274, 356
Wahrhaftigkeit 31
Wahrheit 13, 52, 166
wahrnehmbar 26
wahrnehmen 25
Wahrnehmung 25, 143
Wahrsager 164
Wahrsagerei 164
wahrscheinlich 160
Wahrscheinlichkeitsrechnung 246
Währung 304
Währungspolitik 304
Währungsunion 117, 304
Waisenhaus 51
Waise(nkind) 51
Wald 219, 225
Waldbrand 230
Wäldchen 219
Waldgebiet 219
Walfänger 291
Wal(fisch) 291
Walnuss 56
Walzer 174
Wand 178
Wandel 145
Wanderer 188
wandern 188
Wandern 83, 199
Wanderung 139, 188
Wandschrank 89
Wanduhr 90
Wanze 234
Ware(n) 27, 285, 289, 296, 298, 300, 301, 302
Warenaustausch 296
Warenbestand 301
Warenbörse 304
Warenhaus 193
Warenlager 301
Warensendung 301
Warenverkehr 296
warm 227
warm halten 74
Wärme 241
wärmer 227

Wärmewirkungsgrad 258
Warmluftfront 227
Warmwasserbereiter 90, 91
Warnstreik 315
Warnung 229
Warteliste 290
warten 38, 275, 279
warten auf 297
Wartesaal 288
Wartung 258
Waschbecken 90
Wäsche 38, 39, 92, 93
waschen 38, 39, 92, 93
Waschen 92
Wäscherei 39
Waschlappen 38
Waschmaschine 90
Waschmittel 93
Waschpulver 93
Waschsalon 39
Waschzettel 266
Wasser 243, 261
Wasserfahrzeuge 291
Wasserfall 217
Wasserhahn 90
Wasserkessel 90, 91
Wasserlassen 75
wasserlöslich 243
Wasserschildkröte 234
Wasserskilaufen 199
Wasserspeicher 91
Wasserstoff 207, 243
Wasserstoffbombe 119
Wasserstraße 292
Wasserverschmutzung 225
Watt 259
Watte 39
Wattestäbchen 38, 39
Weben 198
Webseite 279
Wechseljahre 20
Wechselkurs 190, 304
wechseln 190, 286, 302
Wechselstrom 259
Wechselstromgenerator 259
Wechselstube 190
Wechselwähler 104
wecken 192, 238
Wecker 13, 90
Weckruf 192
weder … noch 204
weg 182
Weg 285

weggehen 185, 200
weglaufen 19
wegräumen 93
Wegwerfkamera 171
wegziehen 97
Wehen 50
Wehr 133
Wehrdienst 118
Wehrpflicht 118
Wehrpflichtige 118
wehtun 12, 78
Weibchen 232
weiblich 11, 14
weich 27, 128, 233, 299
weich gekocht 58
weich landen 206
weicher Porno 37
Weichholz 254
Weide 219, 220, 235
Weideland 218, 220
weiden 221
Weihnachten 183
Weihnachtsfest 183
Weihnachtsgratifi- kation 316
Weihnachtstag 183
Wein 28, 63, 200, 261
Weinberg 219
weinen 30, 136, 234
Weinkarte 62
Weinkellner 63
Wein(rebe) 236
Weinstube 61
Weintraube 56
Weise 165
Weisheit 31
Weisheitszahn 79
Weißbrot 54
weißhaarig 16
Weiterbildung 149
weitere 271
weiterführend 148
weitergehen 155
weitsichtig 25
Weitsprung 196
Weitwinkelobjektiv 171
Weizen 54, 221
Weizenernte 221
Welle 256
Welle(nlänge) 241
Wellensittich 233
wellig 218
Wellnesscenter 82
Welpe 232
Welt 97, 165, 204, 214, 215
Weltall 160, 204, 206
Welten 208

Weltkrieg 236
Weltmarkt 296
Weltmeister 195
Weltraum 204, 206
Weltraumfahrt 206
Weltraumflug 206
Weltraummüll 206
Weltraumstation 206
Weltreich 96
Weltreise 188
Weltrekord 195
Weltsicht 164
weltweit 228
Weltwirtschaftskrise 297
Wendekreis 214
wenden 285
weniger 153, 250, 348
wenigsten 52
wenigstens 92
wenn 356
Werbeabteilung 305
Werbeagentur 305
Werbeantwort 273
Werbeanzeige 305
Werbebranche 305
Werbeetat 305
Werbefeldzug 305
Werbegeschenk 306
Werbegrafik 170
Werbegrafiker 170
Werbegutschein 306
Werbeindustrie 305
Werbekampagne 299, 305, 306
Werbekonzeption 305
Werbeleiter 305
Werbematerial 306
Werbemittel 305
Werbemüll 280
Werbepraktiken 305
Werbeschrift 306
Werbeslogan 305
Werbespot 94, 271, 305, 306
Werbetext 305
Werbetexter 305
Werbeträger 305
Werbetrommel 306
Werbeunterlagen 306
Werbezettel 306
Werbung 305, 306
werden 20, 227
werdend 50
werfen 91, 119, 134
Werfen 196
Werft 291
Werftarbeiter 291
Werk 169, 258, 315
Werkmeister 309

Werkstatt 258, 286
Werkstoff 254
Werkstoffkunde 254
Werkzeug 254, 255
Werkzeugmaschine 255
Wert 166
wertlos 32
Wertpapier 304
wertvoll 213
Wesen 22, 161, 164, 166
Wespe 234
West- 214
Weste 64
Westen 158, 214
Westernisierung 139
Westeuropa 214
westeuropäisch 214
westlich 214, 228
Westufer 217
Wettbewerb 177, 187, 195, 296
Wette 195
Wetter 227, 228
Wetteramt 227
Wetterbericht 227
Wetterfrau 271
Wetterkarte 227
Wettermann 271
Wettersatellit 207
Wettervorhersage 227
Wettkampf 187, 195
Wettlauf 195
Wettspiel 195
Whirlpool 82, 83
wichtig 82, 100, 142, 182, 306
wickeln 50
widerspruchsfrei 165
Widerstand 107, 119, 131, 241
wie immer 201
wie wär's mit 200
wiederverwerten 226
wiederaufladen 259
wiederbeleben 72
Wiedereintritt 206
Wiedergabeliste 281
wiederherstellen 116
wiederholen 156
Wiederholung 84, 156, 271
wiederverarbeiten 226
Wiederverkäufer 298
Wiege 17, 41
wiegen 11, 251
Wiegenlied 51
Wiese 220, 221
wild 232, 315

Wild 55, 233
Wildblume 235
Wilderei 131
Wilderer 132
Wildnis 219
Wildpark 219
Wildpflanze 235
Wildreservat 233
Wildschwein 55
Wille 43, 165
Wind 215, 228
Windel 50
windig 228
Windkraft 226
Windpocken 69
Windsurfen 199
Winkel 247
Winkelgeschwindig- keit 241
Winter 196
Wintergarten 88
winterhart 235
Wippe 18
Wirbelsäule 74, 245
Wirbelsturm 229
Wirbelwind 229
wirken 243
wirklich 13
Wirklichkeit 166
wirksam 305
Wirkung 29, 166
Wirkungsgrad 258
Wirt 15
Wirtschaft 295, 296
Wirtschafterin 311
wirtschaftlich 292, 296
Wirtschaftlichkeit 296
Wirtschaftsauf- schwung 127
Wirtschaftsflüchtling 134
Wirtschafts- geschichte 140
Wirtschaftskrise 297
Wirtschaftsleistung 296
Wirtschaftspolitik 100, 296
Wirtschaftsprüfer 114, 310
Wirtschaftsredakteur 269
Wirtschaftssanktio- nen 117
Wirtschaftssystem 296
Wirtschaftsteil 269
Wirtschaftstheorie 296
Wirtschaftswachs- tum 296

Wirtschaftswissen-
schaft 296
Wirtschaftswissen-
schaftler 296
wischen 92, 282
Wischnu 160
Wissenschaft 142,
239, 240, 242, 254
Wissenschaftler 146
wissenschaftlich
165, 242
Witterung 227
Witwe 40, 49
Witwer 49
witzig 170
Witzzeichnung 170
WLAN-Internet-
zugang 279
Woche 182, 221
Wochenende 182
wochenlang 80
wöchentlich 113
Wochenzeitschrift
268
Wochenzeitung 268
Wohl 186
Wohlfahrtsstaat 115
wohlgeformt 15
Wohlstand 297
Wohnblock 86
wohnen 97, 188,
191, 192
Wohngeld 115, 124
Wohngemeinschaft
124
Wohnhaus 86
Wohnheim 125
Wohnhochhaus 87
Wohnküche 88
Wohnmobil 87
Wohnort 10
Wohnraum 86, 124
Wohnraumbewirt-
schaftung 124
Wohnschlafzimmer
86
Wohnsiedlung 86
Wohnung(en) 85,
86, 87, 124, 250
Wohnungs- 124
Wohnungsamt 124
Wohnungsanzeigen
124
Wohnungsbau 124
Wohnungsbauge-
nossenschaft 124
Wohnungsbau-
gesellschaft 124
Wohnungsmangel
124
Wohnungsmarkt
124
Wohnungsnot 124
Wohnungssuche 124
Wohnwagen 87

Wohnzimmer 87,
93, 215
Wolf 233, 238
Wolke 228
Wolkenbruch 228
wolkenbruchartig
228
Wolkenkratzer 87
wolkenlos 228
wolkig 228
Worcestersoße 55
World Cup 197
Wort 180
Wörterbuch 264
Wörterverzeichnis
264
Wortspiel 180
Wuchs 15
Wunde 70, 72
wunderschön 15
Wunsch 29
wünschen 183
Würdenträger 121
Wurm 234, 280
Wurst 55, 192
Wurzel 236
Wurzelbehandlung
79
Wüste 218, 225
wütend 30

Y
Yoga(übungen) 83

Z
zäh 24
Zahl 230, 246, 248
zahlen 62, 111,
300, 302
zählen 246
Zähler 247, 259
Zählung 145
Zahlungsbilanz 297
zahlungsunfähig 304
Zahlungsunfähigkeit
304
zahm 232
Zahn 12, 27, 78, 79
Zahnarzt 78
Zahnbehandlung 78
Zahnbelag 79
Zahnbürste 38
Zähne 38
Zahnersatz 79
Zahnfleisch 78
Zahnklinik 78
Zahnpasta 38, 194
Zahnprothese 79
Zahnrad 256
Zahnradfräs-
maschine 256
Zahnschmerzen 78
Zahnseide 38, 79
Zahnspange 79
Zahnstein 79

Zahnstocher 38
Zange 255
Zapfen 235
zappen 270
zart 21
Zauberei 164
Zauberer 164
Zaun 88
z. B. 94
Zebrastreifen 285
Zecke 234
Zeckenbiss 234
Zeh(e) 12
Zehnerkarte 288
Zehntausende 124
Zeichen 278, 280
Zeichenerkennung
278
zeichnen 168
Zeichner 168
Zeichnerin 168
Zeichnung 168, 170
zeigen 168, 175
Zeit 92, 166, 292
Zeitalter 141, 164,
206, 211, 212
Zeitarbeit 127
Zeitarbeitskraft 127
Zeitgeist 141
zeitgenössisch 140
Zeitgeschichte 140
Zeitschrift 268
Zeitung 268, 272
Zeitungshändler
194, 268
Zeitungskiosk 268
Zeitungsstand 268
Zeitungsverkäufer
268
Zeitvertreib 198, 199
Zeitzone 214
Zelle 237
Zellteilung 237
Zelt 87
Zementwerk 258
Zensus 145
Zentimeter 250, 251
zentral 296
Zentralbank 304
Zentralbankrat 304
Zentrale 268, 275
Zentralheizung 91
Zentralnervensystem
245
Zentrifugalkraft 241
Zentrum 100, 158,
224
Zeremonie 184
Zeremoniell 139
Zerfall 79
zerknittert 16
zerren 72
Zerrung 72
zersetzen 243
zerstören 120, 225

Zerstörer 120
Zerstörung 120
zerstritten 105
zerzaust 16
Zeuge 43, 110
Zeugnis 140, 153,
156
Ziegelstein 178
Ziegenkäse 54
ziehen 79, 97, 215
Ziel 142, 188
Zielbahnhof 188
Zielflughafen 188,
289
Zielgruppe 306
ziemlich 24, 124,
227, 302
Zigarette 201
Zigarettenautomat
201
Zigarettenetui 201
Zigarettenpapier
201
Zigarettenspitze 201
Zigarre 201
Zigeuner 135
Zimmer 87, 188
Zimmer frei 191
Zimmerbestellung
191
Zimmergenosse 124
Zimmermädchen
311
Zimmermann 310
Zimmerreservierung
191
Zimmerservice 192
Zink 212
Zinn 212
Zinsen 297, 308
Zirkeltraining 84
Zirkus 187
Zitrone 27, 56
Zoll 189, 250, 251
Zollabfertigung 189
Zoll(abgabe) 114,
189
zollfrei 189
Zone 294
Zoo 94, 234
zoologisch 234
Zoom(schalter) 171
Zopf 16
Zorn 32, 144
zu Hause 19, 27, 51,
86
Zubehör 66, 172
zubereiten 56
züchten 221
Züchtigung 19
zucken 12
Zucker 59
Zuckerplantage 220
Zuckerrüben 221
Zuckerwatte 271

zuerst 186
Zufallsfehler 241
Zuflucht 125
zufolge 269
zufrieden 22
Zug 25, 28, 118, 287, 288, 291, 293, 294
Zugang 277, 279
Zugbegleiter 288
zugeben 136
zugetan 28
zugreifen auf 277
Zugriff 279
Zugverbindung 287
Zugverkehr 294
Zugvogel 233
Zuhälter 132
Zuhälterei 131
zuhören 26, 271
Zukunft 52, 262
Zulage 316
zulassen 227
zulegen 46, 199
Zulieferer 258
zumachen 155
zumute 28
zunächst 228
Zunahme 25, 125
Zuname 10
Zündkerze 259
zunehmen 76, 110, 126
Zunehmen 131
zunehmend 204
Zuneigung 29, 34
Zunge 12, 13, 78

Zurechnungs-
fähigkeit 111
zurechtkommen 33
zurückgeben 155
zurückgeblieben 51, 73, 144
zurückgehen 70, 126, 299
zurückhaltend 24
zurücklassen 208
zurücklehnen 78
zurückrufen 274
zurückschicken 257
zurückscrollen 277
zurückstellen 90
zurücktreten 106
zurückzahlen 303
zurückziehen 120
zurzeit 26, 82, 191
Zusammenarbeit 34, 186
zusammenarbeiten 34
zusammenbrechen 68
Zusammenbruch 304
zusammenfaltbar 190
zusammenfassen 155
Zusammenfassung 146, 155
zusammengeschla-
gen 133

zusammenheften 313
zusammenkommen 185
Zusammenkunft 185
zusammenrechnen 246
Zusammenschluss 99
Zusammensetzung 210, 242
Zusammenstoß 71
zusammenstoßen 35, 71
Zusätze 80
Zusatzleistungen 316
zusätzlich 313
Zuschauer 176, 271
Zuschlag 294
zuschneiden 172
zusehen 25
zuspammen 280
zusprechen 49
Zustand 72
zustellen 273
Zustellung 273
zutiefst 158
zuverlässig 22
Zuverlässigkeit 144, 146
Zuwanderer 134
zuziehen 68, 72, 74, 91

Zwangspfand 226
Zwangsräumung 125
Zweibettzimmer 191
zweifach 241
Zweifamilienhaus 87
zweifarbig 170
Zweifel 164
zweifeln 164
Zweig 52, 236
Zweigstellen 106
Zweigstellenleiter 303
zweijährig 236
zweimal 249
zweireihig 64
zweistellig 297
Zweistellungs-
schalter 278
Zweite 195
zweiten Grades 71
Zweitplatzierte 195
Zwickmühle 222
Zwiebel 56
Zwilling 50
zwischen 275
Zwischenablage 278
Zwischenaufenthalt 288
Zwischendeck 292
Zwischenspeicher 279
Zwischenstecker 260
Zylinder 65, 256

Die Zeichen der Lautschrift

Die Transkriptionen geben in der Regel die Aussprache wieder, die von Sprecher(inne)n der modernen britischen Standardaussprache (*RP = Received Pronunciation*) mehrheitlich benutzt wird.

[ʌ]	cut	[kʌt]
[æ]	fat	[fæt]
[e]	let	[let]
[ə]	about	[əˈbaʊt]
[ɪ]	fit	[fɪt]
[i]	happy	[ˈhæpi]
[ɒ]	lot	[lɒt]
[ʊ]	good	[gʊd]
[u]	manual	[ˈmænjuəl]
[ɑː]	far	[fɑː]
[iː]	see	[siː]
[ɔː]	law	[lɔː]
[ɜː]	first	[fɜːst]
[uː]	too	[tuː]
[aɪ]	light	[laɪt]
[eɪ]	late	[leɪt]
[ɔɪ]	boy	[bɔɪ]
[aʊ]	now	[naʊ]
[əʊ]	no	[nəʊ]
[eə]	fair	[feə]
[ɪə]	dear	[dɪə]
[ʊə]	tour	[tʊə]
[s]	so	[səʊ]
[z]	zone	[zəʊn]
[θ]	think	[θɪŋk]
[ð]	though	[ðəʊ]
[ʃ]	show	[ʃəʊ]
[ʒ]	measure	[ˈmeʒə]
[tʃ]	cheese	[tʃiːz]
[dʒ]	jet	[dʒet]
[j]	yet	[jet]
[f]	fine	[faɪn]
[v]	vine	[vaɪn]
[w]	wine	[waɪn]
[ŋ]	sing	[sɪŋ]
[x]	loch / lough	[lɒx] (Aussprache wie dt. Lo*ch*)

Das Zeichen [ˈ] steht vor der Silbe, auf der die Hauptbetonung liegt:
welfare [ˈwelfeə] – *welfare state* [welfeə ˈsteɪt]
Downing Street [ˈdaʊnɪŋ striːt] – *one-way street* [wʌn weɪ ˈstriːt]